# Resources for Teaching Young Children with Special Needs

# Resources for Teaching Young Children with Special Needs

## Penny Low Deiner

**Harcourt Brace Jovanovich College Publishers**

Fort Worth   Philadelphia   San Diego   New York   Orlando   Austin   San Antonio
Toronto   Montreal   London   Sydney   Tokyo

*To my husband, John, without whose love, encouragement, and babysitting this book could not have been completed*

ISBN: 0-15-576627-9
Library of Congress Catalog Card Number: 82-84254
Printed in the United States of America

Individualized education programs and case studies in Chapters 6–15 were prepared by Sandra Kay Morris.

The quotation on page 271 is from *Stretching Their Minds: The Exciting New Approach to the Education of the Gifted Child Pioneered by the Sands Point Country Day School* by Benjamin Fine. Copyright © 1964 by Benjamin Fine. Reprinted by permission of the publisher, E. P. Dutton, Inc.

# *Preface*

This is a resource book designed to help teachers prepare programs for children with special needs who are taught in a regular class. The book provides general curriculum adaptations and guidelines as well as over three hundred activities designed to help children meet their needs.

The book is written in a nontechnical style, and its focus is application. The scope of this book is broader than that of most books in the field; it covers temporary as well as long-term needs (e.g., children with broken legs as well as those with cerebral palsy). The philosophy is that all children sometimes have special needs. The view is that needs, not children, should be labeled and that the purpose of labeling needs is better programming.

The book is divided into two parts. Part 1 focuses on the changing role of teachers and gives information on necessary skills and how to develop them. These skills include working with parents, writing and implementing individualized education programs, and teaching children with special needs in the regular classroom. Ten chapters are devoted to programs for children with special needs. The needs covered are speech and language, hearing, visual, learning, physical, health, adjustment, culturally distinct, gifted and talented, and intellectual. In situations where children have needs in more than one area, it is important to read several chapters to gain the necessary information; for example, a child with asthma (health) may be having problems in school (adjustment). The glossary at the end of each chapter defines specific terms, and the annotated bibliography at the end of each chapter contains suggestions for further reading.

The second part of the book offers activities to meet the needs assessed in Part 1. The activities are organized by curriculum area. Although the activities are designed for all children, there is a section at the end of each activity that describes children for whom the activity is especially good and changes to accommodate children with specific needs.

The indexes in the book are designed to save time. The general index at the back of the book lists all the activities. The index at the end of each special needs chapter in Part 1 lists the activities in the book that are especially good for those children. The index at the beginning of each chapter in Part 2 presents the activities in that chapter. In all three indexes, activities are listed by the goals they meet.

This is a down-to-earth book that translates theory into practice. It assumes teachers have basic teaching skills and helps them apply these skills to children with special needs. It is my hope that through this book education for children with special needs can be enhanced and become more enjoyable for teachers and students.

I want to acknowledge the contribution of the students who took my course and who, instead of just taking notes, asked questions that jogged my thinking and forced me to clarify my ideas. Several students deserve special acknowledgment: Valerie Zingler Martin initially organized from my notes much of the material used in the book; Bernadette Metz Gilmore helped prepare the indexes; Linda Foster helped with activities in the motor area; Charlene Ann Dolgos helped shape the chapter on children with visual needs; Jane Friedman helped expand and update the chapter on gifted and talented children; and Joanne Sinclair contributed ideas to the activities section.

I am grateful to Sandra Kay Morris, who wrote the case studies and the individualized education programs, and who read and criticized the manuscript at various stages and provided encouragement.

I wish to thank Clifford Smith, whose training influenced my thinking and increased my awareness of the psychological and emotional needs of myself and others. He influenced the tone more than the content of the book.

My special thanks go to Alice P. Eyman and Camille B. Schiffman, directors of the University of Delaware Laboratory School, for allowing us to observe and take pictures; teachers Beverly Leute, Susan Raphelson, Connie Fisher, Jane Davidson, and Cindy Paris, and the student teachers not only for allowing us to take pictures but also for being enthusiastic about this book and its purpose; and the children for their willingness to be photographed. When I hit a tough spot, I was able to look out my window, see the children playing, and be inspired. I am grateful to the Eyman Children Center and head teacher JoAnn Springsteen for the same privileges.

I wish to acknowledge members of the Community Nursing and Developmental Programs, in particular Patricia A. Childs, who reached out to children in their homes and shared photographs of these children and their families; and the parents who encouraged this and who believe that the book will be useful to them and their children's teachers.

I am grateful to the photographers, Patricia A. Childs, John T. Deiner, and Charles C. Miller, who spent time watching children to get pictures that weren't posed and who took pictures that focused on ability not disability.

I want to thank the able staff at Harcourt Brace Jovanovich who guided the book through its many stages. I also wish to acknowledge the reviewers who read and criticized the manuscript. Their comments helped me to focus the book. The reviewers were Patrick Allinger, Patricia A. Childs, Vernon L. Clark, Elizabeth Grasier, Alison Malone, Kathleen McNellis, Dianne Nichols, Marilyn K. Little, Betsy Reeves, Marjorie B. Van Gulick, Francis L. Whaley, and Linda Whitehead.

Special thanks are also due Mary E. Ball and Sherry Rowland, who typed the manuscript at least twice. Their personal concern was overwhelming, and their ability to read and fill in the words of a tired author is greatly appreciated.

I am grateful to the reference librarians at the University of Delaware Library, in particular Margaret G. Bronner and Laura A. Shepard, who helped me locate elusive material.

My husband, John, and our children, Jamie, Michael, and Paige, who ate on paper plates when we couldn't find the kitchen table and who never asked when the book would be finished but believed that someday it would end, also deserve thanks.

Finally, I owe a great deal to the children I have taught, who in reality taught me—not so much the easy ones, but those who *wouldn't* learn.

Penny Low Deiner

# Contents

# Part 1

# Resources for Meeting Children's Special Needs

# 1

# *Teaching Children with Special Needs*

I teach children who have been labeled handicapped and are handicapped, and children who have been labeled handicapped but are only mildly inconvenienced. In the same class, I teach normal children who also have special needs. How do I teach all these children? That is the question this book is to answer. This book is intended to be a practical aid for those who teach or will be teaching a preschool or kindergarten class in which one or more members have special needs.

Children with special needs are those who require that adjustments be made in their curriculum or classroom. For example, one child, unhappy about a new baby sister, may need to express his feelings through play. The intensity of the need may result in his spending most of his time, over several days, in the free play area, while his work on readiness skills is postponed. Responsive programming is flexible; it allows "additional free play" to become temporarily the child's regular program. When, after a period of time, the child's need changes, the child may resume the previous regular program. A child with spina bifida who is in a walker requires long-range planning: Has enough time been allotted for changing to a new activity? Is the furniture spaced far enough apart to allow the walker to pass through easily? Will the motor requirements of large group activities present problems? All children have special needs some of the time. Some children have special needs all of the time. My goal is to help you meet special needs within the normal classroom routine.

In order to accomplish that goal, this text provides basic information on exceptionalities (supplemented with numerous resources) and a wealth of flexible methods and activities.

## ABOUT YOU

I assume, since you are (or plan to be) a teacher, that you already know general techniques of teaching, and you understand how children develop and learn.* You can recognize the rate at which a child is learning and identify where in the learning process a child is having problems. However, changes in educational philosophies have given rise to *mainstreaming,* the placing of slightly-to-moderately disabled children in the mainstream, or regular classroom. Now you need additional knowledge about impairments and their effect on the children's growth and learning. You need to know how to program the curriculum for the special needs of these children. You are probably somewhat anxious about meeting this new challenge.

What you require, at least initially, is not in-depth expertise, but a basic understanding of disabilities.† You need new or adapted methods and

* If you wish to review child development, see the references at the end of this book.
† For additional information on specific disabilities, see the references at the end of each chapter.

*3*

You are a model for the children.

activities that are not only designed to meet special needs but are good for all children. In short, you need a guide on how to best teach, cope with, and enjoy children with special needs while you meet the special needs of the normal children in your classroom.

In addition to being their teacher, you are a model for the children in your class. Both your verbal and nonverbal behavior indicate to the class your feelings toward special needs children. If you view these children as odd or as needing too much extra help or as requiring that many exceptions be made for them, all the children will also. You probably have many concerns about being a positive role model, as well as about mainstreaming in general. We will discuss the issues further in Chapters 2 and 3.

## ABOUT CHILDREN

All children are individuals, yet all have much in common. They all have strengths as well as needs. In some cases, strengths may be elusive, but they can be found. All children have special needs some of the time. One child may have a cast on his broken leg for several months, while another may forget her toilet training because of stress at home. Are they handicapped, or do they simply have special needs during a crucial period in their lives?

When children have special needs, there is a danger that we will consider only how different those needs make them; we lose sight of how much they resemble other children. When that happens, we forget that exceptional children have their classmates' usual needs as well. All of a child's needs must be taken into account, not just those that are exceptional. A child with a hearing loss needs to learn to speech read and to use residual hearing. However, the child also needs to learn how it feels to wear a fireman's hat and how to roll out clay. In fact, most children have needs in more than one area.

School is a new and frightening experience for many children. A special needs child may fear rejection by you or by peers. This child may have had fewer experiences away from the family, and those may have been painful. More than other children in your class, this child may need your reassurance and may take some time to develop a trusting relationship with you.

You can help classmates accept this child by developing in them an awareness of the strengths and needs of others. As their understanding of other children grows, so will their self-awareness. Through the awareness of others and themselves, children can learn strategies for dealing with people who are different from them—a valuable skill, for we are all different.

## THE PROBLEM OF LABELING

The practice of categorizing, or labeling, children based on their primary disability evolved gradually; no one planned it. One way labeling has been encouraged is through federal law. In 1958 the federal government allocated money to improve the education of the mentally retarded. Funding was expanded in 1963 to include the hearing impaired, speech impaired, visually impaired, emotionally disturbed, and crippled or health impaired; the learning disabled were added to this list in 1970. In order to receive federal money, educators were, and still are, required to label exceptional children. Unfortunately, the practice of labeling is carried into the children's daily lives.

Labeling picks out a single part of a child (usually not a strength) and calls attention to this part. A deaf child, for example, may be viewed as a pair of ears rather than as a child with all the feelings, wants, and needs of a normal child. The child as a whole is lost sight of. Another problem is that our diagnostic skills are not that accurate, and the child may in fact be mislabeled. I am especially concerned when young children are involved, as a label given at age three may be on a child's record for the entire educational career whether or not the need still exists. Future teachers may be biased by the label before they even meet the child. The expectations of both the teacher and the child may be lower because the child is labeled.

In an attempt to be more descriptive and more accurate, labeling often includes the level of severity of the child's problem. For example, a child who has what is called a "situational, short-term adjustment problem" (perhaps due to a new baby, moving, starting school, or divorce) would be labeled *mild*. A more tenacious problem (such as school phobia, persistent acting out, or withdrawal) would be labeled *moderate*. A behavior disorder such as autism would be labeled *severe*. In your classroom you are likely to encounter only children with mild to moderate impairments.

Labeling by level of severity is helpful, but it is only a starting point. I've used it to determine what subjects should be covered by this book. You will use it early in your process of screening children to learn what their needs are. The kind and severity of exceptionality may indicate general areas in which to check for needs. You will find, however, that labels are too general; you cannot program for a label. You can program for needs.

I have found the most useful and positive approach is to identify each child's needs and then to

All children have strengths as well as needs.

build programming to meet these needs. Saying "John has a visual impairment and can distinguish only light and dark" will not help you design an appropriate program. You are only labeling the disability. But when you describe the needs—"John will need an alternative method for handling projects that require visual skills"—you imply two possible actions. Either adapt the approach John must use or adapt the project so that all the children can enjoy it and learn from it. With a simple statement of need, you have already begun to program. I will be demonstrating the process of translating needs into program goals and then into activities throughout this book and particularly in Chapter 4, "Individualized Education Programs."

The process of programming for needs is a dynamic one. A child who is labeled visually impaired may in fact be visually impaired for life, but that child's needs will change—not merely each year, but perhaps each week or day. Your programming must be responsive to the changes.

## ABOUT THE TEXT

This book is divided into two parts. In the first part, Chapters 1–5 introduce the text and discuss such teaching related concerns as the reasons for and effects of mainstreaming, the changing roles of teachers, working with parents and specialists, and writing individualized education programs (IEPs). Chapters 6–15 focus on the needs of children in ten areas of disability. The second section consists of activities designed to help children gain needed skills. These activities are grouped into chapters by curriculum areas, and are also indexed at the beginning of each chapter by the goals the activities are designed to meet.

### Areas of Need

In each of Chapters 6–15, the disability is briefly defined and its major characteristics given, including the levels of severity that you may encounter. Each chapter gives information on the characteristics of children by listing their greatest needs, which then become your teaching goals. Then follow guidelines for working with the children and ways to adapt your curriculum to fit their needs. These adaptations are arranged by curriculum area.

Each discussion of an exceptionality and children's corresponding needs is followed by a child study team report. This is a short biography/history of a child with the impairment under discussion. Although the names have been changed, the reports are based on real children. In some cases, information on more than one child has been combined to make the report more illustrative. The report is similar in form and content to the information you might receive before a special needs child enters your classroom. These represent neither the best nor the worst reports I have read, but are merely typical.

An individualized education program for this child follows the report. Each IEP is a sample designed to show you the process of meeting a child's special needs by individualizing programming in a regular classroom. Although the sample is a good IEP for the child in the case study, it will not perfectly fit any child in your class. It will, however, be a valuable guide when you write your own IEPs.

After the IEP comes the glossary. Nontechnical terms are intentionally used in the text. However, as you read technical reports and talk with specialists, you will need to know the technical terms. These are defined in the glossary.

Each of the ten chapters generally has two annotated bibliographies. The first, readings for teachers, has a section on technical books that provide more detailed information on the disability. It is followed by a fiction and biography section, which is designed to increase your understanding of the ways families and individuals have coped with disabilities. The children's bibliography lists books to be read to and looked at by young children. It first lists books about children with the disability and then books that meet the needs of the children with that disability.

Teaching Resources, which precedes the bibliographies, lists national, and some regional, organizations that can give you more information about a disability. Also listed are sources of specialized materials that may be helpful in your classroom.

At the end of each chapter is an Index to the activities in the second part of the book. The index is organized by annual goals (for example, "To increase body awareness"), which are grouped under the general teaching goals they comprise. Under each annual goal appear the activities designed to accomplish that goal. The curriculum area of each activity is given, as well as its page number.

### Activities for Meeting Children's Special Needs

The second part of the book gives the materials and directions for the activities and is organized by curriculum area. Preceding each curriculum area is an index by goals of the activities, with the page number on which the activity appears. At the beginning of each area, I describe how these activities fit in with the total preschool/kindergarten program. Activities follow that—although good for all the children—are particularly appropriate and effective for meeting the needs of exceptional children. The activities have this general format:

*Name of Activity*
*Goal:* What the activity does, for example: To increase body awareness. This is similar to the annual goal in an IEP.
*Objective:* A statement in behavioral terms of what the child will be expected to do at the end of or during the activity, for example: The child will point to at least five body parts on request. This is similar to the objectives needed to carry out the annual goal in the IEP.
*Materials:* A list of the materials necessary to perform the activity.
*Procedure:* How to carry out the activity.
*Continuation:* Ideas for varying and expanding this activity.
*Comment:* Additional remarks, such as: how to adapt this activity for different impairments; exceptionalities the activity is especially good for, and why; which parts of the activity to emphasize with different children.

The book may be used flexibly to fit your own needs. If you are already knowledgeable about a disability, you might want to omit the description in Chapters 6–15 and go directly to the guidelines and curriculum adaptations. However, you may find it useful to review a chapter before meeting with parents, not to gain new information, but because the level of presentation will be appropriate for parents who are nonexperts.

# Mainstreaming

The word *mainstreaming* represents both an ideal and a process. The ideal is that children with special needs be educated in a way that enables them to join the mainstream of society. The process of mainstreaming is the placing of these children in the mainstream of the educational system. According to the Council on Exceptional Children:

> Mainstreaming is a belief which involves an educational placement procedure and process for exceptional children, based on the conviction that each such child should be educated in the least restrictive environment in which his educational and related needs can be satisfactorily provided for. This concept recognizes that exceptional children have a wide range of special educational needs, varying greatly in intensity and duration; that there is a recognized continuum of educational settings which may, at a given time, be appropriate for an individual child's needs; that to the maximum extent appropriate, exceptional children should be educated with non-exceptional children; and that special classes, separate schooling, or other removal of an exceptional child from education with non-exceptional children should occur only when the intensity of the child's special education and related needs is such that they cannot be satisfied in an environment including non-exceptional children, even with the provision of supplementary aids and services. (Council on Exceptional Children, 1976, p. 3)

Put more simply, children who become part of the mainstream may sometimes leave for alternate channels for short or long periods of time. They may, for example, take alternate routes past rapids, but these detours are based on the children's needs as individuals, not on impersonal labels assigned to them. Some routes take longer than others, some are more grueling, but the common goal is the development of skills, attitudes, and behavior that will allow all children to deal effectively with the world in which they live. Mainstreaming, then, is designed to keep children in or as close to the mainstream as possible while meeting their individual needs.

A graphic model of the mainstreaming process is depicted in Figure 2–1. The figure shows the different educational situations available to exceptional children. They are arranged hierarchically into levels according to how well they integrate the children into the mainstream of education. The components that vary from level to level are time, subjects, and location. In other words, how much time do the children spend in the regular classroom, how many subjects do they share with normal children, and how close are they to other children in the regular classroom? Our intent is to place children in the highest level at which they can function well, to work with them, and, through regular reassessment, to move them into higher levels as their rate of learning comes closer to that of their age mates.

One objective of mainstreaming, then, is to help special needs children be part of a typical school experience. Another is to help nonexceptional children broaden their concept of *normal* to include children who can't see or hear as well as they can, but who can tell funnier stories or turn a somersault straighter. In fact, *normal* doesn't refer to a single

**FIGURE 2–1**

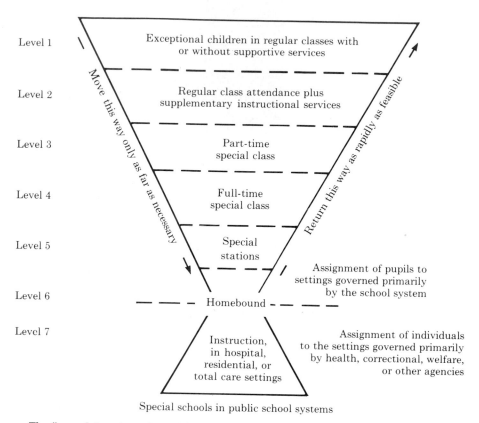

The "cascade" system of special education service. Reprinted from Deno, E., "Special education as developmental capital," *Exceptional Children,* 37 (1970), pp. 229–37. By permission of The Council on Exceptional Children.

ideal. As we commonly use it, it covers a broad range of abilities and differences. A third objective is to increase children's awareness of individual differences without their making judgments about people being "better" or "worse" than others because of these differences.

Why was mainstreaming chosen as the best method for educating children with impairments? Why wasn't the solution more and better special schools? The answer may be learned by following events and changes in the past twenty years. Separate forces—social, legal, and educational—created a favorable environment for, and finally created a demand for, mainstreaming.

## THE DEVELOPMENT OF MAINSTREAMING

The concept of mainstreaming is relatively recent. Historically, we have separated exceptional children in America from the rest of society. Separating these children reinforced society's view that to be excep-

tional was to be bad. The future for these children was a dead end, out of public view. The corresponding educational philosophy led to the building of "special" hospitals and schools (often with distinctive names such as "School of Hope") that were located far from population centers. In addition, some regular schools had "special" classes. As much as possible, "special" children were dealt with only by specialists. Parents were even warned not to become too attached to their "special" child because that would make the "inevitable" institutionalization process even more difficult to bear. The current concept of mainstreaming developed partly in reaction to the "out of sight, out of mind" position.

The forces that led to mainstreaming are tightly interwoven. For the purpose of surveying them, however, I have grouped them into three broad areas: social, legal, and educational.

### Social

In America, as in all countries, the schools are used to impart not only information but social values. To the extent that children are segregated from regular schools and classrooms, whether because of visual impairment or skin color, they are stigmatized; they are seen as deficient. Separate is not equal.

In the past, individuals sometimes opposed the philosophy of separation, but with little effect. In the 1960s some of the stigma of having a disabled child was removed when such public figures as President John F. Kennedy and Vice President Hubert H. Humphrey openly acknowledged their affection for handicapped family members. Perhaps encouraged by this, and by the social activism of the 1960s, parents and professionals began to band together to form organizations and to take legal action. Parent organizations, such as the National Association for Retarded Citizens, and professional organizations, such as the Council on Exceptional Children, that were founded in those years actively promoted their cause. They succeeded in making the general public (and eventually the legislatures) aware that "it can happen to anyone." Society learned of the immediate and concrete need of the disabled for more trained professionals and teachers. Even more fundamentally, people began to realize that the disabled were being deprived of their constitutional and human rights.

A very different influence was also at work changing social attitudes and creating a demand for a solution. In the 1960s and 1970s the cost of general education was outstripping the funds available to pay for it. Constructing and maintaining buildings to provide school, or day, programs for the disabled multiplies the cost to parents and taxpayers. Consider, too, the cost of salaries for a separate set of teachers, administrators, custodians, and other personnel. As more children get closer to the mainstream, the need for residential and other separate facilities decreases. If we eliminate some of the special schools, the savings are tremendous.

Even after spending more money on support services, such as temporary foster care, family counseling, and the traditional therapies, we come out ahead financially. Further savings are possible if, through early identification and appropriate programming, these children learn to be contributing members of society. More important, the personal and social gains to all of us are incalculable.

## Legal

Mainstreaming is required by Public Law 94-142 (1975) and enforced by Section 504 of the Rehabilita-

Mainstreaming requires adaptability. A block under the table may be all that is necessary to participate in lunchtime.

tion Act of 1973. These laws were passed to protect the rights of people with handicapping conditions to equal educational opportunities. What led to these laws being passed?

As parents of exceptional children became increasingly dissatisfied with the educational plight of their children, they sought legal remedies as a way of making the educational system more responsive to their needs. Encouraged by an increasingly receptive public and strengthened by better organization and cooperation among parent and professional groups, parents successfully pressed their cases in court.

In one classic case, *Pennsylvania Association for Retarded Children, et al.* v. *Commonwealth of Pennsylvania, David H. Kurtzman, et al.* (1971), a class action suit was brought by PARC on behalf of the parents of thirteen retarded children. PARC argued that the denial of a free public education for retarded children was a violation of the Fourteenth Amendment of the Constitution of the United States. Education for some had to be education for all. In an out-of-court settlement, the state of Pennsylvania agreed to provide education to all school-age, mentally retarded children living in the state (including those in state institutions) within one year. A parallel decision, *Mills* v. *The District of Columbia* (1972), added the stipulation that lack of funds was not an acceptable reason for excluding exceptional children.

Other decisions concerned children who had been misplaced by the system. In *Diana* v. *State Board of Education of Monterey County, Ca.* (1970), the court ruled that children must be tested in their primary language. Previously, children whose primary language was not English had been tested in English and had sometimes been wrongfully declared mentally retarded.

The many court decisions were, in fact, so consistent and so consistently upheld in higher courts, that litigation gave rise to legislation. Through 1981 the most important single legislative enactment has been Public Law 94-142: The Education of All Handicapped Children Act of 1975. The presence of exceptional children in your classroom is one step toward the implementation of this law.

*Public Law 94-142.* Public Law 94-142, the act with the greatest impact to date, consists of four major parts: the *findings* of Congress, the general *purpose* of the act, *definitions* of terms (including *individualized education program*), and a list of the *rights* of children and parents. (I will be quoting directly from the public registry.) Congress found the following to be true:

SEC. 3. b. 1. There are more than eight million handicapped children in the United States today;

2. the special educational needs of such children are not being fully met;

3. more than half of the handicapped children in the United States do not receive appropriate educational services which would enable them to have full equality of opportunity;

4. one million of the handicapped children in the United States are excluded entirely from the public school system and will not go through the educational process with their peers;

5. there are many handicapped children throughout the United States participating in regular school programs whose handicaps prevent them from having a successful educational experience because their handicaps are undetected;

6. because of the lack of adequate services within the public school system, families are often forced to find services outside the public school system, often at great distance from their residence and at their own expense;

7. developments in the training of teachers and in diagnostic and instructional procedures and methods have advanced to the point that, given appropriate funding, State and local educational agencies can and will provide effective special education and related services to meet the needs of handicapped children;

8. State and local educational agencies have a responsibility to provide education for all handicapped children, but present financial resources are inadequate to meet the special educational needs of handicapped children; and

9. it is in the national interest that the Federal Government assist State and local efforts to provide programs to meet the educational needs of handicapped children in order to assure equal protection of the law.

It is in combination with Section 504 of the Rehabilitation Act of 1973 that PL 94-142 gets its power of enforcement. Section 504 states that no person can be discriminated against by any program that receives federal funds. In most states this includes the school system. The following familiar statements refer to Section 504:

It is the policy of the [name of organization] that no person shall be subjected to discrimination on the grounds of race, color, creed, age, sex, or ethnic or national origin.

or more positively stated:

The [name of organization] is an Equal Opportunity Employer which Encourages Applications from Qualified Minority Groups and Women.

Note especially the words *free appropriate public education* in the following stated purpose of the act:

SEC. 3. c. It is the purpose of this Act to assure that all handicapped children have available to them, within the time periods specified, . . . a free appropriate public education which emphasizes special education and related services designed to meet their unique needs, to assure that the rights of handicapped children and their parents or guardians are protected, to assist States and localities to provide for the education of all handicapped children, and to assess and assure the effectiveness of efforts to educate handicapped children.

Next, the act carefully defines the key terms and concepts, thereby setting the minimum standards that must be met in order to achieve compliance. Following are the four definitions I consider most informative:

Sec. 4. 16. The term "special education" means specially designed instruction, at no cost to parents or guardians, to meet the unique needs of a handicapped child, including classroom instruction, instruction in physical education, home instruction, and instruction in hospitals and institutions.

17. The term "related services" means transportation, and such developmental, corrective, and other supportive services (including speech pathology and audiology, psychological services, physical and occupational therapy, recreation, and medical and counseling services, except that such medical services shall be for diagnostic and evaluation purposes only) as may be required to assist a handicapped child to benefit from special education, and includes the early identification and assessment of handicapping conditions in children.

18. The term "free appropriate public education" means special education and related services which (A) have been provided at public expense, under public supervision and direction, and without charge, (B) meet the standards of the State educational agency, (C) include an appropriate preschool, elementary, or secondary school education in the State involved, and (D) are provided in conformity with the individualized education program required. . . .

19. The term "individualized education program" means a written statement for each handicapped child developed in any meeting by a representative of the local educational agency, . . . the teacher, the parents or guardian of such child, and, whenever appropriate, such child, which statement shall include (A) a statement of the present levels of educational performance of such child, (B) a statement of annual goals, including short-term instructional objectives, (C) a statement of the specific educational services to be provided to such child, and the extent to which such child will be able to participate in regular educational programs, (D) the projected date for initiation and anticipated duration of such services, and

(E) appropriate objective criteria and evaluation procedures and schedules for determining, on at least an annual basis, whether instructional objectives are being achieved.

Number 19 is the subject of Chapter 4. The act goes on to define what is meant by the terms *excess costs, native language,* and *intermediate educational unit,* either directly or in terms of previous legislation.

The act further establishes a minimum level of compliance with regard to the rights of disabled children and their parents. The section begins as follows:

Sec. 615. a. Any State educational agency, any local educational agency, and any intermediate educational unit which receives assistance under this part shall establish and maintain procedures in accordance with subsection (b) through subsection (e) of this section to assure that handicapped children and their parents or guardians are guaranteed procedural safeguards with respect to the provision of free appropriate public education by such agencies and units.

b. 1. The procedures required by this section shall include, but shall not be limited to—

A. an opportunity for the parents or guardian of a handicapped child to examine all relevant records with respect to the identification, evaluation, and educational placement of the child, and the provision of a free appropriate public education to such child, and to obtain an independent educational evaluation of the child:

B. procedures to protect the rights of the child whenever the parents or guardian of the child are not known, unavailable, or the child is a ward of the State, including the assignment of an individual (who shall not be an employee of the State educational agency, local educational agency, or intermediate educational unit involved in the education or care of the child) to act as a surrogate for the parents or guardian;

C. written prior notice to the parents or guardian of the child whenever such agency or unit—

(i) proposes to initiate or change, or

(ii) refuses to initiate or change,

the identification, evaluation, or educational placement of the child or the provision of a free appropriate public education to the child;

D. procedures designed to assure that the notice required by clause (C) fully inform the parents or guardian, in the parents' or guardian's native language, unless it clearly is not feasible to do so, of all procedures available pursuant to this section; and

E. an opportunity to present complaints with respect to any matter relating to the identification, evaluation, or educational placement of the child, or the provision of a free appropriate public education to such child.

The intent of the rest of the section on rights can be more quickly grasped in a brief paraphrase. If they have a complaint with regard to the five procedures stated immediately above or if they are not in agreement with the school's proposed program, "the parents or guardian shall have an opportunity for an impartial due process hearing." The hearing may *not* be conducted by anyone employed by the agency the complaint is against. Either party to a hearing may appeal the findings, in which case an officer of the state educational agency will review the case and decide accordingly. The parties to hearings have the right to be "accompanied and advised" by a lawyer and by specialists in the field of handicapped children. Equally explicit are the following: "the right to present evidence and confront, cross-examine, and compel the attendance of witnesses"; the right to a "verbatim record" of the hearing; and "the right to written findings of fact and decisions." The decision is usually final, although in some cases subject to appeal. If dissatisfied with the decision, but not (under the law) eligible to appeal, a party may pursue the case further by bringing civil action in court.

What happens to the child during this process? After all, hearings and court cases may take a lot of time. The act addresses the problem as follows: "the child shall remain in the then current educational placement . . . or if applying for initial admission to a public school, shall, with the consent of the parents or guardian, be placed in the public school program." In other words, the child is not left in limbo.

We've seen, now, how social pressure and legal action in the courts led to the enactment of new laws protecting the rights of children with special needs. Public Law 94-142 was extended by Congress and will be in effect at least through 1984. As laws will continue to be enacted and amended, it is important for teachers to note the changes that affect education.

## Education

Interwoven with social and legal change is change in the field of education itself. Much of this change has come about as a combined result of research, experimentation, and law. For example, findings in psychology have affected our philosophy of what education is and how it takes place. As a result, we have come to recognize the importance of individualizing our teaching. This has facilitated our providing the attention to individual needs that is essential when working with exceptional children.

Most educational research has focused on how (and what) to teach rather than how children learn. After the work of Swiss psychologist Jean Piaget was published in English in the early 1950s, educators began to focus on how children learn. According to Piaget, the teacher's role is to set up an environment that a child can actively explore. In addition, classroom activities, which are part of the environment, should incorporate both familiar and new aspects. From Piaget's work, we concluded that a child must actively interact with the environment and that the activities in the environment must be individualized to match and then expand the child's experience. To go from individualizing for average children to individualizing for all children is a natural step.

Individualization has also been encouraged by court rulings. *Hobson* v. *Hansen* (1967) made tracking systems (putting all the "A" students in one class) unconstitutional. As a result teachers are regularly taught, through revamped undergraduate programs and in-service training, to deal with individual differences and to program for them within the group.

The work of Albert Bandura and others on how children learn by modeling other children has also affected the education of special needs children. Because exceptional children were segregated at an early age, the only peers available as models were also exceptional. This segregation effectively resulted in teaching handicapped children to imitate their handicapped peers. Now we are finding that with teacher support those children can learn to model normal peers. Both exceptional and normal children are gaining experience from an early age in dealing with a wide range of people. Piaget's work helped make mainstreaming possible by changing our philosophy and methodology of education. Bandura's work may have helped make mainstreaming imperative by demonstrating that segregation deprived exceptional and average childen alike of a full education.

New teaching methods, support services, and technology used in the regular classroom have also prepared us for mainstreaming. For example, team teaching, now a common practice with young children, can help the teacher who has had little experience with exceptional children. The advantage of team teaching is that a teacher trained to work with these children can be added to the team. Increasing the number of children in the class makes this approach economically feasible. The ratio of students to teachers may be improved, and the transition to mainstreaming is made easier and swifter for the regular teacher.

Mainstreaming is more than just placing exceptional children in regular classes. For it to be done well, there must be support services for both the teacher and the child. When exceptional children were channeled off into special schools, these services were primarily diagnostic. As soon as a child was identified as exceptional, the child was moved; the task of support services was finished. Despite their original limited function, school support services have grown to meet the needs of normal chil-

*optimal,* education, but rather an appropriate education. In any given situation different people may have different ideas as to what is appropriate. Sally's parents may think it is appropriate for her to have speech therapy five times a week. The school district sees that as optimal, saying it is appropriate that she have speech therapy once a week. The teacher may well be caught in the middle—understanding both positions.

This problem has a socioeconomic base. Specialists are often overburdened with high case loads and therefore unable to spend much time with any one child. One obvious solution is to hire more specialists. But that is expensive, and taxpayers are voting against tax referendums to give the schools more money. The shortage of specialists is even more acute in rural areas, for some specialists are reluctant to take jobs in areas where they may be the only therapist for miles.

Because of the limitations and expense of specialists, some schools have invested in "hardware" as a means of individualizing and otherwise enhancing education. A computer, a talking typewriter, educational television, or some other form of recently developed hardware may or may not be available to the teacher. Some of these items have applications for helping special needs children. But an entire grade school may have to share one talking typewriter, while several schools may share limited (and expensive) access to computer time. Some items are highly successful but others are quickly dropped. Still, where available, technological advances have also eased the way for mainstreaming.

## THE EFFECTS
## OF MAINSTREAMING

Many of us feel sorry for people with impairments. We also feel somewhat uncomfortable around them. As teachers confronting mainstreaming, we may sometimes ask ourselves: What would I do if

Sarah had a convulsion and I was the only adult around?
David got lost and couldn't hear me calling him?
Jane fell and hurt herself on something she didn't see that I forgot to pick up?

These are disconcerting thoughts, and the easiest way to deal with them is to avoid situations where they are likely to occur. We tend to avoid children with handicaps because we feel inadequate around them. I am afraid that, given the tenor of the times, we will have to confront those feelings and replace them with accurate knowledge about strengths and needs.

Such knowledge not only gives us the confidence

to work with special needs children; it enables us to help average children accept their exceptional classmates. If knowledge about strengths and needs is passed on to them, young children can learn to deal with their peers as individuals: "Hey, if Sam isn't looking at you, he can't hear you." Integration provides children with the opportunity for positive experiences that build a good foundation for lifelong learning about others. Mainstreaming is intended to decrease isolation from and prejudice toward those who are different. However, its effects are more complex than that. It has changed the roles of teachers, children, and parents.

## On Teachers

As a teacher, you are probably the most important element in successful mainstreaming. You are expected to be able to teach not only normal children, but exceptional children as well. And you cannot specialize in one exceptionality, but must be prepared to teach any exceptional child who comes to your classroom.

It is not possible to anticipate what exceptionalities you are likely to get and with what frequency. You will have to learn about each exceptionality as you encounter it. Indeed, you will actually have an important function in the process of identifying exceptional preschoolers.

You need also to be able to explain each exceptionality to the other children in the class (and to their parents) in terms that are easily understood but not stereotyped.

You must be familiar enough with the terminology of an exceptionality to understand technical written reports and to talk with specialists and the parents of the exceptional child. You will have to write an individualized education program (IEP) for the diagnosed special needs child in your class. This requires you to write annual goals and instructional objectives. All of the above will be discussed in more detail in Chapters 3, 4, and 5.

You must believe in providing equal opportunity for all the children. Remember, too, you serve as a model for the children in dealing with a child who has an impairment. If you accept, understand, and are sensitive to the needs of that child, the students will follow your lead. Your attitude toward children is as important as your ability to plan and carry out those plans.

One way to demonstrate acceptance of children is to focus on their positive characteristics. Children need to be encouraged to do what they are able to, not reminded about those things that they cannot do. Encouraging children effectively requires setting realistic goals and planning activities to meet those goals, combined with daily or weekly record keeping. Objective information about where a child is in the learning process is necessary for further planning.

to a........
may have to
with this child

## On Parents

Parents may
pity for a chil
cerned that t
mannerisms f
mal children c
viors; when th
then ignored,
exceptional ch
after school or
play at their h
responsible for
home. They m
needs or worri
emergency. P
questions thei
child. Parents
time-consumin
whether their
teacher's time.

Parents of e
well qualified
training may n
about how thei

dren tease him, and how you feel about having their child in the classroom.

All parents should be encouraged to discuss their fears and, if possible, to participate in the classroom for first-hand experience of mainstreaming.

## CONCLUSION

Mainstreaming in and of itself is neither good nor bad. Many people fear at first that mainstreaming will result in all children being "dumped together" in the rather arbitrary way they were previously separated out. And, if mainstreaming is poorly done, that could happen. Mainstreaming optimally involves placing children in an educational setting that meets their needs and is as close to normal as possible. It involves periodic reevaluation and reas-

signment of children so that their academic placement rises with their educational achievement.

The purpose of mainstreaming is to help both exceptional and normal children gain skills in interacting with each other that will be valuable throughout life, as well as to provide an appropriate education for all.

Mainstreaming has resulted from changing social, legal, and educational philosophies that have led to individualized programming for all children. Of particular importance are the legal requirements of PL 94-142, which mandate that all children have a free, appropriate public education.

Crucial to the success of mainstreaming is your underlying support of equality for all. Mainstreaming depends, too, on your ability to measure and program for children's learning, for their strengths and needs, at many points along the developmental path.

## BIBLIOGRAPHY

Allen, K. Aileen. *Mainstreaming in Early Childhood Education.* Albany, N.Y.: Delmar Publishers, 1980.

Blackwell, Robert B., and Robert R. Joynt. *Mainstreaming: What to Expect—What to Do.* Johnstown, Pa.: Mafex Associates, 1980.

Brooks, Kenneth W., and Carol Deen. "Improving Accessibility of Preschool Facilities for the Handicapped." *Young Children.* (March 1981), pp. 17–24.

Burbach, Harold, ed. *Mainstreaming: A Book of Readings and Resources for the Classroom Teacher.* Dubuque, Iowa: Kendall-Hunt, 1980.

Council on Exceptional Children. "Delegate Assembly Issues Mainstreaming Challenge." *CEC Update 7,* No. 4 (Summer 1976), p. 3.

Dickerson, Mildred G., and Michael D. Davis. "Implications of PL 94-142 for Developmental Early Childhood Teacher Education Programs." *Young Children.* (January 1977), pp. 28–31.

Dunlop, Kathleen. "Mainstreaming: Valuing Diversity in Children." *Young Children.* (May 1977), pp. 26–32.

Gearheart, Bill R., and Mel Weishahn. *The Handicapped Child in the Regular Classroom.* St. Louis, Mo.: C. V. Mosby Co., 1976.

Guralnick, Michael, ed. *The Directory for Exceptional Children: A Listing of Educational and Training Facilities.* 9th ed. Boston: Porter Sargent Publishers, 1981–82.

———, ed. *Early Intervention and the Integration of Handicapped and Nonhandicapped Children.* Baltimore: University Park Press, 1978.

Haglund, E., and V. L. Stevens. *A Resource Guide for Mainstreaming.* Springfield, Ill.: C. C. Thomas, 1980.

Hart, Verna. *Mainstreaming Children with Special Needs.* New York: Longman, 1980.

McLoughlin, James A., and Susan M. Kershman. "Mainstreaming in Early Childhood: Strategies and Resources." *Young Children.* (May 1979), pp. 54–66.

Meisels, Samuel J. "First Steps in Mainstreaming: Some Questions and Answers." *Young Children.* (November 1977), pp. 4–13.

Meyen, Edward L., Glenn A. Vergason, and Richard J. Whelan, eds. *Alternatives for Teaching Exceptional Children: Essays from Focus on Exceptional Children.* Denver: Love Publishing Co., 1975.

Procopio, Mary A. *Enabling Our Children to Learn: Early Education Curriculum.* Andover, Mass.: Charisma Press, 1980.

*Readings in Mainstreaming.* Special Education Series. Guilford, Conn.: Special Learning Corp., 1978.

Turnbull, Ann P., and Jane B. Schulty. *Mainstreaming Handicapped Students: A Guide for the Classroom Teacher.* Boston: Allyn and Bacon, 1979.

# *Teachers' Roles*

Teachers' roles have changed tremendously over time—from adding wood to the furnace, feeding the horses, and teaching grades 1–8 in one classroom, to being part of an educational team that serves the needs of both average and exceptional children in the same class.

New roles require new knowledge and new abilities. No longer is basic information about child development and materials and methods of teaching enough for them.

Teachers today must have or develop skills for

1. Dealing with both average children and special needs children in one classroom
2. Playing a major role in the early diagnosis of special needs children
3. Writing (with parental input) and implementing individualized educational programs (IEP) for children
4. Holding individual conferences with parents about their children and cooperating with them to design a program for their children
5. Working with school psychologists, physical therapists, occupational therapists, speech and language therapists, and others to develop programs for children
6. Conducting parent meetings that parents of both average and exceptional children will attend
7. Keeping abreast of legislation that pertains to teaching
8. Becoming a child's advocate when a child's needs are not being adequately met

The necessary skills listed above do not include others that I assume you already possess (e.g., you are competent at general classroom management and curriculum planning, and you have developed your own philosophy of teaching).

## TEACHING AVERAGE AND SPECIAL NEEDS CHILDREN TOGETHER

How can you teach children with both regular and special needs in the same classroom? In fact, you already have, even if you have taught only a few classes. Since many young children have not had their special needs diagnosed, chances are you have already had one or more unlabeled exceptional children. If you trace the careers of the children you have known, you may well discover that some of them were eventually diagnosed as having a special need. It is unlikely that their special need suddenly occurred after these children left your class unless they experienced a particular trauma. So, in reality, you have probably dealt with exceptional children already.

Since you will be teaching children with a wide variety of needs, you must be able to teach in a way that is beneficial to all. It takes careful planning to develop activities and materials that can be useful on many levels at one time. Using fingerpaint, for example, you can plan to

Strengthen the weaker arm of a child with cerebral palsy

Teach color mixing to gifted children

Add sand to one color to give a visually impaired child a tactile experience

Teach vocabulary (colors, shapes) to a child with language delays.

You will be teaching children with a wide variety of needs.

All children will learn the feel of the paint and the effect of using different body parts to make a mark, and they will all have participated in a creative art experience. Such programming allows the children to work together while each child learns what is appropriate for him. All the fingerpaint pictures may look similar, but each child benefits differently from the process of doing them. Developing a *process orientation,* as this type of programming is called, is not difficult and will help you with a mainstreamed class. You will need only two skills: the ability to choose good, flexible activities that will allow you to program for differences and the ability to adapt those activities to different needs. As you will soon learn, the activities need not be expensive, exotic, or new. With practice, a process orientation becomes habit. You will even forget there was a time when you could not do it.

## EARLY DIAGNOSIS

Young children are delightful and unpredictable—and difficult to make conclusive statements about. The child who "acts out" daily may be angelic when you ask someone to come and observe; the child who is withdrawn cooperates beautifully during the observer's visit. When parents seek to have their children examined, they too have problems. If one child shuts his eyes during an eye examination, it is difficult to determine what he sees. If another cries when earphones are put on, it is difficult to determine what she hears.

You already have some expectations about what normal, or average, behavior is. When you first suspect a problem in a child, you may have only a vague feeling of uneasiness. You may feel that something about this child is outside your category of normal. Trust yourself. Watch this child more closely, noting down what you observe in order to determine what is bothering you. Your notes may resemble these: "Suzy often spills her juice (more often than the other children?). She cannot (will not?) put simple puzzles together, and she does not sit for an entire group time." Does Suzy have a learning disability? Maybe she does, maybe she doesn't, but it is unlikely that you will have confirmation either way while she is still in your class. In any case, it really does not matter whether she is labeled learning disabled or not; you do not need a label to program. What does matter is how you program for her as a child who is displaying a special need. Your observations can be translated into needs for which you can program. As long as two years may elapse between officially expressed concern about a problem and medical or diagnostic confirmation. Those are two very important years for a child! If a child appears to have a problem, the best time to start programming for it is now.

After you've made your preliminary observations, what happens next? In order to gain more information about the nature and extent of a child's problem, a formal diagnostic process is necessary. Once you decide to confirm your observations with testing, the first thing you should do is talk with the parents. (See also pp. 47–52.) In a conference, discuss your concern with the parents and explain why you believe their child will benefit from a formal diagnosis. You need the information a diagnosis provides—and not the label—in order to meet this child's needs in your program planning. If the parents do not share your knowledge and concern, this process may take several conferences and some structured observation.

Once the parents have agreed to testing, the exact procedure depends on the age of the child, whether or not the child is in a public or private school, and your opinion on the nature of the problem.

If the child is enrolled in a public school or is old enough (according to state and federal law), the parents can have the child evaluated at public expense. You would then refer the child to the school psychologist or the department of social services or other organization functioning in this role.

If the parents choose private evaluation, your role would consist of telling them about the type of specialist that you feel would be the most helpful; sharing your written observations with the specialist of their choice (this may be on a referral form); allowing that person to observe in your classroom, if possible; and with the parents' permission, obtaining a copy of the testing results and incorporating the child's strengths and needs into your programming. When the test results are obtained, use them to refine the plan you will already have put into action.

Early diagnosis is the key to an exceptional child's development. Without early diagnosis, a child may experience years of failure before an official diagnosis is reached. The original disability is then compounded by a poor self-concept. Early diagnosis and good programming can give an exceptional child experience in success instead of failure.

## DIAGNOSED CHILDREN

If a child has an official diagnosis before arriving in your classroom, the procedure is covered by PL 94-142 and is very different. In this case, a preliminary IEP must be completed before the child begins class. This means that you have to write an IEP for a child you have never seen! Your information on the child may consist of test results and specialists' evaluations, and these may be in the form of a child study team evaluation. (The child study team is composed of diagnosticians and specialists who determine what level of programming is appropriate for the child.) Members of the child study team may help you write the initial IEP. Sample reports are given at the end of each of Chapters 5–15, followed by an IEP designed to fit that child. The preliminary IEP will be in effect for thirty days, by which time you must have an IEP for the full twelve months.

If the child has been diagnosed and has been in a classroom before, the existing IEP can be used until it runs out. IEPs are usually written to cover October 1 to the following September 30.

## WRITING AND CARRYING OUT AN INDIVIDUALIZED EDUCATION PROGRAM

In the past, teachers were generally accountable for preparing children to enter the next grade level. They made weekly plans for class activities but were rarely asked to plan for individual children or to plan with parents. The parents had something to say about the curriculum only when children's needs were blatantly not being met. Writing an IEP is a new task for both you and the parents.

Too often the teacher and specialists write the IEP, then present it to the parent, who is asked to glance at it and sign it. The conference is then over. In addition to violating the spirit of the law, teachers who do this miss an opportunity for getting useful programming information from parents about the child and what they want him to learn. The step-by-step writing of the IEP is covered in Chapter 4.

## PARENT-TEACHER CONFERENCES

While you are programming for a child, you need to seek information from and share information with the child's parents. Parental knowledge can be valuable. Because they live with the child, they know the child's likes and dislikes as well as strengths and needs. Parents' cooperation at home is equally valuable. As the child is with you only part of the time, it is important that you and the parents work together to achieve goals.

There are three occasions on which you will have parent-teacher conferences. The first traditionally occurs at the beginning of the year. All of the parents are invited to an "open house" to meet the teacher and schedule individual conferences. These are usually routine conferences, the basic technique for which you have already learned. It is a three-step process.

1. Talk about the child's positive qualities and how much progress the child is making.
2. State your concerns about the child and give concrete examples.
3. Conclude on a positive note.

A second routine conference may occur at the end of the year.

On other occasions you will request a conference with the parents or they with you to discuss a particular concern. These conferences are different from the routine ones in that they are problem-related and have one definite topic. You need to schedule a parent-teacher conference when you notice a consistent change in a child's behavior that interferes with learning, in other words, when a child deviates far enough from the norms of academic and social behavior to come to your attention. You need a different technique for these conferences.

### Scheduling the Conference

When you have decided you need a conference with parents, you may request the conference by telephone or when they pick up or drop off the child. Make the time between asking for and having the conference as short as feasible, within two or three days. Parents are likely to be anxious in the interval, wondering what is wrong and trying to "pump" the child about what is happening at school. You can share with them the general topic of the conference, but don't be too specific or you will end up having the conference on the spot, before you are fully prepared.

When parents request a conference, ask them for the general topic so that if necessary you can pull any relevant records or materials.

### Planning the Conference

The next step is preparing yourself and your materials for the conference. First, ask yourself "What do I want?" Answering is not as easy as you may expect; greater care is required for the nonroutine conference. If you say "I want Suzy to sit still during group time," you risk setting yourself up as an adversary of the child (thus alienating her parents). Furthermore, the statement is a procedural dead end; it doesn't suggest an action to take. If you say "I want to plan and control group time so that Suzy will sit through it," you will have taken a constructive approach, one that encourages ideas and shows you are on the side of the child and her parents. The difference is an important one because it changes the whole focus of the conference. The conference is to help you, not to shape up Suzy. Although getting

Suzy to cooperate is your goal, in order to reach it you take responsibility for what is happening rather than blaming Suzy.

After you have carefully described what you want from the conference, you should collect information, including your notes and records and examples of the child's work, to help parents understand your concern. Note, too, what you have tried and share that information as well: "We have group time for about twenty minutes each day. This is a difficult time for Suzy. I have tried reading shorter stories and singing songs since she really likes to sing, but even then I can only keep her attention for about ten minutes."

You should have some questions in mind to ask the parents: "What are Suzy's favorite books? What does she like to do at home?" In addition, be prepared to suggest additional solutions.

### Conducting the Conference

Thank the parents for coming, and then begin discussing your concerns. Parents are expecting bad news. They are waiting for the "but" or "however" after each positive remark. Don't keep them in suspense. Make a brief statement praising qualities you admire in the child, then tell the parents why their child's behavior concerns you. Document that behavior with examples of the child's work and with your notes and records. Then ask the parents if they see similar conduct from the child at home. For example:

I'm really glad Julie is in my class. I've never taught a child that enjoys music as much as she does. However, I'm concerned about the way she has been interacting with the other children recently. For the past two weeks she has chosen to play alone for almost half of the free play period. And she hasn't used the art materials I have set out, even when I planned some of her favorite activities. She almost seems to be avoiding me, especially when I try to talk with her. I wonder if there are any changes in what's happening at home that might be related to this behavior (a relative visiting, a new baby, a sick family member)? Have you noticed any change at home?

Whatever the parents tell you, believe them! If they are observing the same behavior you are, and are also concerned, discuss a plan to work on together. If they are seeing the same thing you are and are not concerned, stress the situational aspect of the behavior, that is, stress that some behavior is fine at home but not appropriate at school and vice versa. Then see if they are willing to support your position at school. If they don't see the behavior you do, try to learn why that is true. Do they not notice it, is there no opportunity to see it, or are they doing something at home to prevent or correct the behavior? If the latter, you may want to try their solution in your classroom.

It is especially important at this phase of the conference for you to take responsibility for the situation. Take care in expressing your ideas to the parents. "I am having problems controlling Suzy during group time" is an "I" statement. It is much less likely to make parents defensive than this statement: "Suzy can't sit still during group time." The second statement invites a response like "Well, maybe she is bored." An unsympathetic reaction like this can easily lead off the subject. Furthermore, blaming Suzy isn't going to change her behavior.

Ask the parents for their suggestions and for their reactions to your suggestions. Discuss a plan that may work through combined effort. A plan for Suzy might begin with the parents reading stories to her and her friends at home "nursery school style" to see what occurs. Both you and the parents should agree in advance on how you will react to Suzy's behavior: For example, you might plan to say, "Suzy, you need to sit for one more page," and then reward Suzy with a hug when she does. Her parents should encourage and reward her in the same manner at home.

When the major part of the conference is over, agree to call or meet with the parents again when you both have had time to try the suggestions. At the second conference, you and the parents will evaluate your experiences and plan from there. Remember, parents have more influence on a child than teachers do. To make changes, parental support at home really helps.

### Summarizing the Conference

Thank the parents for coming, for being concerned, and for sharing their suggestions. Express your eagerness to put their ideas to use and mention your interest in discussing the results at your next conference. You need to be sure they see this conference as part of a problem-solving process. If the solutions were easy, you would have already found them. You are searching along with the parents, and unlike the routine conference, this one requires follow-up. Above all, *do not* tell them you are certain the problem is solved. You need to keep your avenue to information open in the event the suggestions fail.

Depending on the content of the conference, your summary will vary from a review of the suggestions you discussed and the agreements you reached to an expression of how you feel about the parents' perception of the situation.

### After the Conference

In the conference, at least four goals should have been reached. You have voiced your concerns while alerting the parents to one or more of the child's be-haviors. You have shared information and suggestions and have shown your willingness to try possible solutions. After the conference, your responsibility is to put the suggestions into action. If the solutions do not work, another conference should be called and something else tried. When a reasonable number of techniques have been tried—honestly tried—you might then suggest that the child be evaluated by a psychologist or other specialist to determine strengths and weaknesses so that programming can be done more effectively. Do not make this suggestion at the initial parent-teacher conference. You need more information than you have at that point. Also, if parents have not seen what you have, they need time to observe. If you start out asking that children be tested, parents often become defensive and may simply stop listening. Remember, if they refuse to sign the papers, the child cannot be tested. You need to alert them to the problem and discuss intermediate solutions. First, lay the groundwork and try techniques that might work. At the same time, individualize programming to meet this child's needs. Let the parents know you care about their child.

## WORKING WITH SPECIALISTS

As you encounter children who have special needs, you will also come in contact with specialists. In general, to benefit from your dealings with specialists, you should develop two sets of skills. First, learn enough of the specialists' jargon to talk with them about a child and to interpret their technical reports. Second, learn to use the reports in your programming.

Mastering the jargon is not an easy task. Prepare yourself ahead of time by looking up terms in the glossaries in this book. If you have a report to decipher, use a medical dictionary or talk with a friend or colleague who knows the terminology. If the meaning of some words or concepts is still obscure, call the specialist and ask. Specialists are experts in their field, but sometimes jargon is so much a part of their everyday vocabulary that their explanations are difficult to understand. If a specialist's explanation is unclear, you might ask for a demonstration of the concept.

Once you understand the report, you must be able to translate it into needs for which you can program. In practice the two skills might work like this: The occupational therapist reports that a child "fell off the nystagnius board following rotation." You, after doing some research, decide that the child was probably dizzy! This child probably needs practice changing directions and starting and stopping to better develop her vestibular sense (pertaining to balance and the inner ear). You might plan some creative movement with initial slow turns as well as some work on body awareness and flexibility.

When you are planning a child's program, it is important to keep the child as a whole in mind. You need to look at the child's needs in physical therapy, for example, in light of the needs of a four-year-old. Thus, if the physical therapist wants the child to sit in a way that strengthens certain muscles, you might use group story time for that purpose, but not if the posture is so uncomfortable the child cannot concentrate on the story. If discomfort occurs, ask the specialist about alternative positions for the child. If a required posture interferes with a child's full participation in, or feeling of belonging to, the group, inquire about alternatives or have the child use the posture when it is more appropriate. Regardless of the therapeutic benefits, group time is not a good time for a child to be alone at a standing table when all the other children are sitting on the floor.

## PARENT-TEACHER GROUP MEETINGS

Meeting with the parents of normal and exceptional children in a large group requires different skills than does dealing with only one child's parents, particularly if this is the first time the parents are encountering mainstreaming. Be prepared to make some initial statements about your personal philosophy of teaching, what you expect to have happen in your classroom, and what mainstreaming is. While the first two topics are probably familiar to you, the last, mainstreaming, may not be.

Think through beforehand some statements that you will make at the meeting. Although what you say will be affected by your own circumstances, the tone and content might resemble the following:

As we continue to study how children learn, we are discovering that it is beneficial to have a variety of children this age in the same classroom, rather than to match up similar children. This variety encourages the children to learn about their own and others' strengths and needs.

In this particular class, there is a child who prefers to play alone most of the time, who rarely joins the group. The other children are learning skills for approaching this child as well as an appreciation of the fact that there are times when all of us want to be alone. When I require most of them to participate in group time yet don't require one or a few to be part of the group, the children are learning to be flexible and to allow exceptions to rules when appropriate.

These are difficult concepts for young children to learn, yet their efforts will be rewarded, for children's appreciation of individual differences in other children helps them learn more about themselves.

Try to avoid labeling children or citing children by name unless you do it while discussing many children. This becomes easier as you learn to habitually view special needs as one aspect of individual differences.

You need to be prepared for questions that parents will ask. Following are some typical questions with possible answers:

*Parent:* Why doesn't *my* child get an IEP?
*Teacher:* I take the individual needs of all the children into account when I plan my program. In some cases the exact form of programming that I use is dictated by law. In other cases I use a system of my own. I'd like to share this with you during an individual conference.

*Parent:* Do you have enough time to teach all the children in your class when some of them have special needs?
*Teacher:* I think all the children in the class have special needs some of the time, so on a particular day or week I may spend more time with one child than others, but overall I think it evens out. I'm lucky to have Mrs. C. as an aide in the class. Her presence allows us far greater flexibility in programming. We can always use more help, so if any of you have time on a regular basis, I'd enjoy having your help in the room as well.

*Parent:* Isn't it hard to teach children at so many different levels of ability?

Plan activities that can be used at different levels by children who are playing together.

*Teacher:* I think the key to teaching children with varying abilities and interests is to plan activities that can be used at several different levels by children who are playing together. Many of the materials I use fall into this category. The playdough, for example, can be manipulated by all the children. Some children make specific shapes and then count them, others make impressions with cookie cutters, and some even make a "tea set." For some children, using playdough is primarily a creative activity; for others the main benefit lies in developing motor skills or in having a sensory experience. There are many other activities like this that I use for multilevel teaching.

*Parent:* My child says there is a child who cannot walk in his class. How does this affect the class?
*Teacher:* Yes, we do have a child in our class who needs a wheelchair or a creeper to get around. We make sure that this child's toys are placed so that he can reach them, and we have added ramps to make it easy for him to get outside. He needs some help getting out of the wheelchair and down on the floor, but in the same way that your child is working on tying his shoes, this child is working toward independence in movement.

Answers like those above help parents see the process you use in teaching as well as the product. More detailed techniques for working with parents are given in Chapter 5.

## KEEPING ABREAST OF LEGISLATION

The need for keeping up with current law is partly met by reading the newspaper and some professional journals, such as those published by The National Association for the Education of Young Children and The Council on Exceptional Children. In addition, both of these groups have annual conferences that are informative.

## CHILD ADVOCATE

Your teaching role these days includes being an advocate for children. This means more than programming for them in your classroom or participating in their diagnosis where appropriate. Part of your job is to make sure that children get the special services they need. This may mean taking the initiative to find out from parents or specialists how to best serve this child in your class. The parents may need your knowledge of who provides services their child needs and how those services are best acquired. As their advocate, you may find yourself standing up to bureaucrats and fighting to cut red tape. See yourself as an active "doer" rather than as one who waits to be told what to do. Young children cannot be advocates for themselves; they need your help.

## SUMMARY

The introduction of mainstreaming has increased the challenge of teaching. You are now expected to teach both regular and exceptional children in one classroom. You may well be the one to start the early diagnostic process for a child as a result of your keen observations. Your work with parents in both routine and problem-centered conferences has increased as has your responsiveness to parents' needs and demands. You need to develop new skills that will enable you to interpret test results, talk with specialists, and integrate the information you obtain from them in such a way that you can plan activities that children enjoy while their needs are being met.

## BIBLIOGRAPHY

Davis, William. *Educator's Resource Guide to Special Education: Terms, Laws, Tests, Organization.* Rockleigh, N.J.: Longwood Division, Allyn and Bacon, 1980.

Haslam, Robert H., and Peter J. Valetutti, eds. *Medical Problems in the Classroom: The Teacher's Role in Diagnosis and Management.* Baltimore: University Park Press, 1976.

Hildebrand, Verna. *Guiding Young Children.* New York: Macmillan, 1975.

Michaelis, Carol T. *Home and School Partnerships in Exceptional Education.* Rockville, Md.: Aspen Systems Corp., 1980.

Nedler, Shari, and Oralie McAfee. *Working with Parents: Guidelines for Early Childhood and Elementary Teachers.* Belmont, Calif.: Wadsworth, 1979.

Rutherford, Robert B., Jr., and Eugene Edgar. *Teachers and Parents: A Guide to Interaction and Cooperation.* Boston: Allyn and Bacon, 1979.

Safford, Philip. *Teaching Young Children with Special Needs.* St. Louis, Mo.: C. V. Mosby Co., 1978.

# Individualized Education Program

When a child in your class has been identified as exceptional, Public Law 94-142 specifies certain procedures and requirements that must be followed. We discussed the law in Chapter 2. In this chapter we will be discussing some of its practical implications in detail.

The law requires that a specialized education program be designed *in writing* for each child with special needs. This program must be developed *jointly* by the teacher, specialists, the parents or guardians, and if possible, the child. Many parents felt in the past that they had been made promises that were not kept. Putting the program in writing is meant to ensure that it will be carried out and that agreement has been reached between parents and teachers about its content. Some parents believe the teacher knows best, and they are willing to agree with anything the teacher says. Others believe they know their children better than the teacher does; they would like to contribute to program planning. The law guarantees parents a voice in the education program designed for their child. Older children also may participate in their own program planning.

Parents have the right to examine all relevant school records regarding the identification, evaluation, and educational placement of their child. This right enables parents to examine the data that decisions are based on; they no longer simply have to accept the official verdict. Parents are now entitled, on request, to see test results and receive copies of reports.

The school district must provide the parents with information *in writing,* in a language they can understand, about the identification, evaluation, and placement of their child. The parents must be notified in writing of contemplated program changes as well. In the past, some parents were not informed when their children were placed in or removed from special education classes.

An individualized education program (IEP) must be developed for each identified exceptional child and must have the following components:

1. Statement about the child's present level of performance
2. Annual goals set for the child
3. Short-term instructional objectives
4. Specific educational services to be provided
5. Extent to which the child will participate in the regular education program
6. Dates on which special services will begin and end
7. Evaluation criteria to be used to determine whether or not the instructional objectives are being met

As you are learning the elements of an IEP, the fine points of writing good objectives, or how to work well with specialists, you may ask yourself, "Is this worth the effort for just one or two children?" In fact, in the process of learning to comply with these legal requirements, you can learn a great deal about individualizing instruction for all children and about getting the maximum benefit from the resources you have. For the other children in the class, especially any exceptional children who have not yet been officially identified, you can incorporate into your customary planning the principles used to design IEPs.

Training programs are being funded to help both special education and regular teachers learn the requirements of Public Law 94-142. If you are a public school teacher, training may be available to you through your school district. If you are a private school teacher with an exceptional child referred to you from the public sector, you may also receive training through the school district. But even if you are not officially eligible, you can usually find some way to be included in the training offered in your area. Whatever your situation, you are sure to find this chapter helpful.

## INTRODUCTION TO THE IEP FORM

There are probably as many different IEP forms as there are school districts in the United States. All of them must conform to the guidelines stated in Public Law 94-142, but they may include information not required by law. The following IEP was developed for illustrative purposes. You will be able to adapt without any difficulty the information it asks for to the particular form you are required to use.

### The IEP Form: Cover Page

There are typically six sections on the first page of the IEP, as shown on page 25. On the top left, you will see space for *identification* of the child. *Current test data*—habitually used to assess present levels of performance—must also be included in an IEP. It is located here on the top right.

You may encounter results from a variety of tests used by specialists. The most common tests are listed below. Note they fall into three categories—intelligence, achievement, and specialized. The results are usually stated in grade-level equivalents (5-5; fifth grade fifth month) or age equivalents (AE 4.7; four years seven months).

#### Intelligence (Ability) Tests
Stanford-Binet (2 years–adult)
Wechsler Intelligence Scale for Children (WISC) (4–6½ years)
Slosson Intelligence Test (2 weeks–adult)
McCarthy Scales of Children's Abilities (MSCA) (AE 2.6–8.6)

These tests generally yield an intelligence quotient (IQ) as well as a mental age (MA). Some yield a full-scale IQ that can be broken down into a verbal scale (VS) and a performance scale (PS). This break-

down can be useful in assessing relative strengths and needs.

#### Achievement Tests
Basic School Skills Inventory (BSSI) (AE 4–7)
Boehm Test of Basic Concepts (Grades K–2)
Learning Accomplishment Profile (LAP) (AE 2–6)

Achievement tests are intended to test knowledge. They are designed to reveal what skills children have learned relative to expectations for their age and grade level.

#### Specialized Tests
Developmental Indicators for the Assessment of Learning (DIAL) (AE 2.6–5.6)
Illinois Test of Psycholinguistic Ability (ITPA) (AE 3–10)
Kindergarten Auditory Screening Tests (KAST) (Grades late K–early 1)
Adaptive Behavior Scale (AE 3.0–6.9)
Peabody Picture Vocabulary Test (2 years–adult)

These tests are designed to focus on specific aspects of an impairment (for example, auditory discrimination, language skills, eye-hand coordination). They are especially useful in determining learning strengths and needs of a child with an impairment.

In many cases the examiner's remarks indicating quality of the child's behavior are as helpful as the test results themselves. They will often tell you about a child's strengths and needs, and usually give information about cooperation, motivation, response to failure, persistence, and so on.

In the middle right of the form, you will find the section "Recommended Special Services." These are developmental, corrective, and supportive services that are necessary to provide the child with the adequate education the law requires. They include speech and language therapy, psychological services, physical therapy (PT), and occupational therapy (OT). For information on what different specialists do, see pp. 30–31.

Some school districts also provide pediatric medical personnel, social workers, home-school visitors, and other special services. The available specializations and the amount of time specialists can devote to special needs children vary from school to school.

The IEP cites the kinds of services required (such as occupational therapy), the type (group versus individual), and the amount of time to be spent with each service (a half-hour a week, for example). This section also includes a statement about the amount of time spent in the regular class and in a special education setting. (As children get older, subject matter areas involved are usually included.)

Observe, now, the middle left of the form. The

## INDIVIDUALIZED EDUCATION PROGRAM

NAME _____ DOB ___/___/___

AGE _____ GRADE _____

SCHOOL _____

PARENTS/GUARDIANS _____

ADDRESS _____

PHONE _____

### CURRENT TEST DATA

TEST/DATE/RESULTS

_____ ___/___/___

_____ ___/___/___

_____ ___/___/___

_____ ___/___/___

On _____, the IPRD Committee
     (Date)

met to review all current data and

recommends Level _____ placement.

Date of next review _____

Exceptionality: _____

Recommended Special Services (Hrs/Wk):

_____ ___/

_____ ___/

_____ ___/

Total Hours/Week: _____

Special Education Classroom _____

Regular Classroom _____

Present at meeting:

Parents _____ Representative of District/Agency _____

Others: Name/Position _____ ___/ _____ ___/

The committee has determined the following learning strengths and needs to be reflected in the IEP:

| STRENGTHS | NEEDS |
|---|---|
| | |
| | |
| | |
| | |

IPRD Committee (Identification, Placement, Review, and Dismissal) may be named differently in your district. It is similar to the child study team (see p. 33); however, its responsibilities are long term, extending in some cases until the child reaches adulthood. The IPRD Committee identifies a child's special needs, determines the child's level of placement, and continues reviewing the case periodically until it decides the child no longer needs special educational programming. Committee members include education administrators, teachers, and specialists. After the committee meets initially, by law it must meet again within a year to discuss the child. The level of placement is usually determined by the amount of special services the child requires. The more services given, the higher the number. School districts or states determine their own system. Typically, Level I is a regular class; Level II, a regular class with resource room; Level III, a part-time special class; Level IV, a full-time special class.

In the lower middle are spaces where those present at the IEP meeting must sign the form. In general, parents and teachers also sign each page of the IEP. Parents have five days in which to sign the form, which gives them some time for careful consideration.

For programming purposes, the section at the bottom of the page—learning strengths and needs—is the meat of the first page. The information about individual strengths and needs should help you write and implement goals and objectives.

### The IEP Form: Goals and Objectives

The tasks for the IEP's first page require compilation and interpretation. The second and following pages require synthesis, creativity, and perseverance. Here the teacher sets forth the actual programming for one special needs child. The programming task involves stating annual goals, instructional objectives, and activities.

*Writing Annual Goals.* These are statements (one to a page) of long-range goals. They are based on the strengths and needs given on the first page of the form and your observations of the child, as well as on your general knowledge about the child's exceptionality and appropriate developmental levels. Here are some examples of annual goals: to improve auditory discrimination skills, to improve math concepts, to improve eye-hand coordination, or to increase body awareness. Annual goals are too broad for practical application and must be broken down into instructional objectives.

*Writing Instructional Objectives.* Writing instructional objectives is not difficult after you have written a few. Some writing of objectives is based on common sense and trial and error, but for writing other objectives there are actually procedures, such as breaking the task into its component parts and sequencing these. The instructional objectives separate the annual goal into smaller, teachable bits of behavior. They are written in such a way that you, or anyone else, can tell whether the child has learned the behavior. To help satisfy this empirical requirement, there are rules for writing instructional objectives.

The first step is easy. You must decide who is going to do the action stated by the objective. The child, the teacher, or the parents may be the "doer." Second, determine what is going to be done. This is more difficult, as you must be able to measure (see) what is done. This means that some words—such as, *understand, know, appreciate, try, feel, discover,* and *think*—cannot be used. Teachers of young children have more difficulty with this step than other teachers because young children have such a small repertoire of behavior that traditional words—such as, *write, list, translate, read, predict,* and *compare*—represent skills the children in their class have not yet achieved. A starter list of doing words might include the following:

| | |
|---|---|
| point to | set up |
| match | state |
| select | arrange |
| tell | locate |
| order | define |
| say | look at |
| label | draw |
| repeat | circle |
| name | hop |
| pick out | run |
| choose | jump |
| find | walk |
| color | cut out |
| copy | count |
| dramatize | nod |
| dictate | demonstrate |

In the third step of writing instructional objectives, state the object of the action. Fourth, impose conditions to make the task easier or more difficult. Here is what a sample objective might look like so far:

John (doer) / will hop (action) / for ten feet (object) / on left foot (condition).

The conditions may also determine what will or will not be available to the child. They can be set forth at the beginning or end of the instructional objective. This is usually a matter of the writer's style and how the sentence best makes sense.

The fifth and final step is to develop an evaluation criterion. How well or how often does this objective need to be achieved for you as the teacher to decide that it has been mastered? Here are some examples

STUDENT _____ DATE _____

GOAL _____

PARENT SIGNATURE _____ TEACHER SIGNATURE _____

| INSTRUCTIONAL OBJECTIVES | EDUCATIONAL METHODS | DATE Begin | DATE End | Eval. | PERSONS RESPONSIBLE Name | PERSONS RESPONSIBLE Position |
|---|---|---|---|---|---|---|
| | | | | | | |

of criteria: using at least two colors, within ten seconds, two out of three times, or 80 percent of the time.

Because of human variability it is unwise to decide on a 100 percent performance, even when you think this can be achieved. For a variety of reasons, children often decide not to comply with requests. You need to build flexibility into your evaluation criterion.

Putting it all together then, an instructional objective might look like this: Given paper and crayons, the child will draw a picture using at least two colors.

Condition: Given paper and crayons
Doer: the child
Action: will draw
Object: a picture
Evaluation: using at least 2 colors

For the purpose of illustrating the process of writing an instructional objective, I have used a concrete and somewhat over-specific example. In practice, your objectives can often benefit by being more general.

Objectives with enough flexibility to allow for individual differences lend themselves more readily to variety in programming. For example, in order to improve a child's social skills with peers, you may want to have that child interact with others. Your objective may read:

Given paper and watercolor paints, Cathy will paint a mural of a rainy day with two other children for ten minutes.

However, you have put a lot of wasted thought and time into Cathy's IEP if she happens to hate painting, and hates painting rainy-day scenes most of all. A more general objective that achieves the same purpose reads:

Given the appropriate materials, Cathy will participate in an art project with two other children for ten minutes.

This gives you and the child the option of using clay, paint, corn starch, playdough, fingerpaint, collage, or papier-maché to fulfill the objective. There is room for experiment, which makes the IEP more workable.

Several things may become apparent as you review this procedure. You may find that it is much simpler to write trivial objectives than important ones. Furthermore, some of the qualities you value most and want to teach are almost impossible to put into behavioral terms, for example, empathy, creativity, cooperation, joy, and interest. Finally, in order to determine whether or not these criteria have been fulfilled, you will have to develop some system

To improve auditory discrimination . . .

of record keeping. Put such nagging thoughts aside for a while. The answers to these questions will become apparent to you as you grow familiar with the process of writing an IEP.

Try to order the objectives from simple to more difficult, as well as from high to low priority. For example, if your annual goal is to improve auditory discrimination, your objectives will concern listening skills. Perhaps you decide you want the child to distinguish between a bell and a siren. This is a relatively easy task—providing the child has the prerequisite skill of auditory identification; that is, the child can identify each sound by itself. To test the child on auditory identification, ring the bell and ask, "What is this?" Sound the siren and ask the question again. Repeat the sounds behind a screen. Can the child identify the sound without a visual cue? If so, the child can auditorily identify the bell and siren. This does not mean, however, that he can distinguish between the two sounds when played together. Once the child demonstrates the prerequisite skills, you may proceed with more difficult tasks. Be sure you have included enough objectives, in terms of both quantity and scope, to attain your goal.

Setting priorities, deciding what to do first, is often complicated. There is no one way to set them. Parental concerns and the child's wishes influence your decision. If those are not apparent, ask yourself about each objective: How difficult will it be in the future if the child doesn't learn ____ ? The more the child will need this skill, the higher the priority you could assign the corresponding objectives to meet the annual goal.

Your priorities, as well as your assessment of the difficulty of the task, will be reflected in the dates you expect to initiate and complete the objectives. For example, your IEP might reflect the following progression:

Given an easel and paints in three primary colors, the child will point to the correct color when named.  Oct. 1–Nov. 1

Given an easel and paints in three primary colors, the child will name the colors on request.  Nov. 1–Jan. 1

Given an easel and paints in three primary colors, the child will mix two colors to make another color and name that color.  Jan. 1–April 1

The law requires you to state on the IEP form when an objective will be reached. This makes teachers more accountable for the child's learning. In most cases, the date you pick will be your best guess as to when the child will be able to perform that particular task. Some tasks are easier than others. If a child can already point to one color, you might expect that sometime in the fall the child will learn several others. If, however, you decide on June of the following year, a parent may well question your teaching ability. Setting dates requires you to think through what you will teach a child and how many opportunities in a day, week, or month the child will have to practice these skills. If the dates are not met, the parents must be informed. Obviously the dates you choose and the difficulty of the task will depend on the individual child.

*Choosing Activities.* The next step in the process is the most challenging. It involves choosing and adapting activities that meet the objectives you have set. You need to think in terms of the underlying principles of activities: Why do you use them in your program? As you implement the instructional objectives, remember:

1. Choose activities that use as many modalities as possible (vision, taste, touch, hearing, smell).
2. Choose several activities that reinforce the objective. Repetition helps children master a concept.
3. Use variety when presenting the same information. Color for example, can be shown through clothing, painting, bingo, gelatin, and nature walks, to name just a few.

Implementing objectives with regard to different exceptionalities is discussed in Chapters 6–15 of Part One.

*Completing the Form.* To complete the IEP form, you must write who is to carry out the objective. In most cases your name and your position (teacher) will be placed in those columns. Some objectives, however, will be the responsibility of specialists.

Both you and the parents or guardian sign each page of the completed IEP. Additions and changes made in the course of the year must also be signed for by all parties.

There are ten different IEPs in Part One; one at the end of each chapter on an exceptionality (6–15). The IEPs vary with exceptionality, age, and amount of involvement. All are preceded by a case study that gives information about the child, as well as sample test data.

## RECORD KEEPING

Good record keeping is indispensable for implementing an IEP for an exceptional child. You need accurate records documenting development or the lack of it in order to evaluate your program. Your record keeping will be partly informal—quick notes to yourself—and partly formal—a weekly or monthly report. This may sound like a lot of extra time and work, but once you establish a system, you will be amazed at your proficiency.

Notes kept throughout the week will help your memory, for example: 9/28 J. & Sally block 5 min. Weekly (or monthly) reports may be in outline or anecdote form. Outline form corresponds directly to the child's IEP. Numbers and key words identify the goals (1 Fine motor) and objectives (1.1 beads). The check, plus, and minus signs (see *key*) are also helpful shorthand for daily notes.

The second type of formal record keeping, anecdotal, is also based on the notes you take during the week or month.

There are advantages and disadvantages to each

**FIGURE 4-1.** Weekly Report (Outline)

| John H. | 9/15 | 10/15 | Evaluation criteria 11/15 |
|---|---|---|---|
| 1. Fine Motor | | | |
| 1.1 beads | ✓ − | ✓ − | 5 of 10 correct |
| 1.2 copy forms | ✓ − | ✓ + | 3 of 5 correct |
| 1.3 5 block tower | ✓ | ✓ | 4 blocks |
| | | | |
| 2. Language Concepts | | | |
| 2.1 colors | ✓ | ✓ | 5 of 8 receptive |
| 2.2 numbers | ✓ | ✓ + | 1-5 expressive |
| 2.3 prepositions | ✓ − | ✓ | on, under beside, in/recep. |

KEY:  NA  No attempt
  ✓ −  Attempted, little success
  ✓  Attempted, shows progress
  ✓ +  Attained criterion

**FIGURE 4–2.**   Weekly Report (Anecdotal)

```
John H.                          11/15/82
   Fine Motor: J. is still demonstrating
needs in this area. He can now build a
four-block tower and copy 3/5 (three out
of five) forms, including _____, ○, □.
Bead stringing is still very difficult
for J.
   Language: J.'s language quality has
improved since September. He is now
speaking in 4-5 word sentences and
nearly always expresses himself in full
sentences. He can identify 5/8 colors
and can recite the numbers 1-5. He can
follow a one-step direction containing
the following prepositions: on, under,
beside, in.
```

of these record-keeping methods and the decision to use or adapt one or the other will be based on personal preference. Of course, you may already have developed your own workable method.

## WORKING WITH SPECIALISTS

In the process of writing and implementing an IEP, you will be expected to work as part of an interdisciplinary team that includes specialists who may work with the child outside the classroom. Observe the child in therapy, if you can, or ask for a brief description and explanation of the activities that occur during therapy. The therapist can help you understand how a child's therapy needs will affect classroom behavior. Ask how you can carry out the therapist's goals in your classroom. Conversely, you can help the specialist understand what you are doing with the child and why. (For example, he or she may not have any idea why a housekeeping corner could be important.) Remember that a specialist is also a consultant. A child does not have to be in therapy to benefit from a specialist's knowledge.

The jargon specialists use is often difficult for others to understand. To confirm or clarify points, restate (in your own words) what the specialist said. Ask questions to further ensure that your interpretation is accurate. You will sometimes want to ask questions you already know the answers to, particularly on behalf of the parents. Misunderstandings will be prevented, to the benefit of the entire team.

### Major Specializations

Following are brief descriptions of specialists who provide some services you may encounter while teaching young children with special needs.

*Physical Therapist.*   The physical therapist is a state-licensed health professional who has completed an educational program accredited by the American Physical Therapy Association. The program, largely medically-based, includes the study of biological, physical, medical, and psychosocial sciences, as well as more in-depth course work in neurology, orthopedics, therapeutic exercises, and treatment techniques.

Physical therapy is actually directed toward preventing disability, that is, developing, improving, or restoring more efficient muscular functioning and maintaining maximum motor functioning for each patient. A physical therapist would most likely work with any child requiring prosthetic management training, wheelchair mobility training, or measurement for or use of other medically prescribed mobility devices. The physical therapist is also concerned with the child's gross motor skills and through exercises helps the child learn to move body parts more efficiently.

*Occupational Therapist.*   Occupational therapists work from a developmental rather than a medical base. They hold a degree from a school accredited by the American Occupational Therapy Association and the American Medical Association. Course work for this degree includes biological and psychosocial sciences, foundations of medicine, sensory integration, psychiatry, and prevocational skill development. Therapy is based on the age of the child in order to enhance his potential for learning. It emphasizes vestibular (balance as determined by the inner ear), tactile, kinesthetic (sensory knowledge of one's body movements), and perceptual motor (mental interpretation of sensation and movement based on these sensations) development; gross and fine motor coordination; and self-help skills. An occupational therapist may see children with the same special needs as are seen by a physical therapist.

*Speech and Language Therapist.*   A speech and language therapist is state licensed and has completed a degree program with a college accredited by the American Speech and Hearing Association (ASHA). A therapist working in the schools may or may not also hold a Certificate of Clinical Competency (C.C.C.), but a therapist in private practice is required to have this certificate in most states. The certificate is earned by working approximately three hundred clinical hours and passing a test. Course work includes psychology, education, and anatomy with an emphasis on speech and language development. Speech and language therapy is directed toward remediation of language disorders; it includes the development of both receptive and expressive language, the development of syntax and grammar, auditory processing, and articulation. Therapy can be either classroom or home based, individual or small group.

*School Psychologist.* A school psychologist is state certified and has completed either a bachelor, master, or doctoral degree in school psychology. Course work varies from state to state but may include psychology, counseling, standardized testing and its interpretation, child development, children with handicaps, and education. Most psychologists must complete an internship or praticum under a practicing psychologist. The duties of a psychologist in a school setting vary with the number of psychologists in the district and their individual skills.

Most school psychologists spend a great deal of time testing and observing children referred to them because of a suspected exceptionality. They must write the formal reports that are usually required to place children into any special education program. The psychologist may act as a consultant to the teacher or parents, which includes discussing test results or observations. Some psychologists emphasize individual therapy; they counsel either a child or a parent. Others make family therapy their primary function; they work with the child as part of the family unit.

Testing usually occurs in a small, quiet room where the child and psychologist are alone. At times parents stay with the child during evaluations. For the very young child, testing may take two, three, or even more sessions. If possible, the psychologist and child may get to know each other in the classroom prior to testing. Information provided by both parents and teacher is essential to the psychologist working with the very young child. Because children at this age can be uncooperative, the parents or teacher are sometimes asked if the child can perform tasks on the test.

The school psychologist tests children who are suspected of having an exceptionality. Federal law requires new testing and documentation of exceptional children every three years. These test results are helpful in measuring growth and planning programs for individual children, as well as in writing the IEP.

## WRITING THE IEP

Knowing in general how to fill out an IEP and actually doing it for a specific child are two different things. Full-time special educators and specialists who work only with exceptional children may have to write anywhere from eight to ninety IEPs a year, depending on their caseload. You may have to write only one or two. The specialists have usually received training in writing IEPs, and because they do it so often, they have developed a technique and aids that may include goal and objective checklists or data banks.

You, on the other hand, have this book. In the indexes at the end of each of Chapters 5–15 are the annual goals and activities that are most applicable for those needs discussed in the chapter. The activities used to implement these goals are a source of instructional objectives.

As we discussed earlier, when preparing for the IEP conference, you must organize your thoughts and ideas in writing. The following worksheet is designed to help you do this. It can be used for any child and is a valuable resource at an IEP meeting. Instead of shuffling through notes and reports, you will have one sheet of paper outlining the essential information you already have and pointing out information you need to obtain at the meeting.

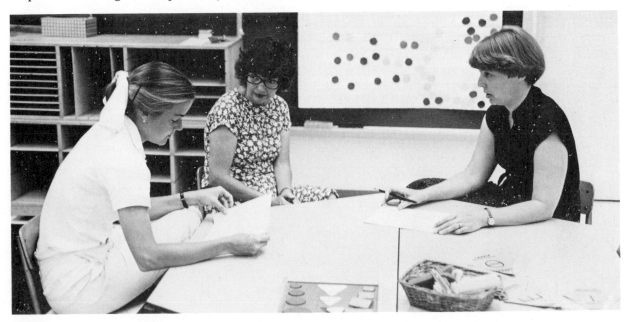

Parents, teachers, and specialists will work together to develop the IEP.

## IEP WORKSHEET

NAME _____   AGE _____

EXCEPTIONALITY _____

### TESTING/OBSERVATION RESULTS

*STRENGTHS*                                    *WEAKNESSES*

_____     _____

_____     _____

_____     _____

_____     _____

### PERSONAL INFORMATION

SPECIAL CONSIDERATIONS (Family, medication, etc.) _____

_____

*LIKES*                                         *DISLIKES*

_____     _____

_____     _____

_____     _____

**GENERAL**

---

PLACEMENT RECOMMENDATIONS _____

_____

*SKILL NEEDS*                                   *GOALS*

_____     1. _____

_____     2. _____

_____     3. _____

_____     4. _____

_____     5. _____

_____

_____

**SPECIFIC**

---

### PRELIMINARY OBJECTIVES FOR GOALS

1. _____

2. _____

3. _____

4. _____

5. _____

## Using the IEP Worksheet

We are going to demonstrate how to fill in an IEP worksheet. Our sources of information are three reports on tests and observations of a child. In the following pages are reports by a psychologist, an occupational therapist, and a child study team on a child, Joanna P. The reports are typical of those you may receive about a child. They illustrate neither extremely good nor bad reports, but are simply average. The reports throughout this book are adaptations or composites of actual cases, making them good general examples of the reports you can actually expect to receive.

The child study team report consolidates the information obtained at a meeting of the child study team—the specialists who have evaluated the child, and sometimes the parents and teachers. Although the name of this group may vary, its functions are to: (1) interpret test results, (2) relate its interpretations to observations of the child, (3) determine the significance of the data for the child's education, and (4) recommend teaching strategies.

## PSYCHOLOGICAL EVALUATION

STUDENT: Joanna P.

DATE OF BIRTH: 8/2/77

EXAMINER: Mrs. F.
School Psychologist

DATE OF EVALUATION:
2/10/82

AGE: 4.6

REASON FOR REFERRAL:
Unpredictable behaviors (varies between physical aggression and withdrawal). Poor peer relationships.

PROCEDURES USED:
Peabody Picture Vocabulary Test (PPVT), Form A
McCarthy Scales of Children's Abilities (MSCA)
Observational Data (classroom observation)

## BACKGROUND OBSERVATION:

This four-and-a-half year old girl was referred for a psychological evaluation by her Headstart teacher, who felt her behavior was "agressive at times and withdrawn at other times." An occupational therapist's evaluation was also recommended by this examiner and has been completed, with therapy prescribed. It is reported that Joanna is an asthmatic who has attacks when she is upset. It is also reported that she may feign attacks on occasion. The family has moved three times in the past two years.

A classroom observation by this examiner was conducted prior to testing. Some aggression noted by this examiner seemed to occur immediately following activities that may have been frustrating for Joanna. One example: After being unable to snap a doll's dress in the housekeeping corner, Joanna hit another child and proceeded to cry. A contrast to this behavior was seen on the day examinations were administered, when Joanna's mother brought her to this examiner's office.

Rapport was quickly established. She separated easily from her mother, offering her hand and a shy smile. The quality and intelligibility of her speech were good, but she spoke very little spontaneously. Near the end of the evaluation, she said "I want my mommy" several times. When allowed to see her mother, she immediately returned to the testing area quite happily. She did begin to tire, however, as the testing drew to a close. She became so tired that, when her mother was talking afterward, she fell sound asleep on the mother's lap.

Joanna was generally cooperative and attentive throughout testing.

## INTELLECTUAL FUNCTIONING:

As measured by the PPVT, this little girl's receptive vocabulary is at a "high average" level, being equivalent to that of a child of 5.0 years. Her general cognitive ability, as assessed by the McCarthy Scales, is equivalent to that of a child of 4.0 years, a delay of six months. Her most highly developed skills are in verbal expression and understanding. Quantitative and memory skills fall within the average range. Her perceptual performance and motor skills are lower, falling in the borderline range. Her relational thinking ability is at a "high average" level as measured on the Opposite Analogies subtest, being equivalent to that of a child of five years ten months. Her ability to count and sort blocks is "average." Her memory skills and understanding of quantitative words are "average."

## CONCLUSIONS AND RECOMMENDATIONS:

Although this child's general level of functioning at the present time is only equivalent to the mental age of a child of 4.0 years, there is evidence that her intellectual potential may be higher. Her perception of spatial relationships and her manipulative skills, rated on the Block Building subtest are her least developed abilities. These learning disabilities could be dealt with in a prekindergarten program with occupational therapy included.

In addition, it is recommended that Joanna participate in counseling in order to enhance her peer relationships and help her deal with frustration more effectively.

Mrs. F.
Psychologist

# OCCUPATIONAL THERAPY EVALUATION

NAME: Joanna P.

EXAMINER: Mr. M.
Occupational Therapist

DATE OF BIRTH: 8/2/77

DATE OF EVALUATION:
2/16/82

AGE: 4.6

Joanna P. was seen for an occupational therapy evaluation, as recommended by a psychologist. Scores from a recent psychological examination indicate weakness in motor skills and perceptual performance.

Joanna P. was brought to the evaluation by her mother. She went readily with the examiner. During the evaluation she tended to wander from the task and had to be repeatedly refocused to the testing. She exhibited some testing behavior, such as scratching her nails on the blackboard and then looking to the examiner for a reaction. Joanna worked best with manipulative materials.

The examiner administered a developmental assessment and the Developmental Test of Visual Motor Integration.

and all graphic reproductions were shifted to the right side of the paper—further evidence of inadequate flexibility. Gross motor planning was found to be adequate.

Fine motor planning activities, such as tapping sequence, were stressful for Joanna. Joanna was able to use both sides of the body together in a coordinated fashion.

During block manipulation tasks, Joanna was able to build a cube bridge and a tower of nine blocks (36-month skills). She was unable to copy an oblique bridge (42-month skill).

Visual motor performance was at the 26-month level, a year below age expectancy. Visual-perceptual performance was also below Joanna's chronological age. She is beginning to use insight to nest and stack rings and blocks. She was unable to nest cans or tower blocks (36- and 42-month skills). She was able to sort blocks according to big–little (42-month skill).

Joanna holds a pencil high on the shaft and does not have a refined, adultlike grasp.

## RESULTS:

Joanna's performance on the tactile portion of the developmental assessment indicated that she has awareness of touch and pressure input and can localize tactile input (for example, she knows which finger is touched). Joanna was able to identify correctly four out of four basic textures.

Joanna's gross motor performance was found to vary from that of a three- to four-year-old. Response to vestibular input was within normal limits, but Joanna fell off the nystagnius board following rotation. This response suggests that Joanna has difficulty stabilizing her body in dynamic movement experiences. Joanna tended to use each hand on the same side of the body, suggesting inadequate postural flexibility or difficulty in crossing the midline. For drawing tests, Joanna preferred her right hand,

## SUMMARY
## AND RECOMMENDATIONS:

Joanna's sensorimotor needs include the following:

1. Improve postural stability and flexibility
2. Improve fine motor planning
3. Improve visual-perceptual performance

Occupational therapy is suggested to meet these needs.

Joanna can be easily engaged in an activity and just as easily distracted. It is recommended that she be placed in an extremely structured program that will provide firm behavioral controls.

Mr. M., O.T.R.
Occupational Therapist

## CHILD STUDY TEAM REPORT*

### Joanna P.

In attendance: Mrs. F., psychologist; Mr. M., occupational therapist; Mrs. P., mother; Ms. R., preschool teacher.

Joanna P. is a *four-and-a-half year old girl* who recently moved to this suburban area from a rural setting. Joanna's father has obtained a job as a salesman with a local firm. Prior to this, Joanna's *family moved quite often,* three times in the past two years, as Mr. P. was transferred frequently.

Records from Joanna's former preschool identify her as *learning disabled with secondary social and emotional problems.* Joanna also has *asthma.* Joanna does not have a current IEP, but testing was completed. The report in the file states that Joanna was referred because of extreme *moodiness* and frequent *physical agression.* Observations by the school psychologist and by the teacher confirm this, reporting both *elation or withdrawal from day to day.* The psychological report notes that Joanna is *easily frustrated* and frequently *cries* and throws *temper tantrums* when she cannot do something. One example is a temper tantrum after Joanna could not snap a doll's dress in the housekeeping corner.

Testing was completed by the psychologist in one session, during which Joanna was cooperative and attentive. Aptitude testing identifies Joanna as being *average in ability* with some variation in test scores. *Pencil and paper tasks and those requiring concentration (such as block designs and motor skills) are more difficult for Joanna.* She seems to *enjoy* more *verbal* subtests, *such as vocabulary and even digit span* (repeating digits presented orally).

Joanna was referred by the psychologist for an occupational therapy evaluation. During this evaluation session, Joanna was *slightly more resistive. Tactile development and gross motor planning were adequate, while gross and fine motor performance and visual motor performance were below age level. Occupational therapy was recommended.*

Joanna, according to her former teacher's reports, was *frequently absent* from school. (She had several asthma attacks at school, which seemed to increase in frequency when Joanna learned the family was moving.) The *other children generally did not respond well* to Joanna due to her unpredictable behavior, and because they did not want to provoke an asthma attack. Joanna *feigned attacks when she didn't get her way* with the other children. Joanna *enjoyed one-to-one attention* from *adults* and *older children.* She worked best in a *small group* and needed a lot of *verbal praise and affection.* The teacher felt Joanna needed to learn ways to *express frustration, anger, and fear.* She also felt Joanna needed to develop *healthy peer relationships.* Based on the preschool teacher's observations as well as her own, the psychologist recommended *small group counseling* for Joanna.

Joanna lives at home with her father, mother, older sister, and younger brother. Mr. P. plans to remain in the area longer than his previous job allowed.

Now that you have a little more information about Joanna, filling out the form will be easier. The top portion is relatively easy.

After filling out this section of the form, you can easily see that this child has as many nonclinical "special considerations" as she has tested clinical needs. And although you have a general idea of Joanna's low frustration level, you could benefit from information on what she specifically dislikes.

The next section of the worksheet requires more of your knowledge and experience as an educator of young children. Looking back at the weaknesses under "Testing/Observation," you can determine some skills needing improvement. Your task is to translate the report's jargon into your own, for example:

Visual-motor skills: eye-hand coordination
Gross motor–fine motor: large and small muscle
  coordination
Easily frustrated: poor self-concept

From "Personal Information," you can assume two things about Joanna. First, she does not have good peer relationships; and second, because of the family moves and her illness, she feels she doesn't have much control over her environment. These can also be interpreted like so:

Poor peer relationships: increase feelings of group
  belonging

---

* The italicized comments in the Child Study Team Report are key words or phrases that apply to Joanna's IEP. Highlighting the report with a transparent colored marker will help you to locate pertinent data quickly when you fill out the IEP worksheet.

```
┌─────────────────────────────────────────────────────────────────────────────┐
│                            IEP WORKSHEET                                      │
├──────────────────────────────────────────────────────────────────────┬──────┤
```

**IEP WORKSHEET**

NAME _____ JOANNA P. _____ AGE _____ 4.6 _____

EXCEPTIONALITY Social/Emotional Maladjustment (Asthma) _____

### TESTING/OBSERVATION RESULTS

| *STRENGTHS* | *WEAKNESSES* |
|---|---|
| Verbal (vocabulary) | Easily frustrated |
| Expressive language | Visual-motor |
| Memory (auditory) | Gross motor |
| | Fine motor |

### PERSONAL INFORMATION

SPECIAL CONSIDERATIONS (Family, medication, etc.) Family moved a lot; other children avoid her; medication for asthma (has feigned attacks).

| *LIKES* | *DISLIKES* |
|---|---|
| One-to-one attention | |
| Verbal praise from adults | |

*(Right margin vertical label: G E N E R A L)*

Little control over environment: needs to increase awareness of feelings and to express feelings

Thus far, the "specific" half of the worksheet looks like the one shown.

The next step is to write the goals, which should reflect the needs. First, generate from five to ten goals for Joanna; second, try to consolidate them; finally, eliminate some and rank the remainder.

To improve large motor coordination

To improve eye-hand coordination
To improve small motor coordination

To improve self-concept
To increase feelings of group belonging
To increase awareness of feelings
To express feelings

PLACEMENT RECOMMENDATIONS ___ Headstart, small group counseling, ___ occupational therapy

| *SKILL NEEDS* | *GOALS* |
|---|---|
| eye-hand coordination; | 1. To improve eye-hand coordination |
| large and small muscle | 2. To increase feelings of group belonging |
| coordination; self-concept; | 3. To increase awareness of feelings |
| group belonging; awareness of | 4. _____ |
| feelings; expression of | 5. _____ |
| feelings | |

*(Right margin vertical label: S P E C I F I C)*

The grouped goals have similarities and can be consolidated. Eye-hand coordination and fine motor coordination may incorporate some of the same objectives.

The last four are all related to improving Joanna's social skills. Although your judgment may differ, I would eliminate "self-concept" and consolidate awareness and expression of feelings. My reasoning for this is that Joanna's needs seem to stem from her inability to express herself rather than simply from her poor self-concept, and that teaching her alternatives to temper tantrums and feigned asthma attacks will, in effect, help to solve the problem of poor self-concept. After Joanna becomes aware of her feelings, alternate ways of expressing those feelings can be more easily taught. Therefore, the goal "To express feelings" is better added to the IEP later. In addition, I have chosen to eliminate "small motor" and "large motor" in order to concentrate on the three most important goals. In the normal cause of events, Joanna will be given a more than adequate number of opportunities to practice small and large motor coordination in occupational therapy and with her peers.

The *Goals* section of the IEP worksheet now reads:

1. To improve eye-hand coordination
2. To increase feelings of group belonging
3. To increase awareness of feelings

Under "Preliminary Objectives," the last section of the IEP worksheet, you should jot down ideas about skill levels, activities, and ways of measuring progress. At the IEP conference, these may be assigned to the IEP headings "objectives," "educational services," and "evaluation." It is here that you need to be knowledgeable about the skill levels and abilities of different age groups. For example, the psychologist testing Joanna found her abilities to be average, while the occupational therapist found her slightly below average in eye-hand coordination. You have to know what skills or tasks an *average* four-year-old would be capable of in order to know what Joanna needs. Child development texts are the best source for this information. A brief summary of some typical development patterns is included at the end of this chapter. The preliminary objective for goal 3, for example, is simply a description of the age-appropriate tasks:

3 (group belonging): Group of 2–4; 20–30 min. attn. span; needs adult approval—wants to do things "right."

These are legitimate expectations for an average four-year-old.

Now you are prepared for the IEP conference. The actual IEP should be filled out at the conference. An example of what might finally result follows.

| PRELIMINARY OBJECTIVES FOR GOALS |
|---|
| 1. _____ |
| 2. _____ |
| 3. (group belonging): Group of 2-4; 20-30 min. attn. span; needs adult approval--wants to do things "right." _____ |
| 4. _____ |

# INDIVIDUALIZED EDUCATION PROGRAM

NAME ___Joanna P.___ DOB _8_ / _2_ / _77_

AGE ___4–6___ GRADE ___Preschool___

SCHOOL ___Upland Day School___

PARENTS/GUARDIANS ___Mr. & Mrs. P.___

ADDRESS ___14–C Holly Hill Apts.___

PHONE ___626–2888___

On _2/30/82_, the IPRD Committee
___(Date)___
met to review all current data and

recommends Level __I__ placement.

Date of next review ___2/30/83___

Exceptionality: ___Social/Emotional Maladjustment___

Present at meeting:

Parents ___Mrs. P.___

Others: Name/Position _____ / _____

## CURRENT TEST DATA

TEST/DATE/RESULTS

MSCA ___/ 2/82 /___ Some variation in test scores; strengths
___/ ___ /___ in verbal; area-weaknesses in perceptual,
___/ ___ /___ visual, motor.
O.T. Eval. _2/16/82_ / Therapy recommended to improve postural
___/ ___ /___ and visual-perceptual and motor performance.

Recommended Special Services (Hrs/Wk):

Occupational therapy ___ / ___ 1 x/wk. (30 min.)

Small group counsel ___ / ___ 1 x/wk. (30 min.)

___ / ___ / ___

Total Hours/Week:

Special Education Classroom __.5__

Regular Classroom __11.5__

(Child Study Team held at former preschool.)

Representative of District/Agency ___Ms. L., Teacher___

___ / ___

The committee has determined the following learning strengths and needs to be reflected in the IEP:

| STRENGTHS | | NEEDS | |
|---|---|---|---|
| Verbal abilities | Tactile skills | Visual-perceptual skills | |
| Attentive during one-to-one | Auditory memory | Acceptable emotional | |
| activity | | responses | |
| Vocabulary | | | |

STUDENT    Joanna P.        DATE     2/30/82

GOAL    To improve eye–hand coordination

PARENT SIGNATURE           TEACHER SIGNATURE

| INSTRUCTIONAL OBJECTIVES | EDUCATIONAL METHODS | DATE Begin | DATE End | Eval. | PERSONS RESPONSIBLE Name | Position |
|---|---|---|---|---|---|---|
| Given a choice of art medium of wire, clay, or string, Joanna will complete three projects to take home. | Salt Putty Beads, String Mobile, String Painting, Wire Sculpture, Clay | 2/30 | 4/30 | | Ms. L. | Teacher |
| Given a target 5' away, Joanna will hit the target with a beanbag in 4/5 trials. | Noisy Toss, Variations on Throwing | 2/30 | 6/30 | | Ms. L. | Teacher |
| Joanna will be able to build a block structure with 1" cube blocks piled at least 5 high. | Cuisenaire Rods, Block play | 2/30 | 6/30 | | Ms. L. | Teacher |
| Joanna will be able to cut simple shapes (○, □, △, □, ◯) from construction paper. | Torn Paper Flowers, Letter Collage, Eye–Hair Collage | 2/30 | 6/30 | | Ms. L. | Teacher |

STUDENT _____ Joanna P. _____ DATE _____ 2/30/82 _____

GOAL _____ To increase feelings of group belonging _____

PARENT SIGNATURE _____

TEACHER SIGNATURE _____

| INSTRUCTIONAL OBJECTIVES | EDUCATIONAL METHODS | DATE Begin | DATE End | Eval. | PERSONS RESPONSIBLE Name | Position |
|---|---|---|---|---|---|---|
| Joanna will actively participate in large group lessons 4/5 days per week. | My Day, My Song, Parachute Games, Puppets, Music | 2/30 | 6/30 | | Ms. L. | Teacher |
| Joanna will actively participate in structured outdoor games with at least 3 other children 3/5 days per week. | Seesaw, Noisy Toss, Parachute Games | 2/30 | 4/30 | | Ms. L. | Teacher |
| Joanna will participate in unstructured free play with 3–4 other children for 15 min. each day. | Blocks, Dramatic play, Housekeeping | 2/30 | 6/30 | | Ms. L. | Teacher |

STUDENT  Joanna P.

GOAL  To increase awareness of feelings

PARENT SIGNATURE _____

TEACHER SIGNATURE _____

DATE  2/30/82

| INSTRUCTIONAL OBJECTIVES | EDUCATIONAL METHODS | Begin | End | Eval. | Name | Position |
|---|---|---|---|---|---|---|
| Joanna will be able to identify pictures of children and adults depicting the following feelings: sad, happy, angry, frightened, worried, with 80% accuracy. | Matching Expressions, Matching Faces | 2/30 | 4/30 | | Ms. L. | Teacher |
| Given an art medium, Joanna will be able to create 5 pictures that represent events that make her feel: happy, frustrated, excited, scared, angry. | My Book, My Puzzle, Best and Worst, Easy/Hard, Peek Pictures | 2/30 | 6/30 | | Ms. L. | Teacher |
| Joanna will be able to describe the pictures to one peer and one adult, using 3–4 word sentences. | | 2/30 | 6/30 | | Ms. L. | Teacher |

Column groups: DATE (Begin, End); PERSONS RESPONSIBLE (Name, Position)

## Summary of Development

| | 18–24 MONTHS | 24–36 MONTHS |
|---|---|---|
| MOTOR DEVELOPMENT | Hand coordination is increasingly steady—can build tower of six or seven blocks.<br>Climbs into adult chair.<br>Runs with good coordination, wide stance.<br>Climbs stairs, using rail.<br>Uses body actively in mastering and exploring surroundings—an active age.<br>Scribbles with crayon in imitation of adults' strokes on paper. | Shows strong interest in investigating the functions and details of household objects.<br>Will imitate simple large motor movements, such as jumping, running, and walking.<br>Can control rate of large motor movements, such as fast running, slow walking.<br>Can follow simple directions with body parts, such as putting hands up high, touching knees, sitting down, standing up.<br>Enjoys variety of large motor activities. Cannot stay with one activity too long.<br>Beginning to show interest in sensory materials, such as sand, paints, clay; but needs supervision for use. |
| LANGUAGE-CONCEPT DEVELOPMENT | Uses two-word sentences.<br>Has vocabulary of 20 to 50 words.<br>Begins to use "me," "I," and "you."<br>Follows simple directions.<br>Listens to simple stories.<br>Says the names of familiar objects in pictures.<br>Begins to play pretend games.<br>Recognizes body parts on a doll.<br>Identifies parts of own body.<br>Likes parents' possessions and play that mimics parents' behavior and activities. | Can name many objects.<br>Begins to grasp meaning of numbers.<br>Memory span is longer.<br>Ability to reason, solve problems, make comparison develops.<br>Grasps concepts of color, form, and space.<br>Uses language as a way of communicating thoughts and developing social relationships.<br>Enjoys using language, gains satisfaction from expressing self and being understood.<br>Understands and uses abstract words such as up, down, now, later. |

| THREE YEARS | FOUR YEARS | FIVE YEARS |
|---|---|---|
| Sure and steady in walk. (Has lost "toddler sway.")<br><br>Can run smoothly with moderate speed. Has ability to start and stop quickly, turn corners, change rate of speed.<br><br>Jumps and climbs with coordination.<br><br>Learns to ride tricycle with great skill.<br><br>Alternates feet going upstairs and still "marks time" descending.<br><br>Is interested in using fine motor skills for short periods. (Puzzles, blocks, painting, screwing things together, hammering, fitting one thing inside another.)<br><br>Independent in routines. Feeds self with fork with little spilling. Washes face and hands, buttons large front or side buttons. Undressing with more ease than dressing.<br><br>Often attempts activities that are beyond abilities and needs close supervision for safety. | Very active and growing rapidly. Beginning a variety of movements including skipping, jumping, running, walking, climbing, hopping—frequent changes of position.<br><br>Cannot sit still comfortably for more than five minutes.<br><br>Can control arm, body, and leg muscles much better than hands and feet. (Needs large materials for work and play.)<br><br>Tumbles and twirls for sheer pleasure.<br><br>When overactive and irritable, may be fatigued or getting sick. | Has good control of arms and legs, so enjoys activities that will strengthen these large muscles—running, jumping, skipping, dancing, climbing, using tricycles, wagons, and large balls.<br><br>Has only fair control of the small muscles of hands and feet (e.g., has difficulty lacing or tying shoe laces).<br><br>Is noisy and active with a sense of purpose in activity.<br><br>Is interested in the activity rather than in the result or what is made. |
| Beginning to be interested in people other than self and close family group.<br><br>High interest in learning about world by sensory exploration.<br><br>Vocabulary increasing rapidly. Loves new words.<br><br>Still talks to self while playing—but language becomes more and more socially directed.<br><br>Beginning to ask many questions for information and for making social contacts.<br><br>Play becomes more imaginative.<br><br>Concepts of distance, space, height, and weight are still limited. Therefore close supervision still required.<br><br>Shows increased creativity in use of raw materials. Crude elements of design begin to appear. The *doing* is still more important than the product.<br><br>Enjoys stories, poetry, rhymes.<br><br>Average attention span may be as long as 8–12 minutes for an activity of own choice. | Can make decisions. Needs time for deciding which socks to wear or which book to read.<br><br>Can think things through by self or in a group.<br><br>Can explain why he or she wants to do something a certain way.<br><br>Developing a longer attention span.<br><br>Can carry out simple commands.<br><br>Has a vivid imagination and can pretend well, using themes from favorite books, dress-up objects, clay, paint, and blocks.<br><br>Talks a lot—not always to tell or ask something important, but to seek attention and companionship.<br><br>Does not understand money values. Doing or making something for others is more important than giving money or things purchased with money. | Has a beginning interest in own community. (Should have trips to the store, firehouse, library, bakery.) Likes association with adults.<br><br>Is curious and asks many questions about things.<br><br>Is ready for facts, not fiction. Often asks, "Is it true?"<br><br>Thinks of object words in terms of what they do, such as "a spoon is to eat with" and "a wagon is to ride."<br><br>Can usually print first name, count by ones, distinguish traffic signals by their color, name colors and pieces of money, and identify some cars and airplanes.<br><br>Is ready to learn the beginning of safety habits.<br><br>Can use complete sentences and give full information; thus needs opportunities to talk with someone who is interested and who will listen attentively. |

| | 18–24 MONTHS *(Cont.)* | 24–36 MONTHS *(Cont.)* |
|---|---|---|
| SOCIAL-EMOTIONAL DEVELOPMENT | Follows simple directions.<br>Controls others, orders them around.<br>Tests, fights, resists adults when they oppose or force him to do something.<br>Increasingly able to differentiate between people.<br>Takes a more self-sufficient attitude, challenges parents' desires, wants to "do it myself."<br>Sense of self-importance is intense—protests, wants to make own choices.<br>Desires to be independent, feed self, put on articles of own clothing.<br>Shows intense positive or negative reactions.<br>Likes to please others, is affectionate.<br>Shows some aggressive tendencies—slaps, bites, hits.<br>Shows greater desire to engage in problem solving and more persistence in doing so.<br>Develops triumphant delight and pride in own actions.<br>Becomes frustrated easily. | Tests own limits in situations involving other people.<br>Says "no" but submits anyway.<br>Shows trust and love.<br>Enjoys wider range of relationships and experiences, enjoys meeting many people other than parents.<br>Becomes aware of self as a separate person, can contrast self with another.<br>Expresses preferences strongly.<br>Expresses pride in achievement.<br>Values own property.<br>Expresses confidence in own activities.<br>Begins to respect and obey rules.<br>Strives for mastery over objects.<br>Can tolerate more frustration, more willing to accept a substitute for forbidden objects.<br>Shows strong desire for independence in actions.<br>Gradually channels aggressive tendencies into more constructive activities.<br>Uses language to express wishes and feelings toward others.<br>Shows a developing sense of humor at surprises, unusual actions, etc. |

| THREE YEARS *(Cont.)* | FOUR YEARS *(Cont.)* | FIVE YEARS *(Cont.)* |
|---|---|---|
| Showing more awareness of and interest in other people. | Still enjoys being independent, but begins to seek the companionship of other children. When with one or two compatible friends, will exclude others from this group. | Is able to concentrate in quiet activity for twenty to thirty minutes. |
| Quickly tires or is overstimulated by a group. Plays best with one other child, much of the time in parallel play. | | Needs quiet times to balance active periods. |
| Still likes and needs to play alone. | | Home is still of major importance. |
| Beginning to form friendships. By the age of three-and-a-half, may have "best" friend although these friendships may shift quickly. | Has a strong feeling for home and family. Talks freely about what happens at home. | Can begin to enjoy younger sister and brother more than before. |
| Indicates insecurity in social relationships by discriminating against those who are not the "best" friend. | Is often jealous, particularly of brothers and sisters. | Wants to conform—to do things "right," to act as others act. Often asks for adult approval and support. |
| Better understanding of concepts of sharing, and taking turns. Still finds these hard to do. | Talks "big"—brags, boasts, threatens. Is not as brave inwardly as he or she sounds, but is feeling own powers and trying them out. | Has a good sense of fair play, but still quarrels and fights on occasion. |
| Learning to ask for things rather than just grabbing them. | Wants to be liked by adults and often seeks attention by showing off. | Wants to help adults, but resists things that are too difficult, rather than being challenged by them as he or she will be when older. |
| Quite cooperative with adults. Seems to want to please and conform. Some by three-and-a-half may enter more negative period again. | Some four-year-olds still resist authority by withdrawal from the group by hitting, pushing, and saying "I won't." | Wants to do what the rest of the group does. |
| Can be reasoned with because verbal ability has improved as well as ability to understand what others say. | | Can work in a group of two to four children, as well as with one child. |
| Striving to be independent, to prove that he or she is big, but still very much needing to know an adult's support and affection are available. | | |
| If things don't go own way, may get upset, but temper outbursts are less frequent, less violent, and recovered from more quickly. | | |
| May show anger by name calling, by saying, "I don't like you!", rather than by striking out physically. | | |

# BIBLIOGRAPHY

Arena, John. *How to Write an I. E. P.* Novato, Calif.: Academic Therapy Publications, 1978.

Cross, Lee, and Kenneth Goin, eds. *Finding and Helping Handicapped Children: A Guide to Casefinding, Screening, Diagnosis, Assessment, and Evaluation.* New York: Walker and Co., 1977.

Lillie, David L. *Early Childhood Education: An Individualized Approach to Developmental Instruction.* Chicago: Science Research Associates, 1975.

Mori, Allen A. and Jane E. Olive. *Handbook of Preschool Special Education: Programming, Curriculum, Training.* Rockville, Md.: Aspen Systems Corp., 1980.

Neisworth, John T., Sara J. Willoughby-Herb, Stephen J. Bagnato, Carol A. Cartwright, and Karen Laub. *Individualized Education for Preschool Exceptional Children.* Rockville, Md.: Aspen Systems Corp., 1980.

Petrone, Fred R. *The Developmental Kindergarten: Individualized Instruction Through Diagnostic Grouping.* Springfield, Ill.: C. C. Thomas, 1976.

"Report from Closer Look." Parents Campaign for Handicapped Children and Youth. Box 1492, Washington, DC 20013. This is a free publication published several times a year.

U.S. Department of Health, Education, and Welfare. Office of Education. *Progress Toward a Free Appropriate Public Education: A Report to Congress on the Implementation of Public Law 94-142: The Education for All Handicapped Children Act.* HEW Pub. No. (OE) 79-05003. January 1979.

U.S. Department of Education. *"To Assure the Free Appropriate Public Education of All Handicapped Children."* Second Annual Report to Congress on the Implementation of Public Law 94-142: The Education for All Handicapped Children Act, 1980.

# Working with Parents

Children with special needs are children first, impaired children second. In the same way, the parents of these children are parents first, and parents of an exceptional child second. You probably don't need special techniques for working with those parents—use the techniques that are a part of your repertoire already. However, telling parents that their child has a problem can sometimes be difficult. We are going to discuss techniques to use when you tell parents information that they do not want to hear.

## BROACHING PROBLEMS

If someone told you your new car had just been hit in the parking lot and was now on fire, what would you say? "It can't be my car. Are you sure? How can this happen to me?"

Such reactions are not unlike those of parents when they learn something may be wrong with their child. Their first response is a denial. "That can't be true. He'll grow out of it. I'd like another opinion." These responses are normal and natural. They are our way of gaining time to absorb the information and to prepare ourselves to deal with the problem. Such a pattern of parental response has special meaning to you, the teacher. Some parents deny information longer than others. You will have to work differently with parents who deny their child is impaired or potentially impaired than with parents who have accepted the exceptionality. To complicate the situation, each parent may react differently to the information. You need to be very careful not to

get in the middle or to appear to be taking sides. You are not a trained psychological counselor. Your goal in working with parents is to get the best possible education for their children, not to help the parents emotionally accept a diagnosis.

No one wants to be the bearer of bad news, but your role in the early diagnosis of children is a crucial one. You need to develop confidence in your ability to determine when a child's needs require special techniques. You then need to convince the parents of the validity of your concerns in such a way that they will seek a formal diagnosis. A delay in detection and programming penalizes a child. Teachers have an awesome responsibility for both obtaining a diagnosis and informing the parents.

I have found the following three techniques most useful in initially discussing negative information.

### Reinforcement

*Reinforcement* is more than saying nice things about people and what they do (Satir, 1972). As a technique it can help build good working relationships with parents. When parents who are separating tell you how they have explained this to their children, you respond, "I'm really glad you took the time to tell me how you have discussed the separation with the children. It makes it easier for me to answer the questions that arise in class." Your response does not mean you necessarily agree or disagree with what they have told their children. It means you are glad to know *what* they told them. You are reinforcing the sharing of information.

When you reinforce others, be specific about what

it is you are citing. You might have said, "I'm really glad you took the time to tell me *this*." Spell out what *this* is. You need to specify what the behavior is that you appreciate and want to continue.

If you had to persuade the person to give you information, you may now feel you should be thanked for your perseverance rather than expected to praise the other person! The technique may seem awkward or unnatural at first, but the results—warm, effective working relationships—are worthwhile.

## Broken Record

*Broken record* is a technique of persistence that is especially useful when parents deny something is wrong (Smith, 1975). When paired with reinforcement, it is an effective way of gaining information or compliance. It involves coming back to an issue again and again until it is resolved.

A conversation using the broken record technique is illustrated below.

*Teacher:* I have been watching Kenneth, and he seems like one of the youngest children in the class to me, yet he is really one of the oldest. He is often restless during group time, he has problems putting pegs in the pegboard, and he hasn't yet learned his colors and shapes. Have you noticed this at home?

*Parent:* Well, you know he's an only child and hasn't played with other children very much. He's probably just shy.

*(The parents just gave you an easy out that is tempting, but if you are really concerned, you need to keep pressing.)*

*Teacher:* Although Kenneth was shy at the beginning of the year, now he seems to be quite comfortable in the class. However, he still does not seem to be learning as fast as the other children.

*Parent:* Well, we've read that boys are always slower at things like school, and he's "all boy."

*(Again, they have given you a way out. They don't want to hear what you are saying any more than you want to say it. Don't judge them as being unobservant, unconcerned, or negligent, but rather as being normal—persist.)*

*Teacher:* I agree that boys often have more small motor problems than girls do at this age; however, he has more problems than the other boys his age do as well. I would really like you to come in and observe your son. I am genuinely concerned about him.

*Parent:* You are the best teacher Kenneth has ever had. He likes you, and he likes school for a change. I'm not sure I really want you to change anything.

*(If at this point you feel that you are getting nowhere, you are right. You want the parents to be concerned about Kenneth's developmental prog-*

*ress. It is difficult for parents who think their child is actually developing normally, or even for those who think there may be something wrong, to absorb all your information in a short conference. Their behavior is healthy, not obstinate. You have just planted a seed; it needs time to germinate. But don't give up, take another approach.)*

*Teacher:* Thank you. I really like Kenneth too. Perhaps that is why I'm so concerned about him. Maybe at this point the best thing would be for the three of us to watch Kenneth carefully for two weeks. I'll watch him at school, where perhaps you could join me one day, and you can watch at home so that we can decide whether Kenneth is behaving about the same way in both places. Then we can meet again at the end of the two weeks to talk about our observations and see where we are. How does that sound to you?

*Parent:* OK, but I'm really not sure all this is necessary.

*Teacher:* I really feel it is necessary, and it would make Kenneth feel very special for you to come to class. He has often said that he wishes you could see what he does in school.

*Parent:* Well, I guess we can arrange it.

*Teacher:* Good, what day will be the best for you? We are going on a field trip Tuesday, but any other day next week is fine.

*Parent:* I'm not sure, maybe we should think about this a bit more.

*Teacher:* I agree we need to think about it, and I think careful observation would really help us make some plans. Would next Thursday be a good day?

*Parent:* Well, maybe I should call you and let you know.

*Teacher:* Why don't we set the date for Thursday at 1:00, and then if you must change that, call me. And once we've observed Kenneth together, we'll meet to discuss our observations in two weeks.

*Parent:* I guess so.

*Teacher:* Thanks so much for coming. Kenneth is really lucky to have concerned parents like you.

*(It was a bit tedious, but you persisted and were a marvelous example of a broken record. When the parents backed off or avoided the subject, you continuously sought your goal, only modifying your responses according to their statements and current attitude.)*

## Verbal Cues

Most of us have a preferred way of learning (Cameron-Bandler, 1978). For some people, this is visual; for others, auditory; and for some, tactile. In other words, we prefer to receive information through one of our senses rather than others. These preferred modalities are important in communicating with people, especially under stressful conditions, as people will often stay in their preferred modality under stress. If you do not match the modality of the people you are communicating with,

Auditory people may tune you out.
Visual people will not picture what you are discussing.
Tactile people cannot get a feel for what is going on.

To reach people effectively, you need to develop an awareness of their preferred way of communicating and to match yours to theirs. Some complex ways of doing this are quite successful, but they require training. There is a simplified approach that may work for you.

Listen to the parents as they talk and note mentally key words that may give you some indication of which sense they favor in receiving and giving information. Words like *think* and *know* are not useful indicators.

| *Auditory* | *Visual* | *Tactile* |
|------------|----------|-----------|
| Listen | See | Touch |
| Hear | Picture | Feel |
| Say | Colored | Rough |
| Tune | View | Warm |
| Talk | Scope | Reach |
| Ask | | Hard |

After you have made a guess about the preferred modality, match your choice of words to the parents'.

Visual:

> *Parent:* I can't really *picture* Stan as having a handicap.
> *Teacher:* How do you *see* him?

Auditory:

> *Parent:* I just get tired of *listening* to these doctors go on and on.
> *Teacher:* After a while it is difficult to *hear* what they're *saying*.

Tactile:

> *Parent:* I *feel* so out of *touch* with the world right now.
> *Teacher:* It's *hard* to *feel* that way.

By matching the modality that people use and using similar terminology, you make it easier for them to talk to you. Remember, too, that each parent may well have a different preferred modality—good communication is a challenge.

### Ending the First Conference

While each of the three techniques is useful, they do not ensure immediate success. Parents rarely come right out and say they do not believe what you are telling them. Rather, they make statements from which you may extrapolate that they are unconvinced.

A home visit can be useful.

"All the boys in our family talk late."
"Oh, she can do all those things; she's just stubborn."

Such statements in and of themselves may be true, or they may indicate that parents are not yet ready to cope with your information. You can probably get them to agree to further observation and consideration. In the meantime, start programming for the child's needs and schedule another conference!

## GATHERING AND SHARING INFORMATION

When the reality of the problem can no longer be denied, most parents go through a stage where they want more information. If we go back to the car: "How did it happen? Who is going to pay for the repairs? Who did this?" Again, parents ask the same kinds of questions. They are concerned about why and how the child became impaired. They may be especially concerned if they have or plan to have other children. They are also very much concerned about the impact their child's impairment will have on their lives and other members of the family. As with any new experience, their first attempts at coping with the situation may go badly. We don't train people to be parents, let alone the parents of children with special needs.

Once parents accept that their child has a disability, they usually look at this cognitively. The parents seek information about the disability and its long- and short-term effects. They may also actively participate in therapy with their child. This is usually an active phase, where people try to adjust their roles and expectations.

Parents may ask you about special programs, developmental norms, long- and short-term expectations for their child, how he fits in with his peers, and so on.

You don't need to be an expert on each exceptionality, but you do need to be able to get relevant information. Once you've mastered the skill of information getting, you will want to share your techniques with parents. Six techniques that are especially useful follow.

### Agree and Ask Again

Often when people are under stress, they stop taking in information. This may happen to parents when you tell them things they do not want to hear. It can also happen to you. If you feel that parents blame you for the situation, you may get defensive and quit listening. You may later realize that the information they can provide is essential to you. If you

ask a question and they tell you that they answered it ten minutes ago, you should *agree* and *ask again:* "I agree that you did tell me that information, but I wasn't ready to hear it. I still need to know, and I'm ready to listen now."

In much the same way, parents may have been intimidated by doctors or specialists and have not followed up on information, or they may not have understood what was said. Ask the parents to get the information you need from the doctor, or, with parents' written permission, call the doctor yourself for the information. Ask them to give you a copy of the medical report to study. (You may need the doctor's help to interpret the results.) Parents may have been frightened of asking for copies of medical reports or may not have known they have access to them. It is not routine to send copies of reports to parents. Therefore, it may be easier at times to get the information directly from the doctor or specialist. After studying the report, talk with the parents again. It is unlikely that all of you will agree on all the interpretations and implications. That's fine, but you can help the parents make a list of questions that need amplification to take to the doctor or specialist on their next visit.

### Accepting Responsibility

*Accepting responsibility* is a simple yet successful way to put people in a frame of mind that allows mutually effective interaction (Fensterheim, 1975). It consists of making "I" statements instead of "you" statements.

"I'm really glad you told me that today."
"I wish I had known that before."

*versus*

"You should have told me that before."

The latter statement is a blaming statement. The person that you blame often becomes defensive and responds with another blaming statement: "You weren't listening; I have told you before." This is a difficult cycle to break once it starts.

Despite the temptation to point blame, "you" statements are rarely useful.

### Workable Compromise

There will be occasions when, regardless of how persistent you are, you will not be successful in gaining the information you need or the services you want. In that case you must reach a *workable compromise* (Fensterheim, 1975). Perhaps you want the parents to sign a release form giving you access to their child's medical report, but they refuse your request.

When this occurs, after a reasonable amount of persistence, it is often best to back up and reevaluate the situation. Do you really need this information? Does anyone else have it? Is there another way of getting it? If I were this person, why wouldn't I want to give the information out? Then try another approach. If you have been asking to see test results without success, you might now ask, "I'm wondering if there is some reason why you don't want me to see these test results?" This will come as an abrupt change from your previous pattern and may result in a useful answer. You might then learn what the parents are willing to do that is acceptable to you. Might they summarize the results or discuss them? With a workable compromise both parties win.

### Matching Style

*Matching style* involves watching the parents and matching your verbal and emotional style to theirs (Berne, 1961). Are they being ultrareasonable (calm, cool, collected) when you are talking about some potentially distressing topic? If the parents are dealing with the information in a clinical way, take that as a cue. It may be that they are very private people who do not show emotions in public, or they may be feeling vulnerable and using feigned calm to protect their private selves. For some it is less painful to adopt the role of an unemotional clinician than feel the emotional involvement of a parent. At this point, you should respect their right to be detached. Adopt the same style when you talk to them. Have data available to back up your points; show them records and charts. Appeal to their organizational abilities. (Prepare yourself ahead of time so that you are completely comfortable with any technical terms you must use.) Remember, your goal is not to provide therapy for parents but programming for a child.

### Self-disclosure

*Self-disclosure* involves revealing to the parents something about yourself that is of a personal nature, for example:

> When I first learned that Jack was going to be in my class, I was really scared. I'd never taught a child in a wheelchair before. Actually, I guess I thought more about the wheelchair than I did about Jack. I can't imagine how I could have felt that way. Now he sometimes has to remind me of the things he can't do. Before, I hardly let him breathe without asking him if he was OK.

A self-disclosure statement can help parents see your emotional acceptance of their child. That is useful for developing a good working relationship.

### Giving Permission

*Giving permission* allows parents to make comments to you that they might otherwise be unwilling to make.

> *Teacher:* I wonder if there is anything I could do in my room that might make it easier for Jack to get around?
> *Parent:* Well, if you moved his locker to the far end of the row, it would keep him out of the traffic pattern a little more.

This technique is a bit more subtle than asking direct questions. It can be done in an open-ended way as well.

> *Teacher:* I really hope that if you think of some useful things that I can do in the classroom for Jack, you'll tell me. I may not be able to do all of them, but I would like to hear your ideas and learn what has been useful in the past.

Statements like this do not force the parents to follow through, but do encourage them to make suggestions. In addition, you have reassured the parents that you will think carefully about what they say. Because you will not automatically do whatever they suggest, some of their burden of responsibility will be relieved.

## TECHNIQUES TO AVOID

There are some techniques that are almost guaranteed to be counterproductive in dealing with parents (or with anyone).

### Avoid Judging or Blaming

Most of us don't like to be judged unless we have agreed to be in a formal competition. Words like *should* and *ought* that are commonly used to judge others evoke negative, defensive feelings (Berne, 1961). In a phrase like "you should have . . ." blame is implicit. Judging and blaming statements will not encourage others to cooperate with you.

### Avoid Mind Reading

"Mind reading," as you might guess is assuming what another person wants to know or should know, without their telling you (Bandler, Grinder, and Satir, 1976).

*Teacher:* What do you want to know about your son's program?
*Parent:* Whatever you think we need to know.

After such an exchange, teachers may be led to talk about what they find interesting or what they would want to know if they were the parents. This may not be at all what the parents want to know! If the parents aren't interested, they may simply tune the teacher out. Unless you help the parents make clear statements about what they want, at the end of the conference you will sense they are dissatisfied, but you won't know why. Here is a more productive follow-up to the earlier exchange:

*Teacher:* It is more useful to be able to tell you what you want to know. Not what I think you need to know. Do you want to know what the diagnosis is technically, do you want me to try to explain it to you, or both? Do you want the test reports? Do you want to know my best guess about the short- and long-term effects of this illness? I want to know what *you* want to know.

Leading questions may still not get the results you want, but, you can start by making your requests clearly and then query points you are not satisfied about.

### Avoid Giving Advice

Most parents don't want you to tell them how to raise their children. However, if you are going to offer positive, constructive suggestions (which should be rare), first gain enough information about the situation to make the advice relevant (McMurrian, 1977). Suppose the problem is plate-throwing. The parents say that their three-year-old son, Bob, frequently throws his plate on the floor when he does not like dinner. First, get the facts you need: "What do you usually do when Bob throws his plate? . . . Have you tried other things? . . . What? . . . Have they worked?" Next, check your perception of the situation. (Just because something is a problem for you doesn't necessarily mean that it is a problem for the parents and vice versa.) "Is it OK with you that Bob does this, or is it a problem?" Then offer advice tentatively, in a nonjudgmental way, by suggesting some specific actions that might be taken. "Have you tried telling him that when he throws his plate, he will not get it back and will get no snacks? You might see if that works for you."

### Avoid the Word *Understand*

Eliminate *understand* from your vocabulary (McMurrian, 1977). If a parent tells you about a problem, do not respond, "I understand exactly what you mean." Such a reponse is likely to trigger the following thoughts in a parent: "How can he understand? He is not me. He does not get up in the middle of the night. . . ." People who respond by "understanding" usually convey the impression to others that they really don't understand.

The alternative is an empathetic response, such as: "It must be really hard to have to get up in the middle of the night."

## WORKABLE RELATIONSHIPS

It is difficult for people to find the right level of expectations for their child. Some people decide that a child with a handicap has enough problems already. These people feel, therefore, that if the child likes TV and popcorn, the best solution is to allow this child to watch TV and eat popcorn as long as he is happy. Other parents view disabilities as something to be overcome. They may expect their child to excell beyond what even an average child is capable of. And to them the therapy, extra hours of work, persistence, and, perhaps, pain that are necessary to achieve that goal are worth the cost. Most parents are somewhere between those two extremes.

Knowing how the parents feel will help you, especially in adjusting your expectations regarding the parents' role. Thus, if you automatically expect parents to be actively involved in the education of their child, both in and out of school, a parent like the first one I described will not fulfill those expectations. On the other hand, you might find the second parent a bit pushy and at times more like a clinician than a parent. A home visit might be particularly useful in ascertaining the role parents are prepared for.

Developing a good working relationship with all parents is important, but it is crucial in the mainstreamed classroom. All parents have the potential to learn and grow with their children. Parents of an exceptional child are, more than most parents, forced to confront individual similarities and differences, and to reexamine their own value systems. Your goal is to reach these parents and help them become contributing members of your educational team.

# BIBLIOGRAPHY

Arnold, Eugene L., ed. *Helping Parents Help Their Children*. New York: Brunner/Mazel, 1978.

Bandler, Richard, John Grinder, and Virginia Satir. *Changing with Families: A Book About Further Education for Being Human*. Palo Alto, Calif.: Science and Behavior Books, 1976.

Baruth, Leroy, and Margaret Burggraf. *Readings in Counseling Parents of Exceptional Children*. Guilford, Conn.: Special Learning Corp., 1978.

Berne, Eric. *Games People Play*. New York: Grove Press, 1964.

———. *Transactional Analysis in Psychotherapy*. New York: Ballantine Books, 1961.

Buscaglia, Leo. *The Disabled and Their Parents: A Counseling Challenge*. New York: Charles B. Slack, 1975.

Cameron-Bandler, Leslie. *They Lived Happily Ever After: A Book About Achieving Happy Endings in Coupling*. Cupertino, Calif.: Meta Publications, 1978.

Chinn, Philip, et al. *Two-Way Talking with Parents of Special Children: A Process of Positive Communication*. St. Louis, Mo.: C. V. Mosby Co., 1978.

Fensterheim, Herbert, and Jean Baer. *Don't Say Yes When You Want to Say No*. New York: Dell, 1975.

Ginott, H. G. *Between Parent and Child*. New York: Macmillan, 1969.

Gordon, Thomas. *P. E. T. Parent Effectiveness Training*. New York: New American Library, 1970.

———. *T. E. T. Teacher Effectiveness Training*. New York: Longman, 1977.

Heward, L. William, Jill C. Dardig, and Allison Rossett. *Working with Parents of Handicapped Children*. Columbus, Ohio: Charles E. Merrill, 1979.

Koth, Roger L. *Communicating with Parents of Exceptional Children: Improving Parent-Teacher Relationships*. Denver: Love Publishing Co., 1975.

McMurrian, T. Thomas. *Intervention in Human Crisis: A Guide for Helping Families in Crisis*. Atlanta: Humanics Limited, 1975.

Rutherford, Robert B., Jr., and Eugene Edgar. *Teachers and Parents: A Guide to Interaction and Cooperation*. Boston: Allyn and Bacon, 1979.

Satir, Virginia. *Peoplemaking*. Palo Alto, Calif.: Science and Behavior Books, 1972.

Smith, Manuel J. *When I Say No, I Feel Guilty: How To Cope—Using the Skill of Systematic Assertive Therapy*. New York: Dial Press, 1975.

Stewart, Jack C. *Counseling Parents of Exceptional Children*. Columbus, Ohio: Charles E. Merrill, 1978.

# Needs: Speech and Language

Some children come to school as "talkers." They immediately want to know where the crayons are, why they are in school, why they can't go outside now . . . until you think you may change your profession if you hear one more question. These children stick in your mind from day one. Then there are the "slow to warm up" children, who appear shy and immature and who you probably still won't have a clear picture of, even after a few weeks. It is in this group, those who quietly go along but don't really exert an influence, that you may find speech and language needs.

The first question to ask when you suspect a problem is this: Can the child communicate in a way that can be understood by others? Then think back over events of the week. When you dismiss the children from group time by the color of their clothes, does this child need to be prompted? When you give simple directions, can this child follow them? How about more complex directions? Does this child seldom volunteer comments to you? Does the child rarely speak up during group time? When this child speaks, can you understand most of the words or only some of them? Given free choice, does this child seek out activities requiring language, or does the child avoid them? How can you tell whether the child falls in that wide range called average and normal, or is exceptional?

## CLASSIFICATION OF SPEECH AND LANGUAGE NEEDS

Language development depends upon the ability to receive, understand, integrate, and express language. Problems can occur at four levels: inner (ideas and concepts), receptive (listening), integrative (processing skills), or expressive (speech). A child's language is impaired when there are deviations in the formation, expression, or understanding of language. Characteristics of impaired language include poor concepts, inability to follow directions, speechlessness, speech confusion, and poor word comprehension.

A child's *speech* is impaired when it deviates so far from the speech of other children that it calls attention to itself, interferes with communication, or causes the child to be self-conscious. Typical speech impairments include poor *articulation* (mispronunciation), difficulties with *phonation* (vocal malfunctions), and *stuttering* (rhythm problems).

To determine the nature and extent of a suspected speech or language impairment, you must first be familiar with the stages of normal speech and language development. (The appendix following Chapter 4 is a useful summary of key indications of development level.) Then look up the child's birth date. This alone might solve the problem. If this child is one of the youngest in the class and your basis for comparison is the older children, the difference between them may be a strictly developmental one that will disappear with time. In early childhood, even a few months has a considerable effect. As a further check, find out if this child was premature and is therefore developmentally younger.

If you are still concerned, assign the child to a small group with several others who are close in age. (Don't include children that have already been designated as intellectually gifted or delayed). While doing language activities with the children (choose activities from Part Two of this book or others you like), note who volunteers the most and least often. Take language samples from each child and compare them for sentence length, sentence structure, vocabulary and concepts, and articulation (note omissions, distortions, or substitutions of sounds). An easy way to obtain language samples is by recording small group time. Do this on at least two occasions to allow for a child's having a bad day. If the child you are concerned about is in the top to middle of this group, there is no cause for concern. If the child is at the bottom, continue gathering information.

As you continue your observation, note how the child uses materials not related to language. How many different materials are used? Are the materials used appropriately? This information will help you decide if the child is delayed in other areas. If so, the child's speech and language problems may have a more profound cause, such as mental retardation.

The next step is to determine the gap between the child's comprehension and production of language. All children at this stage have a greater ability to understand language than to speak it; you are looking for a significantly wider gap between the two than age mates have.

Analyze the child's speech carefully. If the child is having trouble pronouncing words, note exactly which sounds are difficult. Vowels and the consonants *p, b, m,* and *w* are easiest for a young child to pronounce, followed by *t, d, n, k, g, f,* and *v.* The more difficult sounds are *s, z, l, r, ch, th, sh, j, bl,* and *cr.* If the child has problems with the last set of sounds, which children normally take longer to learn, reevaluate a few months later. Be sure to look for the obvious. If the child doesn't have front teeth, some sounds are not possible for him.

After carefully observing the child alone and with others, if you still feel there is a problem, schedule a conference with the parents. Alert them to the problem, then accept whatever they say. Your goals in the first conference are to gather more information and to begin to make the parents aware of the problem. Schedule a class visit for them in about two weeks. Have them observe their own child with an age mate, just as you did. At your second conference discuss and compare their observations with your own.

Consider making a home visit. You will have an opportunity to watch and listen to the family interact more informally. You may learn that the child's speech or language is modeled after the family pattern, which means you are unlikely to convince the parents there is a problem. If you still feel the problem exists, discuss it, but be prepared for the parents not to cooperate. There is still much you can do with classroom programming to foster this child's speech and language development.

If you and the parents agree there is reason to believe the child has a special need, you might suggest that the child be tested. The family physician is probably the first choice, since there may be a medical reason for the problem. The physician might then refer the child to an audiologist to test hearing and to a speech pathologist. You or the doctor might refer the child to the school psychologist for testing in social adjustment and intellectual development. Some communities may have a child diagnostic clinic or a counseling clinic.

No matter how you and the parents choose to obtain further information about the child's needs, there often is a long lag between your initial concern and a final diagnosis. Often as long as a year or two may elapse. Young children can be difficult to diagnose. The test results are often inconclusive, and many times the decision is made to wait awhile and try again. In the meantime, you can develop ideas for helping this child within your classroom.

### Language

In order to program effectively for children with speech and language needs, you need to know the sequence of language development. (See the Appendix following Chapter 4.) Next you must determine where in the sequence they are having problems. Within the sequence are four processes. Ask yourself, in which process does the problem lie? Each process can be broken down into small steps to be mastered in turn from simple to complex. These steps are your teaching goals. Once you have defined your goals, you are ready to choose activities. Let us examine the processes of language more closely.

| Process | Characteristic | Criterion for Evaluation |
|---|---|---|
| Inner language | The ability to communicate with oneself. Developed by actively interacting and manipulating one's environment. Requires opportunity. Does not require adult intervention. | Given a ball, the child rolls, bounces, throws it. (The child doesn't eat it or sit on it.) |

| *Process* | *Characteristic* | *Criterion for Evaluation* |
|---|---|---|
| Receptive language | The ability to understand others. The child uses symbols to connect objects with their names. | Given the command "Show me the ball," the child does in fact show you the ball, not a hand or shoe. |
| Integrative language | The ability to synthesize information. After receiving information the child classifies it (coding, sorting, selecting, organizing, and retaining). Involves more than short-term memory. The child must hold the concept in mind while performing other tasks. | Given the command "Go get the ball" (from across the room), the child brings back the ball, not a crayon or eraser. (The child remembered the task while crossing the room.) |
| Expressive language | The ability to make oneself understood verbally: speech. | Given the question "What is this?", the child responds "ball," not "bell" or "hand." |

The order in which concepts are introduced must correspond to the developmental sequence of learning. The child must first actively experience something, have it named, and then interact further with the named item before being expected to express the name and any ideas about it. When a very young child has been denied sufficient interaction with the environment—because of illness or other disability, overprotective parents, or lack of role models—language impairments are likely to develop.

For each of the four processes described above, rate the child in overall language development. Is the child above, about the same, or below others of that age? If, for example, the child is average in inner and receptive language but below average in integrative language, the point in the sequence at which you start teaching skills is receptive language. Start from where the child is experiencing some success (or just a little frustration) and work toward gradually developing the next process.

### Speech

Speech disorders fall into three categories, poor articulation being the most prevalent. *Articulation* errors occur when sounds are omitted, added, distorted, or substituted. Take, for example, *spaghetti*:

| | |
|---|---|
| paghetti | (*s* is omitted) |
| spaghettiti | (extra *ti* is added) |
| spēghetti | (*a* is distorted to ē) |
| basaghetti | (*ba* is substituted for *p* and put at the beginning) |

Articulation errors can happen at the beginning, middle, or end of a word. They may be the result of indistinct articulation. Slow, labored speech and rapid, slurring speech are both articulation problems. Some articulation problems are a natural part of a child's development. While children may, in fact, outgrow some problems, care must be taken to determine whether therapy is indicated.

*Phonatory* speech disorders are less common and effect voice quality (nasal, breathy, husky, guttural), pitch (high, low, monopitch, uncontrolled switches in pitch), and intensity (soft, loud, uncontrolled switches in intensity).

*Rhythm* speech disorders, although far less frequent than articulation disorders, cause much concern in parents and teachers. All young children have some problem with repetition. However, abnormal repetitions of sounds and words, as well as irregular rhythm (e.g., cluttering), frequent and long hesitations, and speech blocks are serious enough to be classified as disorders. Stuttering is a rhythm speech disorder.

You are likely to encounter many children with speech and language needs, most of them undiagnosed. You will probably play a major role in the identification process.

## CHILDREN'S NEEDS— TEACHING GOALS

Related annual goals may be grouped under broad categories called "teaching goals." Outlined under each teaching goal below are the most important needs of speech and language impaired children. A child may have some or all of these needs, and additional needs as well. The exact configuration of goals and objectives is reflected in the IEP for that child. Suggestions on what you might consequently teach them are included. Often, a course of action is implicit in the description of the need.

### Language Skills

Children with speech problems may talk only when absolutely necessary because of the negative feedback they have received in the past ("You talk funny"). Speaking in front of others is a threatening experience for these children. When asked questions in a group situation, they will respond with a shrug or "don't know." It is easier for them not to know something than to risk ridicule by the other children. Start encouraging speech one-to-one and in

Working with a speech and language therapist.

small groups before you work on large groups. Reinforce spontaneous speech.

Which speech skills to emphasize will depend on the needs of each child. Skills include rhythm, breath control, rhyming, and vocabulary sound production. A speech and language therapist can tell you what skills a child needs the most help with.

## Sensory Skills

*Visual Skills.* Because speech and language needs are often reflected later in reading problems, these children need a solid base in the prereading skills. All the visual skills—discrimination, memory, closure, to name a few—need special attention.

*Auditory Skills.* It is important to provide children with a wide variety of auditory experiences in order to foster development of listening skills. These skills range from the simple identification of a sound (a word) with an object (receptive) to the more sophisticated following of directions (integrative).

*Sensory Integration.* These children need help in understanding information received, whether through visual, auditory, or tactile means. They need particular work with sensory integration—interpreting information received simultaneously through two or more senses.

## Awareness

*Body Awareness.* Under stress, these children will frequently display tics, facial grimaces, unusual body postures, or a characteristic gesture (head nodding, hair twirling). They may need to increase their body awareness. Help them to learn relaxation skills and to become aware of nervous mannerisms.

*Self-concept.* These children are rarely leaders. They often receive instructions from classmates rather than give them, and as they are often reluctant to argue with the leader as others might, they end up with the least desirable roles. As their self-concept improves, teach them ways to be assertive.

*Group Belonging.* Typically, these children do not seek out other children. They frequently play alone or near one other child. Encourage cooperative play so that children can learn to interact comfortably with peers.

## Guidelines

If the child has been diagnosed, try to get a copy of the diagnosis. Talk with the speech and language therapist. Find out what the diagnosis means to the child's total development. (Example: Is language delay a symptom of something else?) Whether the child is diagnosed or not, you must assess where in the language process the problem is and its severity. Although each child's situation will be different, the following guidelines to meeting the child's special needs will be helpful.

1. Begin programming at the appropriate level (inner, receptive, integrative, expressive), where the child is just beginning to have problems.
2. Set aside a time each day for language development. (The activity may vary but the intent shouldn't.)
3. Increase the child's interest in himself and his environment. Encourage the child's desire to communicate.
4. Provide a secure and consistent environment.
5. Set up activities that provide noncompetitive peer interaction.
6. Include the child in group activities. The child need not have a speaking role if that is anxiety-provoking. Nonverbal group participation may be prerequisite to verbal participation.
7. Create a need for speech. If the child uses gestures instead of speech, deliberately (but not obviously) misunderstand briefly and name other objects. Before the child becomes frustrated, give the child what was requested, but use the word in one or two phrases or sentences. Gradually, over several encounters, increase the number of misunderstandings and incorrect guesses until the child is slightly frustrated by your "stupidity."
8. Do a lot of running commentary. Out loud, give a play-by-play description of what either you or the child is doing. Children learn to talk by listening.

9. Be a good listener. Give the child your undivided attention or explain that you can't listen then, but will soon. Arrange to do it as soon after as possible.
10. Reward the child for correct speech, but do not criticize or punish for lack of speech or incorrect speech.
11. Be a good speech and language model.
12. Differentiate between speech and language, and reinforce appropriately. For example, you might tell a child, "I'm glad you want to tell me about your picture, but I'm having trouble understanding what you are saying. Can you tell me with different words?" Therapists traditionally teach the child to understand the difference between "good language but poor speech."
13. Reinforce learning through visual and tactile experiences.
14. Structure lessons to provide children with more successes than failures.
15. Be aware that other class members may develop speech problems as a consequence of imitating defective speech and do not reinforce them.

The following guidelines will help you foster children's development in the four language processes.

*Inner Language.*   Expand the child's awareness of the environment. Lack of stimulation may be a factor in underdeveloped inner language. Use field trips and many "hands-on" experiences that provide concrete learning experiences and materials to introduce and reinforce concepts. It is important the children not be expected to talk about something they have no knowledge of. When providing opportunities to actively explore the environment, remember it often takes several experiences for a child to gain the necessary information.

*Receptive Language.*   Provide varied listening experiences to help the child discriminate and associate sounds. Describe the child's behavior out loud: "Now you are going up the stairs." Use concrete examples or picture cues when possible, and reinforce learning through nonauditory experiences.

*Integrative Language.*   Use simple one-step directions; gradually work up to more complex ones. If necessary, have the child repeat or verbally "walk through" the directions before actually doing an activity.

*Expressive Language.*   Encourage the child to speak and reinforce attempts to do so. Don't rush the child when speaking or criticize the child's speech. If a child mispronounces a word, don't correct it. Instead, use it correctly in a sentence in response. Provide visual cues to speech sounds; if you are asking about a red shirt, point to it. Reinforce newly learned speech patterns (often done in coordination with the speech therapist).

## CURRICULUM ADAPTATIONS

Children with needs in speech and language require few curriculum adaptations. Following are some general adaptations organized by curriculum area. This is not a complete list, but it will help you to begin programming for these children.

### Expressing Language, Listening, and Reading Readiness

The language arts curriculum areas of listening, expressing language, and reading readiness should be the ones most emphasized for speech and language impaired children. In particular, these children need to develop and refine listening, attention, and memory skills. Language arts can be used to increase voluntary speaking as well as to develop readiness skills. Check with the child's speech and language therapist for more specific advice and additional activities.

Provide the child with firsthand experiences followed by discussions and opportunities for internalizing concepts and expanding key ideas. Using farm as an example, you might:

Plan a trip to a farm.
Generate a language experience story about the trip to the farm.
Read a book about a farm at storytime.
Play farm animal lotto.
Discuss and imitate the sounds that farm animals make.

These suggestions are ordered on the principle that children learn the concrete before the abstract and that gradually increasing exposure to a concept increases learning.

Young children with speech and language needs are likely to have difficulty learning to read later (Kirk and Gallagher, 1979). While they are concentrating on pronunciation, their comprehension of the reading material suffers. Their reading rate will be slower than average and their phrasing will be poor. In fact reading may become so unpleasant they will avoid it whenever possible. Particular care should be taken to develop their reading readiness skills in order to forestall these problems.

When you teach reading readiness skills, you will most often use visual and auditory means. Children need to see and say a letter regardless of where it is positioned in the word. Ear training, the ability to listen well, is one prerequisite speech and language impaired children may find difficult to master. Yet it is essential to the development of reading readiness and the ability to communicate. Other skills, including letter recognition, letter memory, and so forth, are discussed in greater detail in Part Two, Chapter 18, "Reading Readiness."

Stories expand the child's world as well as provide a fun opportunity to practice different sounds. Initially use stories about events familiar to the child. Books about children, family, and animals may fill this criteria.

Read stories that emphasize specific sounds, ones that are easy or hard for the child, depending on your objectives. *Sammy Snake* is an example of a story emphasizing the *s* sound. Read stories that emphasize rhyming words (for example, *Each Peach Pear Plum*), voice control (*The Whispering Rabbit and Other Stories*), and listening skills (*What I Hear in My School*).*

Fingerplays are good for children with speech and language needs. Although done with a group, fingerplays cause children to lose their self-consciousness, in part because they can participate in the motions without speaking. The motions also provide visual cues that help children understand the words. Fingerplays that rhyme are good for ear training. Those that have the sounds the child is working on are most useful. Use fingerplays to stimulate body awareness. Those that involve the face and mouth area especially benefit the child. Fingerplays such as "Teensy, Weensy Spider" facilitate eye-hand coordination as well as motor and manual control.

Matching and sorting tasks are either perceptual or conceptual in nature or combine elements of both. Perceptual matching requires the children to match like letters to each other. They don't need to know what the letters stand for. When the task is a conceptual one, the children are required to abstract the idea and generalize it to another instance, for example, when going from small letters to capital letters or when going from script to printing. Conceptual matching can be used not only in reading readiness but also in other curriculum areas. Examples of both follow.

1. Develop a picture file set up in a flexible format that will allow for later expansion.

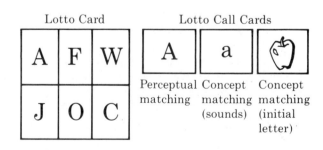

Divide the file into three sets: beginning consonant sounds, medial consonant sounds, and ending consonant sounds. Include the consonant

*Complete references as well as additional titles are given at the end of the chapter.

blends (*bl*ouse, pu*mp*kin, sta*nd*) in each set. Vowels may be omitted because children rarely have problems with them. Organize the sets alphabetically and store them in three file boxes. Once you have developed the three basic sets, you are prepared for a variety of activities.

a. Have children find all the pictures with a specified beginning sound. (When ending an exercise, call out the sounds in alphabetical order. The pictures will automatically be organized for putting away.) Do the same thing for beginning consonant blends. Repeat the process for the middle and final position. When you introduce this activity you might have the name on the front of the card; the activity is easier when the child can match the initial letters as well as the sound. When the sounds are easier for the children, take off the word.

b. Set out four picture cards (three of which have the same ending sounds), say the words, then have the children identify the one that is different. Gradually give the children more responsibilities, thereby increasing the level of difficulty. You might have the children say the words, have them create sets for each other, and so on.

c. A more challenging and creative activity is making sound books. Introduce one sound at a time. Write the sound at the top of a piece of paper. Have the children find magazine pictures of objects that have that sound and have them paste the pictures on the page. When each child has a page for each sound, the pages can be made into books.

d. Letter lotto (or variations of bingo) is a fun way to teach letter recognition. When children can match identical letters, add pictures as well as lower-case letters to the game.

Lotto Card | Lotto Call Cards

| A | F | W |
|---|---|---|
| J | O | C |

Perceptual matching | Concept matching (sounds) | Concept matching (initial letter)

e. The development of letter memory can be facilitated by making two sets of the lotto call cards and playing "Concentration." Start by turning four to six pairs of cards face down. If this is too easy add more pairs.

f. To foster ear training, read stories and fingerplays that have rhymes until the children are familiar with them. Then read the stories with pauses to let the group fill in the rhyming word. The children will also enjoy nonsense rhyming games. You say a word and have the children call out real and made-up rhyming words for you to write on the board.

### Social Studies

Speech and language skills can be integrated into the social studies curriculum through conversation and role playing. Help the children identify similarities and differences throughout the immediate environment, the region, the country, and the world. Your goal is to promote the concept of diversity. At the same time you are promoting the children's awareness of differences and similarities in speech and language without their making judgments.

1. Have a foreign language speaker visit your class and label common objects for the children. Have roll call in another language:

|  |  |  |  |
|---|---|---|---|
| English: | John | French: | Jacques |
|  | Frances |  | Françoise |
| Spanish: | Juan | German: | Johann |
|  | Francisca |  | Franziska |

   You might also make reversible bilingual name tags for the children.
2. Make a tape recording of people from different regions in the United States (with the characteristic accent). If possible have them all say the same sentences so that the children can more readily grasp the differences.
3. Act out situations that require the children to assume roles that have different speech patterns associated with them: for example, cowhand, police officer, father, mother, baby.

### Science/Discovery

Science activities require few verbal skills. Therefore, the risk of failure by the speech and language impaired is minimized. Science topics, such as those outlined below, can enhance children's understanding of the mechanics of speech and language. Although fewer verbal skills are required by science than by some other subjects, interest is usually very high and stimulates language use.

1. Teach some anatomy, especially the organs that produce sound (lips, tongue, teeth, throat, diaphragm).
2. Use mirrors to help children see the articulatory organs while exploring the concept of mirror reversing.
3. Discuss the sounds different animals make and how they make them. (Crickets, for example, rub their legs together.) Have children experiment making sounds by using different body parts

(clap, stomp, slap thighs). Make a tape recording of animal sounds; see if children can pair the picture of the animal with the sound.
4. Talk about how sound is made in nature (thunder, water moving, wind) and how humans make noise (music, talking, working). Discuss how noise cues us to what is happening in our environment. These sounds may be presented on tapes or on records. Use pictures when you first present the sounds; the visual reinforces the aural.
5. Discuss the properties of air and its function in speech. Use a balloon to make air more tangible.

### Mathematics

Children with speech and language problems usually have math skills comparable to their classmates'. They often enjoy math, as it can be learned with a minimum of speech. Math, then, can give these children a feeling of achievement. When they count or discuss concepts, they are working through a strength (math) to meet a need (facility with language and speech).

1. Use math concepts that facilitate speech and language development. Have children count and sort objects that make sounds and objects that don't. Or, have them count the number of times a sound is made.
2. Make number books by having children cut out a specified number of pictures beginning with the same sound. You might have, for example, one *T*, two *R*s, three *S*s, four *TH*s, and so on.

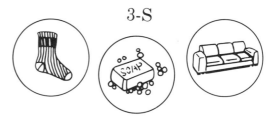

3-S

3. Apply the math vocabulary (big/little, more/less, equal) to sounds and body awareness. Tell children to make their bodies as big as they can, then as little. Have them find pictures of an animal with a big tail and of one with a little tail. Do those animals make big/loud sounds or little/soft sounds?
4. Present pictures of geometric shapes and have children draw these shapes in the air with various parts of their bodies. Once they have shown they understand by tracing the shapes with their hands, have them outline the shapes with their jaw, head, tongue, and finally by moving only their eyes.
5. Compare the chest measurements of children after they inhale and after they exhale. This can

be done with string or measuring tape, although string is more effective with younger children because they can see which string is longer.

## Health and Safety

Speech and language production requires the coordination of muscles from the waist up, the speech organs, and the brain. It is one of the most complicated human processes. Children need to be made aware of the body parts involved while they learn how to take care of their body. Listening to someone who has a stopped-up head helps children learn the nose's function. A sore throat demonstrates the throat's contribution to speech.

*Teeth.* Discuss how to care for teeth. Invite a dentist to visit the class. As children begin to lose their baby teeth, discuss what sounds become difficult. Have them discover the role teeth play in making sounds.

*Jaw.* Use scissors to illustrate the hingelike action of the jaw. Have children use their fingers to feel the bones and muscles as they drop their jaw. Again, experiment with sound as the jaw lowers and rises.

*Tongue.* Do tongue exercises with the class. Let the children use mirrors to watch their tongue move. Have them pair off and watch each other.

*Vocal Cords.* Have children place their hands on their throat to feel the vocal cords vibrate. See if they can feel a difference in sounds. Use a rubber band to show how the vocal cords work, stretching it tight for high sounds and only slightly for low ones.

## Art

Children have the opportunity in art to develop fine motor skills. They also get satisfaction from having a product to show for their efforts. Art activities provide a constructive nonverbal way of expressing feelings and working off energy.

1. Children can learn to recognize differences in how a pencil, a crayon, paint, and chalk sound and feel.
2. Blow painting, or straw painting, develops the muscles of the mouth, gives practice in closing off the palate and throat, and teaches breath control.
3. Encourage children to talk about their pictures (not in response to "What is it?" or, as a naive graduate student once said to a three-year-old, "What does this picture represent to you?"). Start out with a comment such as "I like the way you use red in this picture." That's an invitation—you may have shown enough interest to get a response. You might ask, "Does your picture have a story?" Be prepared for the fact that it may not!
4. Make puppets to be used in dramatic play. Often shy children will vocalize more with puppets.

## Music

Music offers many fun opportunities for non-threatening speech and language training. Music requires children to develop and use different vocal patterns. Blowing instruments and singing stimulate the palate and musculature of the mouth. Because some speech problems don't carry over into singing, this is one vocal activity that can be rewarding for speech impaired children.

1. Have children make musical instruments to develop listening skills. Make paper plate tambourines filled with stones, beans, and rice. These can be played in a group as well as paired according to the different sounds they make. Also make balloon squeakers and rubber band whistles. Have children make musical instruments that emphasize mouth movements.
2. Children become more aware of their voices as they whistle, hum, and sing high and low, loud and soft. Help them note tension in the lips and the feel of air coming in and out. Help them relate what they learn to speaking.
3. Music is a natural way to teach the concepts of high and low. Reinforce the concepts by having the children stretch their bodies high for the high notes, crouch low for the low notes, and be somewhere in between for the middle notes.
4. Holding notes for long or short periods of time increases breath awareness and improves breath control.
5. Music with movement provides an avenue for interpreting or expressing moods.
6. The rhythm of music also applies to speech and language, especially for children who stutter. Interestingly enough these children can often sing things they cannot say. To create more awareness of rhythm you can have children brush teeth, lower jaws (as if chewing), or even click tongues to a rhythm pattern.
7. Songs with action allow children to participate whether or not they know the words. Actions provide visual cues for learning the words.
8. Records and tapes enhance listening skills, but they should be used with visual aids to help children comprehend the content.

## Movement

Use movement to increase body awareness (especially of speech organs) and to provide relaxation.

1. For relaxation have children be clothes fluttering on the line in the wind. To relax the throat and neck, have the children drop their head forward (chin toward chest).
2. To improve articulation, put milk or juice in a bowl and have children lap it up, like a cat, with

their tongue. Licking designs in ice cream will also exercise the tongue.

## Dramatic Play

Dramatic play provides a safe outlet for energy and an opportunity for children to try out roles without fear of judgment. It also allows children to be a part of a group.

1. At the beginning of the year the dramatic play area should be an easy, familiar, nondemanding place. Children with speech and language needs will often drift toward this area, as it represents a tie with home. (This is particularly true of three-year-olds.)
2. These children are often fearful of new situations, such as a field trip or moving to a new house. (The parents may tell you of a new experience the child is going to encounter.) Take advantage of dramatic play to have children rehearse the experience beforehand to gain knowledge of what to expect.
3. Puppets encourage speech in a nonthreatening way. Play a recording of Donald Duck or Mickey Mouse to reassure children that it is alright for puppets to sound different.

## Small Motor Play

Children having difficulty with speech and language need to develop their ability to listen in coordination with seeing and touching. Sensory integration and eye-hand coordination can be accomplished through small motor play.

1. Use activities that pair listening skills with visual or tactile skills. ("Turn the page when you hear the tone.")
2. Use activities that help establish a hand preference (coloring, turning nuts on bolts, eating). (It is irrelevant which hand is preferred.)

## Large Motor Play

Large motor play is usually a pleasure for these children and should be encouraged. Because their language problem rarely interferes, this may prove one of their strengths.

1. Use large motor play to foster a sense of belonging to the group.
2. Help classmates see the child's strengths in this area.
3. Blocks are one activity where speech requirements are few but opportunities for speech are

many. As cooperative play increases, children talk more to each other.

4. By telling children what they are doing, in a play-by-play commentary, large motor play can be made a language-enriching experience.

## Transitions

As children end one activity and prepare to go on to another, there is often some confusion. Turn the confusion into opportunities for learning by taking advantage of transitions.

1. Combine movement and sound to help children get from one area to another. ("Walk like a duck and quack as you go to the art area.") Ask children to walk as quietly or to make as much noise as they can while going to the learning center of their choice.
2. Increase body awareness and sense of self. Dismiss children by hair and eye color.

# CHILD STUDY TEAM REPORT

## Jeannie H.

In attendance: Ms. P., speech and language clinician; Mr. S., psychologist; Ms. L., day care teacher.

Jeannie H. is a four-year, four-month-old girl who was referred for speech and language and psychological testing by her day care teacher. Mrs. H. brought her for testing, but was unable to take another day of work off to be at this meeting. She asked that Ms. L. represent her.

On the day of testing, Mrs. H. reported that Jeannie lives at home with her mother and two younger siblings, aged two years and six months. Jeannie's mother works full time and has placed all three children in a day care center close to their home.

Jeannie reportedly was a full-term baby, weighing seven pounds at birth. According to her mother, Jeannie crawled at nine months, walked at about one year, and was completely toilet trained, including nighttime, at about age three. Jeannie has a history of ear infections. As a result, tubes were placed in her ears at age two. However, an audiological evaluation at that time showed hearing to be in the normal range. Jeannie appears to have pollen allergies, occurring primarily in the spring months. Jeannie began talking (understandable to her mother) at age two and a half. She used one-word utterances, and began to put two words together about a year ago. Mrs. H. realizes that Jeannie is difficult to understand. She was hopeful that being around other children and participating in a "school" (day care) would help her speech.

Mrs. H. reported that she is a single parent. She has been separated from Jeannie's father for about one year, although Jeannie does see him periodically. Jeannie has always been very quiet and seems afraid of her father, who sometimes talks loudly, according to Mrs. H. Mrs. H. feels that if she could spend more time with Jeannie, the child might not be having speech problems. She also feels that the two younger children take a major portion of her time, and that Jeannie has always been "left on her own." Mrs. H. would like to know how she can help Jeannie, but says she really does not have as much time to spend with her as she would like.

Ms. L. stated some of the reasons the referral was made. The day care center staff has expressed concern about Jeannie's "speech and ability to understand." The staff feels Jeannie tries very hard to participate in the activities at the center, yet does not always seem able to follow directions or to get the other children to understand her.

Ms. P, (the speech and language clinician), reports that Jeannie's speech, as tested on the Goldman-Fristow Test of Articulation, is full of substitutions, omissions, and distortions. Oral mechanisms for sound production are adequate. Speech therapy was recommended.

In addition, Ms. P. administered language tests to measure receptive and expressive language and some auditory skills. On the Peabody Picture Vocabulary Test, Jeannie demonstrated a receptive vocabulary language age of one year one month below her chronological age. Analysis of a language sample revealed that Jeannie's grammatic structure and word usage resembled that of a two-and-a-half to three-year-old. Ms. P. noted that most of Jeannie's language was unintelligible. On the Zimmerman Preschool Language Scale, Jeannie had difficulty following one-step directions consistently. She could repeat one digit or one word, and at times could repeat two. Her auditory comprehension of language was about one year below her chronological age. Language therapy was also recommended.

Ms. P. felt that Jeannie was very cooperative during testing and did not frustrate easily. She also referred Jeannie for psychological testing to further identify Jeannie's learning strengths and needs.

The psychologist, Mr. S., who tested Jeannie had

difficulty understanding her. Therefore, he tried to administer tests that did not require a great deal of verbalization. Some subtests of the McCarthy Scales of Children's Abilities and the Weschler Preschool and Primary Scales of Intelligence were administered. He felt Jeannie's difficulty in following his directions depressed her extrapolated intelligence quotient and mental age, which fell in the dull-normal range. On tasks requiring imitation and visual attentiveness, Jeannie demonstrated relative strength, scoring at age level. Weaknesses for Jeannie included auditory attentiveness, verbal concepts, and general knowledge (though it was felt that these weaknesses are related to her communication problem). Mr. S. requested to see Jeannie one year after therapy has been ongoing. He feels her learning strength is in imitation, particularly visual, and gave Jeannie's mother and the day care staff ideas for working with Jeannie. Mr. S. felt Jeannie was cooperative, as does the day care staff. He suggested that verbal directions be held at a minimum length for Jeannie and that visual cues be used whenever giving directions. He stressed the importance of gaining her visual attention when working with her one-to-one or in a group. He felt that peer interaction would be good for Jeannie, and alerted her mother and the day care staff to watch for signs of frustration or giving up when trying to communicate.

Ms. P. will begin to work with Jeannie immediately, in both speech and language. She recommended the day care staff help Jeannie begin to develop auditory skills, such as identification of environmental sounds, listening to short stories, and remembering short songs and rhymes. Ms. P. will work with the staff closely as she works with Jeannie. Ms. P. agreed with Mr. S.'s suggestions on gaining Jeannie's attention and gave Ms. L. a home therapy program for Mrs. H. to follow. This plan incorporated chores, such as table setting, and simple games, like "I'm thinking of something . . . ," that will improve Jeannie's auditory skills.

A therapy schedule was discussed with the day care staff. Jeannie will be seen for two one-half hour sessions per week. She will be reevaluated by Ms. P. every six months, and by Mr. S. at the end of one year. A meeting with Mr. S., Ms. P., Ms. L., and Mrs. H. may have to be held after 5:00 P.M. in order to develop an IEP.

# INDIVIDUALIZED EDUCATION PROGRAM

NAME ___Jeannie H.___ DOB __5__ / __11__ / __79__

AGE ___4-4___ GRADE ___Preschool___

SCHOOL ___Wind in the Willows Day Care___

PARENTS/GUARDIANS ___Mrs. H.___

ADDRESS ___14-B Sycamore Street___

PHONE ___235-9876___

On __9/24/83__, the IPRD Committee
(Date)
met to review all current data and

recommends Level ___I___ placement.

Date of next review ___4/8/84___

Exceptionality: ___Speech and language impaired___

Present at meeting:

Parents ___Mrs. H.___

Others: Name/Position ___Ms. P., Speech and Lang.___

## CURRENT TEST DATA

TEST/DATE/RESULTS

Sp. & Lang. / 9/9/83 / Many substitutions, omissions, and distortions
/ in speech; receptive 1 year delay; expressive
/ 1½ year delay.

WPPSI MSCA / 9/11/83 / Overall score depressed by communication
/ difficulties

Recommended Special Services (Hrs/Wk):

Sp. & Lang. Therapy / 1 hr. (2 half hr. sessions)
/ per week
/

Total Hours/Week:

Special Education Classroom ___0___

Regular Classroom ___40___

Representative of District/Agency ___Ms. L., Day Care Teacher___

___Mr. S., Psychologist___

The committee has determined the following learning strengths and needs to be reflected in the IEP:

| STRENGTHS | NEEDS |
|---|---|
| Imitation | Articulation |
| Visual attentiveness | Receptive language |
| Cooperativeness | Expressive language |
| | Auditory comprehension |
| | Auditory attentiveness |

STUDENT ___Jeannie H.___  DATE ___10/4/83___

GOAL ___To improve expressive language___

PARENT SIGNATURE _____  TEACHER SIGNATURE _____

| INSTRUCTIONAL OBJECTIVES | EDUCATIONAL METHODS | DATE Begin | DATE End | Eval. | PERSONS RESPONSIBLE Name | Position |
|---|---|---|---|---|---|---|
| Jeannie will expressively identify her teacher and at least 5 classmates with 100% accuracy. | Who Are You?, Name songs, Name games, Dramatic play | 10/4 10/4 | 4/8 4/8 | | Ms. L. Ms. L. | Teacher Teacher |
| Jeannie will express at least 4 of the following needs in 3–4 word sentences: toilet, wash hands, thirst, uncomfortable, coldness or warmth, illness, injury, desire to use particular material, on 5 occasions. | Sentences, Puppet Hands, Symptoms, Puppets | 10/4 | 4/8 | | Ms. L. | Teacher |
| Jeannie will increase use of nouns, verbs, and adjectives in language sample by 25% (baseline data to be taken week of 11/1). | Dress Up and Tell, Telephone, Feelings, Dramatic Play, Flannel Board Stories | 11/1 | 4/8 | | Ms. L. | Teacher |
| Jeannie will decrease use of gestures by 50% (baseline data to be taken week of 10/20). | Same as Above | 10/20 | 4/8 | | Ms. L. | Teacher |

STUDENT  Jeannie H.  
GOAL  To increase vocabulary  
PARENT SIGNATURE  

DATE  10/4/83  
TEACHER SIGNATURE  

| INSTRUCTIONAL OBJECTIVES | EDUCATIONAL METHODS | Begin | End | Eval. | Name | Position |
|---|---|---|---|---|---|---|
| Jeannie will receptively identify the following colors: red, blue, yellow, orange, green, purple, white, black; 4/5 of the following shapes: circle, square, rectangle, triangle, oval; 10/12 of the following adjectives: fast, slow, big, little, empty, full, short, long, hot, cold, smooth, rough; 12/14 of the following body parts: head, eye, nose, ear, mouth, elbow, shoulder, ankle, wrist, hip, waist, foot, hand, knee, on 3 separate occasions. | Carpet Shapes, Pockets, Colored Fingernails, Soap Crayons, Picnic, Ordering Objects, Traveling, Cast It, Be the Body, Hands and Feet, Flannel board stories, Movement songs | 10/4 | 12/20 | | Ms. L. | Teacher |
| | | 10/4 | 12/20 | | Ms. L. | Teacher |
| | | 10/4 | 12/20 | | Ms. L. | Teacher |
| Jeannie will expressively identify the above concepts. | | 1/1 | 4/8 | | Ms. L. | Teacher |
| Jeannie will be able to place a block in 4/6 of the following positions: on top of (object), beside, under, in front of, in back of, over, on 3 occasions. | Obstacle Course, Circles | 1/1 | 4/8 | | Ms. L. | Teacher |

STUDENT Jeannie H. DATE 10/4/83

GOAL To improve auditory discrimination

PARENT SIGNATURE ____________ TEACHER SIGNATURE ____________

| INSTRUCTIONAL OBJECTIVES | EDUCATIONAL METHODS | DATE Begin | DATE End | Eval. | PERSONS RESPONSIBLE Name | PERSONS RESPONSIBLE Position |
|---|---|---|---|---|---|---|
| Jeannie will expressively label sounds as fast or slow, loud or soft 9/10 tries on 3 occasions. | Drumbeats, Instruments, Whisper | 10/4 | 4/8 | | Ms. L. | Teacher |
| Given a visual and auditory stimulus, Jeannie will point to the picture of the object that makes the appropriate environmental sounds 8/10 of the times: car (starting), dog (barking), person brushing teeth), cat (meowing), footsteps (running and walking), clock (ticking), children playing), siren, bells (ringing), on 3 occasions. | Noisemakers, Tape It, Sounds, Noisy Steps, Sound and Tell, Sound Cues, Warning Sounds | 10/4 | 1/30 | | Ms. L. | Teacher |
| Jeannie will be able to label the above with no visual stimuli. | | 2/1 | 4/8 | | Ms. L. | Teacher |

STUDENT ___Jeannie H.___ DATE ___10/4/83___

GOAL ___To improve auditory memory___

PARENT SIGNATURE _____  TEACHER SIGNATURE _____

| INSTRUCTIONAL OBJECTIVES | EDUCATIONAL METHODS | Begin | DATE End | Eval. | PERSONS RESPONSIBLE Name | Position |
|---|---|---|---|---|---|---|
| Jeannie will follow a one-step direction given once orally 4/5 trials on 3 separate occasions. | Johnny Hear, Johnny Do, Director, In and Out, Listen Before You Move, Listening Walk | 10/4 | 12/20 | | Ms. L. | Teacher |
| Jeannie will be able to follow a 2-step direction given once orally 4/5 trials on 3 separate occasions. | Same as Above | 1/1 | 4/8 | | Ms. L. | Teacher |
| Jeannie will repeat: 2 digits, 2 unrelated words, a 4-word sentence, 4/5 trials on 3 separate occasions. | Drumbeats, Animal Sounds | 10/4 11/4 12/4 | 4/8 | | Ms. L. | Teacher |
| Jeannie will recite at least 2 fingerplays and 2 songs from memory with half of the words being accurate. | Sequencing Songs, Fingerplays, Songs | 10/4 | 4/8 | | Ms. L. | Teacher |

# GLOSSARY

**Aphasia**   An inability to use words as a way of communicating ideas. This condition is usually the result of a brain lesion.

**Articulation**   The production of speech sounds.

**Auditory skills**   Identification, discrimination, memory, closure, association, comprehension. *See* Activities: Listening Skills.

**Babbling**   An early stage of speech when the child uses meaningless sounds as though talking.

**Cleft palate**   A disorder in which there is no closing between the mouth and the nasal cavity. This gap can vary in size and may include only a portion of the roof of the mouth or include the gum ridge and upper lip. Children with this problem usually have trouble with high pressure sounds, such as /s/, /z/, /p/.*

**Cluttering**   A rhythm disorder sometimes confused with stuttering. The child speaks so rapidly that sounds are omitted or slurred.

**Dyspraxia**   A term used to refer to articulation problems involving the planning and carrying out of voluntary movements. Dyspraxic speech is usually inconsistent and unpredictable.

**Dysarthria**   A term used to refer to articulation problems that are caused by nerve disorders. The result is usually weak or uncoordinated muscles that affect articulation. These conditions cause slow, labored speech that has consistent articulation errors.

**Echolalia**   The repetition of what is said by another person as if echoing them. (Teacher; "Hello John," Child; "Hello John.")

**Jargon**   (When used to refer to speech and language impaired children) confused unintelligible speech sometimes called jargon aphasia.

**Lisping**   An articulation problem in which /th/ is substituted for /s/.

**Morphemes**   The smallest units of a language that contain meaning. These are usually words.

**Phonation**   The production of sound, usually speech.

**Phonemes**   The smallest units of a language that distinguish meaning. They are usually letter sounds. The meanings of ca*t* and ca*p* are distinguished by the phonemes /t/ and /p/.

**Semantics**   The relationship between words or phrases and their meanings.

**Stuttering**   A rhythm disorder characterized by repetitions, hesitations, and prolongations. As the child becomes aware of the disorder, grimaces or other movements not related to speech often appear.

**Syntax**   The arrangement of words into phrases or sentences.

**Visual skills**   Identification, discrimination, memory, closure, association, comprehension. *See* Activities: Reading Readiness.

# TEACHING   RESOURCES

In some situations you may want or need additional information. There are many national as well as regional, state, and local organizations that can help you. The following annotated list of national organizations should be useful in helping you decide where to get the information you need.

American Speech and Hearing Association
9030 Old Georgetown Road
Washington, DC 20014

American Speech-Language-Hearing Association
10801 Rockville Pike
Rockville, MD 20852
   Professional society of specialists in speech-language pathology and audiology.

Center for Applied Linguistics
1611 North Kent Street
Arlington, VA 22209

Serves as a national and international research and resource center in the application of linguistic science to social and educational problems.

National Association of Hearing and Speech Action
814 Thayer Avenue
Silver Spring, MD 20914

National Association of Hearing and Speech Agencies
919 18th Street, N.W.
Washington, DC 20006
   Makes referrals to member affiliates and conducts public education campaigns through its bimonthly magazine and films.

National Council of Stutterers
c/o Speech and Hearing Clinic

---

*When letters are referred to, they are written in italics. When the sound of a letter is being referred to, it is written thus: /s/.

Catholic University of America
Washington, DC 20064

Promotes programs and studies of interest or benefit to adult stutterers.

## BIBLIOGRAPHY

Anderson, Virgil A., and Hayes A. Newby. *Improving the Child's Speech*. 2nd ed. New York: Oxford Univ. Press, 1973.

Bangs, Tina E. *Language and Learning Disorders of the Pre-Academic Child*. Englewood Cliffs, N.J.: Prentice-Hall, 1968

Bar-Adon, Aaron, and Werner F. Leopold, eds. *Child Language: A Book of Readings*. Englewood Cliffs, N.J.: Prentice-Hall, 1971.

Blake, Katherine Reed. *Ideas That Work with Young Children*. Washington, D.C.: National Association for the Education of Young Children, 1972.

Bryant, John E. *Helping Your Child Speak Correctly*. New York: Public Affairs Committee, 1970.

Cazden, Courtney, ed. *Language in Early Childhood Education*. Washington, D.C.: National Association for the Education of Young Children, 1972.

Cohen, Monroe D., ed. *Literature, Creativity, and Imagination*. Washington, D.C.: Association for Childhood Education International, 1973. Reprints from *Childhood Education*.

Eisenson, Jon. *Is Your Child's Speech Normal?* Reading, Mass.: Addison-Wesley, 1976.

Felder, Emma Guy. *Beginning Phonics for Parents*. St. Petersburg, Fl.: Johnny Reads, 1974.

Kirk, Samuel, and James Gallagher. *Educating Exceptional Children*. 3rd ed. Boston: Houghton Mifflin, 1979

Liebergott, Jacqueline, et al. *Mainstreaming Preschoolers: Children with Speech and Language Impairments. A Guide for Teachers, Parents, and Others Who Work with Speech and Language Impaired Preschoolers*. Washington, D.C.: U.S. Government Printing Office, 1978.

Longhurst, Thomas M., ed. *Functional Language Intervention*. 2 vols. Edison, N.J.: Mss Information Corp., 1974.

Mecham, Merlin, and Mary L. Willbrand. *Language Disorders in Children: A Resource Book for Speech-Language Pathologists*. Springfield, Ill.: Charles C. Thomas, 1979.

Murphy, John F., and Charles A. O'Donnell. *Developing Oral Language with Young Children: A Parent-Teacher Inventory*. 6 workbooks. Cambridge, Mass.: Educator's Publishing Service, 1975.

Pizzo, Peggy Daly. *How Babies Learn to Talk*. Washington, D.C.: Georgia Appalachian Outreach Project, 1974.

Platts, Mary E. *Launch: A Handbook of Early Learning Techniques for the Preschool and Kindergarten Teacher*. Stevensville, Mich.: Educational Service, 1972.

Rosolack, Mary N. *Speech Improvement in Early Childhood Through Auditory Awareness and Discrimination*. Danville, Ill.: Interstate, 1975.

Sanders, Lois J. *Procedure Guides for Evaluation of Speech and Language Disorders in Children*. 4th ed. Danville, Ill.: Interstate, 1979.

Schneider, Marie J. *A Guide to Communication Development in Preschool Children: Birth–Five Years*. Danville, Ill.: Interstate, 1979.

Sime, Mary. *A Child's Eye View*. New York: Harper & Row, 1973.

*Speech, Language and Hearing Program: A Guide for Head Start Personnel*. Washington, D.C.: Project Head Start, Office of Child Development, 1973. For sale by Superintendent of Documents, U.S. Government Printing Office.

Staff of Developmental Language and Speech Center, Norman Collins et al. *Teach Your Child to Talk: A Parent Handbook*. Cincinnati: CEBCO/Standard Publishing Co., n. d.

Terango, Larry. *Early Recognition of Speech, Hearing and Language Disorders in Children Under Six Years of Age*. Danville, Ill.: Interstate, 1977.

Van Riper, Charles. *Speech Corrections: Principles and Methods*. 6th ed. Englewood Cliffs, N.J.: Prentice-Hall, 1978.

White, James D. *Talking with a Child*. New York: Macmillan, 1976.

Wilson, D. *Voice Problems of Children*. 2nd ed. Baltimore: Williams and Wilkins, 1979.

Zwitman, D. *The Disfluent Child*. Baltimore: University Park Press, 1978.

## BIBLIOGRAPHY FOR CHILDREN

*Awareness*

Brenner, Barbara. *Faces*. New York: E. P. Dutton, 1970.

Describes the parts of the face and what each does. Uses large black and white photographs.

*Rhyming and Sound Books*

Ahlberg, Janet, and Allan Ahlberg. *Each Peach Pear Plum: An "I-Spy" Story*. New York: Viking Press, 1978.

Uses rhyming phrases based on Mother Goose. "Tom Thumb in the cupboard, I spy mother ——."

Alexander, Anne. *ABC of Cars and Trucks*. Garden City, N.Y.: Doubleday, 1956.

Contains the alphabet and also many repetitive sentences and rhyming words.

Latham, Jean L. *Who Lives Here?* Champaign, Ill.: Garrard Publishing Co., 1974.

As they approach each dwelling, animals try to guess from a rhyme who lives there.

McCord, David. *Every Time I Climb a Tree*. Boston: Little, Brown, 1967.

Contains 25 verses with a lot of rhyming and repetition.

Mosel, Arlene. *Tikki Tikki Tembo.* New York: Holt, Rinehart and Winston, 1968.

Great for kids having trouble pronouncing /t/ as an initial consonant. Fun play with nonsense words. Adaptation of a Chinese folktale.

Spier, Peter. *Gobble, Growl, Grunt.* New York: Scholastic Book Service, n. d.

A picture book of animals and the sounds they make.

Supraner, Robyn. *Higgly-Wiggly, Snickety-Snick.* New York: Parent's Magazine Press, 1978.

Nonsense words, rhymes, and collages are combined to produce a book that children will want to hear many times.

Tremain, Ruthven. *Fooling Around with Words.* New York: Greenwillow Books, 1976.

The riddles, stinky pinkies, and other word games are an entertaining way to learn language.

Tudor, Tasha. *Mother Goose: Seventy-seven Verses.* New York: Oxford Univ. Press, 1944.

Traditional children's stories and poems. Lots of rhyming words.

Wiseman, Bernard. *Morris Tells Boris Mother Moose Stories and Rhymes.* New York: Dodd, Mead, 1979.

A delightful book of Mother Moose Stories that will bring giggles to many children and adults.

### Listening Books

Behrens, June. *What I Hear in My School.* Chicago: Children's Press, 1976.

Uses photographs to show some of the common sounds you might hear if you became more aware of your environment. Have children make the sounds they think an object makes.

Brown, Margaret Wise. *Indoor Noisy Book.* New York: Harper and Row, 1966.

Muffin, a little dog with sharp ears, has a cold and is confined to his room. He can't see, but he hears what is going on.

——*The Whispering Rabbit and Other Stories.* New York: Golden Press, 1965.

A sleepy rabbit catches a bumble bee in his throat while yawning. He finally gets the bee to fly out of his mouth. After reading the book have the children whisper their reactions to the story.

Gaeddert, Lou Ann. *Noisy Nancy Norris.* Garden City, N.Y.: Doubleday, 1965.

A little girl makes so much noise that the landlady is ready to evict the family from their apartment. Nancy then makes quiet noises and feels sad. Ultimately she makes average noises indoors and loud noises outdoors.

Kuskin, Karla. *All Sizes of Noises.* New York: Harper and Row, 1962.

Emphasizes sound contrasts. Children can join in making the different sounds.

——*Roar and More.* New York: Harper and Row, 1956.

Discusses words related to sounds that animals make—loud, soft, and in between. Makes voice control fun.

# INDEX

| *Annual Goals* | *Activity* | *Curriculum Area* | *Page* |
|---|---|---|---|
| | Vibrations | Music | 466 |
| | Water Tones | Listening | 355 |
| | Whisper | Listening | 353 |
| To improve auditory memory | Animal Sounds | Listening | 358 |
| | Drumbeats | Listening | 358 |
| | Johnny Hear, Johnny Do | Listening | 359 |
| | Instruments | Music | 465 |
| | Rhythmic Patterns | Music | 464 |
| | Say It | Listening | 352 |
| | Sequencing Songs | Music | 468 |
| | Whisper | Listening | 353 |
| To improve auditory closure | Rhyming Pictures | Listening | 360 |
| To improve auditory association | Drumbeats | Listening | 358 |
| | Fast and Slow | Listening | 361 |
| | Sound Bingo | Listening | 353 |
| To localize sound | Sound and Tell | Listening | 350 |
| To improve visual identification | Alphabet Lotto | Reading Readiness | 366 |
| | Letter Day | Listening | 352 |
| To improve visual discrimination | Alphabet Lotto | Reading Readiness | 366 |
| | Letter Collage | Art | 460 |
| | Warning Signs | Health and Safety | 437 |
| To improve visual memory | Hidden Objects | Mathematics | 416 |
| To improve visual closure | What's Missing? | Reading Readiness | 373 |
| To improve visual association | Match 'em | Reading Readiness | 376 |
| | Opposite Lotto | Reading Readiness | 376 |
| To improve visual comprehension | Peek Pictures | Expressing Language | 337 |
| To improve tactile identification | Letter Day | Listening | 352 |
| To improve tactile discrimination | Barefoot | Outdoor Play | 530 |
| | Food Sense | Science/Discovery | 405 |
| | Feeling Track | Large Motor Play | 519 |
| | Feely Bag | Small Motor Play | 499 |
| | Feely Box | Small Motor Play | 503 |
| To improve discrimination of smells | Food Sense | Science/Discovery | 405 |
| To improve taste discrimination | Food Sense | Science/Discovery | 405 |
| To improve sensory integration | Body Parts | Social Studies | 386 |
| | Bonnie | Music | 467 |
| | Cereal Balls | Mathematics | 429 |
| | Colored Fingernails | Art | 457 |
| | Fast and Slow | Listening | 361 |
| | Popcorn | Science/Discovery | 402 |
| | Weighty Movements | Movement | 478 |

## LANGUAGE SKILLS

| | | | |
|---|---|---|---|
| To improve expressive language | Bookstore | Dramatic Play | 488 |
| | Dress Up and Tell | Dramatic Play | 492 |

| *Annual Goals* | *Activity* | *Curriculum Area* | *Page* |
|---|---|---|---|
| | Interviews | Expressing Language | 339 |
| | Peek Pictures | Expressing Language | 337 |
| | Puppets | Dramatic Play | 492 |
| | Puppet Hands | Art | 457 |
| | Sentences | Expressing Language | 333 |
| | Telephone | Expressing Language | 338 |
| | Who Are You? | Health and Safety | 441 |
| To increase vocabulary | Barefoot | Outdoor Play | 530 |
| | Cat and Mouse | Expressing Language | 342 |
| | Object File | Listening | 354 |
| | Rhyming Words | Expressing Language | 340 |
| | Symptoms | Health and Safety | 439 |
| | Synonyms | Expressing Language | 339 |
| | Will It Fit? | Mathematics | 427 |
| To follow directions | Obstacle Course | Large Motor Play | 515 |
| | Tense Me | Movement | 480 |
| To improve breath control | Bird-in-a-Hole | Science/Discovery | 401 |
| | Blowing Bubbles | Outdoor Play | 531 |
| | Bubble Machine | Outdoor Play | 527 |
| | Director | Music | 465 |
| | Ping-Pong Blow | Small Motor Play | 508 |
| | Pinwheel | Science/Discovery | 403 |
| | Straw Painting | Art | 450 |
| To increase understanding | Opposite Lotto | Reading Readiness | 376 |
| | Traveling | Expressing Language | 344 |
| | Synonyms | Expressing Language | 339 |

## THINKING AND REASONING SKILLS

| | | | |
|---|---|---|---|
| To improve cause and effect reasoning | Bird-in-a-Hole | Science/Discovery | 401 |
| | Blowing Bubbles | Outdoor Play | 531 |
| | Director | Music | 465 |
| | Dress Up and Tell | Dramatic Play | 492 |
| | Food Forms | Social Studies | 391 |
| | Picnic | Outdoor Play | 530 |
| | Pinwheel | Science/Discovery | 403 |
| | Popcorn | Science/Discovery | 402 |
| | Straw Painting | Art | 450 |
| | Vibrations | Music | 466 |
| | Warnings Signs | Health and Safety | 437 |
| | What Would You Do If? | Health and Safety | 438 |
| | Water Tones | Listening | 355 |
| | What's Missing? | Reading Readiness | 373 |
| | Who's Been Here? | Social Studies | 387 |
| To increase logical reasoning | Will It Fit? | Mathematics | 427 |
| To improve classification skills | Match 'em | Reading Readiness | 376 |
| To improve sequencing skills | Scrambled Eggs | Science/Discovery | 404 |
| To improve color concepts | Colored Fingernails | Art | 457 |

| *Annual Goals* | *Activity* | *Curriculum Area* | *Page* |
|---|---|---|---|
| To make predictions | Food Sense | Science/Discovery | 405 |
| | Pinwheel | Science/Discovery | 403 |
| | Scrambled Eggs | Science/Discovery | 404 |
| | Straw Painting | Art | 450 |
| | Who's Been Here? | Social Studies | 387 |
| To improve decision making | No Name | Dramatic Play | 494 |

## MATHEMATIC SKILLS

| | | | |
|---|---|---|---|
| To improve number concepts | Hidden Objects | Mathematics | 416 |
| To improve measurement concepts | Cereal Balls | Mathematics | 429 |
| To improve spatial concepts | Cat and Mouse | Expressing Language | 342 |
| | From Your House to Mine | Social Studies | 393 |
| | Letter Collage | Art | 460 |
| To improve size concepts | Object Sizes | Mathematics | 425 |
| | Will It Fit? | Mathematics | 427 |

## SOCIAL SKILLS

| | | | |
|---|---|---|---|
| To take turns | From Your House to Mine | Social Studies | 393 |
| To increase sharing skills | Solutions | Social Studies | 385 |
| To broaden concepts of families | Animal Families | Social Studies | 384 |
| | Food Forms | Social Studies | 391 |
| | Photograph Story | Social Studies | 389 |
| To increase survival skills | Symptoms | Health and Safety | 439 |
| | Warnings Signs | Health and Safety | 437 |
| | What Would You Do If? | Health and Safety | 438 |
| | Who Are You? | Health and Safety | 441 |
| To increase awareness of roles people play | Audiologist | Dramatic Play | 489 |
| | Bookstore | Dramatic Play | 488 |
| | Circus | Dramatic Play | 486 |
| | Dentist | Dramatic Play | 485 |
| | Eye Doctor | Dramatic Play | 490 |
| | Patient in the Hospital | Social Studies | 388 |
| | Photograph Story | Social Studies | 389 |
| | Stick Puppets | Art | 459 |
| | Visitor | Social Studies | 388 |
| To cooperate with peers | Audiologist | Dramatic Play | 489 |
| | Cereal Balls | Mathematics | 429 |
| | Eye Doctor | Dramatic Play | 490 |
| | From Your House to Mine | Social Studies | 393 |
| | Hug Tag | Outdoor Play | 531 |
| | No Name | Dramatic Play | 494 |

| *Annual Goals* | *Activity* | *Curriculum Area* | *Page* |
|---|---|---|---|
| **AWARENESS** | | | |
| To increase body awareness | Barefoot | Outdoor Play | 530 |
| | Be the Body | Movement | 473 |
| | Body Mural | Art | 454 |
| | Body Parts | Social Studies | 386 |
| | Body Sounds | Listening | 356 |
| | Circus | Dramatic Play | 486 |
| | Colored Fingernails | Art | 457 |
| | Feeling Track | Large Motor Play | 519 |
| | Hand Plaster | Art | 455 |
| | My Puzzle | Small Motor Play | 503 |
| | Ping-Pong Blow | Small Motor Play | 508 |
| | Puppet Hands | Art | 457 |
| | Relaxation Stories | Movement | 476 |
| | Rhythm Walk | Music | 464 |
| | Slings | Dramatic Play | 494 |
| | Symptoms | Health and Safety | 439 |
| | Tense Me | Movement | 480 |
| | Variations on Running | Outdoor Play | 524 |
| | Weighty Movements | Movement | 478 |
| To improve self-concept | Interviews | Expressing Language | 339 |
| | Johnny Hear, Johnny Do | Listening | 359 |
| | My Puzzle | Small Motor Play | 503 |
| To increase awareness of individual differences | Body Mural | Art | 454 |
| | Hand Plaster | Art | 455 |
| To increase awareness of speech and language needs | No Words | Awareness | 535 |
| | Talking | Awareness | 534 |
| | Tongue Twisters | Awareness | 535 |
| To increase awareness of hearing needs | Audiologist | Dramatic Play | 489 |
| To increase awareness of visual needs | Eye Doctor | Dramatic Play | 490 |
| To increase awareness of physical needs | Slings | Dramatic Play | 494 |

# *Needs: Hearing*

When a hearing impaired child joins your class, you will suddenly become aware of the many times during the day that children must listen. They have to listen for roll call, opening exercise, and directions for activities and cleanup. They must listen for music time, story time, and even fire drills. Answers to the many questions you will have about these children may not all be easy to obtain. You may wonder whether the child will talk and, if so, whether you and the other children will be able to understand. How much can this child hear and how will this affect your classroom routine? How much individual time will this child require? What will you tell the other children (and their parents) about this child?

Hearing is important in developing communication skills. Children learn to talk by listening and imitating others and by hearing themselves. The hearing child enters kindergarten with a vocabulary of about 5,000 words. The hearing impaired child may understand and speak only a few basic words, and even the few words spoken may be hard to understand. Our society assumes that people can convey their wants and needs verbally. In school, children are expected to ask to go to the bathroom, to tell the teacher if they are hurt, and to talk with their playmates. They are also expected to put away their toys when told to, and to line up or come when called. Hearing impaired children have trouble following instructions and discussion. They may be mistaken for children who daydream or choose not to listen, and they are sometimes seen as being stubborn, disobedient, or lazy.

Hearing allows a person to gain cognitive information about the world. We use hearing to monitor our physical and social environment. Children who cannot hear danger signals may find themselves in hazardous situations that others can avoid. Being out of touch with moment-to-moment ordinary sounds has a social-emotional impact of equal magnitude. Hearing impaired children must be taught to use other cues in order to be in touch with their world.

## CLASSIFICATION OF HEARING NEEDS

Before you begin programming, it is important for you to find out how impaired the child's hearing is. A deaf child cannot understand speech by using only the ears, even with a hearing aid. A child who is hard of hearing can understand speech (with difficulty) using only the ears, either with or without a hearing aid. The effects on the child vary according to the severity of hearing loss and can be summarized as follows (Smith and Neisworth, 1975; Garwood, 1979):

| *Severity of Loss* | *Effects* |
|---|---|
| Mild/Slight (hard of hearing) 35 to 54 dB (decibel loss) | Will have a more limited vocabulary than peers. If faced and spoken to within 3–5 feet, will probably understand. If in a large group and voices are faint, |

Moderate/Marked (hard of hearing) 55 to 69 dB — Will have a limited vocabulary and may have speech problems. Loud conversations, face-to-face, will probably be understood. Will have a great deal of trouble understanding large-group discussions.

Severe (deaf) 70 to 89 dB — Will have little comprehensible speech. May hear loud voices one foot from ear. May hear warning signals (alarms, sirens).

Extreme/Profound (deaf) 90 dB and above — Will have very little comprehensible speech. Will be more aware of vibrations than of speech itself. Will rely on vision rather than hearing.

The two ears can have different amounts of loss and, typically, the child can function at the level of his better ear. In other words, if a child has a 55 dB (decibel) loss in the right ear and an 80 dB loss in the left, he may function as a moderately hard-of-hearing child.

However, the difference between hearing sound and hearing words is a big one. Consider the following sentence (Bryan and Bryan, 1979, p. 226):

"Let's go camping in a state park next August."

The child may hear:

"Le   o   amp n   a      ar ne  Au u ."

At the same time, the child may see by speech reading:

"Let's  o  ampi   in a state par  ne t Au ust."

Even using a combination of hearing and vision, understanding is still difficult for children with hearing needs. Because of this, some people believe that children with severe to profound losses should use a *total communication* approach— using what hearing they have, signing, and speech reading in combination.

The prevalence of hearing impairment is difficult to estimate. The diagnosis varies somewhat according to the method of testing and criteria used by the investigator. Mild hearing losses in particular are not easily detected and, consequently, the child is not even referred for testing. It has been estimated that between three and five percent of school-age children have hearing needs severe enough to require special educational programming. Of these, one in 1,000 could be classified as deaf (Bryan and Bryan, 1979). These children have losses greater than 70 dB and are referred to as having severe, extreme, or profound losses. These children will learn to communicate using visual and tactile cues, not auditory ones.

The sense of balance (vestibular sense) is located in the inner ear, and children with hearing needs often need more practice than others developing balance skills. They need practice at starting, stopping, and changing directions while maintaining balance.

## Hearing Aids

The ears receive sound waves or vibrations in the air and convert them into electrical signals the brain can understand. When the ear is defective, it sends weak or distorted signals. A hearing aid only amplifies sounds, and it magnifies all sounds, not just speech. Because it doesn't correct distortion, it is not useful for all types of hearing impairments.

Hearing aids are individually prescribed by audiologists and purchased from commercial dealers. Using the aids properly requires training. (The child must actually be taught how to listen; speech may be gobbledygook to someone who has never heard it before.)

Although the hearing aid is beneficial, that doesn't mean the child will willingly wear it. Parents and teachers are frequently frustrated by children who pull out their hearing aids. For young

An ear-level aid can help children understand and enjoy their environment.

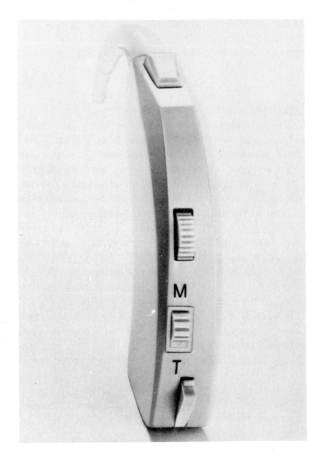

An ear-level aid (ear piece not shown).

3. Know how to move the controls. When the hearing aid "whistles," turn it down.
4. Hearing aids should not be abused, but they are sturdy enough to allow the child to participate in most activities. Try to keep them from getting soaked or sandy.

Remember that hearing aids do not make a child hear perfectly. Be sure the other children also understand this. A hearing aid works well for a radius of only ten feet. Even then it amplifies *all* sounds.

The model of hearing aid a child has is determined by the type and amount of his loss. In general, the greater the loss the more powerful the hearing aid must be. Most young children will have one hearing aid that is worn on their chest with a Y-shaped cord going to ear molds in each ear. These body-worn aids are more powerful than ear-level aids, but they don't compensate for different losses in each ear. They are also conspicuous and a bit cumbersome. As children get older, Y-aids are often replaced with ear-level aids, much smaller hearing aids that fit behind the

The child is unimpeded by the Y-shaped aid he is wearing.

children especially, the aid may feel strange. They will try to make themselves feel more comfortable, often by taking it out. If children were previously unaware of most sounds and speech, the hearing aid may be delivering what to them is meaningless noise. Again, their solution is to remove the aid. Once children see the advantages of hearing with the aid they are usually willing to wear it. Until then, however, much encouragement is needed. If you force the child to wear the aid, the child will associate you with the hated process and you will become ineffective as a teacher. Don't be in awe of the hearing aid, the parents, or the audiologist. Work out a compromise with the parents about what each of you will and will not do about this problem.

You need to develop some skills in working with a hearing aid. The child's parents can help you. You should be able to do certain things the child may not yet have mastered.

1. Put the ear piece back in when it falls out or is pulled out.
2. Check if batteries are dead and replace them. (Keep a supply in the child's locker.)

ear itself. Two aids may be required. However, the aids are almost unnoticeable, especially under long hair.

### Total Communication

The total communication approach uses the auditory, visual, and tactile senses in combination to provide children with as much information as possible. In this system the sender of the message, or speaker, verbalizes the message while simultaneously signing or finger spelling.

American Sign Language (Ameslan or ASL) consists of a set of standard hand signs used in relation to other parts of the body. Each sign represents an idea or concept. Grammatically and conceptually, ASL is a shorthand system. It is fleshed out with fingerspelling, in which twenty-six different finger configurations are used, one for each letter of the alphabet. (See the Glossary for an illustration of this alphabet.)

Not everyone believes in total communication. "Oralists" favor using speech and whatever residual hearing there is. They fear that because signing is easier than speech reading or talking, children will not develop these skills and hence will be able to communicate only with people who can sign and not the majority of society. "Manualists" favor signing and finger spelling with less emphasis on speech reading or talking than is advocated by total communication. Although you should be aware of the issues, you will not have to take a side in the controversy. Teach the hearing needs child in accordance with the parents' choice.

## CHILDREN'S NEEDS— TEACHING GOALS

Related annual goals may be grouped under broad categories called "teaching goals." Outlined under each teaching goal below are the most important needs of hearing impaired children. A child may have some or all of these needs and additional needs as well. Suggestions on what you might consequently teach them are included. Often, a course of action is implicit in the description of the need.

### Sensory Skills

*Visual Skills.* Hearing impaired children need to replace some of the auditory skills they lack with visual skills. Speech reading depends on fine visual discrimination bolstered by visual closure, which fills in some of what speech reading misses. Interpreting signs and finger spelling is both a visual task and a reading readiness skill. Plan numerous activities that require fine visual discrimination. Introduce variety into activities by using three-dimensional objects, pictures, line drawings, and even people.

*Auditory Skills.* Hearing impaired children often have poor listening skills; they haven't developed what hearing they do have. They often listen with their head tilted, to favor the stronger ear. They have difficulty understanding the speech of others, especially when in groups, when the speaker is far away, or when the speaker is looking in another direction. These children need practice in using their residual hearing. Be sure the auditory tasks are presented clearly and loudly enough so that children can hear them.

*Sensory Integration.* Characteristically, when these children explore the environment, they rely more on vision and touch than do their peers. Their visual and tactile skills need to be refined so that they can gain as much information from the environment as possible.

### Language Skills

Hearing impaired children have limited or impaired speech. They often run words together and have a peculiar voice quality that might be described as a flat, high-pitched monotone. Even when they can speak, they often don't because of difficulties in being understood and their embarrassment. When they do speak, the volume may be inappropriate (e.g., shouting in church or whispering at a football game). They often use gestures to express themselves. Encourage these children to speak in small groups first where they feel safe. Be sure to reward their speaking even if it is labored and difficult to understand.

These children frequently lack experience compared to other children their age. Their lack is compounded if overprotective parents don't allow participation in certain activities (perhaps vigorous outdoor play, swimming, climbing, or riding tricycles) out of fear of worsening the hearing loss through falls or infections. Participation in new experiences will help them increase their inner language. (See Chapter 6 for a discussion of inner language.) You must be concerned about the children's safety yet encourage participation as well.

### Awareness

Because of difficulty in communicating with the outside world, hearing impaired children often have highly developed self-feedback systems (e.g., teeth grinding, mouth breathing, masturbation). Such actions result from their need to receive information from other senses. You will need to teach them body awareness.

Children can feel part of a group while developing tactile skills.

In general, these children have usually had more negative experiences compared to other children their age, both medically and personally. They need to learn to view themselves positively and to develop skills in dealing with others, especially when they are being treated unkindly.

### Feelings

These children need to increase their feelings of group belonging. Previous unsuccessful experiences in interacting with children and adults will cause children to withdraw or to avoid participating with others. When interacting, hearing impaired children are further encumbered by their lack of experience. Because they are often not aware of the tone of the events taking place, they frequently lack or have an inappropriate facial expression. When possible, they watch for cues and are therefore followers not leaders. Hearing impaired children rarely reach out toward others and often feel rejected. When they do reach out, their approach is often physical and inappropriately vigorous. Help the children develop the skills to approach others and give them cues for roles that they might play.

### Guidelines

Some children may know how to speech read and may depend on it to various extents. Others, with milder hearing loss, may not have learned speech reading, but will still benefit from picking up cues by watching lips.

1. Don't obscure your lips; wear lipstick; shave a beard or mustache. If your hair is long, tie it back so that it doesn't fall in your face while you talk. Don't talk with your hand over your mouth or with anything in your mouth.
2. Face the child and, whenever possible, bring yourself to the same eye level. Sit in front of the child when helping him, not beside him. Don't talk to the hearing impaired child from another room, while looking in a closet, or while writing on the board. Don't walk around the room or pace back and forth when you talk.
3. See that the light is not shining in the eyes of the child.

Once you are certain the child can see your lips,

1. Attract the child's attention before speaking. Call his name and wait to make eye contact. (You may

even use a prearranged signal, such as flicking the lights.) Otherwise you will have to repeat your first few words.

2. Speak in a normal voice without shouting or exaggerating. It is impossible to speech read when the mouth is distorted. Even if you whisper loudly, the sounds and lips are distorted.

3. Aid the child's understanding of your speech by using appropriate body language (use gestures, point).

4. Reduce background noise when carrying on a conversation. When this is not possible, realize that the child is likely to miss much of what you say. (Hearing aids pick up all noises not just relevant ones.)

5. Some words are more difficult to speech read than others. If you find different ways of saying something rather than merely repeating the sentences exactly, these children will have a better chance of getting the information. It is important to repeat concepts. However, initially be consistent on word usage (*cat*, not *kitty* or *kitten*).

Similar principles are reflected in the use of audio-visual aids.

1. Use as many visual aids as possible (e.g., picture cards of daily routines, charts, hand gestures).

2. Remember that this child will miss much of what is said on TV and in films because the actors often turn their faces away from the camera.

3. Use an overhead projector instead of a blackboard, if possible. This way you do not have to turn your back to the child.

4. Try not to talk in the dark during a filmstrip or slide presentation. If this is necessary, seat the child close enough to see you. Use a flashlight to illuminate your face when you talk. Repeat important answers that other students give.

5. Don't expect the child to react to a tape recorder, phonograph record, radio, or intercom just because you turn up the volume. He still may not understand.

During group activities the following adaptations will help.

1. Let the child with a hearing need sit where he has the best view of the teacher and class. This is in front of, not beside, the teacher and not facing a window. It is best to seat the group in a circle.

2. Call names during a discussion so that the child will know who is speaking next and can follow the conversation. If the children have hand signs for their names, sign the speaker's name. Have other children raise their hands (not call out) so that the child with hearing needs can see who to look at.

3. Remember that the child is often so intent on catching the main points of the discussion that he cannot think about the concepts at the same time. If you call on the child to participate, give extra time to think; don't demand an immediate answer.

4. Summarize and repeat points other children have made.

5. Encourage other children to use gestures and signs when they talk to this child. Ask them to show him what you want.

If the child knows how, signing and finger spelling are aids to communication, whether individually or in groups.

1. Teach the other children some signs and especially the sign for their name. Learn significant signs (drink, bathroom). (Ask the help of the child and his parents or a teacher of the deaf in making up signs for each child's name, and draw these on the back of your roll cards.)

2. Learn to finger spell. When a child cannot understand a spoken word, help by finger spelling the first letter or the whole word. Keep a visual finger spelling alphabet in the room, so you can point if necessary for children who sign and finger spell.

Finally, there are two points of caution. Remember that only about one-fourth of the speech sounds are visible on the lips. The best speech reader only gets about one word in four. Hearing impaired children are great bluffers. They do not want to ask the teacher to repeat. If the teacher asks them if they understand, they will often say yes when in fact they do not. Learn to recognize when a child is bluffing. Ask the child to repeat the instructions if necessary.

*Generalization and Differentiation.* Developing ideas about their world through generalization and differentiation is difficult for children with hearing needs because they learn primarily from direct experience. If a child is shown an armchair labeled "chair," the child may not immediately make the generalization that a rocking chair also belongs in the "chair" class. Because of this, it is important that hearing impaired children be given a larger variety of visual stimuli to help them generalize to an abstract concept. For "chair," you would want to compare as many different chairs as you could think of.

*Introducing the Class.* People disagree on the best way to introduce a hearing impaired child into a classroom. Some teachers have the child not come until the second day. On the first day they tell the children about the child during a group time. Others send letters home and have the parents tell their children before school starts. I recommend that you start school with all the children (having already allowed the hearing impaired child an advance visit to become familiar with the classroom). Then carefully introduce the concept of the exceptionality. When warned in advance about a hearing impaired child, the others conjure up fantastic ideas about what the child will look like. Sometimes they expect the child to have no ears! As your first activity, plan a group time game emphasizing similarities and differences. For example:

"Will all the children with hair stand up?"
"Will all the children with brown hair stand up?"
"Will all the children with red shoes stand up?"
"Will all the children with hearing aids stand up?"
"Will all the children with blue eyes stand up?"

In the process, emphasize that *all* of the children have hair, *some* have brown hair, *one* has red shoes, *one* has a hearing aid, and a *few* (or *some*) have blue eyes.

*Awareness of Special Needs.* If children ask questions, answer them simply and honestly. Encourage the child with the hearing loss to help answer the question if possible.

*"What's wrong with John?"* "There's nothing *wrong* with John. He can't hear as well as others."
*"Why does he wear that box?"* "To help him hear better."
*"Does he sleep with it?"* "No."
*"If I play with him can I catch that?"* "No, it isn't like a cold or chicken pox. John was born that way (or however it occurred)."
*"Can I have a box too?"* "No, ear doctors decide who needs these boxes, just as eye doctors decide who needs glasses. We'll have a box in class someday that you can try out."
*"I don't like it when John hits me."* "I can understand that. John is telling you in his way that he wants to play with you. What could he do that would be better for you?"
*"Can't he talk?"* "He can only say a few words. It is hard to learn to talk when you can't hear other people talk."
*"I hate John."* "Today that is true for you. Someday you might like him."

You might also give the children hints on how to communicate with the child, such as: "Be sure John is looking at you when you talk to him. Can you show him what you want? What can he do that doesn't require talking? What kind of game do you think John would like?"

## CURRICULUM ADAPTATIONS

Many of the adaptations and activities in this section may be minor modifications of your current practices, while others may not have occurred to you yet.

### Expressing Language, Listening, and Reading Readiness

Language arts cause the most problems for hearing impaired children. They have difficulty with both receiving and expressing language. Nevertheless language arts can be made enjoyable for these children.

After reading this section, be sure to read the chapter on children with speech and language needs and to consult a speech and language clinician for additional activities.

1. Label everything in the classroom (tables, chairs, lockers, crayons, paints, easel, and so on).
2. Emphasize some of the basic vocabulary words in each curriculum area. Post the words where they will best be seen or hang them on a string from the ceiling so that all teachers and aides use the same vocabulary. If you have a doctor's office in the dramatic play area, you might emphasize the following four words, backing the labels with pictures (avoid stereotyping by using several pictures).

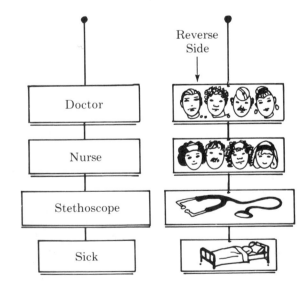

3. Use as many visual aids and gestures as possible to help the child understand.
4. To teach concepts, use materials that interest the child. If you are teaching number concepts to a football fan, you can put the numbers on

checkers, set up a checkerboard as a football field with the checkers as players, and then call the plays: "Give the ball to number 3 and have him run around number 5 and then between 1 and 7." The child scores only if he follows the correct pattern. If the child cannot hear or speech read, use your fingers or cards to show the plays.

5. You can use the concrete to demonstrate the abstract. Use conceptual matching cards; shoe–slipper, clock–watch, lamp–flashlight, shirt–blouse, jacket–coat.

6. Point out objects in the room that are used in the same way but look different: crayons versus paint, short versus long brushes.

7. Show visual analogies and have the child choose the correct card. (See the activities in Part Two for a more complete description.)

8. Have children classify and reclassify objects in different ways. For example: Using small and large shapes, some of which are black and the others white, ask the child to sort them into two piles; when the task is complete, ask the child to sort another way. Demonstrate what you mean, if necessary.

9. Teach situationally, describe verbally what is happening at that moment ("I'm sitting in front of you").

10. Emphasize activities that require fine visual discrimination (alphabet matching lotto) because this skill is needed for speech reading.

Stories help expand the child's world. Start with stories about familiar events before using more creative ones.

1. Choose books that depict familiar sights and actions.

2. Use illustrations that are simple, large, and uncluttered.

3. Choose scratch and smell, or touch books, which have extra olfactory or tactile appeal.

4. Provide the child with auditory cues and visual aids when reading. For example, during *The Three Little Pigs*, squeal, change rhythm, and huff and puff. You might even bring in straw, wood, and bricks and let the children huff and puff at them at the science table.

5. Use flannelboard stories, as these usually have simple, graphic plots.

6. Have the children act out simple stories.

7. Allow the hearing impaired child to preview the story.

8. Place picture books with a clear, sequential story line in the book corner.

9. Avoid using blackboard stories. If you draw on the overhead projector, the child will have an unobstructed view of your face.

10. Choose books with realistic, not abstract illustrations, when teaching language arts. Abstract illustrations are more appropriate for art time.

Fingerplays are excellent for children with hearing needs; they can participate whether or not they can speak. The "choral" aspect of fingerplays sometimes reduces their self-consciousness about speaking. This is an excellent way to teach visual memory and sequencing.

1. Choose short, simple fingerplays at first.

2. Demonstrate the actions as you sing or say the words.

3. Encourage the children to imitate you, move slowly so the children can keep up.

Early reading readiness skills include: habitually looking at words and letters from left to right, making fine visual discriminations, and recognizing a sense of pattern (letters versus spaces).

1. Demonstrate left to right progression. For example, point a marker at the left side before starting and move it to the right as you read.

2. When writing stories of the children's experiences, draw or paste in pictures illustrating significant words.

We went to a store.

3. Use activities that require perceptual (visual matching) skills, such as lotto, bingo, and puzzles.

### Social Studies

The child with hearing needs has to learn the skills to cope with a hearing world.

1. When teaching these children to generalize, use illustrations of diverse families (those with single parents, working mother, grandparent in the home, and so on).

2. Emphasize firsthand experiences but use follow-up activities as well. Take your class to a police station. Later, read stories about police and use police props in dramatic play.

3. Prepare children with hearing needs for social situations they may encounter.
4. Use family celebrations and holidays to talk about similarities and differences.
5. Making maps is an excellent way to familiarize a hearing impaired child with a new situation. Start with maps of known places (the classroom, the play yard) before you branch out into less familiar places (the whole school).

### Science/Discovery

Few other curriculum areas have the potential for discovery, satisfaction, and interaction with materials that science has. Provide hearing impaired children with the right materials and offer well-timed visual hints, instead of asking questions as you normally would.

1. Help the child generalize by providing abundant materials.
2. Allow plenty of time to process hypotheses and conclusions.
3. Help the child understand that things can exist in more than one state. Compare corn on the cob, frozen corn, canned corn, creamed corn, and popped and unpopped corn.
4. Use visual demonstrations.
5. Have the child go through the action when there are directions to be followed.
6. Use a variety of media. For example, to teach about plants: visit a farm, nursery, or plant store; plant seeds, varying the water, light, and soil; look at books on plants; show a filmstrip on how plants grow; invite a florist to speak to the class.
7. Use regularly occurring natural events like seasonal change to teach a sense of predictability in the world.
8. Use items made of different materials, such as wood, cardboard, styrofoam, to broaden the child's understanding of the concept of matter.

### Mathematics

Math goals for the hearing impaired child are directed toward developing a concrete base of fundamental math concepts to prepare the child for abstract concepts that will come later.

1. Use three-dimensional materials (cubes, balls) before progressing to two-dimensional squares and circles.
2. Develop the language skills that serve as the foundation for math, such as understanding the relationships equal/more/less.
3. Use naturally occurring situations to teach math, such as the number of chairs at the table or the one-to-one correspondence between children and napkins. Cooking, sand play, and water play provide many opportunities for learning math concepts.
4. Use human three-dimensional illustrations. For example, have four children form a square; three, a triangle; and so on.
5. Measure with different instruments (ruler, metal tape, cloth tape). Compare relative amounts, using both conventional and nonconventional measures. Some nonconventional measures you might use are sponges and bottles for liquids, the children's feet or paces for length.

Water play provides opportunities for learning math concepts through firsthand experience.

### Health and Safety

Because hearing impaired children may miss some warning signals, their safety is jeopardized more often than other children's. In addition, they often have fewer skills in dealing with dangerous situations.

1. Use traffic warning signals outside with the tricycles, wagons, and so on. Teach the meaning of traffic lights (play Red Light-Green Light).

2. Practice crossing streets.
3. Take field trips to police stations and fire stations. Have the children play being police officers or firefighters.
4. Discuss what to do if the child is lost or hurt, then dramatize the emergency (using dialog) or pantomime it.
5. Use snack or lunchtime to instill good eating habits, and toileting to teach good hygiene.
6. Familiarize the hearing impaired child with the procedure for fire alarms. Incorporate a visual cue (flickering lights or a red flag) into your usual procedure. Try to keep the hearing impaired child in sight during a fire alarm to ensure that the child neither wanders off nor misses later instructions. With older children you might use a buddy system as well.

### Art

Art needs the fewest adaptations for the hearing impaired. Follow the general guidelines for communicating with these children.

1. Help the child with hearing needs learn to use art as an emotional release when necessary. An additional outlet is especially useful in bad weather, when large motor activities are restricted.
2. Post any rules, adding illustrations and the word NO or an X through the picture. Also, post pictures of some of the things the child is allowed to do. Visual reminders of how to carry scissors and put paint away will be helpful to the entire class.
3. Have three-dimensional art materials available.
4. The child may tend to overgeneralize as a result of limited experience. Know that this child will probably learn the qualities of materials (paint versus paste, for example) through trial and error as well as from your demonstrations and watching peers.
5. If the child has a Y-cord hearing aid, put it on his back or outside of the apron to optimize hearing. The noise made by an apron rubbing will make it difficult for him to hear.
6. Give simplified directions because following instructions is more difficult for a child with a hearing impairment.

### Music

Accompanied by visual cues, music can be a positive experience for hearing impaired children. Don't eliminate them from the group because they can't sing.

1. Use percussion instruments (children can feel vibrations and see the beat).
2. Take the front off the piano, so the children can see how and when the piano hammers strike.
3. Choose songs that incorporate motion, so the child can participate in the movement if not in the singing.
4. Show pictures to set the mood for songs and creative movement. If you want the children to pretend they are walking through leaves, use a fall picture with leaves. If they are to be flowers growing, show both buds and flowers in full bloom.
5. Use the piano with a mildly hearing impaired child to teach the concepts of high/low, fast/slow, and other types of auditory discrimination. With a moderately to severely hard-of-hearing child, use a more visual method—drums or clapping.
6. When you sing, use your hand to show when the song goes up or down in pitch.
7. Use rhythmic dance and free dance.
8. Learn to sign some favorite songs. The class may find this more challenging and fun than some fingerplays.

### Dramatic Play

Through dramatic play hearing impaired children can express some feelings and concerns. They can also try out roles (mother, father, teacher, and so on) without fear of being judged. Dramatic play provides some of the experiences necessary for developing inner language.

1. Include a traditional home living area in your classroom initially. (This fosters some sense of security.)
2. Use the dramatic play area to expand the child's environment.
3. Provide play props appropriate to the activities.

### Small Motor Play

Hearing impaired children interact with the world primarily through vision, touch, smell, and the integration of these senses. It is particularly important to help these children develop good fine motor control in conjunction with vision and smell.

1. Use activities that require both visual and fine motor skills (puzzles, assorted nuts and bolts to put together, wood working, bead stringing.)
2. Use activities requiring only the sense of touch, such as sorting graded sandpaper or playing with a feeling box. In case the child is not able to name the feeling box objects, have a tray with a second set of the objects, so the child can choose the matching one.
3. Provide some relatively unsupervised activities to give the hearing impaired child opportunities to make discoveries on his own.
4. Use fingerplays to develop awareness of the hands and fine motor control, which are necessary for learning sign language.

### Large Motor Play

There are a few restrictions placed on the hearing impaired child when large motor activities are taking place. If there is damage to the semicircular canals, the child will have problems with dizziness, with obvious implications. High climbing should be discouraged (falling on a hearing aid hurts). Rough tumbling may also cause damage. Remember, too, that the child's difficulty in hearing verbal instructions poses some safety concerns. The child should stay fairly near you, and you should have an unobstructed view of him if the child is in a relatively dangerous area (near the swings, seesaw, blocks, and so on).

1. Choose activities that help develop the child's sense of balance.
2. Choose activities that require stopping, starting, and changing directions. (Inability to do these without losing balance is a weakness related to the inner ear.)
3. Use activities such as obstacle courses to teach language skills (crawl *through* the tunnel, jump *over* the bar, run *around* the pole).
4. Help the child perfect the skills of running, leaping, jumping, skipping, and so on.
5. Have the children imitate animal walks (with pictures as cues) to help them identify different styles of walking.
6. Help the child use large motor skills to safely relieve pent-up energy and frustration.
7. Use props to help this child realize the intent of the group if it appears a change of plans has been missed by the child.

### Transitions

Transition periods are often not particularly fun for any child. They can become quite unpleasant for the hearing impaired child, who may not have grasped the verbal directions or the other children's intentions.

1. Be sure the hearing impaired child knows the daily sequence. Use a picture poster and point to what will happen next.
2. Keep your schedule fairly standard once it is set. Knowing that some things are predictable gives the hearing impaired child a sense of security.
3. Use visual signs to announce upcoming changes. (One light blink for a five-minute warning, two blinks for cleanup time.)
4. Demonstrate what is going to happen (start picking up, get your coat, and so on).

## CHILD STUDY TEAM REPORT

### John H.

In attendance: Mr. and Mrs. H.; Mr. R., psychologist; Ms. A., speech and language therapist.

John H. is a five-year eight-month-old boy with a moderate bilateral sensorineural loss. John's parents report that they took John to a specialist at age eighteen months for hearing testing. His loss was determined at that time to be moderate, caused by high fevers during early infancy. John crawled at eight months and walked alone at twelve months. Language development has been delayed.

John's parents report he has a younger sibling, Karen, age three, whom he teases and fights with. His social development is of increasing concern to them. They report John does not get along well with other children in the neighborhood. There is one child John's age, but he rarely initiates play with her. When visiting relatives, John stays close to adults. Mrs. H. has attempted to set up play situations for John, but she says these usually end up with John being punished. John enjoys cartoons on television, simple puzzles, and picture books.

The school psychologist, Mr. R., tested John in order to provide an assessment of his learning strengths and needs. Instruments used included the Leiter International Performance Scale, the Developmental Test of Visual-Motor Integration, and the Vineland Social Maturity Scale. John arrived at the testing session with both his parents. He separated easily from them and performed most tasks willingly. Overall, John's abilities lie in the above-average to superior range. John's weakest abilities, although they fell within the normal age range, were in coordination and in copying block designs and geometric designs with paper and pencil. He had an age score of 4.9 on the VMI.

John appeared reluctant to talk to the psychologist. He demonstrated above-average abilities in visual memory tasks and nonverbal activities such as analogies of verbal concepts presented visually. The psychologist recommended a classroom where John could develop his above-average abilities, become more socially adept, and become more comfortable with his use of language. He also recommended an evaluation by an occupational therapist.

The occupational therapist's report was interpreted by Mr. R., as the therapist, Ms. T., was unable to attend. The Purdue Perceptual-Motor Survey was completed. Ms. T. found John's tactile, gross motor, and fine motor skills to be age-appropriate. John demonstrated some difficulties in balance and visual-perceptual-motor skills. Therapy was not recommended. However, Ms. T. will be available to John's teacher as a consultant for implementation of programming to meet his needs in this area.

John has been receiving speech and language therapy since he was two-and-a-half, and Mr. and Mrs. H. have had him involved in a home extension program for the hearing impaired since he was eighteen months old. The speech and language clinician working with John, Ms. A., has updated her therapy report to include the last six months of therapy. Recent test scores from the Zimmerman Preschool Language Scale and the Test of Language Development indicate a receptive language age of 4.0, with verbal usage approximately in the same range. John can identify common nouns, verbs, and adjectives receptively and expressively. He can follow a two-step direction during therapy. John is resistive to using expressive language and seems embarrassed by his speech. During therapy, John will use three-word phrases to identify and talk about pictures and to express his needs. Mrs. H. reports that this is consistent with her observations at home, but also said that John talks less with people that he does not know.

Current goals for John in therapy include an improvement in articulation skills and an increase in his use of expressive language. Ms. A. and Mr. and Mrs. H. feel that a stimulating learning environment is very important for John in order to keep him interested in learning. Speech and language therapy is very important to his development and should be continued. Sessions should be scheduled twice a week on an individual basis for thirty minutes each.

John's parents report that John is very aware of the fact that he has reached kindergarten age and is anxious to attend. Mr. and Mrs. H. want to make certain that John will not be frustrated by kindergarten because of his delayed language development. They also feel that his self-concept and social development are very important now, and they do not want to inhibit John by placing him in a preschool setting. The psychologist and speech and language clinician agree that John's abilities indicate he should have a successful kindergarten experience, but his progress should be carefully watched.

In summary, John's parents and the specialists agree that John will benefit from educational placement in a regular kindergarten with support services in speech and language therapy and occupational therapy. Goals for John should include improvements in social skills, expressive language, balance, and visual-motor skills. Mrs. A. noted that preferential seating is a priority for John, and that he works best in small groups with minimal visual distraction.

Mr. and Mrs. H. would like to involve John in some counseling if his vocalizations and peer interactions do not increase. They are afraid that he is placing a lot of pressure on himself to talk perfectly, or not at all. They feel this will ultimately affect his academic development and is now starting to affect him through moodiness and unhappiness, particularly with peers. Progress in this area will be checked by the kindergarten teacher and John's parents in about three months, when another conference will be held. Scores from speech and language testing will also be available at that time.

# INDIVIDUALIZED EDUCATION PROGRAM

NAME ___John H.___ DOB _12_/_17_/_76_

AGE ___5-8___ GRADE ___K___

SCHOOL ___Windy Hills Elementary___

PARENTS/GUARDIANS ___Mr. & Mrs. H.___

ADDRESS ___1923 New Brook Avenue___

PHONE ___453-0620___

On _8/15/82_, the IPRD Committee
(Date)
met to review all current data and

recommends Level ___I___ placement.

Date of new review ___8/15/83___

Exceptionality: ___Hearing impaired___

Present at meeting:

Parents ___Mr. & Mrs. H.___

Others: Name/Position ___Mr. R., Psychologist___

## CURRENT TEST DATA

| TEST | DATE | RESULTS |
|---|---|---|
| Psych. | 8/1/82 | Above-average to superior intelligence |
| Purdue | 8/6/82 | Balance and visual-motor integration are both needs |
| TOLD, | 8/6/82 | Expressive lang. and articulation |
| Zimmerman | | needs; reluctant to use language |

Recommended Special Services (Hrs/Wk):

Speech & Language / 2 x/wk. (30 min. each)

_____ / _____

_____ / _____

Total Hours/Week:

Special Education Classroom ___0___

Regular Classroom ___12½___

Representative of District/Agency

___Ms. A., Speech & Language Therapist___

The committee has determined the following learning strengths and needs to be reflected in the IEP.

| STRENGTHS | NEEDS |
|---|---|
| Above-average to superior intelligence | Social skills |
| Visual memory | Balance |
| Analogous thinking (verbal concepts presented visually) | Visual-motor skills |
| | Expressive language |
| | Articulation |

STUDENT   John H.    DATE   8/15/82

GOAL   To improve eye-hand coordination

PARENT SIGNATURE _____    TEACHER SIGNATURE _____

| INSTRUCTIONAL OBJECTIVES | EDUCATIONAL METHODS | DATE Begin | DATE End | Eval. | PERSONS RESPONSIBLE Name | Position |
|---|---|---|---|---|---|---|
| Given five beanbags, John will be able to throw them to a classmate a distance of 5' in 4/5 trials. | Hit the Can, Balloon Badminton | 8/15 | 1/15 | | Ms. T. | Teacher |
| Given five beanbags thrown to him at a distance of 5', John will be able to catch them 4/5 times. (Beanbags should be aimed at chest.) | Variations on Throwing, Noisy Toss, Target Bounce | 8/15 | 1/15 | | Ms. T. | Teacher |
| Given block patterns presented visually, John will be able to reproduce the following block patterns with 1" cube blocks. | Torn Paper Flowers, Wire Sculpture, Pouring Peanuts, Cuisenaire Rods, Peg Design | 11/15 | 1/15 | | Ms. T. | Teacher |
| Given paper and pencil, John will be able to reproduce the following shapes with a pass score according to guidelines in VMI* score booklet: ○:△:□:+:/:\:×. | Pockets, Disability Puzzle, Lock Box, Rubbings, Sandwick Tricks, Shape Pictures, Touch Shapes | 11/15 | 1/15 | | Ms. T. | Teacher |
| Given pencil and paper, John will be able to copy his full name on primer paper with a maximum of 3 errors in each trial. | Printing, Language Experience Stories | | | | | Teacher |

*Developmental Test of Visual Motor Integration

STUDENT ____John H._____    DATE ____8/15/82____

GOAL ____To improve balance skills_____

PARENT SIGNATURE _____    TEACHER SIGNATURE _____

| INSTRUCTIONAL OBJECTIVES | EDUCATIONAL METHODS | DATE Begin | DATE End | Eval. | PERSONS RESPONSIBLE Name | Position |
|---|---|---|---|---|---|---|
| John will be able to stand on a line, one foot in front of the other, for 5 seconds in 4/5 trials. | Balancing, Circus, Freeze, Ladder Walk, Seesaw | 8/15 | 1/15 | | Ms. T. | Teacher |
| John will be able to stand on one foot, with no support, for a total of 5 seconds each foot in 3/5 trials. | Balancing, Creative Movement | 11/15 | 1/15 | | Ms. T. | Teacher |
| John will be able to walk on a balance beam, placed on the floor, one foot in front of the other, for 5 feet in 3/5 trials | Obstacle Course | 11/15 | 1/15 | | Ms. T. | Teacher |

STUDENT  John H.                                    DATE  8/15/82

GOAL  To improve expressive language

PARENT SIGNATURE _____        TEACHER SIGNATURE _____

| INSTRUCTIONAL OBJECTIVES | EDUCATIONAL METHODS | DATE Begin | DATE End | Eval. | PERSONS RESPONSIBLE Name | Position |
|---|---|---|---|---|---|---|
| John will increase number of expressive responses during large and small group activities by 50% (baseline data to be obtained during second week of school). | Best and Worst, Flannel Board Stories, Interviews, My Shoes, Puppets, Telephone, Who Are You? | 8/15 | 1/15 | | Ms. T./Ms. A. | Teacher/ Speech and Language Therapist |
| John will increase length of average expressive response during large and small group times to 4–5 words (baseline data as above). | | 8/15 | 1/15 | | Ms. T./Ms. A. | Teacher/ Speech and Language Therapist |
| John will increase number of expressive interactions with peers in dramatic play and block area by 50% (baseline data as above). | Traveling, Dentist, Who am I?, Emergency Room | 8/15 | 1/15 | | Ms. T./Ms. A. | Teacher/ Speech and Language Therapist |

STUDENT ____ John H. ____   DATE ____ 8/15/82 ____

GOAL ____ To improve self-concept ____

PARENT SIGNATURE ____   TEACHER SIGNATURE ____

| INSTRUCTIONAL OBJECTIVES | EDUCATIONAL METHODS | DATE Begin | DATE End | Eval. | PERSONS RESPONSIBLE Name | Position |
|---|---|---|---|---|---|---|
| John will be able to independently lead a small group (3 peers) in a game for 10 minutes on 5 occasions. | Color Lotto, Food Lotto, Alphabet Lotto, Matching Faces, Matching Expressions, Color Concentration | 8/15 | 1/15 | | Ms. T. | Teacher |
| John will be able to name 3 activities each week that he felt he did very well. | Nutty Sort, Hidden Objects, Red Light/Green Light, Traffic Sign Hunt, Scavenger Hunt, Match 'em, What Doesn't Belong? | 8/15 | 1/15 | | Ms. T. | Teacher |

# GLOSSARY

**Air-conduction tests** A measure of the child's ability to hear sound through the air. For testing, the soundwaves are delivered to the child's ear by earphones connected to a pure-tone audiometer.

**Audiogram** A graph on which levels of hearing are recorded. Frequency is plotted horizontally, and intensity vertically. Each ear is plotted separately.

**Bilateral (or binaural) hearing loss** Loss in both ears. The amount of loss in each ear may differ.

**Audiologist** A professional trained in the identification and measurement of hearing impairments. The audiologist also aids in the rehabilitation of the hearing impaired.

**Audiology** The study of hearing and disorders of hearing.

**Audiometer** An instrument that generates sound electronically. The intensity and frequency of tones can be controlled to determine how much or how little someone hears. The results of the testing are charted on an audiogram. Earphones are used to test air-conduction hearing. Bone-conduction hearing is tested with a vibrator that is attached to the head. The difference in hearing scores between air and bone conduction has diagnostic significance.

**Bone-conduction test** A measure of the ability to hear through vibrations of the bones in the skull. These bones can directly cause movement in the fluid of the inner ear. The test is performed with a bone-conduction vibrator attached to a pure-tone audiometer.

**Cycles per second (cps or Hz)** A measure of frequency (pitch). The greater the number of cycles per second, the higher the pitch.

**Conductive impairment** A dysfunction of the outer or middle ear. Sound doesn't get into the inner ear.

**Decibel (dB or db)** A measure of sound intensity (loudness). The higher the number of decibels, the louder the sound.

**Ear** As illustrated in the diagram, there are three parts to the ear: the outer ear, the middle ear, and the inner ear. Vibrations travel through the ear canal and then hit the eardrum, causing it to vibrate back and forth. The eardrum is attached to one of the small bones in the middle ear, the malleus (hammer), through which vibrations are transmitted to the incus (anvil) and stapes (stirrup), until they reach the oval window, the beginning of the inner ear. As the vibrations push the oval window (a thin membrane) back and forth, the fluid in the cochlea moves, sensitizing its tiny hair cells inside. These hair cells send electrochemical impulses through the nerve fibers, through the auditory nerve, and to the brain. The brain then must interpret the signals.

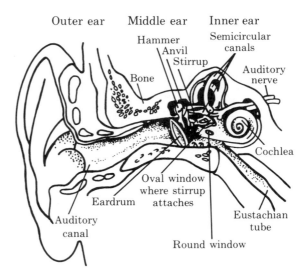

**Eustachian tube** A slender tube from the middle ear to the pharynx. Its purpose is to equalize pressure on both sides of the eardrum.

**Frequency** Cycles per second; pitch.

**Hearing aids** Battery-operated mechanical devices that amplify sound over a limited frequency range. They are composed of three main parts: receiver, amplifier, and speaker. The sound always has some distortion. Hearing aids have volume and tone controls. A *body worn aid* is usually worn in a sling around the neck and chest. *Ear-level aids* are worn behind the ears.

**Hertz (Hz)** A measure of frequency (pitch). *See also* cycles per second.

**Impedance Bridge Test** An audiometric test that measures pressure on either side of the ear drum. It does not require a verbal response and is often used with infants and young children.

**Intensity** The carrying power of speech.

**Manualists** People who believe that the deaf should be taught to finger spell and use conventional signs. They feel the effort required for learning speech shortchanges the child's overall academic and social development.

**Nerve loss** Same as sensorineural impairment.

**Oralists** People who believe that the deaf should be taught only to talk and speech read, not to use signs or finger spell. The deaf can then communicate with hearing people.

**Otology (Otologist)** A medical speciality that deals with the diagnosis and treatment of ear diseases.

**Perceptive impairment** Same as sensorineural impairment.

**Pitch** Relative highs and lows as measured in cycles per second: frequency.

**Semicircular canals** Three loop-shaped tubes of the inner ear that serve to maintain balance.

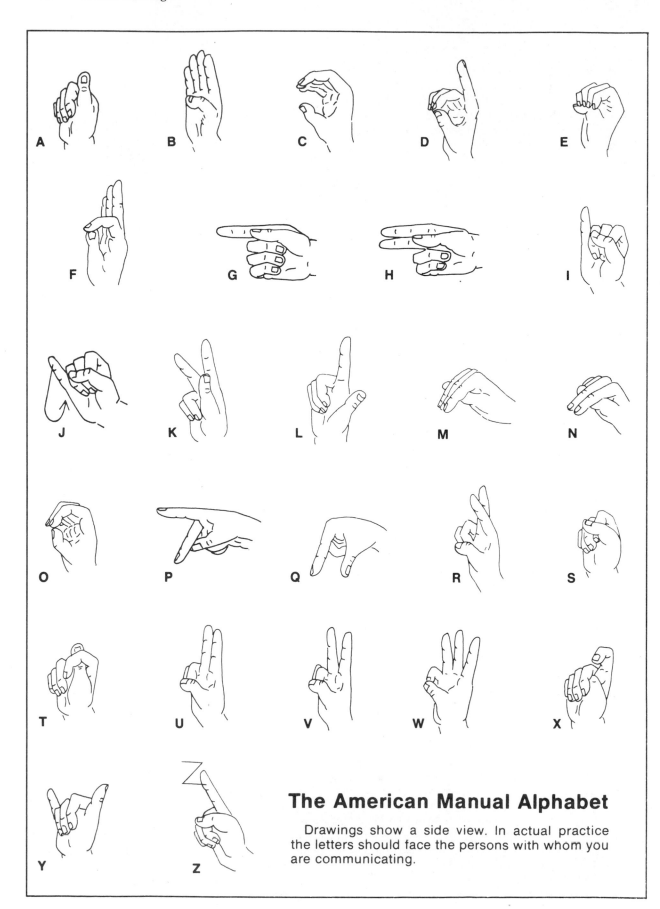

# The American Manual Alphabet

Drawings show a side view. In actual practice the letters should face the persons with whom you are communicating.

**Sensorineural impairment** A type of hearing loss caused by a defect in the inner ear or the nerve to the brain stem (not curable by surgery). Perceptive impairment and nerve loss are synonyms.

**Sign language** The American Sign Language, *Ameslan,* is a system of visual communications using the hands; alphabet is on opposite page.

**Speech pathology** The diagnosis and treatment of people with oral language disorders.

**Tinnitus** A ringing or other sensation of sound in the ear not resulting from an external stimulus.

**Total communication** Simultaneous use of oral and manual methods of speaking.

**Threshold (absolute)** The intensity at which someone can detect a sound at least half the time.

**Unilateral hearing loss** Loss in one ear. Because of the duplication of the hearing mechanism this does *not* decrease hearing by half. It creates difficulty in locating sound and some difficulty in hearing.

## TEACHING RESOURCES

In some situations you may want or need additional information. There are many national as well as regional, state, and local organizations that can be helpful to you. The following annotated list of national organizations should be useful in helping you decide where to get the information you need.

The Alexander Graham Bell Association for the Deaf
3417 Volta Place, N.W.
Washington, DC 20007
  Publishes many useful materials for parents and teachers.

American Annals of the Deaf
The Convention of American Instructors of the Deaf
5034 Wisconsin Avenue, N.W.
Washington, DC 20016
  The American Annals of the Deaf is a directory that lists schools and classes for the deaf, clinics, organizations, publications. Gives information about current research. Send $5.00 to above address.

American Tinnitus Association
P.O. Box 5
Portland, OR 97207
  Physicians, audiologists, hearing aid dispensers, and individuals who suffer from tinnitus. Disseminates information about tinnitus; provides referrals; supports research; sponsors monthly workshops for testing and evaluating.

Ear Research Institute
256 S. Lake Street
Los Angeles, CA 91345
  Develops conceptual and technically feasible approaches to resolving hearing and balance disorders through applied research. Conducts research; offers seminars; maintains library.

International Foundation for Children's Hearing Education and Research
871 McLean Avenue
Yonkers, NY 10704
  Parents and professionals concerned with public awareness of hearing impairments. Supports research; seeks to improve educational facilities for the deaf.

International Parent's Organization
c/o Alexander Graham Bell Association for the Deaf
1537 35th Street, N.W.
Washington, DC 20007
  Encourages and supports parent group action and programs on behalf of hearing impaired children; works for auditory/oral teaching of hearing impaired children.

The John Tracy Clinic
806 W. Adam Avenue
Los Angeles, CA 90007
  Specializes in infant stimulation programs for hearing impaired.

Junior National Association of the Deaf
Gallaudet College
Washington, DC 20002
  Provides a resource directory.

National Association of the Deaf
905 Bonifant Street
Silver Springs, MD 20910
  National headquarters works for improved educational and employment opportunities for the deaf. Serves as an information and referral center. Does not concern itself with the medical aspects of deafness other than to serve as a source of information in medical research.

National Organization for Hearing and Speech Action
814 Thayer Avenue
Silver Springs, MD 20910
  Political action group.


For specialized materials, request catalogs from the following companies.

Sign Language Store
8753 Shirley Avenue
P.O. Box 4440
Northridge, CA 91328

Joyce/Ideal
Ideal School Supply Company
11000 South Laverne Avenue
Oak Lawn, IL 60453

# BIBLIOGRAPHY

Blackwell, Peter M., et al. *Sentences and Other Systems: A Language and Learning Curriculum for Hearing Impaired Children.* Washington, D.C.: Alexander Graham Bell Association for the Deaf, 1978.

Bryan, James H., and Tanis H. Bryan. *Exceptional Children.* Sherman Oaks, Calif.: Alfred Publishing Co., 1979.

Garwood, S. Gray. *Educating Young Handicapped Children: A Developmental Approach.* Germantown, Md.: Aspen Systems Corp., 1979.

Kannapell, Barbara M., Lillian B. Hamilton, and Harry Barnstein. *Signs for Instructional Purposes.* Washington, D.C.: Gallaudet College Press, 1969.

Katz, Lee. *The Deaf Child in the Public Schools: A Handbook for Parents of Deaf Children.* Danville, Ill.: Interstate, 1974.

LaPorta, Rita Ann, et al. *Mainstreaming Preschoolers: Children with Hearing Impairment. A Guide for Teachers, Parents, and Others Who Work with Hearing Impaired Preschoolers.* Washington, D.C.: U.S. Government Printing Office, 1978.

Ling, Daniel, and Agnes H. Ling. *Basic Vocabulary and Language Thesaurus for Hearing Impaired Children.* Washington, D.C.: Alexander Graham Bell Association for the Deaf, 1977.

Miller, A. L. *Hearing Loss, Hearing Aids and Your Child.* Springfield, Ill.: Charles C. Thomas, 1980.

Nix, Gary W., ed. *The Rights of the Hearing Impaired Child.* Washington, D.C.: Alexander Graham Bell Association for the Deaf, 1977.

Northcott, Winifred H. ed. *The Hearing Impaired Child in a Regular Classroom: Preschool, Elementary and Secondary Years: A Guide for the Classroom Teacher and Administrator.* Washington, D.C.: Alexander Graham Bell Association for the Deaf, 1973.

Rampp, Donald L. *Classroom Activities for Auditory Perceptual Disorders.* Danville, Ill.: Interstate, 1976.

Smith, Robert M., and John T. Neisworth. *The Exceptional Child: A Functional Approach.* New York: McGraw-Hill, 1975.

Weintraub, Frederick J., Allan R. Abeson, and David L.
Braddock, eds. *State Law and Education of Handicapped Children: Issues and Recommendations.* Arlington, Va.: Council for Exceptional Children, 1971.

*Biography/Autobiography/Fiction*

Brown, Helene. *Yesterday's Child.* New York: Signet Books, 1977.

Karen is deaf, mentally retarded, and has cerebral palsy. The story tells of the struggles of Karen and her parents, how the problem breaks up the family, and how the mother then deals with Karen and a normal son.


Greenberg, Joanne. *In This Sign.* New York: Holt, Rinehart and Winston, 1970.

The story of a deaf couple—their married life, their adjustments to living in a normal society, and the difficulties they face in trying to raise two "hearing" children. It gives an excellent insight into the world of the deaf and the special problems of normal children reared by deaf parents.


Smithdas, Robert J. *Life at My Fingertips.* New York: Doubleday, 1958.

Bob Smithdas was stricken with spinal meningitis at age five. He lost his vision at once and his hearing by the end of the fourth grade. Through determination and perseverance, he became the second deaf-blind person to graduate from college (the first being Helen Keller). He went on to pursue a career and a fully independent life.


Tidyman, Ernest. *Dummy.* Boston: Little, Brown, 1974.

A deaf lawyer attempts to give legal assistance to a black deaf-mute, who's twice accused of murder. It raises philosophical and practical questions concerning the rights of an individual who lacks the means to communicate with others. Thought provoking and just plain good reading.

# BIBLIOGRAPHY FOR CHILDREN

*Awareness*

Castle, Sue. *Face Talk, Hand Talk, Body Talk*. Garden City, N.Y.: Doubleday, 1977

This text, with accompanying photographs, shows children communicating through facial expressions and gestures.

Levine, Edna S. *Lisa and Her Soundless World*. New York: Human Sciences Press, 1974.

Lisa's life changes dramatically after she gets a hearing aid.

Litchfield, Ada B. *A Button in Her Ear*. Chicago: A Whitman, 1976.

A little girl relates how her hearing deficiency is detected and corrected with the use of a hearing aid.

Peter, Diana. *Claire and Emma*. New York: John Day, 1977.

This story of two girls, ages two and four, who were born deaf is written by their mother.

Peterson Jeanne W. *I have a Sister, My Sister is Deaf*. New York: Harper and Row, 1977.

An account of what a deaf child can and cannot do and how she experiences everyday events.

Saulnier, Karen Luczak. *Mealtime at the Zoo*. Prepared under the supervision of the staff of the Preschool Signed English Project. Washington, D.C.: Gallaudet College Press, 1973.

A description of what various zoo animals eat is accompanied by diagrams showing how to form the sign for each word of the text.

Wolf, Bernard. *Anna's Silent World*. Philadelphia: Lippincott, 1977.

Anna, a deaf child, learns to talk and is eventually able to attend school with hearing children.

*Picture Books*

Anno, Mitsumasa. *Anno's Alphabet*. New York: Thomas Y. Crowell, 1975.

This is an alphabet book with large colorful pictures. No words.

Carle, Eric. *Do You Want to Be My Friend?* New York: Thomas Y. Crowell, 1971.

A mouse searches for a friend. The book helps teach right-left progression, and that not everyone wants to be friends.

Funk, Tom. *I Read Signs*. New York: Holiday House, 1962.

A boy finds the post office by reading and following signs. The only dialog is in the first few pages.

Hutchins, Pat. *Changes, Changes*. New York: Macmillan, 1971.

In this brightly colored book, blocks become various things (boat, house, and so on). No words.

Kent, Jack. *The Egg Book*. New York: Macmillan, 1975.

A chicken watches another chicken sit on an egg and hatch a chick. The first chicken sits on different eggs and hatches a turtle, an alligator, an ostrich, and finally a chick. No words.

———. *Jack Kent's Hop, Skip and Jump Book: An Action Word Book*. New York: Random House, 1974.

Illustrations of children jumping, skipping, waving, and so on, have the word describing the action printed below.

Sears, Nancy. *Farm Animals*. New York: Random House, 1977.

This pop-up book about a farmer and the different jobs he has to do is good for cause and effect reasoning.

Thackray, Patricia. *Big Bird's Rhyming Book*. New York: Random House, 1975.

This colorful pop-up book uses simple (three- and four-letter) rhyming words such as *cat* and *bat*. The pull tabs make it gamelike.

Turkle, Brinton. *Deep in the Forest*. New York: E. P. Dutton, 1976.

The Goldilocks story is turned around making the little bear the intruder. No words.

*Scratch and Sniff, and Touch and Feel Books*

These delightful books allow the child to develop the olfactory and tactile senses.

Berenstain, Stan and Jan. *Papa's Pizza: A Berenstain Bear Sniffy Book*. New York: Random House, 1978.

Fulton, Mary J. *Detective Arthur on the Scent*. New York: Golden Press, 1971.

Hays, Anna J. *See No Evil, Hear No Evil, Smell No Evil: Sesame Street*. New York: Golden Press, 1975.

Hazen, Barbara S. *A Nose for Trouble*. New York: Golden Press, 1973.

Howard, Katherine. *Little Bunny Follows His Nose*. New York: Golden Press, 1971.

———. *Max, the Nosey Bear*. New York: Golden Press, 1972.

Kent, Jack. *Supermarket Magic*. New York: Random House, 1978.

Long, Ruthanna. *Once-Upon-a-Time Scratch and Sniff Book*. New York: Golden Press, 1978.

McHargue, Georgess. *What's in Mommy's Pocketbook: A Touch and Feel Book*. rev. ed. New York: Western Publishing Co., 1971.

McKie, Roy. *The Sniff and Tell Riddle Book*. New York: Random House, 1978.

Mayer, Mercer. *Professor Wormbog's Gloomy Kerploppus: A Book of Great Smells.* New York: Golden Press, 1977.

Miller, J. P. *Sniffy the Mouse.* New York: Random House, 1980.

Ottum, Bob, and JoAnne Wood. *Santa's Beard Is Soft and Warm.* New York: Western Publishing Co., 1974.

Scarry, Patricia M. *The Sweet Smell of Christmas.* New York: Golden Press, 1970.

Scarry, Richard. *Egg in the Hole.* New York: Western Publishing Co., 1964.

———. *Is This the House of Mistress Mouse?* New York: Western Publishing Co., 1964.

Smollin, Michael J. *Sweet Smell of Strawberryland.* New York: Random House, 1978.

Thackray, Patricia. *Big Bird Gets Lost.* New York: Golden Press, 1978.

———. *Raggedy Ann's Sweet & Dandy, Sugar Candy.* New York: Golden Press, 1977.

Walt Disney Studio. *Bambi's Fragrant Forest.* New York: Golden Press, 1975.

Walt Disney Studio. *Mickey Mouse and the Marvelous Smell Machine.* New York: Golden Press, 1979.

Walt Disney Studios. *Winnie the Pooh Scratch and Sniff Book.* New York: Golden Press.

Witte, Eve, and Pat Witte. *Look, Look Book.* New York: Western Publishing Co., 1961.

———. *Touch Me Book.* New York: Western Publishing Co., 1961.

# I N D E X

| Annual Goals | Activity | Curriculum Area | Page |
|---|---|---|---|
| **SENSORY SKILLS** | | | |
| To improve auditory identification | Magician | Listening | 349 |
| To improve auditory discrimination | Body Sounds | Listening | 356 |
| | Instruments | Music | 465 |
| | Object File | Listening | 354 |
| | Rhyming Words | Expressing Language | 340 |
| | Vibrations | Music | 466 |
| To improve auditory memory | Animal Sounds | Listening | 358 |
| | Instruments | Music | 465 |
| | Drumbeats | Listening | 358 |
| | Listen Before You Move | Listening | 360 |
| | Number Tapping | Mathematics | 414 |
| | Rhythmic Patterns | Music | 464 |
| | Sequencing Songs | Music | 468 |
| | Traffic Sign Hunt | Health and Safety | 439 |
| To improve auditory closure | Rhyming Pictures | Listening | 360 |
| To improve auditory association | Drumbeats | Listening | 358 |
| | Fast and Slow | Listening | 361 |
| To improve visual identification | Alphabet Lotto | Reading Readiness | 367 |
| | Look Closer | Science/Discovery | 408 |
| | Sandpaper Letters | Reading Readiness | 367 |
| To improve visual discrimination | Alphabet Lotto | Reading Readiness | 367 |
| | Color Lotto | Reading Readiness | 369 |
| | Expressions | Reading Readiness | 368 |
| | Fishing for Faces | Reading Readiness | 368 |
| | Food Lotto | Science/Discovery | 407 |
| | Follow That Line | Reading Readiness | 370 |
| | Letter Collage | Art | 460 |
| | Matching Faces | Reading Readiness | 370 |
| | Nuts and Bolts | Small Motor Play | 505 |
| | Peg Design | Mathematics | 417 |
| | Texture Paint | Art | 449 |
| | Traffic Sign Hunt | Health and Safety | 439 |
| | Warning Signs | Health and Safety | 437 |

| *Annual Goals* | *Activity* | *Curriculum Area* | *Page* |
|---|---|---|---|
| To improve visual memory | Changes | Reading Readiness | 372 |
| | Changing Objects | Reading Readiness | 371 |
| | Color Concentration | Reading Readiness | 372 |
| | Color Lotto | Reading Readiness | 369 |
| | Hidden Objects | Mathematics | 416 |
| | Scavenger Hunt | Reading Readiness | 371 |
| To improve visual closure | I'm Thinking Of | Social Studies | 392 |
| | What Is It? | Reading Readiness | 372 |
| | What's Missing? | Reading Readiness | 373 |
| To improve visual association | Flannel Board Stories | Reading Readiness | 374 |
| | Food Lotto | Science/Discovery | 407 |
| | Match 'em | Reading Readiness | 376 |
| | Natural Sequencing | Reading Readiness | 377 |
| | Visual Analogies | Reading Readiness | 377 |
| | What Doesn't Belong? | Mathematics | 424 |
| To improve visual comprehension | Peek Pictures | Expressing Language | 337 |
| | Picture Shapes | Mathematics | 424 |
| To improve tactile discrimination | Barefoot | Outdoor Play | 530 |
| | Buttoning Sequences | Small Motor Play | 504 |
| | Buttons | Small Motor Play | 498 |
| | Cave Exploration | Outdoor Play | 528 |
| | Feeling Track | Large Motor Play | 519 |
| | Feely Bag | Small Motor Play | 499 |
| | Feely Box | Small Motor Play | 503 |
| | Food Sense | Science/Discovery | 405 |
| | Grading Sandpaper | Small Motor Play | 504 |
| | Nature Feely Board | Science/Discovery | 404 |
| | Nuts and Bolts | Small Motor Play | 505 |
| | Sandpaper Letters | Reading Readiness | 367 |
| | Texture Classification | Science/Discovery | 406 |
| | Texture Paint | Art | 449 |
| | Texture Playdough | Art | 449 |
| | Touch Shapes | Mathematics | 422 |
| To improve tactile memory | Nature Feely Board | Science/Discovery | 404 |
| To improve discrimination of smells | Food Sense | Science/Discovery | 405 |
| | Wiggly Worms | Science/Discovery | 406 |
| To improve taste discrimination | Food Sense | Science/Discovery | 405 |
| To improve sensory integration | Cereal Balls | Mathematics | 429 |
| | Fast and Slow | Listening | 361 |
| | Listen Before You Move | Listening | 360 |
| | Popcorn | Science/Discovery | 402 |

## LANGUAGE SKILLS

| | | | |
|---|---|---|---|
| To improve expressive language | Di-Vergent | Expressing Language | 335 |
| | Dress Up and Tell | Dramatic Play | 492 |
| | Puppets | Dramatic Play | 492 |
| | Who Are You? | Health and Safety | 441 |
| | What Shall We Make? | Dramatic Play | 495 |

| *Annual Goals* | *Activity* | *Curriculum Area* | *Page* |
|---|---|---|---|
| To increase vocabulary | Barefoot | Outdoor Play | 530 |
| | Object File | Listening | 354 |
| | Peek Pictures | Expressing Language | 337 |
| | Rhyming Words | Expressing Language | 340 |
| | Room Shapes | Mathematics | 425 |
| To follow directions | Listen Before You Move | Listening | 360 |
| | Maze | Large Motor Play | 516 |
| | Obstacle Course | Large Motor Play | 515 |
| | Tactile Gameboard | Small Motor Play | 500 |
| To interpret body language | Body Language | Expressing Language | 344 |
| | Expressions | Reading Readiness | 368 |
| | Feelings | Expressing Language | 342 |
| | Matching Faces | Reading Readiness | 370 |
| | Who Am I? | Dramatic Play | 491 |
| To improve breath control | Bird-in-a-Hole | Science/Discovery | 401 |
| | Blowing Bubbles | Outdoor Play | 531 |
| | Bubble Machine | Outdoor Play | 527 |
| | Director | Music | 465 |
| | Ping-Pong Blow | Small Motor Play | 508 |
| | Pinwheel | Science/Discovery | 403 |
| | Straw Painting | Art | 450 |
| To increase understanding | Feelings | Expressing Language | 342 |
| | Traveling | Expressing Language | 344 |
| | Visual Analogies | Reading Readiness | 377 |

## THINKING AND REASONING SKILLS

| | | | |
|---|---|---|---|
| To increase attention span | Changing Objects | Reading Readiness | 371 |
| | Color Concentration | Reading Readiness | 372 |
| | Color Lotto | Reading Readiness | 369 |
| | Red Light/Green Light | Health and Safety | 434 |
| To improve cause and effect reasoning | Bird-in-a-Hole | Science/Discovery | 401 |
| | Blowing Bubbles | Outdoor Play | 531 |
| | Cornstarch Playdough | Science/Discovery | 402 |
| | Director | Music | 465 |
| | Dress Up and Tell | Dramatic Play | 492 |
| | Food Forms | Social Studies | 391 |
| | Gelatin | Science/Discovery | 400 |
| | Grading Sandpaper | Small Motor Play | 504 |
| | Nature Feely Board | Science/Discovery | 404 |
| | Picnic | Outdoor Play | 530 |
| | Pinwheel | Science/Discovery | 403 |
| | Planting Seeds | Science/Discovery | 398 |
| | Popcorn | Science/Discovery | 402 |
| | Red Light/Green Light | Health and Safety | 434 |
| | School Moods | Art | 447 |
| | Shoe Store | Dramatic Play | 487 |
| | Straw Painting | Art | 450 |
| | Texture Paint | Art | 449 |
| | Texture Playdough | Art | 449 |
| | Vibrations | Music | 466 |
| | Warning Signs | Health and Safety | 437 |

| *Annual Goals* | *Activity* | *Curriculum Area* | *Page* |
|---|---|---|---|
| | What Shall We Make? | Dramatic Play | 495 |
| | What Would You Do If? | Health and Safety | 438 |
| | What's Missing? | Reading Readiness | 373 |
| | Who Has Been Here? | Social Studies | 387 |
| To increase logical reasoning | Scavenger Hunt | Reading Readiness | 371 |
| To improve classification skills | Food Lotto | Science/Discovery | 407 |
| | Match 'em | Reading Readiness | 376 |
| | Picture Shapes | Mathematics | 424 |
| | Room Shapes | Mathematics | 425 |
| | Sorting | Small Motor Play | 500 |
| | Texture Classification | Science/Discovery | 406 |
| | Texture Playdough | Art | 449 |
| | What Doesn't Belong? | Mathematics | 424 |
| | Wiggly Worms | Science/Discovery | 406 |
| To improve sequencing skills | Buttoning Sequences | Small Motor Play | 504 |
| | Natural Sequencing | Reading Readiness | 377 |
| | Scrambled Eggs | Science/Discovery | 404 |
| To improve color concepts | Color Scavenger Hunt | Outdoor Play | 531 |
| To make predictions | Food Sense | Science/Discovery | 405 |
| | Matching Rods | Mathematics | 427 |
| | Pinwheel | Science/Discovery | 403 |
| | Planting Seeds | Science/Discovery | 398 |
| | Scrambled Eggs | Science/Discovery | 404 |
| | Straw Painting | Art | 450 |
| | Who Has Been Here? | Social Studies | 387 |
| To increase problem-solving skills | Follow That Line | Reading Readiness | 370 |
| | Gelatin | Science/Discovery | 400 |

## MATHEMATIC SKILLS

| | | | |
|---|---|---|---|
| To improve number concepts | Abacus | Mathematics | 412 |
| | Cuisenaire Rods | Mathematics | 414 |
| | Hidden Objects | Mathematics | 416 |
| | Matching Dots | Mathematics | 412 |
| | Maze | Large Motor Play | 516 |
| | Number Tapping | Mathematics | 414 |
| | Peg Design | Mathematics | 417 |
| | Spacy Dots | Mathematics | 415 |
| To improve measurement concepts | Arm's Length | Mathematics | 428 |
| | Cereal Balls | Mathematics | 429 |
| | Jump over the Creek | Outdoor Play | 526 |
| | Matching Rods | Mathematics | 427 |
| | Topless Popcorn | Mathematics | 428 |
| To improve spatial concepts | From Your House to Mine | Social Studies | 393 |
| | Letter Collage | Art | 460 |
| | Spacy Dots | Mathematics | 415 |
| To improve shape concepts | People Shapes | Mathematics | 423 |
| | Picture Shapes | Mathematics | 424 |
| | Room Shapes | Mathematics | 425 |

| *Annual Goals* | *Activity* | *Curriculum Area* | *Page* |
|---|---|---|---|
| | Touch Shapes | Mathematics | 422 |
| | What Doesn't Belong? | Mathematics | 424 |
| To improve size concepts | Matching Rods | Mathematics | 427 |
| | Object Sizes | Mathematics | 425 |
| | People Shapes | Mathematics | 423 |

**SOCIAL SKILLS**

| | | | |
|---|---|---|---|
| To take turns | From Your House to Mine | Social Studies | 393 |
| To increase sharing skills | Solutions | Social Studies | 385 |
| To increase survival skills | Red Light/Green Light | Health and Safety | 434 |
| | Traffic Sign Hunt | Health and Safety | 439 |
| | Warning Signs | Health and Safety | 437 |
| | What Would You Do If? | Health and Safety | 438 |
| | Who Are You? | Health and Safety | 441 |
| To improve self-help skills | Buttoning Sequences | Small Motor Play | 504 |
| To broaden concepts of families | Food Forms | Social Studies | 391 |
| | Photograph Story | Social Studies | 389 |
| To increase awareness of roles people play | Audiologist | Dramatic Play | 489 |
| | Circus | Dramatic Play | 486 |
| | Dentist | Dramatic Play | 485 |
| | Patient in the Hospital | Social Studies | 388 |
| | Photograph Story | Social Studies | 389 |
| | Shoe Store | Dramatic Play | 487 |
| | Stick Puppets | Art | 459 |
| | Visitor | Social Studies | 388 |
| | Who Am I? | Dramatic Play | 491 |
| To cooperate with peers | Audiologist | Dramatic Play | 489 |
| | Cereal Balls | Mathematics | 429 |
| | Changes | Reading Readiness | 372 |
| | Color Concentration | Reading Readiness | 372 |
| | Color Scavenger Hunt | Outdoor Play | 531 |
| | Follow That Line | Reading Readiness | 370 |
| | From Your House to Mine | Social Studies | 393 |
| | Hug Tag | Outdoor Play | 531 |
| | People Shapes | Mathematics | 423 |
| | Share Your Feelings | Social Studies | 392 |
| | Variations on Throwing | Outdoor Play | 526 |
| To cooperate with adults | My Shadow | Art | 456 |
| | Visitor | Social Studies | 388 |
| | Who Are You? | Health and Safety | 441 |

**MOTOR SKILLS**

| | | | |
|---|---|---|---|
| To improve large motor coordination | Jump over the Creek | Outdoor Play | 526 |
| | Maze | Large Motor Play | 516 |
| | Obstacle Course | Large Motor Play | 515 |

| *Annual Goals* | *Activity* | *Curriculum Area* | *Page* |
|---|---|---|---|
| | Parachute Games | Outdoor Play | 525 |
| | Picture Relays | Outdoor Play | 526 |
| | Variations on Hopping | Large Motor Play | 513 |
| | Variations on Running | Outdoor Play | 524 |
| | Variations on Throwing | Outdoor Play | 526 |
| To improve small motor coordination | Buttons | Small Motor Play | 498 |
| | Feely Bag | Small Motor Play | 499 |
| | My Puzzle | Small Motor Play | 503 |
| | Sorting | Small Motor Play | 500 |
| | Tactile Gameboard | Small Motor Play | 500 |
| To improve eye-hand coordination | Bubble Machine | Outdoor Play | 527 |
| | Cuisenaire Rods | Mathematics | 414 |
| | Fishing for Faces | Reading Readiness | 368 |
| | Follow That Light | Small Motor Play | 506 |
| | Letter Collage | Art | 460 |
| | Nuts and Bolts | Small Motor Play | 505 |
| | Peg Design | Mathematics | 417 |
| | Stick Puppets | Art | 459 |
| | Variations on Throwing | Outdoor Play | 526 |
| | What Shall We Make? | Dramatic Play | 495 |
| To improve balance skills | Balancing | Large Motor Play | 517 |
| | Flopsy | Movement | 480 |
| | Freeze | Outdoor Play | 528 |
| | Variations on Balancing | Large Motor Play | 518 |
| | Variations on Hopping | Large Motor Play | 513 |
| To encourage creative movement | Be It | Movement | 474 |
| | Flopsy | Movement | 480 |
| | Movement Exploration | Movement | 474 |
| | Moving Colors | Movement | 481 |
| To increase sense of rhythm | Director | Music | 465 |
| | Rhythmic Patterns | Music | 464 |
| | Rhythm Walk | Music | 464 |

## CREATIVITY

| To encourage creativity | Foot Painting | Art | 450 |
|---|---|---|---|
| | Mood Colors | Art | 453 |
| | Puppets | Dramatic Play | 492 |
| | Traveling | Expressing Language | 344 |
| | Who Am I? | Dramatic Play | 491 |
| To encourage creative problem solving | Di-Vergent | Expressing Language | 335 |
| | Hands and Feet | Social Studies | 385 |
| | Solutions | Social Studies | 385 |
| | What Would You Do If? | Health and Safety | 438 |
| | Who Has Been Here? | Social Studies | 387 |
| To stimulate curiosity | Cornstarch Playdough | Science/Discovery | 402 |
| | Look Closer | Science/Discovery | 408 |

| *Annual Goals* | *Activity* | *Curriculum Area* | *Page* |
|---|---|---|---|
| **FEELINGS** | | | |
| To increase awareness of feelings | Matching Faces | Reading Readiness | 370 |
| To express feelings | Feelings | Expressing Language | 342 |
| | Share Your Feelings | Social Studies | 392 |
| To increase feelings of group belonging | Circles | Movement | 479 |
| | Color Scavenger Hunt | Outdoor Play | 531 |
| | Dress Up and Tell | Dramatic Play | 429 |
| | Flannel Board Stories | Reading Readiness | 374 |
| | Hug Tag | Outdoor Play | 531 |
| | I'm Thinking Of | Social Studies | 392 |
| | Parachute Games | Outdoor Play | 525 |
| | Picnic | Outdoor Play | 530 |
| | Picture Relays | Outdoor Play | 526 |
| | Puppets | Dramatic Play | 492 |
| | Share Your Feelings | Social Studies | 392 |
| | Traveling | Expressing Language | 344 |
| **AWARENESS** | | | |
| To increase body awareness | Arm's Length | Mathematics | 428 |
| | Balancing | Large Motor Play | 517 |
| | Barefoot | Outdoor Play | 530 |
| | Be It | Movement | 474 |
| | Be the Body | Movement | 473 |
| | Body Language | Expressing Language | 344 |
| | Body Sounds | Listening | 356 |
| | Cave Exploration | Outdoor Play | 528 |
| | Changes | Reading Readiness | 372 |
| | Circles | Movement | 479 |
| | Circus | Dramatic Play | 486 |
| | Eye-Hair Collage | Art | 455 |
| | Feeling Track | Large Motor Play | 519 |
| | Flopsy | Movement | 480 |
| | Foot Painting | Art | 450 |
| | Freeze | Outdoor Play | 528 |
| | Hands and Feet | Social Studies | 385 |
| | Jump over the Creek | Outdoor Play | 526 |
| | Mixed-Up People | Art | 456 |
| | Movement Exploration | Movement | 474 |
| | My Puzzle | Small Motor Play | 503 |
| | My Shadow | Art | 456 |
| | Ping-Pong Blow | Small Motor Play | 508 |
| | Rhythm Walk | Music | 464 |
| | Variations on Balancing | Large Motor Play | 518 |
| | Variations on Hopping | Large Motor Play | 513 |
| | Variations on Running | Outdoor Play | 524 |
| To improve self-concept | My Puzzle | Small Motor Play | 503 |
| To increase awareness of individual differences | Eye-Hair Collage | Art | 455 |
| | I'm Thinking Of | Social Studies | 392 |
| | Mixed-Up People | Art | 456 |
| To increase awareness of moods | Mood Colors | Art | 453 |
| | Moving Colors | Movement | 481 |
| | School Moods | Art | 447 |

| *Annual Goals* | *Activity* | *Curriculum Area* | *Page* |
|---|---|---|---|
| To increase awareness of hearing needs | Audiologist | Dramatic Play | 489 |
| | Charades | Awareness | 537 |
| | Finger Spelling Lotto | Awareness | 537 |
| | Muffles | Awareness | 536 |
| | No Words | Awareness | 535 |
| | Special Dolls | Awareness | 537 |
| | Voiceless Roll Call | Awareness | 536 |

# 8

# *Needs: Visual*

One of my memories of being in first grade is of Charles, whose mother once asked our teacher whether or not we teased him about his patch. The teacher's startled response was, "What patch?" Charles went out of the house each morning with a patch over his left eye, put it in his pocket, and arrived at school without it. He put it back on before he got home. I don't know if we would have teased him when he wore it, but the fear of being teased or different made him avoid the possibility. It is a very powerful concern that causes a six-year-old to do that kind of planning and remembering. Teaching visually impaired children means dealing not only with those who have noncorrectable problems but also with those who refuse to wear glasses or corrective patches out of fear of ridicule and with those whose visual impairments have not yet been discovered. The child with glasses has visual needs, and so does the child who is blind.

You will have a number of important questions about children with visual needs. First, of course, you will need to determine the extent of the impairment and what the needs of each child are. Can the child deal with everyday classroom tasks or should special methods and materials be used? How do the needs affect the child's development and the programing of the class? Should the room be rearranged to make it easier to get around? Should special care be taken in play areas to protect the child from injuries? How do you head off or deal with other children's jokes and taunts about glasses and patches and the inability to move as quickly and skillfully as they do? And how do you recognize a child with an undiagnosed visual need and discuss the issue with the child and parents?

## CLASSIFICATION OF VISUAL NEEDS

There are a variety of ways of classifying children with visual needs. For our purposes they will be categorized according to the likelihood of having them in your classroom. You are more likely to encounter mild or correctible visual impairments. Before we discuss the categories, it is important to understand in general how the eye works. The eye does not actually "see." It receives light, turns light into electrical impulses, and sends them to the brain. It's the brain that actually perceives visual images. If the part of the brain that sees is severely damaged, a child may not be able to see, even though the eye is completely normal. Damage in the brain or the optic nerve is not correctable. Defects in the eye itself, however, often are. The purpose of most visual aids is to compensate for defects in the eye so that a correct message can be sent to the brain.

### Correctable Visual Needs

The following visual conditions are correctable if caught during early childhood. In some cases if these conditions are not diagnosed and treated the loss becomes a permanent one.

*Amblyopia* is the reduction or loss of vision in one eye due to disuse of that eye. This is caused by a muscle imbalance. The weak eye may turn in toward the nose (*estropia*), away from the nose (*exotropia*), or upward (*hypertropia*). The brain, seeing a double image, will turn off the vision of the weaker eye to compensate. If this imbalance is not treated by the time the child is about six years of age, the vision in that eye will be very poor for the rest of the child's life. Amblyopia is treated either by surgery or by wearing a patch over the stronger eye to force the weaker eye to work.

*Astigmatism* is an error in refraction caused by the lens or cornea being slightly bumpy instead of completely smooth. The image is out of focus because it falls in the wrong place on the retina. Astigmatism can usually be corrected by glasses that compensate for the irregular shape. This condition can also occur with other visual conditions. A child can be nearsighted and have an astigmatism.

*Cataracts* are caused by the clouding of the lens inside the eye. If the lens is clouded, light cannot reach the back of the eye and cannot be sent by electrical impulses to the brain. Some children are born with cataracts (*congenital* cataracts). Cataracts can be removed surgically. Children who have had cataracts removed will wear very thick glasses that help bend and focus light rays in place of the missing lens.

*Cornea damage*, usually punctures or scars, results in impaired vision. Known as "the window of the eye," the cornea protects the lens and the iris. It is possible in some cases to have a cornea surgically replaced. This is the only kind of eye transplant possible to date.

*Detached retina* is usually the result of an injury. The retina comes loose from the back of the eye. As a result, the retina loses its ability to function. This can be corrected by burning the retina back on to the eye with a laser beam. There will be a permanent blind spot where the laser beam reattaches the retina.

*Glaucoma* is a condition in which the fluid in the eye does not drain properly, causing pressure to build up. The pressure will slowly destroy the retina. However, there are eyedrops that control the pressure if the problem is diagnosed early.

*Hyperopia* is the technical term for *farsighted*. The child can see distant things better than relatively close things. The eye is too short, and the focused image that should fall on the retina falls behind it. The shorter the eye the more out of focus the image and the more convex the lenses in the glasses will be.

*Myopia* is the technical term for *nearsighted*. This is the opposite of hyperopia. The child can't see things that are far away. The eye is too long, causing the image to be in focus before it reaches the retina. Myopia is corrected with the use of concave lenses.

*Strabismus* is an error of refraction where the eyes are not able to focus simultaneously on one

Hyperopia, myopia, and normal vision

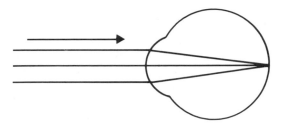

Normal vision

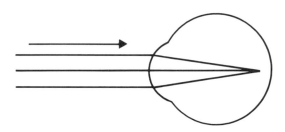

Myopia (nearsighted)

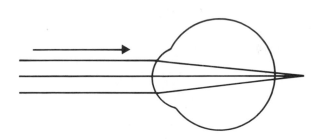

Hyperopia (farsighted)

point. One or both eyes squint all or some of the time. This is typically dealt with by corrective eye glasses and orthoptic training (exercise that works on developing the eye muscles).

### Noncorrectable Visual Needs

*Achromatopsia* refers to a color deficiency or *color blindness*. Children who have it are unable to identify one or more of the primary colors. This deficiency is hereditary and is caused by a recessive gene that affects males. The term *color deficient* is technically correct and preferable to use because young children are often frightened by the use of the term *blindness*.

*Cortex damage* results in loss of vision because of lesion in the visual area of the cerebral cortex. The exact location and size of the lesion determine the amount of vision lost.

*Eyeball damage*, damage to the eye itself, can result in permanent loss of vision. This can be the result of infection or injury. Damage can result from large particles getting into the eye. The longer a partical remains in the eye, the deeper it becomes embedded, and the greater the likelihood of permanent damage.

*Optic nerve damage* is usually associated with the incomplete development of the optic nerve or damage to it from disease or trauma. The optic nerve carries the electrical impulses from the eye back to the brain for processing. If this nerve is not developed properly, it will not be possible for the signals to get to the brain so that the child can see. The effects on vision vary depending on the amount and place of the damage.

*Nystagmus* is the involuntary movement of the eye. It is not a disease but a symptom of another eye condition and is usually an indication of poor visual acuity. Nystagmus does not allow the child to see clearly. Contrary to popular misconceptions, the child will not see objects as being jerked back and forth. Rather, things will look blurry. Since nystagmus is only a symptom, it is important to diagnose the real condition.

Use the senses of touch and hearing to teach concepts.

### Visual Acuity

Visual acuity is the resolving power of the eye. We usually measure this by having children identify or match letters or pictures in various sizes, a standard distance from the chart. That distance is 20 feet (6.1 meters). A person who can see at 20 feet what most people see at 20 feet has normal vision. Normal vision is expressed in a fraction: 20/20. For children below third grade, vision of 20/40 or better in each eye or vision of 20/30 or better when using both eyes is considered normal.

*Low Vision (Partially sighted).* Legally, a partially sighted person is one with a corrected visual acuity between 20/200 and 20/70. The American Foundation for the Blind, as well as most educators, prefer to use the term *partially sighted* for those with degrees of visual impairment, but with enough usable vision for learning through the help of magnification and large print books.

*Blind.* A person is legally blind who has a visual acuity no better than 20/200 in their better eye with correction. The legally blind person sees at 20 feet what people with normal vision can see at 200 feet

or has a field of vision restricted to 20 degrees or less (tunnel vision). Educationally, a person who is blind will learn using the auditory and tactile modes.

Although we have no accurate figures for how many preschool children have noncorrectable visual disorders, the United States Office of Education estimates that approximately one-tenth of one percent of school-age children are in this category. However, if you add noncorrectable to correctable visual disorders, the estimates are as high as 20 percent. Of every twenty-five children then, five are likely to have vision problems of some sort (Garwood, et al, 1979).

In addition to accommodating programming to those with visual needs, the preschool teacher plays an active role in early diagnosis. Unless we have a particular reason to suspect that a child has a visual problem, it usually doesn't occur to us to have the child's vision checked by an eye doctor. Children themselves are usually no help, since they assume that whatever vision they have is normal. There are, however, some things that you may observe or hear that will lead you to suspect a visual impairment. If your observations support your suspicion, point out the symptoms to the parents, state your concerns, and ask them to take the child to an eye doctor (ideally a pediatric or developmental ophthalmologist).

First, look at the child's eyes to see if they are red,

watery, or appear to have a discharge; if they are not coordinated (one eye remains still while the other follows the object); if the eyelids are red, swollen, crusted, or droopy; if the pupil is white; or if there are frequent (recurring) styes. Any child with these symptoms should have an eye examination *soon*.

Other general signs of visual impairment include frequent frowning, squinting, or eye rubbing; shutting or covering one eye; tilting the head to one side or the other; and frequently complaining about headaches, stomachaches, or being unable to stand up because of dizziness.

In addition to these symptoms, there are behaviors and complaints that may indicate vision problems. When doing close work such as looking at books, puzzles, or games, a child with visual needs may blink continually, hold a book (or place himself) too close or too far away, keep changing the distance of the book, or over- or underestimate distance when working with puzzles or pegboards. When doing visual work at a distance (such as during group time, films, or slides) the child may seem inattentive or lose interest after a brief time. (This is, of course, more significant in a child who usually attends well during other activities.)

Other symptoms to look for during activities that require distance vision or when outside are the inability to identify parents, friends, or teachers at a distance; not noticing objects from across the room or playground; difficulty in such activities as calendar reading or blackboard games; bumping into things; or misjudging distances in games.

One thing to watch out for, however, is that the frequent complaint "I can't see" is usually unrelated to visual needs. Sometimes it seems as if *no* child can "see" during group time. Keep in mind that, unless they are just chiming in with the others, children who really can't see are not likely to tell you that.

One of the most common screening tests with very young children is the Flash-Card Vision Test, which uses three symbols (apple, house, and umbrella) that can be either verbally or manually matched. Another common test, the Snellen (grades K–3), is a chart with the letter E in different spatial arrangements. These are relatively easy tests to give and are often used by the school nurse.

The question is, what can you, as a teacher, do to help children use the vision they have and the vision aids they need? When you are working with a child with correctable vision problems, the dilemma is that you want the child to wear the patch or glasses *and* to enjoy learning. You can't afford to be cast in the role of the villain who *makes* the child wear these things. First check with the parents or, if necessary, the ophthalmologist to be certain of what the child is supposed to do. Then the trick is to make the child *want* to do what he is supposed to.

## CHILDREN'S NEEDS—
## TEACHING GOALS

Related annual goals may be grouped under broad categories called "teaching goals." Outlined under each teaching goal below are the most important needs of visually impaired children. A child may have some or all of these needs, and additional needs as well. The greater the impairment, the more likely it is that teaching modifications will have to be made. Suggestions on what you might consequently teach these children are included. Often, a course of action is implicit in the description of the need.

### Sensory Skills
All children with visual needs will benefit from practice in using what vision they have and from developing their other senses.

*Visual Skills.* Fostering visual skills means encouraging children to use their vision in a way most advantageous to them. This means encouraging children to wear their glasses or patch. Help children compensate for reduced vision by regulating the light levels in the room. Allow them to hold books and other visual material at the best place for them even if it seems odd to you. Remember, they will not hurt their eyes through use.

Within their ability to see, teach them visual discrimination. Start with gross discrimination paired with tactile reinforcement (shapes and sizes), then progress to finer distinctions. Because these children may miss details, work on visual closure. It will help them make better guesses about what is missing.

*Auditory Skills.* Children with visual needs are more dependent on hearing to deal with their environment, to master (advanced) language skills, and to guard their personal safety. It is important that they learn to identify and discriminate between sounds. Help children develop better skills in this area through the use of sound eggs and listening tapes. Tapes and records of stories and music are good for classifying sounds (long, short, high, low) and for identifying who or what might make that sound and in what situations; children also need practice locating sounds.

### Language Skills
Children with visual needs may rely more on auditory cues to learn speech, whereas other children can more easily see and imitate movements of the lips, mouth, and jaw. Encourage children to ask what things are and help them to broaden their understanding of labels used. When enhancing lan-

guage skills, use real objects and field experience to help clarify points and build inner language. Encouraging feedback from the children about their perceptions will enable you to clarify misunderstandings and foster increased verbalization.

Following verbal directions is another important language skill. Start with simple one or two step directions. Remember to keep them concrete.

## Thinking and Reasoning Skills

Children must develop many concepts, but most of these are useless unless they know when to use them. For example, children can learn to identify moving cars by ear and by sight, but this isn't much help unless they listen and look before crossing a street. Learning to make predictions about what will happen under a specified set of circumstances is important as a way of developing independence and creating a sense of predictability in their world.

## Awareness

Children with limited vision tend to develop body awareness more slowly because of lack of confidence or having fewer examples to emulate. Exercises in naming body parts and the ways in which they move are helpful. Hold the child's hands in your own as you point and demonstrate, if necessary. Encourage children to explore a variety of methods of moving from place to place. Have them talk about when they could use these different methods. They need to become more aware of their body in relation to their surroundings. Provide an environment of acceptance and experimentation that will build these children's self-confidence.

## Guidelines

The modifications that you will need to make in your classroom depend on the needs of the particular children you have. These guidelines are divided into two sections. The first deals with the techniques that you will use to encourage children to wear the glasses or patch that allow them to use their vision. The second section provides guidance in how to modify your room for children whose corrected vision still qualifies them as being partially sighted or blind.

*Corrected Visual Needs.*

1. Find out when and for how long glasses must be worn. For example, are the glasses to be worn at *all* times? Sometimes the correction is for specific use only. A nearsighted child wears glasses to see at a distance, but because this correction may dis-

tort the child's vision for close work, it would be inappropriate to keep the glasses on during seat work.

2. Observe the child's behavior with aids. Does the child continually take the glasses off or look over them? Such actions may mean the correction is not helping and further consultation with the ophthalmologist or optometrist may be necessary. Young children can be difficult for the ophthalmologist to test and an incorrect prescription sometimes results.

3. If a child refuses to wear glasses, try to create a situation in which the child needs to wear the glasses to succeed. How you actually do this depends on the problem. If, for example, a child is farsighted, find an intriguing book or game that requires close vision. Then, depending on the circumstances, say something like: "Before you got your glasses we couldn't have played this," or "I'd like to play this game with you, but you forgot your glasses. If you wear them tomorrow, we can play." You might also make appropriate statements like: "You've learned to do this so much faster since you got your glasses," or "I like the way you look with your glasses." The child will feel rewarded not only by the activity, but also by your attention.

4. Create a need to see. For example, if a nearsighted child will not wear glasses, you might have that child sit as far away from you as possible during group time. Then, when the child realizes that there is a need to see (in the middle of a story with pictures or during a fingerplay), have an aide bring the child's glasses.

   This sounds like a manipulative thing to do and the child will have a harder time learning, but if you and the parents agree that it is important to wear the glasses, you must create a definite need and then reinforce the change in behavior that occurs. This process may be repeated many times before the behavior is established. You may have a farsighted child sit as close to you as possible during group time and then follow the procedure described above. Be careful to do this subtly and in a matter-of-fact way so as not to bring the attention of the group to the child.

5. A unit on feelings may be necessary to increase other children's awareness of visual needs, and the child involved might be asked to explain his reactions to taunting. At first, you may have to lead the discussion and state some typical reactions, but you should gradually help the child learn to speak up. Perhaps a session on assertiveness training will help. Children must learn to say, "I don't like it when you call me 'four eyes.'"

6. A unit on sight may also help all children better understand how they see. Discuss the sense of vision as well as a variety of visual problems. Simulating various visual needs creates awareness

and is educational as well. Suggestions for appropriate activities are given in the activities section of this book.

7. Don't fall into the trap of saying, "I'll bet you can see much better since you got your glasses." A child who doesn't want to wear glasses will probably respond, "No, I can't," even when you know he can. Sometimes reality is irrelevant. Remember, if it is important that a child learn a particular thing, such as safety rules, make sure that he can learn it with or without glasses.

## Uncorrected Visual Needs

*Partially Sighted.* Children who are partially sighted need additional accommodations.

1. Be aware of lighting conditions and your source of light. Use shades to regulate the amount of natural light in your room. (Ideally, for all children, illumination should be between 70 and 100 foot-candles.) Light switches with dimmers can be helpful (but most cannot be used with fluorescent lights). Don't stand or sit with your back to the light source.
2. Arrange seating so that lighting conditions favor those who need it most. (Check the eye specialist's report. For some children maximum illumination is best, and for others lower-than-normal levels are optimal.)
3. Light-colored tables (or dishes) should have a dull finish; glare is fatiguing.
4. Where possible, paint the rims of bookcases, tables, and door frames with a lighter or darker color that will make the edges easier to see. Use a dark light switch against light-colored walls so that it will stand out.
5. Use a heavy black marking pen to outline the boundaries of the paper so that the child knows where the edges are. Look at the books you have in your reading area. Make sure that some of them have clear, simple pictures and large print.
6. Try to use materials with distinctive shapes and textures and bright, high-contrast colors.
7. Try to keep the general noise level down. A child with visual needs relies heavily on auditory cues, and these will be masked by noise. (If your room is beside the playground or cafeteria, you might try to have it changed.)
8. Avoid excessive detail on bulletin boards. Be aware of the child's vision when you display the children's work. The work of partially sighted children should be hung at their eye level. They can see it displayed and they can point it out to others.
9. Think about what you do to reinforce children's behavior. Do you rely on smiles, gestures, body cues, and eye contact? These are visual cues.

With the partially sighted, you need to talk and touch for reinforcement.

*Blind.* Children who are blind need even more accommodations.

1. A well-arranged classroom is a great help to all children but especially to those with visual needs. Eliminate clutter and confusion! Keep things neat and make sure that toys are picked up as soon as the children are finished with them and that chairs are pushed under the tables. Eliminate unnecessary obstacles in the classroom. Those that are necessary should have a consistent location. Consolidate items where possible. (For example, have one large wastebasket rather than many little ones.) Keep doors fully open or completely shut. Even children with excellent vision tend to run into partly opened doors. Round tables are safer than rectangular ones because there are no corners to bump into. If rectangular ones are all you have, pad sharp edges with foam. If you are a person who likes to arrange and then rearrange your classroom, *don't!* It takes a while for children with visual needs to get their bearings and feel comfortable in a room. If possible, give these children the chance to become acquainted with the arrangement of the room before the other children come in.

   Use auditory, olfactory, and tactile cues to structure the room. The bubbling of an aquarium might identify the science area; a rug could mark the story area; wind chimes would indicate that the outside door is open, and so on.
2. Encourage independence. When you assign lockers or coat hooks, be sure to give this child one that is easy to locate—an end one that's out of the traffic pattern. Don't move objects around after this child has placed them. Moving something two inches may mean that it is "gone," since the child can't visually scan the area.
3. Encourage the child to find things without help. Use a label maker to put raised labels on materials where possible. It is more important to label favorite toys with something easy to find than to make a descriptive label. (A puzzle of the Three Little Pigs might have just the raised number *3* on it rather than the entire title.) Make sure the materials are put away so that the label is facing out. Use rubber bands as labels on round objects. You might put one rubber band on the red paint, two on the blue, and three on the yellow. (This is good for children with color deficiencies also.)

   Be careful not to give a blind child *unnecessary* special treatment. Before you give this child help that you would not give others, ask the child if he needs it. Do offer help, but don't take over or allow the other children to do the task for the child.
4. Your teaching techniques will also have to be

modified slightly. When you enter a room, especially if the child is alone, tell the child that you are there. Encourage the children to do the same. Also make it clear when you leave, especially if you are wearing soft-soled shoes—it is rarely necessary with clogs! Use the other children's names during group time when possible. Have you ever talked to an unidentified person on the telephone who assumes you know who is speaking? It's disconcerting until you identify the person. It is important for the blind child to know who is present, especially at the beginning of the year. Use auditory cues—such as a short tune, a chord on the piano, or a song—to signal regular activities, such as cleanup time. Be consistent in using the signals, so the children learn to associate the activities and cues. Help out with an ongoing monolog about what is happening during an activity. If the class is making cookies, say "Susie has finished sifting the flour, and now Harry is going to beat the batter." This also helps the child learn to identify sounds.

5. When talking to this child, keep your voice within normal limits. (Some of us assume that those who don't see well also don't hear well.) When a blind child is present, talk directly to the child, not about him. Don't ask Gloria's father if she wants to play in the block area, ask her. (Her father may answer, but that is a different problem.) Don't eliminate the words *see* and *look* from your vocabulary—use them when they are appropriate. When giving directions, use characteristics that can be felt or counted rather than seen.

   Make sure that the instructions you give really help. "It's right over there" is not enough. You have to name places and specify ways of doing things. It helps if the child knows right from left. If not, have the child wear something (rings, bracelet, watch, ribbon) on one hand or arm so that you can say, "Reach up with the hand with the ribbon on it."

6. When walking with a blind child, you may go in front, but never behind. If you want to walk alongside, let the child hold your arm or wrist; don't hold his. This allows a greater sense of the movement of your body, especially when you turn or go up or down steps.

## CURRICULUM ADAPTATIONS

The amount of visual acuity a child has will determine which, if any, curriculum modifications have to be made. The less vision the child has, the more the auditory and tactile channels must be used and the use of any residual vision encouraged.

### Expressing Language, Listening, and Reading Readiness

Children who are visually impaired have a greater need for understanding speech than their normally sighted peers since they are often dependent on verbal information to perform certain tasks. Even children with corrected vision problems don't always wear their glasses and may often be dependent on speech. They all need to be encouraged to use vision.

1. Use language to help children focus their vision, as well as to get feedback. "Can you see that wheel? Do you see what's inside the wheel? Those are spokes. Can you count them?"
2. Go from gross to fine discriminations, and from situations where you supply the language to those where you ask for the child to express language.
3. Use words that refer to things that can be smelled, touched, heard, seen, tasted, or experienced directly. Try to make the words you use as concrete as possible, using real examples whenever you can. Then move on to more abstract language concepts such as *time, friendship,* and so on.
4. Use functional definitions of objects as well as descriptive ones. "A ball rolls" or "a ball bounces" should be used in addition to the definition "a ball is round." Reinforce the concept by letting the child roll and bounce the ball.
5. In order to move freely, the low-vision child needs to be able to follow verbal directions. Words like *stop/go, high/low, big/little, in/out/on,* and *hard/soft* are useful. Games like "Simon Says" and "May I" work well for teaching directions.

Stories are a useful way of expanding the children's world, but it is important to start with themes children are familiar with. It is preferable to use pictures that illustrate the story's major points in a simple way. Point out to the children the relationship of the picture to the story. Create a need to see within their ability to discriminate. For low-vision children:

1. When you read stories, you might pass around small replicas of the major objects (rabbits, carrots, trains) for the children to feel. The same can be done with textures and smells. "Scratch 'n' Sniff" books and "Touch and Feel" books are useful, but they tend to wear out quickly.
2. Use cassette tapes or records of books at a listening center. These allow more individualization and choice in the books available. You can make your own recordings of favorite books. You might even bring in blank cassettes so that the children can "write" their own books.
3. Have books with large type and in braille. Even if

the child does not require braille, it broadens their range of experience and understanding to develop the idea that braille is a form of writing. "Talking books" may prove useful. (These are available from the National Chapter of the Visually Impaired. A new series for four-to-five-year-old children was recently released.)

Fingerplays incorporate language as well as fine motor skills.

1. Begin with simple, short fingerplays that have more large than small movements. (In other words, teach "Head, Shoulders, Knees, and Toes" before "Thumbkin.")
2. For children who aren't picking up the details and sequence, try to teach the fingerplays to parents so the children can practice them at home or while traveling.
3. Children with low vision find fingerplays difficult because they can't see some of the finer details. When teaching fingerplays to these children, have someone help the child respond at the appropriate time so that the child begins to associate the movement with the words.

In the area of reading readiness, the emphasis is on developing and refining visual skills. If children are having problems developing these skills, you may suspect visual needs. It is not unlikely that you will find children who can't make the necessary distinctions to develop reading skills. Confer with the parents and refer those children for visual screeing.

1. Start with large objects that have gross distinctions. Simple shapes are fine, such as circles, triangles, and squares. Encourage children not only to label and distinguish among shapes, but also to point out salient characteristics (a circle doesn't have any corners, a triangle has three). Have children trace the shapes with their index finger to gain a motor as well as a visual sense of these distinctions.
2. When children can make gross distinctions, work on finer ones. Even when you teach these, try to point out significant features. Use large letters and have the children trace them with their fingers. Teach that *A* has straight lines, *O* has curved lines, and *P* has straight and curved lines. Teach by contrasting *A*, *O*, and *P* and use other contrasting groups of shapes before you have the children attempt to differentiate among *A*, *K*, *W*, for example, which have only straight lines.

Children with low vision may have to combine their usable vision with tactile skills to learn reading readiness. If the amount of usable vision decreases, the need for more tactile discrimination will increase since this is a prebraille skill. Among the things that can be used to help these children are sandpaper letters and texture cards (for matching practice). Be sure the visual discrimination activities you employ are possible for the children. If not, find ways to adapt them, such as outlining significant features with a wide marking pen.

## Social Studies

All children need to learn about the world around them, and field trips are a pleasant and effective way to accomplish this. Visual needs children in particular can use many hands-on experiences in order to make accurate generalizations. Even children who have fully corrected vision have spent some large portion of their life without optimal vision. (If the corrective lenses were worn at age two and the child is now four, that is *half* of her lifetime.)

1. Try to plan many field trips with *small* groups of children so that all of them can participate in the experience. It isn't enough just to see a cow, especially if the child can't see it well. The child has to feel it and feel enough of it to avoid the classic errors of the blind men with the elephant.
2. Always provide follow-up activities with stories and dramatic play after field trips. Have the children describe with all their senses what they remember. Drink milk, smell and handle hay, make farm sounds, and sing farm songs.
3. Help children become aware of the role the medical profession plays in assessing visual acuity, as well as prescribing corrective lenses. This can be done with a field trip, a visit from an eye doctor, or both.
4. If you know a blind person who would be comfortable with the children, have the person visit. (A seeing eye dog always makes an impression.)

## Science

Science activities can help children learn about the sense of vision and the other senses. Emphasize creative problem solving and discovery.

1. Help children learn about the eye and how it works.
2. Talk about the purpose of lenses. Have magnifying glasses and binoculars available in the science area. Talk about the difference in the amount of detail that can be seen with the naked eye and with magnification. A field trip to visit a planetarium or observatory would also be interesting.
3. Have children participate in experiences in which materials change form, such as making

butter or melting ice. Be sure to let low vision children feel the changes as well.

4. Discuss the weather and appropriate dress for different types of weather. Talk about and feel fabrics used in warm versus cold weather clothing. Examine materials designed for use in the rain. Let children have time and opportunity to really handle these materials.

## Mathematics

Number concepts are necessary for all children to learn. The fun is in using them creatively to help children explore and classify their world. For children with low vision, the tactile-motor aspect of learning these concepts can be added with a few modifications.

1. When teaching number concepts, start with real objects. Food works well because it can be used informally during snack time and eaten afterward. Everyone gets *one* carton of milk, *two* crackers, *ten* raisins, and so on. An abacus is also useful for counting. One can both see and feel the placement of the beads and check back if necessary. Encourage children to count. Have them count the days in the month, the number of children in the classroom, the number of boys, girls, children wearing pants, children with tie shoes, and so on. Have them even count the steps between places they are likely to go often.
2. Matching together large dominoes with indented dots is a good activity that teaches fine motor skills as well as number concepts.
3. Use actual objects for teaching geometric shapes and the concept of size. When the basics have been mastered, go on to pictures of these objects and then to finding specific shapes and sizes within complex pictures (a traffice signal light—three circles on a cylinder).
4. Have children use their body and other devices to measure. Record these measurements. Special modifications should be made to help low vision children understand distances—an arm's length, two paces, three handspans. Glue pieces of string on the paper to make graphs with lines that can be felt.

## Health and Safety

This is an important and difficult area of learning for all young children. It requires them to consciously inhibit their spontaneous curiosity and think through the implications of actions *before* doing them. For children with low vision, the possibility of falling or bumping into things, or stooping over and hitting something, is far greater than for other children, yet the price of overprotection is great also. Greater coordination problems exist when learning skills because the children are more dependent on tactile cues for learning than on visual ones. Bear in mind that they need the confidence and esteem that come from learning self-help skills to motivate further exploration.

1. Help all children develop independence in self-help skills. Use buttoning, lacing, and snapping frames to teach these skills. Montessori materials are excellent, but you can make your own fairly easily. Keep soap, paper towels, and the wastebasket in the same places in the bathroom and at a level the child can reach.
2. Teach safety, looking, and listening skills. Make sure children can identify such sounds as cars, sirens, and fire bells, and that they know what they should do when they hear these sounds.
3. Teach all children to do deep knee bends as a way of getting down to pick things up. It is especially important when they lift heavy objects, and it decreases bumped heads.
4. When children are playing very actively, have those who wear eyeglasses use a safety strap to keep the glasses from falling off.
5. In outdoor play areas, fence in the swings, seesaws, or any other heavy moving equipment. Keep tricycles and wagons on specified paths. For low vision children, add bells to any moving objects (tricycles, wagons, even balls) so the child can hear them and learn to avoid their path.

## Art

Although children with very little residual vision face limitations in some areas of art, there arc many highly tactile materials (such as clay) that allow a great deal of manipulation. The potential that art activities and materials offer for the release of emotions make them doubly valuable experiences for all children with visual needs.

1. Use a variety of modeling materials to provide different tactile experiences. Among the most popular materials are playdough (made of salt and flour), clay (use the powdered type and let the children help mix it), cornstarch, papier-mâché, and plastic-coated wire.
2. Have children fingerpaint right on the table if they are using actual fingerpaint. You can then print the picture when a child makes one he wants to keep. In addition, try fingerpainting with pudding, shaving cream, Ivory Snow Flakes (a clean feeling for those who are reluctant to get dirty), or laundry starch. Fingerpainting to music is another good variation.
3. Add textured materials such as sand or sawdust to easel paint and fingerpaint. Make the paint thicker so that it can be more easily felt and controlled.
4. Make textured boundaries for work areas. (This is a good idea for any child who tends to use too

much space.) Use masking tape to divide the table into areas, depending on your needs.

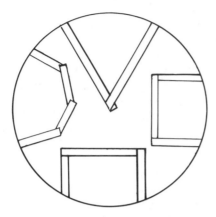

Use place mats to define each child's space. Put glue around the outside edge of a sheet of paper and sprinkle a little sand on it.

5. If you are using white paper on the easel, first cover the easel with dark construction paper so that the child can easily see where the paper ends. If the child cannot see, use a textured material for the board, such as coarse sandpaper or cork so the child can feel the boundaries.

6. Use a heavy lead pencil or a dark marking pen to print names on papers and, obviously, remember to *print big*.
7. Hang the child's art work in a place where the child can find it easily, see it, and point it out to others. Hang it low and near the beginning or the end of the line.
8. If you have a child who is wearing a patch over one eye, have the class make patches and then decorate and wear them. For long-term decoration, put a figure on the patch that is the same size and intensity as the other eye. (A star works well.)
9. Make a texture collage with a specific theme: for *nature*, use feathers, pine needles, leaves, and grass.

## Music
Music is usually a particularly enjoyable activity for these children and, with the number of famous visually impaired musicians (such as Ray Charles, Stevie Wonder, or Joaquin Rodrigo), it is not difficult to find encouragement to do well in this area. Music study is a good way to develop finer auditory discrimination and to facilitate the development of memory skills—both of which are particularly important to the visually impaired. The best music games to play are those in which none of the children use vision.

1. Play an instrument or ring a bell and have the children (who have their backs to you and eyes closed) guess what area of the room you are in. A variation of this is to have them search for a ticking kitchen timer, which you set to go off in a short time. A wind-up music box can be placed inside a small foam pillow and thrown or kicked and then found.
2. Teach the concepts of *high* and *low* with music pitch games. Have children practice using *loud* and *soft* volume as cues to distance (for finding a hidden object, for example). *Fast* and *slow* are also easily taught through musical games—the faster the music, the closer the child is to the hidden object.
3. Songs that have motions are often a great way to teach labels (especially those of body parts and actions). Extra time, however, must be devoted (at school or home) to teaching low vision children the motions that go with songs.
4. Moving creatively to music is good because it encourages varieties of movement and gracefulness, and because there is no right or wrong. Dancing, from the waltz to the twist to disco, is good exercise and great for developing coordination.

## Dramatic Play
Dramatic play allows children to learn about, experience, and control situations. They can make new experiences more familiar by playing through them first. Working through some frightening experiences will take the sting out of them.

1. Provide a lot of props. Be sure that at least some of them give obvious cues (tactile as well as visual) about the activity going on. For example, tea cups and saucers mean a tea party, but add a tea pot and appropriate clothing for the occasion to set the mood.
2. When children dress up, check to be sure there are no dangling belts or scarves that could cause tripping.
3. Set up an optometrist's office and have children test each other's vision. (The purpose is to teach a process, not to get accurate visual acuity results for each child.)

## Small Motor Play
The development and refinement of fine motor skills and eye-hand coordination requires extra

practice for those with visual needs. Start with experiences that they are likely to be successful at so that they don't get discouraged and quit trying. This is especially important for those who are just learning to use corrective aids. They may tell you they can do it better without the aids and, if they have learned good compensatory skills, they may be right! Encourage the use of the aids and ensure success also.

1. Fit-in puzzles (those with large pieces that go into specific places) and knob puzzles are good for teaching fine motor skills.
2. Three-dimensional building toys are very helpful (but get the type that interlock in some way, so they won't fall apart when bumped). Encourage children to start with larger pieces and work toward using the smaller ones. Keep the pieces in a tray so that children can keep track of them.
3. Sewing cards with large holes around the perimeter of the image allow a child to both feel and see the outline of the images. These cards can be easily made by pasting pictures on cardboard and using a hole punch.
4. Tactile skills can be developed with everyday materials (such as satin, felt, and cotton) that can be used for texture-matching games. Try different grades of sandpaper, which the children can try to arrange in order of fineness.
5. The pegboard offers opportunities for both fine motor and prereading activities, especially for those with failing vision who will eventually

need to learn braille. It is also good for teaching simple geometric shapes and concepts like *straight*. Low vision children should be taught to use their left hands for finding the holes and their right hands for manipulating the pegs (reverse this for left-handers). Start with large holes that can be easily located and low pegs so that there is less likelihood of flipping the pegs out. Eventually children should be able to copy any uncomplicated pattern an adult makes.

6. Tracing shapes will help the child progress from using actual items to learning to represent them. Children can begin by tracing the actual shape (using a piece of very heavy cardboard) and can then fill in the space with colors.

## Large Motor Play

Using the large muscles of the body is one way for children to increase their knowledge of their own body, as well as a way to explore their environment. Children who have recently had visual correction and those with low vision will probably have less refined skills in this area than their age mates. They will need encouragement as well as practice.

1. Balancing "tricks" are especially useful. Start with static balance. The child stands or sits still and balances a particular object. (Bean bags are easier to start with than books.) For dynamic balance, have the children walk, jump, or crawl

Larger objects may be easier to handle.

Encourage practice in large motor skills.

while balancing an object on their heads. As children become more skillful, see how long or how far they can balance things. Walking on a balance board or beam is also useful.

2. Relay races where children run, walk, jump, hop, or skip while holding hands with partners are great for developing both large motor skills and cooperating with peers. (Emphasize not speed and winning but completion of the task.)

3. Walking between the rungs of a ladder placed flat on the ground or floor helps children establish spacing, and they learn to realize whether or not they are walking in a straight line. As children become more skillful, have them do this blindfolded.

## Transitions

Transition times are difficult for all children because a lot of movement and change occurs. You can slow the process down, make it more fun, and teach spatial awareness concepts such as *over*, *under*, and *around* by having the children go over a chair, under the table, or around other children as they are dismissed from the group. Use nonvisual cues as one means of dismissal: for example, "Everyone with a shirt that buttons can get their coats." You can use types of clothing, fabrics, or the first letters of names. (Try not to use the girls/boys division very often.) It is a good idea to dismiss children with visual needs either early or late, when there will be the least amount of confusion.

## CHILD STUDY TEAM REPORT

### *Melissa T.*

In attendance: Ms. T., Mr. P., preschool teacher, Ms. F., psychologist.

Melissa T. is a three-year, two-month-old girl who had cataracts and now wears bifocals to correct the problem. Melissa was referred for testing by a pediatrician at the local well-baby clinic. Melissa lives at home with her mother and fifteen-month-old brother.

Melissa arrived for testing with her mother and brother. Ms. T. reported to the psychologist that she has difficulty "controlling Melissa," who frequently refuses to wear her glasses. Ms. T. feels Melissa has always "talked well," and says that she started at about a year of age and was speaking in three-to-four-word phrases by about two or two and a half. However, Melissa was a late walker; she began at twenty months. Since then, Ms. T. says, Melissa has "to be watched constantly and is into everything."

Melissa would not leave her mother, so Ms. T. and the younger child entered the examination room. After playing with trucks with the psychologist for a few moments, Melissa consented to have her mother and brother wait outside—but throughout the testing Melissa ran to the door frequently, calling for her mother. While working with the psychologist, she often made comments like "all done," "no more," or "put those away."

Overall, Melissa's mental age appeared to be one year below her chronological age, as measured on the Stanford-Binet Intelligence Scale. Her attention span was extremely short, and she generally resisted all tasks presented. When left to play with the materials in the room, Melissa moved from one toy to another, staying with a toy only long enough to pick it off the shelf. While viewing toys and materials, Melissa looked over her glasses rather than through them. She removed her glasses twice but was able to put them back on herself.

Ms. T. reported to the psychologist that Melissa can button and unbutton her own clothes, dress herself somewhat independently, and feed independently, but is not toilet trained and cannot ride a tricycle. Ms. T. added that Melissa frequently refuses to do those tasks she is capable of.

Ms. T. would like to place Melissa in a preschool program, but has not, since her daughter is not toilet trained. Ms. F. feels that Melissa would benefit from preschool and should begin in a program that can help increase her attention span and cooperativeness and allow her to be part of a group. By increasing the amount of time Melissa wears her glasses, proper vision can also be restored, which may help her visual attentiveness provided she receives help in learning how to see through her bifocals. Melissa would also benefit from a program providing a wide range of experiences and materials—as long as the class was small enough to allow the teacher to give her extra help in the use of materials. Melissa would do well with children slightly younger than herself, preferably two-year-olds, since she does not appear to be ready for the structure a program for older children may have. Both speech and language and occupational therapy evaluations are recommended for Melissa after a period of three months in preschool, when she may be more ready to respond to testing. The psychologist will reevaluate Melissa after six months.

Family counseling is recommended, since it may alleviate some of the tensions at home by helping the parents learn how to involve Melissa constructively. Ms. T. is not sure how her husband will react to this or if he will be available, since he works varying shifts. She wishes to begin counseling as soon as possible and will try to involve Mr. T. as well.

## INDIVIDUALIZED EDUCATION PROGRAM

NAME ___Melissa T.___ DOB ___4 / 19 / 79___

AGE ___3-2___ GRADE ___Preschool___

SCHOOL ___Mother Goose Preschool___

PARENTS/GUARDIANS ___Mr. & Ms. T.___

ADDRESS ___137 Long Lane___

PHONE ___245-6890___

### CURRENT TEST DATA

TEST/DATE/RESULTS

Stanford-Binet ___/___ / Approximate 1 year delay overall

Intelligence Scale ___/___ / mental age (affected by short attention span)

Vineland Social ___/___ / Social quotient slightly below

Maturity Scale ___6/15/82___ / chronological age.

___

On ___6/30/82___, the IPRD Committee
(Date)
met to review all current data and

recommends Level ___I___ placement.

Date of new review ___12/30/82___

Exceptionality: ___Visually impaired___

Recommended Special Services (Hrs/Wk):

___None___ ___/___

___ ___/___

___ ___/___

Total Hours/Week:

Special Education Classroom ___0___

Regular Classroom ___6___

Present at meeting:

Parents ___Ms. T.___

Others: Name/Position ___Ms. F., Psychologist___    Representative of District/Agency ___Mr. P., Preschool Teacher___

The committee has determined the following learning strengths and needs to be reflected in the IEP:

| STRENGTHS | NEEDS |
|---|---|
| Self-help skills | Cooperativeness with adults |
| Proper vision restorable | and peers |
|  | Attention span |
|  | Wearing of corrective lenses |

STUDENT     Melissa T.              DATE     6/30/82

GOAL     To cooperate with adults and peers

PARENT SIGNATURE _____

TEACHER SIGNATURE _____

| INSTRUCTIONAL OBJECTIVES | EDUCATIONAL METHODS | DATE Begin | DATE End | Eval. | PERSONS RESPONSIBLE Name | PERSONS RESPONSIBLE Position |
|---|---|---|---|---|---|---|
| Upon entering the classroom, Melissa will remove her hat and coat/sweater and hang it on a designated hook, 4/5 of the times she wears a coat/sweater. | Buttoning Sequences, Counting Cherries, Dramatic Play, Dress-Up | | | | Mr. P. | Teacher |
| a. with teacher direction | | 6/30 | 9/30 | | | |
| b. independently | | 9/30 | 12/30 | | | |
| When leaving the classroom, Melissa will put her coat/ sweater on, 4/5 of the times she wears a coat/sweater. | Same as Above | | | | Mr. P. | Teacher |
| a. with teacher direction | | 6/30 | 9/30 | | | |
| b. independently | | 9/30 | 12/30 | | | |
| Given a snack, Melissa will throw away wastes and clean her area of the table with a sponge 4/5 days per week. | Snack | | | | Mr. P. | Teacher |
| a. with a teacher assisting | | 6/30 | 9/30 | | | |
| b. with classmates assisting | | 9/30 | 12/30 | | | |
| Melissa will actively participate in fingerplays and songs during group time 50% of the time. | Group, Music, Fingerplays | 6/30 | 12/30 | | Mr. P. | Teacher |
| Melissa will participate in dramatic play, housekeeping, <u>or</u> block corner with at least one other child once a day for 5 minutes. | Dramatic Play, Housekeeping, Blocks | 6/30 | 9/30 | | Mr. P. | Teacher |

STUDENT _____ Melissa T. _____  DATE _____ 6/30/82

GOAL _____ To increase attention span

PARENT SIGNATURE _____  TEACHER SIGNATURE _____

| INSTRUCTIONAL OBJECTIVES | EDUCATIONAL METHODS | Begin | DATE End | Eval. | PERSONS RESPONSIBLE Name | Position |
|---|---|---|---|---|---|---|
| Given a supervised activity, Melissa will actively participate for 5 minutes for a total of 15 consecutive days. | Nuts and Bolts, Texture Paint, Nature Feely Board, Crayon Rubbing, Cornstarch Playdough, Gelatin, Dyeing Macaroni | 6/30 | 9/30 | | Mr. P. | Teacher |
| Melissa will sit on the floor with peers in a designated space and attend to a story for 15 days over a 1 month period. | Flannel Board Stories, Stories | 9/30 | 12/30 | | Mr. P. | Teacher |
| Given an age-appropriate book or toy, Melissa will increase the time spent actively playing with the toy independently by 50% (baseline data to be taken week of 9/15/82). | Salt Putty Beads, Inch Cubes, Snap-together Blocks, Books | 9/30 | 12/30 | | Mr. P. | Teacher |

STUDENT    Melissa T.      DATE    6/30/82

GOAL    To increase wearing time of corrective lenses

PARENT SIGNATURE _____    TEACHER SIGNATURE _____

| INSTRUCTIONAL OBJECTIVES | EDUCATIONAL METHODS | DATE Begin | DATE End | Eval. | PERSONS RESPONSIBLE Name | Position |
|---|---|---|---|---|---|---|
| Melissa will wear her corrective lenses during 100% of small group activities. | Preschool placement Behavior modification techniques--verbal praise (oral rewards, if necessary) | 6/30 | 7/30 | | Mr. P. | Teacher |
| Melissa will wear her corrective lenses during 100% of large group and small group activities. | | 7/30 | 9/30 | | Mr. P. | Teacher |
| Melissa will wear her corrective lenses during the entire time she is at school. | | 9/30 | 11/30 | | Mr. P. | Teacher |
| Melissa will look through her corrective lenses (rather than over them) during the entire time she is at school. | | 11/30 | 12/30 | | Mr. P. | Teacher |

# GLOSSARY

**Achromatopsia**   See color deficient.

**Amblyopia**   The dimness or loss of vision in one eye due to the disuse of the eye. Correctable through surgery and/or wearing a patch over the stronger eye to prevent muscle deterioriation and double vision.

**Ametropia**   Errors of refraction (hyperopia, myopia, and astigmatism). In all cases and for a variety of reasons, the best focal point is not on the retina.

**Astigmatism**   A visual impairment caused by variations in the curvature of the cornea or lens that prevent the light rays from coming to a single focal point on the retina. It can be corrected with glasses.

**Braille**   A system of touch reading. The characters are in combinations of six dots arranged in a cell, two dots wide and three dots high. The symbols are embossed on heavy manila paper and read from left to right. There are 63 possible dot combinations, and special notations for mathematics, music, scientific problems, and numbers make almost any academic subject possible.

**Cataracts**   A disease in which the lens of the eye becomes opaque. Vision can only be restored by an operation in which the lens is removed and rather thick glasses are prescribed.

**Color deficient (blindness)**   Achromatopsia. The inability to identify one or more primary colors. There is no way to correct this.

**Cornea damage**   The cornea is the "window" of the eye that protects the lens and iris. Scars or punctures of the cornea can obstruct vision, but it is possible to have the cornea replaced. This is the *only* kind of eye transplant possible to date.

**Cross-eye (Strabismus)**   The inability of the eyes to focus together because the muscles that control movement are not equally strong. One or both eyes may be affected, vertically and/or horizontally. An inward-turning condition is called *cross-eye*, an outward-turning one is called *walleye*. Because a double image is perceived, there is a tendency to use only one eye. Strengthening exercises are needed, and a patch is sometimes worn primarily over the stronger eye although occasionally over the weaker. If necessary, an operation can be performed.

**Diplopia**   Double vision in either one or both eyes.

**Eye**   The organ of vision. When light enters the eye it passes through the *cornea* (a transparent membrane), the *aqueous humor* (a watery fluid), the *lens*, and the *vitreous humor* (a jellylike substance that fills the eyeball). The amount of light that enters is controlled by the *iris*, a set of muscles that expand or contract the *pupil*, the hole through which the light enters. The light focuses on the *retina*, a layer of nerves that transmits impulses

to the brain through the *optic nerve*. The most sensitive part of the retina is the *fovea*; the only insensitive part is the *blind spot*, which is where the nerve fibers come together.

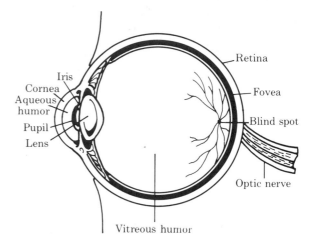

**Farsightedness (hyperopia)**   A defect in which things at a distance can be clearly seen but things that are nearby cannot. It is the result of a short eyeball or a lens problem that causes the image to focus beyond the retina. It can be corrected with glasses.

**Glaucoma**   If the fluid in the eye does not drain properly, pressure will build up and impede the entry of blood. This can lead to the destruction of nerve cells in the retina. Special eye drops can be used to control the pressure. The disease is extremely rare in children.

**Nearsightedness (myopia)**   A defect in which images that are near the viewer can be seen clearly but things that are distant cannot. It is the result of a long eyeball or a lens problem that causes the image to focus in front of the retina. It can be corrected with glasses.

**Nightblindness**   Less-than-normal vision in dim light. The eyes cannot adjust easily from light to dark stimuli. It is a symptom of vitamin A deficiency. If the condition continues to exist for more than a few months it becomes permanent.

**Oculist**   A physician who specializes in eye problems and writes prescriptions for lenses (glasses) (ophthalmologist).

**Ophthalmologist**   Physician specializing in the anatomy, function, and diseases of the eye.

**Optacon**   A device that scans print and converts it into patterns transmitted by 144 tactile pins that produce an image of the letter against a finger.

**Optic Nerve**   The second cranial nerve. It carries impulses from the retina to the occipatal lobe of the brain.

**Optometrist** Specialist who can examine eyes and write prescriptions for lenses, but who does not have a medical degree.

**Orthoptics** The science of using exercises that use the eye muscles to correct faulty eye coordination.

**Retina, detached** One that has been torn loose from the next layer of the eyeball. It can be reattached surgically with very little loss of vision.

## TEACHING RESOURCES

In some situations you may want or need additional information; there are many national as well as regional, state, and local organizations that can be helpful to you. The following annotated list of national organizations should be useful in helping you decide where to get the information you need.

Association for Education of the Visually Handicapped
919 Walnut Street, 4th Floor
Philadelphia, PA 19107
  Teachers, administrators, and parents of blind children interested in the education, guidance, vocational rehabilitation, or occupational placement of the visually handicapped.

Better Vision Institute
230 Park Avenue
New York, NY 10017
  Sponsors preschool screening programs by Junior Chamber of Commerce, primarily aimed at amblyopia: "To keep public aware of the need for more adequate vision care."

American Foundation for the Blind, Inc.
15 West 16th Street
New York, NY 10011
  Serves as a consultant to local agencies and refers individuals to local agencies where they can receive direct help. Write the Foundation for addresses of regional offices.

National Society for the Prevention of Blindness, Inc.
79 Madison Avenue
New York, NY 10016
  The National Society and its affiliates carry out a comprehensive program for service, education, and research dealing solely with blindness prevention.

The Talking Book Service Division for the Blind and Physically Handicapped
Library of Congress
Washington, DC 20542
  The service provides talking books for those who need them.

## BIBLIOGRAPHY

Alonso, Lou, et al. *Mainstreaming Preschoolers: Children with Visual Handicaps. A Guide for Teachers, Parents, and Others Who Work with Visually Handicapped Preschoolers.* Washington, D.C.: U. S. Government Printing Office, 1978.

Bishop, Virginia E. *Teaching the Visually Limited Child.* Springfield, Ill.: Charles C. Thomas, 1978.

Chapman, Elizabeth K. *Visually Handicapped Children and Young People.* Boston: Routledge and Keegan, 1978.

Garwood, S., et al. *Educating Young Handicapped Children: A Developmental Approach.* Germantown, Md.: Aspen Systems Corp., 1979.

Halliday, Carol. *The Visually Impaired Child: Growth, Learning, Development, Infancy to School Age.* Louisville, Ky.: Instructional Materials Reference Center, American Printing House for the Blind, 1970.

Hardy, Richard E., and John G. Cull, eds. *Social and Rehabilitation Services for the Blind.* American Lectures in Social and Rehabilitation Psychology Series, No. 846. Springfield, Ill.: Charles C. Thomas, 1972.

Harley, Randall K., and Lawrence G. Allen. *A Visual Impairment in the Schools.* Springfield, Ill.: Charles C. Thomas, 1977.

Jan, James E., et al., eds. *Visual Impairments in Children and Adolescents.* New York: Grune and Stratton, 1977.

Kukurai, Shiro. *How Can I Make What I Cannot See?* New York: Van Nostrand Reinhold, 1974.

Library of Congress. Division for the Blind and Physically Handicapped. *Sources of Reading Materials for the Visually and Physically Handicapped.* Washington, D.C.: 1970.

Lowenfeld, Berthold. *Our Blind Children: Growing and Learning with Them.* 3rd ed. Springfield, Ill.: Charles C. Thomas, 1977.

————, ed. *The Visually Handicapped Child in School.* John Day Books in Special Education. New York: John Day, 1973.

————, Georgie Lee Abel, and Phillip H. Hatlen. *Blind Children Learn to Read.* Springfield, Ill.: Charles C. Thomas, 1974.

Martin, Glenda J., and Mollie Hoben. *Supporting Visually Impaired Students in the Mainstream: The State of the Art.* Reston, Va.: Council for Exceptional Children, 1977.

Scott, Eileen, James Jan, and Roger Freeman. *Can't Your Child See?* Baltimore: University Park Press, 1977.

Spungin, Susan J. *Competency Based Curriculum for*

Teachers of the Visually Handicapped: A National Study. New York: American Foundation for the Blind, 1977.

Stratton, Josephine. *The Blind Child in the Regular Kindergarten*. New York: Charles C. Thomas, 1977.

Taylor, Billie Wesley. *Blind Preschool: A Manual for Parents and Educators*. rev. ed. Colorado Springs: Industrial Printers of Colorado, 1974.

U.S. Children's Bureau. *The Preschool Child Who Is Blind*. Washington, D.C.: U.S. Government Printing Office, 1968.

*Biography/Autobiography/Fiction*

Caulfield, Genevieve. *The Kingdom Within*. Ed. E. Fitzgerald. New York: Harper Brothers, 1960.

The autobiography of a woman who was accidentally blinded at the age of two and had only faint light perception in one eye through her life. She graduated from college as a teacher and traveled to both Japan and Thailand to work with the blind.

Hartwell, Dickson. *Dogs Against Darkness: The Story of the Seeing Eye*. New York: Dodd, Mead, 1960.

Seeing eye dogs and their training.

Sullivan, Tom, and Derek Gill. *If You Could See What I Hear*. New York: Harper & Row, 1975.

An autobiography on blindness from infancy to adulthood. Contrasted with his mother's overprotective attempts to isolate him and his father's equally extreme belief that his son could accomplish all that other boys could, if not more, are Sullivan's ongoing attempts to live a normal life and become a part of the mainstream.

Ulrich, Sharon. *Elizabeth*. Ann Arbor, Mich.: Univ. of Michigan Press, 1972.

A brief description of the life of a preschool blind child. The first section of the book was written by the director of the child-development project Elizabeth participated in. The second section was written by Elizabeth's mother, who explains methods used in toilet training, learning to walk, and learning how to deal with basic problems.

# BIBLIOGRAPHY FOR CHILDREN

*Awareness*

Hartwell, Dickson. *Dogs Against Darkness: The Story of the Seeing Eye*. New York: Dodd, Mead, 1960.

Seeing eye dogs and their training. (May be paraphrased for younger children.)

Heide, Florence Parry. *Sound of Sunshine, Sound of Rain*. New York: Scholastic Book Services, 1970.

The experiences and sensations of a blind black boy as he maneuvers in his small world.

Keats, Ezra Jack. *Apartment Three*. New York: Macmillan, 1971.

Two young brothers develop a friendship with a blind man who plays the harmonica, and they develop an understanding of the meaning of visual impairment.

Litchfield, Ada. *A Cane in Her Hand*. Chicago: Whitman, 1977.

Valerie longs to be treated normally by others.

MacLachlan, Patricia. *Through Grandpa's Eyes*. New York: Harper and Row, 1980.

John's grandfather is blind, but he can see things in a special way.

Peterson, P. *Sally Can't See*. New York: John Day, 1974.

Twelve-year-old Sally uses a cane and braille to help her lead an active life swimming, riding horses, and playing the organ, among other things.

*For low-vision children*

These books were chosen because they depict familiar

events in an interesting yet straightforward manner and use simple pictures with high contrast.

Brown, Margaret Wise. *The Noisy Book*. New York: Harper and Row, 1939.

A classic story about Muffin, a dog who got a cinder in his eye and all the noises he heard when he couldn't see.

———. *The Quiet Noisy Book*. New York: Harper & Row, 1950.

Another book about Muffin and the sounds he hears while waking up.

Hoban, Tana. *Count and See*. New York: Macmillan, 1972.

A black-and-white photograph book with numbers, dots, and corresponding objects.

Kalan, Robert. *Freight Train*. New York: Greenwillow Books, 1978.
———. *Rain*. New York: Greenwillow Books, 1978.

Both books use vibrant colors to portray the motion of rain, the following rainbow, and the train tooting through city and country.

Keats, Ezra Jack. *Skates*. New York: Franklin Watts, 1973.

A simple story of two colorful dogs who find some skates and try them out.

Miles, Betty. *A House for Everyone*. New York: Alfred A. Knopf, 1958.

A colorful, high-contrast book that shows houses in many places and the people that live in them.

Munari, Bruno. *ABC*. Cleveland, Ohio: World Publishing Co., 1960.

A traditional alphabet book with large black letters and colorful pictures.

*Touch and Feel Books*

The stories vary, but all of these books allow children to develop the tactile sense as they touch the pages of the books.

Hillbert, Margaret. *The Sleepy Time Book*. New York: Golden Press, 1975.

Kunhardt, Dorothy. *Pat the Bunny*. New York: Golden Press, 1962.

Kwitz, Mary D. *Whose Baby?* New York: Golden Press, 1978.

Ottum, Bob. *Busy Days with Raggedy Ann and Andy*. New York: Golden Press, 1976.

Showers, Paul. *Find Out by Touching*. New York: Thomas Y. Crowell, 1961.

Thomas, Anthony. *Things We Touch*. New York: Franklin Watts, 1976.

White, Mary S. *Touch and Tell*. Nashville, Tenn.: Broadman, 1962.

Witte, Pat and Eve. *Who Lives Here?* New York: Golden Press, 1961.

# INDEX

| *Annual Goals* | *Activity* | *Curriculum Area* | *Page* |
|---|---|---|---|
| | My Yard | Outdoor Play | 527 |
| | Sandpaper Letters | Reading Readiness | 367 |
| To improve visual discrimination | Alphabet Lotto | Reading Readiness | 366 |
| | Letter Collage | Art | 460 |
| | Nuts and Bolts | Small Motor Play | 505 |
| | Texture Paint | Art | 449 |
| | Traffic Sign Hunt | Health and Safety | 439 |
| To improve visual memory | Hidden Objects | Mathematics | 416 |
| To improve visual closure | I'm Thinking Of | Social Studies | 392 |
| To improve visual association | Classify It | Reading Readiness | 379 |
| | Color Words | Expressing Language | 342 |
| | Flannel Board Stories | Reading Readiness | 374 |
| | Matrix | Reading Readiness | 374 |
| | What Doesn't Belong? | Mathematics | 424 |
| To improve tactile discrimination | Barefoot | Outdoor Play | 530 |
| | Buttoning Sequences | Small Motor Play | 504 |
| | Buttons | Small Motor Play | 498 |
| | Cave Exploration | Outdoor Play | 528 |
| | Feeling Track | Large Motor Play | 519 |
| | Feely Bag | Small Motor Play | 499 |
| | Feely Box | Small Motor Play | 503 |
| | Food Sense | Science/Discovery | 405 |
| | Grading Sandpaper | Small Motor Play | 504 |
| | Nature Feely Board | Science/Discovery | 404 |
| | Nuts and Bolts | Small Motor Play | 505 |
| | Pick-a-Pair | Small Motor Play | 504 |
| | Sandpaper Letters | Reading Readiness | 367 |
| | Texture Classification | Science/Discovery | 406 |
| | Texture Paint | Art | 449 |
| | Texture Playdough | Art | 449 |
| | Touch Shapes | Mathematics | 422 |
| | Tracing Pictures | Art | 446 |
| To improve tactile memory | Nature Feely Board | Science/Discovery | 404 |
| To improve discrimination of smells | Food Sense | Science/Discovery | 405 |
| | Smell Cues | Health and Safety | 436 |
| | Wiggly Worms | Science/Discovery | 406 |
| To improve taste discrimination | Food Sense | Science/Discovery | 405 |
| To improve sensory integration | Body Parts | Social Studies | 386 |
| | Cereal Balls | Mathematics | 429 |
| | Listen Before You Move | Listening | 360 |
| | Mirror Movement | Movement | 477 |
| | Movement Songs | Music | 468 |
| | Painting to Music | Art | 454 |
| | Popcorn | Science/Discovery | 402 |
| | Tempo | Movement | 477 |

## LANGUAGE SKILLS

| | | | |
|---|---|---|---|
| To improve expressive language | Di-Vergent | Expressing Language | 335 |
| | Dress Up and Tell | Dramatic Play | 492 |

| *Annual Goals* | *Activity* | *Curriculum Area* | *Page* |
|---|---|---|---|
| | Telephone | Expressing Language | 338 |
| | Treasure Hunt | Expressing Language | 338 |
| To increase vocabulary | Barefoot | Outdoor Play | 530 |
| | Locomotion | Expressing Language | 340 |
| | Object File | Listening | 354 |
| | Seasonal Clothing | Health and Safety | 435 |
| | Synonyms | Expressing Language | 339 |
| To follow directions | Color Graphs | Small Motor Play | 499 |
| | Directions | Expressing Language | 343 |
| | In and Out | Movement | 478 |
| | Ladder Walk | Outdoor Play | 529 |
| | Listen Before You Move | Listening | 360 |
| | Locomotion | Expressing Language | 340 |
| | Obstacle Course | Large Motor Play | 515 |
| | Sandwich Tricks | Mathematics | 418 |
| | Tactile Gameboard | Small Motor Play | 500 |
| To interpret body language | Who Am I? | Dramatic Play | 491 |
| To increase understanding | Color Words | Expressing Language | 342 |
| | Directions | Expressing Language | 343 |
| | Synonyms | Expressing Language | 339 |
| | Traveling | Expressing Language | 344 |

## THINKING AND REASONING SKILLS

| | | | |
|---|---|---|---|
| To increase attention span | Red Light/Green Light | Health and Safety | 434 |
| | Treasure Hunt | Expressing Language | 338 |
| To improve cause and effect reasoning | Balance It | Large Motor Play | 519 |
| | Contour Maps | Science/Discovery | 401 |
| | Cornstarch Playdough | Science/Discovery | 402 |
| | Corrugated Collage | Art | 446 |
| | Dress Up and Tell | Dramatic Play | 492 |
| | Dyeing Macaroni | Art | 446 |
| | Food Forms | Social Studies | 391 |
| | Gelatin | Science/Discovery | 400 |
| | Grading Sandpaper | Small Motor Play | 504 |
| | Listening Obstacle Course | Listening | 361 |
| | Nature Feely Board | Science/Discovery | 404 |
| | Popcorn | Science/Discovery | 402 |
| | Red Light/Green Light | Health and Safety | 434 |
| | Seasonal Clothing | Health and Safety | 435 |
| | Smell Cues | Health and Safety | 436 |
| | String Mobile | Art | 447 |
| | Texture Paint | Art | 449 |
| | Texture Playdough | Art | 449 |
| | Tracing Pictures | Art | 446 |
| | Vibrations | Music | 466 |
| | Warning Sounds | Health and Safety | 437 |
| | Water Tones | Listening | 355 |
| | Where Is It? | Music | 467 |
| | Who Has Been Here? | Social Studies | 387 |

| Annual Goals | Activity | Curriculum Area | Page |
|---|---|---|---|
| To increase logical reasoning | Matrix | Reading Readiness | 374 |
| | Title | Listening | 362 |
| To improve classification skills | Classify It | Reading Readiness | 379 |
| | Pick-a-Pair | Small Motor Play | 504 |
| | Sorting | Small Motor Play | 500 |
| | Sounds | Listening | 362 |
| | Texture Classification | Science/Discovery | 406 |
| | Texture Playdough | Art | 449 |
| | What Doesn't Belong? | Mathematics | 424 |
| | Wiggly Worms | Science/Discovery | 406 |
| To improve sequencing skills | Buttoning Sequences | Small Motor Play | 504 |
| | Going to the Beach | Listening | 358 |
| To improve color concepts | Color Scavenger Hunt | Outdoor Play | 531 |
| To make predictions | Food Sense | Science/Discovery | 405 |
| | Matching Rods | Mathematics | 427 |
| | Noisy Toss | Large Motor Play | 517 |
| | Who Has Been Here? | Social Studies | 387 |
| To increase problem-solving skills | Gelatin | Science/Discovery | 400 |
| To improve decision making | Title | Listening | 362 |

## MATHEMATIC SKILLS

| | | | |
|---|---|---|---|
| To improve number concepts | Abacus | Mathematics | 412 |
| | Hidden Objects | Mathematics | 416 |
| | Matching Dots | Mathematics | 412 |
| | Number Tapping | Mathematics | 414 |
| | Spacy Dots | Mathematics | 415 |
| To improve measurement concepts | Areas | Mathematics | 420 |
| | Cereal Balls | Mathematics | 429 |
| | Matching Rods | Mathematics | 427 |
| | Salt Putty Beads | Art | 459 |
| | Topless Popcorn | Mathematics | 428 |
| To improve spatial concepts | Contour Maps | Science/Discovery | 401 |
| | Letter Collage | Art | 460 |
| | Spacy Dots | Mathematics | 415 |
| To improve shape concepts | Areas | Mathematics | 420 |
| | Pockets | Mathematics | 417 |
| | Sandwich Tricks | Mathematics | 418 |
| | Touch Shapes | Mathematics | 422 |
| | What Doesn't Belong? | Mathematics | 424 |
| To improve size concepts | Areas | Mathematics | 420 |
| | Matching Rods | Mathematics | 427 |
| | Pouring Peanuts | Small Motor Play | 507 |

## SOCIAL SKILLS

| | | | |
|---|---|---|---|
| To broaden concepts of families | Food Forms | Social Studies | 391 |
| To increase survival skills | Red Light/Green Light | Health and Safety | 434 |

| *Annual Goals* | *Activity* | *Curriculum Area* | *Page* |
|---|---|---|---|
| | Seasonal Clothing | Health and Safety | 435 |
| | Smell Cues | Health and Safety | 436 |
| | Traffic Sign Hunt | Health and Safety | 439 |
| | Warning Sounds | Health and Safety | 437 |
| To improve self-help skills | Buttoning Sequences | Small Motor Play | 504 |
| | Pouring Peanuts | Small Motor Play | 507 |
| To increase awareness of roles people play | Audiologist | Dramatic Play | 489 |
| | Circus | Dramatic Play | 486 |
| | Eye Doctor | Dramatic Play | 490 |
| | Visitor | Social Studies | 388 |
| | Who Am I? | Dramatic Play | 491 |
| To cooperate with peers | Audiologist | Dramatic Play | 489 |
| | Cereal Balls | Mathematics | 429 |
| | Color Scavenger Hunt | Outdoor Play | 531 |
| | Directions | Expressing Language | 343 |
| | Eye Doctor | Dramatic Play | 490 |
| | Hug Tag | Outdoor Play | 531 |
| | Seesaw | Large Motor Play | 520 |
| | Share Your Feelings | Social Studies | 392 |
| | Telephone | Expressing Language | 338 |
| | Variations on Throwing | Outdoor Play | 526 |
| | Who's There? | Listening | 357 |
| To cooperate with adults | Visitor | Social Studies | 388 |

**MOTOR SKILLS**

| *Annual Goals* | *Activity* | *Curriculum Area* | *Page* |
|---|---|---|---|
| To improve large motor coordination | Crashing | Large Motor Play | 511 |
| | Noisy Toss | Large Motor Play | 517 |
| | Obstacle Course | Large Motor Play | 515 |
| | Parachute Games | Outdoor Play | 525 |
| | Target Bounce | Outdoor Play | 524 |
| | Variations on Jumping | Large Motor Play | 513 |
| | Variations on Running | Outdoor Play | 524 |
| | Variations on Throwing | Outdoor Play | 526 |
| To improve small motor coordination | Buttons | Small Motor Play | 498 |
| | Color Graphs | Small Motor Play | 499 |
| | Feely Bag | Small Motor Play | 499 |
| | My Puzzle | Small Motor Play | 503 |
| | Sorting | Small Motor Play | 500 |
| | Tactile Gameboard | Small Motor Play | 500 |
| To improve eye-hand coordination | Classify It | Reading Readiness | 379 |
| | Corrugated Collage | Art | 446 |
| | Dyeing Macaroni | Art | 446 |
| | Letter Collage | Art | 460 |
| | Noisy Toss | Large Motor Play | 517 |
| | Nuts and Bolts | Small Motor Play | 505 |
| | My Yard | Outdoor Play | 527 |
| | Pockets | Mathematics | 417 |
| | Pouring Peanuts | Small Motor Play | 507 |
| | Salt Putty Beads | Art | 459 |
| | String Mobile | Art | 447 |
| | String Painting | Art | 451 |
| | Target Bounce | Outdoor Play | 524 |

| *Annual Goals* | *Activity* | *Curriculum Area* | *Page* |
|---|---|---|---|
| | Variations on Throwing | Outdoor Play | 526 |
| | Wire Sculpture | Art | 451 |
| To improve balance skills | Balance It | Large Motor Play | 519 |
| | Balancing | Large Motor Play | 517 |
| | Freeze | Outdoor Play | 528 |
| | Ladder Walk | Outdoor Play | 529 |
| | Seesaw | Large Motor Play | 520 |
| | Variations on Balancing | Large Motor Play | 518 |
| | Variations on Jumping | Large Motor Play | 513 |
| To encourage creative movement | Be It | Movement | 474 |
| To increase sense of rhythm | Rhythmic Patterns | Music | 464 |
| | Rhythm Walk | Music | 464 |
| To relax at will | Relaxation Stories | Movement | 476 |

## CREATIVITY

| | | | |
|---|---|---|---|
| To encourage creativity | Foot Painting | Art | 450 |
| | Painting to Music | Art | 454 |
| | String Painting | Art | 451 |
| | Traveling | Expressing Language | 344 |
| | Who Am I? | Dramatic Play | 491 |
| | Wire Sculpture | Art | 451 |
| To encourage creative problem solving | Body Parts | Social Studies | 386 |
| | Di-Vergent | Expressing Language | 335 |
| | Our Town | Social Studies | 384 |
| | Treasure Hunt | Expressing Language | 338 |
| | Who Has Been Here? | Social Studies | 387 |
| To stimulate curiosity | Cornstarch Playdough | Science/Discovery | 402 |
| | Look Closer | Science/Discovery | 408 |

## FEELINGS

| | | | |
|---|---|---|---|
| To express feelings | Share Your Feelings | Social Studies | 392 |
| To increase feelings of group belonging | Circles | Movement | 479 |
| | Color Scavenger Hunt | Outdoor Play | 531 |
| | Dress Up and Tell | Dramatic Play | 492 |
| | Flannel Board Stories | Reading Readiness | 374 |
| | Hand/Foot Painting | Art | 458 |
| | Hug Tag | Outdoor Play | 531 |
| | I'm Thinking Of | Social Studies | 392 |
| | Our Town | Social Studies | 384 |
| | Parachute Games | Outdoor Play | 525 |
| | Share Your Feelings | Social Studies | 392 |
| | Traveling | Expressing Language | 344 |

## AWARENESS

| | | | |
|---|---|---|---|
| To increase body awareness | Balance It | Large Motor Play | 519 |
| | Balancing | Large Motor Play | 517 |
| | Barefoot | Outdoor Play | 530 |

| *Annual Goals* | *Activity* | *Curriculum Area* | *Page* |
|---|---|---|---|
| | Be It | Movement | 474 |
| | Be the Body | Movement | 473 |
| | Body Mural | Art | 454 |
| | Body Parts | Social Studies | 386 |
| | Cave Exploration | Outdoor Play | 528 |
| | Circles | Movement | 479 |
| | Circus | Dramatic Play | 486 |
| | Crashing | Large Motor Play | 511 |
| | Feeling Track | Large Motor Play | 519 |
| | Foot Painting | Art | 450 |
| | Freeze | Outdoor Play | 528 |
| | Hand/Foot Painting | Art | 458 |
| | Hand Plaster | Art | 455 |
| | In and Out | Movement | 478 |
| | Ladder Walk | Outdoor Play | 529 |
| | Mirror Movement | Movement | 477 |
| | Movement Songs | Music | 468 |
| | My Puzzle | Small Motor Play | 503 |
| | Relaxation Stories | Movement | 476 |
| | Rhythm Walk | Music | 464 |
| | Tempo | Movement | 477 |
| | Variations on Balancing | Large Motor Play | 518 |
| | Variations on Jumping | Large Motor Play | 513 |
| | Variations on Running | Outdoor Play | 524 |
| To improve self-concept | My Puzzle | Small Motor Play | 503 |
| | Tape It | Listening | 356 |
| | Who's There? | Listening | 357 |
| To increase awareness of individual differences | Body Mural | Art | 454 |
| | Hand Plaster | Art | 455 |
| | Hand/Foot Painting | Art | 458 |
| | I'm Thinking Of | Social Studies | 392 |
| To increase awareness of moods | Painting to Music | Art | 454 |
| To increase awareness of visual needs | Eye Doctor | Dramatic Play | 490 |
| | Moving in the Dark | Awareness | 539 |
| | Simulated Glasses | Awareness | 540 |
| | Who Is It? | Awareness | 541 |

# Needs: Learning

My concern for the child with specific learning needs, or disabilities, started fifteen years ago when we thought in terms of children who *wouldn't* behave.

At the beginning of the school year, three-year-old Sam was "acting out." He hit other children without provocation. He would neither print his name nor remember where his locker was (despite the animal sticker on it). He wouldn't sit still during group time, but would wander around the room being disruptive. He was reminded so often that "it hurts when someone hits you" that by the end of the school year no matter where he was in the room, if a child cried, Sam would go up to that child and say, "I'm sorry I made you cry." He believed he caused others to cry even when he wasn't responsible.

Now I wonder if Sam was a child who *wouldn't* or *couldn't* behave. We didn't have a label for "learning disabilities" then; there were only "difficult" children who were "behavior problems." Sam was in fact diagnosed as learning disabled after he had repeated first grade and was having trouble in second grade. By then, he had not only a learning disability but also a poor self-concept. Sam is only one of the children I wonder about. I have had others; perhaps you have too. This chapter is designed to help you find and teach the children who "can't" but who "should be able to."

## CLASSIFICATION OF LEARNING NEEDS

There is no one definition of what a learning disability is. For teaching purposes, the following is true of most children with learning needs.

1. The children have average to above-average intelligence. They are not mentally retarded.
2. The learning problems are not caused by visual, aural, emotional, or environmental problems. The problems occur in the processing of information more often than in the reception of it.
3. The children have problems understanding or speaking or reading and writing language or any combination of these. Both speaking and understanding speech are delayed.
4. There may or may not be irregularities in the brain.

These are children who look normal and have all of the normal senses, yet who do not function as well as they should. More than ninety terms have been used to describe the problems that we now call learning disabilities. (Some of these are in the Glossary, including the legal definition of learning disabilities.) The label encompasses a broad spectrum of needs, but they can be summed up by the title of a book written by Louise Clarke: *Can't Read, Can't Write, Can't Talk Too Good Either*. Learning disabilities are still not completely understood.

It is difficult to determine the prevalence of learning disabilities in children. Examiners use different tests or even different criteria for evaluating the same test. In addition, the definition is broad enough for learning disability to be a catchall category for children who defy the labeling system. Estimates of the numbers of learning needs children range from 1–3 percent of the school population to 7–10 percent, depending on the screening procedure and definition used. This translates into 500,000 to 1,500,000 school-age children (Bryan and Bryan,

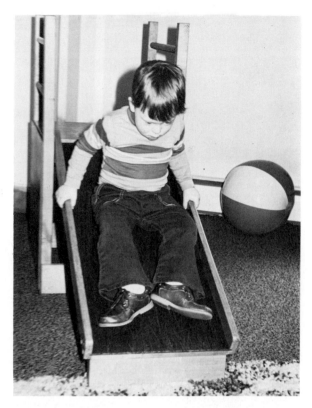

This child is hesitant to touch the slide and even more reluctant to go down it. The child needs more time to process sensory input.

1979). There are few estimates of how many preschool children fall into this category. No doubt the problem exists at this age; it just hasn't been diagnosed this early in most cases. You may be the first, then, to suspect an exceptionality. You may have to base your programming on your own diagnosis because as much as a year may pass before the diagnosis is confirmed.

In most cases, the causes of learning disabilities are not known. Learning disabilities seem to occur with greater frequency in some families than others, but the contributions of heredity and environment have not yet been determined. It is currently held that learning disabilities can be present at birth, can result from an accident, or can be caused by environmental factors.

Medically, a learning disability is a strange phenomenon. At one time, children had to have electroencephalographic (EEG) irregularities to be classified as learning disabled, but given two children with the same characteristics, one may have an irregular EEG and the other a normal one. While medical doctors claimed the latter child was normal, teachers disagreed. Now we rely on an educational definition of learning disability based on "soft" signs (behavior) rather than "hard" signs (blood count, EEGs).

Hyperactivity, which frequently occurs in con-junction with a learning disability, may need to be treated by a physician. Hyperactive children are calmed down through drugs and sometimes diet so that they are able to learn. You may be asked to provide observations on the effects of these treatments or to comply with the recommended diet. It is important that you understand a child's individual regimen.

The use of drugs for hyperactivity is problematic. The medical profession does not agree on the implications of the long-term use of medication. In addition, children respond differently to the same drug, making it difficult to find a drug that works and to determine the least dosage that will give the desired result.

Your responsibility is not to decide whether the child needs medication (that's the parents' and doctor's decision), but rather to give useful reports to parents, especially when correct dosage is being determined. Use a simple checklist to record not whether the child is "good or bad" but whether there is "improvement, no change, or additional problems" as a result of medication.

## CHECKLIST FOR RATING BEHAVIOR OF CHILD ON MEDICATION

Date _____

Child _____

Medication (with dosage)* _____

Age _____

Rating scale:

| | | | |
|---|---|---|---|
| −3 | much worse | +3 | much improved |
| −2 | somewhat worse | +2 | somewhat improved |
| −1 | slightly worse | +1 | slightly improved |
| 0 | no change | N | not observed |

| *Behavior or Activity* | Rating | Comment |
|---|---|---|
| 1. Attention span | | |
| 2. Impulsiveness | | |
| 3. Acting out | | |
| 4. Large motor coordination | | |
| 5. Small motor coordination | | |
| 6. Speech (understandability) | | |
| 7. Peer relations | | |
| 8. Group time behavior | | |
| 9. Snack behavior | | |
| 10. Restlessness | | |
| 11. Distractability | | |

*As advance knowledge of a change in the child's medication may influence your judgment, wait until after the observation to find out and fill in the medication and dosage.

The drugs that you are most likely to encounter may be categorized as stimulants or tranquilizers. The most commonly used stimulants are dextroamphetamine (Dexedrine) and methylphenidate (Ritalin). Paradoxically, these stimulants have a calming effect on prepuberty-age children. There is no "standard" dosage. Children may use from 2.5 mg to 200 mg daily. The stimulants are effective for three to four hours; you may need to consult with the parents to coordinate your activity schedule with the timing of the child's medication. The most commonly used tranquilizers are thioridazine (Mellaril) and chlorpromazine (Thorazine). They are effective over longer time periods than stimulants, so the timing of the medication will concern you less.

Medication does not "cure" these children, it makes them more manageable and available for you to teach. Sometimes the drugs make these children so calm they fall asleep in class. This needs to be reported to the parents. The doctor can reduce the dosage if necessary.

The Feingold diet is another method some doctors use to control hyperactivity. Although double-blind studies have found diet unrelated to hyperactivity, it does work for some. Essentially the diet eliminates all artificial food colors, flavors, and additives. Ask the child's parents for a complete list of permitted and forbidden foods so that you can adapt your snack and lunch programs. For more extensive information, see *Why Your Child Is Hyperactive* by Dr. Ben Feingold.

You have a rare opportunity to participate in changing a child's life from one of academic failure and poor self-esteem to one of promise. Children with learning needs who are helped at the preschool level can usually function as normal adults when they grow up. The later intervention to help them starts, the less the probability of success. Working with learning disabled children is exhilarating and also somewhat frightening because your efforts make such a difference.

## CHILDREN'S NEEDS— TEACHING GOALS

Related annual goals may be grouped under broad categories called "teaching goals." Outlined under each teaching goal below are the most important needs of learning disabled children. A child may have some or all of these needs, and additional needs as well. Suggestions on what you might consequently teach them are included. Often, a course of action is implicit in the description of the need.

A learning disability is usually not a single problem but rather a combination of problems. Learning disabilities are diverse; two children may be labeled learning disabled and one's strengths might be the other's weaknesses. Be alert to "need clusters" that indicate areas to concentrate on. (For example: If a child is clumsy, has poor eye-hand coordination, and has balance and rhythm problems, concentrate on teaching this child motor skills.) It is also important to keep in mind the developmental level of the child.

Because these children have problems with gross motor skills, balance, spatial awareness, and sensory integration, they may need help with climbing.

(Is the attention span really short for a three-year-old?) Look for uneven development characterized by average to above-average development in one or more areas, but noticeable developmental lags in other areas. (The child can discuss trains, the roles of the various people on the train, and how trains work, but cannot put a toy train beside, in front of, or above a block.)

### Sensory Skills

*Visual Skills.* It is difficult for children with learning needs to recognize similarities and differences (visual discrimination). Their problems are magnified when they try to learn to recognize numbers and letters, as the differences are slight. The letters that are reversible are especially difficult (*b*, *d*), as are the ones with "tails" (*p, q, j, g*). Part-whole relationships (visual closure) cause problems. Relating the pieces of a puzzle to the whole puzzle is a real challenge. These children have trouble identifying missing parts; a picture of a three-legged chair would appear normal to them. They also have trouble remembering sequences and images (visual memory). Because of the difficulty they have in sorting out foreground and background, these children often focus on irrelevant details. Have these children practice identifying and matching shapes and colors before they proceed to letters and numbers. Needed memory skills can be built by games that require children to remember the original order of objects that have been moved.

*Auditory Skills.* These children have difficulty recognizing differences in sounds or words (auditory discrimination); hence they often misinterpret meanings. They also have problems identifying the rhyming elements of words. They find classifying words next to impossible (for example, finding all the words that start with *a*). Hierarchical classifications are generally beyond their capability. As you might guess, these are children who do not enjoy sound and word games and who often cannot express thoughts and ideas clearly.

Because it is important that they develop auditory skills, choose topics that are of particular interest to them and reinforce their attempts at communicating. Don't avoid areas that are difficult, but keep the time spent on them short and praise the children's attempts. Work to increase concentration and attention span as well.

### Thinking and Reasoning Skills

They need practice in logical reasoning. Demonstrate first with objects and then by drawing attention to the child's own behavior that it is possible to make predictions about what will happen. In this way they will gradually develop cause and effect reasoning skills. Start with short, obvious examples, such as putting weights on a balance. Work toward tasks requiring higher-level reasoning skills, such as figuring out the need plants have for water and sunlight. Include activities in which children can cause change—the harder they press their crayons, the darker the color. Then (in combination with the work on body awareness) help children learn how they cause their environment to change.

### Motor Skills

Learning needs children are often clumsy or awkward; their large motor coordination is poor. While walking or running, these children appear disjointed. They get where they want to go but they appear inefficient and they don't move smoothly. They lack the necessary coordination for hopping, jumping, and skipping and show an irregular rhythm when clapping or tapping. Their balance is poor as a result of the motor problems.

They may need your encouragement to participate in large motor activities, especially if others have teased them in the past. Plan opportunities both indoors and out for children to practice large motor

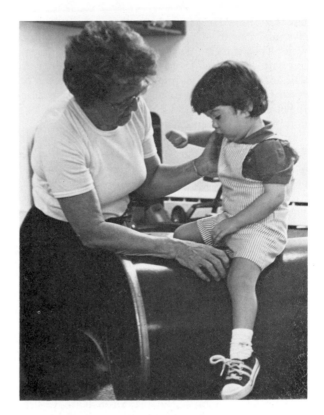

Moving through space and maintaining balance can both be difficult. Going back and forth on a barrel is practice for the swing and jungle gym.

skill in a noncompetitive way. Walking on a line or balance beam and stepping through the rungs of a ladder lying on the floor are both useful. Riding a tricycle and climbing a jungle gym provide opportunities to develop large motor coordination.

Using small motor and eye-hand coordination to hold chalk, a crayon, or a pencil properly may be a challenge. Learning needs children find coloring inside the lines or pasting in a specific area difficult and cutting with scissors impossible. They also have trouble catching a ball, especially if it bounces first. It is difficult for these children to decide when the ball will reach them and how high the ball will be when it does. Hence, they rarely catch it. Use underinflated beach balls as well as large balls to increase the possibility for success. Provide scissors that work by squeezing a circular handle. Large crayons and large chalk and simple designs all help. Your concern is to ensure that these children experience success in this area so that they don't quit trying.

### Feelings

They need to increase their awareness of their own feelings and those of others as well. They also need experience in differentiating between feelings and behavior: "It's OK to be mad at Chunga; it is not

OK to hit her." Help them learn to express both positive and negative feelings in socially acceptable ways. They can run, poke playdough, or hit a punching bag. They need to consciously decide how they will deal with their feelings. They may also need to learn the expressions and gestures to show others that they are happy and like them. They need help making and keeping friends.

In general, these children dislike change. Special school events are often stressful. They have trouble handling feelings of anticipation, as will become apparent when you are preparing the class for a field trip. The anxiety often takes the form of questions: These children ask many more questions than their peers, and they ask the same questions over and over. Help them learn other ways of coping with anxiety.

### Awareness

*Body Awareness.* Learning disabled children show poor knowledge of their own body whether they are asked to label parts on a doll or identify a body part of their own that is being touched. They need to become more aware of themselves in relation to their surroundings. Help children learn to use spatial terms that define where they are—*near*, *far*, *in front of*, *behind*, *above*, *below*.

*Self-concept.* Identifying learning needs early benefits both you and the children. Once children have already experienced failure, you have to deal with a poor self-concept in addition to the learning disability. You can help them become aware of their individual strengths even while working on needs.

### Guidelines

The following guidelines should prove generally useful when teaching children with learning needs. Two key words to keep in mind are consistency and preparation.

1. Be consistent, not only in the class rules you set but also in the daily schedule of activities.
2. Prepare children for changes in routine. Announcement of a change will set off a flood of questions, which you may have to control. The third time you hear the same question, you might respond, "I understand your concern about the trip to the orchard. I'll answer the question this last time, but not again." From then on you can usually discourage the questions with one of those "teacher" looks.

It will be necessary to simplify the program and make it as concrete as possible. Work very gradually toward a more challenging program.

1. Eliminate as many distractions as possible when it is important that the child concentrate. For example, don't have a group activity in a place where this child can look out the window and see others playing on the playground.
2. Begin with simple activities dealing with one concept and move to more complex concepts as the child seems ready, for example, from *taking turns* to *friendship*, from *counting* to *estimating*.
3. Make directions simple, short, and clear; if necessary, give them a step at a time. "It's cleanup time" may not be enough. Try "Put the doll clothes back in the drawer" and when that is completed continue with "Put the dolls in their bed," and so on. When the child has done as you requested, be sure to reinforce the behavior: "I liked the way you folded the doll clothes and put them away." A specific and concrete reinforcement is more effective than one as general as "That's a good job."
4. If a child has problems learning a particular task, check if he has mastered the prerequisite skills. For example, if a child can't pick out the square from a group of circles, he probably can't find the *p* among similar looking letters.
5. As young children begin to reason concretely, be sure to use concrete objects when teaching. For example, count children, fingers, boys, girls, windows, teachers, but don't just count.
6. All children have a preferred way of learning information (visual, auditory, or kinesthetic/tactile). It can be particularly helpful to know and use the learning needs child's preference. For example:

   Visual: Have a poster in the block corner demonstrating the proper and improper use of blocks.
   Auditory: Tell the child, "Blocks are to build with" or "You may not throw the blocks."
   Kinesthetic/Tactile: Take the child to the block corner and show the child what to do, then have the child demonstrate the appropriate behavior to you.

7. Provide numerous and varied learning experiences that teach the same idea in many different ways. For example, you can teach body awareness through art, movement, listening, music, and health activities.
8. Provide many activities that encourage movement, especially during large group times. Don't expect these children to sit as long as some of their peers might.

Discipline, or classroom management, is rarely easy; children with learning needs present an additional challenge. Because their behavior is inconsistent, it is difficult to know whether these children are refusing or are unable to behave as they should.

(Parents have the same dilemma.) The traditional solution is *behavior modification*. This may involve token rewards for good or "on task" behavior and sitting in a "time out" area or loss of token rewards for inappropriate behavior. Others have successfully used *logical consequences*. For example, if a child knocks all the plastic blocks off a table, he needs to help pick them up. If she spills juice, she should help clean it up. (If the child spills juice persistently and purposefully, you might try not giving him any more. If he claims to be thirsty, you could give him water.) A combination of the two methods works best. You want the child to learn internalized self-control in order to stop inappropriate behavior.

Ignoring inappropriate behavior (especially when you think that getting attention is the child's purpose) is ideal when it works. However, it doesn't always work in the classroom, particularly if the child is doing something dangerous or is disturbing the other children. In those cases, removing the child from the situation is probably the best solution.

The use of "time out" for learning disabled children has its proponents and opponents. "Time out" is removing the child from the ongoing activities to a specified location off to one side of the room or playground. It is designed to give children time to regain their self-control. It is not a punishment. Space can be designated by placing a chair in a taped-off square or in a large (refrigerator size) carton. When the child is ready, he or she can easily rejoin the group.

Keep in close touch with the parents. Change can take place daily, and knowing that a child had a "good day" may be the support a parent needs.

I once taught a little girl who was particularly disruptive during group time. I had an aide take her out into the hall whenever she acted up. Instead of decreasing, the disruptive behavior increased, and it began to occur closer to the beginning of group time. I decided to trade roles with the aide to see what was happening. The next time Andrea created a disturbance, I took her out into the hall. Once there, she told me to sit down, plopped herself in my lap, and said, "This is the book I want to read today." She then hauled out her book, and I read it. Now I knew why this child disrupted my group! The next day Andrea went to the hall with *no* book, and the aide was instructed to ignore her. The following day she sat through most of group time! The point of the story is, make sure your consequence is not rewarding.

*Satiation* is another way of dealing with inappropriate behavior. The child is made to continue the behavior when he or she no longer wants to. This is particularly effective for something physical, like falling off a chair. In one case I required a child to sit down, fall off, and get up repeatedly for twenty minutes! As you might guess, this behavior lost its charm when I not only encouraged but also required it. To discourage acts that are likely to be contagious in a classroom, satiation is far more effective than ignoring.

An additional method of stopping a behavior is to set up *incompatible alternatives*. I used this technique successfully with a child who frequently masturbated in class. After all my attempts had failed in discussing the difference between private and public behavior with the child, reviewing my program to see if he could be bored, checking to see if his pants were too tight, and asking his mother if he had a rash—I changed tactics. I planned a program of messy table activities requiring two hands. It really is difficult to finger paint with pudding with both hands and masturbate at the same time!

## CURRICULUM ADAPTATIONS

Children with learning disabilities can usually make do with few adaptations. However, if you adapt your programs to meet their needs in the preschool years, chances are these children's problems can be corrected.

### Expressing Language, Listening, and Reading Readiness

Because most learning disabled children will have problems learning to read, it is imperative to make language arts a successful and enjoyable experience for them at the preschool level. To be motivated to overcome their problems in this area they need to know it can and *will* be fun.

Stories can be entertaining and enlightening for children or they can become totally frustrating. Children with learning needs are often the ones who hit the person beside them and are eliminated from the group for not listening—an unpleasant experience.

1. Keep stories short. It is better to read a five-page story that the children sit through attentively than to read a twenty-page story with twenty interruptions.
2. Establish boundaries for the children during story time. Put strips of tape on the floor or carpet, or have each child sit on a carpet square.
3. Use stories that allow participation. Children can move the flannel board characters to follow the story.
4. Sometimes read stories in small groups, where you can individualize the story and your attention.
5. Choose stories that deal with hostile or unhappy feelings as well as happy ones.
6. Choose stories that deal with individual differences. (For suggestions see the Bibliography for Children at the end of this chapter.)

Fingerplays are great for learning disabled children. They are actively involved and able to learn through the kinesthetic/tactile sense. Also, hands that are busy doing fingerplays are less likely to be bothering the person next to them.

1. Use fingerplays to teach concepts where appropriate.
2. Quiz the children in a way that is fun but that also makes them think about what they are saying: For example, sing "Where Is Thumbkin" while holding up your index finger. Ask them what is wrong with doing it that way. Ask them for another word for thumbkin (thumb), pointer (index finger), tall man (middle finger), ring man, and pinkie. Can the children tell you how the fingers got these nick names?

Children are expected to be ready to read when they are about five or six years old. However, many children with learning needs don't seem to be ready when their peers are. If this is the case, check that they have the prerequisite skills necessary. Use the activities in Part Two to informally diagnose at what level the children are functioning. You might even devise for yourself an informal check sheet to ascertain what skills the children have acquired. This way you can match your teaching to the children's level of skill. Challenge but don't overwhelm children with the necessary visual and auditory skills that are prerequisites to reading.

### Social Studies

Social studies can be used to create awareness of other people and of the roles they play.

1. Try setting up a "society" in your class based on the strengths and needs of the individual children: "Gina will take the messages to others because she is a good runner. Barbara will print the messages. Kenzi will call us all together because he has a good strong voice."
2. Emphasize group belonging and the courtesy extended to other group members, property rights, space to play, including others, and so on. Discuss how people feel when they are not included, their toys are taken, or their space is intruded on. Also discuss ways of dealing with these feelings.

### Science/Discovery

Science activities may create enthusiasm in learning needs children if a basic discovery approach is taken.

1. Let children examine items (orange, cup, mirror) and describe as many details of the item as they can (color, shape, size, texture, function, parts). This is a great way for children to learn comparison. Two items may be alike in some ways and different in others.
2. Cause and effect reasoning is important. It may help children develop inner controls and curb impulsivity. Encourage children to answer questions like: "What happens if . . . ? What could you do about . . . ? Is there anything else you could do?" And then, when practical, have them test out their answer.

### Math

Helping these children at this age develop a sensorimotor experiential awareness of math will help alleviate future problems in math. Doing math, not just looking or hearing about it, is the key.

1. Use concrete objects to teach number concepts, and employ as many variations as you can think of. Use food (raisins, miniature marshmallows) for teaching these concepts: *same/different, numbers, sets, equal, one-to-one correspondence,* and *more/less/same.* (Somehow, children learn faster when another child is going to get "more" than they are!)
2. Provide running commentary whenever possible: "You've had half of your juice. You have one cookie yet to eat. We have two empty chairs at this table."
3. Create situations where children must come up with mathematical solutions: "What if you run out of large blocks and you need to make another wall the same length as the first?" Discuss relative length.

### Health and Safety

This is an important curriculum area for learning disabled children, who, even at this early age, may have seen a variety of specialists, perhaps had an EEG, and taken drugs and who may have some fears about health professionals. Because these children must cooperate in testing and report their reactions to drugs they may be taking, developing good rapport between children and medical personnel is important. Increase body awareness so the children can successfully locate body parts and then respond about how specific parts feel.

Other important health and safety areas need work.

1. As these children are more likely than others to become lost, teach them to state their name, telephone number, and parents' names early in the year.
2. Work on traffic signs and try to teach these children to control impulsive behavior that may lead to accidents.
3. Help children see the relationship between ac-

tions and results (e.g., what may happen if some-one runs in front of a car).

4. State and post class safety rules, especially those related to situations in which children could be hurt (standing on chairs and tables, walking with scissors, throwing blocks).

### Art

With learning needs children, the focus of art should be on the *process*, not the product. Leave them free to be spontaneous and creative. When they begin to feel that their work should "be something" or look like something specific, and the emphasis is on a product, the potential for failure is greater.

1. Use three-dimensional materials (clay, play-dough). They can be good for releasing tension, and because they are reusable and easily stored, they are available on short notice.
2. Use large paintbrushes and finger paint. They require less eye-hand coordination than small brushes.
3. Be sure to use some art materials that accommodate expansive work: Color or paint on very large paper without restriction or use finger paint on the table, then print the pictures.
4. Colored marking pens are easier for these children to use than crayons, since either light or heavy pressure leaves an impression and looks fine.

### Music

Music allows children to be actively part of a group. Here are some suggestions.

1. Use songs with motions: "My Bonnie Lies over the Ocean," "Hey, Betty Martin."
2. Use songs that create body awareness: "Put Your Finger in the Air," "Head, Shoulders, Knees, and Toes."
3. Combine music and movement to give children the opportunity to translate an auditory stimulus (record, music) into movement. Be sure to discuss the mood of the music and what types of actions this mood evokes.
4. Music can be used to release energy. If bad weather has kept the children indoors, play salsa or a Sousa march. Music also helps children settle down. If the children are excited before a rest period, help them relax with some "easy listening" music.

### Dramatic Play

Dramatic play allows children to try out roles and perhaps work through fearful experiences. It gives children the chance to be in control.

1. Holidays and special events are particularly stressful; play through some of these.
2. Because children with learning needs often have as much trouble expressing pleasure as pain, have them practice being happy and sad. Discuss how others know you are happy. Have the children pretend to open a package that contains something they really want.
3. Help children play through field trips, visits to the doctor, and so on. Discuss what could happen as well as what behavior is expected of them.

### Small Motor Play

All young children need practice in fine motor skills. Children with learning needs should receive extra attention in this area. Because they are often uncoordinated, they may avoid small motor activities.

1. Pick some activities that may especially intrigue the particular child. If the child likes cars, provide a car drawing to color. (This to me is not creative art, but rather practice in small motor skills.) Provide a maze for small toy cars to follow. Have the child practice lining the cars up in specified patterns. Magnets can be used to attach metal cars to one another.
2. Have children practice the self-help skills of buttoning, snapping, and tying. Discuss the pride of being able to "do it myself."
3. Avoid small motor play if a child is having a "bad" day or seems to have excessive amounts of energy. One sweep of the arm can scatter endless numbers of small items all over the classroom.

### Large Motor Play

Children with learning needs use large motor activities as a means of releasing frustration, tension, and anger. Participating in these activities with minimal conflict will help children develop feelings of belonging to a group.

1. Help children develop concepts of space and direction by having them pace off distances or see how far they can run in five seconds compared to walking or crawling.
2. Have children do variations on skills that they already know, like walking, jumping, throwing, rolling, and crawling.
3. Include activities that develop the lateral muscles of the trunk: crawling, climbing, and crashing. It is generally believed that children can't develop fine motor coordination until these lateral muscles have been strengthened. Therefore, it is futile to expect a child to color within the lines until the lateral muscles are sufficiently developed.)
4. Help the learning disabled child learn to use

The children are developing their tactile skills and spatial awareness. They can be successful at this firsthand experience because they don't have to deal with gravity or balance—both of which can be problematic for learning needs children.

large motor activities as a tension release.

5. In a doorway, hang up an old laundry bag stuffed with pillows, scrap materials, or anything soft. Encourage children who feel like hitting to hit the punching bag (not just to hit once or tap lightly but as hard and often as they can).

6. Provide a large rubber ball for kicking. Encourage children to kick the ball and then run after it and kick it again, or kick the ball and try to hit a target like a bowling pin.

7. Include activities that require children to use both sides of the body together, such as throwing or catching a ball or balloon with both hands, hopping or jumping with both feet together, clapping, and doing jumping jacks. (An underinflated beach ball is easier for the child to catch.)

8. Include activities that require children to use both sides of the body alternately, such as going up steps with alternate feet on each tread, climbing a ladder, riding a tricycle, walking a line or balance beam, running, walking, and skipping. Place a string in various configurations (straight, curved, with angles) and have the children walk on this.

9. Include activities that require children to cross the midline (the imaginary line through the center of the body, which divides it into right and left sides). When playing "Simon Says" request children to put the *right* hand on the *left* shoulder and so on. Have children throw balls or bean bags while standing sideways to the target. Have them touch the toes of the opposite foot while standing. Don't force a child to cross the midline, and when doing these activities, focus children's attention on the activity, not on whether or not they are crossing the midline.

### Transitions
Use transitions for learning and for burning off energy.

1. Without being obvious about it, dismiss the learning needs child early in the transition—this should be thought of as prevention, not favoritism.

2. Use transitions to increase body awareness and feelings of being part of the group. "All children with brown eyes and blonde hair may *jump* to their centers."

## CHILD STUDY TEAM REPORT

### Scott D.

In attendance: Mrs. D., Ms. L., preschool teacher, Ms. R., psychologist, Mrs. C., occupational therapist.

Scott D. is a four-and-one-half year old boy who was referred for testing by his pediatrician at the request of his mother. Scott has two older siblings at home. A ten-year-old brother is in the third grade and attends a resource room for learning disabled children, where he receives instruction in reading, spelling, and adaptive physical education. A seven-year-old sister attends second grade.

Scott lives at home with his siblings, father, and mother. His paternal grandmother also lives with the family. Mrs. D. reports that Scott sat up alone at seven months, walked at about fifteen months, and began speaking in two-word phrases at about eighteen months.

Scott has been attending a neighborhood play group for about six months. Mrs. D. and four other mothers rotate planning for the group. Mrs. D. reports that Scott is not interested in the things the other children are, especially in more structured activities like painting, coloring, cutting, and pasting. He is less coordinated than the other children and appears to have a somewhat shorter attention span. Mrs. D. says that one of the other mothers noticed these things also.

Mrs. D. also reports that both Mr. D. and his mother, as well as her pediatrician, were reluctant to agree to have Scott tested. They think she is making "a big deal out of nothing," and that Scott is "immature." Mrs. D. says that she is concerned because of the learning problems of her first son. She thinks that Scott may not be ready for kindergarten next year. She says that although Scott is bright and has a very good vocabulary, he is "different" from other children his age.

The psychologist who saw Scott for testing administered an intelligence (Weschler Preschool and Primary Intelligence Scale) and a developmental criterion test. The intelligence test indicated a significant difference between Scott's verbal abilities, which were in the high-average range, and his performance scores, which were in the low to low-average range. Scott's lowest scores occurred in subtests that involved perceptual tasks like copying geometric shapes, copying block designs, and completing mazes. Scott's strongest score was in vocabulary.

Scott's drawing of a person was immature for his age, which may have been at least partially due to the fact that his pencil control was poor. The items on the criterion test that Scott excelled on included vocabulary and concepts. Weaknesses occurred in the areas of fine motor and visual-motor tasks. The psychologist felt Scott's attention span was age appropriate, at least working one to one in the testing environment with minimal distractions. The psychologist referred Scott to the occupational therapist for a sensorimotor evaluation.

After administering the Purdue Perceptual-Motor Survey, the occupational therapist reported that Scott's gross motor skills are age appropriate. Scott appears to have a lot of confidence in this area. She noted that Scott is right-hand, right-foot, and right-eye dominant. His weaknesses were in spatial relations and fine motor coordination. She reports that some of Scott's primitive postural reflexes have not been integrated, which affects muscle tone and eye-hand coordination. She recommends individual therapy for Scott at least once a week.

Both the psychologist and occupational therapist recommend Scott attend a preschool program five mornings a week, with supplemental occupational therapy once a week. At the end of six months, a conference can be held to discuss kindergarten enrollment or alternative placements for next year.

The preschool staff should be made aware of Scott's needs in the visual-motor and perceptual areas. A copy of the reports will be sent to them. At home, Mrs. D. can provide Scott with opportunities to explore a variety of materials including preschool-size blocks that snap together, clay, crayons or markers and paper (as opposed to coloring books), scissors, and a large, soft ball for ball play. Mrs. D. inquired about swimming. Everyone agreed this would be a good activity for Scott. A therapy schedule for occupational therapy was discussed.

Mrs. D. feels that her husband and mother-in-law will disagree with therapy, but not preschool. She will try to get them involved with the staff at the preschool and with the occupational therapist. The psychologist and occupational therapist assured Mrs. D. that her observations of Scott were valid, and that in view of family history, she really was wise to bring Scott for testing.

# INDIVIDUALIZED EDUCATION PROGRAM

NAME __Scott D.__ DOB __6__ / __3__ / __78__

AGE __4-6__ GRADE __Preschool__

SCHOOL __Flanders Field Day School__

PARENTS/GUARDIANS __Mr. & Mrs. D.__

ADDRESS __23 New Hope Lane__

PHONE __456-7891__

On __1/6/83__, the IPRD Committee
   (Date)
met to review all current data and
recommends Level __I__ placement.

Date of new review __6/30/83__

Exceptionality: __Learning disabled__

Present at meeting:

Parents __Mrs. D.__

Others: Name/Position __Ms. R., Psychologist;__

## CURRENT TEST DATA

TEST/DATE/RESULTS

WPPSI / 12/6/82 / Verbal: high-average to high;
                  / Performance: low to low-average

Criterion/ 12/6/82 / High: vocabulary, concepts;
                   / Weak: fine motor, visual motor

Purdue / 12/13/82 / OK: gross motor; Weak: spatial relations,

P-N Survey         fine motor coordination

Recommended Special Services (Hrs/Wk):

Occupational Therapy / 1 hr./wk
                     /
                     /

Total Hours/Week:

Special Education Classroom __0__

Regular Classroom __12½__

Representative of District/Agency __Ms. L., Preschool Teacher__

__Mrs. C., Occupational Therapist__

The committee has determined the following learning strengths and needs to be reflected in the IEP:

| STRENGTHS | NEEDS |
|---|---|
| Above-average verbal abilities | Lack of reflex integration |
| Vocabulary | Fine motor skills |
| Concepts (language) | Spatial relations |
| Gross motor skills | Eye-hand coordination |
| Right established dominance | |

STUDENT _____ Scott D. _____ DATE _____ 1/6/83 _____

GOAL _____ To improve eye-hand coordination _____

PARENT SIGNATURE _____

TEACHER SIGNATURE _____

| INSTRUCTIONAL OBJECTIVES | EDUCATIONAL METHODS | DATE Begin | DATE End | Eval. | PERSONS RESPONSIBLE Name | Position |
|---|---|---|---|---|---|---|
| Scott will be able to construct a tower of 8 1" cubes. | Cuisenaire Rods, Block play | 1/6 | 6/30 | | Ms. L. | Teacher |
| Given 4 patterns to copy, Scott will be able to string at least 8 beads on a shoestring on 2 occasions. | Salt Putty Beads, Nuts and Bolts, String Mobile | 1/6 | 6/30 | | Ms. L. | Teacher |
| Scott will be able to trace simple shapes from a template and color the shape, remaining within the lines for 75% of surface area. | Touch Shapes, Picture Shapes, Pockets, Sandwich Trick, Color Graphs | 1/6 | 6/30 | | Ms. L. | Teacher |
| Given heavy paper marked with a straight and curved ½" line, Scott will be able to cut on the line, staying on the line 75% of the time. | Torn Paper Flowers, Place Mat Collage | 1/6 | 6/30 | | Ms. L. | Teacher |

STUDENT _____ Scott D. _____  
GOAL _____ To improve spatial concepts _____   DATE _____ 1/6/83

PARENT SIGNATURE _____   TEACHER SIGNATURE _____

| INSTRUCTIONAL OBJECTIVES | EDUCATIONAL METHODS | DATE Begin | DATE End | Eval. | PERSONS RESPONSIBLE Name | Position |
|---|---|---|---|---|---|---|
| When given verbal instructions, Scott will be able to place a book in 6/6 of the following positions relative to a chair: next to (beside); on; under; over; in front of; in back of; on 3 occasions. | Cat and Mouse, Contour Maps, Obstacle Course | 1/6 | 4/6 | | Ms. L. | Teacher |
| Given a block and box in positions in the above task, Scott will be able to verbally express the position of the block relative to the position of the box. (5/6 positions on 3 occasions.) | same as above | 4/6 | 6/30 | | Ms. L. | Teacher |
| Scott will be able to point to the side, top, bottom, middle of his body on 3 occasions. | Body Mural, Body Parts, Movement Songs, Mixed-up People | 3/6 | 6/30 | | Ms. L. | Teacher |
| Given crayons and paper, Scott will be able to mark the paper to designate 6/6 of the following positions: side; top; bottom; top corner; bottom corner; middle; on 3 occasions. | same as above | 4/6 | 6/30 | | Ms. L. | Teacher |

STUDENT ___ Scott D. ___    DATE ___ 1/6/83 ___

GOAL ___ To improve small motor coordination ___

PARENT SIGNATURE ___    TEACHER SIGNATURE ___

| INSTRUCTIONAL OBJECTIVES | EDUCATIONAL METHODS | DATE Begin | DATE End | Eval. | PERSONS RESPONSIBLE Name | PERSONS RESPONSIBLE Position |
|---|---|---|---|---|---|---|
| Scott will construct a simple object from clay, wire, or string on 2 occasions. | Corrugated Collage, String Painting, Wire Sculpture, Clay | 1/6 | 6/30 | | Ms. L. | Teacher |
| Given a 10-piece puzzle, Scott will complete it independently without being timed. | Disability Puzzle, Natural Sequencing, My Puzzle | 1/6 | 6/30 | | Ms. L. | Teacher |

# GLOSSARY

**Behavior modification**   A systematic technique for changing someone's behavioral responses to specific stimuli. See Conditioning, Reinforcement.

**Conditioning**   A technique for establishing a specific behavior. The most common type used in education is instrumental, or operant, conditioning. When an appropriate behavior occurs, it is reinforced.

**Developmental aphasia**   Inability from an early age to use or understand the spoken or written word.

**Distractibility**   How easily a person's attention is drawn to extraneous stimuli.

**Dyscalculia**   The inability to perform mathematical functions, usually associated with neurological dysfunction.

**Dysgraphia**   Extremely poor handwriting or the inability to perform the motor movements required for handwriting.

**Dyslexia**   The partial inability to read or to understand what one reads.

**Echolalia**   The parrotlike repetition of words, phrases, or sentences spoken by another person, without understanding the meaning.

**EEG**   Electroencephalogram. A graphic record of the wavelike changes in the electric potential observed when electrodes are placed on the skull. Irregular patterns in an EEG are used to locate lesions in the brain.

**Enuresis**   Bed-wetting.

**Frostig**   A test and/or materials designed by Dr. Marianne Frostig to test for and train perceptual ability.

**Laterality**   An internal awareness of the two sides of the body. Usually there is a dominant side (left-handedness, right-handedness). There is concern about the relationship of laterality to learning disabilities.

**Learning disabilities**   "Children with learning disabilities exhibit a disorder in one or more of the basic psychological processes involved in understanding or using spoken or written languages. These may be manifested in disorders of listening, thinking, talking, reading, writing, spelling, or arithmetic. They include conditions which have been referred to as perceptual handicaps, brain injury, minimal brain dysfunction, dyslexia, and developmental aphasia. They do not include learning problems which are due primarily to visual, learning, or motor handicaps, to mental retardation, emotional disturbance, or environmental disadvantage." (National Advisory Committee on Handicapped Children [PL 91–230] uses this definition.)

**Minimal brain dysfunction (MBD)**   The medical term for "learning disabilities."

**Perceptual handicap**   The inability to integrate sensory information.

**Perseveration**   The tendency to continue in any activity, once it is begun, beyond its logical conclusion. This is caused by relative difficulty in shifting from one task to another or in changing methods to suit a change in conditions.

**Reversal**   The tendency to read or write backward (*was* for *saw*, for example).

**Reinforcement**   The giving or withholding of a reward in order to increase the likelihood of a response.

**Syndrome**   A set of symptoms that occur together.

**Underachievement**   Educational attainment below one's evidenced ability.

# TEACHING   RESOURCES

In some situations you may want or need additional information. There are many national as well as regional, state, and local organizations that can be helpful to you. The following annotated list of national organizations should be useful in helping you decide where to get the information you need.

Association for Children with Learning Disabilities (ACLD)
5521 Grace Street, Lower Level
Pittsburgh, PA 15236
   Refers inquiries to state affiliates and publishes newsletters.

Foundation for Children with Learning Disabilities
99 Park Avenue, Second Floor
New York, NY 10016
   Provides direct financial assistance to various programs that aid learning disabled children and their families academically and socially.

Perceptions, Inc.
P.O. Box 142
Millboro, NJ 07041
   Publishes a newsletter that serves as an information source for parents wishing to develop expertise in meeting the educational, social, and emotional needs of their learning disabled child.

Research and Demonstration Center for the Education of Handicapped Children and Youth
Box 223
Teachers College
Columbia University
New York, NY 10027

"Addresses itself to the identification of psycho-educational characteristics of the handicapped learner and the development of instructional methods and materials which will be effective in bridging existing gaps between these learners and school tasks."

# BIBLIOGRAPHY

Adamson, William C., and Katherine K. Adamson, eds. *A Handbook for Specific Learning Disabilities*. New York: Halsted Press, 1979.

Adler, Sidney Jacson, with Keith C. Terry. *Your Overactive Child: Normal or Not?* New York: Williams and Wilkins, 1972.

Ansara, Alice, ed. *Our Challenge: The Right to Know*. Pittsburgh, Pa.: Association for Children with Learning Disabilities, 1975.

Baren, Martin, et al. *Overcoming Learning Disabilities: A Team Approach (Parent-Teacher-Physician-Child)*. Englewood Cliffs, N.J.: Reston, 1978.

Brutten, Milton, et al. *Something's Wrong with My Child: A Parent's Handbook About Children with Learning Disabilities*. New York: Harcourt Brace Jovanovich, 1979.

Bryan, James H., and Tanis H. Bryan. *Exceptional Children*. Sherman Oaks, Calif.: Alfred Pub., 1979.

Bush, Clifford L., and Robert Andrews. *Dictionary of Reading and Learning Disabilities Terms*. Los Angeles: Western Psychological Services, 1978.

Crook, William Grant. *Can Your Child Read? Is He Hyperactive?* rev. ed. Jackson, Tenn.: Professional Books, 1977.

Cruickshank, William M., ed. *Learning Disabilities in Home, School and Community*. Syracuse, N.Y.: Syracuse Univ. Press, 1979.

Durkin, Dolores. *Teaching Your Children to Read*. 2nd ed. Boston: Allyn and Bacon, 1980.

Faas, Larry A. *Children with Learning Problems: A Handbook for Teachers*. Boston: Houghton Mifflin, 1980.

Feingold, Ben F. *Why Your Child Is Hyperactive*. New York: Random House, 1974.

Fisher, Joanna. *A Parent's Guide to Learning Disabilities*. New York: Scribner, 1979.

Gardner, Richard A. *MBD: The Family Book About Minimal Brain Dysfunction*. New York: Aronson, 1973.

Hobbs, N. *The Futures of Children: Categories, Labels, and Their Consequences*. San Francisco: Jossey-Bass, 1974.

Kephart, Newell C. *Learning Disability: An Educational Adventure*. West Lafayette, Ind.: Kappa Delta Pi Press, 1968.

Lahey, Benjamin B., ed. *Behavior Therapy with Hyperactive and Learning Disabled Children*. New York: Oxford Univ. Press, 1979.

McCarthy, Jeanne McRae, ed., with Samuel A. Kirk. *Learning Disabilities: Selected ACLD Papers*. Boston: Houghton Mifflin, 1975.

Osman, Betty B. *Learning Disabilities: A Family Affair*. New York: Warner Books, 1979.

Patterson, Gerald R., and M. Elizabeth Gullion. *Living with Children: New Methods for Parents and Teachers*. Champaign, Ill.: Research Press, 1976.

Smith, Deborah D. *Teaching the Learning Disabled*. Englewood Cliffs, N.J.: Prentice-Hall, 1981.

Stevens, Suzanne H. *The Learning Disabled Child: Ways That Parents Can Help*. Winston-Salem, N.C.: Blair, 1980.

Stewart, Mark A., and Sally Weendkos Olds. *Raising a Hyperactive Child*. New York: Harper and Row, 1973.

Szasz, Suzanne. *The Unspoken Language of Children*. New York: W.W. Norton, 1980.

Tarnopol, Lester, ed. *Learning Disorders in Children: Diagnosis, Medication, Education*. Boston: Little, Brown, 1971.

Velten, Emmett C., Jr., and Carlene Sampson. *Rx for Learning Disabilities*. Chicago: Nelson-Hall, 1978.

Wagner, Rudolph F. *Dyslexia and Your Child: A Guide for Parents and Teachers*. New York: Harper and Row, 1979.

Waugh, Kenneth W., and Wilma J. Bush. *Diagnosing Learning Disorders*. Columbus, Ohio: Charles E. Merrill, 1971.

Wender, Paul H. *The Hyperactive Child—A Handbook for Parents*. New York: Crown, 1973.

———*Minimal Brain Dysfunction in Children*. New York: Wiley, 1971.

Wepman, J. M., and W. M. Cruickshank. "Learning Disabilities." *Issues in the Classification of Children*. Ed. Nicholas Hobbs. 2 vols. San Francisco: Jossey-Bass, 1975, pp. 300–17.

Wyatt, Gertrude L. *Language Learning and Communications Disorders in Children*. New York: Free Press, 1969.

*Biography Autobiography/Fiction*

Browning, Elizabeth. *I Can't See What You're Saying*. New York: Coward, McCann and Geoghegan, 1973.

A mother's account of the medical and educational history of her son's language disability.

Brutten, Milton, et al. *Something's Wrong with My Child: A Parents' Book About Children with Learning Disabilities*. New York: Harcourt Brace Jovanovich, 1973.

An easily read, comprehensive work on learning disabilities. Information and advice to parents for dealing with doctors, educators, and agencies. Background information for teachers. (Appendix A, Facilities for the Developmentally Disabled; Appendix B, Associations for Children with Learning Disabilities; Appendix C, Sources of Information; Appendix D, National Organizations; Reading List; indexed.)

Clarke, Louise [pseud. for Thelma Purtell]. *Can't Read, Can't Write, Can't Talk Too Good Either: How to Recognize and Overcome Dyslexia in Your Child.* New York: Walker and Co., 1973.

A mother writes of her son's struggle to overcome a handicapping condition characterized by difficulty in reading, writing, spelling, and speaking. Mrs. Clarke

gives a vivid picture of what she considers to be the social and economic implications of the untreated dyslexic.

Cohen, Martin E., with Barbara Davidson. *Bets Wishz Doc: A Dynamic Approach to Learning Disabilities* New York: Penguin Books, 1975.

An informative book concerned with the education of learning disabled children. The book itself is divided into four parts: (1) case histories; (2) the defining of learning disability and perception training, and the explanation of an educational program; (3) a daily account of the program in operation at a private school; and (4) a section designed for parents providing guidelines for dealing with their exceptional child in the home.

# BIBLIOGRAPHY FOR CHILDREN

*Awareness*

Cohen, Miriam. *No Good in Art.* New York: Greenwillow Books, 1980.

A first grader is convinced he can't draw, but when encouraged, he finds he can.

———. *When Will I Read?* New York: Greenwillow Books, 1977.

A good book for children who are anxiously awaiting the time that they will learn to read.

Fassier, Joan. *One Little Girl: A "Slow Child" Finds Her Strengths.* New York: Human Sciences Press, 1969.

While Laurie is slow at doing some things, she is fast at doing others. When the adults realize this, Laurie is at last happy to be herself.

Hatch, Jean. *School Makes Sense Sometimes.* New York: Human Sciences Press, 1980.

The author covers every aspect of early education as she helps children to appreciate many of the confusing experiences of school.

Lasker, Joe. *He's My Brother.* Chicago: Albert Whitman, 1974.

A young boy sensitively describes the experiences of his slow-learning younger brother at school and at home.

*Body Awareness*

Brenner, Barbara. *Bodies.* New York: E. P. Dutton, 1973. A look at all kinds of bodies—all shapes, colors, and sizes. It shows the differences and similarities and stresses the uniqueness in everyone.

Corey, Dorothy. *Tomorrow You Can.* Chicago: Albert Whitman, 1977.

An understanding book about growing up and all the things that children may be ready to participate in later on.

Harris, Robbie H., and Elizabeth Levy. *Before You Were Three: How You Began to Walk, Talk, Explore and Have Feelings.* New York: Delacorte Press, 1977.

Children and adults can read this book together and explore the process of growing during the first three years of life.

Showers, Paul. *Follow Your Nose.* New York: Thomas Y. Crowell, 1963.

This gay book carefully gives young readers an understanding of smelling and other functions of the nose.

———. *How Many Teeth?* New York: Thomas Y. Crowell, 1962.

Every child loses teeth and wonders what has happened.

———. *How You Talk.* New York: Thomas Y. Crowell, 1967.

The reader learns how sounds are made with the nose, larynx, and mouth.

*Siblings and Family Relationships*

Conford, Ellen. *Impossible Possum.* Boston: Little, Brown, 1971.

A little boy possum's older sister uses her wits and helps him overcome a problem.

Waber, Bernard. *Good-bye, Funny Dumpy Lumpy.* Boston: Houghton Mifflin, 1977.

Five vignettes reveal how a mother, father, and their three children negotiate common family problems.

Zolotow, Charlotte. *Big Brother*. New York: Harper and Row, 1960.

When big brother won't stop teasing his small sister—a gentle lesson with a happy ending shows how brothers and sisters can share their play and work activities.

*Friendship and Feelings*

Auglund, Joan Walsh. *Love Is a Special Way of Feeling*. New York: Harcourt Brace Jovanovich, 1960.

A small book about things.

Krauss, Ruth. *The Bundle Book*. New York: Harper and Row, 1951.

This quickly and easily read story narrates a guessing game between a mother and her child. Expressively illustrated.

———. *The Carrot Seed*. New York: Harper and Brothers, 1945.

A classic story of a little boy who plants a carrot seed that everyone says won't come up. Good for sequencing and discussing discouragement.

Udry, Janice. *Let's Be Enemies*. New York: Harper and Row, 1961.

About an argument with a friend. The simply phrased pages explain the trials of friendship.

———. *The Mean Mouse and Other Mean Stories*. New York: Harper and Row, 1962.

All the main characters of the story are mean, but each one gets his comeuppance before the story is over.

———. *What Mary Jo Shared*. Chicago: Albert Whitman, 1966.

Mary Jo never shared at school because she was shy and could never find anything different to share. Finally, she found someone very special to share with the class.

Wiseman, B. *Morris Goes to School*. New York: Harper and Row, 1970.

A humorous story about a moose who goes to school. Despite his mistakes and differences, the class still likes him.

Zolotow, Charlotte. *The Hating Book*. New York: Harper and Row, 1969.

A little girl asks her friend why they hate each other.

———. *If It Weren't for You*. New York: Harper and Row, 1966.

Older brother muses about all the advantages he would have if he were an only child—until he comes to one major disadvantage.

———. *My Friend John*. New York: Harper and Row, 1968.

The story of two friends. A boy compares himself to his friend. He tells the good, bad, and secret aspects of their personalities and families.

———. *Someday*. New York: Harper and Row, 1965.

The essence of childhood longing is reflected in one little girl's dreams.

———. *The Unfriendly Book*. New York: Harper and Row, 1975.

Bertha is jealous when Judy, her best friend, plays with other people.

*Building Concepts*

Emberley, Barbara. *Drummer Hoff*. Englewood Cliffs, N.J.: Prentice-Hall, 1967.

A simple picture book describing how to fire a cannon. Excellent for sequencing and rhyming.

Gay, Zhenya. *Look!* New York: Viking Press, 1965.

A nicely illustrated book describing different animals. Told in rhyme with counting skills integrated in the reading.

Hoban, Tana. *Look Again!* New York: Macmillan, 1971.

Pages with cutouts that reveal part of the picture on the next page. Good for part/whole relationships. No words.

———. *Shapes and Things*. New York: Macmillan, 1970.

Uncommon visual presentation of common articles found in the home. No words.

Oxenbury, Helen. *ABC of Things*. New York: 1971.

Pictures and words enhance understanding of the alphabet.

*The Sesame Street Book of Shapes*. Created in cooperation with the Children's Television Workshop, producers of *Sesame Street*. New York: New American Library, 1971.

Introduces children to shapes and shows how shapes can be combined in different ways.

# I N D E X

| *Annual Goals* | *Activity* | *Curriculum Area* | *Page* |
|---|---|---|---|
| To improve visual association | Flannel Board Stories | Reading Readiness | 374 |
| | What Doesn't Belong? | Mathematics | 424 |
| To improve visual comprehension | Comics | Reading Readiness | 379 |
| | My Books | Reading Readiness | 380 |
| | Picture Shapes | Mathematics | 424 |
| To improve tactile identification | Letter Day | Listening | 352 |
| To improve tactile discrimination | Barefoot | Outdoor Play | 530 |
| | Buttoning Sequences | Small Motor Play | 504 |
| | Cave Exploration | Outdoor Play | 528 |
| | Feely Bag | Small Motor Play | 499 |
| | Feely Box | Small Motor Play | 503 |
| | Food Sense | Science/Discovery | 405 |
| | Nature Feely Board | Science/Discovery | 404 |
| | Nuts and Bolts | Small Motor Play | 505 |
| | Sandpaper Letters | Reading Readiness | 367 |
| | Texture Classification | Science/Discovery | 406 |
| | Texture Paint | Art | 449 |
| To improve tactile memory | Nature Feely Board | Science/Discovery | 404 |
| To improve discrimination of smells | Food Sense | Science/Discovery | 405 |
| | Wiggly Worms | Science/Discovery | 406 |
| To improve taste discrimination | Food Sense | Science/Discovery | 405 |
| | Taste Sort | Science/Discovery | 408 |
| To improve sensory integration | Bonnie | Music | 467 |
| | Cereal Balls | Mathematics | 429 |
| | Colored Fingernails | Art | 457 |
| | Crayon Rubbing | Art | 448 |
| | Fast and Slow | Listening | 361 |
| | Listen Before You Move | Listening | 360 |
| | Mirror Movement | Movement | 477 |
| | Movement Songs | Music | 468 |
| | Music and Movement | Movement | 480 |
| | Musical Colors | Music | 470 |
| | Painting to Music | Art | 454 |
| | Popcorn | Science/Discovery | 402 |
| | Tempo | Movement | 477 |

## LANGUAGE SKILLS

| | | | |
|---|---|---|---|
| To improve expressive language | Best and Worst | Expressing Language | 335 |
| | Dress Up and Tell | Dramatic Play | 492 |
| | Is–Is Not | Expressing Language | 333 |
| | My Shoes | Expressing Language | 334 |
| | Puppets | Dramatic Play | 492 |
| | Telephone | Expressing Language | 338 |
| | Treasure Hunt | Expressing Language | 338 |
| | What Shall We Make? | Dramatic Play | 495 |
| To increase vocabulary | Barefoot | Outdoor Play | 530 |
| | Cat and Mouse | Expressing Language | 342 |
| | Locomotion | Expressing Language | 340 |
| | Room Shapes | Mathematics | 425 |
| | Seasonal Clothing | Health and Safety | 435 |
| | Will It Fit? | Mathematics | 427 |

## THINKING AND REASONING SKILLS

| Annual Goals | Activity | Curriculum Area | Page |
|---|---|---|---|
| To increase logical reasoning | Scavenger Hunt | Reading Readiness | 371 |
| | Title | Listening | 362 |
| | Will It Fit? | Mathematics | 427 |
| To improve classification skills | Picture Shapes | Mathematics | 424 |
| | Room Shapes | Mathematics | 425 |
| | Sorting | Small Motor Play | 500 |
| | Sounds | Listening | 362 |
| | Taste Sort | Science/Discovery | 408 |
| | Texture Classification | Science/Discovery | 406 |
| | What Doesn't Belong? | Mathematics | 424 |
| | Wiggly Worms | Science/Discovery | 406 |
| To improve sequencing skills | Buttoning Sequences | Small Motor Play | 504 |
| | Comics | Reading Readiness | 379 |
| | Day Play | Dramatic Play | 490 |
| | Scrambled Eggs | Science/Discovery | 404 |
| To improve color concepts | Color Scavenger Hunt | Outdoor Play | 531 |
| | Colored Fingernails | Art | 457 |
| | Musical Colors | Music | 470 |
| To make predictions | Balloon Badminton | Outdoor Play | 528 |
| | Food Sense | Science/Discovery | 405 |
| | Matching Rods | Mathematics | 427 |
| | Mixing Colored Water | Science/Discovery | 403 |
| | Noisy Toss | Large Motor Play | 517 |
| | Pace It Off | Mathematics | 430 |
| | Planting Seeds | Science/Discovery | 398 |
| | Problems | Social Studies | 386 |
| | Scrambled Eggs | Science/Discovery | 404 |
| | Straw Painting | Art | 450 |
| | Temperature | Science/Discovery | 400 |
| To increase problem-solving skills | Follow That Line | Reading Readiness | 370 |
| | Mixing Colored Water | Science/Discovery | 403 |
| To improve decision making | Title | Listening | 362 |

## MATHEMATIC SKILLS

| Annual Goals | Activity | Curriculum Area | Page |
|---|---|---|---|
| To improve number concepts | Abacus | Mathematics | 412 |
| | Counting Cherries | Mathematics | 413 |
| | Cuisenaire Rods | Mathematics | 414 |
| | Hidden Objects | Mathematics | 416 |
| | Matching Dots | Mathematics | 412 |
| | Maze | Large Motor Play | 516 |
| | Number Tapping | Mathematics | 414 |
| | Peg Design | Mathematics | 417 |
| | Spacy Dots | Mathematics | 415 |
| To improve measurement concepts | Cereal Balls | Mathematics | 429 |
| | Jump over the Creek | Outdoor Play | 526 |
| | Matching Rods | Mathematics | 427 |
| | Pace It Off | Mathematics | 430 |
| | Salt Putty Beads | Art | 459 |
| | Topless Popcorn | Mathematics | 428 |

| *Annual Goals* | *Activity* | *Curriculum Area* | *Page* |
|---|---|---|---|
| To improve spatial concepts | Cat and Mouse | Expressing Language | 342 |
| | Contour Maps | Science/Discovery | 401 |
| | From Your House to Mine | Social Studies | 393 |
| | Letter Collage | Art | 460 |
| | Pace It Off | Mathematics | 430 |
| | Spacy Dots | Mathematics | 415 |
| To improve shape concepts | Carpet Shapes | Mathematics | 417 |
| | Inside Out | Mathematics | 422 |
| | Little Shadows | Mathematics | 422 |
| | Musical Colors | Music | 470 |
| | People Shapes | Mathematics | 423 |
| | Picture Shapes | Mathematics | 424 |
| | Pockets | Mathematics | 417 |
| | Room Shapes | Mathematics | 425 |
| | What Doesn't Belong? | Mathematics | 424 |
| To improve size concepts | Inside Out | Mathematics | 422 |
| | Matching Rods | Mathematics | 427 |
| | Object Sizes | Mathematics | 425 |
| | People Shapes | Mathematics | 423 |
| | Will It Fit? | Mathematics | 427 |
| To improve time concepts | Day Play | Dramatic Play | 490 |
| | Timed Race | Large Motor Play | 519 |

## SOCIAL SKILLS

| | | | |
|---|---|---|---|
| To take turns | From Your House to Mine | Social Studies | 393 |
| To increase sharing skills | Solutions | Social Studies | 385 |
| To increase survival skills | Red Light/Green Light | Health and Safety | 434 |
| | Seasonal Clothing | Health and Safety | 435 |
| | Traffic Sign Hunt | Health and Safety | 439 |
| | Warning Signs | Health and Safety | 437 |
| To improve self-help skills | Buttoning Sequences | Small Motor Play | 504 |
| | Counting Cherries | Mathematics | 413 |
| To increase awareness of roles people play | Be the Teacher | Social Studies | 390 |
| | Cast It | Dramatic Play | 486 |
| | Circus | Dramatic Play | 486 |
| | Day Play | Dramatic Play | 490 |
| | Dentist | Dramatic Play | 485 |
| | Doctor's Office | Dramatic Play | 485 |
| | Eye Doctor | Dramatic Play | 490 |
| | Who Am I? | Dramatic Play | 491 |
| To cooperate with peers | Cereal Balls | Mathematics | 429 |
| | Color Concentration | Reading Readiness | 372 |
| | Color Scavenger Hunt | Outdoor Play | 531 |
| | Directions | Expressing Language | 343 |
| | Eye Doctor | Dramatic Play | 490 |
| | Follow That Line | Reading Readiness | 370 |
| | From Your House to Mine | Social Studies | 393 |

| *Annual Goals* | *Activity* | *Curriculum Area* | *Page* |
|---|---|---|---|
| | Ladder Walk | Outdoor Play | 529 |
| | Seesaw | Large Motor Play | 520 |
| | Variations on Balancing | Large Motor Play | 518 |
| | Variations on Hopping | Large Motor Play | 513 |
| | Variations on Jumping | Large Motor Play | 513 |
| To encourage creative movement | Be It | Movement | 474 |
| | Body Maneuvers | Movement | 479 |
| | Flopsy | Movement | 480 |
| | Moving Colors | Movement | 481 |
| | Music and Movement | Movement | 480 |
| To increase sense of rhythm | Mood Songs | Music | 464 |
| | Rhythmic Patterns | Music | 464 |
| To relax at will | Rag Doll | Movement | 476 |
| | Relaxation Stories | Movement | 476 |
| | Tense Me | Movement | 480 |

## CREATIVITY

| | | | |
|---|---|---|---|
| To encourage creativity | Clay | Art | 451 |
| | Foot Painting | Art | 450 |
| | Mood Montage | Art | 453 |
| | My Shoes | Expressing Language | 334 |
| | Painting a Feeling | Art | 452 |
| | Painting to Music | Art | 454 |
| | Puppets | Dramatic Play | 492 |
| | Who Am I? | Dramatic Play | 491 |
| To encourage creative problem solving | Our Town | Social Studies | 384 |
| | Problems | Social Studies | 386 |
| | Solutions | Social Studies | 385 |
| | Treasure Hunt | Expressing Language | 338 |

## FEELINGS

| | | | |
|---|---|---|---|
| To increase awareness of feelings | Matching Faces | Reading Readiness | 370 |
| To express feelings | Best and Worst | Expressing Language | 335 |
| | Feelings | Expressing Language | 342 |
| | My Books | Reading Readiness | 380 |
| | Painting a Feeling | Art | 452 |
| | Share Your Feelings | Social Studies | 392 |
| To increase feelings of group belonging | Circles | Movement | 479 |
| | Color Scavenger Hunt | Outdoor Play | 531 |
| | Dress Up and Tell | Dramatic Play | 492 |
| | Flannel Board Stories | Reading Readiness | 374 |
| | I'm Thinking Of | Social Studies | 392 |
| | Hug Tag | Outdoor Play | 531 |
| | Our Town | Social Studies | 384 |
| | Parachute Games | Outdoor Play | 525 |
| | Picture Relays | Outdoor Play | 526 |
| | Puppets | Dramatic Play | 492 |
| | Share Your Feelings | Social Studies | 392 |

| *Annual Goals* | *Activity* | *Curriculum Area* | *Page* |
| --- | --- | --- | --- |
| **AWARENESS** | | | |
| To increase body awareness | Balancing | Large Motor Play | 517 |
| | Balance It | Large Motor Play | 519 |
| | Barefoot | Outdoor Play | 530 |
| | Be It | Movement | 474 |
| | Be the Body | Movement | 473 |
| | Body Language | Expressing Language | 344 |
| | Body Maneuvers | Movement | 479 |
| | Body Mural | Art | 454 |
| | Body Noises | Expressing Language | 345 |
| | Cave Exploration | Outdoor Play | 528 |
| | Circles | Movement | 479 |
| | Circus | Dramatic Play | 486 |
| | Colored Fingernails | Art | 457 |
| | Crashing | Large Motor Play | 511 |
| | Eye-Hair Collage | Art | 455 |
| | Flopsy | Movement | 480 |
| | Foot Painting | Art | 450 |
| | Freeze | Outdoor Play | 528 |
| | Hand Plaster | Art | 455 |
| | In and Out | Movement | 478 |
| | Jump over the Creek | Outdoor Play | 526 |
| | Ladder Walk | Outdoor Play | 529 |
| | Little Shadows | Mathematics | 422 |
| | Mirror Movement | Movement | 477 |
| | Mixed-Up People | Art | 456 |
| | Movement Songs | Music | 468 |
| | Moving Balloons | Movement | 478 |
| | My Puzzle | Small Motor Play | 503 |
| | Rag Doll | Movement | 476 |
| | Relaxation Stories | Movement | 476 |
| | Robot | Listening | 360 |
| | Soap Sticks | Art | 455 |
| | Tempo | Movement | 477 |
| | Tense Me | Movement | 480 |
| | Timed Race | Large Motor Play | 519 |
| | Variations on Balancing | Large Motor Play | 518 |
| | Variations on Crawling | Large Motor Play | 512 |
| | Variations on Hopping | Large Motor Play | 513 |
| | Variations on Jumping | Large Motor Play | 513 |
| | Variations on Running | Outdoor Play | 524 |
| | Variations on Rolling | Large Motor Play | 512 |
| | Variations on Walking | Large Motor Play | 515 |
| To improve self-concept | My Puzzle | Small Motor Play | 503 |
| | Who's There? | Listening | 357 |
| To increase awareness of individual differences | Body Mural | Art | 454 |
| | Eye-Hair Collage | Art | 455 |
| | Hand Plaster | Art | 455 |
| | I'm Thinking Of | Social Studies | 392 |
| | Mixed-Up People | Art | 456 |
| To increase awareness of moods | Mood Montage | Art | 453 |
| | Moving Colors | Movement | 481 |
| | Painting to Music | Art | 454 |
| | Soap Sticks | Art | 455 |

| *Annual Goals* | *Activity* | *Curriculum Area* | *Page* |
|---|---|---|---|
| To increase knowledge of foods | Taste Sort | Science/Discovery | 408 |
| To increase awareness of learning needs | Cutting Cardboard | Awareness | 542 |
| | Fast Talk | Awareness | 542 |
| | Noisy Tasks | Awareness | 541 |
| | Pens | Awareness | 542 |

# Needs: Physical

All children want to move—for some it is easy, for others it is more difficult—but move they can and will in their own ways. While most preschool children can climb and run, children with physical impairments may be limited to walking and crawling. Because of these limitations they may have different firsthand knowledge and experiences than their peers. They may show an unevenness in physical, sensory, mental, and social-emotional growth.

Each child with a physical impairment is unique. However, there are some common problems that affect all children with physical impairments, whether the impairments are long term—such as cerebral palsy, spinal cord injuries, and amputations—or short term—such as broken limbs. Obviously, the more severe the impairment and the longer it lasts, the more impact it will have on your programming. Physical limitations may interfere with school attendance and may require special equipment and educational services.

## CLASSIFICATION OF PHYSICAL NEEDS

In general, impairments are classified according to three considerations: severity of the impairment, the clinical type of impairment, and the parts of the body that are affected.

Children with a *mild* impairment can walk (with or without crutches, walker, or other prosthetic device, use their arms and communicate well enough to make their wants and needs known. They may take more time to do things, but with adaptations, can in fact do what most other children can. Their problems involve mostly fine motor skills.

Children with a *moderate* impairment require some special help with locomotion and need more assistance than their peers with self-help and communication skills.

Children with a *severe* impairment are usually not able to move from one place to another without the aid of a wheelchair or someone carrying them. Their self-help and communication skills are very weak. You are not likely to have children with a severe impairment in your classroom. About five in one thousand school-age children have long-term physical impairments (Garwood et al., 1979).

The actual name given to an impairment is often a partial description of it. The names and subcategories are usually only meaningful for those in the field. There are, however, some common terms that will be useful for you to know. Several are discussed later in this chapter; others appear in the Glossary.

Following are some terms often used to describe the areas of the body affected.

Hemiplegia: one side of the body is involved
Diplegia: legs more involved than arms
Quadraplegia: all four limbs are involved
Paraplegia: only the legs
Monoplegia: only one limb
Triplegia: three limbs are involved

Physical impairment can have a variety of causes—some of which are unknown. Lack of oxygen in the child's brain either while the mother is pregnant or during birth can cause physical impairment. Diseases that affect the brain, such as meningitis or encephalitis, or prolonged high fevers can also cause permanent damage. Poisoning and other conditions that lead to lack of oxygen in the brain, as well as head, neck, and back injuries, sometimes cause paralysis or abnormal movement patterns. Some chronic health problems like arthritis or muscular dystrophy may ultimately result in physical impairments, but, since such impairments usually occur only after repeated acute attacks, they are less likely to be apparent at the preschool level. (Chronic health problems are therefore dealt with in another chapter.)

Before explaining in detail the implications of various impairments, it may be helpful to look at movement in general. Knowledge of how we move and the importance of muscle tone in movement aids in the understanding of some of the problems encountered by children with physical needs.

In order to move, we increase the tension in specific groups, or patterns, of muscles. For example, if you are lying on your back on the floor and want to sit up, you will probably lift your head and shoulders first. You then bend your back and afterward your hips. (Try sitting up by raising your head and shoulders but keeping your back straight.) One reason why children with physical impairments have trouble moving is that various muscle groups do not function in coordination. These children need to learn to use alternate muscle groups as well as to gain more control over affected muscles.

With your back on the floor again, tense all of your muscles (make fists, squinch up your face, tense your legs, trunk, and back) and try to sit up. You will find that your movements are jerky and stiff and that you probably cannot sit up. Now relax. Let your arms become floppy as you pretend to be a rag doll. Try to sit up without tensing any of your muscles. That doesn't work either. The first situation will give you an idea of the problems *hypertonic* children have; the second will help you understand *hypotonic* children.

Some physically impaired children (primarily those with cerebral palsy) have abnormal muscle patterns because of brain damage. The result is inefficient, uncoordinated movements. These children must learn compensatory patterns in much the same way that you discovered that when someone held your feet down you could still sit up by using other muscle groups.

Muscle tone is the amount of tension, or resistance to stretch, in muscles. "Normal" muscle tone is the condition of the muscles at rest. Children with high muscle tone (hypertonic) move with stiff, jerky movements. In some cases, depending on the exact area of the brain involved, a child's motor problems are compounded by faulty internal communications. The child may think, "Let go of the cup," but the

brain does not send the appropriate message to the muscles in the hand for the child to let go.

Children with low muscle tone (hypotonic) may have problems picking up the cup in the first place. One who did pick it up successfully may unexpectedly drop it later because it was held too loosely. Grasping very small objects is especially difficult for hypotonic children.

If children have high, low, or inconsistent muscle tone, you can expect that they have difficulty picking up and holding small, hard objects, screwing on paint-jar lids, turning the water off and on, and doing a different thing with each hand (for example, holding a music box in the left hand while winding it with the right). These latter skills require *rotation*, the ability to twist a part of the body. Rotation is of primary importance in learning to write because writing requires rotating the wrist and fingers. For a better understanding of the problem, attempt to take the lid off a container while keeping your fingers and wrists stiff. (Try handling all classroom materials and doing all classroom procedures with stiff muscles to check how difficult each task is for physically impaired children.) In general, hard objects are more difficult to handle than soft, small more difficult than large, and slippery more difficult than rough. Your awareness of the child's strengths and needs and your creativity and willingness to try things that are different are the key to good programming for children with physical impairments.

## Common Impairments

Regardless of the exact diagnosis, general information on the child's muscle tone and ability to move is important to both your programming and your expectations. Here is some information on physical impairments children may have.

*Amputation.*  The child is missing one or more limbs. These may not have been present at birth or may have been surgically removed because of injury. Children are now usually fitted with an artificial limb, or prosthesis, almost immediately. In general, the younger a child gets an artificial limb, the easier and more natural adjustment is. However, fit is very important, in terms of both comfort and the ability to use the device. A prosthesis must be adapted as the child grows.

You need to have some basic understanding of how the prosthesis works in case the child needs help making adjustments, and so that you can plan activities that do not totally frustrate the child who must use one. Being accepted as a whole person is extremely important, so don't refer to this device as the child's *bad* arm or leg. If you notice abnormal postures or motor patterns developing, discuss them with the parent and physical therapist so that they can decide what to do. Exercising the joints nearest

With a prosthesis this boy can climb a ladder as well as his classmates can.

the amputation is important; ask for information about that as well.

*Brittle Bone Disease (Osteogenesis Imperfecta).* Brittle bone disease is a condition in which the bones are very susceptible to breaking. It may result in skeletal deformities or frequently broken bones that need to be rethreaded into a rod to mend. This condition usually improves after puberty.

Encourage the child to participate in as much activity as the parents and medical staff feel is safe. Emphasize fine motor skills, especially eye-hand coordination, and social skills.

*Correctable Orthopedic Impairments.* There are a variety of relatively short-term orthopedic problems that are dealt with during the preschool years to facilitate normal future growth. These conditions usually require surgery, bracing, casting, and physical therapy. The prognosis is generally good if the condition is treated at an early age. If not treated, orthopedic problems result in some degree of physical disability.

Bowlegs and inwardly rotated feet are common when a child first begins to walk. They are usually cured by normal growth. In extreme cases, however, braces and casts and/or surgery are used to correct the problem.

Clubfeet are usually treated with casts and splints and physical therapy, or surgery. Flat feet may be treated with arch supports.

Congenital hip problems are usually characterized by improper fit of the femur in the socket joint of the hip. They are most often treated by a webbed brace, traction, cast, or surgery. Usually, hip problems are treated in infancy. In severe cases, they can have long-term implications.

The prognosis for these correctable orthopedic impairments is good, yet from the child's perspective the restriction of movement is frustrating and "mean." Some children need a lot of help expressing this anger. Prepare children for medical procedures where possible; discuss their fears and feelings; help them express emotions while they are physically restricted; give them activities they can participate in; and try to explain the purpose of the medical treatment in terms they understand.

*Cerebral Palsy.* This is a nonprogressive disorder in which people cannot control some of their movements. It is caused by damage to the brain either before or during birth, or in early childhood. The disease is typically classified by the clinical manifestations as well as the location.

Depending on the severity of the disorder, these children may need wheelchairs or other help in moving around the classroom. Consult with the parents and physical therapist to learn what activities the children can participate in, what kinds of bowls and cups are easiest for them to use, and what special toileting procedures, if any, are required.

Because children spend a lot of time sitting, it is important that they sit in the most beneficial position. This is often not the easiest one. If you hold a child with cerebral palsy in your lap, have his legs straddle one of yours and hold him around the middle. If the child sits on the floor, cross-legged, or tailor-style, sitting is not recommended. Have the child sit with his legs in front and together, bent at the knee if the child is athetoid, straight if spastic. The child with cerebral palsy already has abnormal patterns of movement that should not be exaggerated or reinforced. (See Finnie, 1975, for details and illustrations.) These children need a lot of practice to develop fine motor skills. You need to plan more time for them in this area than for other children.

*Spina Bifida.* Spina bifida is the common term for a condition in which the spinal cord is not closed or protrudes at birth or both. The degree of severity varies. In *myelomeningocele*, the most severe form, a cystlike formation containing part of the spinal cord occurs on the spinal column. *Meningocele* is the term

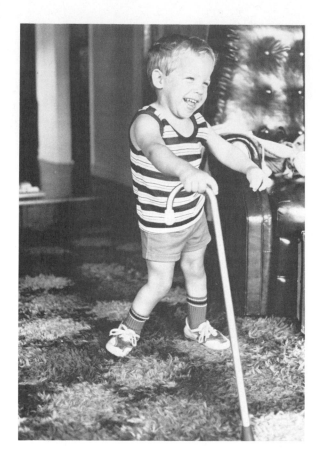

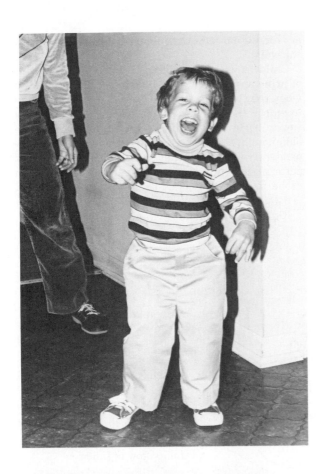

Five-year-old Jeff has made great strides since he was diagnosed four years ago as having cerebral palsy. This progress is due in large part to the help of therapists and the devoted care and determination of his parents.

Jeff started seeing a physical therapist when he was nine months old and a speech and language therapist when he was two years old. More than continuing these therapies with specific exercises at home, his parents encouraged the routine use of both hands in order to strengthen the left side of his body. They also gave him large toys and balls to play with and arranged for swimming lessons.

Although Jeff's parents wanted him to walk, he was reluctant to try. Despite great excitement when he took a first step at three and a half years of age, he didn't want to take any more steps. After his parents provided a cane (and a padded cap for outdoors), Jeff felt secure enough to take short walks. He was progressing nicely until he fell and refused to walk any more.

Loving encouragement failed to persuade Jeff, so after several weeks and a conversation with the physical therapist, Jeff's mother designed a harness for him. The harness gave Jeff the security he needed to try again and helped him to maintain balance rather than favoring his right side. Shortly thereafter Jeff began to wear a brace that was designed especially for him. The brace fits around his hips, under his clothes, and keeps his left leg from crossing over his right leg as he walks. Jeff also wears light plastic braces in his shoes to keep his heels on the ground.

Jeff's speech is appropriate for his age level. For the past two years he has attended a typical kindergarten program. Twice a week he attends speech and physical therapy sessions and does exercises at home with his parents.

used when only the covering tissue (meninges) protrudes in the sac. In *spina bifida occulata* there is no protrusion and often the problem is only discovered by x-rays.

The sac is usually surgically repaired so that the child's brain will not become infected. *Hydrocephalus*, an abnormal amount of fluid in the head, often occurs. If it does, the head is usually surgically shunted (drained) to relieve pressure on the brain cells.

Manifestations vary, with some children having only bowel and bladder dysfunction, some having weakness and sensory loss below the knee, and others having no feeling or motor control at all below the waist.

Children with spina bifida are usually incontinent of urine and, since they have no feeling, cannot tell when they are wet. Catheterization is the usual way to empty the bladder, which means the child may wear a bag and collecting device. When children are old enough, they learn to insert the catherter independently—but until that time, trained adults must perform the procedure. These children are also prone to fractures, since their bones are thin and brittle.

Rigorous treatment is extending life expectancy.

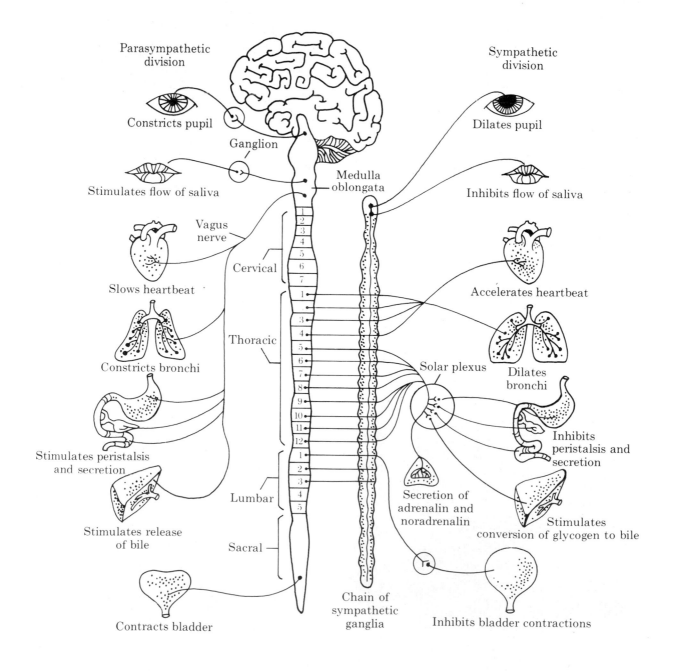

Some of these children will learn to walk with braces and crutches or to use a wheelchair for locomotion.

During the early preschool years, incontinence is not a significant problem because the child can usually just wear diapers. The parents and surgeons later make some decision about how to manage this problem. Because of concern over urinary infection, it is often recommended that these children drink four ounces of liquid every hour. Spina bifida children may have weight problems due to lack of movement, which must be kept in mind, along with the need for liquids, when choosing snacks. If you notice any changes in personality or if the child complains of headaches or double vision, notify the parents. These may be signs of increased pressure on the brain.

*Spinal Cord Injuries.* Although young children do get spinal cord injuries, these injuries are most common in adolescent boys, and accidents are the most common cause. If the spinal cord is not completely cut, some feeling may remain below the lesion, but in general, anyone who has a spinal cord injury is permanently paralyzed and unable to feel pressure or pain. These children literally cannot tell whether or not their feet are on the ground. The ultimate effect of an injury usually cannot be ascertained with certainty for about two months.

The spinal cord is divided into three major areas (see page 166). Starting from the bottom, there are five lumbar vertebrae, twelve thoracic vertebrae, and seven cervical vertebrae—which are sometimes referred to as *L*, *T*, and *C*. The closer to the head, the more severe the injury. Each inch of spine or vertebra is important in bodily function (Travis, 1976).

If a child has movement in the arms and shoulders, work should be done to strengthen these, since future mobility may depend on them—ultimately the child has to learn to lift his own weight. Another important consideration is the prevention of pressure sores ("bed sores"). These seem innocuous, but pressure sore infections can cause death. Sometimes it takes weeks or months for them to heal, and they may have to be closed surgically. Because the child lacks feeling, be concerned about sunstroke, overheating, and frostbite. Insect bites may also occur and not be noticed.

## CHILDREN'S NEEDS— TEACHING GOALS

Related annual goals may be grouped under broad categories called "teaching goals." Outlined under each teaching goal below are the most important needs of physically impaired children. A child may have some or all of these needs, and additional needs as well. Suggestions on what you might consequently teach them are included. Often, a course of action is implicit in the description of the need.

### Language Skills

Children develop language by actively interacting with their environment. To the extent that this firsthand experience has been limited, they may need more real experiences to spur language development. Field trips followed by stories, both those written by the children about the experience and those written by others to expand the experience, may be necessary to develop a functional understanding of language. Bringing a pet to class and using realistic props for dramatic play will also help.

### Thinking and Reasoning Skills

Because these children are less mobile than others and may require more energy to carry out tasks, it is important that they learn to think about tasks before attempting them rather than use a trial-and-error approach. They must learn to predict how long it will take to cross the path to the swings if someone is approaching on a tricycle. They must develop cause and effect reasoning skills—for example, the sun may make their skin red even if they can't feel it. They can learn to prevent or slow down this process by using suntan lotion or by regulating the amount of time they stay in the sun. Help them develop problem-solving skills to compensate for things they may not be able to do. For example, have them think of how many different ways they can get across the room, paint a picture, or play with blocks. Encourage unconventional solutions.

### Motor Skills

Most self-help skills as well as prewriting skills require small motor skills. These are essential for growing independence. Large motor skills and building up of strength are necessary to learn to move from one place to another with crutches or a wheelchair. The children need more time to accomplish large and small motor tasks and they need practice, so be sure to schedule flexibly. Talk with the parents and physical therapist for help planning activities that will aid the child's development while staying within his capabilities.

### Awareness

These children need awareness of their bodies not only to achieve a good self-concept but also to maintain health and safety. Children need to be able to assess what they can and can't do physically. They must also be taught to notice sores on areas of the body that lack feeling. A full-length mirror in the classroom helps, and so do songs and fingerplays that use body parts.

## Feelings

Children with physical impairments cannot do all the things other children can—or all the things they want to do—and this may result in frustration. Children need to become aware of these feelings and, since they have difficulties actively working them off, must learn ways of venting them. Help children learn the vocabulary to express their feelings. Talk about individual differences, stressing that differences are not good or bad.

All children need to feel that they are part of the group. This is especially true when physical distance from other children is sometimes required because of special equipment. Be sure to plan activities where children can move creatively as part of a group. Choose movements that the children are able to do, such as sitting on the floor, swaying to music.

## Guidelines

School can provide a broader range of experiences for children with physical needs than they have had. Therefore, it is important to include these children in firsthand experiences when possible and to provide a wide variety of materials and equipment. Foster independence in any way you can.

1. These children learn early what others can do that they can't. To motivate children, give them tasks they *can* accomplish.
2. Be sure that they get to touch things as well as see them. Where necessary, bring things to them so that they too can explore.
3. If the child doesn't seem interested, demonstrate how things can be used. Some children really don't know what to do and are simply too shy to ask for help.
4. These children often have a self-concept that is in dire need of strengthening. Our society is a mobile one that values beauty and strength. Because body image greatly influences self-concept, these children need special help integrating body image into a healthy self-concept.
5. Work on developing language skills, especially those necessary to express feelings and to meet personal needs. Provide activities that help children release energy and work out feelings.
6. Be sure to help them establish a sexual identity. For some reason people with physical impairments are often treated as if they were asexual. An appropriate sex role identification is important to their developments.
7. Keep in contact with the child through get-well cards, audio tapes, and visits if the child is out of school for an extended period of time.

For children with physical impairments the classroom itself may need to be modified.

1. Provide ample space for activites, since crutches and wheelchairs often need extra room.
2. Use lighter equipment—this child may not be as strong as others of the same age.
3. Borrow a wheelchair or use a regular chair to determine how accessible classroom equipment is for the physically impaired. Check doors and passageways to be sure wheelchairs can get through.
4. Where possible, move sand and activity tables away from walls so that each child can get to them from all sides. Put materials on the floor; lower sand and water tables to floor level if necessary.
5. Be sure there are many different chairs a child can sit in. If necessary, modify a chair. Usually an abduction block—a chunk of something padded that the child's legs can straddle—will prevent the child from sliding onto the floor. You may have to add a footstool so that the child's feet can be flat, but this should be done only at the recommendation of the child's therapist.
6. Temporary ramps may need to be added to help the child enter and leave the classroom.
7. Use nonslip floor coverings (no highly waxed floors or shag rugs). If you have carpets, be sure they are attached by a metal strip, so they won't slide and so children don't trip over the edges. Also make sure that toys are kept off the floor when not in use to prevent children from tripping over them.
8. Toilet cubicles may present a problem. They should be wide enough to accommodate the child in a wheelchair, with handrails to make the transfer an easy one. Although lifting a young child is not difficult, it does hinder early development of self-help skills.
9. Tables with semicircular "bites" out of them allow the children to get closer to the table, and a rim around the edge prevents small objects from being knocked off easily.

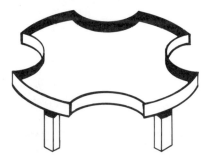

10. Lengthen the handles on paintbrushes, rackets, and paddles to make them easier for the physically impaired child to use.

11. For snacks, use deep-sided bowls instead of plates and two-handled mugs instead of cups. Serve a lot of finger foods.

12. Have bolsters, wedges, and beanbag chairs to provide a change for the children, as well as scooters to encourage movement.

13. Attach small bicycle baskets to walkers and provide around-the-neck carriers for children on crutches. (Knapsacks also work, but something in the front is handier.) Most wheelchairs can have their own trays.

14. Use larger versions of manipulative toys. Especially helpful are toys that have a built-in tolerance for error—blocks that fit together even if the child doesn't match them perfectly.

15. Remove equipment that is easily overturned.

16. Wagons are great for outside and field trips.

17. Be careful of rectangular tables, sharp edges, scissors, and spilled liquids.

## CURRICULUM ADAPTATIONS

The actual physical limitations a child has will determine the number and degree of adaptations necessary. In general, encourage the child to do as much as possible independently—but not to the point of frustration.

### Expressing Language, Listening, and Reading Readiness

Language is a necessary and useful skill for all children. For the physically handicapped, the ability to express oneself is essential in order to compensate for the lack of motor skills. (If you are able to go get something you want, you don't need language as much as if you depend on asking others to fetch what you need.)

Some children with physical impairments have special speech and language problems that will be dealt with by a speech and language therapist. Consult these specialists for more information.

A friend to carry artwork helps when hands are needed for crutches.

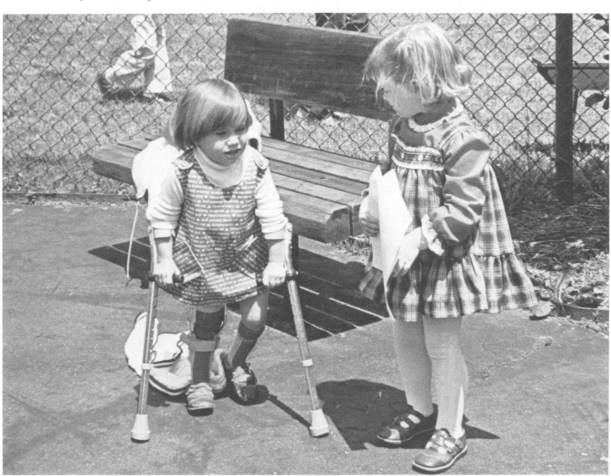

1. Use puppets to encourage expressive language. Have puppets that talk and move in many different ways. Finger puppets, as well as hand puppets, can encourage body awareness and the use of weak body parts. If the child favors one hand, encourage using a puppet on each hand and having them "talk" to each other. Sock puppets, or puppets on sticks that just need to be moved up and down, may be easier for children with hand impairments to operate.
2. Expand children's utterances, especially when they use "telegraphic speech." If a child says "get doll," you might respond, "Which doll do you want me to get you? Oh, you want the one with the red dress." When children ask for objects by pointing, help them learn vocabulary by filling in the words they need. "That's the doll." However, if children are able to respond with only "yes" or "no," phrase your questions accordingly: "Do you want the blue one?" not "Which one do you want?"

Be sure that books are stored in a place that is accessible to the physically impaired child. Select stories that have a variety of characters, some of whom wear glasses and perhaps have handicaps.

1. Either have all children sit in chairs for group time or, if the class sits on the floor, take the child out of the wheelchair so that he is part of the group. If a child needs to sit a special way, be sure he does so at this time. Provide proper support for the child, if necessary.
2. Read stories and show pictures of children who are physically impaired, choose stories that emphasize the senses the child can use. Present a balance of disabilities in your selections.
3. Use flannel board stories to help focus attention and to increase participation.
4. Add background music to stories to enhance the mood for children who haven't experienced the events described (circus music, waves breaking, and so on).
5. For children who have difficulty turning pages, get a specialized page turner. Also provide a listening center with headphones.

Fingerplays are especially recommended because they encourage children to use both hands in a controlled fashion.

1. When you introduce a new fingerplay, encourage children to do only the actions at first, if they need a lot of concentration to follow those.
2. Keep the actions simple and slow enough for everyone to keep up.
3. Do variations, when you can, so that the children don't forget—and aren't always starting something new.
4. Many children with physical impairments have fine motor delays. Use fingerplays that allow the child to use the whole hand rather than just the fingers.
5. Remember that this child may need the help of an aide or friend in order to make certain movements.
6. Fingerplays that require different motions with each hand are sometimes too difficult.

Reading readiness skills are those necessary for children to learn to read and write. Listening and visual activities can easily be adapted to children with physical needs. Writing skills are far more difficult if the children have coordination problems.

1. Since these children may lack experiences other children have had, be sure that they can visually and verbally identify objects before you work on discrimination and other higher level skills.
2. When teaching fine motor skills, have them use materials that create some resistance, such as a pencil used to draw on clay, so that the children can feel the resistance as well as see the results.
3. To teach prewriting skills, use activities that require finger and wrist movement, especially rotation. (Use, for example, activities requiring children to lock boxes, screw bolts onto nuts, or twist jar lids.)
4. Clothespins that must be squeezed to open can be put around the edge of a can or used to hang up doll clothes. Their use develops necessary finger strength.
5. Puzzle pieces that have knobs are easier to insert and remove. Start with shapes that go in easily, for example, a circle before an octagon.

### Social Studies
Community awareness is important for the physically impaired child. Start by familiarizing the child with the immediate environment.

1. If you are doing a unit on transportation, include wheelchairs, crutches, walkers, and so on in your discussion.
2. Help children personalize their equipment. Wheelchairs can be decorated with license nameplates, bicycle bells, or horns and streamers. Walkers may be painted (with parents' permission) or wrapped with ribbon. Casts can be decorated with marking pens or paints.
3. Have appropriate community visitors (i.e., those who play a role in this child's life: osteopath, physical therapist, social worker, surgeon, neurologist).

### Science/Discovery

Science has great potential for the physically impaired child because it teaches cause and effect reasoning that is necessary for safety and encourages children to devise adaptations for their needs.

1. Magnets are fun and potentially useful. Attach a string to a stick, tie a magnet on the end of the string, and go fishing. Catch paper fish that have paper clip mouths. This activity is good for eye-hand coordination. Show children how they can pick up metal objects with a magnet attached to a stick. A child who is confined to a wheelchair can then pick up some things without calling for help.
2. Work on simple causal relationships. (The faster I move my hands on the wheel, the faster the wheelchair moves. If I only move the right wheel forward, I turn left!)
3. Help children learn to use simple machines such as wheels and pulleys with ropes as a way of moving objects that they otherwise might not be able to move.
4. Use objects that vary in weight for sorting activities. Take a ping-pong ball, tennis ball, hard ball, empty cup, cupful of peanuts, and cupful of sand and see if the children can arrange them in order. Discuss the relationship between an object's weight, the distance someone throws it, and the thrower's strength.
5. Use objects that vary in shape, size, and texture. Help children decide the easiest and most difficult to move.

### Mathematics

Physically impaired children have been exposed to many concepts that are classified under the heading of math. They know something about time concepts: It may take them longer to do some things than it takes to do others. They know something about distance and how far they can go before they get tired. Math in school helps them quantify these experiences and build on them.

1. Physically impaired children need to know something about distance and the relationship between speed and distance. "I can go 20 feet (here to the door) as fast as I can and I'm tired. I can go 80 feet (the length of the room) slowly. It takes longer, but I can do it."
2. Measuring and weighing children helps them understand why braces no longer fit and need to be replaced.
3. Discuss shapes that roll and those that don't. Relate them to concepts like *brakes* and *moving*—round shapes are used for wheels; a triangular block of wood can be used to stop a wheel from moving.

### Health and Safety

Health and safety are especially important for the physically impaired and can make a difference not only to them but to other children and to you the teacher.

1. Teach the physically impaired child to put crutches or other aids in a place where others won't trip over them.
2. Help children learn to take care of bruises and scrapes and to spot pressure sores.
3. This child may need assistance during a fire drill. Be sure the child is familiar with the procedures and the routes to be taken. Have your own drills in preparation for the official ones.

### Art

Children with poor muscular control of arms and hands often find art difficult and discouraging. Others with better control may find it a release.

1. Choose activities that require two hands, like fingerpainting and modeling playdough. Encourage children to use both hands as a way of building strength.
2. Tape drawing paper to the table so that children can concentrate on what they are putting on the paper, not the paper itself.
3. Use marking pens. They require little pressure, are easy to grip, and are colorful. Build up thin ones with masking tape or place sponge hair curlers around them so that they are easier to use.
4. Adapt other drawing materials where necessary. For easier gripping, use large pieces of chalk, push pens or pencils through rubber balls, and insert crayons wrapped in paper into roll-on deodorant bottles (with the ball removed).
5. Make paint jars easier to handle: Put a thick rubber band (or a thin sheet of foam or sponge) around them, and glue sandpaper on the lids.
6. Use extra large easels and paper.
7. Paint large objects, like boxes.
8. Outside, have the child "paint" the sidewalk with a bucket of water and a broom (if the child is in a wheelchair) or large brush.
9. Make clay, varying the moisture to meet the strength and motor skills of the child (the moister the clay, the easier to manipulate). Encourage the use of a rolling pin or blunt knife as well as hands to mold clay. If you want, allow the clay to dry out, and fire it. It is then ready for painting. Be sure to allow adequate time for exploration since the physically impaired child may be slower. This activity will help build strength and coordination.
10. Get special scissors called easy-grip loop scis-

sors (they have a squeezeable loop instead of finger holes) or scissors with four holes so that you can help the child cut.

11. Have children stick objects in and take them out of clay and playdough—cookie cutters and rolling pins work well for this.

### Music

Use music to increase body awareness and encourage movement. Music can also be used to teach concepts.

1. Sing the song "Put Your Finger in the Air" and substitute words for *finger* and *air*. Be sure to take into account the abilities of the physically handicapped child as you adapt this song. Some variations might be: nose on your shoulder, tongue on your lip, and wrist on your cheek. Other songs also teach body awareness.
2. Have children play rhythm instruments in an informal way to create a mood. This is a nondemanding way for children to be part of a group.
3. Movement activities can be used if you allow for individual differences and creativity. Make your suggestions in relation to the child's abilities.
4. Activities that require two hands to be coordinated—such as clapping—are good practice, but may be difficult, so go slowly.
5. If a child has difficulty holding on to specific instruments, adapt them. On finger cymbals, have elastic attachments that go around the hand rather than knobs. If a child cannot hold a stick to tap a xylophone, have the child wear a mitten with Velcro in the palm and glue Velcro to the stick. Weight down objects like drums or xylophones with beanbags to help them stay in one place.

### Dramatic Play

Children can use this type of activity to play different roles as well as to express fears and concerns. Children with physical impairments need to learn to use dramatic play to acknowledge and act out their feelings. They cannot "run it off," and feelings that are denied eventually take a toll.

1. Help other children become more aware of the problems of being in a wheelchair or on crutches by having these available for the children to play with if possible.
2. Play hospital with casting tape (available in most

Providing dolls with braces and casts can make a child less fearful of an operation and help other children understand what it might be like to use braces.

drugstores). Have children cast dolls' legs or their fingers (use blunt-nosed scissors to cut the casts off).
3. Use a full-length mirror to encourage children to explore their individual characteristics. Be sure to show children how you use the mirror to see parts of you that are difficult to see otherwise. (Put a dot or a cutout on each child's back and have him try to see it in the mirror.)

### Small Motor Play

For some children, traditional large motor activities are not possible. These children need to concentrate on fine motor skills as well as eye-hand coordination.

The ability to grasp, manipulate, and release objects is basic to using materials in the classroom and lifelong independence skills.

1. Buy or make a tetherball. Using a small table as a base, secure a thirty-inch pole in the center and attach a string. Attach a rubber ball to the string. The children try to wind the ball around the pole by hitting it with their hands or a paddle. This

game can be played in a wheelchair with ease. It develops the child's eye-hand coordination.

2. Make "Freddie the Frog" or "Katie Kangaroo" or some such animal from a large, limp beanbag. Putting this beanbag on the child's head and seeing how long it will stay there before it jumps off is a fun way to strengthen neck muscles and to help children hold their heads erect.

3. Blocks that snap together and those that are held together with bristles can be built into structures that are not easily knocked apart unintentionally by children with poor control of their hands.

4. Pegboard play improves the child's ability to grasp and aim, and to control involuntary motion. The size, number, and spacing of the pegs should vary according to the child's needs. Larger pegs are easier to grasp. Holes distantly spaced suit some children because children are less likely to knock over one peg when inserting another. Rubber pegboards are good for strengthening fingers because they offer some resistance.

5. Playing with popbeads helps develop coordination.

6. If a child has trouble holding a lacing card for stringing, you might use a stand-up pegboard or a piece of cardboard that is perpendicular to the table (and therefore does not require wrist rotation). (Pasting pictures on cardboard helps to make them sturdier.) Reinforce the end of the string with tape or glue so that it is stiff, or use colored shoelaces.

7. Activities that require performing two separate motions or a different action with each hand are difficult. For example, a child's problems in holding a juice cup with one hand while pouring juice with other hand can be gotten around if you hold the cup while the child pours with two hands. Or have him hold the cup while you pour.

## Large Motor Play

Physically impaired children must be given a chance to discover their own physical limitations and abilities. Allow children to use all equipment and participate in all activities normally provided in preschool, unless you have been told otherwise. It's best to check with a child's therapist to see if an activity is permissable. Specialists are one of your prime resources, too, for ideas on adapting equipment and activities.

1. Supervise carefully. Children with poor muscular control are in more danger of falling. Someone must be on hand to catch them.

2. If muscular control is unsteady, secure feet to tricycle pedals with giant rubber bands from an inner tube or with toe straps.

3. When you use toss games (beanbags, balls, ring throws), attach the objects to the child's chair with a string so that the child can retrieve them.

4. If the game cannot be otherwise adapted, allow the child to be scorekeeper with an abacuslike counter, attached to the chair if necessary. Instances in which a physical need can't be accommodated should be rare.

5. A child with poor balance and motor coordination may increase his mobility if you have him push something as he moves forward, such as a toy carriage weighted with sand bags.

6. Mounting toys on walls at a child's height facilitates hand coordination, balance, and grasping. If a child needs practice standing, mounted objects provide the incentive and the opportunity.

7. The child in a wheelchair can participate with little or no difficulty in any game that requires sitting down. Tossing and catching are skills in which this child needs practice. Use soft balls of yarn or foam for safety. Balloons or underinflated beach balls are good too. Scoopers for catching the balls in can be easily made from bleach bottles. You can use tossing games to teach concepts such as *over*, *under*, *low*, and *high*.

## Transitions

Transitions are often confusing. Be sure these children know where they are going and for what purpose.

1. Use transitions to teach simple concepts, such as color or clothing texture.

2. Because these children need more time to move around, dismiss them no later than the middle of the transitional activity.

3. Always tell the children what you are planning to do *before* you begin doing it. If you simply lift them onto the rug, for example, they may become frightened at suddenly being taken out of a secure position. Even if they have limited speech, talk to them, and make them aware of any change about to take place.

## CHILD STUDY TEAM REPORT

### *Kent L.*

In attendance: Mr. and Mrs. L.; Mrs. R., preschool teacher; Mrs. O., physical therapist; Mrs. K., kindergarten teacher.

Kent L. is a five-year one-month-old boy with mild to moderate cerebral palsy. Kent has been attending preschool three mornings a week for the past year. He has been participating in physical therapy for the past three years. Kent's parents requested a meeting in order to familiarize the kindergarten staff with Kent's needs before he enters public school. No recent test scores are available for Kent because his progress in preschool has been average and therefore has not warranted additional testing. However, therapy reports are available.

Kent lives at home with his mother, father, and infant sister. He was diagnosed as ataxic cerebral palsied at eighteen months of age, shortly after learning to walk. Kent's cerebral palsy affects his gait, gross and fine motor movements, balance, and to a much smaller degree his speech.

The preschool staff working with Kent last year found him to be a very verbal child. They identified his vocabulary, ability to express himself, and ability to learn verbal concepts as very strong. At the same time, they noted Kent will use his verbal skills to avoid fine and gross motor tasks. He will attempt to involve those around him in conversation rather than complete the requested task The preschool teacher also noted that some math skills, including number and spatial concepts, have been difficult for Kent. She feels Kent is much more inclined to socialize with adults than with children his own age. She mentioned that Kent's speech is slow and deliberate, although articulation is not affected.

Kent's parents added that Kent's difficulty with movement probably helped him develop some language skills, while inhibiting others. They feel Kent is very frustrated by his inability to move as quickly as his peers and to participate in activities. Mrs. L. reported that Kent will sometimes talk about this frustration. He especially dislikes days he has to get the milk for snacktime, since the other children have to wait for him. Mrs. L. feels his dislikes and fears are justified because the other children are in-

clined to complain or to offer help "to hurry things along." Kent is sensitive, and his parents are not really sure what is the best way to approach this.

The physical therapist will continue to see Kent once a week for individual therapy in order to improve his movement quality and efficiency. She commented that the problems with speed, balance, and awkwardness will continue. Therapy is not designed to cure cerebral palsy, and the type of improvements Kent may make in a year of therapy will not drastically change the quality or speed of his movements. She added that Kent will probably fall down frequently, especially during outside play. Any teacher working with Kent should allow him extra time to complete tasks that are more difficult for him. In addition, he may tire more quickly than other children when asked to walk long distances on field trips or participate in any similarly extended activity.

Mr. and Mrs. L. are interested in arranging physical therapy for Kent through the school. Mr. L. is often out of town on business for periods of time ranging from two weeks to one month, and Mrs. L. works part time two days a week. With the addition of their infant daughter, it has been difficult for them to provide transportation to and from therapy. They added that they realize the importance of therapy and will continue to take responsibility for this if the school does not.

Mrs. K., who will be Kent's kindergarten teacher, said she is concerned about how to make Kent feel as comfortable as he can with other children. She also wants to learn which activities would be helpful for Kent. The physical therapist offered to provide consulting time to the teacher and added that Mr. and Mrs. L. are the real experts on Kent and should be used as a valuable resource.

## INDIVIDUALIZED EDUCATION PROGRAM

NAME ___Kent L.___ DOB _7_ / _16_ / _77_

AGE ___5-1___ GRADE ___K___

SCHOOL ___Monroe Place Elementary___

PARENTS/GUARDIANS ___Mr. & Mrs. L.___

ADDRESS ___2013 Jefferson Avenue___

PHONE ___987-7665___

On _8/15/82_ , the IPRD Committee
(Date)
met to review all current data and
recommends Level ___I___ placement.

Date of new review ___1/15/83___

Exceptionality: ___Physically impaired/cerebral palsy___

### CURRENT TEST DATA

| TEST/DATE/RESULTS | |
|---|---|
| Physical therapist report | Poor fine and gross motor skills; slow; tires easily |
| Preschool teacher report | Strong verbal skills; speech slow though articulation good; weak number and spacial concepts. |

Recommended Special Services (Hrs/Wk):

| | | |
|---|---|---|
| Physical Therapy | / | 45-60 min./wk. |
| | / | |
| | / | |

Total Hours/Week:

Special Education Classroom ___0___

Regular Classroom ___12½___

Present at meeting:

Parents ___Mr. & Mrs. L.___

Others: Name/Position ___Mrs. O., Physical Therapist___

Representative of District/Agency ___Mrs. K., Kindergarten Teacher___

___Mrs. R., Preschool Teacher___

The committee has determined the following learning strengths and needs to be reflected in the IEP:

| STRENGTHS | NEEDS |
|---|---|
| Vocabulary | Fine motor skills |
| Expressive language | Gross motor skills |
| Verbal concepts | Social skills with peers |
| Social skills with adults | (self-concept) |
| | Frustrated by difficulty with movement |
| | Math skills |

STUDENT _____ Kent L. _____    DATE _____ 8/15/82

GOAL _____ To improve number and spatial concepts _____

PARENT SIGNATURE _____

TEACHER SIGNATURE _____

| INSTRUCTIONAL OBJECTIVES | EDUCATIONAL METHODS | Begin | End | Eval. | Name | Position |
|---|---|---|---|---|---|---|
| | | DATE | DATE | | PERSONS RESPONSIBLE | PERSONS RESPONSIBLE |
| Kent will be able to identify the number of objects in sets, and pictures of sets, of 1 to 10 objects with 90% accuracy. | Tactile Gameboard, Spacy Dots | 9/5 | 1/15 | | Mrs. K. | Teacher |
| Kent will be able to group objects in sets of 1 to 10 objects with 90% accuracy. | Peg Design, Matching Dots, Counting Songs | 9/5 | 1/5 | | Mrs. K. | Teacher |
| Kent will be able to expressively identify the numerals 1–10 when shown numeral flashcards in random order with 90% accuracy. | Abacus, Color Graphs, Cuisenaire Rods | 9/5 | 1/5 | | Mrs. K. | Teacher |
| Given a choice of 3 pictures, Kent will be able to correctly identify one(s) representing 7/8 of the following concepts: longer, shorter, larger, smaller, more, less, empty, full, on 3 occasions. | Color Graphs, Cereal Balls, Matching Rods, Will It Fit?, Ordering objects | 9/5 | 1/5 | | Mrs. K. | Teacher |
| Kent will be able to receptively and expressively identify 6/7 of the following concepts: on top of, under, beside, over, next to, close to, far away, on 3 occasions. | Cat and Mouse, Contour Maps, Noisy Toss | 9/15 | 1/5 | | Mrs. K. | Teacher |

STUDENT ____Kent L.____   DATE ____8/15/82____

GOAL ____To improve self-concept____

PARENT SIGNATURE _____   TEACHER SIGNATURE _____

| INSTRUCTIONAL OBJECTIVES | EDUCATIONAL METHODS | DATE Begin | DATE End | Eval. | PERSONS RESPONSIBLE Name | Position |
|---|---|---|---|---|---|---|
| Kent will be able to name 3 ways he resembles 3 of his peers, on 2 occasions. | Body Mural, Eye—Hair Collage, Roles, Who Am I? | 9/5 | 1/15 | | Mrs. K. | Teacher |
| Given any art medium, Kent will be able to create 3 projects that represent 3 activities he is very good at doing and enjoys. | Easy/Hard, My Day, My Song, Interviews, Tape It | 9/5 | 1/15 | | Mrs. K. | Teacher |
| Given a tape recorder and tape, Kent will be able to name 2 peers who like him, and tell why, on 3 occasions. | Who Is It?, Who Are You?, Telephone | 9/5 | 1/15 | | Mrs. K. | Teacher |

STUDENT ___ Kent L. ___ DATE ___ 8/15/82 ___

GOAL ___ To improve small motor coordination ___

PARENT SIGNATURE ___ TEACHER SIGNATURE ___

| INSTRUCTIONAL OBJECTIVES | EDUCATIONAL METHODS | DATE Begin | DATE End | Eval. | PERSONS RESPONSIBLE Name | PERSONS RESPONSIBLE Position |
|---|---|---|---|---|---|---|
| Kent will participate in 5 indoor supervised fine motor activities per week for 4 weeks<br>a. with teacher direction<br>b. as an independent choice | String Mobile, String Painting, Pockets, Clay, Torn Paper Flowers, My Puzzle, Lock Box, Pouring Peanuts, Feely Bag, Buttons | 9/5<br>1/15 | 1/15<br>6/30 | | Mrs. K. | Teacher |
| Kent's completion of fine motor activities will increase by 25% (data to be taken week of 10/1/82). | same as above | 11/5 | 1/15 | | Mrs. K. | Teacher |

STUDENT _____ Kent L.

GOAL _____ To improve large motor coordination

DATE _____ 8/15/82

PARENT SIGNATURE _____

TEACHER SIGNATURE _____

| INSTRUCTIONAL OBJECTIVES | EDUCATIONAL METHODS | DATE Begin | DATE End | Eval. | PERSONS RESPONSIBLE Name | Position |
|---|---|---|---|---|---|---|
| Given outdoor time (or during gym class), Kent will actively participate in 5 supervised games per week for 4 weeks. | Flopsy, Obstacle Course, Parachute Games, Balloon Badminton, Target Bounce, Freeze | 9/5 | 1/15 | | Mrs. K. | Teacher |
| Kent's participation in free-play large muscle activities will increase by 25% (data to be taken week of 10/1/82). | Outdoor play equipment, unstructured outdoor play | 10/1 | 1/15 | | Mrs. K. | Teacher |

# GLOSSARY

**Abduction**    The movement of the limbs away from the middle (midline) of the body.

**Adduction**    The movement of the limbs toward the center (midline) of the body.

**Asymmetry**    Inequality of the two sides of the body. One side may be stronger and larger.

**Ataxia**    Primarily a balance and motor coordination problem. These children have a characteristic high-stepping walk, fall frequently, and are a bit unsteady (as if drunk). Eye coordination problems are common.

**Athetosis**    A condition in which the muscles move involuntarily. Thus children with athetosis are able to get their hand to their mouth, but they may go through a variety of unnecessary uncontrollable movements to get it there. During rest, these children show no abnormal behaviors. The more excited or upset the children become, the less control they have.

**Atrophy**    The deterioration of muscle or nerve cells. They become smaller and weaker through disuse. Atrophy may result from wearing a cast or from a child's desire for voluntary inactivity to avoid pain.

**Cerebral Palsy**    A condition that affects the motor system of the body as a result of lesions in the brain. There are many different types of cerebral palsy depending on the size and location of the lesion.

**Chiropodist**    A specialist in foot disorders.

**Contracture**    Permanent tightness of muscles and joints that limits their full range of motion.

**Cyanosis**    A bluish tinge to the skin caused by lack of oxygen in the blood. The tinge is most easily seen in the lips and fingernails.

**Deformities**    The body or limbs are fixed in abnormal positions.

**Equilibrium**    Sense of balance.

**Extension**    The straightening of any part of the body.

**Flaccid**    Body postures or movements lacking normal firmness. Also described as "floppy."

**Flexion**    The bending of any part of the body.

**Hydrocephalus**    A condition in which the buildup of spinal fluid in the brain causes pressure on the brain cells. Unless the fluid is drained, permanent damage will occur.

**Hypertonic**    Having high or increased muscle tension (similar to tightness and stiffness).

**Hypotonic**    Having low or decreased muscle tension. Standing and walking is difficult because the muscles are not tense enough to combat gravity.

**Midline**    An imaginary dividing line that runs vertically through the center of the body.

**Neurologist**    A physician who specializes in the nervous system.

**Occupational therapy**    Prescribed activities designed to restore, reinforce, and facilitate fine motor skills that are important in self-help.

**Oral surgeon**    A physician who specializes in surgery of the mouth.

**Orthopedically impaired**    Having a severe orthopedic impairment that adversely affects educational performance (as defined by PL 94-142). The term includes impairments caused by congenital anomaly, disease, and other causes, such as fractures or burns that cause contractures.

**Osteopath**    A physician who specializes in the musculo-skeletal system. He or she uses mechanical manipulation, medicine, and surgery to correct malfunctions.

**Paralysis, forms of**

*Diplegia*. The whole body is paralyzed, but the legs more than the arms. Diplegic children usually have some head control and moderate to slight paralysis of the upper limbs. Speech can be affected. This term is primarily used with cerebral palsy.

*Hemiplegia*. Paralysis of the upper and lower extremity on the same side of the body. In cerebral palsy, hemiplegics are usually of the spastic type.

*Monoplegia*. Only one arm, or, less frequently, only one leg is paralysed.

*Paraplegia*. Lower extremities are involved. Paraplegics are commonly found among spinal injuries and spina bifida and rarely in cerebral palsy.

*Quadraplegia*. Paralysis of all four limbs. Head control is poor and, in cerebral palsy, there is usually impairment of speech and eye coordination. With spinal cord injuries, speech is often not affected.

*Triplegia*. This condition involves three extremities, usually both lower extremities and one arm. It may also be a combination of paraplegia and hemiplegia.

**Passive therapy**    Therapy done without the child's help.

**Physical therapy**    Prescribed activities or exercises designed to restore, reinforce, and teach compensatory large motor skills.

**Physiotherapy**    The treatment of movement disorders by physical, mechanical, and electrical means. (Part of physical therapy.)

**Podiatrist**    A specialist in foot disorders.

**Range of Motion**    The normal range, measured in degrees, within which any joint can be moved.

**Righting**    The ability to return one's head and body to normal and natural positions from abnormal or uncomfortable ones.

**Rigidity**    A condition in which the muscles involuntarily resist each other and the limbs become stiff and difficult to move.

**Shunt**    A plastic tube inserted in the brain that redirects excessive cerebrospinal fluid into the peritoneal cavity. This helps prevent retardation. The shunt must be lengthened as the child grows.

**Spasticity** Jerky, uncontrollable movements caused by an obstruction in the brain that suppresses certain nerve impulses, resulting in an imbalance between opposing muscle groups.

**Spina bifida** A condition in which the spinal cord is not closed or protrudes at birth. The degree of severity varies from bowel and bladder dysfunction to paralysis below the waist.

**Tremor** A type of cerebral palsy similar to the spastic type. While motor control is better, there is an involuntary, vibrating, rhythmic motion to the muscles. This is usually most obvious in the hands.

## TEACHING RESOURCES

In some situations you may want or need additional information. There are many national as well as regional, state, and local organizations that can be helpful to you. The following annotated list of national organizations should be useful in helping you decide where to get the information you need.

National Rehabilitation Association
1522 K Street, N.W.
Washington, DC 20005
Encourages an interdisciplinary approach. Interested in increasing public understanding of the physically and mentally handicapped.

Parents Campaign for Handicapped Children and Youth
Closer Look
Box 1492
Washington, DC 20013
Provides information in a free newsletter about educational programs and special services to parents and professionals who work with physically, mentally, and emotionally handicapped children.

Services for Crippled Children
U.S. Department of HEW
Bureau of Community Health Services
Rockville, MD 20852
Provides information about programs available for physically impaired children.

The National Easter Seal Society for Crippled Children and Adults
2023 West Ogden Avenue
Chicago, IL 60612
Administrative headquarters for Easter Seals affiliates that operate direct service programs for handicapped children and adults. They treat speech, hearing, and related disorders; learning disorders; and psychological disorders, in addition to physical ones.

United Cerebral Palsy Association, Inc.
66 East 34th Street
New York, NY 10016
National headquarters. Provides guidance and services to affiliates and supports extensive medical research programs.

## BIBLIOGRAPHY

Best, Gary A. *Individuals with Physical Disabilities: An Introduction to Educators.* St. Louis, Mo.: C. V. Mosby Co., 1978.

Bleck, E.D., and Donald A. Nagel, eds. *Physically Handicapped Children: A Medical Atlas for Teachers.* New York: Grune and Stratton, 1975.

Cruickshank, William M., ed. *Cerebral Palsy: A Developmental Disability.* 3rd rev. ed. Syracuse, N.Y.: Syracuse Univ. Press, 1976.

Deppe, Phillip, and Judith Sherman. *The High Risk Child: A Guide for Concerned Parents.* New York: Macmillan, 1981.

Edington, Dorothy. *The Physically Handicapped Child in Your Classroom: A Handbook for Teachers.* Springfield, Ill.: Charles C. Thomas, 1976.

Feingold, Ben F. *Why Your Child Is Hyperactive.* New York: Random House, 1974.

Finnie, Nancy. *Handling the Young Cerebral Palsied Child at Home.* 2nd ed. New York: E. P. Dutton, 1975.

Garwood, S. Gray, et al. *Educating Young Handicapped Children: A Developmental Approach.* Germantown, Md.: Aspen Systems Corp., 1979.

Hale, Glorya, ed. *The Source Book for the Disabled.* New York: Paddington Press, 1979.

Love, Harold D. *Teaching Physically Handicapped Children: Methods and Materials.* Springfield, Ill.: Charles C. Thomas, 1978.

Travis, Georgia. *Chronic Illness in Children: Its Impact on Child and Family.* Stanford, Calif.: Stanford Univ. Press, 1976.

*Biography/Autobiography/Fiction*

Baker, Louise. *Out On a Limb.* New York: McGraw-Hill, 1946.

A humorous and practical autobiographical account by an amputee of her adjustment problems and her experiences with crutches, an artificial leg, and a peg leg.

Brown, Christy. *Down All the Days*. New York: Stein and Day, 1970.

A novel written by a man with cerebral palsy. He traces growing up as one of a family with twenty-two children living in a Dublin slum. He typed the manuscript of this novel with one left toe.

Carlson, Earl R. *Born That Way*. New York: John Day, 1941.

The autobiography of Earl Carlson who despite his own cerebral palsy, became a doctor specializing in treating others with that disability.

Eareckson, Joni, and Joe Musser. *Joni*. Grand Rapids, Mich.: Zondervan, 1980.

Autobiography of a girl who becomes a quadraplegic from a diving accident.

————, and Estes, Steve. *A Step Further*. Grand Rapids, Mich.: Zondervan, 1980.

A sequel to *Joni*, her further trials and triumphs.

Joel, Gil S. *So Your Child Has Cerebral Palsy*. Albuquerque, N.M.: Univ. of New Mexico Press, 1975.

Written by a man who has cerebral palsy, focuses on parent's reaction and feelings and gives advice.

Killilea, Marie. *Karen*. Englewood Cliffs, N.J.: Prentice-Hall, 1963.

A mother's story of the life and upbringing of her cerebral palsied daughter.

————. *With Love from Karen*. New York: Dell, 1980.

Another book about Karen.

Marx, Joseph Lawrence. *Keep Trying*. New York: Harper and Row, 1974.

This practical story, about and for the physically handicapped, is written by a man who had polio as an infant and who has since led a full and active life.

Neufield, John. *Twink*. New York: New American Library, 1970.

The story of a sixteen-year-old girl with cerebral palsy, told for the most part by her sister and mother.

Russell, Harold. *Victory in My Hands*. New York: Creative Age Press, 1949.

A young man's adjustments after an explosion in which both his hands were blown off. It is an absorbing chronical of the emotional obstacles he faced and conquered.

Viscardi, Henry, Jr. *The Phoenix Child*. Middlebury, Vt.: Eriksson, 1975.

The true story of Darren, a black orphan child with severe facial deformities, and the Human Resource Center on Long Island, which educates severely disabled children who cannot attend neighborhood schools.

# BIBLIOGRAPHY FOR CHILDREN

*Awareness*

Adams, Barbara. *Like It Is: Facts and Feelings about Handicaps from Kids Who Know*. New York: Walker and Co., 1979.

A group of six children talk about how they learned to deal with their handicaps and have full, satisfying lives. The photographs may be useful for starting a conversation with younger children.

Burger, G. *Physical Disabilities*. New York: Watts, 1979.

Describes specific disabilities and the treatment used for them. Attitudes toward handicaps are also discussed.

Fassler, Joan. *Howie Helps Himself*. Chicago: Albert Whitman, 1975.

Howie has cerebral palsy and more than anything wants to be able to move his wheelchair by himself.

Kamien, Janet. *What If You Couldn't . . . ? A Book About Special Needs*. New York: Scribner, 1979.

Encourages children to imagine themselves with different disabilities and discusses several ways to overcome the problems that go along with each disability.

Mack, Nancy. *Tracy*. Chicago: Children's Press, 1976.

Tracy, a victim of cerebral palsy, talks about school and activities and how she overcomes her handicap in every way she can.

O'Reilly, Edward. *Brown Pelican at the Pond*. San Rafael, Calif.: Manzanita Press, 1979.

Children discover a pelican with a broken wing and nurse it back to health. This book is sensitively written and very appealing to children.

Pursell, Margaret Sanford. *A Look at Physical Handicaps*. Minneapolis, Minn.: Lerner Publications, 1976.

This factual, photographic book about physical handicaps provides a simple, honest introduction to the subject.

Stein, Sara Bonnet. *About Handicaps*. New York: Walker and Co., 1974.

Vivid photographs and a simple, direct text characterize the child's version of the story, while the parents and teachers can follow in a more detailed accompanying text.

Sullivan, M. B., A. Brightman, and J. Blatt. *Feeling Free*. Reading, Mass.: Addison-Wesley, 1979.

A group of children get together to explore what it would be like to be disabled.

White, Paul. *Janet at School*. New York: Thomas Y. Crowell, 1978.

Five-year-old Janet has spina bifida; she has no movement in her legs. Although at school she can't do everything the others can, she finds her own way to join in.

Wittman, Sally. *A Special Trade*. New York: Harper and Row, 1978.

Nelly and Bartholomew have a special friendship. Bartholomew pushes Nelly in her stroller. They trade roles when Bartholomew comes out of the hospital and Nelly pushes him in his wheelchair.

Wolf, Bernard. *Don't Feel Sorry for Paul*. Philadelphia: Lippincott, 1974.

Paul rides a bike, plays football, goes to school, and loves baseball games. Some people feel sorry for Paul; others laugh at him and call him Captain Hook. Paul has artificial feet and a hand that is a two-part hook. Even though the text is advanced for preschool, the incredible photographs will capture the children's interest.

Wolff, Angelika. *Mom! I Broke My Arm!* New York: Lion Press, 1969.

About bones, x-rays, castings, and how it feels to have a broken bone.

*Being Different*

Alexander, Martha. *Blackboard Bear*. New York: Dial, 1969.

A little boy is left out of games because he is too small. He creates an enormous bear on his blackboard to play pretend with.

Anderson, Hans Christian. *The Ugly Duckling*. Minato-tu, Tokyo: Zokersha Pub., 1968.

The classic story that deals with being different.

Beim, Jerrold. *The Smallest Boy in the Class*. New York: Morrow, 1949.

The smallest boy in class tries to get everyone's attention, but he is giving and the children realize he has the biggest heart.

Bendick, Jeanne. *Why Can't I*. New York: Scholastic Books, 1969.

Discusses why we can't do all of the things that animals do and some of the things we can do that animals can't.

Brennar, Barbara. *Mr. Tall and Mr. Small*. New York: Young Scott Books–Addison-Wesley, 1966.

Mr. Tall is a giraffe and Mr. Small is a mouse. They each

have special abilities and use them to help each other during a fire.

De Regniers, Beatrice S. *The Giant Story*. New York: Harper and Row, 1953.

Tommy imagines that he's larger than the world. He imagines all the things a giant can do until he gets sleepy and becomes small again.

Ets, Marie Hall. *Just Me*. New York: Viking Press, 1965.

A little farm boy tries to walk like the different farm animals. He finds the best way to get around is to run just like himself.

Ginsburg, Mirra. *The Chick and the Duckling*. New York: Macmillan, 1972

A chick and a duckling are born at the same time and do everything together. When the duck goes into the water, the chick follows and promptly sinks. When the duckling returns for a second swim, the chick says "not me."

Greenberg, Polly. *I Know I'm Myself Because . . .* New York: Human Sciences Press, 1981.

A thoughtful book that captures the moments that awaken a child's sense of identity. Depicting the familiar experiences and emotions of childhood with humor and sensitivity, the author celebrates the wonder of a child's world.

Greene, Laura. *Help*. New York: Human Sciences Press, 1980.

Through a simple text and colorful illustrations, this book portrays the many ways we give and receive help and that it is all right to need help.

Krasilovsky, Phyllis. *The Very Tall Little Girl*. New York: Doubleday, 1969.

Upset in the beginning of the story because she is six-inches taller than most girls her age, a girl soon finds lots of reasons for being glad she is tall.

Kent, Jack. *Just Only John*. New York: Parents' Magazine Press, 1968.

John has been John for four years now and is getting tired of it. He learns what comes of wanting to be something you are not.

LeSieg, Theodore. *I Wish That I Had Duck Feet*. New York: Beginner Books-Random House, 1965.

A boy wishes for different things—duck feet, a tiger tail, a trunk, horns—all to help him show up big Bill, the bully. He finally concludes it is best to just be himself.

Strauss, Joyce. *How Does It Feel . . . ?* New York: Human Sciences Press, 1981.

Thought-provoking questions explore the many feelings and emotions experienced in memory, fantasy, and everyday situations. This enlightening book will enable children to understand and express their emotions more effectively.

# I N D E X

| *Annual Goals* | *Activity* | *Curriculum Area* | *Page* |
|---|---|---|---|
| To increase understanding | Traveling | Expressing Language | 344 |
| | Controller | Expressing Language | 336 |

## THINKING AND REASONING SKILLS

| | | | |
|---|---|---|---|
| To increase attention span | Changing Objects | Reading Readiness | 371 |
| | Red Light/Green Light | Health and Safety | 434 |
| To improve cause and effect reasoning | Balance It | Large Motor Play | 519 |
| | Balloon Badminton | Outdoor Play | 528 |
| | Cornstarch Playdough | Science/Discovery | 402 |
| | Crayon Rubbing | Art | 448 |
| | Creature | Art | 448 |
| | Dress Up and Tell | Dramatic Play | 492 |
| | Magnets | Science/Discovery | 398 |
| | Mixing Colored Water | Science/Discovery | 403 |
| | Red Light/Green Light | Health and Safety | 434 |
| | Temperature | Science/Discovery | 400 |
| | Torn Paper Flowers | Art | 445 |
| | Tracing Pictures | Art | 446 |
| | Warning Sounds | Health and Safety | 437 |
| | What Would You Do If? | Health and Safety | 438 |
| | Where Is It? | Music | 467 |
| To increase logical reasoning | Bring Me | Expressing Language | 336 |
| | Measure It | Mathematics | 430 |
| To improve classification skills | Classify It | Reading Readiness | 379 |
| | Nutty Sort | Science/Discovery | 407 |
| | Sorting | Small Motor Play | 500 |
| To improve sequencing skills | Buttoning Sequences | Small Motor Play | 504 |
| | Natural Sequencing | Reading Readiness | 377 |
| To improve color concepts | Color Scavenger Hunt | Outdoor Play | 531 |
| | Musical Colors | Music | 470 |
| | Shape Pictures | Mathematics | 419 |
| To make predictions | Balloon Badminton | Outdoor Play | 528 |
| | Magnets | Science/Discovery | 398 |
| | Matching Rods | Mathematics | 427 |
| | Measure It | Mathematics | 430 |
| | Mixing Colored Water | Science/Discovery | 403 |
| | Noisy Toss | Large Motor Play | 517 |
| | Temperature | Science/Discovery | 400 |
| To increase problem-solving skills | Mixing Colored Water | Science/Discovery | 403 |

## MATHEMATIC SKILLS

| | | | |
|---|---|---|---|
| To improve number concepts | Counting Cherries | Mathematics | 413 |
| To improve measurement concepts | Areas | Mathematics | 420 |
| | Arm's Length | Mathematics | 428 |
| | Matching Rods | Mathematics | 427 |
| | Measure It | Mathematics | 430 |
| | Salt Putty Beads | Art | 459 |
| To improve shape concepts | Areas | Mathematics | 420 |
| | Musical Colors | Music | 470 |

| *Annual Goals* | *Activity* | *Curriculum Area* | *Page* |
|---|---|---|---|
| | My Yard | Outdoor Play | 527 |
| | Noisy Toss | Large Motor Play | 517 |
| | Pockets | Mathematics | 417 |
| | Pouring Peanuts | Small Motor Play | 507 |
| | Salt Putty Beads | Art | 459 |
| | String Painting | Art | 450 |
| | Target Bounce | Outdoor Play | 524 |
| | Torn Paper Flowers | Art | 445 |
| | Variations on Bouncing | Outdoor Play | 524 |
| | Throwing Games | Small Motor Play | 506 |
| | Velcro Toss | Small Motor Play | 506 |
| | Wire Sculpture | Art | 451 |
| To improve balance skills | Balance It | Large Motor Play | 519 |
| To encourage creative movement | Movement Exploration | Movement | 474 |
| | Music and Movement | Movement | 480 |
| To increase sense of rhythm | Rhythm Walk | Music | 464 |
| To relax at will | Tense Me | Movement | 480 |
| | Relaxation Stories | Movement | 476 |

## CREATIVITY

| | | | |
|---|---|---|---|
| To encourage creativity | Clay | Art | 451 |
| | Foot Painting | Art | 450 |
| | Mood Montage | Art | 453 |
| | Painting to Music | Art | 454 |
| | String Painting | Art | 451 |
| | Traveling | Expressing Language | 344 |
| | Wire Sculpture | Art | 451 |
| To encourage creative problem solving | Body Parts | Social Studies | 386 |
| | Creature | Art | 448 |
| | Di-Vergent | Expressing Language | 335 |
| | Hands and Feet | Social Studies | 385 |
| | Our Town | Social Studies | 384 |
| | What Would You Do If? | Health and Safety | 438 |
| To stimulate curiosity | Cornstarch Playdough | Science/Discovery | 402 |

## FEELINGS

| | | | |
|---|---|---|---|
| To express feelings | Share Your Feelings | Social Studies | 392 |
| To increase feelings of group belonging | Color Scavenger Hunt | Outdoor Play | 531 |
| | Dress Up and Tell | Dramatic Play | 492 |
| | I'm Thinking Of | Social Studies | 392 |
| | Our Town | Social Studies | 384 |
| | Picture Relays | Outdoor Play | 526 |
| | Share Your Feelings | Social Studies | 392 |
| | Traveling | Expressing Language | 344 |

## AWARENESS

| | | | |
|---|---|---|---|
| To increase body awareness | Arm's Length | Mathematics | 428 |
| | Balance It | Large Motor Play | 519 |
| | Body Parts | Social Studies | 386 |

# Needs: Health

A chronic health need can be any one of several illnesses. Although their illnesses are different, children with chronic health needs have the following characteristics in common. They will miss more school, spend more time convalescing at home, and be in the hospital more frequently than most other children. The repeated separation and trauma experienced during early childhood affect them both physically and emotionally. The cycles of "good" and "bad" health are often related to stress. Stress may bring on an acute stage of the disease or make an existing acute stage more severe. Their family's physical, emotional, and financial resources may be severely taxed as they attempt to cope with the effects and limitations imposed by a child's long-term illness.

Parents are often expected to take on the role of clinician, or therapist-in-training, in addition to the traditional parental role. They perform daily much of the therapy that the specialists prescribe each week or month. They monitor the child's health, seeking medical help in acute phases. When medical treatment is required, they are the ones to chauffeur the child to and from the appointments. The extra work and responsibility places an added burden on the parent-child relationship.

Health needs make up the largest single category of special needs. Although there is no consensus on what illnesses should be classified chronic health problems and, therefore, no agreement on a figure, a representative study concluded that about 23 percent of children under seventeen years of age have one or more chronic conditions (Travis, 1976).

A chronic health problem is an illness that affects one or more organs of the body and persists for a long period of time (from months to perhaps a lifetime). Some chronic health problems shorten life span, others do not. All are potentially life-threatening. Almost all have periods of activity and remission. In some cases, the disease is progressive, getting increasingly worse, or it weakens other body systems, making the child more susceptible to other illnesses.

## COMMON CHRONIC HEALTH PROBLEMS

Brief descriptions of the most common chronic health problems follow. Remember you will not be expected to be an expert on each disease, but rather you need to be aware of typical characteristics and how they will influence your programming. (The illnesses are in alphabetical order.)

### Allergies

Allergies are the most common chronic health problem of children. They account for one-third of all chronic health conditions that occur during the preschool years. Only about 35 percent of children with allergies have been diagnosed and treated. About 10 to 24 percent of the population has serious allergies; another 26 percent experience minor allergies. Most allergies begin before age fourteen (Travis, 1976).

An allergy is a sensitivity to something that most other people find harmless. In an allergic reaction caused by pollen, for example, the body acts as if it is being invaded and must defend itself. It produces antibodies, which stimulate (in the case of hayfever) the white blood cells to produce a chemical called histamine. Histamine causes the hayfever symptoms, and the drugs used to combat this reaction are called *anti*histamines. Allergenic substances fall into four categories. The most common items are listed below.

*Air-borne* (inhalants). These are substances taken into the body through the mouth and nose: plant pollen, fungi spores, mold, dust, feathers (down), animal dander (Travis, 1976).

*Foods and Drugs* (ingestants). These are substances that are taken into the gastrointestinal tract. Early in the school year, before you have gotten to know your students, you may want to avoid using common problem foods for snacks. The following foods are responsible for 90 percent of food allergies: legumes (peas, beans, and nuts, especially peanuts), chocolate, citrus fruit (especially oranges), cereal and grain products (including corn, corn syrup, corn starch, and wheat), fish/shellfish, milk, eggs, cola drinks, berries, tomatoes, cinnamon, food colors. These oral drugs are common offenders: aspirin, sulfa drugs, penicillin.

*Contact* (contactants). These substances come in contact with the surface of the skin: ingredients in cosmetics, starch, wool, some detergents.

*Some Drugs and Chemicals* (injectables). These substances enter the body through the skin: penicillin (injected), mosquito venom, venom from bee stings. Insect bites can be fatal. A bee sting often results in localized swelling and redness, which indicates only a mild allergy. A serious allergic reaction causes more generalized swelling and/or hotness about the face and neck, followed by difficulty in breathing and more severe bodily reactions. A sting can result in death if treatment is not immediate.

*Implications.* You will play an important part in diagnosing allergies in very young children. Particularly difficult to spot are symptoms that seem to be related to the season or weather.

Nose: Frequent runny nose, sniffling, rubbing the nose, frequent nosebleeds, frequent sneezing (four or five times in a row), wrinkling up the nose.

Mouth: Dry hacking cough, wheezing, mouth breathing.

Eyes: Red puffy eyes, rubbing the eyes, dark circles under the eyes.

Skin: Skin irritations and rashes.

If a child is diagnosed allergic to common inhalants, you should have the classroom scrubbed and vacuumed frequently. (Dusting merely redistributes the dust.) If you have an air conditioner, be sure the filter is cleaned often. Do the same for the heating system filter. Consider adding a humidifier or air cleaner if necessary (Voignier and Bridgewater, 1980).

Be sure to ask all of the parents whether their children have known allergies. The information will help you screen lunch and snack menus, choose a class pet, and prepare in advance against insect bites and other potential allergens encountered during field trips. Find out what reaction the child is likely to have, what you should do if the reaction occurs, and what the side effects of the child's medication are.

Because a child's first allergic reaction may occur during school hours, it is important that you establish emergency procedures. (See the discussion under Guidelines.)

## Asthma

Asthma is the leading cause of school absences in young children. It is a respiratory problem caused by an obstruction of the small bronchial tubes that occurs because of a swelling of the tubes themselves or the membrane linings. Asthma can also result from the contraction of the muscles around the tubes or by the plugging of the tubes with mucus. The symptoms are generally the same regardless of the cause—shortness of breath, coughing, wheezing, and choking. The lungs become enlarged because more air can be inhaled than can be exhaled. The chest expands, the neck muscles strain, and the veins tend to swell. This condition is twice as common in boys as girls.

Asthma has a variety of causes; the most common are allergies. Emotional excitement (good or bad) as well as overexertion or even ordinary activity can trigger an attack. Since these attacks occur without warning, they may be frightening to the child who is having one as well as to the other children. Attacks are most likely to come in the early morning hours. Children usually have prescribed medication (in pill or inhaler form) to take. You need to have it available and to know how to help the child use it. Generally, the most comfortable positions for the child having an attack are sitting backwards straddling a straight chair or planting the elbows on the knees. These positions are easiest to breathe in. Lying down is not helpful and in some cases may actually be harmful.

*Implications.* Asthmatic young children are commonly allergic to dust. If possible, have the floor

After a strenuous activity like running, plan time for the child to rest or participate in a quiet activity.

of your room damp-mopped and eliminate rugs or curtains. If not, have the room vacuumed at night so that dust can settle. Try to balance strenuous activities with less strenuous ones. You should arrange a way to keep in contact with this child at home, since he will frequently be absent. The severity of attacks will vary from time to time. The child will probably not "outgrow" asthma during the preschool years.

## Cancer

Cancer is an umbrella term for a group of diseases, all of which produce malignancies in some part of the body (skin, muscle, nerve, lining of stomach, and so on). Most commonly affected in children are the nervous system, the genitourinary system, the system of connective tissues, and the blood-forming system.

Cancer is treated with surgery, radiation, chemotherapy, or a combination of those methods. The prognosis depends on how early the disease is detected, what type of cancer it is, and which system is affected. Although cancer occurs rarely, it causes more deaths in children between one and fourteen than any other disease (Travis, 1976). (Only accidents cause more deaths.)

Leukemia is the most common form of cancer found in young children. Although people think of leukemia as a blood disease, it is actually a disease of the tissues that produce the white blood cells. When affected by leukemia, these tissues produce copious abnormal white cells. The cells are ineffective in fighting infection, and they disrupt the production of red blood cells and prevent blood from clotting properly.

There are two types of leukemia—acute and chronic. Most afflicted children have acute leukemia. In the past that meant they would normally have only several months to live once the disease was diagnosed. Today a child may live an additional two to five years. Children with chronic leukemia may live as long as ten years (Travis, 1976).

Because leukemia is not localized, surgery is not effective. Early diagnosis and treatment cannot prevent the disease from spreading. Various chemicals, hormones, and sometimes x-rays are used to combat this disease. Platelet transfusions, gamma globulin, and other blood products are helpful in managing the disease. Being cured of leukemia is rare, although with new research there is new hope. Currently no way of preventing leukemia is known.

Although medical advances can increase the life span and even hold out the hope of an ultimate cure, leukemia is still a fatal illness in most cases. The decrease in red blood cells causes anemia, which results in the child being lethargic, tired, and pale much of the time. Because of decrease in platelets, the child bleeds excessively and bruises from minor causes. Heavy nosebleeds are frequent. The low "normal" white cell count decreases the child's resistance to infection and makes getting well more difficult. Many children also have pain and discomfort from both the disease and the treatment. Often one side effect of the treatment is loss of hair; another is stiffness in the joints.

*Implications.* After the initial diagnosis, a period of intensive treatment follows and then a first remission in which the child looks well and has energy. This may be the time the child is in your program. Discipline should be "normal" at home and at school, but given the circumstances, disciplining this child will be hard to do. Adequate nutrition for growth is a problem because the drugs decrease appetite. (In some cases, the drugs must be reduced so that the child's appetite can improve.) Be sure your snacks and lunches are nutritious, as this child cannot afford empty calories. School, despite the dangers of infection and taunting by peers, has great psychological value to both the child and the family. Often hospitals or community agencies will offer seminars on death and dying which may be helpful for teachers and parents to attend.

### Cystic Fibrosis

Cystic fibrosis is a hereditary chronic disease in which the mucus-secreting and sweat glands produce a mucus so thick and sticky that it interferes with the functioning of the respiratory and digestive systems. It affects boys and girls equally and occurs in about one in every 2,000 Caucasian births (Travis, 1976). Often cystic fibrosis is diagnosed in infancy by analyzing the concentration of sodium and chloride in the sweat. However, it is difficult to diagnose because it can be confused initially with asthma, food allergies, failure to thrive, and even maternal overanxiousness, to name but a few.

Symptoms vary, but some common ones are below-average height and weight despite a voracious appetite; frequent coughing (wheezing is common), throat clearing, sinus infections and respiratory problems; foul-smelling stools; and gastrointestinal problems (upset stomach and diarrhea).

Currently, with improved treatment, about 75 percent of children with cystic fibrosis live until at least middle or late adolescence. Parents live with the constant knowledge of impending death. This psychological strain is accompanied by a financial one. Estimated costs of treatment range from $4,000 to $12,000 per year. Medication alone can cost $3,000 per year. The actual treatment and caring for the equipment often takes two hours a day. Children's lives depend on their family's ability to put them first.

*Implications.*    Some special arrangements have to be made. There can be no smoking in the classroom. See that the child takes enzyme pills before snack and lunchtime. Develop a plan for maintaining contact when the child is home sick or hospitalized. See that the child is encouraged to bring up phlegm, not stigmatized for doing so. Some signs of emotional difficulty to look for in the child are depression and withdrawal, fear of death, fear of losing control (dependence), and acting out. Have an emergency plan (see Guidelines).

Provide matter-of-fact explanations for other children: "This child has trouble breathing, like you do when you have a cold, only Leroy has this all the time. He also has a tummyache a lot."

### Juvenile Diabetes

Juvenile diabetes, by definition, begins before a child is fifteen years old. In young children it is almost always severe. (Diabetes causes the highest rate of hospitalization among white children.) Common symptoms are extreme thirst, frequent urina-

Properly planned snacks allow the diabetic child to be part of the group and to learn more about food and its effects.

tion, constant hunger, loss of weight, itching, easy tiring, changes in vision, and slow healing of cuts and scratches. However, it is possible for a child to be a diabetic without having all these symptoms, and some children have no obvious symptoms.

Diabetes is a metabolic disorder in which the body either does not produce enough insulin (a hormone made by the pancreas that helps the body use glucose) or the insulin produced is not effective. In juvenile diabetes, the pancreas produces no insulin at all. Therefore the child can not eat carbohydrates in great quantity. The goal is to manage the disease by developing a predictable relationship between the child's diet, insulin, and the amount of exercise. Diabetes can lead to many serious medical complications (kidney disease, blindness), as well as a shortened life span.

Insulin injections are necessary for almost all children with diabetes. The painful injections must be given daily and are probably the most hated part of the treatment. Urine testing (usually before breakfast and dinner) is also necessary each day. This procedure is embarrassing for a child striving toward independence. Charting the test results provides the basis for changes in insulin dosage and gives clues to why some diabetes goes out of control. Diabetic children are allowed to have slowly digestible sweets like ice cream, but are not allowed to eat candy bars and other carbohydrates that burn quickly. (An exception to this rule occurs when the child needs quick sugar to avert an insulin reaction.)

Brittle or "labile" diabetic children are those who are difficult to keep under medical control. In other words, it is difficult to determine the correct amount of insulin to prevent either shock or coma. These children are usually hospitalized until management techniques are worked out.

Although most juvenile diabetics are on a "free" diet, it is by no means unstructured. The "free exchange system" used by adults is often used with children. This system divides foods into six groups based on the calories and the grams of carbohydrates, proteins, and fats. Thus, if the child is allowed one bread exchange, the choice of any one of the following could be made: a piece of bread, one-half cup cereal, two graham crackers, one-half cup mashed potatoes, and one-fourth cup baked beans (Travis, 1976). The number of exchanges is determined by the individual's needs. The parents will tell you what exchanges the child requires.

*Implications.* You need to have snack and lunch at about the same times each day. Each should provide about the same food values every day. The child need not eat the same things every day, but the foods should be of equivalent groups and values.

Because of the possibility of insulin reaction (hypoglycemia), you must always have some quick-burning sugar on hand to give the child if you suspect a reaction is about to occur. Most children have some warning signs, but young children rarely can identify these. The child may be dizzy, shaky, trembling, or having an emotional outburst before the insulin reaction occurs. Find out in advance what the child's favorite sources of sugar are: You need to offer something especially tempting because the child may not feel like eating at this time. Some traditional quick sugar sources are orange juice, soda, a sugar cube, small chocolate bars. Always carry one of these on a field trip. If you miss the warning signs and the child becomes unconscious, do not try to get the child to drink, since choking might result. Discuss emergency measures with parents before the trip. (They will probably want to be informed and have the child taken to the emergency room of a hospital. You may even need to learn to give a shot of glucagon to the child.)

Too much sugar in the body for the amount of insulin is indicated by very frequent urination, thirst, hunger, weakness, drowsiness, vomiting, and finally coma. Call the parents when you notice any of the early signs. This condition can result from eating "forbidden foods," sleeping more, less active playing, or illness. If children know they have done something wrong to bring on the attack, they may be reluctant to tell. An unconscious child must be taken to the emergency room of a hospital.

The parents supervise and regulate the child's insulin and diet, and they can usually accommodate any situation if they know about it ahead of time. Send them a list of your snacks for the week or month, or at least post them on a bulletin board for the parents to check when they drop off or pick up their child. If another child will have a birthday party with cupcakes, tell the parents. The diabetic child can have one too, if it is planned.

The child should wear a Medic-Alert bracelet or locket at all times.

Being different is often a problem. Diabetic children often have a low self-esteem and tend to be loners. Remember to work toward improving their self-concept.

## Epilepsy

Epilepsy is technically not a disease but a symptom of a neurological disorder which manifests itself as a seizure. The seizure itself is caused by too much energy being discharged from the cells of the brain. There are two major types of seizures: *generalized* seizures and *focal* seizures. Generalized seizures involve the whole body. Focal seizures involve specific parts of the body, but may progress to generalized seizures.

*Grand mal* is a type of epilepsy in which generalized convulsions occur. The child loses consciousness, appears out of control for a period of time, and is tired afterwards. Some children get a warning or "aura" before a grand mal seizure. *Petit mal* seizures are generalized and occur almost without notice and as often as one hundred times a day. They may appear as a brief period of rapid blinking or as a glazed look. Afterward the child will continue on as if nothing had happened. They are unaware they have had a seizure. These seizures may often pass unnoticed by you and the other children. Focal seizures can be psychomotor or autonomic. Ask the parents for their child's special symptoms. A child with a psychomotor seizure, for example, might smack the lips and stare into space for about five minutes. The child may not remember having the seizure (Weiner, 1973).

An electroencephalogram (EEG) is one useful diagnostic tool. Each type of epilepsy has a characteristic irregular brain wave pattern that can be detected by an EEG. After the EEG is completed, the skull is x-rayed and a spinal tap is done. These tests help the physician select the most effective anticonvulsant drug for the particular type of seizure the child is having. It is difficult to predict which drug or combination of drugs will control seizures in individual children. While medical personnel are trying different medications, the seizures will probably not be under control. About 20 percent of epilepsy patients have seizures that cannot currently be controlled by drugs.

*Implications.* People who don't understand epilepsy often have negative feelings that may take the form of social ostracism of the child. As a result, children with epilepsy need help improving their self-concept.

You need to be prepared to deal with a seizure if one occurs. If the child gets a warning, help the child lie down on a blanket on the floor in some out-of-the-way place in the room. Remove any nearby objects or furniture so that the child can avoid injury during the convulsion. Generally, it is better to lie a child on the side rather than the back to decrease the chance of the child gagging on the tongue. Place a soft object like a folded handkerchief or a tongue depressor wrapped in gauze between the child's upper and lower back teeth. (If the seizure has already started, don't try to put anything in the mouth.) When the seizure is over, cover the child and let him sleep until ready to get up. An explanation for the other children might be: "Maria sometimes looks like she is having a temper tantrum when she is having a seizure. She is not angry; this is something that sometimes happens to her. It takes a lot of energy, so when she is done, she wants to rest."

### Heart Problems

Defective hearts and rheumatic fever are the two major causes of heart problems in young children. In rheumatic fever, the child's heart often becomes enlarged and the pumping action weakened. Sometimes the valves (especially on the left side) become inflamed. If these heal with a scar, or if the enlarged heart does not return to normal, there is permanent damage. Healing can occur so that the child is able to lead a normal life. Rheumatic fever is only one-tenth as common now as in the past.

You may encounter a child with a heart murmur. Heart murmurs are unusual sounds produced by the blood as it circulates through the heart. This sound is caused by the incomplete closing of the heart valves. Heart murmurs are harmless for about half of the preschool children who have them. In other cases, restricted activity or heart surgery may be required.

About three-dozen different heart defects have been identified. These may occur separately or in combination. Surgery is the usual treatment. Most heart conditions in children can be either completely or partially corrected by surgery, although some conditions are inoperable (Travis, 1976).

Preschool children with heart problems may show the following symptoms: poor physical development, frequent respiratory infections, squatting (this is a natural way of increasing circulation), clubbed fingers and toes, shortness of breath on exertion, and perhaps even fainting. Insufficient oxygen may sometimes cause these children to turn a bluish color around the lips and eyes, or cheeks and fingertips may become reddened. Young children with symptomatic cardiac defects may want to be held more, cry and whine more, eat poorly, and, with repeated

serious illness, be difficult to establish a relationship with.

*Implications.* Although these children may need some limitations in their activity, there is generally not a problem if you alternate strenuous activities with restful ones and let children rest when they are tired. If you avoid strenuous competitive games, the children need not exert themselves unduly to win. Children who are subject to blackouts should be distracted from excessive activity that causes breathlessness. (Children may resist being distracted if they realize your intent, but their well-being may depend on it, so be creative.)

There is a tendency for families to overprotect these children, denying them the opportunity to build inner controls. It's important for you to be responsive to their needs within a framework that requires the children to learn responsibility. For example, if a child is too tired to help pick up the dolls he played with, the first time have the child rest. If you suspect the child is using his illness to avoid cleaning up, have the child rest the second time, but leave things to be put in their proper places later so that he learns that this is not a way to get out of cleaning up. If the child is genuinely tired, shorten the activity time.

### Hemophilia

Hemophilia is a genetic blood disease that usually affects only males. It is transmitted by a recessive gene of the mother's. In hemophilia, the child's blood lacks one of the essential ingredients for clotting. The old fear was that the child would get a cut and bleed to death. The real threat is from internal hemorrhaging, with death resulting from bleeding into the brain, air passages, or other vital organs. This is now rare. Almost all children with hemophilia live into adulthood.

With early diagnosis and treatment using a clotting factor that can be isolated from blood plasma, many of the dangers of hemorrhaging are eliminated. However, this treatment is not a cure; it must be used whenever hemorrhaging from an injury occurs (Travis, 1976). Over the long term, bleeding into the joints can cause crippling. The more severe the disease (there are a wide range of clotting deficiencies within hemophiliacs) and the longer the time span between hemorrhaging and treatment, the greater the possibility of long-term crippling. As you might guess, surgery is not an easy solution to correct these deformities. Even dental work causes concern. This disease is very painful. Aspirin cannot be used in treating the pain since it further reduces the blood's ability to clot.

*Implications.* Parents and teachers should work out what equipment the child can safely use. If possible, tag the equipment this child cannot use as a visual reminder. Find out what the parents want you to do if the child is injured. Also decide how acting out and temper tantrums will be dealt with. If the child is experiencing a lot of pain or seems to be very tired, you might make arrangements for him to go home early. Use noncompetitive physical activities to reduce the dangers of overexertion and injury.

### Juvenile Rheumatoid Arthritis

Rheumatoid arthritis is the most common crippling disease of childhood. It can appear as early as six months (although peak incidents occur between the ages of two and four, and eight and ten) and is more common in girls than boys. The joints are inflamed, which results in pain, fever, soreness, and stiffness.

The cause is unknown; one theory is that a virus causes the inflammation by triggering chemical reactions. Children experience flare-ups without warning as well as periods of improvement (remission). During a flare-up, the children feel pain and stiffness. Some wake up at night and cry from the pain. They may need a hot bath to relieve stiffness. Children are usually treated with drugs called salicylates, the most common of which is aspirin. In about one-third of children, the disease is active into adulthood. Rheumatoid arthritis stops in about two-thirds of the children by the end of ten years (Travis, 1976). In most children, growth is stunted. Some may have crippling, but with medical improvements this is becoming less severe. Physical therapy is used to prevent or rectify deformities. The prescribed exercises are repetitious, painful, and little fun. Ordinarily, the parents and child do these activities at home on a daily basis.

*Implications.* This child will often be tired and lack muscular strength. Care needs to be taken to allow the child time to do things. Realize that the child is probably in some pain. (The drugs reduce inflammation and pain but don't cure.) The child should not participate in competitive sports, in activities that continuously use the same joints (typing, piano playing), or in jarring, twisting play.

### Muscular Dystrophy

Muscular dystrophy is an umbrella term for a group of chronic progressive diseases that affect the voluntary muscles. The process, which can occur quickly or slowly, leads to increased disability and ultimately death (usually by age twenty). About two-thirds of the people affected in the United States are children between three and fifteen (Travis, 1976). Although its cause is not certain, it appears to be a metabolic birth disorder, and is at least partly hereditary. An enzyme that converts food into tissue and energy is apparently lacking.

We do not know how to correct the metabolic disorder or halt the progression of the disease. The earlier the symptoms appear, the more severe the disease is likely to be and the earlier death will occur. As muscles deteriorate, the child becomes weaker and more helpless. Death usually results from respiratory or heart failure (Travis, 1976).

Children with muscular dystrophy have normal feeling in their limbs even though they cannot always move them (unlike a child with a spinal cord injury, who has little or no feeling in the limbs). As the disease progresses, the child becomes like a quadraplegic because leg problems are compounded by weakness in the upper arms and shoulders. The disease itself is painless. Once the disease has started there are no remissions and its progress over time is predictable. These children will have a waddling gait, fall frequently and have trouble getting up, climb stairs with difficulty, and often walk up on their toes. As preschoolers, they will be able to walk. Around age ten to twelve, the children will be confined to a wheelchair.

Although too much exercise is painful, appropriate stretching exercises are helpful (be sure to consult the physical therapist and/or parents to find the right exercises). Because the child's physical activities are limited and added weight is an additional burden, a low-calorie diet is recommended.

*Implications.* Blowing and breathing activities maintain the chest muscles that are essential in coughing. Snacks and lunches should be planned with the child's diet in mind. At preschool age, this child looks weak, not ill, and hence is often made fun of. Work to develop both the child's self-image and peer relationships.

School, especially at an early age, is invaluable psychologically for both the child and the parents. These children pose few problems at this age.

### Obesity

Obesity in young children is a serious problem. It affects their health, their self-concept, and the way others feel about them. Obesity is an excessive accumulation of fat; body weight exceeds "normal" by at least 20 percent. About thirteen percent of preschool children are obese (Collipp, 1980). Obesity is commonly caused by eating too much. Overeating may result from poor dietary habits or from difficulties in coping with everyday problems. Rarely do inherited disorders or metabolic and endocrine abnormalities contribute to obesity. Few children are referred for medical advice at this age. It is assumed that they will outgrow their baby fat. However, in many cases they never stop being fat. Children who are classified as obese are likely to have one or two obese parents. It is difficult to tell if children become obese because of eating patterns in the home or because of a genetic tendency in the family or because of a combination of the two.

Our society looks scornfully at obesity. Even from three-year-olds, the taunts of "tubby," "fats," and "fatso" are heard. These children are discriminated against by peers and teachers. They grow up expecting rejection and usually get it. They grow more isolated and unhappy and often react by eating more. Those children who are obese not from high caloric intake but from lack of activity need to be encouraged to participate in active play.

If lifelong obesity is to be avoided, along with the accompanying complications of heart disease, hypertension, diabetes, and emotional distress, programs to stem obesity must be started at the preschool level.

*Implications.*   Obese children exercise less than other children. They seem to be able to do single, nonrhythmic activities like climbing, but have problems with repeated rhythmic activities like running. Playing loud music with a distinct beat during activities helps them improve this skill. To help burn calories and tone muscles, these children should be encouraged to participate in large motor play. As obese children are usually loners, plan special activities to bring them into the group and foster a sense of group belonging.

They and their parents also need education on nutrition. Praise and other noncaloric rewards should be used, never sweets.

## Sickle-Cell Disease

Sickle-cell disease is a painful, inherited blood disorder that primarily affects blacks. There is a major distinction between sickle-cell trait and sickle-cell anemia. The trait exists when the child inherits the disease from only one parent, the anemia when it is inherited from both. The child with the trait is not ill, but instead is a carrier of the disease. The trait occurs in about one in ten black Americans, the anemia in about one in four hundred. The actual proportion of the sickle-shaped cells varies from child to child. The higher the proportion, and the earlier the symptoms appear, the more severe the disease is likely to be. Diagnosis is usually made between the second and fourth year. Characteristically, this child will be chronically sick with infections of one sort or another, be weak, and experience abdominal pain. He may also suffer from painful swelling of the hands and feet.

Red blood cells are normally shaped like a donut with a hole in the middle that does not go through completely. In sickle-cell disease, cells take on a crescent, or sickle, shape. This shape impairs the oxygen-carrying capacity of the cells and is also condu-

cive to clogging. The result is pain and chronic fatigue. There is no known cure, and frequent blood transfusions are necessary to replace the destroyed red blood cells. Children afflicted with severe forms of the disease usually die in childhood or early adult life from a blood clot, which does not allow enough oxygen to reach the brain.

*Implications.*   Toddlers and preschool children are more prone to crisis and, hence, hospitalization than are older children. Crises are precipitated by a variety of circumstances—infection, chilling, dehydration, strenuous exercise, sweating, cold (especially cold, damp weather). Use this knowledge to take preventive measures. This child needs a high-protein, high-vitamin, adequate iron diet. You can plan snacks and lunches to meet that need. He also needs to drink a great deal of fluids, especially water and juice. The forced intake of liquids means the child frequently urinates. Encourage the child to drink more by having fluids readily available. Make sure the child has easy access to the bathroom.

Fatigue is a major factor, as this child tires easily and a general lassitude is always present. Be aware of the balance of active and quiet activities in the classroom. Be sure to alternate these activities and to have available alternatives to those activities that are physically demanding. Stress cooperation, not competition. This is likely to be a small, fragile-looking child who needs help building a good self-concept.

## CHILDREN'S NEEDS— TEACHING GOALS

Related annual goals may be grouped under broad categories called "teaching goals." Outlined under each teaching goal below are the most important needs of chronic health needs children. A child may have some or all of these needs, and additional needs as well. Suggestions on what you might consequently teach them are included. Often, a course of action is implicit in the description of the need.

### Feelings

Chronically ill children may develop phobias; they may be fearful and anxious, always awaiting the next crisis situation, the next painful experience. They cannot even enjoy their periods of health because of the fear of doing something that will bring on a bad period. These children may suffer from loneliness, boredom, and depression.

Also, many of these children have shortened life expectancies, so the fear of death and dying is a major issue that may often be on their minds as well as on their parents'. (This seems to be true whether or not they have been told they have years ahead of them.) Teachers can help children become more aware of their feelings, help them learn to express them, and give them the skills to work through them.

### Language skills

Many of these children lack experience and hence a good inner language base. Especially in the case of terminal illness, parents are frequently overprotective both because of the disease itself and because most diseases weaken the child and bring increased susceptibility to contagious diseases. In addition to expanding their overall language base, these children need to develop the vocabulary to express their fears and concerns. They need to be aware of their symptoms and how to label them, know the body parts, and be able to put the two together to give more accurate information about their current state of health.

### Awareness

These children need to become aware of their own uniqueness. Because they look normal, other children and adults may not understand or remember their problems. Because they have periods when they are fine and periods when they are not, others wonder if it is just a game they are playing. These children may be misunderstood at school. Often they cannot participate in some of the more strenuous activities. Because of frequent absences it is difficult for them to build relationships with other children and to complete projects. Especially if the child is experiencing pain or some side effects from drugs, the child may not be fun to be with. Teachers have to remind the other children of these circumstances. Emphasize quality, not quantity, and decrease the emphasis on speed. It's not how fast something is done that counts, but how well.

### Guidelines

1. Use activities that allow the children to be in control or adapt activities so that children have more control. For example, let the children decide what color paint to add to the shaving cream finger paint—and how much. Putting the paint in a large salt shaker allows children to shake out just the amount they want.
2. Encourage independence and allow the children to do as much as possible for themselves. Because it is very easy for these children to become dependent on adults, you must encourage age-appropriate independence.
3. Arrange the class schedule so that vigorous activities are followed by less strenuous ones, and, when necessary during strenuous activities, provide rest periods that are built in, not obvious.
4. Be flexible in scheduling the children's day so that if they have to leave for pills, shots, or therapy, this can become part of the routine. If you accept the children's therapy and its importance, it will be easier for them. Some children find a full day tiring, especially when they return after an illness. Allow them to come for part of the day.
5. Plan activities that are open-ended and do not require excessive amounts of time to complete, or plan ones that can be completed at home if necessary. Since these children often work more slowly and miss more school than others, they easily decide not to start things they may never complete. If, for example, the class is doing wire sculpture, put the child's sculpture in a bag labeled *Sam's Wire Sculpture*. Ask the parents to put it in a place at home where the child can get it when ready. This will help him feel that he is still part of the group.
6. Learn about these children by being a good observer. Watch for mood changes, as these are often cues to well-being. Be aware of the children's body language. Often these children will grimace or give other signs that will alert you to possible pain. Young children have trouble recognizing and verbalizing their needs; you can help them.
7. Find out as much as you can about the illnesses children in your class have and how it affects them. Read books on the subject and talk to the parents, therapists, and doctors. Be informed about the children's diet, physical restrictions, medication, possible side effects of the medicine, and the behaviors that indicate when the chronic illness is turning acute. You also need to know what children have been told about their illness and its implications. Since the other children in your class may repeat things, you need to be prepared to respond to comments, such as: "I don't want to play with you. You have leukemia. You're going to die." You need to know how the parents are dealing with the concept of death and exactly what they call the illness. Even with that knowledge, handling the situation is not easy. Children at the preschool age are not capable of abstract thinking. Death to them is like going to sleep, and it is reversible. This doesn't mean, however, that they are any less fearful of it. While the child's classmates may seem unfeeling, they are only displaying curiosity and lack of knowledge.
8. Help children learn about the implications of their health problems. Verbalize for them what happens under certain circumstances: "You are allergic to peanuts. If you eat them, it will be hard for you to breathe. There are other things

that are crunchy like peanuts that you can eat. These are sunflower seeds. I like them. Do you?" (Obviously, be sure a child is not allergic to the substitute.)

9. Provide an open atmosphere where children can discuss fears and problems freely. One thing that children know even at this age is that if it is "taboo" it is bad. Be honest when you do not know an answer; say you don't know and then find out the answer. In general, don't tell children more than they ask. They are the best guide about what they need to know.

10. Develop a plan for keeping in touch with absent children. You could send get-well cards through the mail. Another child could deliver an audio tape. The child could be called on the phone by other children. (Find out good times to call or let the child phone school.) Send home a "fun bag" or develop a lending library of books and toys. The best plan is one that is tailored to your situation and the child's needs.

11. Certain illnesses require certain privileges such as free access to the toilet, extra time for task completion, special food for snack, scheduling time to take medication, and so on.

12. Classroom stress can bring on crises in some chronic illnesses (asthma, diabetes), so play down competitive games and deadlines. Make the classroom as pressure-free as possible.

13. Special events (Christmas, birthdays, field trips) may lead to flare-ups, as there is almost always some psychosomatic element in the timing or severity of acute bouts. Prepare children for events. Talk about what is likely to happen. This is a time to watch for stress-related reactions.

14. Learn to recognize warning signs that may signal an emergency. Discuss with parents what they want you to do in case of an emergency. If you are to call, call when you suspect something is wrong—do not wait for full confirmation. Tape the numbers near the phone you will use. Know the location of the nearest emergency room and the fastest way to get there. Take a first aid course. Be sure it includes the Heimlich hug and cardiopulmonary resuscitation.

Because a child with chronic health needs spends a lot of time at home, it is important to develop a system for keeping in touch with the child. One way is to provide the same kinds of toys at home and at school.

## CURRICULUM ADAPTATIONS

Children with chronic health problems require few curriculum adaptions as long as they are allowed to work at their own pace. While working in each curriculum area emphasize helping children feel part of the group and improving their self-concept. In addition, develop a means of communication and support to bridge long absences.

### Expressing Language, Listening, and Reading Readiness

Language arts is important to these children because they need to learn a vocabulary to communicate.

1. Use field trips to the grocery store, farm, post office, and so on, to help the child gain the firsthand experiences that are often lacking in children with chronic health needs.

2. When the child is home for extended periods of time, exchange language experience stories. Have the mother and child write a story about "Going to the Hospital" or "Things I Can See Out My Window."

3. Send a "Get Well Soon" audio tape to the child. Have children who want to share send a message to this child on the tape. If you set this up as an activity area, you might put a picture of the child beside the tape and encourage the children to talk to the absent child. The child who is ill may wish to send an answer tape back.

Readiness skills are extremely important to the child with chronic health needs. Because the disability may not permit the child to have all the experiences other children do, the child may depend far more on reading to learn about the world. Reading can help a child pass many a lonely hour. If strong reading skills are developed early, absences in later years will have a less profound effect on the child's education. Teach parents how to help the child develop readiness skills in order to keep up with the class even during long absences.

1. If the child is likely to be hospitalized, make a listening tape of hospital sounds. This will make a strange place a bit more familiar. If the child has to stay in bed, do a listening tape of things one might hear from bed.
2. Have the child help draw and fill in a map of the route from his room to the playroom in the hospital. Include other significant places in the map.
3. Have children match line-drawing faces showing different expressions. Then talk about what these people might be feeling or doing.

4. Play hospital or medical lotto.

Stories are a great way to make the unknown a little more familiar, to help children know they are not the only ones with fears, and perhaps to help them put themselves and their situation into perspective. Choose stories that relate to the specific situation the children you are dealing with might face. (See the children's bibliography at the end of this chapter for appropriate titles.)

1. Read stories about children in hospitals.
2. Read stories about children or animals who are different.

Fingerplays can be used to teach concepts and are especially good for those who are in bed frequently. Fingerplays are active, yet not tiring. Parents can easily learn them and thus form another link with school.

1. Use fingerplays that are repetitive, so children only have to learn minor changes in order to participate: "Where is Thumbkin?"

2. Use fingerplays to increase body awareness: "I put my finger on my face."
3. Use fingerplays to teach concepts: "A Little Ball."

## Science/Discovery

Since most of these children take medicine to alleviate symptoms, it is important to develop their cause-and-effect reasoning skills. They need to understand why they should take the medicine even when they feel well.

1. Plant seeds. Discuss conditions for growth. Put some plants in the dark. Do not water some. Discuss the implications of the various conditions and "treatments."
2. Use experiments that require children to make predictions. Help children apply this skill to their particular situation. (I have trouble breathing when I run fast. If I run slower, I can run farther.)

## Mathematics

It is especially important for children who have had some physical limitations to start with a sensorimotor concept of mathematics. This involves active interaction with materials like blocks, cuisenaire rods, and pegs. Then move on to more abstract number concepts.

1. Use three-dimensional objects like unit blocks to teach basic math concepts; don't rely on rote memory.
2. Use music and rhythmic activities to reinforce math concepts (clap four times).
3. Make math relevant. Children need to know how many pills they must take, and when. This is a step toward independence as well as toward learning number concepts.

## Social Studies

Because chronically ill children spend most of their life in the community, not the hospital, it is important that they have some knowledge about the community. Children need to know and role play not only the traditional occupations but also the variations.

1. Nurses—public health nurses who visit in homes.
2. Teachers—itinerant teachers who visit children who cannot attend school.
3. Social workers or others who may serve as a support system to the family.
4. Emphasize ways of approaching others. Have the children practice introducing themselves to others.

## Health and Safety

Another major emphasis in programming for children with chronic health needs is health and safety. Children particularly need to learn about foods, those that are good for them and those they must avoid.

1. Work on the food groups, on what is in each and how they are related.
2. Help all the children enjoy the foods that are allowed. Sharing is part of the fun of food.
3. Explain, using illustrations, what happens when people eat food they are allergic to.
4. Because these children should be protected from contagious diseases, it is important that all children cover their mouths when coughing and sneezing, wash hands after toileting, and follow all forms of good hygiene.
5. Emphasize body awareness. The child needs to be able to name body parts. If the children are older or gifted, you might include some of the internal body parts. Start with those they can feel (bones) and commonly known ones (stomach).

## Art

Art is both a means of creative expression and a tension reliever. If children do not have the energy to participate in large motor activities or cannot do so for other reasons, art may be their only channel for releasing tension.

1. Concentrate on the process. If you can convince children to use arms and fingers they might not otherwise use, you are succeeding. It really does not matter what the result is.
2. Use many three-dimensional art materials. Again, the goal is manipulation, not a final product.
3. Use art materials that do not require good fine motor skills. Coloring within the lines may promote good eye-hand coordination, but it doesn't serve to release tension.

## Music

Music alone and in combination with movement or small motor play is a great tool for learning as well as a release for feelings.

1. Have children toss balloons into the air and hum or sing one note until the balloon touches the floor.
2. Do movement exploration activities, especially those that emphasize relaxation skills: "Move like a rag doll." "Move like a flag blowing in the breeze."

3. Teach some colors and numbers with songs: "Who Has Red On," "Ten Little Children."
4. Use songs that call children by name.

## Dramatic Play

Dramatic play, given appropriate props, allows children to act out fears and gives them control over frightening situations. Set up situations chronically ill children may encounter.

1. Emergency room: Discuss and play scenes that might be going on in an emergency room, emphasizing the sense of urgency.
2. Doctor's office/clinic: Talk about routine visits and visits when children are sick.
3. Surgery: Discuss operations. Allow the children to operate on dolls to "fix" them. Make finger casts so that children can learn that this is not a painful process.
4. Hospital: Set up a hospital. Talk about being scared, about strange hospital sounds, about being left alone.
5. Encourage children to build a hospital, using blocks in conjunction with the dramatic play area.

## Small Motor Play

Small motor play is not physically taxing and can therefore be a potential strength. Many activities that fall into this category use materials that can be placed in jellyroll pans (cookie sheets with four raised sides). These can serve as storage trays and can also be used in a wheelchair, on the floor, or in bed.

1. Choose toys that are washable. If one child has a contagious disease, it may be passed to others if the toys cannot be disinfected.
2. Use a variety of fine motor toys. Children need much practice in this area and, without sufficient variety, they may become bored before they acquire the necessary skills.

## Large Motor Play

Children with chronic health needs typically have problems with large motor play. Try to keep these activities noncompetitive and pressure-free.

1. Emphasize the quality of movement, not speed.
2. Use exercises, especially those done to music. Select a body part (or combination) and have the children move it back and forth at a slow tempo.
3. Modifications may need to be made to some games. Reduce the distance to be traveled. Slow

the pace by having children walk, not run. Institute intermissions. (All children must clap ten times between events.)

4. Have children jump on a trampoline (or mattress with dust cover). This improves drainage of the respiratory tract.

## Transitions

Many disabilities cause children to move more slowly than other children. Remind them early about cleanup time. Dismiss them early, among the first few, from the group.

1. Transitions may be a good time to have children take necessary medication. Other children are less likely to notice because there is a lot going on at this time.
2. This is a good time to emphasize similarities—all children with brown hair and blue eyes, all children with plaid shirts, all children with buckle shoes.

## CHILD STUDY TEAM REPORT

### *Christi J.*

In attendance: Mrs. J.; Ms. T., public health nurse; Ms. S., preschool teacher.

Christi J. is a four-year five-month-old girl entering preschool for the first time. Christi has cystic fibrosis. Her condition has prevented any previous preschool experience. Her mother is anxious to have Christi begin, since she has been in fair health for about six months. The public health nurse, who has been involved with Christi since she was two years old, and Christi's mother arranged a meeting with the preschool staff in order to inform them about Christi's condition.

Christi's cystic fibrosis was diagnosed at twenty-two months. She had suffered repeated lung infections and digestive problems as an infant. Christi lives at home with her mother and ten-year-old sister. Christi's parents have been divorced for two years. Mrs. J. receives public assistance and help with medical expenses from the state public health department and the local chapter of the Cystic Fibrosis Foundation.

Christi's doctor, the nurse, and Mrs. J. all feel Christi is a very bright girl who would benefit from the opportunities for growth provided by a preschool program. The nurse explained that although Christi is slightly smaller in stature than other children her age and has slightly enlarged fingertips and slightly discolored teeth (from medications), she will not appear any different from other children her age. However, Christi will cough frequently in order to expell mucus. She will also need to take some of her medication during school hours, along with a large snack. The nurse explained that CF is a disease affecting the lungs and digestion. The thick, sticky mucus that clogs bronchial tubes, making it difficult for Christi to breathe, also plugs ducts of the pancreas, interfering with the flow of digestive enzymes.

Mrs. J. said that Christi's treatment involves chest therapy in the morning and evening to loosen mucus. Christi may also use aerosol mist medication, depending on her condition. Salt tablets may be needed during hot weather. She added that although Christi may tire more easily than her peers, physical activity within limits facilitates breaking up mucus in the chest.

The nurse stated that the medication does not affect Christi's attitudes or behavior. Mrs. J. added that Christi avoids taking pills at times. She tries to hide them in a napkin or under her plate and then volunteers to clear the table. She also dislikes attention drawn to her coughing, pill-taking, and need for rest during strenuous activity. It was suggested that some discreet ways be developed to signal Christi when she should slow down or rest.

Mrs. J. feels that Christi would benefit from talking more about her feelings. When her condition improves, Christi tends to think that she is "all better," refuses to take her pills, and overexerts herself. The nurse offered to talk to the class about general health topics in order to help Christi become comfortable talking about her own illness. In addition, some play situations with a medical theme would be helpful for Christi.

Mrs. J. said that she tends to lead a day-to-day existence and that with the time involved in doing chest therapy, cleaning the equipment, paying for the pills, and so on, she really has not talked with Christi about the implications of CF for her future. She agrees that is important, but it is difficult for her to deal with.

# INDIVIDUALIZED EDUCATION PROGRAM

NAME _____ Christi J. _____ DOB 8 / 12 / 78

AGE _____ 4-5 _____ GRADE _____ Preschool

SCHOOL _____ Center City Preschool

PARENTS/GUARDIANS _____ Mrs. J.

ADDRESS _____ 15-C Newport Pike

PHONE _____ 239-0711

On 1/15/83 , the IPRD Committee
         (Date)
met to review all current data and

recommends Level _____ I _____ placement.

Date of new review _____ 7/15/83

Exceptionality: _____ Cystic fibrosis

Present at meeting:

Parents _____ Mrs. J.

Others: Name/Position _____ Ms. T., Public Health Nurse

## CURRENT TEST DATA

TEST/DATE/RESULTS

Medical _____ / _____ / _____ /

reports _____ / _____ / _____ /

_____ / _____ / _____ /

Recommended Special Services (Hrs/Wk):

_____ Medical support as needed _____ / _____ / _____ /

Total Hours/Week:

Special Education Classroom _____ 0

Regular Classroom _____ 12½

Representative of District/Agency _____ Ms. S., Preschool Teacher

The committee has determined the following learning strengths and needs to be reflected in the IEP:

| STRENGTHS | NEEDS |
| --- | --- |
| Average (or above) abilities | Cooperation with adults |
| Treatment has been effective | Expressing feelings |
|  | Awareness of medical needs |

STUDENT    Christi J.       DATE    1/15/83

GOAL    To cooperate with adults

PARENT SIGNATURE      TEACHER SIGNATURE

| INSTRUCTIONAL OBJECTIVES | EDUCATIONAL METHODS | DATE Begin | DATE End | Eval. | PERSONS RESPONSIBLE Name | Position |
|---|---|---|---|---|---|---|
| Christi will expressively identify implications of her illness including 3/4 of the following: need to take medication, physical limitations, diet, chest therapy, in a discussion with an adult of her choice. | My Puzzle, Dramatic play, 1-1 teacher/child interactions, Visiting nurse, Medical play, Stories/books, Interviews | 1/15 | 4/15 | | Ms. S. | Teacher |
| Christi will take her medication as needed at school 4/5 times<br>a. with teacher direction<br>b. independently | Graph taking medication | 1/5<br>4/15 | 4/15<br>7/15 | | Ms. S. | Teacher |
| Christi will expressively identify her symptoms of overexertion in a discussion with an adult of her choice | same as first objective above, Symptoms, Doctor's Office | 1/15 | 4/15 | | Ms. S. | Teacher |
| Christi will independently choose an alternative activity 3/5 times as needed<br>a. with adult intervention<br>b. independently | Graph choosing activity as needed | 1/15<br>5/15 | 5/15<br>7/15 | | Ms. S. | Teacher |

STUDENT _____ Christi J. _____  DATE _____ 1/15/83

GOAL _____ To increase awareness of roles people play _____

PARENT SIGNATURE _____

TEACHER SIGNATURE _____

| INSTRUCTIONAL OBJECTIVES | EDUCATIONAL METHODS | DATE Begin | DATE End | Eval. | PERSONS RESPONSIBLE Name | PERSONS RESPONSIBLE Position |
|---|---|---|---|---|---|---|
| Christi will expressively identify 6/8 of the following medical tools and their function on 2 occasions: doctor's bag, pill vial, stethoscope, reflex mallet, tongue depressor, cotton ball, swab, hypodermic needles | Medical tools, Stick Puppets, Dramatic play, Eye Doctor, Emergency Room, Audiologist, Patient in the Hospital, Stick Puppets | 1/15 | 7/15 | | Ms. S. | Teacher |
| Christi will role play appropriately with these tools on at least 3 occasions. | Patient in the Hospital, Emergency Room, Doctor's Office | 1/15 | 7/15 | | Ms. S | Teacher |
| Christi will be able to describe to the adult of her choice procedures likely to occur during an upcoming doctor visit, on 3 separate occasions. | Cast It, Doctor's Office, Emergency Room, Dramatic play with medical equipment | 1/15 | 7/15 | | Ms. S. | Teacher |

STUDENT  Christi J.                     DATE  1/15/83

GOAL  To express feelings

PARENT SIGNATURE _____   TEACHER SIGNATURE _____

| INSTRUCTIONAL OBJECTIVES | EDUCATIONAL METHODS | DATE Begin | DATE End | Eval. | PERSONS RESPONSIBLE Name | Position |
|---|---|---|---|---|---|---|
| Given a visual stimulus (face), Christi will expressively identify 5/6 of the following feelings: sad, angry, happy, excited, scared, frustrated, lonely, on 3 occasions. | Expressions, Matching Faces | 1/15 | 7/15 | | Ms. S. | Teacher |
| Given a story, Christi will identify the proper emotion (from above) the main character may be feeling on 5 occasions | Same as above, Stories | 1/15 | 7/15 | | Ms. S. | Teacher |
| Given the above, Christi will expressively identify the reason(s) the main character may feel that way on 5 occasions. | Same as above | 3/15 | 7/15 | | Ms. S. | Teacher |
| Christi will identify expressively at least 1 situation in which she feels sad, angry, happy, excited, scared, frustrated, lonely, on 2 occasions. | My Books, Painting a Feeling, Best and Worst, Share Your Feelings | 3/15 | 7/15 | | Ms. S. | Teacher |

# GLOSSARY

**Acquired**   A condition that is not genetic, rather the result of some external trauma or influence after birth.

**Allergen**   Any substance that brings on an allergic reaction. What one is allergic to.

**Anesthesiologist**   A physician specializing in drugs or gases that cause partial or complete loss of sensation or consciousness.

**Arthogryposis**   Children with this condition are born with stiff joints and weak muscles. The hips, knees, elbows, and wrists are the most commonly affected. The trunk is usually not affected.

**Aura**   A sensation that often precedes an epileptic attack. The nature of the sensation varies with each person.

**Benign**   A growth that is nonmalignant and nonrecurring.

**Cardiologist**   A physician specilizing in heart disease.

**Cerebrospinal fluid** (CSF)   The fluid that surrounds the brain and spinal cord. (A spinal tap is used to test this fluid.)

**Chronic health problems**   According to PL 94–142: Health impaired means having limited strength, vitality, or alertness due to chronic or acute health problems, such as a heart condition, epilepsy, tuberculosis, rheumatic fever, asthma, nephritis, sickle-cell anemia, hemophilia, lead poisoning, leukemia, or diabetes, which adversely affect a child's educational performance.

**Congenital**   A condition that is present at birth.

**Enzyme**   A substance that accelerates or helps the breakdown of certain chemicals. When enzymes are not present in the body, they must be supplied. (This would be done orally in the case of cystic fibrosis.)

**Geneticist**   A physician specializing in the study of genes.

**Genetic counselor**   A specialist in genes who talks with parents and others concerned about the likelihood of their offspring being born normal or with genetic defects.

**Glucagon**   A hormone that increases blood sugar.

**Hematologist**   A specialist in the study of blood and blood-forming tissue.

**Hereditary**   A condition that is genetically transmitted from a parent or parents to the child.

**Lead poisoning**   Poisoning that results from eating lead or products containing lead, especially lead-based paints used to coat plaster, window sills, or toys. Abdominal cramps are the most common result. In chronic cases it eventually causes impairment of the nervous system.

**Malignancy**   A tumor that grows or spreads into other parts of the body; cancer. It can reoccur.

**Nephritis**   An inflamation of the kidneys that can be either acute or chronic.

**Orthopedist**   A physician specializing in the skeletal structure, especially the joints and muscles.

**Otorhinolaryngologist**   A physician specializing in the ear, nose, and throat.

**Pancreas**   A gland that lies behind the stomach. It produces digestive enzymes and insulin.

**Periodontist**   A physician specializing in gums. (Children on some seizure-prevention medicine have periodontal problems.

**Platelet**   A round disk found in the blood. Platelets help the blood coagulate by adhering to each other and forming a plug when an injury occurs.

**Radiologist**   A physician specializing in the use of radiation for diagnostic and treatment procedures.

**Systemic**   A condition affecting the whole body.

**Transplantation**   The transfer of an organ or tissue from one person to another, or from one place within a person's body to another place.

**Thrombosis**   A blood clot that prevents oxygen from getting to vital body organs.

# TEACHING    RESOURCES

In some situations you may want or need additional information. There are many national as well as regional, state, and local organizations that can be helpful to you. The following annotated list of national organizations should be useful in helping you decide where to get the information you need.

Allergy Foundation of America
801 Second Avenue
New York, NY 10017
    Has national and regional programs to educate the public through printed literature. Gives lists of qualified, practicing allergists in any part of the country.

The Arthritis Foundation
1212 Avenue of the Americas
New York, NY 10036
    Offers grants to medical schools and hospitals to help support Clinical Research Centers. The local affiliates provide the complete spectrum of total care including diagnosis, treatment, orthopedic surgery, and rehabilitation services.

American Cancer Society
219 East 42nd Street
New York, NY 10017

National Headquarters refers to its affiliates and prints literature. It does not operate medical or laboratory facilities, treat cancer patients, or pay physician's fees.

Leukemia Society of America, Inc.
211 East 43rd Street
New York, NY 10017

National headquarters conducts the research support program and public and professional education programs; it also makes referrals to local chapters, which provide many medical services.

Association of State Maternal and Child Health and Crippled Children's Directors
Division of Maternal and Child Health
301 Centennial Mall S.
P.O. Box 95007
Lincoln, NE 68502

Active in efforts to define health needs of mothers and children, including crippled children. Conducts studies; makes recommendations to U.S. Public Health Service, the Child's Bureau, and Congress.

Children in Hospitals
31 Wilshire Park
Needham, MA 02192

Parents, educators, and health professionals who seek to minimize the trauma involved in a child's hospitalization by supporting and educating parents and medical personnel regarding the needs of children while hospitalized.

Cooley's Anemia Blood and Research Foundation for Children, Inc.
3366 Hillside Avenue
New York, NY 11040

Maintains and distributes a blood credit; promotes means of obtaining funds for the blood credit program and research programs; and publicizes the nature of the disease and the needs of these children.

National Cystic Fibrosis Research Foundation
3379 Peachtree Road, N.E.
Atlanta, GA 30326

National headquarters: coordinates and funds Foundation programs for research, education, and care. Refers inquiries to their local chapters and Cystic Fibrosis Centers.

American Dental Association
211 East Chicago Avenue
Chicago, IL 60611

A professional service organization with informational and referral services for the public.

American Diabetes Association
18 East 48th Street
New York, NY 10017

National headquarters is concerned with maintaining and expanding its five basic programs in patient education, professional education, public education, detection, and research. It will make referrals to affiliates and answer questions.

Juvenile Diabetes Foundation
23 East 26th Street
New York, NY 10010

This foundation funds research, provides counseling and support services, educates the public.

Epilepsy Foundation of America
1828 "L" Street, N.W.
Suite 406
Washington, DC 20036

This foundation conducts programs in research, employment, public information, and patient services.

American Heart Association
44 East 23rd Street
New York, NY 10010

The national office does not operate a direct patient service or referral program; however, inquiries and requests are forwarded to the appropriate affiliation which aids in maintaining or developing heart centers and clinics.

The National Hemophilia Foundation
25 West 39th Street
New York, NY 10018

This foundation stimulates and assists chapters in development of social service programs in the community. It makes referrals to treatment centers and provides publications.

National Tay-Sachs and Allied Disease Association, Inc.
200 Park Avenue South
New York, NY 10003

This association makes referrals to clinics for diagnosis and carrier and prenatal detection throughout the U.S. It provides information about social services and nursing care.

National Tuberculosis and Respiratory Disease Association
1740 Broadway
New York, NY 10019

This association makes referrals to affiliates and makes available literature and films.

National Kidney Foundation
116 East 27th Street
New York, NY 10010
> This association gives referrals to affiliates; it also distributes public and professional educational materials.

Muscular Dystrophy Association of America, Inc.
1790 Broadway
New York, NY 10019
> National headquarter services include direct payments for all authorized services for patients who don't live in areas with local chapters; edu-

cation of the public, publishing of literature and films, and sponsoring of national research conferences.

The Foundation for Research and Education in Sickle-Cell Disease
421–431 West 120th Street
New York, NY 10027
> Professional group concerned with making the public aware of sickle-cell disease. It assists in establishing special treatment clinics in the New York area, but accepts requests for referrals throughout the U.S.

# BIBLIOGRAPHY

Collipp, Platon J., ed. *Childhood Obesity*. 2nd ed. Littleton, Mass.: PSG Publishing Co. 1980.

Cooper, Irving S. *Living with Chronic Neurologic Disease: A Handbook for Patient and Family*. New York: W.W. Norton, 1976.

Debuskey, Matthew. *The Chronically Ill Child and His Family*. Springfield, Ill.: Charles C. Thomas, 1970.

Klinzing, Dennis R., and Dene G. Klinzing. *The Hospitalized Child: Communication Techniques for Health Personnel*. Englewood Cliffs, N.J.: Prentice-Hall, 1977.

Pless, Ivan B. and Philip Pinkerton. *Chronic Childhood Disorder. Promoting Patterns of Adjustment*. Chicago: Year Book Medical Publishers, 1975.

Reinisch, Edith H., and Ralph E. Minear, Jr. *Health of the Preschool Child*. New York: Wiley, 1978.

Strauss, Anselm L. *Chronic Illness and the Quality of Life*. St. Louis, Mo.: C.V. Mosby Co, 1975.

Sultz, Harry, et al. *Long-Term Childhood Illness*. Pittsburgh, Pa.: Univ. of Pittsburgh Press, 1972.

Travis, Georgia. *Chronic Illness in Children: Its Impact on Child and Family*. Palo Alto, Calif.: Stanford Univ. Press, 1976.

Voignier, Ruth, and Sharon C. Bridgewater. "Allergies in Young Children." *Young Children*, 35, No. 4 (1980).

Weiner, Florence. *Help for the Handicapped Child*. New York: McGraw-Hill, 1973.

*Biography/Autobiography/Fiction*

Baruch, Dorothy W. *One Little Boy*. Medical Collaboration by Hyman Miller. New York: Julian Press, 1952.

> An account of the emotional life of an asthmatic eight-year-old, written by his psychologist. As Kenneth works out his problems, his asthma all but disappears.

Gunther, John. *Death Be Not Proud: A Memoir*. New York: Harper and Row, 1949.

> The struggles and triumphs of Johnny Gunther, who died of a brain tumor at age seventeen.

Lund, Doris. *Eric*. Philadelphia: Lippincott, 1974.

> A moving account of a young man's struggle to live a fulfilling life despite the diagnosis of leukemia, written by Eric's mother after his death.

Massie, Robert K., and Suzanne Massie. *Journey*. New York: Knopf, 1975.

> The Massie family's struggle to deal with the hemophilia of Robert Massie, Jr. *Journey* dispels commonly held myths about hemophilia.

# BIBLIOGRAPHY FOR CHILDREN

*Awareness*

Corbin, William C. *The Day Willie Wasn't*. New York: Coward, McCann and Geoghegan, 1971.

> A light-hearted look at the problem of juvenile obesity. After Willie's weight is made fun of, he goes on a starvation diet until he can't be seen anymore.

Silverstein, Alvin and Virginia B. Silverstein. *Itch, Sniffle & Sneeze: All About Asthma, Hay Fever and Other Allergies*. New York: Four Winds Press, 1978.

> A serious and informative discussion about allergies and their causes.

*The Body and How It Works*

Maguire, Leslie. *You: How Your Body Works*. New York: Platt and Munk, 1974.

> Working from the outside in, it illustrates sneezing, jumping, climbing, and more, then explores the internal hows, whys, and whats. There is also a lesson on how to take care of your body.

Showers, Paul. *Hear Your Heart*. New York: Thomas Y. Crowell, 1976.

In simple yet precise language, the structure of the heart and what it does are discussed. It contains light-hearted yet scientifically accurate pictures.

*Being Sick*

Ardizzone, Edward. *Diana and Her Rhinoceros*. New York: Oxford Univ. Press, 1979.

Diana nurses a sick rhinoceros that has escaped from the zoo and then fights off armed men who come to take it back.

Brandenberg, Franz. *I Wish I Was Sick, Too!* New York: Greenwillow Books, 1976.

When Edward gets sick and the family waits on him, Elizabeth wants to be waited on too. When she does get sick, she realizes that it is more fun being well.

Lobel, Arnold. *Frog and Toad Are Friends*. New York: Harper and Row, 1970.

Toad and Frog take care of each other.

MacLachlan, Patricia. *The Sick Day*. New York: Pantheon, 1979.

Emily and her father trade roles as they take turns getting sick and caring for each other.

Wiseman Bernard. *Morris Has a Cold*. New York: Dodd, Mead, 1978.

A delightful story of Boris the Bear's attempts to help Morris the Moose get well. Children with colds or allergies will find this book fun to read.

*Doctors, Hospitals*

Althea. *Going into Hospital*. Cambridge, England: Dinosaurs Publ., 1974.

An excellent book for three- to five-year-olds who will be facing hospitalization. It deals with discomforts but stresses that the children manage the situation well.

Bemelmans, Ludwig. *Madeline: Story and Pictures*. New York: Puffin Books 1977.

Madeline, the smallest girl in boarding school, braves an appendectomy.

Charlip, Remy, and Burton Supree. *Mother, Mother, I Feel Sick, Send for the Doctor, Quick, Quick, Quick: A Picture Book and Shadow Play*. New York: Four Winds Press, 1980.

The doctor finds all kinds of unexpected things in a child's stomach, from spaghetti (plate and all) to a two-wheeled bike. This story can be adapted for flannel board.

Chase, Francine. *A Visit to the Hospital*. New York: Grosset and Dunlap, 1957.

Helps overcome a child's fears of going into a hospital for a tonsillectomy or any minor operation. There is an introduction for parents.

Clark, Bettina. *Going to the Hospital*. New York: Random House, 1971.

Imaginative play will be encouraged by this activity pop-up book.

Fassler, Joan. *The Boy with a Problem*. New York: Behavioral Publications, 1971.

Johnny is deeply troubled about his problems in the hospital. He feels much better when he reveals his problems to a friend.

Froman, Robert. *Let's Find Out About the Clinic*. New York: Watts, 1968.

Describes a step-by-step visit to a clinic for a routine check up. Talks about the role of nurses and doctors.

Garn, Bernard. *A Visit to the Dentist*. New York: Grosset and Dunlap, 1959.

Helps answer questions and relieve fears a child may have.

Meeker, Alice M. *How Hospitals Help Us*. Chicago: Benefic Press, 1962.

One of the "how" series, this informative book introduces children to all aspects of the hospital. It includes real photographs of the hospital, including x-ray, the emergency room, the operating room, food service, and laundry.

Paullin, Ellen. *No More Tonsils!* Boston: Beacon Press, 1958.

Good photographs of a little girl going to the hospital to have her tonsils out.

Reit, Seymour. *Jamie Visits the Nurse*. New York: McGraw-Hill, 1969.

Jamie cuts his finger and is sent to the nurse. The photographs present a real school situation and provide a good introduction to a nurse's office.

Rey, Margaret, and Hans Rey. *Curious George Goes to the Hospital*. In collaboration with the Children's Hospital Medical Center, Boston. Boston: Houghton Mifflin, 1966.

Hospitalization results from a swallowed puzzle piece. The book includes illustrations of an x-ray machine and other aspects of a hospital.

Rockwell, Harlow. *My Doctor*. New York: Macmillan, 1973.

A doctor's office from a child's viewpoint. The doctor is a woman.

Rogers, Fred. *Mr. Rogers Talks About the New Baby, Moving, Fighting, Going to the Doctor, Going to School, Haircuts*. New York: Platt and Munk, 1974.

Addresses the fears a child may have before going to the hospital or doctor's office and introduces common procedures.

Sharmat, Marjorie Weinman. *I Want Mama.* New York: Harper and Row, 1974.

A little girl's mother goes to the hospital. Helps children realize that anyone may have to go the hospital and although the stay may seem to last forever, they will eventually return home.

Shay, Arthur. *What Happens When You Go to the Hospital?* Chicago: Reilly and Lee, 1969.

Karen cries and expresses her fears about her tonsillectomy.

Sobol, Harriet. *Jeff's Hospital Book.* New York: H.Z. Walck, 1975.

A young boy has eye surgery, a realistic portrayal of the operation.

Sonneborn, Ruth. *I Love Gram.* New York: Viking Press, 1971.

Ellie, a little black girl, is waiting impatiently for her grandmother to come home from the hospital.

Stein, Sara Bonnett. *A Hospital Story: An Open Family Book for Parents and Children.* New York: Walker and Co., 1974.

A young girl's tonsillectomy, covers many hospital procedures.

Tamburine, Jean. *I Think I Will Go to the Hospital.* Nashville: Abingdon, 1965.

Susie doesn't want to go to the hospital, but after a preadmissions visit where she practices procedures on a pet, she feels much better.

Weber, Alfons. *Elizabeth Gets Well.* New York: Crowell. 1970.

Fear and pain are acknowledged as Elizabeth prepares for her appendectomy.

Wolde, Gunilla. *Betsy and the Doctor.* New York: Random House, 1978.

Betsy's feelings before and after she goes to the doctor for the first time.

### Death and Dying

Aliki. *The Two of Them.* New York: Greenwillow Books, 1979.

One of the finest books available for children about grandparents and the aging process. Adults may find this book meaningful also.

Bartoli, Jennifer. *Norma.* Waterside Plaza, N.Y.: Harvey House, 1975.

A beloved grandparent's death portrayed from the child's viewpoint.

Bernstein, Joanne E., and Stephen Gullo. *When People Die.* New York: E.P. Dutton, 1977.

What happens when people die, why people die, and how a child responds to death (black and white photos).

Borack, Barbara. *Someone Small.* New York: Harper and Row, 1969.

A low-keyed story about a new sibling and a new pet growing together and the death of the pet.

Brown, Margaret Wise. *The Dead Bird.* New York: W. R. Scott, 1958.

Children find a dead bird and bury it in a quiet spot.

DePaola, Tomie. *Nana Upstairs and Nana Downstairs.* New York: Puffin Books, 1978.

A child's love for her grandmother and her adjustment to the grandmother's death.

Dobrin, Arnold. *Scat!* New York: Four Winds Press, 1971.

A story of a small black boy growing up in a house full of adults. When his grandfather dies the young boy serenades his grandmother with a harmonica, hoping to ease the pain. The boy describes all the sadness around him.

Fassler, Joan. *My Grandpa Died Today.* New York: Behavioral Publications, 1971.

A boy talks about his grandpa, what they did together, and his feelings about the death.

Gackenbach, Dick. *Do You Love Me?* New York: Seabury Press, 1975.

A boy accidentally kills a bird while trying to catch it.

Gauch, Patricia Lee. *Grandpa and Me.* New York: Coward, McCann and Geoghegan, 1972.

A young boy remembers his grandfather and how they loved to do things together.

Hammond, Janice M. *When Mommy Died: A Child's View of Death.* Ann Arbor, Mich.: Cranbrook, 1980.

This commendable book emphasizes the need for understanding the emotions of a child feels toward the deceased and makes suggestions for guiding the child through the experience.

Harris, Audrey. J. *Why Did He Die?* Minneapolis: Lerner Publications, 1965.

Poetry explaining the death of a grandfather.

Lamorisse, Albert. *The Red Balloon.* Garden City, New York: Doubleday, 1956.

A boy becomes attached to his balloon. The other boys tease him, throw rocks, and it breaks. (Many children see the balloon as dying.)

Little, Jean. *Home from Far.* Boston: Little, Brown, 1965.

When Jenny's twin brother is killed in an automobile accident, she must deal with the loss. Her emptiness is filled when her family takes in a foster brother and sister.

Miles, Miska. *Annie and the Old One*. Boston: Little, Brown, 1971.

Annie's grandmother tells her she will die before the rug they are making is completed. When Annie tries to stop the completion of the rug, her grandmother explains that natural events cannot be changed.

Silverstein, Shel. *The Giving Tree*. New York: Harper and Row, 1964.

A beautiful tree gives its parts to a boy. As the boy gets older he wants more from the tree. Eventually there is just a stump left and the now old man rests on it.

Smith, Doris B. *A Taste of Blackberries*. New York: Thomas Y. Crowell, 1973.

A boy's best friend dies and he feels guilty when he thinks he might have prevented it. The boy successfully works out his feelings.

Stoddard, Sandol. *Growing Time*. Boston: Houghton Mifflin, 1969.

Jamie mourns the death of her collie.

Tobias, Tobi. *Petey*. New York: Putnam, 1978.

Emily's parents help her deal with the illness and death of Petey the gerbil.

Tresselt, Alvin R. *The Dead Tree*. New York: Parents' Magazine Press, 1972.

After a tree dies and falls, animals come to live in it. In the spring a new tree grows from a fallen acorn. A good introduction for kindergarteners to the concept that everything dies eventually.

Viorst, Judith. *The Tenth Good Thing About Barney*. New York: Atheneum, 1971.

A boy mourns the death of his cat, and at the funeral he tells his friends ten good things about Barney.

Zim, Herbert S., and Sonia Blecker. *Life and Death*. New York: Morrow, 1970.

A well-written book for all ages that explains how life exists, what medical procedures help determine the cause of death, how the body is prepared for burial, and what happens at a funeral.

Zolotow, Charlotte. *My Grandson Lew*. New York: Harper and Row, 1974.

Lew and his mother find they are less lonely when they share their memories of grandfather.

*Growing and Changing*

Baum, Arline, and Joseph Baum. *On Bright Monday Morning*. New York: Random House, 1973.

A picture book tale of what a child sees on the way to school. Helps children realize that, even if all they can do is look, there is a lot that is interesting.

Krauss, Ruth. *The Growing Story*. New York: Harper and Row, 1947.

Tells how each animal, flower, and child grows and changes in its own special way.

Kuskin, Karla. *The Bear Who Saw the Spring*. New York: Harper and Row, 1961.

Illustrates the regular changes in the seasons.

McCloskey, Robert. *Time of Wonder*. New York: Viking Press, 1957.

The changing seasons.

Tresselt, Alvin R. *White Snow, Bright Snow*. New York: Lothrop, Lee and Shepherd, Co. 1947.

Seasonal change.

———. *It's Time Now!* New York: Lothrop, Lee and Shepherd, 1969.

The sights, sounds, and smells of each season as it passes over the urban scene.

Zolotow, Charlotte. *Someone New*. New York: Harper and Row, 1978.

An especially sensitive book about a child's changing and growing—a book of self-discovery.

# I N D E X

| *Annual Goals* | *Activity* | *Curriculum Area* | *Page* |
|---|---|---|---|
| **SENSORY SKILLS** | | | |
| To improve auditory identification | Sound Cues<br>Warning Sounds | Listening<br>Health and Safety | 351<br>437 |
| To improve auditory discrimination | Say It<br>Tape It<br>Where Is It? | Listening<br>Listening<br>Music | 352<br>356<br>467 |
| To improve auditory closure | Rhyming Pictures | Listening | 360 |
| To improve auditory association | Sound Cues | Listening | 351 |

| *Annual Goals* | *Activity* | *Curriculum Area* | *Page* |
|---|---|---|---|
| To improve visual identification | Alphabet Line | Reading Readiness | 367 |
| | Alphabet Lotto | Reading Readiness | 366 |
| | My Yard | Outdoor Play | 527 |
| To improve visual discrimination | Alphabet Line | Reading Readiness | 367 |
| | Alphabet Lotto | Reading Readiness | 366 |
| To improve visual memory | Changes | Reading Readiness | 372 |
| | Changing Objects | Reading Readiness | 371 |
| | Color Concentration | Reading Readiness | 372 |
| To improve visual closure | I'm Thinking Of | Social Studies | 392 |
| To improve auditory memory | Going to the Beach | Listening | 358 |
| | Say It | Listening | 352 |
| To improve visual association | Natural Sequencing | Reading Readiness | 377 |
| | Place Mat Collage | Art | 458 |
| To improve visual comprehension | Bring Me | Expressing Language | 336 |
| | Class Book | Reading Readiness | 380 |
| | Comics | Reading Readiness | 379 |
| | Peek Pictures | Expressing Language | 337 |
| To improve tactile discrimination | Food Sense | Science/Discovery | 405 |
| To improve discrimination of smells | Food Sense | Science/Discovery | 405 |
| To improve taste discrimination | Food Sense | Science/Discovery | 405 |
| | Taste Sort | Science/Discovery | 408 |
| To improve sensory integration | Body Parts | Social Studies | 386 |
| | Colored Fingernails | Art | 457 |
| | Music and Movement | Movement | 480 |
| | Tempo | Movement | 477 |

## LANGUAGE SKILLS

| | | | |
|---|---|---|---|
| To improve expressive language | Best and Worst | Expressing Language | 335 |
| | Bring Me | Expressing Language | 336 |
| | Controller | Expressing Language | 336 |
| | Dress Up and Tell | Dramatic Play | 492 |
| | Ideas | Expressing Language | 334 |
| | Interviews | Expressing Language | 339 |
| | Puppet Hands | Art | 457 |
| | Peek Pictures | Expressing Language | 337 |
| To increase vocabulary | Controller | Expressing Language | 336 |
| | Room Shapes | Mathematics | 425 |
| | Symptoms | Health and Safety | 439 |
| To follow directions | Moving Balloons | Movement | 478 |
| | Obstacle Course | Large Motor Play | 515 |
| | Tense Me | Movement | 480 |
| To improve breath control | Bird-in-a-Hole | Science/Discovery | 401 |
| | Ping-Pong Blow | Small Motor Play | 508 |
| | Pinwheel | Science/Discovery | 403 |
| | Straw Painting | Art | 450 |

| *Annual Goals* | *Activity* | *Curriculum Area* | *Page* |
|---|---|---|---|
| To increase understanding | Controller | Expressing Language | 336 |
| | Class Book | Reading Readiness | 380 |

## THINKING AND REASONING SKILLS

| | | | |
|---|---|---|---|
| To increase attention span | Changing Objects | Reading Readiness | 371 |
| | Color Concentration | Reading Readiness | 372 |
| | Red Light/Green Light | Health and Safety | 434 |
| To improve cause and effect reasoning | Balloon Badminton | Outdoor Play | 528 |
| | Bird-in-a-Hole | Science/Discovery | 401 |
| | Cornstarch Playdough | Science/Discovery | 402 |
| | Dress Up and Tell | Dramatic Play | 492 |
| | Gelatin | Science/Discovery | 400 |
| | Pinwheel | Science Discovery | 403 |
| | Planting Seeds | Science/Discovery | 398 |
| | Red Light/Green Light | Health and Safety | 434 |
| | Straw Painting | Art | 450 |
| | String Mobile | Art | 447 |
| | Temperature | Science/Discovery | 400 |
| | Warning Sounds | Health and Safety | 437 |
| | Where Is It? | Music | 467 |
| To increase logical reasoning | Bring Me | Expressing Language | 336 |
| | Measure It | Mathematics | 430 |
| To improve classification skills | Place Mat Collage | Art | 458 |
| | Room Shapes | Mathematics | 425 |
| | Taste Sort | Science/Discovery | 408 |
| To improve sequencing skills | Comics | Reading Readiness | 379 |
| | Going to the Beach | Listening | 358 |
| | Natural Sequencing | Reading Readiness | 377 |
| To improve color concepts | Colored Fingernails | Art | 457 |
| | Shape Pictures | Mathematics | 419 |
| To make predictions | Balloon Badminton | Outdoor Play | 528 |
| | Food Sense | Science/Discovery | 405 |
| | Measure It | Mathematics | 430 |
| | Pace It Off | Mathematics | 430 |
| | Pinwheel | Science/Discovery | 403 |
| | Planting Seeds | Science/Discovery | 398 |
| | Straw Painting | Art | 450 |
| | Temperature | Science/Discovery | 400 |
| To increase problem-solving skills | Gelatin | Science/Discovery | 400 |

## MATHEMATICS SKILLS

| | | | |
|---|---|---|---|
| To improve number concepts | Time Cards | Mathematics | 416 |
| To improve measurement concepts | Measure It | Mathematics | 430 |
| | Pace It Off | Mathematics | 430 |
| To improve spatial concepts | From Your House to Mine | Social Studies | 393 |
| | Pace It Off | Mathematics | 430 |

| *Annual Goals* | *Activity* | *Curriculum Area* | *Page* |
|---|---|---|---|
| To improve shape concepts | Room Shapes | Mathematics | 425 |
| | Shape Pictures | Mathematics | 419 |
| To improve time concepts | Time Cards | Mathematics | 416 |
| | Timed Race | Large Motor Play | 519 |

**SOCIAL SKILLS**

| | | | |
|---|---|---|---|
| To take turns | From Your House to Mine | Social Studies | 393 |
| To broaden concepts of families | Photograph Story | Social Studies | 389 |
| To increase survival skills | Emergency Room | Dramatic Play | 487 |
| | Red Light/Green Light | Health and Safety | 434 |
| | Symptoms | Health and Safety | 439 |
| | Warning Sounds | Health and Safety | 437 |
| To improve self-help skills | Lock Box | Small Motor Play | 502 |
| To increase awareness of roles people play | Audiologist | Dramatic Play | 489 |
| | Cast It | Dramatic Play | 486 |
| | Circus | Dramatic Play | 486 |
| | Connections | Dramatic Play | 488 |
| | Doctor's Office | Dramatic Play | 485 |
| | Emergency Room | Dramatic Play | 487 |
| | Eye Doctor | Dramatic Play | 490 |
| | Patient in the Hospital | Social Studies | 388 |
| | Photograph Story | Social Studies | 389 |
| | Stick Puppets | Art | 459 |
| | Visitor | Social Studies | 388 |
| To cooperate with peers | Audiologist | Dramatic Play | 489 |
| | Changes | Reading Readiness | 372 |
| | Color Concentration | Reading Readiness | 372 |
| | Eye Doctor | Dramatic Play | 490 |
| | From Your House to Mine | Social Studies | 393 |
| | Hug Tag | Outdoor Play | 531 |
| | Peek Pictures | Expressing Language | 337 |
| | Share Your Feelings | Social Studies | 392 |
| To cooperate with adults | Interviews | Expressing Language | 339 |
| | Visitor | Social Studies | 388 |

**MOTOR SKILLS**

| | | | |
|---|---|---|---|
| To improve large motor coordination | Obstacle Course | Large Motor Play | 515 |
| | Variations on Bouncing | Outdoor Play | 524 |
| | Variations on Jumping | Large Motor Play | 513 |
| To improve small motor coordination | Lock Box | Small Motor Play | 502 |
| | My Puzzle | Small Motor Play | 503 |
| | Puppet Hands | Art | 457 |
| To improve eye-hand coordination | Alphabet Line | Reading Readiness | 367 |
| | Balloon Badminton | Outdoor Play | 528 |

## CREATIVITY

## FEELINGS

## AWARENESS

| *Annual Goals* | *Activity* | *Curriculum Area* | *Page* |
|---|---|---|---|
| | Colored Fingernails | Art | 457 |
| | Flopsy | Movement | 480 |
| | Foot Painting | Art | 450 |
| | My Song | Music | 469 |
| | Moving Balloons | Movement | 478 |
| | My Puzzle | Small Motor Play | 503 |
| | Place Mat Collage | Art | 438 |
| | Ping-Pong Blow | Small Motor Play | 508 |
| | Puppet Hands | Art | 457 |
| | Rag Doll | Movement | 476 |
| | Relaxation Stories | Movement | 476 |
| | Slings | Dramatic Play | 494 |
| | Symptoms | Health and Safety | 439 |
| | Tempo | Movement | 477 |
| | Tense Me | Movement | 480 |
| | Timed Race | Large Motor Play | 519 |
| | Variations on Balancing | Large Motor Play | 518 |
| | Variations on Jumping | Large Motor Play | 513 |
| To improve self-concept | Interviews | Expressing Language | 339 |
| | My Puzzle | Small Motor Play | 503 |
| | Tape It | Listening | 356 |
| To increase awareness of individual differences | I'm Thinking Of | Social Studies | 392 |
| To increase knowledge of foods | Taste Sort | Science/Discovery | 408 |
| To increase awareness of health needs | Get Well Cards | Awareness | 544 |
| | Medical Tools | Awareness | 544 |
| | Not to Eat | Awareness | 545 |
| | Special Dolls | Awareness | 537 |
| | Tired | Awareness | 545 |

# Needs: Adjustment

"I wonder about Julie. She used to be such a happy, outgoing little girl, and now it seems like she'd rather sit in her locker than do anything else. Even the other children notice it. They ask me what's wrong with Julie. I'm probably overreacting; after all, what could be wrong with a four-year-old?"

That's a good question. What could be bothering a four-year-old? As you contemplate your own problems and worries, the things that might bother a four-year-old seem so inconsequential that you often decide the child's concerns are not worth worrying about. Therefore, you tell the child not to fret. That is like a millionaire telling you not to worry about your inconsequential rent, bills, and so on. Your response might well be a silent or spoken "you don't understand."

To go back to Julie, she has lost interest in everything, including playdough, which used to be her favorite activity. Trying to interest Julie in the playdough is one way you show you don't understand. Julie has been spending more time just sitting in her locker, and that worries you. Rather than enticing her away, show concern by saying, "Julie, *I'm* worried because you are sitting in your locker and not playing the way you usually do." Compare the preceding statement with this one: "Julie, *you* shouldn't be sitting here in your locker, especially when I put out your favorite activity." In the first instance, you make an *I* statement, which reflects your concern about the situation. It requires nothing of Julie, not even a response. In the second statement, you seem to be both judging and blaming Julie for her behavior. "You shouldn't" really means "she shouldn't because I don't want her to." You would be

better off admitting your discomfort than blaming it on her. After expressing concern, give the child permission to talk about her feelings. "Sometimes when I'm sad I want to be alone. I wonder if you're sad about something now?" While still expressing concern, you can offer an opportunity, or invitation, for Julie to talk.

Whether or not she responds, the next move is to tell her how you are willing to help, while giving her some control over the situation: "Would you like to talk about how you feel? (Pause) I can listen now. I'd like. to come and sit beside you for a few minutes whenever I can. Is that OK with you?" Be careful not to make an offer you can't follow through on. Don't offer to sit beside the child all morning even if you think that would be helpful. Your duties as a teacher make an "all morning" offer impossible to fulfill.

The question is, is Julie just having a temporary bad time? Is this teacher's imagination or intuition? Is there, in fact, something wrong with Julie? Let's look at Julie to see what signs or characteristics are significant.

All children have bad days, and so do adults for that matter. Therefore, an important variable is *how long* the unusual behavior has been observed. Obviously the longer the behavior has gone on, the greater the concern. Another factor is *severity*: How different is this behavior from normal? Normality can be ascertained in two ways. If you know this child, you can compare present behavior with past behavior. This is self-comparison. Another way is comparing the child to other children or to theoretical behavioral norms that are age-appropriate. It is important to keep the child's age in mind when emo-

School can be a frightening experience for some children. Lacking adult language skills, these children often comfort themselves with infantile behaviors. Only when these behaviors persist for a long time is an adjustment problem indicated.

tional problems are suspected. (A toilet accident at age six is significantly different from one at age three.) It is also important to look at the social context of the child's behavior. Some aggressive boys who appear to be acting out may be encouraged at home to be "all boy." In addition to knowing the *values* of a family, it is often useful to learn what is currently happening in the family. Children traditionally have problems with the addition of a new family member, separation or divorce, moving (even if it is just across the street), or the death of a close friend or relative. This does not mean that the child's problems are any less real, but they are more understandable in the context of a specific situation.

Children rarely tell you that they are having a hard time; they show you by their behavior. Two general behavior styles that children adopt when in distress are *withdrawal* and *aggression*. As you might guess, children who choose to act out receive more attention and receive it faster. Other behaviors that often accompany either of these two styles have to do with regression to infantile forms of behavior, such as baby talk, thumb sucking, toilet accidents, and clinging. There is also a tendency for children having adjustment problems to develop recurrent physical pains, often in one particular body part, or to become obsessed with one particular fear. Let's discuss the two characteristic behavior styles in more detail.

Aggression in moderation (assertion) is a necessary survival skill. Too much aggressive behavior can, however, be detrimental. Some aggressive behavior is an attempt to gain something or to protect something. (Tom hits Sally because she tries to take

his truck.) It is a different case when the intent is simply to hurt another. Young children often revert to the first kind of aggression because of frustration, lack of experience, and poor communication skills. The latter kind is cause for concern and is more indicative of an adjustment problem. Frequent temper tantrums may also be indicative.

Withdrawal, or passive behavior, is less disruptive in the classroom than aggression, but is also a cause for concern. The withdrawn child always stays on the fringe, doesn't willingly participate in activities (especially ones that are large-group), and often appears to be a loner. In cases of extreme withdrawal you may suspect more long-term psychological problems. These children should be referred to a psychologist or psychiatrist for psychological evaluation and treatment, if indicated.

In both aggression and withdrawal, the child's behavior interferes with learning and with developing good relationships with peers and teachers.

## CLASSIFICATION OF ADJUSTMENT NEEDS

We have no reliable statistics on the prevalence of children with adjustment problems at preschool age. Unless a child is having severe psychological problems (and such a child is unlikely to appear in your classroom), he probably will not have been seen by a psychologist or psychiatrist. Do not rely on getting a diagnosis; instead program for the child's ascertainable needs.

## CHILDREN'S NEEDS— TEACHING GOALS

Related annual goals may be grouped under broad categories called "teaching goals." Outlined under each teaching goal below are the most important needs of children with social and emotional adjustment problems. A child may have some or all of these needs and additional needs as well. Suggestions on what you might consequently teach them are included. Often, a course of action is implicit in the description of the need.

### Feelings
Before children can learn to control feelings, they must become aware of their emotions and how they respond to them. It is important to ask a child how he feels: "When I see you sitting alone in your cubbie, I wonder how you are feeling." Don't tell a child, "You're lonely"; he may not be lonely—he may be sad or angry. Help the child learn that he is the only

one who knows how he feels. Once a child is aware of feelings, he can be taught to express them. If you, as a teacher, accept the feelings and don't judge them, then the child will probably continue to talk. If children are told that it is silly or stupid to feel the way they do, they are likely to quit talking about how they feel.

More than others these children need help in feeling part of the group. They need to be aware of individual differences, know the other children, and know that they too are accepted and belong even when they are isolated or have conflicts with others. Plan activities that don't demand a great deal of social interaction yet allow children to see themselves as part of the group. For example, have each child paint or color an area of a mural, or have each child contribute a page to a class book.

## Language

Children who are having adjustment problems need to develop the language and vocabulary necessary to express their wants, needs, and feelings. Teach children words that facilitate this development: *happy, sad, tense, relaxed, tight,* and so on.

## Awareness

Children need to become more aware of their body and the relationship between their feelings and what their body does. They need help learning how to recognize tension in their body and how to release that tension in a way that doesn't infringe on the rights of others. Children need to know how their body feels just before aggressive interactions and, once this knowledge is attained, you can help children learn to substitute other behaviors. (It is much like toilet training in that respect.) Children need to become aware of their body before they can control it.

Provide experiences in which these children are likely to be successful. Point out things that they do well. Look at the situational aspects of things that don't go well and verbalize these aspects to the child: "It is really difficult for *you and Joey* to play together in the block corner."

## Guidelines

Children with social and emotional needs, whether temporary or long term, need a warm, relaxed, and secure environment. Accept the children as they are, not as you would like them to be, and gear your requirements accordingly. Allow children to work at their own pace. Until children can cope with the world, they may not have the energy to forge ahead academically, even if tests show they have the ability. You can still prod a bit, but keep the whole child in mind when you do.

Perhaps the most important thing you can do for these children is help them accept themselves as good people. The most effective ways to do that are to teach children to control the behaviors that cause other children to avoid them and to provide successful experiences for them in the various curriculum areas.

Set up your classroom in a way that is conducive to this child's learning.

1. Remove objects or toys that cause problems. Make it a rule that if a child brings a squirt gun from home, it must stay in the child's locker until it is time to go home.
2. Consider restructuring the class day, especially if the child seems to have problems at the same times each day. If large group time is at 10:30 and this is a bad time for the child, consider rearranging the schedule so that the class is outside at 10:30 and in group time at 9:30 or 11:00.
3. If a child cannot cope with a situation, take him out of it early, before it worsens. If children are having problems playing together in the dramatic play area and your several solutions to sharing aren't working say, "There are too many children in the dramatic play area now. Who would be willing to play in another area?" If no one volunteers, ask a child. If that doesn't work, close down that area for the day. This is one way of preventing the need for more drastic measures.
4. Be sure the child understands what is expected of him. His definition of sharing the blocks may be very different from yours. You may have to ask questions to determine his perceptions. Be specific: "Which blocks are you sharing with Misha?" (The child points to three small blocks.) "You need to give him some of the big blocks too." (You may need to specify how many as well.)
5. As you learn more about the children in your class, be aware of who is sitting beside whom. Some combinations of children provoke trouble. You might place yourself between these children or ask an aide to sit there or have one of the children move.
6. If you have planned a long story or listening time and some of the children are having problems listening for long periods, change the pace. Break for something active, such as having the children stretch as high and low as they can reach, then come back to your quiet activity.
7. Teach children to distinguish between feelings and behavior and provide them with socially acceptable outlets that are easily accessible. If the child feels like hitting something, then she can hit a punching bag or the playdough, or kick a ball.

*Classroom Management.* Your goals are to strengthen, or reinforce, appropriate behavior and to redirect inappropriate behavior. Let's start with the strengthening goal. It is easy to reinforce children who do the right things. Praise, a smile, a "thank you," a hug, or even a token or cereal or a raisin reward work. But with children who don't do the right things, where do you start? Start with a principle called *successive approximation.* Reinforce the child at each step that brings him closer to the goal. For example, if a withdrawn child like Julie sits in her locker and cries during group time, praise her when she doesn't cry. Then praise her when she progresses (with your encouragement) to sitting on a chair beside her locker, a chair at a table, a chair nearer the group, a chair behind the group, a chair in the group, and then finally the floor in the group. Reward each stage, but don't expect her to go directly from the locker to the middle of the group. This process may take several days or weeks. You might try discussing with Julie where she'd like to sit. Then after you and she reach an agreement, reinforce behavior that conforms to the agreement. As children do things closer to (that approximate) what you want, keep rewarding that behavior until you achieve the goal.

*Modeling*—demonstrating behavior in situations—is also effective, but can be doubled-edged. Children tend to model meaningful people, which in a classroom means they will probably model you over classmates or aides (and model parents over you). You are always on display. If you combat aggression with aggression, you may then serve as an aggressive model for children regardless of your intentions. Be a good model by behaving in a way you would like the children to copy.

*Cueing*—warning children before they are expected to do something—is another effective means of changing behavior. You use cueing when you flick the lights to tell the children it is cleanup time. More specifically, if Amy looks longingly at John's truck, warn her by saying, "Ask John if he is using the truck." Don't wait until Amy has clobbered John and then say, "John was using the truck. It hurts him when you hit him." If you can anticipate that the child is about to do something undesirable, act *before* it happens. When you sense trouble, just moving into the area will do a lot to prevent a child from misbehaving. (Observers comment that they can see children visually locating the teacher before carrying out some aggressive behavior.) Giving a child a "teacher look" is another to cue a child that something the child is doing or plans to do is not appropriate. These nonverbal techniques (frowns, eye contact, throat clearing) are most effective when a child is just beginning to act out. To work, they typically require a relationship with the child.

When children have adjustment needs, it is important to fine-tune your classroom-management techniques. Be consistent, set clear limits, and state the necessary rules only as briefly as possible. However,

Children should be allowed to approach new materials and situations in their own way. While some children are tentative and need support, others require limits.

be prepared to enforce those that you have. Make children aware of both positive and negative consequences. If you don't think you can enforce a rule, don't make it.

If a rule states that everyone who plays with the blocks helps to clean them up, you need to know who played with them. Then if one child is reluctant to help, you need to say, "Tom, you played with the blocks, so you need to help clean them up." If there is no response, you might make an offer: "It's time to pick up the blocks. Do you want to do it by yourself, or would you like me to help you?" If necessary, physically help Tom by opening his hand, placing a block in it, closing the hand, walking with him (or carrying him if need be), to the block shelf, helping him deposit the block in the right place, and then thanking him for helping. The rule was not that children had to clean up *all* the blocks. Time and physical limitations might make such a rule unenforceable. The children are only required to *help*, and even one block put away is a help.

When a child does do something that you want continued, by all means reinforce the child's behavior. Decide what specific behavior you want to reinforce (such as sitting through group time). Tell the children they can have or do something they value if they do the specific behavior you've decided on. The trick in using reinforcement is to discover what is rewarding to particular children. Praise, attention, being able to go outside first, a hug, or some time alone to read in the book corner may be the answers for different children. Make your best guess and then try it out. (If the behavior continues, you are doing something rewarding.) When dealing with adjustment needs, be cautious about being demonstrative at first. Some children find this frightening, and some find it difficult to handle praise. A child may not consider a hug or praise at all rewarding.

Some children will prefer rewards that you don't personally like. Start with their preferences until the behavior is established. Then decide how to change the reward system. For example, if the child finds candy rewarding and you want to use praise, use the following procedures. When Tom does well, praise him, then give him candy. Gradually stop giving the candy. Present the new reward just before you present the old one that you know works but that you want to change.

Reward children's behavior each time only until the behavior becomes established, then reward randomly. This is the way to have behavior continue. If you *always* reward behavior then forget a few times, the child will decide you don't want that behavior to continue—if you did you would keep rewarding it as in the past. Random reinforcement is a proven method for establishing a new behavior. (Regretfully, the same principle works in reverse for setting limits. If you uphold the limits sometimes and not others, the children will *always* test them. It is important to always reinforce limits!)

If you think a child is acting out to get attention, purposefully ignore the behavior (providing the behavior isn't dangerous to the child or other children). Make a mental note to give attention when the child does something that is desired. Give the child cues for acceptable ways of getting your attention: "If you want me to watch you build with the blocks, ask and I'll come over." Praising the child who is next to the disruptive child may also be useful: "I like the way Sara is sitting."

## CURRICULUM ADAPTATIONS

The number and degree of adaptations depend on each child's needs. Your awareness of short-term needs will do a lot toward the child's long-term adjustment.

### Expressing Language, Listening, and Reading Readiness
The language arts area can help children develop the language skills to talk about situations they find difficult and the feelings these situations bring about. Through literature, children learn how other children have dealt with similar feelings and situations.

1. Teach vocabulary for expressing feelings. Use words the child can understand: *mad, sad, happy, tight, ready to hit, tense, excited.*
2. Demonstrate words, especially those associated with feelings. Pretend to be a statue or fashion model. Have the children tell you how to arrange yourself to show a specific emotion, but give them some clues: "I'm angry. Should my hands be open or closed? Should I look up or down? How should my mouth be?"
3. Encourage children to use words to solve problems: "Tell Jack you don't like it when he takes the blocks you are using."
4. Tell stories about a child who learns to deal with feelings: "Once upon a time there was a girl named ___ who . . ."

Mastering reading readiness skills requires the child to make fine auditory and visual distinctions. Although here the needs of this child are similar to those of other children, try to use subject matter that is especially relevant to the adjustment needs of the child.

1. Distinguish and label facial features. Play Lotto by matching faces. Even in simple line drawings, focus attention on the face.

2. Have children discuss moods. Write language experience stories using these as themes. Discuss what might happen to make children happy or sad.
3. Cut pictures of people and situations out of magazines. (Those with obvious themes are easiest.) Have the children make up a story about what might have happened and how the people in-

volved may have felt. Invent a variety of endings and discuss which aspects of situations that could change.

Use stories to help children increase skills in dealing with themselves and others. (See the children's bibliography following this chapter.)

1. Read stories dealing with angry feelings and peer conflict.
2. Select stories that have problem situations pertinent to the child's.

Fingerplays are beneficial for adjustment needs children because they provide opportunities for peer-group acceptance and positive role modeling.

1. If a child has a characteristic behavior such as hand waving, incorporate it into a fingerplay or a set of motions done to music: Do this in a way that helps the child feel part of the group but doesn't draw attention to him. "Shake, shake, shake your hands, Shake your hands together." Then do something else that is incompatible with hand shaking: "Clap, clap, clap your hands, Clap your hands together." Ask for volunteers to do other motions.
2. Use fingerplays to "settle" children. Practice fingerplays ("Open Shut Them") that finish with the hands in the lap. Whether a fingerplay merely quiets the children or has them keep their hands in their lap, they will be less likely to poke their neighbors.

## Social Studies

As children get into the preschool years, interaction with peers and the community at large becomes more important.

1. Adjustment problems often have their basis in the family. Talk about many different types of families: with one or two children, with many children, single parent, step or blended, with relatives living in the home, mixed racial, and with adopted or foster children.
2. Expand the concept of families by talking about the different roles: mother, wife, friend, daughter, teacher, sister. Help the children see their own various roles: son, friend, brother, pupil.
3. Be sure to acquaint the children with community helpers and their roles. Role play such situations as being lost, seeing a fire, and being sick.

## Science/Discovery

A discovery approach has great potential for teaching science to children with adjustment problems. They can be doing what they prefer, yet still be part of a group.

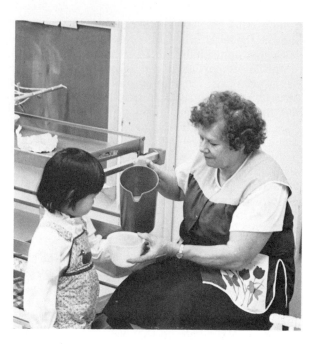

Having children participate in routine activities encourages independence and teaches self-help skills. It also provides a more familiar environment.

1. Help children to understand cause and effect relationships as they learn the physical properties of materials: "Snow melts when it gets warm."
2. Help children make predictions about experiments before they actually do them: "What will happen to the balance when you put the cup on it? Let's try it and see." Eventually you can expand this skill to personal situations: "What might Brad do if you take his book?"

## Mathematics

Math skills can be taught for their own sake, but when taught as part of other activities, they can also be used to increase a child's general awareness.

1. Use math to point out likenesses and differences and to create a sense of group belonging: "There are *three* boys with brown hair, but only *one* boy with brown hair and a plaid shirt."
2. Incorporate math skills into turn taking and sharing: "You can play with the truck for five minutes, then it is Stan's turn." (Set a timer.) "You can ride the trike around the play yard four times, then give it to Linda."
3. Use simple card games like "Fish" to encourage peer interaction.

## Health and Safety

Help the child learn to accept that the world is a basically safe place when you understand how to handle things and when to exercise caution.

1. Label "dangerous" things and discuss ways of dealing with them. Show children how to use the stove light to tell if an electric stove is on. (Use water to teach them the concepts *hot* and *cold* if they do not know them.)
2. Help the child gain independence and self-esteem by teaching self-help skills. To teach dressing, use buttoning and zipping frames as well as natural opportunities such as before and after toileting, coming and going home from school or outside, or playing with large dolls. Be sure children learn to wipe themselves, flush, and wash and dry their hands after using the toilet. Provide a variety of snacks or lunches to help children learn to use eating utensils correctly.
3. Use cleanup time to help the child feel like part of the group, and try to create a sense of responsibility for keeping the room neat.

### Art
Art can teach children about their bodies and how to express their feelings.

1. Use activities that incorporate the child's body or name.
   a. Make body pictures. Trace the outline of the child on a large sheet of paper. Have the child color and cut it out to make a life-sized paper doll.
   b. Use water to paint the child's shadow on the sidewalk.
   c. Use face- or body-shaped paper for painting or coloring.
   d. Make a "Name Book"—a book about the child and what the child does and likes.
   e. Put makeup on a child's face or have the child do it with soap sticks.
   f. Make posters or books using pictures of the children in the class.
   g. Do foot or hand printing or painting.
2. Help children use three-dimensional art media such as clay to work through feelings. Let them pound, roll, and tear the clay.
3. Encourage children to paint their feelings and to use the paintings to talk about these feelings.
4. If children seem reluctant to try messy activities, try some "clean" messy activities. Use shaving cream for finger paint.

### Music
Music can be used to teach the relationship between feelings and sound. Combined with movement, it is good for energy release.

1. If children are particularly wound up and you need to calm them down, start out with a vigorous tune and work toward a slow one. Make a tape of selections ranging from very loud and active to quiet and restful. Condense to save time. Tape only a part of each piece rather than the whole piece.
2. Add movement to make music time more than just a listening experience.
3. Once children have learned songs, use them often to promote a sense of predictability in a changing world. Teach new songs after singing old favorites.
4. Movement requires space. Music activities with movement are good for helping children learn how much space they require not to bump into each other.

### Dramatic Play
Dramatic play can be used to help children build successful peer relations and work out fears about specific issues.

1. If a child wants to play with another child or a group of children but does not know how to join the group, you might join the group with that child, play until the child becomes involved, and then slowly lessen your own involvement.
2. If a child is afraid to join in the play when many children are present, arrange some special times when this child and a child he or she likes can do things together. Arrange some dramatic play time together inside when the rest of the class is outside. Plan a visit to the office or kitchen or other separate room where the two can play together for a while.
3. Let children see how they fit into the various roles and relationships in a family, school, store, hospital, or fire station. Let them try on different roles.
4. Help children reenact fearful experiences in the more supportive class atmosphere, where they can come to grips with the experience.
5. Encourage the children to try on animal roles or roles of things they are afraid of, such as ghosts, monsters, skeletons, and snakes. This helps children feel in control.
6. Use puppets as a way for children to talk indirectly about experiences.
7. Have telephones available. These children may talk more freely when not face to face with their partner.

### Small Motor Play
The timing of small motor tasks is crucial for children having adjustment problems. If a child is already feeling frustrated, problems connected to small motor development may increase the frustration.

1. Encourage the use of small motor toys on children's good days or at good times of the day.
2. Use many varieties of toys, including some of the

*large* small motor toys designed for younger children.

3. If a child appears frustrated by a toy or activity, remove the child, because usually his next step is to dump or throw the materials. Although rarely dangerous, the child's actions can create a real mess, with ensuing problems if you enforce clean-up rules.

### Large Motor Play

Teach adjustment needs children to use large motor play to run off excess energy and frustration. The benefits are obvious to adults who clean house or jog or work out in a gym when angry. Children have yet to learn this. Rather than have them sit in a time-out box or read a book, help them learn to release energy. Encourage them to play hard until they are tired but not exhausted.

1. If children have a long ride to school, plan to do some large motor activities early in the day.
2. Actively encourage these children to participate. It is a good way to learn about oneself. It is also something the child might like and excel at.
3. Large motor play may let an aggressive child be part of a group and accepted in this role.
4. Consider adding a punching bag to your room. When children feel like hitting something, encourage them to hit the punching bag—hard. A duffle bag filled with old clothes and suspended from the ceiling works well. Comment positively on this behavior: "You really can hit that punching bag hard."
5. Use light, large, cardboard blocks. They are less of a problem when a conflict arises.
6. Have children throw Velcro-covered ping-pong balls at a bull's-eye or beanbags at a target.

### Transitions

Use transitions to single children out and build their self-esteem. When you dismiss children from large group time or while you wait for others to join the group, try:

Singing the children's names.
Writing the names on the blackboard.
Calling last names and telephone numbers.
Calling parents' names.
Using initials. (Children often are not aware there are so many different ways of referring to themselves.)
Calling the child who lives at _____ (address).
Calling the child who has two brothers.
Describing an important event or fact about the child.
Calling hair color, eyes, or clothes.

Outside play allows children to work off energy and learn important lessons in sharing and respecting personal property.

# CHILD STUDY TEAM REPORT

## *Gregory S.*

In attendance: Mr. S.; Mr. L., early childhood special education coordinator for Head Start; Mrs. C., teacher.

Gregory S. is a four-year seven-month-old boy who attends a Head Start preschool program. Gregory has been attending Head Start for four months and seemed to like preschool during most of that period. His preschool teacher, Mrs. C., felt he was making average progress and showed special interest in creative art projects and in creative drama activities. Mrs. C. called a conference with Gregory's parents a month ago to discuss some problems Gregory had begun to have. Mr. L. was invited to offer suggestions and to explain services Gregory may be eligible for in Head Start.

Mrs. C. reported that in the last month Gregory has frequently refused to participate in activities and has run out of the classroom threatening to go home on several occasions. Mrs. C. has noticed that Gregory becomes very absorbed in solitary activities (such as painting, playing with puppets, coloring, drawing, and looking at books) and often refuses to leave these activities to participate with the rest of the class.

Mr. S. explained the situation at home. Gregory's parents have recently separated. Gregory now lives at home with his father. His mother and three-year-old sister have moved into Gregory's grandmother's house until they can find suitable housing.

Gregory has not discussed that separation or his feelings about it with his father or teacher. Mr. S. thinks he is unhappy and doesn't fully understand the situation. He thinks Gregory misses his mother and sister (he and his sister shared the same bedroom) and doesn't understand why they cannot all be together. Mr. S. says that he has tried to explain it to Gregory on the boy's level, but he really isn't sure how to approach the issue. Because Gregory and his mother often "went at it," Mr. S. stated, he has trouble understanding why Gregory misses her so much.

Mrs. C. asked if Gregory saw his mother. Mr. S. informed her that Gregory did see his mother on Wednesday evenings and Sundays.

Asked about Gregory's behavior at home, Mr. S. replied that Gregory really doesn't talk about the separation, although his frustration about understanding it has led to tears occasionally. Mr. S. added that most of their time together during the week involves getting ready for school, dinner, or bed. He said that during the weekends, he tries to set aside some time on Saturday for Gregory and his sister. They usually go to a park, shopping, or to Mr. S.'s parents that day. Gregory often asks for his mother to come along.

Mrs. C. suggested Mr. S. ask the public library for some books on divorce written for children. Mr. L. stated that since Gregory's problems seem to relate directly to the changes at home, a full psychological report would probably not be appropriate at this time. It may be helpful if one staff member became very close to Gregory and tried to help him talk about his feelings. Until it is certain that this is a temporary problem, Gregory will be kept under observation and a psychological evaluation may be done at a later date. Some interim family counseling is also recommended.

In the meantime, Mrs. C. will work out some activities that may help Gregory to express some feelings and to vent his frustrations. A regular parent volunteer could work with Gregory on a one-to-one basis. Mrs. C. stated that she will ask Mr. S. to come in to the Head Start Center again and help to draw up a program for Gregory.

## INDIVIDUALIZED EDUCATION PROGRAM

NAME ___Gregory S.___ DOB _5_/_7_/_78_

AGE ___4-7___ GRADE ___Preschool___

SCHOOL ___South Side Head Start___

PARENTS/GUARDIANS ___Mr. S.___

ADDRESS ___16-B Alpha Street___

PHONE ___543-2798___

### CURRENT TEST DATA

TEST/DATE/RESULTS

Teacher observations / Refuses to participate, only plays alone, / runs away

Recommended Special Services (Hrs/Wk):

Family Counseling / 1 hr./wk

Total Hours/Week:

Special Education Classroom ___0___

Regular Classroom ___20___

On _12/20/82_, the IPRD Committee
(Date)

met to review all current data and

recommends Level ___I___ placement.

Date of new review ___3/30/83___

Exceptionality: ___Adjustment problems___

Present at meeting:

Parents ___Mr. S.___ Representative of District/Agency ___Mr. L., Head Start___

Others: Name/Position ___Mrs. C., Teacher___

The committee has determined the following learning strengths and needs to be reflected in the IEP:

| STRENGTHS | NEEDS |
|---|---|
| All learning areas | Self-concept |
| Creative art | Feeling part of the group |
| Creative drama | Understanding own feelings |

STUDENT ___Gregory S.___ DATE ___12/20/82___

GOAL ___To improve self-concept___

PARENT SIGNATURE _____ TEACHER SIGNATURE _____

| INSTRUCTIONAL OBJECTIVES | EDUCATIONAL METHODS | DATE Begin | DATE End | Eval. | PERSONS RESPONSIBLE Name | Position |
|---|---|---|---|---|---|---|
| Given pictures of peers' families and his own, Gregory will be able to expressively identify 2 similarities between the families on 2 occasions. | Animal Pictures, Family Pictures, Roles, Books | 12/20 | 3/30 | | Mrs. C. | Teacher |
| Given 2 pictures of peers' families, Gregory will be able to expressively identify 2 differences between the families on 2 occasions. | Same as above | 12/20 | 3/30 | | Mrs. C. | Teacher |
| Gregory will participate in group games and songs and respond with his name on request. | B-I-N-G-O<br>Who Has Red On<br>I'm Thinking Of | 12/20 | 3/30 | | Mrs. C. | Teacher |

STUDENT Gregory S. DATE 12/20/82

GOAL To express feelings

PARENT SIGNATURE ______ TEACHER SIGNATURE ______

| INSTRUCTIONAL OBJECTIVES | EDUCATIONAL METHODS | DATE Begin | DATE End | Eval. | PERSONS RESPONSIBLE Name | PERSONS RESPONSIBLE Position |
|---|---|---|---|---|---|---|
| Given pictures of children that represent the following feelings: happy, excited, scared, angry, sad, frustrated, Gregory will be able to expressively identify a reason the child may feel that way for 5/6 pictures. | Sad, Expressions, Matching Faces, New Doll | 12/30 | 3/30 | | Mrs. C. | Teacher |
| Given art medium of his choice, Gregory will complete 3 art projects representing 2 of the above feelings. | Mood Colors, Painting to Music, Wire Sculpture, Clay, Texture Paint | 12/30 | 3/30 | | Mrs. C. | Teacher |
| Gregory will role play at least 1 situation in which he has felt the above feelings. | Dramatic play, Housekeeping, Roles | 12/30 | 3/30 | | Mrs. C. | Teacher |

STUDENT _____ Gregory S. _____ DATE _____ 12/20/82 _____

GOAL _____ To increase feelings of group belonging _____

PARENT SIGNATURE _____   TEACHER SIGNATURE _____

| INSTRUCTIONAL OBJECTIVES | EDUCATIONAL METHODS | DATE Begin | DATE End | Eval. | PERSONS RESPONSIBLE Name | PERSONS RESPONSIBLE Position |
|---|---|---|---|---|---|---|
| Gregory will participate in at least 3 small group (3–4 children) activities per day for a period of at least 10 minutes each day for 3 weeks. <br> a. with teacher help <br> b. independently | Cooking, Dramatic play, Housekeeping, Art activities, Blocks, Gross motor activities | 12/30 <br> 2/15 | 2/15 <br> 3/30 | | Mrs. C. | Teacher |
| Gregory will name 3 peers in his class he likes and tell why on 2 occasions. | | 12/30 | 3/30 | | Mrs. C. | Teacher |
| Gregory will actively participate in at least 1 large group activity (10–15 children) per day for at least 10 minutes for 4 weeks. | Group time, Music, Movement, Gross motor play | 12/30 | 3/30 | | Mrs. C. | Teacher |

# GLOSSARY

**Acting out**   Behavior that is physically aggressive when it is not warranted by the situation.

**Autism**   A rare mental disorder characterized by extreme withdrawal, speech and language impairment, and perceptual problems, as well as an inability to relate appropriately to people and objects.

**Behavior disorders**   Behavior that deviates from cultural norms and hence is hard to define specifically. What might be labeled a behavior disorder in one culture or setting might not be so labeled in another.

**Neurosis**   A mild mental disorder that is characterized by generalized anxiety, usually treated on an outpatient basis. These children are often mainstreamed. The neurotic child may be anxious about any or all new experiences.

**Phobia**   A mental disorder that is characterized by specific fears that seem to have no rational basis. School phobia, death phobia, and fear of abandonment are most common in young children.

**Projective test**   A psychological test in which the responses to the standardized materials are open-ended so that the child's particular response can be used to diagnose inner feelings and personality. (Children's Aperception Test—CAT—is an example.)

**Psychiatrist**   A medical doctor specializing in the diagnosis and treatment of mental disorders. The psychiatrist can prescribe drugs when necessary.

**Psychologist**   A specialist in the treatment of mental disorders through analysis, testing, and therapy, but who cannot prescribe drugs.

**Psychosomatic disorders**   Physical symptoms of illness that are caused by, or at least triggered by, emotions.

**Psychosis**   A severe mental disorder in which the child is disoriented and out of touch with reality.

**Regression**   A return to an earlier, more immature behavior, usually related to stress. As a situational, short-term problem it is common in all children.

**Schizophrenia**   A common psychosis that is characterized by extreme withdrawal, inability to establish relationships with others, disorientation, and extreme emotional responses. Hallucinations or delusions often occur as well.

**Self-abusive behavior**   Behavior that is characterized by excessive hitting, banging, or biting oneself on purpose (also called self-mutilation or self-destructive behavior). May sometimes be extinguished by behavior modification.

**Self-stimulation**   Inappropriate behaviors, or mannerisms (hand flapping, masturbation, teeth grinding), which apparently provide some sensory input for the child and are continued for this reason.

**Transient situational personality disorders**   Adjustment problems that usually stem from a traumatic event in the child's life, such as the death of a parent; the most common problem you will encounter among adjustment needs children. The symptoms differ for each child. Whether or not the child needs special help depends on the length and severity of the reaction.

# TEACHING   RESOURCES

In some situations you may want or need additional information. There are many national as well as regional, state, and local organizations that can be helpful to you. The following annotated list of national organizations should be useful in helping you decide where to get the information you need.

Center for Attitudinal Healing
19 Main Street
Tiburon, CA 94920
    Offers help, free of charge, to children and adults suffering from life-threatening diseases or traumatic accidents. Program deals with peace of mind and elimination of fear. Pain and death are openly discussed.

Foundation for Child Mental Welfare
255 West 71st Street
New York, NY 10023

Initiated development of Children's Day Treatment Center and School in New York City, an institution which works with mentally afflicted children and their families; seeks to rehabilitate children and return them to community schools and to a happier family and social life after a three-year program.

International Society for Autistic Children
1A Golders Green Road
London, NW11 8EA
England
    Stimulates understanding of autism; exchanges information; performs research.

National Consortium for Child Mental Health Services
1424 16th Street, N.W., Suite 201A
Washington, DC 20036

Serves as a forum for exchange of information on child mental health services.

National Society for Autistic Children
621 Central Avenue
Albany, NY 12206

The national headquarters makes referrals to local chapters, and works for programs of legislation, education, and research for all mentally ill children.

The National Association for Mental Health
1800 North Kent Street
Rosslyn Station
Arlington, VA 22209

The national office refers individuals to local affiliations; directs a research program and a public information program; and acts as a liaison with governmental and private organizations. Also a source of information on both public and private mental health facilities.

# BIBLIOGRAPHY

Hayes, Rosa, and Merce G. Stevenson. *Teaching the Emotionally Disturbed–Learning Disabled Child: A Practical Guide.* 4 vols. Washington, D.C.: Acropolis Books, 1980.

Crow, Gary A. *Children at Risk: A Handbook of the Signs and Symptoms of Early Childhood Difficulties.* New York: Schocken, 1978.

Hewett, Frank M., and Frank D. Taylor. *The Emotionally Disturbed Child in the Classroom: The Orchestration of Success.* 2nd ed. Boston: Allyn and Bacon, 1980.

Mason, Robert L., et al. *The Emotionally Troubled Child: A Guide for Parents and Teachers in the Early Recognition of Mental and Nervous Disorders in Children.* Springfield, Ill.: Charles C. Thomas, 1976.

Mosier, Doris, and Ruth Pork. *Teacher-Therapist: A Text-Handbook for Teachers of Emotionally Impaired Students.* Santa Monica, Calif.: Goodyear, 1979.

Newcomer, Phyllis L. *Understanding and Teaching Emotionally Disturbed Children.* new ed. Boston: Allyn and Bacon, 1980.

Reinert, Henry R. *Children in Conflict: Educational Strategies for the Emotionally Disturbed and Behaviorally Disordered.* 2nd ed. St. Louis, Mo.: C. V. Mosby Co., 1980.

Wolff, Sula. *Children Under Stress.* Harmondworth, England: Allen Lane–Penguin, 1973.

*Biography/Autobiography/Fiction*

Axline, Virginia Mae. *Dibs: In Search of Self.* Boston: Houghton Mifflin, 1964.

A bright boy who suffered from severe emotional deprivation. The book is based on Dr. Axline's records of the treatment and her later contacts with Dibs as he grew to adulthood. A bit dated, but a classic in the field.

Copeland, James. *For the Love of Ann.* London: Severn House Publishers, 1976.

Within a year of her birth, Ann was demonstrating bizarre autistic behavior and turning her parents' lives into a nightmare. The book recounts the attempts made to alter Ann's behavior so that she could lead a normal life.

Greenfeld, Josh. *A Child Called Noah: A Family Journey.* New York: Holt, Rinehart and Winston, 1972.

The story in diary form of the thoughts and feelings of an autistic child's father, and what goes through his mind when he thinks about Noah's present and future.

Hundley, Joan. *The Small Outsider: The Story of an Autistic Child.* New York: St. Martin's Press, 1972.

A mother's story about discovering autism in her son and the effects on herself and the rest of the family. The last part of the book tells about other autistic children and their families, and how they cope with the problems of living with an autistic child.

MacCracken, Mary. *Lovey, A Very Special Child.* Philadelphia: Lippincott, 1976.

A teacher's account of a school year spent working with four emotionally disturbed children, ages eight to twelve.

Neufeld, John. *Lisa, Bright and Dark.* New York: S. G. Phillips, 1969.

The experience of a teenage girl who feels herself becoming increasingly mentally ill. Three girl friends try to help as her parents and teachers refuse to acknowledge her condition.

Park, Clara. *The Seige: The First Eight Years of an Autistic Child.* Boston: Little, Brown, 1972.

A mother's story of her autistic daughter's life from infancy through adolescence. She depicts the parents' frustrating search for professional help and counselling. The book contains numerous techniques and methods that Mrs. Park found useful with her daughter.

Phillips, Leon. *I Love You, I Hate You.* New York: Harper and Row, 1975.

Phillips writes about his daughter, Andrea, who has an emotional problem, tracing her antisocial behavior from childhood through adolescence. Parts of the book were written by Andrea herself, including passages from her diary, that show the inner torment of her life.

Rubin, Theodore Isaac. *Jordi/Lisa and David.* New York: Ballantine, 1967.

Two separate stories of psychotic children. *Jordi* is about a young autistic boy who suffers from severe anxiety attacks and hallucination, but who possesses superior intelligence. Reluctantly, his parents institutionalize the eight-year-old. He remained there for the next five years.

*Lisa and David* is about adolescents in a residential treatment center over a period of two years.

*Autobiography of a Schizophrenic Girl,* with analytic interpretation by Renée M. Sèchehaye. New York: Grune and Stratton, 1951.

The story of a young girl who went "mad" and was brought back to reality by a psychoanalyst, told in biographical form, with interpretation by the analyst. Good for anyone who has ever wondered what it is like to feel "split" or what analysts look for.

Smith, Bert. *No Language But a Cry,* Boston: Beacon Press, 1964.

Discusses the causes, types, and treatment of childhood mental illness. The author also deals with the needs of the parents and describes the facilities available to help these children find meaningful, useful lives.

Wender, Paul H. *The Hyperactive Child: A Handbook for Parents.* New York: Crown, 1973.

A systematic discussion of hyperactivity and its management practices. A section on educational management is of particular interest to teachers. Treatment with drugs is taken for granted, a view that is disputed by some professionals in the field.

Wexler, Susan Stanhope. *The Story of Sandy.* Indianapolis: Bobbs-Merrill 1955.

The struggles of a severely emotionally disturbed child, told by the boy's foster mother. At the age of three, Sandy came to live with foster parents after having been mistakenly diagnosed a "congenital imbecile."

Wilson, Louise. *This Stranger, My Son: A Mother's Story.* New York: Putnam, 1968.

The story of Tony, a beautiful child who grows increasingly difficult to handle, much to the concern of both his parents and siblings. The parents were blamed for Tony's problem. When they learned of theories of a biological basis for paranoid schizophrenia, they were relieved of their guilt feelings.

# BIBLIOGRAPHY FOR CHILDREN

*Being Afraid*

Alexander, Anne. *Noise in the Night.* Chicago: Rand McNally, 1960.

A child can find reassurance here about things that go bump in the night.

Alexander, Martha G. *I'll Protect You from Jungle Beasts.* New York: Dial, 1973.

Through a child's daydream, we learn of his fears in a dark jungle. He protects his teddy bear from the beasts, and later the bear protects him.

Bacigalupi, Marcella, et al. *It's Scary Sometimes.* New York: Human Sciences Press, 1978.

Discusses children's fears, both rational and irrational. Includes anecdotes and drawings by children.

Bannon, Laura. *The Scary Thing.* Boston: Houghton Mifflin, 1956.

A boy and his farm animal friends are frightened by something that is dark, lumpylike, and hides in the bushes: a newborn calf.

Clifton, Lucille. *Amifika.* New York: E. P. Dutton, 1977.

A sensitive account of a child's fears that her father won't remember her when he returns home from the Army.

Engle, Paul. *Who's Afraid?* New York: Crowell-Collier Press, 1963.

A young boy visits his uncle's farm and finds many things that are new and scary to him. This book could be used to help children express their feelings of fear.

Fassler, Joan. *Don't Worry, Dear.* New York: Behavioral Publications 1971.

Jenny wets her bed, stutters, and sucks her thumb. With the help of her loving mother, she outgrows these behaviors.

Feder, Jane. *The Night-Light.* New York: Dial, 1980.

Kate finds a nightlight she likes that helps her deal with her fear of the dark.

Freeman, Don. *Mop Top.* New York: Viking Press, 1955.

A boy who never wants to get his hair cut finds all kinds of excuses until an old lady mistakes him for a red mop.

Garrett, Helen. *Angelo, the Naughty One.* New York: Viking Press, 1972.

Angelo is a little Mexican boy who is terrified of water. When he must clean up for his sister's wedding, he is so frightened he runs away. This fear is dissipated when soldiers find him, bathe him, and make him the pride of the wedding feast.

Gay, Zhenya. *Who's Afraid?* New York: Viking Press, 1965.

Who's afraid? Even the mighty King of Beasts that's who!

Goldsmith, Howard. *Toto, the Timid Turtle*. New York: Human Sciences Press, 1980.

Young children will easily identify with Toto, who imagines himself to be brave and daring, but keeps his head securely tucked inside his shell. Realizing that withdrawal thwarts needs and ambitions, Toto comes to grips with reality and achieves self-discovery.

Greenberg, Barbara. *The Bravest Babysitter*. New York: Dial, 1977.

A little girl recognizes her babysitter's fear of thunder. They work together to deal with this fear.

Hoban, Russell. *Bedtime for Frances*. New York: Harper, 1960.

Frances, the badger, doesn't want to go to sleep, but gradually gets over her fears.

Kauffman, Lois. *What's That Noise?* New York: Lothrop, Lee and Shepard, 1965.

Joey hears scary noises for several nights. When he finds out what the noise is, it turns out not to be scary at all!

Leaf, Munro. *Boo, Who Used to Be Afraid of the Dark*. New York: Random House, 1948.

Boo was scared of just about everything, but his cat Alexander showed him how not to be scared of dogs, frogs, snakes, thunderstorms, bugs, mice, and even the dark.

Lexau, Joan M. *Benjie*. New York: Dial, Press 1964.

Benjie is too shy to talk with anyone except his grandmother. He overcomes this when helping his grandmother find a lost earring.

———. *Benjie on His Own*. New York: Dial, 1970.

Benjie's grandmother doesn't show up to walk him home from school. He's scared walking home, but finally makes it and discovers that his grandmother is sick. The next day, while she is in the hospital, he walks to school by himself and is not afraid.

Mayer, Mercer. *There's a Nightmare in My Closet*. New York: Dial, 1968.

A boy conquers his fear of the nightmare in his closet by making the nightmare scared of him.

Memling, Carl. *What's in the Dark?* New York: Parents' Magazine Press, 1971.

Helps the child cope with fears of sleeping in the dark by showing the child all of the things where they were left: pants, tee shirt, crayons, and other things the child can identify with that will help to make him feel safe and secure.

Ryan, Cheli D. *Hildilid's Night*. New York: Collier, 1974.

An old woman attempts to chase away the night. She finally realizes that since she can't hurt the night, it can't hurt her.

Schick, Eleanor. *Peter and Mr. Brandon*. New York: Macmillan, 1973.

Deals with a child's fear of being away from home overnight.

Schneider, Nina. *While Suzie Sleeps*. New York: W. R. Scott, 1948.

Deals with a child's fear of the dark by explaining all the things that go on during the night, such as the policeman patrolling, the milkman delivering, and the traffic lights changing.

Schwarty, Julius. *Now I Know*. New York: Whittlesey House, 1955.

Explanations for sounds, sights, and feelings that children may be afraid of.

Sendak, Maurice. *Where the Wild Things Are*. New York: Harper and Row, 1963.

A humorous book about a little boy named Max who gets carried away the night he wears his wolf suit. A novel way to deal with those monster fears.

Shortall, Leonard. *Tony's First Dive*. New York: Morrow, 1972.

Tony's mother enrolls him in swimming lessons. He learns to overcome his fears through the aid of a lifeguard and a facemask and finds a woman's bracelet at the bottom of the lake.

Showers, Paul. *A Book of Scary Things*. Garden City, N.Y.: Doubleday, 1977.

The book focuses on both real and imaginary fears of children.

Smaridge, Norah. *Scary Things*. New York: Abingdon Press, 1969.

The author touches on almost every circumstance that could be frightening for a child—great for helping a child overcome all kinds of fears.

Sonneborn, Ruth A. *The Lollipop Party*. New York: Viking Press, 1967.

A young boy is afraid about being left alone, but everything turns out all right when his mother arrives.

Vogel, Ilse-Margaret. *The Don't Be Scared Book: Scares, Remedies and Pictures*. New York: Atheneum, 1964.

A humorous book that helps children deal with their fears.

Waber, Bernard. *Ira Sleeps Over*. Boston: Houghton Mifflin, 1972.

Two children debate whether or not to share their fears. This story identifies fears of staying away from home at night and at the same time deals with sharing problems.

Wheeling, Lynn. *When You Fly*. Boston: Little, Brown, 1967.

Written in the form of a humorous poem, this book explains the process of going somewhere on a plane from boarding until landing—helpful for a child preparing for his first flight.

Williams, Gweneira. *Timid Timothy. The Kitten Who Learned to be Brave*. New York: W. R. Scott, 1944.

A little kitten who is afraid of everything learns that no matter how brave one becomes, one should not look for trouble.

### Loneliness

Beim, Jerrold. *The Smallest Boy in the Class*. New York: Morrow, 1949.

Jim is the smallest boy in class, but one day he finds there is another way to be big besides height.

Johnson, Elizabeth. *All in Free But Janey*. Boston: Little, Brown, 1968.

A delightful story of a young girl who can't play very well, but uses her imagination to dream of many make-believe friends. Great for children with nothing to do or who are lonely. A book for all ages.

Kennedy, Mary. *Come and See Me*. New York: Harper and Row, 1966.

A little girl living alone and her quest to find a friend.

Krasilovsky, Phyllis. *The Shy Little Girl*. Boston: Houghton Mifflin, 1970.

Anne doesn't like herself until she finds a new friend who gives her confidence.

Meyer, Renate. *Vicki, A Picture Book*. New York: Atheneum, 1969.

Entirely composed of illustrations that show how it feels not to have a friend. Good for the creative parent who can compose his own story.

Scott, Ann Herbert. *Sam*. New York: McGraw-Hill, 1967.

Everybody is too busy to play with Sam. When he starts to cry, they all take notice and find the perfect job for him to do.

Udry, Janice May. *What Mary Jo Shared*. Chicago: Albert Whitman, 1966.

Mary Jo was too shy to take part in show-and-tell until she decided to share her father with the class.

### Feelings

Barret, John M. *Daniel Discovers Daniel:* New York: Human Sciences Press, 1980.

The problem of parental favoritism is the underlying theme.

Berger, Terry. *I Have Feelings*. New York: Human Sciences Press, 1971.

Through photographs and stories, this book discusses different feelings a child may experience in one day.

Hazen, Barbara Shook. *If It Weren't for Benjamin (I'd Always Get to Lick the Icing Spoon)*. New York: Human Sciences Press, 1979.

A sympathetic look at both the older and younger brother's feelings.

Hazen, Nancy. *Grownups Cry Too*. Chapel Hill, N.C. Lollipop Power, 1973.

Grownups are human. Men and women are shown as both sad and happy.

Jones, Penelope. *I Didn't Want to Be Nice*. Scarsdale, N.Y.: Bradbury Press, 1977.

Nettie, a squirrel, didn't want to go to a brithday party at her friend's house, then her mood changes.

Kraus, Robert. *The Little Giant*. New York: Windmill and Dutton, 1977.

A small person makes himself feel he is a giant.

Martin, Bill, Jr. *David Was Mad*. New York: Holt, Rinehart and Winston, 1967.

A pink haze runs across the bottom of the page. It is red when David is maddest, then turns back to pink as he works through some of his anger.

Meyers, Bernice. *My Mother Is Lost*. New York: Scholastic Book Service, 1970.

A boy lost in a store finds another lost boy. When they finally reach Lost and Found, their mothers are there.

Ruffins, Reynold. *My Brother Never Feeds the Cat*. New York: Scribner, 1979.

Anna's brother never helps with chores around the house. A good book for talking to children about the things they can do, which helps in developing a positive self-concept.

Stanton, Elizabeth and Henry Stanton. *Sometimes I Like to Cry*. Chicago: Albert Whitman, 1978.

Several real life situations are portrayed as Joey learns about crying.

Tester, Sylvia Root. *Feeling Angry*. Elgin, Ill.: Child's World, 1976.

A little girl is jealous about the arrival of a baby.

Vigna, Judith. *Anyhow, I'm Glad I Tried*. Chicago: Albert Whitman, 1978.

A witty, sensitive story of a child who treats a disagreeable classmate with kindness even though she feels her effort is in vain.

Viorst, Judith. *Alexander and the Terrible, Horrible, No Good, Very Bad Day.* New York: Atheneum, 1972.

The book describes the events that make Alexander's day horrible and how he deals with it in the end.

Wolde, Gunilla. *This Is Betsy.* New York: Random House, 1975.

Betsy gets in touch with her body parts and her emotions.

*Friendship:*

Boyd, Selma, and Pauline Boyd. *The How: Making the Best of a Mistake.* New York: Human Sciences Press, 1981.

We all make mistakes and there is no reason to feel ashamed. The young hero turns a threatening situation into an opportunity to understand himself better and to make new friends.

Carle, Eric. *Do You Want to Be My Friend?* New York: Thomas Y. Crowell, 1971.

A child looks for and finds a friend.

Cohen, Miriam. *Best Friends.* New York: Macmillan, 1973.

Jim and Paul are best friends. While doing an errand for their kindergarten teacher, their friendship is ruptured; it is eventually mended.

———. *Will I Have a Friend?* New York: Macmillan, 1971.

Jim wonders if he will have a friend at his new school. The school setting of the book will be very familiar to kindergarteners or preschoolers.

Delton, Judy. *Two Is Company.* New York: Crown, 1976.

Duck and bear were very close friends until a newcomer joined them.

Ets, Marie Hall. *Play with Me.* New York: Viking, 1955.

An inquisitive little girl finds many animal friends by a pond.

Gackenback, Dick. *Hound and Bear.* New York: Seabury Press, 1976.

Practical jokes and friendship are given a light-hearted twist.

Hoban, Russell. *Best Friends for Frances.* New York: Harper and Row, 1969.

Frances, a badger, has to convince Albert that he values her friendship. In the process she learns sisters can also be friends.

Hurd, Edith Thatcher. *Who Will Be Mine?* San Carlos, Calif.: Golden Gate Junior Books, 1966.

A photographic story of a little girl in search of a friend. After talking with many animals in the park she finds a friend, a dog.

Ichikawa, Satomi. *Friends.* New York: Parents' Magazine Press, 1977.

People need friends, and some of the different things that friends do together are depicted.

Jaynes, Ruth. *Friends! Friends! Friends!* North Hollywood, Calif.: Bowmar, 1967.

A small girl describes her friends. This may help broaden a child's search for friends beyond just peers.

Kantrowitz, Mildred. *I Wonder If Herbie's Home Yet?* New York: Parents' Magazine, Press, 1971.

A young boy is angry that his best friend has made plans to play with someone else one day. The colorful illustrations are cartoon style and match the story well.

Kraus, Robert. *All the Mice Came.* New York: Windmill and Dutton, 1977.

The story of friendship and trust that was built up between a cat and mouse.

Sherman, Ivan. *I Do Not Like It When My Friend Comes to Visit.* New York: Harcourt Brace Jovanovich, 1973.

When her friend visits, everything she does is right and everything our heroine does is wrong. The situations are reversed the next day when our heroine visits her friend's house and gets to play with all of *her* toys.

Skorpen, Liesel Moak. *Plenty for Three.* New York: Coward, McCann and Geoghegan, 1971.

The contrast between the fun of doing something with a friend and the aloneness of doing it by yourself. At the end of the book the pair of friends invite the one who is alone to join them.

Winthrop, Elizabeth. *That's Mine.* New York: Holiday House, 1977.

Two children fight over blocks only to find that with some cooperation they can build a more beautiful castle.

Zolotow, Charlotte. *The Hating Book.* New York: Harper and Row, 1969.

A little girl decides her friend hates her and doesn't know why until she asks.

———. *The Quarreling Book.* New York: Harper and Row, 1963.

Friends can quarrel, too.

———. *The Unfriendly Book.* New York: Harper and Row, 1975.

Bertha criticizes everyone. Judy has something nice to say about everyone. They discuss their friends while walking their dogs.

*Marriage/Separation/Divorce*

Caines, Jeannette. *Daddy.* New York: Harper and Row, 1977.

A little girl's relationship with Daddy on their weekend get-togethers is highlighted.

Clifton, Lucille. *Everett Anderson's 1-2-3*. New York: Holt, Rinehart and Winston, 1977.

When Everett's mother decides to marry the neighbor, Everett wonders what it will be like to have three people in the house.

Gardner, Richard. *The Boys and Girls Book About Divorce.* New York: Aronson, 1971.

A very useful, encyclopedic work that discusses all aspects of divorce clearly and rationally. It can serve as a reference for both parents and children.

Goff, Beth. *Where Is Daddy? The Story of Divorce.* Boston: Beacon Press, 1969.

The fears and adjustments that children will go through if their parents are going through a divorce are explained. The illustrations are done from a child's point of view.

Hazen, Barbara Shook. *Two Homes to Live In: A Child's-Eye View of Divorce.* New York: Human Sciences Press, 1978.

A little girl explains how she came to terms with her parents' divorce.

LeShan, Eda J. *What's Going to Happen to Me? When Parents Separate or Divorce.* New York: Four Winds Press, 1978.

Children's concerns about themselves during a time when families are separating.

Lexau, Joan M. *Me Day.* New York: Dial, 1971.

A young black boy wakes up on his birthday with one wish—to see his father.

Perry, Patricia, and Marietta Lynch. *Mommy and Daddy Are Divorced.* New York: Dial, 1978.

Young children's feelings about, and adjustment to, their parents' divorce. Explains that reasons for divorce often don't make much sense to young children.

Stein, Sara Bonnett. *On Divorce: An Open Family Book for Parents and Children Together.* New York: Walker and Co., 1979.

A group of children are "playing divorce." A girl who hears the play becomes frightened that her parents will get a divorce. The parents explain that they disagree, but are not getting a divorce.

Stensen, Janet Sinberg. *Divorce Is a Grown-Up Problem: A Book about Divorce for Young Children and Their Parents.* New York: Avon, 1978.

Parents explain to a child why they are getting a divorce, and the child talks about how it feels to have parents who are getting a divorce.

## Moving

Hoff, Syd. *Who Will Be My Friends?* New York: Harper and Row, 1960.

Freddy has just moved into a new neighborhood and wonders who his friends will be. His ability to throw and catch win him the friendship of boys who need a good baseball player.

Tobias, Toby. *Moving Day.* New York: Knopf, 1976.

A child's point of view about moving. The same feeling of being uprooted is often felt by a child who is hospitalized—especially far from home.

Viklund, Alice R. *Moving Away.* New York: McGraw-Hill, 1967.

It can be sad leaving familiar things, but there is some excitement in facing something new and different.

Wise, William. *The House with the Red Roof.* New York: Putnam, 1961.

Jimmy likes his house with the red roof and all the familiar things about his life. After moving, he discovers he doesn't mind his new house with the brown roof after all.

Zolotow, Charlotte. *Janey.* New York: Harper and Row, 1973.

A young girl's best friend moves away.

## Starting School

Amoss, Berthe. *The Very Worst Thing.* New York: Parents' Magazine Press, 1972.

A story told by a little boy who is new in school.

Barkin, Carol, and Elizabeth James. *I'd Rather Stay Home.* Milwaukee, Wis.: Raintree Editions, 1975.

A boy's first day at school is depicted.

Binzen, Bill. *First Day in School.* Garden City, N.Y.: Doubleday, 1972.

An introduction for preschoolers to the kindergarten routine. Photographs show the first day in the classroom.

Breinburg, Petronella. *Shawn Goes to School.* New York: Thomas Y. Crowell, 1973.

Shawn's reaction to his first day at nursery school is shown.

Buckheimer, Naomi. *I Know a Teacher.* New York: Putnam, 1967.

David's first day in kindergarten is exciting. His teacher takes the class on a tour of the building and introduces them to the principal and custodian. A good account of daily classroom routine is given.

Cohen, Miriam. *Will I Have a Friend?* New York: Macmillan, 1967.

A young boy experiences uncertainty on his first day at a child care center.

Hurd, Edith Thacher. *Come with Me to Nursery School.* New York: Coward, McCann and Geoghegan, 1970.

The question "What will I do at my school?" is answered in the text and in over 500 pictures.

Johnson, John E. *My School Book*. New York: Random House, 1979.

The story explains what happens on the first day of school.

Justus, May. *New Boy in School*. New York: Hastings House, 1963.

Minority children adjust to a new school.

Katzoff, Betty. *Cathy's First School*. New York: Knopf, 1964.

A little girl's first school and all the fun things that happen to her there are depicted through photographs.

Marino, Dorothy. *Buzzy Bear's First Day at School*. New York: Watts, 1970.

Buzzy Bear is anxious to go to school, but when he gets there the other animal children are doing things that Buzzy feels he can't do. Finally he learns what he can do.

Rockwell, Harlow. *My Nursery School*. New York: Greenwillow Books, 1976.

A good book for a child who is either hospitalized or at home because it demonstrates through the use of pictures what may be going on at school while the child is away.

Soderstrom, Mary. *Maybe Tomorrow I'll Have a Good Time*. New York: Human Sciences Press, 1981.

Marsha Lou finds the first day of school difficult. This story helps children confront their own feelings of separation and gain a sense of independence and self-confidence.

### New Baby

Alexander, Martha. G. *Nobody Asked Me If I Wanted a Baby Sister*. New York: Dial, 1971.

Oliver tries to give his sister away because she cries all the time.

————. *When the New Baby Comes, I'm Moving Out*. New York: Dial, 1979.

A humorous treatment of ambivalent feelings about a new baby. Oliver discovers all the special things big brothers can do when there is a new baby.

Arstein, Helene S. *Billy and Our New Baby*. New York: Behavioral Publications, 1973.

The new baby takes up most of Mom's time. Billy wants to act like a baby, but Mom shows him it is more fun to be big and do things. Billy accepts the baby though he still doesn't like him part of the time.

Byars, Betsy. *Go and Hush the Baby*. New York: Puffin Books, 1982.

Before he can play baseball, a little boy must try many antics to hush the crying baby.

Clifton, Lucille. *Everett Anderson's Nine Month Long*. New York: Holt, Rinehart and Winston, 1978.

Everett's parents take an understanding view of his feelings as the family welcomes the new baby.

Greenfield, Eloise. *She Came Bringing Me That Little Baby Girl*. Philadelphia: Lippincott, 1974.

A little boy hates his new sister and everyone else because they play with the baby and not him.

Helmering, Doris, and John William Helmering. *We're Going to Have a Baby*. Nashville: Abingdon, 1978.

Jimmy looks forward to a new baby in the family until his friends advise him that babies are no fun. Good for discussing the pros and cons of new babies.

Hoban, Russell. *A Baby Sister for Frances*. New York: Harper and Row, 1964.

Frances isn't sure she wants a new sister because no one seems to have time for her.

Holland, Viki. *We Are Having a Baby*. New York: Scribner, 1972.

At first, four-year-old Dana is happy about having a baby, but when the baby comes home she feels hurt and abandoned. Photos capture the emotions of that phase in a child's life.

Jordan, June. *New Life: New Room*. New York: Thomas Y. Crowell, 1975.

Rudy, Tyrone, and Linda work together, rearranging furniture, painting their room, and weeding through toys: They are making room for the arrival of the new baby.

Keats, Ezra Jack. *Peter's Chair*. New York: Harper and Row, 1967.

A black boy experiences feelings of neglect after the arrival of a new baby—until he gets a chair of his very own.

Knotts, Howard. *Great-Grandfather, the Baby, and Me*. New York: Atheneum, 1978.

A young boy feels sad about the arrival of a new sister. Great-grandfather tells the child a story and comforts him. They leave together to greet the new baby.

Skorpen, Liesel Moak. *His Mother's Dog*. New York: Harper and Row, 1978.

Both the dog and the boy feel rejected when mother comes home from the hospital with a baby. In despair they turn to each other for comfort.

# I N D E X

| *Annual Goals* | *Activity* | *Curriculum Area* | *Page* |
|---|---|---|---|
| **THINKING AND REASONING SKILLS** | | | |
| To increase logical reasoning | Measure It | Mathematics | 430 |
| To improve cause and effect reasoning | Balloon Badminton | Outdoor Play | 528 |
| | Cornstarch Playdough | Science/Discovery | 402 |
| | Mood Songs | Music | 464 |
| | Seasonal Clothing | Health and Safety | 435 |
| | Straw Painting | Art | 450 |
| | Texture Paint | Art | 449 |
| | Torn Paper Flowers | Art | 445 |
| To improve sequencing skills | Day Play | Dramatic Play | 490 |
| To improve color concepts | Colored Fingernails | Art | 457 |
| To make predictions | Ballon Badminton | Outdoor Play | 528 |
| | Measure It | Mathematics | 430 |
| | Problems | Social Studies | 386 |
| | Straw Painting | Art | 450 |
| To improve decision making | No Name | Dramatic Play | 494 |
| **MATHEMATIC SKILLS** | | | |
| To improve measurement concepts | Measure It | Mathematics | 430 |
| To improve shape concepts | Carpet Shapes | Mathematics | 417 |
| To improve time concepts | Day Play | Dramatic Play | 490 |
| | Timed Race | Large Motor Play | 519 |
| **SOCIAL SKILLS** | | | |
| To broaden concepts of families | Roles | Social Studies | 390 |
| To increase survival skills | Seasonal Clothing | Health and Safety | 435 |
| | Traffic Sign Hunt | Health and Safety | 439 |
| | Who Are You? | Health and Safety | 441 |
| To increase awareness of roles people play | Audiologist | Dramatic Play | 489 |
| | Be the Teacher | Social Studies | 390 |
| | Cast It | Dramatic Play | 486 |
| | Connections | Dramatic Paly | 488 |
| | Day Play | Dramatic Play | 490 |
| | Dentist | Dramatic Play | 485 |
| | Doctor's Office | Dramatic Play | 485 |
| | Eye Doctor | Dramatic Play | 490 |
| | Patient in the Hospital | Social Studies | 388 |
| To cooperate with peers | Audiologist | Dramatic Play | 489 |
| | Eye Doctor | Dramatic Play | 490 |
| | Hug Tag | Outdoor Play | 531 |
| | No Name | Dramatic Play | 494 |
| | Share Your Feelings | Social Studies | 392 |
| | Seesaw | Large Motor Play | 520 |
| | Telephone | Expressing Language | 338 |
| | Variations on Throwing | Outdoor Play | 526 |

| *Annual Goals* | *Activity* | *Curriculum Area* | *Page* |
|---|---|---|---|
| To cooperate with adults | Be the Teacher | Social Studies | 390 |
| | Interviews | Expressing Language | 339 |
| | My Shadow | Art | 456 |
| | Who Are You? | Health and Safety | 441 |

## MOTOR SKILLS

| | | | |
|---|---|---|---|
| To improve large motor coordination | Variations on Bouncing | Outdoor Play | 524 |
| | Variations on Throwing | Outdoor Play | 526 |
| To improve small motor coordination | Puppet Hands | Art | 457 |
| To improve eye-hand coordination | Balloon Badminton | Outdoor Play | 528 |
| | Clay | Art | 451 |
| | Fishing for Faces | Reading Readiness | 368 |
| | Torn Paper Flowers | Art | 445 |
| | Variations on Bouncing | Outdoor Play | 524 |
| | Variations on Throwing | Outdoor Play | 526 |
| To improve balance skills | Flopsy | Movement | 480 |
| | Seesaw | Large Motor Play | 520 |
| To encourage creative movement | Flopsy | Movement | 480 |
| | Moving Colors | Movement | 481 |
| | Music and Movement | Movement | 480 |
| To increase sense of rhythm | Mood Songs | Music | 464 |
| | Rhythm Walk | Music | 464 |
| To relax at will | Rag Doll | Movement | 476 |
| | Relaxation Stories | Movement | 476 |
| | Tense Me | Movement | 480 |

## CREATIVITY

| | | | |
|---|---|---|---|
| To encourage creativity | Clay | Art | 451 |
| | Foot Painting | Art | 450 |
| | Mood Colors | Art | 453 |
| | Mood Montage | Art | 453 |
| | Painting a Feeling | Art | 452 |
| | Painting to Music | Art | 454 |
| | Puppets | Dramatic Play | 492 |
| To encourage creative problem solving | Connections | Dramatic Play | 488 |
| | Our Town | Social Studies | 384 |
| | Problems | Social Studies | 386 |
| To stimulate curiosity | Cornstarch Playdough | Science/Discovery | 402 |

## FEELINGS

| | | | |
|---|---|---|---|
| To increase awareness of feelings | Matching Faces | Reading Readiness | 370 |
| To express feelings | Best and Worst | Expressing Language | 335 |
| | Feelings | Expressing Language | 342 |
| | My Books | Reading Readiness | 380 |
| | Painting a Feeling | Art | 452 |
| | Share Your Feelings | Social Studies | 392 |

| *Annual Goals* | *Activity* | *Curriculum Area* | *Page* |
|---|---|---|---|
| To increase feelings of group belonging | Circles | Movement | 479 |
| | Connections | Dramatic Play | 488 |
| | Hug Tag | Outdoor Play | 531 |
| | I'm Thinking Of | Social Studies | 392 |
| | My Song | Music | 469 |
| | No Name | Dramatic Play | 494 |
| | Our Town | Social Studies | 384 |
| | Puppets | Dramatic Play | 492 |
| | Share Your Feelings | Social Studies | 392 |

## AWARENESS

| | | | |
|---|---|---|---|
| To increase body awareness | Body Language | Expressing Language | 344 |
| | Body Mural | Art | 454 |
| | Body Noises | Expressing Language | 345 |
| | Cave Exploration | Outdoor Play | 528 |
| | Circles | Movement | 479 |
| | Colored Fingernails | Art | 457 |
| | Eye-Hair Collage | Art | 455 |
| | Foot Painting | Art | 450 |
| | Flopsy | Movement | 480 |
| | Mirror Movement | Movement | 477 |
| | Mixed-Up People | Art | 456 |
| | Moving Balloons | Movement | 478 |
| | My Shadow | Art | 456 |
| | My Song | Music | 469 |
| | Puppet Hands | Art | 457 |
| | Rag Doll | Movement | 476 |
| | Relaxation Stories | Movement | 476 |
| | Rhythm Walk | Music | 464 |
| | Soap Sticks | Art | 455 |
| | Tense Me | Movement | 480 |
| | Timed Race | Large Motor Play | 519 |
| To improve self-concept | Interviews | Expressing Language | 339 |
| To increase awareness of individual differences | Body Mural | Art | 454 |
| | Eye-Hair Collage | Art | 455 |
| | I'm Thinking Of | Social Studies | 392 |
| | Mixed-Up People | Art | 456 |
| To increase awareness of moods | Mood Colors | Art | 453 |
| | Mood Montage | Art | 453 |
| | Moving Colors | Movement | 481 |
| | Painting to Music | Art | 454 |
| | Soap Sticks | Art | 455 |
| To increase awareness of adjustment needs | My Day | Awareness | 543 |
| | New Doll | Awareness | 543 |
| | Sad | Awareness | 543 |
| To increase awareness of physical needs | Cast It | Dramatic Play | 486 |
| To increase awareness of hearing needs | Audiologist | Dramatic Play | 489 |
| To increase awareness of visual needs | Eye Doctor | Dramatic Play | 490 |

# 13

# Needs: Culturally Distinct

I learned about the American Revolution in Pennsylvania's public schools. My cousin learned about it in Niagara Falls, Ontario. Over the summers, we had long, hard arguments over whether the Tories were heroes or traitors. Native American children might have similar problems seeing Custer as a hero, fighting the "savages." Asian American children might question the wisdom of dropping bombs on Japan.

Because we attempt to transmit the values of our society through education, it is imperative that we look at both our personal and institutional values, and examine how these are portrayed in the books and activities we use and in our style of teaching. If our style of teaching devalues a child's culture and family, it is unlikely that she will learn in our classrooms.

Children from minority groups have been legally part of the mainstream of education since the Supreme Court ruled in 1954 on *Brown* v. *Board of Education* that segregation by race is inherently unequal and therefore unconstitutional. But after three decades, implementation of the philosophy behind that ruling has not been a total success.

From an educational perspective, there have been two very different ways of treating children who are culturally distinct. The first is a model that views the dominant white culture as being "right," with other cultures being deficient and hence their children disadvantaged. The goal of education for the first model is acculturation—wipe out the values the child has and replace them with the values espoused by the school, values that reflect the dominant cul-

ture. Perhaps the best thing that can be said about this model is it hasn't worked.

The second model views children with different cultural backgrounds as *culturally distinct*. Both cultures, the dominant and the distinct, are valid, have advantages and disadvantages in certain circumstances, and are not necessarily mutually exclusive. Education under the second model requires teachers to alter their teaching styles to meet the needs of the individual children, rather than make the children conform to the demands of the school. As is clear from the title, this chapter is written from a distinct, not a deficient, viewpoint.

Regardless of the cultural background children come from, the following generalizations can help you develop a useful perspective before reading about specific cultures.

1. When the school and home cultures are different, it is important that children learn about both cultures. They need to be encouraged to keep the values of their own culture yet gain the skills that enable them to function in school. Your goal is to increase the options children have so that they can function in both cultures.
2. Around the age of three, children become aware of their ethnic background. With this awareness children begin to look at themselves differently. How they view themselves relative to their ethnic background affects their self-concept and their feelings of belonging in the school environment.
3. Your behavior serves as a model for the children

and for other adults in the classroom. Children whom you respect are more likely to learn and enjoy school than those who are shown disapproval and who see school as an unfriendly, threatening place. In order to demonstrate your respect you must acquire and share knowledge about the cultures of the children you teach.

4. Just as there is no one white American culture, there is also no one Asian American, black American, Hispanic American, or Native American culture. Find out which aspects of the culture are important to particular families and which ones are not.

All children are different—different heights, different weights, different personalities, different colors, different cultures. The role of the teacher is to discover differences, appreciate them, and program in a way that allows for and encourages differences as well as similarities.

## CLASSIFICATION OF CULTURALLY DISTINCT NEEDS

The following brief sketches provide some information on the concerns that will be most relevant to your teaching. The resources and bibliographies at the end of the chapter can help you locate additional information.

### Asian Americans

Today there are over one and one-half million Asian Americans. This number is increasing with new immigrations. They are primarily from Japan, China, the Philippines, Vietnam, and Korea. Relative to other minorities, we know little about Asian Americans. As a group they have been very successful in the United States. They have caused few problems and hence been the subjects for few research studies.

In order to facilitate learning and to be more relevant, materials and programming need to take the child's culture into account. Be aware, however, of the differences among Asian cultures. Japanese and Chinese people have both similar and different values. Even among members of one group, there is great variation. Learn about the particular families that you will interact with. Then decide which generalizations apply and which do not.

Typically, the Asian family is very structured with clear roles and authority. The father is the head of the family. Children are expected to be obedient and respectful to their parents, specifically, and to anyone older than they are, generally. Family interactions are less verbal and involve few direct confrontations. The family is seen as a harmonious group and anything, such as strong emotions, that might disrupt this harmony is expected to be suppressed. Children are expected to conform. In order to develop these values in children, parents may teach children that disobedience brings ridicule on the child and shame on the family (Kitano, 1980). Traditional cultural values of patience and persistence are handed down as well. Family dependency is valued over independent achievement and cooperation over competition. Many of these children are bilingual.

Asian American families place a high value on education. The parents generally show teachers respect and expect their children to do the same. As you are an authority figure, children are expected to obey and not question what you say. It is important to teach these children the skill of asking questions of adults without questioning the authority that adults have. As these children are very family oriented they may need to learn skills for getting along with peers. Stress the value of cooperation and helping others rather than one child winning and others losing. Talk about the differences between feelings and how these feelings can be expressed. Children will need your help in learning to express themselves in ways that do not conflict with family values. As you work this out, consult with the parents for their ideas. In addition, the parents are a resource for expanding your knowledge of the Asian culture. Encourage children to use and develop their native language in addition to English.

### Black Americans

Black Americans are currently the largest distinct cultural group and number about 26 million. Black American families are more similar to than different from white families of the same social class. However, a disproportionate number of blacks live below the poverty level. In order to gain a perspective on black Americans today it is important for you to study their history and how it has contributed to their culture.

Although black families are primarily nuclear families, they have a much stronger bond to relatives and are more likely than whites to have relatives living with them. These relatives or "kin" may or may not be blood-related, but in either case, they take an active family role. Within the nuclear family, roles are flexible and tasks are often interchanged. Women may have relatively more power than in other cultures, but the female dominance often portrayed is rarely true, except for single-parent families with a female head of household. Education is valued for upward mobility. Most women work either out of necessity or out of desire to enhance family income. About half of the children between three

Children begin to become aware of racial and cultural differences around age three. Use this as an opportunity to teach children about both similarities and differences.

and five years of age are in preschools or day care centers (*Statistical Abstracts of the United States*, 1980).

Although most teachers are aware of economic and cultural differences between black and white children, to date the most prevalent way of educating black children is to assume they are white children who "happen to be painted black" (Wilson, 1980). We have done little to enhance the children's understanding of their culture. Black Americans are now asking for separate facilities and for some of their differences as well as their similarities to be acknowledged and encouraged. Because the tests that are used to determine learning ability and achievement are standardized on white populations, we don't know how black children learn best. Perhaps because of fear of discriminating, we have been so afraid to teach these children differently we have not reached them. Remember these children have individual strengths and needs when you teach them.

Examine your teaching materials. Do you have stories about black children and black dolls available in the doll area? When you discuss families, include families that have others living with them, single-parent families, and those with working mothers. Emphasize role flexibility in the family. Learn about the black culture and incorporate this knowledge in your teaching. If children use black di-

alect, show you value it as a valid method of communication while you also encourage children to use standard English at school. Stress the situational aspect of language usage.

### Hispanic

The Hispanic population in the United States is increasing rapidly and may soon be the largest minority group. There are approximately 20 million Hispanics in the United States today. Most are American citizens; some are not, but are legal residents; some are here illegally. About 80 percent are Mexican American, Puerto Rican, or Cuban American, and 20 percent come from other countries in Latin America. This Hispanic population is young and primarily urban. About 21 percent of them live below the poverty level (Delgado, 1980).

Because of family values, it is not likely that you will have many very young Hispanic children in preschool programs. Mothers are generally expected to stay home and raise children. When this is not possible, the extended family—brothers, sisters, aunts, uncles, grandparents—takes over the care of the young children. Some families may see sending children to school before kindergarten as a sign of deteriorating family values. Within the family itself there may be more stringent role requirements. The father is the head of the household; he earns the money. The mother traditionally raises the children. The children are respectful and obedient to adults.

Communicating with Hispanic families may be a challenge. Spanish may or may not be the only language spoken in the home. Children may come to school with good language skills in both Spanish and English or with only rudimentary knowledge of English or Spanish.

Families who choose to send their children to preschool need your support. Help them see preschool as an alternative to extended family care. They should not be made to feel that you judge them or that they are not fulfilling their roles as parents. If the parents speak little or no English, it is important to have bilingual/bicultural support for parent-teacher conferences and to translate forms that are to be sent home. If possible, use the parents as a resource to learn about the culture and enrich the class curriculum. Learn about traditional holidays and how they are celebrated. Help children develop their language skills in both languages by labeling objects and teaching songs and fingerplays in both languages.

### Native Americans

It is strange to think that the people native to America could be considered culturally distinct and need specially tailored educational programs, but this is true nonetheless. There are about one million Native Americans in the United States. About half live on reservations and half dwell mostly in urban areas (Thompson, 1978).

Education for Native American children has often been run by the federal Bureau of Indian Affairs. Traditionally, the schools have been boarding schools, located far from the children's homes, with white teachers. The focus of this education was to "de-Indianize" the Native American. It hasn't worked. Native Americans have in many instances not wanted to have their children mainstreamed, but instead have wanted to foster close ties with the tribe. They want to improve the quality of education for their children by changing the standard curriculum to be more responsive to another view of American history.

Some feel that one reason the drop-out rate for Native American children is 50 percent higher than for the rest of the population (Beuf, 1977) is because of the biased view that teachers and textbooks present. For example, many Native Americans view Thanksgiving as a day of mourning, not one of cooperation, celebration, and feasting. Look at the ways in which you celebrate holidays and try some nontraditional approaches.

Other children's ideas of Native Americans may be influenced by traditional "Cowboy and Indian" movies. Replace these ideas with more realistic ones and have children do more than make Indian headbands and give war whoops. Giving an in-depth view of Native Americans will help other children increase their knowledge and decrease their prejudices.

Make your programming responsive to these children's needs. Ask the parents for assistance. If children speak a tribal language, have them share this with the other children. Encourage use of both languages. Learn about each child's background and experiences. Determine whether or not a child has had the firsthand experiences other children in the class have had. If not, provide those experiences—but also value what the child does have. Help these children develop a good self-concept.

## CHILDREN'S NEEDS— TEACHING GOALS

Related annual goals may be grouped under broad categories called "teaching goals." Outlined under each teaching goal below are the most important needs of culturally distinct children. A child may have some or all of these needs, and additional needs as well. Suggestions on what you might consequently teach them are included. Often, a course of action is implicit in the description of the need.

### Language Skills
Children need to develop expressive language skills. If they come to school speaking a language other than English, they may speak less often and have a smaller vocabulary than their peers. Give these children the opportunity to interact with materials, and supply the language for what they are doing in standard English and, if possible, in their native language.

### Awareness
All children come from a culture. It is the goal of this chapter to encourage you to help children become more aware of their own culture and to teach them about other children's cultures. It is important for all children to explore and appreciate a variety of cultures. Children can be taught to respect differences, not judge them.

As you help them view events from a variety of perspectives, increase children's awareness of the uniqueness of "self." Have them become aware of, and appreciate, themselves, their families, and their heritage. Culturally distinct children can do this by sharing their holidays and traditions with the class. Some form of a family tree can help all children become more aware of their extended families.

### Feelings
All children need to feel and be a part of a group some of the time. You can help them develop the skills to do this. Help them develop as well the skills to be and do things alone. Help children label how they feel. Teach them to express those feelings in ways that allow them to be part of your class and that are also acceptable within their culture.

### Guidelines
1. Redirect rather than punish misbehavior. It may result from ignorance of expected behavior. Some children eat playdough or throw blocks because these seem like logical things to do.
2. Help children become aware of the situational aspect of socially acceptable behavior. In the classroom, children can learn to raise their hands before speaking, honor rules for sharing, and take turns.
3. Limits that are set ought to be clear, concise, and consistently upheld. Having children participate in setting the limits increases the likelihood of their being upheld.
4. Provide varied cultural experiences that use visual, auditory, and tactile skills.
5. Remember that you are a role model. If you are excited by having children from a variety of backgrounds in your class, the children will adopt the same positive attitude.

6. Be aware of cultural mores that may influence the children, and know what is acceptable behavior in their culture. Try not to violate these mores at school.
7. When possible, use the family as a resource. Have parents, grandparents, aunts, uncles, or even friends participate in some aspect of the class.
8. Provide opportunities for all children to tell the class about their homes and the things there that are special to them. At the same time, be sensitive to the needs of children who do not want to discuss their home life.
9. Encourage children to develop the necessary skills to play both alone and with others in the class. When possible, allow children to work out their own conflicts. Teach them methods for sharing and taking turns.
10. Help all children to appreciate their uniqueness as human beings as well as their cultural background.
11. Encourage children to try new foods at snacktime, but remember that foods that are familiar and ordinary to us may be strange to these children, and vice versa. Because children have emotional associations with foods, they may take a long time to assimilate their diet.
12. When possible, have a bilingual/bicultural staff that reflects the children in the class.
13. Forms that are sent home should be translated so they can be understood by the parents. When conferencing with parents, have someone available to translate.

## CURRICULUM ADAPTATIONS

In general, the curriculum adaptations are geared toward providing new strategies for learning, teaching the situational aspects of behavior, and enhancing the child's knowledge of her own culture, as well as giving all children information about a variety of cultures.

### Expressing Language, Listening, and Reading Readiness

Language arts offers an easy way both to provide needed stimulation and to enhance cultural differences.

1. Help all children build a functional vocabulary, then add words for the finer points. This is probably most easily done by labeling objects and behavior verbally, in a play-by-play manner: "Rosa, you are rolling the red playdough." Don't expect children to learn the first or even the tenth time around.

2. Label simple objects around the classroom in two languages—one for identification, one for learning.

| Clock | Table | Chair | Book | Rug |
|-------|-------|-------|------|-----|
| Reloj | Mesa | Silla | Libro | Alfombra |

3. Depending on your approach, encourage both languages or only one language, but do encourage language!
4. Look for a child's creative use of language and for children who learn language easily. Because most of our intelligence tests were designed for a white, middle-class, native English-speaking population, we often miss the gifted and talented children who are culturally different. Language fluency may indicate that a culturally distinct child is gifted.

The same visual discrimination skills are necessary for reading all languages. Readiness skills are the same no matter what language a child eventually uses to read and write.

1. When you work on visual identification and discrimination skills, use pictures of objects and scenes that reflect all the cultures represented in your classroom.
2. Play Lotto or Concentration with words, numbers, or significant pictures from relevant cultures.

Books can teach children about a variety of cultures and celebrations within cultures. When choosing children's books, be aware of racist and sexist material. The following general guidelines were adapted from guidelines created by the Council on Interracial Books for Children.

Read the story. Decide if there are "good guys" and "bad guys" and if so, who they are relative to race and sex. If the good guys are always white males, the book may be unrepresentative and may be detrimental to those children who, because their race or sex is different, identify with the bad guys. As you read look for the way words are used—check for firefighters versus fire*men*, ancestors versus forefathers, and so on. Look at the theme. Is it a middle-class white American plot that happens to have other races plopped in it, or is it a realistic portrayal of what life is like? Does it offer insights, or is it so simplistic that it reinforces rather than breaks down stereotypes? Check the illustrations to see if they too reflect the real world or a stereotypic interpretation. In addition to checking stories for prejudicial portrayals, use the following guidelines for choosing books to read in your classroom.

1. Read stories about various cultures: Indian, Chinese, African, Mexican, black, Japanese, and Eskimo. (See the Bibliography for Children at the end of this chapter.)
2. Read stories about different places, such as the city, the desert, and other countries. (See the Bibliography for Children at the end of this chapter.)
3. Read stories about similarities and differences in children. (See the Bibliography for Children for suggestions.)
4. Read stories that are written in two languages. Depending on your background, you may need some help. You could get someone who speaks the other language to read the story or tape record the story for you and your class.
5. As you choose books, be sure they portray a variety of families and environments, including ones relevant to each child in the class.

Fingerplays combine both fine motor skills and language. The concepts taught are simple and descriptive.

Books can teach children about their own culture and the cultures of others. Be sure the books they read are nonracial and nonsexist.

1. Be aware of sterotypic presentations in traditional fingerplays. Look at the general idea and see what you can do to adapt them. Many fingerplays were developed when we were not as aware of the impact of stereotypes as we are now. "Ten Little Indians" can be changed to "Ten Little Children."
2. Adapt fingerplays about families to meet specific family configurations or to enhance language learning.
3. If you have children who speak another language, ask the parents to translate a simple fingerplay for you. Remember that all languages have idiomatic ways of saying things, so don't expect a word-for-word translation.

### Social Studies

Social Studies provides many natural opportunities to discuss cultural differences and is enhanced by having culturally distinct children in the class. Be sure to include special events on holidays, and discuss the different ways people celebrate them. Give information on a variety of cultures and emphasize those represented in your classroom. Include discussions of things that vary with geography (foods, temperatures, seasons), and how cultures adapt to geographical differences.

1. Celebrate holidays on the dates and in the ways it is done in a variety of cultures. Be sure to give children information on the mood, reason for the dates, and types of celebrations.
   Chinese: New Year's Day may fall from January 21 to February 19 (depends on lunar calendar).
   Jewish: Rosh Hashanah, two days in late September or early October.
   Seminole: Chalo Nitka Festival, first Saturday in March.
2. Ask parents or relatives to come to class and talk to the children about some aspect of their culture. Perhaps they could help by preparing a special food, teaching a song or rhyme, or showing some special playthings that are different from those in the preschool. They might also wear the traditional dress of their culture.
3. Using a map or globe, have children share faraway places they have lived in or visited, or where they have family or friends living. Encourage them to talk about things that are different from the United States, and about things that are the same.

### Science/Discovery

Science is a marvelous way of looking at individual differences in a nonjudgmental way.

1. Use a magnifying glass and have the children look at their skin and hair. All skin has pores;

some skins have more or less pigment or even freckles. Put a strand of each child's hair in water and see what happens to straight and curly hair.

2. Use cooking to help children learn about foods and what goes into them. Taste raw and cooked carrots or potatoes. Choose unfamiliar recipes with many ingredients. Then have the children help in the cooking to make the food more familiar and to increase the likelihood of their eating it.

### Mathematics

Math needs few adaptations, and expanding children's awareness of language and math is fun.

1. Teach children to count in another language. (Numbers are relatively easy to learn.)
2. Help children build the language concepts for comparison they need to advance in math: small, big; smallest, largest.
3. Have children measure the distance to the various places their families are from.
4. Develop classification skills and use them to help children realize that they belong to many sets all at the same time: children, boys/girls, black/white/brown.

### Health and Safety

Because people have varying ideas about health and safety practices, it is important to teach these skills situationally. In other words, teach the skills that are appropriate for school.

1. When children initially engage in some unsafe practice, such as climbing the fence instead of the jungle gym, make your limits clear, but situational: "*At school* you may not climb on the fence. If you want to climb, you may climb on the jungle gym." Be prepared to reinforce this statement physically if necessary: Help the child climb down from the fence and walk over to the jungle gym with him.
2. Integrate food preparation into the curriculum through snack and lunch. Discuss nutrition. Help children learn about the relationship between growth, food, and health. Be sure to include cultural variations of "good food." Use foods that are familiar to the children, as well as some that aren't.
3. Suggest a variety of eating situations (picnic, banquet, brown bag lunch, bedtime snack) and have children predict what foods might be served at each.

### Art

You can incorporate the cultural variations present in your class in art. You can also use art for in-creasing an appreciation of cultural variety in general.

1. With the help of their parents, have children make a family tree that includes their family's place of origin. To simplify the project, have the children use only first names and names of states or countries.
2. Colors, like numbers, are easy to learn in a variety of languages.
3. Do activities that demonstrate the unique qualities in all people: thumbprints, handprints, shadow drawings, footprints, body outlines.

### Music

Music is enriched by cultural variation. As cultures and subcultures have developed, all have found music a way to express feelings and to share experiences common to their heritage.

1. Play albums for listening and singing, and also to create moods.
   Compare folk or popular songs of American and other cultures.
   Demonstrate musical styles of different cultures, such as Mariachi band music.
   Contrast music associated closely with particular subcultures, such as jazz/blues, reggae, opera, and rock and roll.
2. Ask parents to teach you (and also have them come into the class and teach the children), traditional children's songs and games from their culture.
3. Have a variety of traditional instruments available from various cultures, such as maracas, castanets, bongo and conga drums, and flutes.

### Dramatic Play

Dramatic play is another way of learning about other cultures.

1. Set up the dramatic play area with props and clothing from a particular culture. Choose ones both within and outside the United States. Be sure to follow up with discussions.
2. People use many types of transportation. Discuss the relationship of various transportation systems to cultures. People can move themselves (walk, run, swim). They can use animals by riding them or having them pull something to ride in (camels, horses, elephants, llamas). People also ride in or on machines (cars, buses, subways, trains, trucks, planes). Discuss and role play the implications of various forms of transportation.
3. Have overnight bags available to take pretend trips to a variety of places. Get travel folders. Decide how you'll get there, what you'll do there, what you need to take, and what language will be

spoken. Then go on your trip. If you have children from other countries in your class, have them pretend to take the class on a trip to their country.

## Small Motor Play

Small motor skills need practice. One way of showing acceptance for cultural differences is to use materials that come from different cultures for small motor play.

1. When you make self-help boards for lacing, buttoning, zipping, and snapping, add hooks and eyes, toggles, and oriental "frogs." If possible, use traditional materials from various countries for the cloth: madras, linen, silk, traditional prints, traditional weaves, gingham, tartan wool plaids. (To make some of the fabrics sturdier, iron on heavy pellon.)
2. Make sewing cards from traditional symbolic shapes, or those that have cultural significance. Then, have children design their own.
3. Teach children how to play Chinese checkers.
4. Teach children some of the simpler forms of origami (paper folding).
5. Set up simple looms and have children weave small articles. Take them on a field trip to visit someone with a large loom.

## Large Motor Play

Different cultures and subcultures have traditional games and large motor activities. Be sure to include these in your planning.

1. Make and fly traditional Japanese kites.
2. Make a piñata and break it at a traditional Mexican Christmas party.
3. Play stick ball.
4. Look at land use and space, a high-rise apartment and a ranch. Make replicas of Native American homes—the Navajo hogans and the long house of the Iroquois—and show how these were responsive to the environment.
5. Encourage children to build structures for various climates and uses. Ask them to suggest additions they need to the construction area, such as fabric, dowels, netting, and so on to build their structures. Have them design
   - a house where it is hot and rainy
   - a school where it is almost always cold
   - a store where the temperature changes
6. Show pictures of buildings from various cultures in the school area, and have children adapt building structures to situations.
   - city (lots of people)
   - country (few people)
   - seashore
   - mountain
7. Show children pictures of buildings and see if they can duplicate the structure.
   - church
   - skyscraper
   - pagoda
   - apartment building
   - pyramid
   - nuclear power plant
   - brownstone
   - clock tower
   - bank

## Transitions

Transitions provide another opportunity for helping children feel the same as other children yet be unique as individuals. Be sure children understand what you want them to do during transitions, especially at the beginning of the school year.

1. Play the "I'm thinking of someone" game to dismiss children: "I'm thinking of someone with brown hair, brown eyes, and a plaid shirt! Yes. Lisa, you can get your coat."
2. Encourage knowledge of full names and addresses by dismissing children by last name, address, or phone number. (Not all children necessarily have a phone number, so you may want to make up some phone numbers or have them learn an emergency number for your area.)
3. Dismiss children with simple commands from another language.

## CHILD STUDY TEAM REPORT

### George P.

In attendance: Mr. and Mrs. P.; Ms. Y., kindergarten teacher; Mr. T., psychologist.

George P. is a five-year two-month-old boy of Hispanic origin. When George started kindergarten, it was soon apparent to Ms. Y. that his primary language was Spanish. She referred him to the school district's Spanish-speaking psychologist for testing. She requested the testing in order to help her in planning for George in her "English-speaking" classroom.

George's father acts as the spokesperson for the family, since Mrs. P. does not speak English. Mr. P. reports that he and his wife are originally from Puerto Rico and speak Spanish at home. However, he feels George understands both languages.

George lives at home with four siblings, ages two, four, seven, and nine. The two older children attend public school. George's seven-year-old sister attends special education classes for the social/emotionally maladjusted children in her school.

George has been hospitalized for removal of his tonsils and adenoids. Mr. P. reports that George suffered frequent colds up until this point. He added that George is allergic to milk, which was discovered when he was "a little over one year," after he had experienced frequent stomach pains. Mr. P. described George as a "fussy baby," but now considers him "quiet."

Ms. Y. believes that George feels uncomfortable in the classroom. Her informal observations confirm Mr. P.'s belief that George understands English well.

According to Ms. Y., George understands directions and has caught on quickly to the routine of the classroom. He speaks to his peers very little. George uses English when he talks to his peers, but only in three-to-four word phrases. She added that George particularly likes the housekeeping area of the room, and assumes the role of father, mother, baby, or big brother when playing there. George does sit and observe during large group time and has just begun to sing along with songs and fingerplays.

Mr. T. stated that testing clearly indicated Spanish was George's primary language. When tested in Spanish, George's full-scale IQ is in the "very superior" range, with a score of 142. He also reported that at times George mixes Spanish and English when talking. His knowledge of English, however, is limited to common nouns and verbs. George demonstrated very mature fine motor skills and knowledge of colors, numerical and quantitative concepts at about a second-grade level, and shapes, when tested in Spanish. George's visual and auditory memory were particular strengths. He was able to remember a total of seven pictures of objects, presented visually, and eight digits forward and six backward when presented orally. Mr. T. suggested that these skills be used in teaching George.

When asked about George's activities at home, Mr. P. reported that George was the only child at home that disliked TV. He stated that George likes to draw, especially with fine markers, and draws pictures of everything he sees. He also likes to build with Tinkertoys. The games he plays at home are usually with his brothers and sisters. They play baseball and hide-and-seek most frequently.

Ms. Y would like to see George participate more with the other children and learn to communicate more effectively with them. The next parent-teacher conference was set for May of this school year.

## INDIVIDUALIZED EDUCATION PROGRAM

NAME ___George P.___ DOB ___10___ / ___5___ / ___77___

AGE ___5-3___ GRADE ___Kindergarten___

SCHOOL ___Harmony Bells Elementary___

PARENTS/GUARDIANS ___Mr. & Mrs. P.___

ADDRESS ___17 Rounding Lane___

PHONE ___None___

On ___1/16/83___, the IPRD Committee
   (Date)
met to review all current data and

recommends Level ___I___ placement.

Date of new review ___6/30/83___

Exceptionality: ___Culturally distinct___

Present at meeting:

Parents ___Mr. and Mrs. P.___

Others: Name/Position ___Mr. T., Psychologist___

### CURRENT TEST DATA

TEST/DATE/RESULTS

Psychological / 12/1/82 / Superior intellectual functioning: tested
          /     / in Spanish
          /     /
          /     /
          /     /

Recommended Special Services (Hrs/Wk):

Total Hours/Week:

Special Education Classroom ___0___

Regular Classroom ___12½___

Representative of District/Agency ___Ms. Y., Teacher___

The committee has determined the following learning strengths and needs to be reflected in the IEP:

| STRENGTHS | NEEDS |
|---|---|
| Superior intellectual functioning | Social skills w/peers |
| Visual & auditory memory | Expressive language/ability |
| Quantitative concepts | to communicate with peers |
| Fine motor skills | and adults |

STUDENT _____ George P. _____ DATE _____ 1/16/83

GOAL _____ To increase vocabulary _____

PARENT SIGNATURE _____

TEACHER SIGNATURE _____

| INSTRUCTIONAL OBJECTIVES | EDUCATIONAL METHODS | Begin | DATE End | Eval. | PERSONS RESPONSIBLE Name | Position |
|---|---|---|---|---|---|---|
| Given 10 pictures at a time of: common household objects; farm animals; zoo animals; colors; numerals (1–20); verb actions; modes of transportation; community helpers; people in occupations; fruits; vegetables; other foods, George will identify them a. receptively in English b. expressively in English with 80% accuracy. | Sounds, Animal Sounds, Food Lotto, Color Lotto, Opposite Lotto, Johnny Hear, Johnny Do, Robot, Controller | 1/16 3/15 | 4/15 6/30 | | Ms. Y. | Teacher |

STUDENT ____George P.____ DATE ____1/16/83____

GOAL ____To cooperate with peers____

PARENT SIGNATURE _____ TEACHER SIGNATURE _____

| INSTRUCTIONAL OBJECTIVES | EDUCATIONAL METHODS | Begin | DATE End | Eval. | PERSONS RESPONSIBLE Name | Position |
|---|---|---|---|---|---|---|
| Given a free play period of 30 min., George will participate in cooperative play with 1 peer or more for 20 minutes on 5 consecutive days. | Barefoot, Puppets, Bookstore, Picnic, Traveling | 1/16 | 6/30 | | Ms. Y. | Teacher |
| Given a small group game or activity of his choice, George will pick 2 peers to play with him and will play for at least 15 minutes on 5 occasions. | Color Concentration, Charades, Peg Design, Matching Faces, Fishing for Faces | 1/16 | 4/30 | | Ms. Y. | Teacher |
| Given a 30-minute outdoor recess or gross motor play, George will participate in group play with 3 peers or more for 20 minutes on 5 consecutive days. | In and Out, Bubble Machine, Balance It | 3/16 | 6/30 | | Ms. Y. | Teacher |

STUDENT  George P.  DATE  1/16/83

GOAL  To increase understanding

PARENT SIGNATURE

TEACHER SIGNATURE

| INSTRUCTIONAL OBJECTIVES | EDUCATIONAL METHODS | DATE Begin | DATE End | Eval. | PERSONS RESPONSIBLE Name | Position |
|---|---|---|---|---|---|---|
| George will be able to follow a 2-step direction given in English in 4/5 trials. | Johnny Hear, Johnny Do, Controller, Transitions, Directions, Tense Me | 1/16 | 4/30 | | Ms. Y. | Teacher |
| George will be able to follow a 3-step direction given in English in 4/5 trials. | same as above | 3/15 | 6/30 | | Ms. Y. | Teacher |
| George will be able to give a 2-step direction to a peer in 4/5 trials. | same as above | 3/15 | 6/30 | | Ms. Y. | Teacher |

STUDENT    George P.    DATE    1/16/83

GOAL    To improve expressive language

PARENT SIGNATURE _____

TEACHER SIGNATURE _____

| INSTRUCTIONAL OBJECTIVES | EDUCATIONAL METHODS | DATE Begin | DATE End | Eval. | PERSONS RESPONSIBLE Name | Position |
|---|---|---|---|---|---|---|
| George will express his needs verbally to adults in 3–4 word English phrases. | Feelings, Dress Up and Tell, Share Your Feelings | 1/16 | 6/30 | | Ms. Y. | Teacher |
| George will increase English verbalization with peers and adults by 50% (baseline data to be taken week of 1/15/83). | Telephone, Peek Pictures, I'm Thinking Of, Awareness Activities, Freeplay & Dramatic Play Activities | 4/16 | 6/30 | | Ms. Y. | Teacher |
| George will increase initiation of English conversation with peers during free play and dramatic play by 50% (baseline data to be taken week of 4/15/83). | Same as those for second objective | 4/16 | 6/30 | | Ms. Y | Teacher |
| George will answer questions appropriately in a. small group discussions (3–4 children) b. large group discussions (10–12 children) 4/5 days per week. | Story, Flannel board story, Group time | 1/83 3/83 | 6/83 6/83 | | Ms. Y | Teacher |

# GLOSSARY

**Acculturation**   The process of adopting the cultural traits or social patterns of another group.

**Alienation**   The process by which people are turned away or offended. To force a child who usually looks at his feet when spoken to by an adult (as is appropriate in his culture) to look you in the eye when you talk with him may alienate the child and his parents.

**Assimilation**   The merging of cultures so that one or both lose some of their distinct traits.

**Bilingual**   The ability to speak two languages with equal fluency.

**Bilingual program**   A program taught in two languages.

**Cultural bias**   A tendency to look at or interpret actions and events from one's own perspective. Achievement and IQ tests that have been given to primarily white, middle-class children to develop norms are biased against those with other cultural backgrounds, such as blacks and Hispanics.

**Cultural deficit**   A viewpoint that judges cultures that are different from the dominant one deficient and that advocates changing the child's value system to conform to the school's.

**Dialect**   A variation of a language that is used by a specific group of people.

**Ethnic**   Characteristic of a particular group or culture, such as speech, food, or dress.

**Ethnocentric**   The belief in the superiority of one's own culture and values over others. Viewing other cultures from the perspective of one's own.

**Immersion language program**   A program that involves the exclusive use of one language, usually the child's second language.

**Institutional racism**   The organization of parts of our society so that individuals of different races are treated unequally.

**Mores**   Folkways that are valued by everyone in a particular group.

**Nonimmersion language program**   Programs where both languages are used in the teaching process. Some versions concentrate on using the native language as a bridge to teach important concepts. Others aim to develop proficiency in both languages.

**Situationally specific behavior**   Behavior that is appropriate in one setting but not in another (yelling is fine outside but not inside).

**Stereotype**   An oversimplification or generalization about a particular group. Stereotypes are usually demeaning in some way.

**Tokenism**   The inclusion of a minority person based on their differences.

**Value conflict**   Differences between expectations about behavior at school and at home. (Parents might see school as the "3 Rs"; you see it including creative arts and social skills.)

# TEACHING RESOURCES

In some situations you may want or need additional information. There are many national as well as regional, state, and local organizations that can be helpful to you. The following annotated list of national organizations should be useful in helping you decide where to get the information you need.

African American Institute
School Services Division
833 United Nations Plaza
New York, NY 10017
   An educational division that helps inform Americans about Africa.

Afro-American Publishing Co., Inc.
1727 South Indiana Avenue
Chicago, IL 60616
   Distributes books and other materials for young children. Request a catalog.

Alternatives
1924 East Third
Bloomington, IN 47401

   Provides information on Native Americans and alternative ways of celebrating Thanksgiving.

Asian American Studies Center
3232 Campbell Hall
University of California, Los Angeles
Los Angeles, CA 90024
   Provides information on current research and on ways of breaking down traditional stereotypes.

Bureau of Indian Affairs
1951 Constitution Avenue, N.W.
Washington, DC 20242
   Has twelve regional offices and distributes materials that it publishes.

The Council on Interracial Books for Children, Inc.
1841 Broadway
New York, NY 10023
   Has extensive and valuable bibliographies, as well as criteria for detecting racism and sexism

in books. Copies of the Council's complete guidelines are available for 10¢ each.

Hispanic-American Institute
100 East 27th Street
Austin, TX 78705
   Provides resources for increasing understanding of the Hispanic people and their culture in the United States and in Latin America.

Indian Cultural/Curriculum Center
Tuba City Public Schools
Tuba City, AZ 86045
   Provides class units on Indian culture, as well as a bibliography.

Indian Education Resources Center
123 Fourth Street, S.W.

P.O. Box 1788
Albuquerque, NM 87103
   Provides information on research and curriculum bulletins.

New York Public Library
The Branch Libraries
8 East 40th Street
New York, NY 10016
   Has annotated lists of books for children in a variety of cultures.

Office of State Superintendent of Public Instruction
Old Capital Building
Olympia, WA 98504
   Provides an extensive list of annotated books on Asian and Asian American cultures suitable for young children.

# BIBLIOGRAPHY

Banks, James A. *Multiethnic Education: Theory and Practice*. Boston: Allyn and Bacon, 1981.

Bender, Michael, and Rosemary K. Bender. *Disadvantaged Preschool Children: A Source Book for Teachers*. Baltimore: Paul H. Brookes, 1979.

Beuf, Ann H. *Red Children in White America*. Phila., Pa: Univ. of Pennsylvania Press, 1977.

Inter American Research Associates. *A Bibliography of Bilingual–Biculture Preschool Materials for the Spanish Speaking Child*. U.S. Department of Health, Education, and Welfare, Office of Child Development, Washington, D.C.: 1977.

Cordasco, Francesco, and Eugene Bucchioni, eds. *The Puerto Rican Community and Its Children on the Mainland: A Source Book for Teachers, Social Workers and Other Professionals*. 3rd revised ed. Metuchen, N.J.: Scarecrow Press, 1982.

Curry, Leah, and Larry A. Rood. *Head Start Parent Handbook*. rev. ed. Ranier, Md.: Gryphon House, 1978.

Dana, Richard H., ed. *Human Services for Cultural Minorities*. Baltimore, Md.: University Park Press, 1981.

Delgado, Melvin. "Providing Child Care for Hispanic Families." *Young Children*. (September 1980), pp. 26–32.

Forbes, Jack D. *Afro-Americans in the Far West: A Handbook for Educators*. Berkeley, Calif.: Far West Laboratory for Educational Research and Development, 1968.

Garcia, Eugene E. "Bilingualism in Early Childhood." *Young Children*. (May 1980), pp. 52–66.

Gold, Milton J., C. A. Grand, and H. W. Rivlen, eds. *In Praise of Diversity: A Resource Book for Multicultural Education*. Washington, D.C.: Teacher Corps, 1977.

Ibuka, Masaru. *Kindergarten Is Too Late*. New York: Simon and Schuster, 1980.

Inui, Lloyd, and Franklin Odo. *The Asian American Experience*. Long Beach, Calif.: California State University, 1974.

Jenkins, Jeanne K., and Pam MacDonald. *Growing Up Equal: Activities and Resources for Parents and Teachers of Young Children*. Englewood Cliffs, N.J.: Prentice-Hall, 1979.

Jones, Reginald L., ed. *Mainstreaming and the Minority Child*. Reston, Va.: Council for Exceptional Children, 1976.

Kitano, Margie K. "Early Education for Asian American Children." *Young Children*. (January 1980), pp. 13–26.

McNeill, Earldene, Judy Allen, and Velma E. Schmidt. *Cultural Awareness for Young Children*. Mt. Rainier, Md.: Gryphon House, 1981.

Mills, Joyce W., ed. *The Black World in Literature for Children: A Bibliography of Print and Non-print Materials*. Atlanta, Ga.: Atlanta University, School of Library Service, 1975.

Nurcombe, Barry. *Children of the Dispossessed: A consideration of the nature of intelligence, cultural disadvantage, educational programs for culturally different people and of the development and expression of a profile of competencies*. Honolulu: Univ. Press of Hawaii, 1976.

Ramsey, Patricia G. "Beyond 'Ten Little Indians' and Turkeys: Alternative Approaches to Thanksgiving." *Young Children*. (September 1979), pp. 28–52.

Schmidt, Velma E., and Earldene McNeill. *Cultural Awareness: A Resource Bibliography*. Washington, D.C.: National Association for the Education of Young Children, 1978.

Staples, Robert. *Introduction to Black Sociology*. New York: McGraw-Hill, 1976.

Thompson, Thomas, ed. *The Schooling of Native America*. Washington, D.C.: American Association of Colleges for Teacher Education, 1978.

United States Bureau of Indian Affairs, *American Indians: Answers to 101 Questions*. Washington, D.C.: U.S. Government Printing Office, Superintendent of Documents. 1974.

*Unlearning "Indian" Stereotypes*. New York: Racism and Sexism Resource Center for Educators, a division of the Council on Interracial Books for Children, 1977.

U.S. Department of Commerce, Bureau of the Census. *Statistical Abstracts of the United States, 1980.* 101st Edition. Washington, D.C.: U.S. Government Printing Office, 1980.

Wilson, Amos N. *The Developmental Psychology of the Black Child.* New York: United Brothers Communications Systems, 1978.

*Biography/Autobiography/Fiction*

*Asian Americans*

Charyn, Jerome. *American Scrapbook.* New York: Viking, 1969.

The story of one family's internment in a concentration camp in the U.S. and the effects this had on each of the six family members.

Lee, Cy. *The Flower Drum Song.* New York: Farrar, Straus & Giroux, 1957.

The story of family life in San Francisco's Chinatown. The pull between tradition and western culture is typified.

Kingston, Maxine Hong. *China Men.* New York: Knopf, 1980.

Mrs. Kingston describes the lives of men who came from China, in particular her father and brothers. She blends myth, legend, and the history of China to help better understand "China Men."

————. *The Woman Warrior: Memoirs of a Girlhood Among Ghosts.* New York: Knopf, 1976.

The autobiography of a girl haunted by the ghosts of her Chinese ancestors and the white-faced American ghosts she met as she grew up in San Francisco. She pictures the collision of cultures as she as a child failed kindergarten and didn't speak in school until the third grade. She goes to Berkeley on a scholarship. The growth is painful.

Shimer, R. H. *The Cricket Cage.* New York: Harper and Row, 1975.

Set in the 1880's, this focuses on the China trade and the problems of the Chinese in Seattle.

*Black Americans*

Angelou, Maya. *Gather Together in My Name.* New York: Random House, 1974.

A sequel to *I Know Why the Caged Bird Sings;* begins where the other stopped. Maya Angelou speaks of the various jobs she had as she tried to support herself and her child. The specific adventures are hers but could have happened to anyone in her generation.

————. *I Know Why the Caged Bird Sings.* New York: Random House, 1970.

An autobiography of Maya Angelou growing up in a small, Southern, rural black community. It is both powerful and sensitive. The story ends when she is 16, unmarried, and has a new baby.

Brown, Claude. *Children of Ham.* Briarcliff Manor, New York: Stein & Day, 1976.

The children are a group of blacks living together in Harlem. They are surviving and each member of the group tells about his past and how he came to join the commune.

————. *Manchild in the Promised Land.* New York: Macmillan, 1965.

The autobiography of a man who grew up in Harlem during the 1940s and 50s. It is brutal and honest and the language and style reflect this.

Ellison, Ralph. *Invisible Man.* New York: Random House, 1952.

A classic novel about a black man's dubious position in a white man's world. Ellison feels the black man is invisible because others refuse to see him.

Hurston, Zora Neale. *I Love Myself When I Am Laughing . . . And Then Again When I Am Looking Mean and Impressive.* Pref. by Alice Walker. A Zora Neale Hurston Reader, Old Westbury, New York: The Feminist Press, 1979.

A compilation of the works of Zora Neale Hurston including her essays "How It Feels to Be Colored Me" and "What White Publishers Won't Print," excerpts from *Their Eyes Were Watching God, Moses, Man of the Mountain,* and more. The introduction helps one get a feel for Zora Hurston, novelist, folklorist, journalist, critic, and for thirty years, one of the most prolific black women writers in America.

Wright, Richard. *Native Son.* 1940; rpt. New York: Harper and Row, 1969.

One of the first books written in the Protest Era of black literature after 1940. The book uses a black male and white female to represent the racial tensions between blacks and whites.

*Native Americans*

Momaday, N. Scott. *House Made of Dawn.* New York: Harper and Row, 1968.

A four-part novel that portrays Abel, a young American Indian, in relation to reservation life both before and after his induction into the army and the white man's civilization. This book is the first novel written by this young Kiowa Indian and depicts the trials of trying to live in two cultures.

————. *The Names. A Memoir.* New York: Harper and Row, 1976.

An extension of *The Way to Rainy Mountain.* Portrays, through the names given to objects, land, animals, birds, and so on, the meaning they had to the Kiowa.

————. *The Way to Rainy Mountain.* Albuquerque: University of New Mexico Press, 1969.

An autobiographical novel that combines the voices of legend, history, and the author's contemporary interpretations of these into a gentle yet conscience-nagging novel.

Sanchez, Thomas. *Rabbit Boss*. New York: Knopf, 1973.

Typifies the change in Indian culture caused by a vanishing wilderness and the greed of the white man. A powerful novel.

Welch, James. *Winter in the Blood*. New York: Harper and Row, 1974.

An unforgettable story of a young Indian living on a reservation in Montana, the tragic death of his beloved grandmother, and the discovery of his own heritage.

*Spanish Americans*

Brawley, Ernest. *Selena*. New York: Atheneum, 1979.

Selena is a chicana labor organizer who shows through her love–hate relationship with the landowner's son what life among the *compeñeros* in California is like. A social protest as well as a moving story.

Lange, Oliver. *Red Snow*. New York: Seaview Books, 1978.

A hunt for a mountain lion brings law officers and a primarily Spanish American local village into conflict. The hate, prejudice, and resentment is unleashed.

Piercy, Marge. *Woman on the Edge of Time*. New York: Knopf, 1976.

Consuelo Ramos, a chicana living in Harlem, is hospital-ized for insanity. Her treatment there and escape are detailed, as is her visualization of a utopic world of 2075.

Rodriguez, Richard. *Hunger of Memory: The Education of Richard Rodriguez: An Autobiography*. Boston, Mass: D. R. Godine, 1982.

Rodriguez enters kindergarten virtually speechless as he is the only Spanish-speaking child in his class. He has a private life at home and a public one once outside. With the emphasis on speaking English, Rodriguez does not easily become bilingual. Eventually, English replaces Spanish; he becomes Americanized. The book talks about his love for Spanish, his loss of intimacy, and the educational system.

Sanchez, Thomas. *Zoot-suit Murders: A Novel*. New York: Dutton, 1978.

Mid-WW II, when there is a lot of chicano distrust, some young men from the barrio are caught in the middle of a murder plot.

Thomas, Piri. *Down These Mean Streets*. New York: Knopf, 1967.

An autobiography that focuses on being an adolescent of Puerto Rican descent growing up in Spanish Harlem.

Wheeler, Richard S. *Beneath the Blue Mountain*. New York: Doubleday, 1979.

In the Arizona Territory of 1873–74 a Puritan family comes to take over the land of a proud Mexican family.

# BIBLIOGRAPHY FOR CHILDREN

*Asian American Children*

Ayer, Jacqueline. *The Paper Flower Tree*. New York: Harcourt Brace Jovanovich, 1962.

When a traveling peddler in Thailand presents little Miss Moon with a blossom from his paper flower tree, she plants its one seed and patiently waits for it to bloom.

Behrens, June. *Soo Ling Finds a Way*. Chicago: Childrens Press, 1965.

Fearing her grandfather's ruin from a laundromat going up across the street from his hand laundry, Soo Ling tells Grandfather to iron in front of the window since he has a magic hand at ironing. Grandfather Soo is so good at the iron, the new owner asks Grandfather to be his partner!

Flack, Marjorie, and Kurt Wiese. *Story About Ping*. New York: Viking Press, 1933.

An old favorite about a little duck who lives on a boat on the Yangtze River and his adventures when he hides from his master in order to avoid getting a spank on the back.

Handforth, Thomas. *Mei Li*. New York: Doubleday, 1938.

The story of a young girl in China.

Issa. *A Few Flies and I*. New York: Pantheon, 1969.

Collection of Japanese haikus.

Johnson, Doris. *Su An*. Chicago: Follett, 1968.

This charming little book presents death, adoption, and leaving one's homeland, in a very touching way. After her mother's death, Su An arrives in America from Korea, her home. She is going to join a new family, but her heart still longs for her mother.

Liang, Yen. *Tommy and Dee-Dee*. New York: Walck, 1953.

A simply written story illustrating how two boys living in different parts of the world, one in America and the other in China, are alike in many ways.

Martin, Patricia Miles. *The Greedy One*. New York: Rand McNally, 1964.

Tells the customs of the traditional Japanese "Boys Day" and what happens when a greedy boy eats the fish being saved for the festival. Red and white ink illustrations.

———. *The Rice Bowl Pet*. New York: Thomas Y. Crowell, 1962.

Jim lives in a crowded apartment in San Francisco's Chinatown. He roams the street looking for a pet small enough to fit in his rice bowl.

Politi, Leo. *Moy Moy*. New York: Scribner, 1960.

A story about life in the Chinese section of an American city and the celebration of the Chinese New Year told through the eyes of Moy Moy, an American-Chinese girl who lives in Los Angeles.

Riwkin-Brick, Anna. *Mokihana Lives in Hawaii*. New York: Macmillan, 1961.

The story of four Hawaiian children and how they spend one day.

Slobodkin, Louis. *Moon Blossom and the Golden Penny*. New York: Vanguard Press, 1963.

A poor child in Hong Kong receives a lucky penny when she helps an old woman.

Yashima, Taro. *Crow Boy*. New York: Viking Press, 1955.

The moving story of Chibi, a shy Japanese boy, whose classmates are helped by their teacher to understand him. This book points up the problems of young children from different backgrounds.

———. *Umbrella*. New York: Penguin Books, 1977.

Momo, a Japanese girl, wants it to rain so that she can use her new birthday umbrella and her beautiful red boots. When it finally rains, she has a marvelous time playing.

### Black American Children

Adoff, Arnold. *Black Is Brown Is Tan*. New York: Harper and Row, 1973.

Poetically phrased picture of a white-black marriage and family.

———. *Mandala*. New York: Harper and Row, 1971.

The story of an African family (MA is mother, DA is father, LA is singing). These sounds and others join over and over in a tuneful way that celebrates the circle of the family and the cycle of life.

Baldwin, Anne Norris. *Sunflowers for Tina*. New York: Scholastic Book Services, 1973.

Tina, a black girl, is determined to grow a garden in the middle of New York City.

Bond, Jean Carey. *Brown Is a Beautiful Color*. New York: Watts, 1969.

A story in simple rhyme that calls attention to all the things around us that are brown.

Cavin, Ruth. *Timothy the Terror*. New York: Harlin Quist, 1973.

A story about a little black boy's revenge on his three sisters.

Clifton, Lucille. *Three Wishes*. New York: Viking Press, 1976.

Written in black English, this story tells about Nobie and Victoria and a magic penny.

Elkin, Benjamin. *Such is the Way of the World*. New York: Scholastic Book Services, 1968.

A young African boy, while minding his father's cattle, loses his pet monkey and goes in search of him.

Feelings, Muriel. *Moja Means One: The Swahili Counting Book*. New York: Dial, 1971.

A Swahili counting book that describes East African culture.

———. *Jambo Means Hello: Swahili Alphabet Book*. New York: Dial, 1974.

An alphabet book that also describes East African culture.

Greenfield, Eloise. *First Pink Light*. New York: Thomas Y. Crowell, 1976.

Tyree is a young black child whose father has been away for a month. Tyree and his mother wait up together for Father, whom they miss so.

Hill, Elizabeth. *Evan's Corner*. New York: Holt, Rinehart and Winston, 1967.

Evan, a young black boy, tries to find privacy by creating his own special corner.

Keats, Ezra Jack. *The Snowy Day*. New York: Viking Press, 1962.

Delightful story of a black child's adventures in the snow.

———. *Whistle for Willie*. New York: Penguin Books, 1977.

A black city boy named Peter finds it difficult to learn to whistle for his dog Willie.

———. *Goggles*. New York: Macmillan, 1969.

Two black children find a pair of motorcycle goggles but have to outsmart a gang of "big guys" in order to keep them.

———. *Hi Cat*. New York: Macmillan, 1972.

Archie, a black city boy, makes friends with a stray black cat. A humorous tale of how the cat follows Archie around.

Lexau, Joan M. *Benjie on His Own*. New York: Dial, 1970.

Benjie, a black boy in a ghetto neighborhood, must walk home from school alone one day when his grandmother doesn't meet him. On the way, he encounters a big dog and some big boys who threaten and tease him. At home, he finds that his grandmother is sick. He finds some people to help, and a friend's mother takes him into her home while his grandmother is in the hospital.

McDermott, Gerald. *The Magic Tree. A Tale From the Congo.* New York: Holt, Rinehart and Winston, 1973.

A traditional African folk tale about making promises and keeping them. The magic tree gives a boy everything provided he keeps it a secret.

Radlaur, Ed, and Ruth Shaw. *Father Is Big.* Glendale, Calif.: Bowmar, 1967.

Close-up photographs by Harvey Mandlin show how a black child looks up to his father.

Randall, Blossom E. *Fun for Chris.* Chicago: Albert Whitman, 1956.

Chris finds a friend his age named Toby. Toby is black, but Chris doesn't attach any significance to the difference in skin coloring until an older friend makes it seem wrong. Chris's mother resolves the situation and Chris keeps his friend.

Scott, Ann Herbert. *Sam.* New York: McGraw-Hill, 1967.

Sam, a little boy, has nothing to do and causes his whole family to be mad at him.

Sonneborn, Ruth A. *Friday Night Is Papa Night.* New York: Viking Press, 1970.

The tender story of a black family looking forward to having Papa come home on Friday night.

Steptoe, John. *My Special Best Words.* New York: Viking Press, 1974.

A little girl uses black dialect to describe her daily life with her family (her brother and father) and her babysitter.

Stone, Elberta H. *I'm Glad I'm Me.* New York: Putnam, 1971.

A little boy, when he is lonely, dreams of all the things that he would like to be. Finally he realizes that he is glad to be himself because he has two arms to hug people with and two legs to walk with. Most important, he will grow up to be what he wants to be.

Udry, Janice May. *What Mary Jo Shared.* Chicago: Albert Whitman, 1968.

A little black girl shares her father during "show and tell."

———. *What Mary Jo Wanted.* Chicago: Albert Whitman, 1968.

Mary Jo, a young black girl, gets her wish: a puppy. She soon discovers that this is a twenty-four-hour-a-day responsibility.

Van Leeuwen, Jean. *Timothy's Flower.* New York: Random House, 1966.

A sensitive story of a small black boy who starts a garden in the middle of a city.

Yolen, Jane. *It All Depends.* New York: Funk and Wagnall, 1969.

A black boy becomes more aware of himself by asking his mother questions: "How tall am I?" "It all depends—to an ant, you are immense, to a whale you are small."

### Native American Children

Baker, Betty. *Little Runner of the Longhouse.* New York: Harper and Row, 1962.

Little Runner is envious of his older brothers who are allowed to participate in the Iroquois New Year's ceremonies.

Blood, Charles L, and Martin Link. *The Goat in the Rug.* New York: Scholastic Book Services, 1978.

Geraldine tells a story of a Navajo rug and the goat hair that was used to make the rug.

Parish, Peggy. *Little Indian.* New York: Simon and Schuster, 1968.

In search of a name, the little Indian goes into the forest to catch an animal so that he can be called by the animal's name. Eventually, a turtle catches him, so he is called Snapping Turtle.

Perrine, Mary. *Salt Boy.* Boston: Houghton Mifflin, 1973.

The story of a Navajo Indian boy's feelings for his father.

———. *Nannabah's Friend.* Boston: Houghton Mifflin, 1970.

A young Navajo girl copes with loneliness while taking her sheep to pasture.

Sleator, William. *The Angry Moon.* Boston: Little, Brown, 1970.

Tlingit Indian legend from Alaska.

Stuart, Gene S. *Three Little Indians.* Washington, D.C.: National Geographic Society, 1974.

The stories of a Cheyenne boy, a Greek girl, and a Nootha boy.

Wiseman, Bernard. *Iglook's Seal.* New York: Dodd, Mead, 1977.

Iglook is an Eskimo who can't bring himself to harpoon a baby seal, so he brings it home as a pet. The seal ultimately catches fish for him.

### Hispanic American Children

Archuleta, Nathaniel, et al. *El Perrioto Perdido; Una Luminaria; Para Mis Palomitas; Ya Perdiste tu Colita, Tita; Perlitas de Ayer y Hoy.* Available from Dr. Nathaniel Archuleta, University of New Mexico, Albuquerque, NM, 1975.

These five books of stories, poems, rhymes, songs, and activities are written in Spanish with an English version in the back. They highlight the Hispanic culture.

Atkinson, Mary. *Maria Teresa*. Chapel Hill, N.C.: Lollipop Power, 1979.

Maria and her mother move to a new town where no one speaks Spanish. With the help of her puppet, Maria helps the other children in the class learn the language.

Blue, Rose. *I Am Here. Yo Estoy Aquí*. New York: Watts, 1971.

A young girl from Puerto Rico makes friends and begins to learn English in her new surroundings.

Brenner, Barbara. *Barto Takes the Subway*. New York: Knopf, 1961.

A Puerto Rican boy explores the sights and sounds of New York's subway.

Brunhoff, Laurent de. *Babar's Spanish Lessons*. New York: Random House, 1965.

Babar gives Spanish lessons to his elephant friends. The text is written in English with Spanish after each English sentence.

Ets, Marie Hall. *Bad Boy, Good Boy*. New York: Thomas Y. Crowell, 1967.

The story of a large Spanish-speaking family. The little boy is always getting into trouble because he has nothing to do. When the mother leaves after a fight with the father, the father is forced to take the little boy to a day care center. At first the little boy hates it there. After a while, he learns to speak English and writes his mother a letter begging her to come home. She does.

————. *Gilberto and the Wind*. New York: Viking Press, 1963.

This Mexican boy makes the wind his playmate. The book shows the many things the wind can do. (Also available in Spanish)

Freeman, Don. *Corduroy*. New York: Viking Press, 1968.

This book shows a young hispanic girl's feelings of loneliness, companionship, and love for a very special teddy bear.

Hautzig, Esther. *In the Park: An Excursion in Four Languages*. New York: Macmillan, 1968.

Written in four languages (English, French, Russian, and Spanish), this book shows pictures of things seen in parks in New York, Moscow, Paris, and Madrid.

Keats, Ezra Jack. *My Dog Is Lost*. New York: Thomas Y. Crowell, 1960.

Juanito, who speaks only Spanish, comes to New York from Puerto Rico and loses his only friend, his dog. His search takes him to Park Avenue, Chinatown, and Harlem. The text introduces some simple Spanish phrases.

Kesselman, Wendy, and Norma Holt. *Angelita*. New York: Hill and Wang, 1970.

Angelita loses her treasured doll as she moves from Puerto Rico to New York City. Photographs depict the land and scenery of each place.

Morrow, Elizabeth. *The Painted Pig*. New York: Knopf, 1930.

Pedro is a young Mexican boy whose greatest wish is to own a china pig. The story of his determined efforts to get his pig gives the readers an understanding of the children and customs of Mexico.

Nielson, Virginia. *Adassa and Her Hen*. Toronto: McKay, 1971.

A little girl in Jamaica has an unusual pet hen.

Politi, Leo. *Rosa*. New York: Scribner, 1963.

Rosa is a little girl who lives in San Felipe, Mexico. Her wish for a doll comes true in a special way when a baby sister is born on Christmas Eve. This book, also available in Spanish, shows the toys and games Rosa plays with as well as the customs of her country.

————. *The Nicest Gift*. New York: Scribner, 1973.

Carlitos's dog has disappeared, but reappears on Christmas Day. Fantastic illustrations of a Mexican neighborhood near Los Angeles.

Schweitzer, Byrd Baylor. *Amigo*. New York: Macmillan, 1973.

A Mexican boy wants a pet, but his family cannot afford to feed one. He decides to tame a prairie dog as a solution.

Serfozo, Mary. *Welcome Roberto! Bienvenido Roberto!* Chicago: Follett, 1969.

A Mexican-American child's first experience in school.

Sonneborn, Ruth. *Seven in a Bed*. New York: Viking Press, 1968.

Mama, the baby, and seven children come from Puerto Rico to join Papa, but they have a sleeping problem the first night.

Williams, Letty. *The Little Red Hen: La Pequeña Gallina Roja*. Englewood Cliffs, N.J.: Prentice-Hall, 1969.

The story of the little red hen told in both English and Spanish.

## Children from Other Cultures

Alder, David A., and Marilyn Hirsh. *The House on the Rook—A Sukkot Story*. New York: Bonim Books, 1976.

A gentle, warm, and humorous story about an old man getting ready for a special Hebrew holiday. Eventually, he must explain his actions to the neighbors.

Floethe, Louise, and Richard Floethe. *The New Roof*. New York: Scribner, 1955.

A Tahitian family needs a new roof on their palm-thatched house. When none of the men has time to fix it, the women decide to do it, and the next day the men decide to finish the project.

Paola, Tomie. *Watch Out for the Chicken Feet in Your Soup*. Boston: Houghton Mifflin, 1959.

Joey takes Eugene to visit his old-fashioned Italian grandmother.

Wim, Marie. *The Fireside Book of Fun and Game Songs*. New York: Simon and Schuster, 1974.

A good book for children of all ages. It offers songs of entertainment from a variety of cultures.

## Differences and Similarities

Evans, Eva Knox. *All About Us*. New York: Golden Press, 1957.

Explains simply the reasons for similarities and differences among children around the world.

Goldin, Augusta R. *Straight Hair, Curly Hair*. New York: Thomas Y. Crowell, 1972.

This is a science book with colorful illustrations that answers questions about hair.

Green, Mary McBurney. *Everybody Eats, Everybody Has a House*. Reading, Mass.: Addison-Wesley, 1967.

Tells what boys, girls, and animals eat, and about the houses they live in.

Keats, Ezra Jack. *Louie*. New York: School Book Services, 1979.

Louie, an alienated little boy, joins his friends Susie and Robert at a magical moment in a puppet show.

May, Julian. *Why People Are Different Colors*. New York: Holiday House, 1971.

Pictures of people of the three major races (Mongoloid, Caucasian, and Negroid). Discusses physical adaptations and their usefulness today.

Miles, Betty. *Around and Around—Love*. New York: Knopf, 1975.

A photographic expression of love among people. The text uses many different words to describe love. Photographs depict many different races and ages.

Simon, Norma. *Why Am I Different?* Chicago: Albert Whitman, 1976.

This story portrays everyday situations in which children see themselves as "different." The book says that it is all right to be different.

Tripp, Paul. *The Little Red Flower*. New York: Doubleday, 1968.

A drab and dusty mining town with dull and drab citizens is brightened up when a newcomer places a red flower in his window. When he gets sick, the townspeo-

ple have to learn to take care of it, and the result is a red flower in every window and a new spirit in the town.

## Cities and Children

Armer, Alberta. *Cherry House*. Boston: Beacon Press, 1958.

A story about slums and the children who live there. Explains the simple beauties of a city through children's dialogue.

Burton, Virginia Lee. *The Little House*. Boston: Houghton Mifflin, 1978.

A tender tale about a house built in the country and how the city grows up around it.

Clymer, Eleanor. *The Big Pile of Dirt*. New York: Holt, Rinehart and Winston, 1968.

A group of city children make a playground out of a lot full of junk. After the lot becomes piled with dirt, the children are told they can't play there. With the help of grownups, the children take a stand and get a playground.

Gaeddert, Lou Ann. *Noisy Nancy and Nick*. New York: Doubleday, 1970.

Nancy's new neighbor is from the Midwest and doesn't like the city. She shows him how to have fun.

Getz, Arthur. *Tar Beach*. New York: Dial, 1979.

In a blistering hot city, children play in the spray of the fire hydrant and use other ideas to stay cool. City summers come to life in this story.

Greene, Robert. *Two and Me Makes Three*. New York: Albert Whitman, 1970.

Three boys—Joey, Juan, and Willie—live in New York City, go to school, play on the streets and in the parks, and make the most of their surroundings.

Grifalconi, Ann. *City Rhythms*. Boston: Charles E. Merrill, 1965.

This book depicts city life through a small black boy's eyes.

Himler, Ronald. *The Girl on the Yellow Giraffe*. New York: Harper and Row, 1976.

The sights of the city become a fantasy world for one little girl.

Hitte, Kathryn. *What Can You Do Without a Place to Play*. New York: Parents' Magazine Press, 1971.

About city children and the different places they find to play.

Hoban, Tana. *Over, Under and Through*. New York: Macmillan, 1973.

Great black and white photographs depict children going over, under, and through different objects found in a city.

Stimulates discussions about going over, under, and through things at school and in the child's immediate environment.

Howell, Ruth Rea. *A Crack in the Pavement*. New York: Atheneum, 1970.

Growing things are everywhere—even in the cities. Grass and dandelions grow in cracks of the sidewalk, and pigeons nest on window sills.

Keeping, Charles. *Joseph's Yard*. New York: Watts, 1969.

A poignant story about a boy who wants his ghetto backyard full of things of nature. When he grows a rose and almost kills it trying to protect it, Joseph learns how too much can be as bad as too little.

Krasilovsky, Phyllis. *Cow Who Fell into the Canal*. Garden City, N.Y.: Doubleday, 1972.

Handrika, a country milk cow, has an eventful and educational fling in the big city.

Merrill, Jean, and Frances Scott. *How Many Kids Are Hiding on My Block*. Chicago: Albert Whitman, 1970.

Great hide-and-seek story written in prose style. Many children from different cultures are shown hiding in unique places.

Steptoe, John. *Stevie*. New York: Harper and Row, 1969.

A young black boy stays with a neighboring black family because his own mother is always at work. Written to help children understand the realities of the ghetto, its setting is realistic and thought-provoking.

———. *Uptown*. New York: Harper and Row, 1970.

A realistic and hardhitting story of two young black boys in Harlem who sit and discuss all the things they can be when they grow up. Their choices are based on the limited things they have seen in their own community.

Ventura, Piero. *Book of Cities*. New York: Random House, 1975.

A book about cities—what you would find in a city, different ways of getting around, and what things there are to do. It also talks about some unique features of various big cities.

*Families*

Blue, Rose. *Grandma Didn't Wave Back*. New York: Watts, 1972.

Debbie feels very special: She has a Grandma right at her apartment. However, one day she notices that Grandma is acting in a strange manner, and forgetting things. Debbie thinks it is temporary but soon discovers she is mistaken. It is a traumatic experience for youngsters to see the signs of aging and the changing of someone special.

Borack, Barbara. *Grandpa*. New York: Harper and Row, 1967.

Though Grandpas can be old, they sure can be fun. Marilyn's Grandpa even plays with her, and his imagination never ceases. The elderly need not be feared.

Brownstone, Cecily. *All Kinds of Mothers*. New York: Mc-Kay, 1969.

There are many different types of mothers and there are many options open to them. Questions put to the reader throughout the book involve children in the story. The detailed illustrations aid in comprehension.

Buckley, Helen E. *Grandfather and I*. New York: Lothrop, 1959.

A story about the relationship between a child and his grandfather. Ideal for ages three to six, it illustrates the closeness that can develop between a grandparent and grandchild.

———. *Grandmother and I*. New York: Lothrop, 1961.

Grandmother's lap is compared to the other laps in the family, each of which is good for different things.

Charnley, Nathaniel, and Betty Jo Charnley. *Martha Ann and the Mother Store*. New York: Harcourt Brace Jovanovich, 1973.

A little girl tries out different kinds of mothers and realizes that her own is best, even if she does make rules, scold, and require some obedience.

Lundgren, Max. *Matt's Grandfather*. New York: Putnam, 1972.

Matt's parents take him to visit his eighty-five-year-old grandfather. They prepare him to see an old and feeble man. Matt and his grandfather take a walk, and the grandfather turns out to be not as old and feeble as Matt expected.

Miziemuru, Kazue. *If I Were a Mother*. New York: Thomas Y. Crowell, 1968.

Animal mothers provide examples of ways of mothering. Each animal treats its baby a certain way, like the mother horse who helps its baby until it can stand on its own feet. The little girl and little boy end the story wanting to be like his or her own mother.

Radlauer, Ruth Shaw. *Mothers Are That Way*. London: Abelard Schuman, 1960.

This book tells from a child's point of view what the difference is between mothers and children. It explains how mothers use water not for making mud pies, but for cleaning. It shows children the difference in the way they and their mothers think.

Schlien, Miriam. *The Way Mothers Are*. Chicago: Albert Whitman, 1963.

With adorable pictures by Lucy Hawkinson of mother and son cat. The son asks his mother if she will love him even when he does something bad. The mother cat explains that because he is her son she will love him in spite of the things he does wrong and will not love him any more if he does good things. The story deals with the fear that many children have of rejection from their parents, especially when they have done something wrong.

Simon, Norma. *All Kinds of Families*. Chicago: Albert Whitman, 1975.

The book reflects the many patterns of traditional and nontraditional families. It stresses the supportive function of families and the child's joyous place in it.

Sonneborn, Ruth A. *I Love Gram*. New York: Viking Press, 1971.

A little girl's grandmother, who lives with her family, is taken to the hospital. The girl is very upset and afraid that her Gram will die like her friend's grandmother. Finally her grandmother comes home.

Young, Eleanor R. *Mothers, Mothers, Mothers*. Minneapolis: T. S. Denison, 1971.

By showing children the universal aspects of mother's role, this book helps a child understand that all people are basically similar. The simple illustrations make the point by showing mothers of different races and nationalities.

Zolotow, Charlotte. *The Sky Was Blue*. New York: Harper and Row, 1963.

A tender story of a little girl who looks through the family album with her mother. As they look back over the years at the pictures of her mother, grandmother, and great grandmother when they were little girls her age, the little girl wonders what it felt like to be a little girl back then. Her mother tells her the really important things don't change. The sky is always blue, the grass always green.

*Nontraditional Family Situations*

Barrett, John M. *No Time for Me: Learning to Cope with Busy Parents*. New York: Human Sciences Press, 1979.

Eight-year-old Jimmy feels rejected because his parents seem to have no time for him. This is a helpful book for a child whose parents are both working and for the parents too.

Blaine, Marge. *The Terrible Thing That Happened at Our House*. New York: Scholastic Book Services, 1975.

A child relates the problems that occur after her mother goes to work and how the family solves them.

Bunin, Catherine. *Is That Your Sister? A Story of a Free Adoption*. New York: Pantheon, 1976.

Catherine, six, talks about the adoption of herself and

her younger sister Carla, both of whom are black, into a white family.

Drescher, Joan. *Your Family, My Family*. New York: Walker and Co., 1980.

A clever look at many different types of families in a variety of settings. Children can recognize their own family group and learn about other people.

Eichler, Margit. *Martin's Father*. Chapel Hill, N.C.: Lollipop Power, 1977.

Martin's father cares for him, and they perform everyday tasks together. Shows the father as a nurturing parent.

Lapsley, Susan. *I Am Adopted*. Scarsdale, N.Y.: Bradbury Press, 1975.

A simple book in which two children describe what it means to be adopted. It means security and belonging.

*The Me and You Book*. Chicago: Encyclopedia Britannica, 1974.

The book talks about different kinds of families and how hard it is to share feelings.

Merriam, Eve. *Mommies at Work*. New York: Scholastic Book Services, 1977.

The story of a woman who is a "mommy" and also has a job.

Rappart, Doreen, et al. *A Man Can Be . . .* New York: Human Sciences Press, 1981.

Through a glimpse into a day shared by a father and his son, this delightful book discusses the ever changing roles and emotional responses of men.

Simon, Norma. *I'm Busy, Too*. Chicago: Albert Whitman, 1980.

A book about the diversity of families both within them and among them. Especially useful for the child who is new to day care, since it discusses three families who attend the community care center.

Surowiecki, Sandra Lucas. *Joshua's Day*. Chapel Hill, N.C.: Lollipop Power, 1977.

Joshua lives in a one-parent home. His mother, who is a photographer, takes him to a day care center where he interacts with both boys and girls.

Zolotow, Charlotte. *William's Doll*. New York: Harper and Row, 1972.

William wants a doll. His father buys him "boy" toys: a basketball, a train, and so on. He likes them but still wants a doll. His grandmother buys him one and explains to his father how important this is in helping him become a caring father.

| *Annual Goals* | *Activity* | *Curriculum Area* | *Page* |
|---|---|---|---|
| | What Shall We Make? | Dramatic Play | 495 |
| | Who Are You? | Health and Safety | 441 |
| To increase vocabulary | Barefoot | Outdoor Play | 530 |
| | Cat and Mouse | Expressing Language | 342 |
| | Controller | Expressing Language | 336 |
| | Object File | Listening | 354 |
| | Seasonal Clothing | Health and Safety | 435 |
| | Synonyms | Expressing Language | 339 |
| | Will It Fit? | Mathematics | 427 |
| To follow directions | Directions | Expressing Language | 343 |
| | Tense Me | Movement | 480 |
| To improve breath control | Director | Music | 465 |
| To increase understanding | Controller | Expressing Language | 336 |
| | Directions | Expressing Language | 343 |
| | Opposite Lotto | Reading Readiness | 375 |
| | Synonyms | Expressing Language | 339 |
| | Traveling | Expressing Language | 344 |

## THINKING AND REASONING SKILLS

| | | | |
|---|---|---|---|
| To increase attention span | Changing Objects | Reading Readiness | 371 |
| To improve cause and effect reasoning | Director | Music | 465 |
| | Dress Up and Tell | Dramatic Play | 492 |
| | Food Forms | Social Studies | 391 |
| | Picnic | Outdoor Play | 530 |
| | Planting Seeds | Science/Discovery | 398 |
| | Popcorn | Science/Discovery | 402 |
| | Seasonal Clothing | Health and Safety | 435 |
| | String Mobile | Art | 447 |
| | Who Has Been Here? | Social Studies | 387 |
| | What Shall We Make? | Dramatic Play | 495 |
| To improve classification skills | Food Lotto | Science/Discovery | 407 |
| | Match 'em | Reading Readiness | 376 |
| | Nutty Sort | Science/Discovery | 407 |
| | People Pictures | Mathematics | 415 |
| | Place Mat Collage | Art | 458 |
| | Taste Sort | Science/Discovery | 408 |
| To improve sequencing skills | Going to the Beach | Listening | 358 |
| To increase logical reasoning | Will It Fit? | Mathematics | 427 |
| To make predictions | Food Sense | Science/Discovery | 405 |
| | Planting Seeds | Science/Discovery | 398 |
| | Problems | Social Studies | 386 |
| | Who Has Been Here? | Social Studies | 387 |

## MATHEMATIC SKILLS

| | | | |
|---|---|---|---|
| To improve number concepts | People Pictures | Mathematics | 415 |
| To improve measurement concepts | Cereal Balls | Mathematics | 429 |

| *Annual Goals* | *Activity* | *Curriculum Area* | *Page* |
|---|---|---|---|
| To improve spatial concepts | Cat and Mouse | Expressing Language | 342 |
| | Letter Collage | Art | 460 |
| To improve size concepts | Will It Fit? | Mathematics | 427 |

## SOCIAL SKILLS

| | | | |
|---|---|---|---|
| To broaden concepts of families | Animal Families | Social Studies | 384 |
| | Food Forms | Social Studies | 391 |
| | Photograph Story | Social Studies | 389 |
| | Roles | Social Studies | 390 |
| To increase survival skills | Seasonal Clothing | Health and Safety | 435 |
| | Who Are You? | Health and Safety | 441 |
| To increase awareness of roles people play | Audiologist | Dramatic Play | 489 |
| | Bookstore | Dramatic Play | 488 |
| | Cast It | Dramatic Play | 486 |
| | Circus | Dramatic Play | 486 |
| | Connections | Dramatic Play | 488 |
| | Dentist | Dramatic Play | 485 |
| | Eye Doctor | Dramatic Play | 490 |
| | Photograph Story | Social Studies | 389 |
| | Visitor | Social Studies | 388 |
| To cooperate with peers | Audiologist | Dramatic Play | 489 |
| | Cereal Balls | Mathematics | 429 |
| | Directions | Expressing Language | 343 |
| | Eye Doctor | Dramatic Play | 490 |
| | Hug Tag | Outdoor Play | 531 |
| | Share Your Feelings | Social Studies | 392 |
| | Variations on Throwing | Outdoor Play | 526 |
| To cooperate with adults | Visitor | Social Studies | 388 |
| | Who Are You? | Health and Safety | 441 |

## MOTOR SKILLS

| | | | |
|---|---|---|---|
| To improve large motor coordination | Parachute Games | Outdoor Play | 525 |
| | Variations on Throwing | Outdoor Play | 526 |
| To improve small motor coordination | Feely Bag | Small Motor Play | 499 |
| | My Puzzle | Small Motor Play | 503 |
| | Nutty Sort | Science/Discovery | 407 |
| To improve eye-hand coordination | Letter Collage | Art | 460 |
| | String Mobile | Art | 447 |
| | Variations on Throwing | Outdoor Play | 526 |
| | What Shall We Make? | Dramatic Play | 495 |
| To encourage creative movement | Be It | Movement | 474 |
| | Music and Movement | Movement | 480 |
| To increase sense of rhythm | Director | Music | 465 |
| To relax at will | Tense Me | Movement | 480 |

| *Annual Goals* | *Activity* | *Curriculum Area* | *Page* |
|---|---|---|---|
| **CREATIVITY** | | | |
| To encourage creativity | Painting a Feeling | Art | 452 |
| | Painting to Music | Art | 454 |
| | Puppets | Dramatic Play | 492 |
| | Traveling | Expressing Language | 344 |
| To encourage creative problem solving | Animal Families | Social Studies | 387 |
| | Connections | Dramatic Play | 488 |
| | Problems | Social Studies | 386 |
| | Who Has Been Here? | Social Studies | 387 |
| **FEELINGS** | | | |
| To express feelings | Painting a Feeling | Art | 452 |
| | Share Your Feelings | Social Studies | 392 |
| To increase feelings of group belonging | Bookstore | Dramatic Play | 488 |
| | Connections | Dramatic Play | 488 |
| | Dress Up and Tell | Dramatic Play | 492 |
| | Hug Tag | Outdoor Play | 531 |
| | Panama | Dramatic Play | 491 |
| | Parachute Games | Outdoor Play | 525 |
| | Picnic | Outdoor Play | 530 |
| | Puppets | Dramatic Play | 492 |
| | Share Your Feelings | Social Studies | 392 |
| | Slings | Dramatic Play | 494 |
| | Traveling | Expressing Language | 344 |
| **AWARENESS** | | | |
| To increase body awareness | Barefoot | Outdoor Play | 530 |
| | Be It | Movement | 474 |
| | Be the Body | Movement | 473 |
| | Body Mural | Art | 454 |
| | Circus | Dramatic Play | 486 |
| | Movement Songs | Music | 494 |
| | My Puzzle | Small Motor Play | 503 |
| | Place Mat Collage | Art | 458 |
| | Slings | Dramatic Play | 494 |
| | Tense Me | Movement | 480 |
| | Weighty Movements | Movement | 478 |
| To improve self-concept | Johnny Hear, Johnny Do | Listening | 359 |
| | My Puzzle | Small Motor Play | 503 |
| To increase awareness of individual differences | Body Mural | Art | 454 |
| To increase awareness of moods | Painting to Music | Art | 454 |
| To increase knowledge of foods | Taste Sort | Science/Discovery | 408 |
| To increase awareness of other cultures | Charades | Awareness | 537 |
| | Foreign Languages | Awareness | 547 |
| | Holidays | Awareness | 547 |
| | International Snack | Awareness | 548 |
| | Lingo's | Awareness | 548 |

# Children Who Are Gifted and Talented

It was a terrible morning. Four degrees above zero. Ice and snow on the ground. A wind that jabbed like a merciless ice pick. Cars stalled on the road. And by 8:30 A.M. three calls had come into my office—three teachers, each of them depressed and speaking haltingly, reporting in sick. Flu, Asian flu, and one of those 24-hour bugs.

At nine, I went up to the classroom that was going to be most affected. "It looks as if you are going to have an unexpected holiday," I told the students.

There were no shouts of "Hurray," no subdued exclamations of happiness. Just silence.

"Why?" a girl finally asked.

I explained that their teachers were all ill. I said that I'd stay with the class during the morning, but that after lunch it might be best for them to go home. Meanwhile I'd have their homes checked by phone to be certain that someone would be there when they arrived.

One of the boys stood up. "Dr. Fine, could we have some privacy, please?"

"Sure," I said. "I'll be next door. Call me when you're ready."

Five minutes passed, and then I was summoned.

Nancy was sitting at the teacher's desk when I re-entered the room.

"I'm class president," she told me. "We've decided that I'll be teacher during the reading. Brenda will be teacher when we do our arithmetic. Andy will be teacher when we have current events. We

can have lunch with Mrs. Gilbert's group. You don't have to send us home, Dr. Fine."

I agreed. We decided that they could come to me if they had any problems they couldn't settle among themselves. I told them that they could join Mrs. Hunter's class for French in the afternoon.

And then I walked out of the room.

I managed to pass their door many times that day. Nancy spotted me once, and called me in. "We've just finished our silent reading. Now we're going to read out loud."

"Oral reading," someone in the classroom corrected her.

Later they asked me in to watch the dress rehearsal of a play they were going to put on the next day. And at about two o'clock in the afternoon I was needed to settle a question about a problem in arithmetic.

And then at the end of the afternoon, the fourteen children went home. Eight boys, six girls.

Who ranged in age from just over four to just over five. (Fine, 1964)

In America today we have just begun to realize that gifted and talented children too may need "special" education. It has been far easier to get funds for children with delays than for the gifted and talented. Federally funded programs such as Head Start are required to include specific percentages of children with handicapping conditions, but they are neither required to have a specific percentage of gifted children nor to individually program for them.

Apparently our deep-down feeling toward gifted and talented children is, why do we have to accommodate children who are so bright? Why can't these children, with all their gifts, accommodate us? To answer that let's ask ourselves another question: Why is it acceptable to single out one group of children and require them to do all the accommodating? Remember our original premise that all children have special needs at least some of the time. Gifted and talented children are doubly handicapped by their very difference and by society's refusal to meet their individual needs.

Traditionally, accommodation for the gifted and talented has consisted of either acceleration or enrichment. *Acceleration* is the process of assigning children to a grade based on their level of mental functioning rather than their chronological age. *Enrichment* consists of offering special programs to enhance learning within the regular classroom. Enrichment and acceleration are also used in tandem. If well done, ungraded primary units (where children can progress at their own rate and perhaps finish the first three years in two), are a way of providing both enrichment and acceleration without leaving gaps in knowledge. For some children, early admission is a good alternative, especially if they have attended preschool and have missed the enrollment age cutoff date by only a short time.

Either solution has both advantages and drawbacks. In the case of acceleration, although the children are able to do well academically, a year or more of age difference can become a social barrier. Enrichment has the potential of meeting children's needs but too often isolates children. Increased feelings of separateness occur when children are repeatedly assigned tasks away from the group. An individualized program of enrichment within the group should meet these children's needs without isolating them. Using flexible materials will help. For example, if clay or playdough is used, some children can pound and roll it, while others can engage in complex creations. Children can use the same materials and work at the same table, but all have their needs met. This approach requires teachers to do a lot of planning that begins with evaluating which materials can be used on how many different levels.

## CLASSIFICATION OF GIFTED AND TALENTED NEEDS

Experts cannot agree on a definition of "gifted," and defining "talented" poses an even greater challenge. Most educators agree that those children who perform about two standard deviations above the mean, (that is, who score 125 or more) on standardized intelligence tests may be considered gifted. Others feel giftedness is more than IQ, but the "more" is difficult to measure. The children usually show some indication of exceptional potential. Talented children, like gifted, are usually above average in intelligence. However, talented children show such fluency and flexibility in their thinking and behavior that their ideas are not just an extension of what they already know, but often "leaps of logic." For a simple example, the average child might say: two + two = four and four + four = eight. However, the child who independently discovers that $2 \times 4 = 8$ would be considered talented for having discovered "fast addition." The world might already know about this "fast addition," but the child performed a leap of logic to think of it. Following are some guidelines to aid you in early identification. Bear in mind that no single child must have all of the following characteristics to be identified as gifted or talented. This list does not differentiate between characteristics attributable to the gifted child and those of the talented child. Such differentiation is difficult, and the results are somewhat arbitrary.

1. Early speech as well as an unusually large vocabulary for their age often indicate gifted and talented children. A good memory and a strong desire to learn may also be indicators.
2. The children can initiate and maintain a meaningful conversation with adults on a wide variety of subjects.
3. Relative to the peer age group, the children are usually most advanced in reading and least advanced in fine motor skills (ultimately penmanship).
4. The children possess a tremendous facility for acquiring English if foreign speaking, or a foreign language if English speaking. This is especially obvious if they are placed in an immersion situation, where most others use the new language.
5. They may be precocious in overall physical development, as well as being advanced socially and academically.

These children may demonstrate particular ability in problem solving.

1. These children like to play with ideas and problems.
2. They rank high in divergent production (reorganizing facts into new and varied relationships).
3. They invent unusual and original solutions to problems.
4. Their thinking is fluent (they have lots of ideas), flexible (they usually have alternatives), and original. They can elaborate on the ideas of others.
5. They are open and often see things others miss.

A gifted and talented child usually displays an early interest in books and the ability to read.

6. They often make suggestions that are valued by their peers.
7. They are frequently called on to mediate disputes, plan strategies, and anticipate outcomes, since these children see things from many points of view.

Gifted and talented children differ from their peers with regard to their attention and interest span.

1. These children have an unusually long interest span for their age.
2. They are quick to grasp ideas and anxious to try them out.
3. They do not always appear to be paying attention. They may daydream because of boredom.

In more general terms, these children present a special personality.

1. These children prefer to do things their own way. They show independence from an early age.
2. They are persistent, inquisitive, flexible, and skeptical.
3. The creative ones often seem to thrive on disorder.
4. They are emotionally responsive and often feel deeply about subjects that do not touch their peers.
5. They are willing to take risks, both intellectually and creatively.

6. They have a good sense of humor.
7. They are usually mature and responsible for their age, and often seek out older friends.
8. They are great imitators and elaborators of adult behaviors—even those you don't want imitated.

## CHILDREN'S NEEDS— TEACHING GOALS

Related annual goals may be grouped under broad categories called "teaching goals." Outlined under each teaching goal below are the most important needs of gifted and talented children. A child may have some or all of these needs, and additional needs as well. Suggestions on what you might consequently teach them are included. Often, a course of action is implicit in the description of the need.

### Awareness

Children may need help in becoming more aware of their bodies. They must learn to accept the fact that they will think of things they want to do but can't because of the gap between their mental and physical development.

These children need to develop a realistic self-concept. They need to learn to value their skills as well as the skills of others. Teach them that being different is fine. Do this by having the gifted child help another child with mathematics, for example, and then have the other child help the gifted child improve a different skill, such as tumbling. Do not set up a one-way system in which only the gifted child helps others. Such a system is unfair and makes normal peer relationships difficult. Help children find acceptable roles with their peers and adults.

### Feelings

Gifted and talented children need to feel part of the group and need to find out how it feels to be both a leader and a follower. If they see themselves as "better" than others or judge others as "stupid," peer relations are hindered. Help them develop the language they need to express feelings and encourage them to do this in appropriate ways.

### Thinking and Reasoning Skills

Gifted and talented children often excel in this area, but their skills need to be challenged in order to expand. Encourage flexibility in thinking by having more than one right answer to problems. Have children think of and evaluate a lot of solutions along with the implications those solutions have for the characters involved. Have them check the answers for themselves rather than rely on adults for confirmation.

### Guidelines

1. Have gifted and talented children develop independent work habits, but don't equate independence with isolation. See if those skills that are best developed independently can be worked on at home. Remember, children come to school to be with other children. Your challenge is to plan basic activities that can be done on many levels so that all children in the class can participate and grown.
2. These children need to learn socially acceptable ways of dealing with emotions. They are not entitled to special privileges with regard to undesirable behaviors.
3. Provide a variety of activities and experiences that will allow children to explore and find an area of interest, but allow children to concentrate their energy in one area if they choose.
4. Provide children with activities that require divergent thinking (for example, have them pretend they are locked out of the classroom and let them figure out how to get back in).
5. Emphasize both how and why something occurs, and how one could make it happen differently.
6. Emphasize both group and individual problem solving.

There are many ways of encouraging creativity. The easiest is to tell children to be creative—obvious, yet it does work.

1. Regard creativity as a process. Do not emphasize the product. Encourage different ways of doing things, regardless of the results (which may look far worse than a classmate's more traditional product).
2. Value achievement in comparison to a personal norm, not a universal one. If a product or process is new for this child, it is creative for him, whether or not society would see it in that light. If a child can read at a fourth-grade level, don't be overenthusiastic about her reading at a second-grade level just because she's reading.
3. Reward creativity!
4. Encourage children to ask questions and to explore materials.
5. Help children learn by asking questions that stimulate creative thinking. Here are some useful statements:
   Start your mind to work on this, but do not tell me yet.
   Do you see anything of interest?
   What can you say about this?
   Is there anything worth talking about?
   Do you get any ideas?
   Does this remind you of anything?
   Let's set up some "ground rules" for the comfort of all.
   Stretch your brain a little.
   Let me watch the wheels going around while you think.
   I will be the audience and let you think for a minute.
   What can we do with this?
   Does this look interesting?
   Can you make a puzzle out of this?
   Would you like to rearrange?
   Do you see any possibilities?
   Can you see some place to start?
   Can you find something here?
   What's funny about this?
   Can you change this to make something else?
   Can you use this for something else?
6. Encourage children to make the commonplace different—don't ask what things are or require that products have a specific purpose.

There are a number of practices you should strive to avoid with children who are gifted and talented. It is often easier to discourage creativity than to encourage it. The following responses and procedures are great discouragers.

1. Putting pressure on children for conformity. This does not mean that children should be excused from following class rules, but that they should not be judged as strange because they act differently. Discipline that demands compliance, discourages understanding and questioning, and values only obedience is disastrous for these children. If children must do things "because I said so," they lose the opportunity to learn and create.
2. Undue emphasis on traditional sex roles. This tends to discourage creativity for both boys and girls because it narrows both roles.
3. Pressuring children to succeed. In a success-oriented culture such as ours, failures present problems. Fear of failure keeps many children from being creative. Stress processes, not products.
4. Insistence on regimen. Having a regimented class day that cannot be expanded or contracted, or requiring all children to finish projects in a specified amount of time, discourages some children.
5. Using highly structured materials. Materials that do it all—that are brightly colored, move, make noise—don't leave as much room for imagination as those that allow the child to implement the movement, function, and noise.
6. Avoid using phrases such as:
   Don't be silly.
   It's a good idea, but . . .
   It won't work.

What's the matter with you?
That's not our problem.
Don't be so sloppy.
Do it the right way.
Do it the way I said to.

Judging children or their activities often discourages creativity. Consider these two statements:

That's a really good picture.

I like the way you used red in that picture.

The first statement is poor because it carries a value judgment. The second is better. It is a personal statement about what *I* like and does not place a value on the child's efforts.

## CURRICULUM ADAPTATIONS

Activities for the gifted and talented preschool child need to be more varied, done in greater depth, and individualized where possible.

### Expressing Language, Listening, and Reading Readiness

This is an area of special strength for many gifted and talented children. They often read early. In fact, they usually teach themselves. Because reading is the basis for learning many subjects, it should be encouraged. Your job is to refine, expand, and enrich the child's language skills.

1. Visit the library and discuss not only its books and records, but also the events this library sponsors. Discuss how the library is organized and how people borrow books. Send a note home to parents about your visit and the availability of library cards.
2. Encourage children to brainstorm. Be sure not to make value judgments or belittle the responses, because children will refrain from making comments freely.
3. Help children think creatively and translate their thinking into expressive language by giving them situations to talk about:
    Describe your life as a five-year-old bicycle.
    You are a gingerbread mix about to be made and then baked. How do you feel?
    You are a camera, what kind of pictures will you take? How do you work?
4. Encourage children to learn a vocabulary and a life perspective that allows for differences by teaching concepts like *some, sometimes, often, frequently, rarely,* as well as *never* and *always.*

5. Encourage both fluency and flexibility in verbal interchanges. Encourage colorful phrases, vivid descriptions, and analogies.

Depending on the skills of the child, reading readiness work may be unnecessary, or it may occur on a level appropriate to older primary children. If children are not reading, readiness skills should be available, as they would be for all children this age.

1. Make some nontraditional puzzles. Paste pictures on heavy cardboard and cut with a jigsaw. Use, for example, a photograph of the child or a picture of the child's favorite animal.
2. Puzzles can be more difficult if the child does two at the same time. Mix the pieces of two puzzles together and have the child work on both. Mark the back of each puzzle differently so that, if necessary, the child can check the backs to sort difficult pieces. This requires more skill and challenges the child who finds your stock of puzzles too easy.

These children generally love stories and books. If they are to be challenged, you need to offer a wide variety of reading materials. Choose books that are unusual or creative, and provide books the children are capable of reading on their own.

1. After reading stories or poems, present simple questions to evoke creative responses.
2. Have records, tapes and film strips available for independent viewing and listening at learning centers. Such materials help you to program individually for this child's needs.
3. These children may want to write their own stories, but they may not have the necessary motor skills. Have a tape recorder available for them or write their stories as dictated. Some of the children may want to try to type. Make a scrapbook of each child's stories after they have been typed on a large-type typewriter.
4. When reading a new story, stop at a critical point and ask the children to make up an ending. Then compare their ending with the one the author wrote. Let them dictate their endings to you. Mail the endings to the author with a note. Have children make up different endings to familiar stories.
5. Dramatize stories, songs, and poems.
6. Have children generate stories to go with the pictures in wordless picture books. (Some good books are given in the bibliography at the back of the chapter on Needs: Hearing.)

Fingerplays combine language with motions. They are a fun way of teaching and a good way for children to express themselves creatively.

Teach small groups of children more intricate fingerplays and encourage them to act out the fingerplays or develop a variation of an old favorite.

1. Have children act out fingerplays with their whole body. Have each child do the action corresponding to a specific finger in the song "Where Is Thumbkin?"
2. Encourage children to make up their own fingerplays.
3. Teach more intricate fingerplays to a small group of interested children.

### Social Studies

Social studies can cover nontraditional roles and occupations and provide information on other ways of doing things. Lessons should be designed that give children understanding of themselves and their role in society.

1. Cook foreign foods and eat them in traditional ways. Tempura and fried rice can be eaten with chopsticks. Pu Pu with two fingers, hors d'oeuvres with toothpicks, shish kebob from skewers, and fondue with a fondue fork.
2. Explore varied occupations such as plumber, computer programmer, baker, physicist, producer, professional athlete, and pest exterminator. Let the children's interest guide your choices. Be sure to give a nonsexist presentation of occupations. (Check the bibliography at the end of this chapter for useful books.)

3. Discuss where different foods grow and compare fresh foods with canned or frozen foods. Introduce some foods that are from other parts of the country or from other countries.

### Mathematics

Children need to develop a functional math vocabulary to keep pace with their mathematical skills. Math activities should be manipulative and game-like, and, at least at the beginning, should have a concrete experiential base. Once that has been established, move in directions that intrigue the children.

1. Help children recognize two or pairs in their environment: shoes, mittens, socks. Teach them the use of the word *pair* for a single object: pair of scissors, pair of pants, pair of glasses.

   Expand the *pair* concept to the concept *three*. Children can group three objects and figure out the names of related objects: trio, tripod, tricycle, triangle.
2. While children are in the process of mastering counting skills, have them count a wide variety of objects: raisins, blocks, children.
3. Once children have used objects for counting, have them group and count by sorting and classifying: seven red buttons, three yellow buttons. Eventually you can teach them addition and hierarchical classification:

   Furniture

   7 beds + 5 chairs + 2 tables = 14 pieces of furniture.
4. Fractions are also fun to teach casually, as the occasion arises: half an apple, a quarter of a sandwich. Give children the entire object. They can count the pieces, put them back together, and take them apart again.
5. Teach children basic measuring skills and the relationships among one quarter, one third, one half and one cup. Have at least four quarter-cup measures. Fill some and have the children compare the number of full to empty measures. (You can do the same thing with teaspoons and tablespoons, but these require better-developed fine motor skills.) These tasks are easily done at a water table, in the sandbox, or when making cocoa, jello, or cookies.
6. Once children have mastered the traditional shapes, teach some of the more unusual ones, as well as the relationship between three-dimensional and two-dimensional ones: oval/egg, circle/ball/globe, combination (oval & rectangle)/cylinder, pentagon, trapezoid.
7. Introduce children to more complex and different measuring systems: yardsticks, meter sticks, centigrade and fahrenheit thermometers, tire pressure gauges.

8. To facilitate individual work in math concepts, have children use the abacus, cuisenaire rods, and Montessori-type materials. These materials help develop fine motor control. They also let children discover and experiment with facts rather than simply memorize them.

### Science/Discovery

Science often provides the structure for gaining new experience and developing reasoning. Start with known concepts and expand on them. Increase the ability of children to hypothesize and make predictions.

1. Use familiar concepts such as the wind, the sun, and water. On a windy day make observations of the winds' effects. Draw on the children's experiences with the wind and their reactions to it. Share with them the tingle of the skin, the watering of the eyes, the tossing of the hair, the bracing and turning of the body to cut through the blowing wind. Have them observe how clothes on a line are pushed by wind; the difference in the way people walk facing the wind or with the wind at their back. Watch the surface of a pond or puddle as wind blows over it; watch rain change direction when the wind changes; listen to the sounds of the wind. Record different wind and blowing sounds. Reenact scenes from a windy day. Have children take a pretend walk on a windy day and have other children guess the direction and strength of the wind. Demonstrate a weather vane or windmill. Discuss machines that create wind, such as hair dryers and electric fans. Bring milkweed to school and blow it apart. Blow a small boat across a pan of water. Blow ping pong balls or balloons. Make pinwheels or kites.
2. Visit an orchard and pick apples. Explore the parts of the apple. Experiment with the effects of heat and cold on apples. Find out what happens when you drop apples and bruise them. Cook apples in different ways. Compare the tastes of applesauce, baked apples, apple juice, and apple butter. See how many ways children can use apples.
3. Children often enjoy learning about animals. Begin with a firsthand experience. Visit a farm or zoo. Show them an animal. Then add depth to the experience. Talk about where the animal might live, how he protects himself, and how and what he eats. Have children invent animals for particular climates or conditions, such as a light animal with large, flat feet that lives near quicksand.
4. Have children focus on a problem. Encourage them to persist in trying various solutions to the problem by having them find a variety of approaches. Try to get children to generalize the problem-solving process to new problems. Show them how to use the information that was obtained to make increasingly more accurate guesses regarding outcomes.
5. Encourage children to think and guess what will happen before they actually do a task. Afterward have them come back to that guess and determine whether it was right or wrong. Have them speculate about why it was right or wrong. Then have children make new guesses to further test their thinking.

    For example, using a candle, try to determine how long it will burn if you place a glass over it. Begin by asking the children what, if anything, will happen. Once they realize the candle will go out, have them predict whether it will go out faster or slower as you change the size of the glass. Expand this with some information about fires. Next, discuss matches and safety and have a fire drill.

### Health and Safety

Health and safety are important for gifted and talented children because their curiosity and experimentation can lead to problems. The "what happens if I swallow a penny" or "will I bubble like the washer if I eat detergent" syndrome can have dangerous side effects. (However, the trip to the poison control center can be stimulating.)

1. Help children read labels and sort them on the basis of whether or not to play with the contents. Add new things and help children learn to classify unknown objects as "not to be played with" or "not to be eaten." Make sure they realize that unknowns are not safe.
2. The safe use of tools and other equipment should be emphasized. Discuss safe use of simple tools such as hammers and screwdrivers. Have safety goggles available and discuss why they are used.
3. Talk about safety devices and their use and what happens if you don't use them: helmets, seat belts, safety glasses.

### Art

Encourage children to explore their world through art. You can introduce activities that allow the children to make their own decisions and exert some control over their world.

1. Set up art activities with enough space around to enable children to work freely either alone or in small groups.
2. *All* children of this age are interested more in the process than the product. Don't stifle creative growth by imposing adult ideas and standards on children, or by expecting children to come up

with a product that *is* something. Don't ask "What is it?" Don't assume you recognize something. (A house may not be a house in the child's eye.)

3. When you repeat activities such as easel painting or making collages, vary the shape, size, and kinds of paper you use.

4. Encourage children to choose colors (paint or food color) and to predict what new colors will be made by mixing them. Add white and black to paint so that children can experiment with shades of color as well.

5. Do some difficult art projects that have several steps, like crayon etching. (Color with a light crayon design. Cover again with black crayon. Etch with a popcycle stick. Use tough paper that resists tearing.) Try crayon and paint (again, light-colored crayon, dark paint). Discuss why the paint doesn't adhere where the crayon is.

6. Supply a wide variety of traditional art implements. Use wide and narrow crayons of many colors. Provide paintbrushes in several widths.

7. Origami—Japanese paper folding—is a great activity for these children. It helps them translate ideas into three-dimensional results.

8. Make lots of variations in the same activity. Fingerpaint with

| | |
|---|---|
| liquid laundry starch | flour, salt, and water |
| cornstarch | shaving cream |
| instant pudding | commercially-made |
| frosting | fingerpaint |
| whipped soap | |

Add texture to fingerpaints with

| | |
|---|---|
| sand | coffee grounds |
| salt | glitter |
| fine sawdust | confetti |

9. Encourage activities that require problem solving, such as Batik. (Drip hot wax on material in any desired pattern and then dip the material in dye. The dye will not be absorbed where the wax was.)

Tie-dyeing is another good problem-solving activity. (The children can knot their material or white tee shirt with marbles and thread or rubber bands.) The complexity of the design will depend on each child. Tie-dyed material can later be used in a sewing project. Have the children help pin the fabric together and baste it. Perhaps some can sew it, either by hand or machine.

## Music

Music can contribute much to a child's physical, aesthetic, and intellectual development. It provides pleasure and creative experience, develops auditory skills, encourages physical development, and increases range and flexibility of one's voice. There should be a wide variety of musical experiences: listening, singing, moving to music, and playing instruments.

1. Have a variety of different instruments available. Help children explore and evaluate the sound of an instrument when it is held and played in different ways. See if they can identify the instruments they know in a recording.

2. Incorporate music and language experiences; have children make up new verses to old songs. Play unusual instrumental records and ask the children to describe what they imagined while listening.

3. Put stories to music. Have children choose background music for stories.

4. Paint to music.

5. Encourage a feeling of group belonging and, at the same time, foster creative movement. Have children "hold up the roof." Children strain together to hold up the roof. They gradually let it down and then push it back up again. They can be ice cubes melting in the hot sun or a balloon deflating. Play "people machines," with or without noises. The children can do this all together or one at a time, slowly or speeding up. Repeat such creative movement experiences until the children are comfortable enough to experiment with their bodies.

6. Have children make musical instruments (cigarbox guitars, coffee-can drums, wax paper and comb). As they participate in this process, they will gain an understanding of how sounds are made, where they come from, and how to change them. See if they can make sounds with different parts of their body.

7. Music that combines creative movement and stories is fun and mind expanding:

*The Story of Peer Gynt*, with the recording of the *Peer Gynt Suite* by Grieg.

*Cinderella*, with the recording of *Cinderella* by Prokofiev.

*Hansel and Gretel*, with excerpts from the opera *Hansel and Gretel* by Humperdinck.

Stories about troubadours and meistersingers, with excerpts from *Die Meistersinger* by Wagner.

The fairy tale *Nutcracker King*, with Tchaikovsky's *Nutcracker Suite*.

*Mother Goose*, with *Mother Goose* Suite by Ravel (Martinson, 1968)

8. Introduce concepts of pitch, loudness, and length.

## Dramatic Play

In the dramatic play area, too much is worse than too little for these children. Challenge these children to create and design the props they need. Use props such as dolls and dishes with fewer details. If you provide all the necessary props, children will not improvise and exercise their creativity.

1. Have a small-group planning session to set up a store. Discuss the props they will need, how they will get them, and when the store should go into business. Create the store and evaluate its success. Use play money and a cash register and/or calculators.
2. Plan a train or plane trip. Look at maps to determine where to go. Explain how to use a compass. Have the children investigate weather conditions there, how long it will take to get there, what they will do when they get there. Take the class to a travel agency that is willing to answer their questions and provide schedules and brochures.
3. These children often love ghost stories. Have them build a ghost house and do a ghost play for Halloween.
4. Have the children set up their own fast food chain. They can make hamburgers, french fries, and chicken out of construction paper. Have them decide who will be the manager, cook, order taker, and customer.
5. Help the children set up a small pup tent (outside if possible). Discuss aspects of backpacking, including the equipment, and take a hike. (They might even pretend to climb a mountain.)

### Small Motor Play

Gifted and talented children will have motor skills closer to their chronological age than their mental age. Their ability to plan and conceptualize products and purposes will be closer to their mental age.

1. Have abundant materials (two or three sets instead of one) so that children's creations are not limited by a scarcity of materials. Have a wide variety of materials, so children can work on small motor skills without being bored.
2. Encourage planning and prediction by the children after they have mastered the motor skills for manipulating the materials. (How many blocks will a planned tower need?)

Gifted children need practice with fine motor skills, because in this area they function closer to their chronological age than their mental age.

3. Using heavy string, teach children knots and simple macramé.
4. Adding manipulative materials to the block or dramatic play areas will encourage children to create props.
5. Provide old clocks, radios, or other equipment for the children to take apart to examine or compare the sizes and shapes of pieces and basic construction.
6. Bring in a bicycle wheel and have the children help change the tire. Discuss air, volume, and shape.

### Large Motor Play

Whether or not children are gifted and talented, their overall motor development is probably closer to their chronological age than to their level of mental functioning. In order to develop a well-rounded child, it is important that you encourage the development of large motor skills.

1. Use an imaginary obstacle course. Have a child climb, dodge, or wade while the other children guess what the obstacles are.
2. Have the children walk through imaginary substances, such as gelatin, deep sand, flypaper, a swamp, or quicksand. Have the others guess what the substances are.
3. Have the children help make an obstacle course either inside or outside.

### Transitions

This is a good time to individualize programming while not drawing attention to a specific child.

1. If you are giving two-step directions to others in the class, add a third step to the child's instructions: "Touch your nose, *stamp your feet*, and get your coat."
2. Because this child may have more complex projects to clean up, provide an early warning for transitions.

## CHILD STUDY TEAM REPORT

### Cynthia V.

In attendance: Mr. and Mrs. V; Mrs. M., kindergarten teacher; Mr. Y., teacher of gifted and talented.

Cynthia V. is a five-year, three-month-old girl who has been identified as intellectually gifted. Her scores on a kindergarten screening instrument administered to all kindergarteners indicated that Cynthia qualifies for a special program for gifted children in her school district. An individual psychological test indicated that Cynthia is functioning in the very superior range of intelligence. She attained an IQ of 145 on the Wechsler Preschool and Primary Scale.

Cynthia is one of four children in her kindergarten class who have been identified as eligible for the gifted program. (This program is designed to supplement the grade-level placement of the children involved.) Cynthia and her three classmates will attend a class of kindergarten and first-grade children for two mornings a week, and attend kindergarten in the afternoon, five days a week. An individualized educational program that can be implemented in both classrooms must be developed for Cynthia by both the regular and supplemental teachers.

Cynthia's particular strengths have been identified to be in the verbal area. Her vocabulary and ability to form verbal concepts are two of her strongest skills. Her abilities in these areas correspond to those of a seven-and-one-half-year-old.

Cynthia's parents attended a parent-teacher conference that was held in order to learn more about her interests and abilities. Cynthia lives at home with her mother and father and maternal grandmother. Mrs. V. works full time as a school administrator's secretary; Mr. V. is an accountant with an office in his home. Cynthia's grandmother has spent a great deal of time with her, transporting her to and from preschool for the past two years and acting as babysitter for two years before that. Mr. V. said they are not sure what the best educational approach is for Cynthia. Mr. V. is concerned that if Cynthia is pushed too hard, she may feel too pressured. On the other hand, he feels if she is not challenged, she will become bored. Mr. V. added that Cynthia's preschool teacher feels she does very well, finishing work quickly. Usually Cynthia finishes before the other children and is given independent time to do puzzles, read books, or paint, all of which she enjoys very much.

At home, Mr. V. said that Cynthia enjoys books, especially craft books with illustrations. Cynthia enjoys making projects following the picture instructions. Cynthia has expressed a great interest in reading, Mr. V. said, but he and Mrs. V. were reluctant to teach her because they thought they might teach her incorrectly. Cynthia reads a few words, especially road signs and words from familiar children's books. She often plays at his typewriter and calculator at home, typing her name, address, and other words.

The teacher of the gifted and talented classroom noted that Cynthia's interest in reading was a very good sign that she was ready to read, and added that reading may be one of the things Cynthia will learn in the class. He also indicated that acceleration was not the sole purpose of the program. The goal was to provide stimulation and opportunity for individual growth for Cynthia, according to her interests and needs. Knowing Cynthia's interests at home was useful for planning school activities. Continuity between the special program and the kindergarten was essential.

The kindergarten teacher and the teacher of the gifted program explained the way the programs work together. The two teachers will meet every two weeks to plan centers and activities for the four gifted and talented children. The other kindergarteners will also be given the opportunity to participate in these activities along with the regular kindergarten curriculum. The activities should be motivating, and each child will be encouraged to work to full potential without being frustrated. Weekly activity cards sent home with Cynthia will illustrate the activities she has worked on that week. Some of the projects and activities will be things Cynthia can actually bring home, while others will not.

Mr. V. said that although he and his wife were excited about Cynthia starting school and the gifted program, they were not familiar with this approach and would like to learn more. He also added that he would like to visit school during the day. (His work schedule allows that kind of flexibility.)

When asked about Cynthia's social abilities, Mr. V. explained that the preschool she attended was really the only opportunity Cynthia had for interacting with other children. There are no other children in the family, and Cynthia plays alone at home. She has always been able to occupy herself. He added that the preschool teachers felt she spent perhaps too much time alone, especially since she finished the activities so quickly. Cynthia is reluctant to play housekeeping, dress up, or blocks, Mrs. V. said, because she feels it is too noisy. Mr. and Mrs. V. think Cynthia feels awkward in large groups.

Mr. V. seemed impressed that Cynthia was going to have an individualized program. He was reluctant to think he and Mrs. V. could contribute to the program as this was really not their field.

## INDIVIDUALIZED EDUCATION PROGRAM

NAME ___Cynthia V.___ DOB _5_ / _20_ / _77_

AGE ___5-3___ GRADE ___K___

SCHOOL ___Indian Road School___

PARENTS/GUARDIANS ___Mr. & Mrs. V.___

ADDRESS ___2112 Tuckahoe Pl.___

PHONE ___366-5173___

### CURRENT TEST DATA

TEST/DATE/RESULTS

Psych. WPPSI / 8/1/82 / Superior intellectual range, strong

_____ / _____ / verbal abilities; IQ 145

_____ / _____ / _____

_____ / _____ / _____

On _8/15/82_ , the IPRD Committee
    (Date)
met to review all current data and

recommends Level ___II___ placement.

Date of new review ___1/15/83___

Exceptionality: ___Gifted & Talented___

Recommended Special Services (Hrs/Wk):

_____ / _____

_____ / _____

_____ / _____

Total Hours/Week:

Special Education Classroom ___5___

Regular Classroom ___12½___

Present at meeting:

Parents ___Mr. and Mrs. V.___

Others: Name/Position _____

Representative of District/Agency ___Mr. Y., teacher of gifted and talented___

___Mrs. M., kindergarten teacher___

The committee has determined the following learning strengths and needs to be reflected in the IEP:

| STRENGTHS | NEEDS |
|---|---|
| Vocabulary | Social skills with peers |
| Verbal concepts | |
| Superior abilities | |

STUDENT _____ Cynthia V. _____ DATE _____ 8/15/82 _____

GOAL _____ To encourage creativity and creative problem solving _____

PARENT SIGNATURE _____ TEACHER SIGNATURE _____

| INSTRUCTIONAL OBJECTIVES | EDUCATIONAL METHODS | DATE Begin | DATE End | Eval. | PERSONS RESPONSIBLE Name | PERSONS RESPONSIBLE Position |
|---|---|---|---|---|---|---|
| Given a hypothetical situation, Cynthia will state a likely result in 4/5 trials. | Di-Vergent, What If?, What Would You Do If?, My Shoes, Solutions | 9/4 | 1/15 | | Mrs. M/Mr. Y | Teacher/ Teacher of Gifted and Talented |
| Given art media (paint, clay, paper, crayons, glue, string, wire, salt putty) Cynthia will create at least 3 projects of her choice. | Clay, String Painting, Wire Sculpture, Creature, Salt Putty Beads | 9/4 | 1/15 | | Mrs. M/Mr. Y | Teacher/ Teacher of Gifted and Talented |
| Cynthia will create a dramatic play corner theme, block corner theme and/or house corner theme on 4 occasions. | Picnic, Puppets | 9/4 | 1/15 | | Mrs. M/Mr. Y | Teacher/ Teacher of Gifted and Talented |
| Given an unfinished story, Cynthia will provide on ending through expressive language, art medium, or creative movement on 5 occasions. | What Would You Do If?, Music and Movement, Body Maneuvers, Comics | 9/4 | 6/1 | | Mrs. M/Mr. Y | Teacher/ Teacher of Gifted and Talented |

STUDENT _____ Cynthia V. _____   DATE _____ 8/15/82

GOAL _____ To improve cause and effect reasoning

PARENT SIGNATURE _____

TEACHER SIGNATURE _____

| INSTRUCTIONAL OBJECTIVES | EDUCATIONAL METHODS | DATE Begin | DATE End | Eval. | PERSONS RESPONSIBLE Name | Position |
|---|---|---|---|---|---|---|
| Given a simple cause-effect activity, Cynthia will be able to identify expressively the cause of the changes seen on at least 5 occasions. | Cornstarch Playdough, Crayon Rubbing, Gelatin, Magnets, Popcorn | 9/4 | 1/15 | | Mrs. M/Mr. Y | Teacher/ Teacher of Gifted and Talented |
| Cynthia will be able to sequence events of a cause-effect activity a. given picture cards b. given verbal statements on 5 occasions. | Comics, Planting Seeds | 9/14 11/15 | 11/15 1/15 | | Mrs. M/Mr. Y | Teacher/ Teacher of Gifted and Talented |
| Cynthia will be able to expressively predict the outcome of cause-effect experiments on 5 occasions. | Mixing Colored Water, Planting Seeds, Temperature, Texture Playdough | 9/4 | 1/15 | | Mrs. M/Mr. Y | Teacher/ Teacher of Gifted and Talented |

STUDENT  Cynthia V.  DATE  8/15/82

GOAL  To increase awareness of individual differences

PARENT SIGNATURE _____  TEACHER SIGNATURE _____

| INSTRUCTIONAL OBJECTIVES | EDUCATIONAL METHODS | DATE Begin | DATE End | Eval. | PERSONS RESPONSIBLE Name | Position |
|---|---|---|---|---|---|---|
| Cynthia will be able to identify 3 likenesses and 3 differences between a peer and herself on 3 occasions (using 3 different peers). | Body Mural, Holidays, Eye-Hair Collage, Family Pictures, International Snack, People Pictures | 9/4 | 1/15 | | Mrs. M/Mr. Y | Teacher/ Teacher of Gifted and Talented |
| Cynthia will be able to identify 2 of her own strengths and weaknesses on 1 occasion. | Easy/Hard, Best and Worst | 9/4 | 1/15 | | Mrs. M/Mr. Y | Teacher/ Teacher of Gifted and Talented |

STUDENT   Cynthia V.          DATE    8/15/82

GOAL    To increase feelings of group belonging

PARENT SIGNATURE _____    TEACHER SIGNATURE _____

| INSTRUCTIONAL OBJECTIVES | EDUCATIONAL METHODS | DATE Begin | DATE End | Eval. | PERSONS RESPONSIBLE Name | PERSONS RESPONSIBLE Position |
|---|---|---|---|---|---|---|
| Cynthia will choose a ''buddy'' for activities requiring 2 children. | Telephone, Field Trips, Mirror Movement | 9/4 | 1/15 | | Mrs. M/Mr. Y | Teacher |
| Cynthia will be able to name all of her classmates with 100% accuracy. | Names | 9/4 | 11/15 | | Mrs. M/Mr. Y | Teacher |
| Cynthia will participate in cooperative play in a play area of her choice for 10 minutes, for 10 consecutive days. | Cast It, Who Am I, Shoe Store | 9/4 | 1/15 | | Mrs. M/Mr. Y | Teacher |

# GLOSSARY

**Achievement test**  A test that measures what a child has already learned.

**Ability grouping**  Grouping children with the same ability level in one class for teaching purposes (special class for gifted, for example).

**Aptitude test**  A test that measures a child's potential for learning in specific areas.

**Cognition**  A term used to denote thinking ability. More specifically, the ability to use information in problem solving.

**Grade equivalent score**  An achievement test score that is related to grade level, not chronological age. A reading score of 2.4 means the child is reading at a level appropriate to the fourth month of second grade. (Achievement test scores are often reported as grade level equivalents.)

**Intelligence**  The ability to understand, recall, and use previously learned information appropriately in new situations.

**Intelligence quotient (IQ)**  A number that indicates the relative level of intelligence that a person has. The Mental Age divided by the Chronological Age multiplied by 100 is an approximation.

**Mental age**  A score on an intelligence test that tells the approximate age level at which a child is thinking and solving problems. A child with an MA of six responds to questions as a six-year-old would, regardless of whether the child's chronological age is two years or twelve years.

**Norms**  These denote normal, average, or typical development. Norms are used to determine above- and below-average performance.

**Percentile**  A way of dividing up groups or information. A child in the 90th percentile did better than 90 percent of the children taking a test, and is in the top 10 percent of the group.

# TEACHING RESOURCES

In some situations you may want or need additional information. There are many national as well as regional, state and local organizations that can be helpful to you. The following annotated list of national organizations should be useful to you.

CEC-TAG Gifted Handicapped Committee
The Council for Exceptional Children
1920 Association Drive
Reston, VA 22091
  A subgroup of the Council for Exceptional Children that publishes materials regarding the gifted.

Foundation for Gifted and Creative Children
395 Diamond Hill Road
Warwick, RI 02886
  Provides counseling for children and parents, and testing of children.

Gifted Child Society
P.O. Box 120
Oakland, NJ 07436
  Parents and educators of gifted children. Provides educational enrichment for gifted, talented, and creative children through the Saturday Workshop Program. Holds conferences for parents and sponsors demonstration workshops.

National Association for Creative Children and Adults
8080 Springvalley Drive
Cincinnati, OH 45236
  Offers In-service Teacher Training Program; sponsors workshops on creativity and international conferences; provides consulting service; conducts research.

National Association for Gifted Children
Marshall University
Department of Educational Foundations
Huntington, WV 25701
  Offers teacher training programs.

National Association for Gifted Children
217 Gregory Drive
Hot Springs, AR 71901
  Seeks to further education of the gifted and to enhance their potential creativity.

Office of the Gifted and Talented
U.S. Office of Education
Washington, DC 20202
  For programs and legislation for the gifted and talented. They also offer grants for research.

# BIBLIOGRAPHY

Barbe, Walter B., ed. *Psychology and Education of the Gifted.* New York: Irvington Publishers, 1980.

Callahan, Carolyn M. *Developing Creativity in the Gifted and Talented.* Reston, Va.: Council for Exceptional Children, 1978.

Hall, Eleanor G., and Nancy Skinner. *Somewhere to Turn: Strategies for Parents of the Gifted and Talented.* New York: Teachers College Press, 1980.

Maker, June C. *Providing Programs for the Gifted Handicapped.* Reston, Va.: Council for Exceptional Children, 1977.

Martinson, Ruth A. *The Identification of the Gifted and Talented.* Reston, Va.: Council for Exceptional Children, 1975.

Renzulli, Joseph S. *The Enrichment Triad Model: A Guide to Developing Defensible Programs for the Gifted and Talented.* Mansfield Center, Conn.: Creative Learning Press, 1977.

Roedell, Wendy C., et al. *Gifted Young Children.* New York: Teachers College Press, 1980.

Torrance, E. Paul. *Discovery and Nurturance of Giftedness in the Culturally Different.* Reston, Va.: Council for Exceptional Children, 1977.

Vail, Priscilla L. *The World of the Gifted Child.* New York: Walker and Co., 1979.

Whitmore, Joanne Rand. *Giftedness, Conflict, and Underachievement.* Boston: Allyn and Bacon, 1980.

## Biography/Autobiography/Fiction

Grost, Audrey. *Genius in Residence.* Englewood Cliffs, N.J.: Prentice-Hall, 1970.

> Mother of a gifted child reveals some interesting experiences from the birth of her son until his college graduation at the age of fifteen.

Hersey, John. *The Child Buyer.* New York: Knopf, 1960.

> A novel in the form of a hearing in which a company tries to buy a poor but gifted boy in order to use his brains for the good of the company.

Jones, Andrew. *Flight Seaward.* New York: Morrow, 1978.

> Documents a calculus child prodigy, his growth, development as a nuclear physicist, and ultimate mental breakdown.

Potok, Chaim. *My Name Is Asher Lev.* New York: Knopf, 1972.

> This novel tells of the family crisis of raising a very talented child who wants only to draw and paint and by family standards is a very odd little boy.

# BIBLIOGRAPHY FOR CHILDREN

## Creative Thinking

Adler, David A. *A Little at a Time.* New York: Random House, 1976.

> A grandfather and his grandson take a day's outing to the museum and take everything "a little at a time." This book could greatly enhance a child's concept of time.

Anno, Mitsumasa. *Topsy Turvies: Pictures to Stretch the Imagination.* Salem, Mass.: John Weatherhill, 1970.

> Intriguing picture book without words that has intricate as well as incongruous pictures.

Baldwin, Anne Norris. *Sunflowers for Tina.* New York: Scholastic Book Services, 1973.

> Tina, a black girl, is determined to grow a garden in the middle of New York City.

Castle, Sue. *Face Talk, Hand Talk, Body Talk.* Garden City, N.Y.: Doubleday, 1977.

> Discusses nonverbal communications. Photographs of children show alternate ways to express words and feelings.

Cauley, Lorinda Bryan. *The Bake-Off.* New York: Putnam, 1978.

> Mr. Hare tries to find a delicious and nutritious dish that will beat Mrs. Beaver's chocolate cake and you can help. Mr. Hare's recipe is included in the end.

Conford, Ellen. *Impossible Possum.* Boston: Little, Brown, 1971.

> Little boy possum's older sister uses her wits to help him overcome a weakness.

dePaola, Tomie. *Andy That's My Name.* Englewood Cliffs, N.J.: Prentice-Hall, 1973.

> Andy carries his name in a wagon. His friends get together and rearrange the letters to make new words. Encourages flexible thinking.

dePoix, Carol. *Jo, Flo and Yolanda.* Chapel Hill, N.C.: Lollipop Power, 1973.

> Three girls have a true adventure.

Freeman, Don. *Tilly Witch.* New York: Viking Press, 1969.

> Tilly goes back to school for a refresher course in scaring people.

Gaeddert, Lou Ann. *Noisy Nancy and Nick.* Garden City, N.Y.: Doubleday, 1970.

> Nancy shows her new neighbor how to have fun. He is from the Midwest and he doesn't like the city.

Galdone, Paul. *The Little Red Hen*. New York: Scholastic Book Services, 1975.

This brave hen takes the role of leader among her animal friends.

Gauch, Patricia Lee. *Christina Katerina and the Box*. New York: Coward, McCann and Geoghegan, 1980.

Christina takes a box that is intended for trash and turns it into a clubhouse, a dance floor, and a racing car.

Gill, Joan. *Sara's Granny and the Goodle*. Garden City, N.Y.: Doubleday, 1969.

Sara goes on an incredible imaginary trip.

Hoban, Lillian. *Arthur's Christmas Cookies*. New York: Harper and Row, 1972.

Arthur the chimp makes surprise Christmas cookies.

Kahn, Bernice. *The Watchamacallit Book*. New York: Putnam, 1976.

Children who read this book will have fun trying to identify and read words that are scrambled over the pages.

Kent, Jack. *Wizard of Wallaby Wallow*. New York: Scholastic Book Services, 1971.

A delightful story about a little mouse who visits the Wizard of Wallaby Wallow and receives a bottle saying that it will turn him "into something else." The little mouse finds something wrong with each creature he imagines himself as becoming.

King, Patricia. *Mabel the Whale*. Chicago: Follett, 1958.

Mabel has to adjust to her new surroundings after she has been captured and put in a tank.

Kroll, Steven. *Gobbledy-Gook*. Northville, Mich.: Holiday House Press, 1977.

The humorous story of a boy getting up in the morning. It is told in mixed-up language. (He squashes his laces; he flushes his teeth.) Great fun to decipher.

Lasker, Joe. *Merry Every After: The Story of Two Medieval Weddings*. New York: Viking Press, 1976.

This book provides a fascinating way to compare medieval life with today's life. It may encourage imaginative dramatic play.

Lewis, Stephen. *Zoo City*. New York: Greenwillow Books, 1976.

This book contains pictures of animals and also pictures of objects you might find in a city that look like these animals. The children can match the real animal with the inanimate lookalike.

McCloskey, Robert. *Blueberries for Sal*. New York: Penguin, 1976.

A mother and daughter encounter a mother bear and cub while picking blueberries on a hill.

Mayer, Mercer. *A Silly Story*. New York: Parents' Magazine Press, 1972.

A clever and comical story about a child's search for his identity. A young boy thinks "perhaps I am not me!" All the while he's wondering about who he really is, he fills his mind with all the silly things he might be.

Miller, Barry. *Alphabet World*. New York: Macmillan, 1971.

This book is made up of transparent pages with a letter of the alphabet on each one overlaying a page with a photograph of an everyday object in which the letter is to be found. (Look at the trafic light sideways and it forms an *E*.)

O'Neill, Mary. *Hailstones and Halibut Bones*. New York: Doubleday, 1961.

Twelve poems about color, written as though color can be heard, touched, and smelled as well as seen.

Perrine, Mary. *Nannabah's Friend*. Boston: Houghton Mifflin, 1970.

A young Navajo girl copes with loneliness while taking her sheep to pasture.

Rockwell, Anne. *Albert B. Cub and Zebra: An Alphabet Story Book*. New York: Thomas Y. Crowell, 1977.

An alphabet book that has hidden pictures of many items starting with one letter of the alphabet. Although wordless, the pictures weave a story.

Ruchlis, Hy. *How a Rock Came to Be a Fence on a Road near a Town*. New York: Walker and Co., 1973.

This "story" of a rock starts 300 million years ago at the bottom of the sea and continues until the rock is where we find it today. An interesting way to look at changing geography and terrain.

Sandberg, Inger and Lasse Sandberg. *What Little Anna Saved*. New York: Lothrop, Lee and Shepherd, 1965.

Anna makes all sorts of things out of odds and ends.

Segal, Lore. *Tell Me a Mitzi*. New York: Farrar, Straus and Giroux, 1970.

Imaginative Mitzi tells three delightful stories about her family life.

Sendak, Maurice. *Where the Wild Things Are*. New York: Harper and Row, 1963.

The story of a boy who is sent to bed without supper. He dreams he goes to an island of monsters who make him King of the Wild Things.

Shulevitz, Uri. *Rain Rain Rivers*. New York: Farrar, Straus and Giroux, 1969.

While listening to the rain, a little girl looks forward to playing in the puddles.

Skarpen, Liesel Moak. *We Were Tired of Living in a House.* New York: Coward, McCann and Geoghegan, 1969.

Imaginative story of kids tired of living in a house, so they try living in a tree, a pond, a cave, and at the seashore. In each place something unusual happens to make them move on to the next place and finally home.

Spier, Peter. *Bored, Nothing To Do.* New York: Doubleday, 1978.

Two bored brothers decide to make an airplane from scraps. Encourages divergent thinking.

Thompson, Susan L. *One More Thing, Dad.* Chicago: Albert Whitman, 1980.

An ingenious counting book in which Caleb packs a healthy lunch. This book has many possibilities for activities and discussions.

Van Woerkom, Dorothy. *Hidden Messages.* New York: Crown, 1979.

Shows how ants give messages to one another in order to find food, attract mates, and warn others. Good lead into nonverbal communication.

Vreeken, Elizabeth. *The Boy Who Would Not Say His Name.* Chicago: Follett, 1959.

A boy who won't answer to his real name because he likes to pretend he is someone else. One day he gets lost and has to tell his real name so that his parents can come find him. Helps teach to differentiate reality from fantasy.

Wahl, Jan. *Wolf of My Own.* New York: Macmillan, 1969.

A little girl thinks her birthday puppy is a "wolf friend."

### Nonstereotypic Roles and Occupations

Babbitt, Natalie. *Phoebe's Revolt.* Garden City, N.Y.: Farrar, Straus and Giroux, 1977.

Phoebe revolts against frills and lace and wants to wear her father's clothes.

Berenstain, Stanley, and Janice Berenstain. *He Bear, She Bear.* New York: Random House, 1974.

Relates that both he and she bears can do anything they like. Shows a variety of occupational roles.

Blaine, Marge. *The Terrible Thing That Happened at Our House.* New York: Scholastic Book Services, 1975.

When a mother goes back to work, her children have to learn to cook and to care for themselves.

Brownstone, Cecily. *All Kinds of Mothers.* New York: McKay, 1969.

An interracial book showing mothers who work both outside and inside the home.

Burton, Virginia Lee. *Katy and the Big Snow.* Boston: Houghton Mifflin, 1974.

Katy, an old red tractor, rescues a snowed-in city.

Chapman, Kim W. *The Magic Hat.* Chapel Hill, N.C.: Lollipop Power, 1976.

Polly finds a magic hat that helps to make the fence disappear that separates boys' toys from girls' toys. The toys are for everyone, no matter what sex they are.

Cohen, Miriam. *Will I Have a Friend?* New York: Macmillan, 1967.

A young boy experiences uncertainty on his first day at a child care center. His father takes him there, which shows that a father can have a nurturing role in his child's life.

Eichler, Margret. *Martin's Father.* Chapel Hill, N.C.: Lollipop Power, 1977.

Martin's father cares for him, and they perform everyday household tasks together.

Godden, Rumer. *Impunity Jane.* New York: Macmillan, 1955.

A young boy takes pride in his china doll.

Goffstein, M. B. *Goldie the Dollmaker.* Garden City, N.Y.: Farrar, Straus, and Giroux, 1980.

Goldie makes wooden dolls for her living.

———. *Two Piano Tuners.* Garden City, N.Y.: Farrar, Straus, and Giroux, 1970.

Debbie decides that she would like to be a piano tuner just like her grandfather.

Goldreich, Gloria, and Ester Goldreich. *What Can She Be? A Newscaster.* New York: Lothrop, Lee and Shepherd Press, 1973.

Photographs and text capture a day in the life of a black woman newscaster.

Goodyear, Carmen. *The Sheep Book.* Chapel Hill, N.C.: Lollipop Power, 1972.

A story of a farmer and her sheep.

Hazen, Nancy. *Grownups Cry Too: Los Adultos Tambien Lloran.* Chapel Hill, N.C.: Lollipop Power, 1978.

Grownups are human and they should be able to express their emotions just as children. Men and women are shown as both sad and happy.

Kingman, Lee. *Georgina and the Dragon.* Boston: Houghton Mifflin, 1972.

Ten-year-old Georgina is an early victim of job discrimination, but she overcomes this and makes life easier for girls in her neighborhood.

Klagsburn, Francine, ed. *Free to Be You and Me.* New York: McGraw-Hill, 1974.

A selection of songs and poems saying that you can be whatever you want to be.

Klein, Norma. *Girls Can Be Anything*. New York: E. P. Dutton, 1975.

This story shows that girls can be doctors, scientists, pilots, or anything that they want to be.

Kraisilovsky, Phylis. *The Girl Who Was a Cowboy*. New York: Doubleday, 1965.

A little girl would rather play cowboys with the boys than dress up and play tea party like little girls. When she finally wears a "girl's" hat and dress she feels funny until one of the little boys compliments her. She then doesn't mind dressing up, but she still plays cowboys too.

Lasker, Joe. *Mothers Can Do Anything*. Chicago: Albert Whitman, 1972.

Mothers are shown in many nontraditional jobs such as doctor, judge, dancer, and ditch digger.

Leaf, Munro. *Story of Ferdinand*. New York: Penguin, 1977.

A gentle bull loves flowers and refuses to fight. The story makes the point that this nonstereotypic bull was very happy doing as he pleased.

Lengstrand, Rolf, and Pierre Rolen. *The Long Pony Race*. New York: Knopf, 1966.

Fia races her pony to victory in the Long Pony Race of Sweden.

Lenski, Lois. *Debbie and Her Pets*. New York: Walck, 1971.

A young girl collects small animals and puts on her own pet show.

Lenthall, Patricia Riley. *Carlotta and the Scientist*. Chapel Hill, N.C.: Lollipop Power, 1976.

Carlotta, a penguin, decides to join a female scientist in her travels. She lets her husband stay behind and care for their family.

McKee, David. *The Man Who Was Going to Mind the House*. New York: Abelard-Schuman, 1973.

A folktale about a man and wife who exchange jobs for a day because the husband is always complaining that he works so hard.

Merriam, Eve. *Mommies at Work*. New York: Scholastic Book Services, 1973.

Working mothers are shown typing letters, building bridges, assembling automobiles, and performing other nontraditional jobs.

Miles, Betty, and Joan Blos. *Do You Have the Time Lydia?* New York: E. P. Dutton, 1971.

Lydia cooks and sews, hammers and nails, and also builds racing cars.

————, and Joan Blos. *Just Think*. New York: Knopf, 1971.

Mother works in a lab while father walks his son to school. Boys and girls are shown playing baseball, cowboys, and dolls together.

Phleger, Frederick. *Ann Can Fly*. New York: Random House, 1959.

Ann learns to fly her father's private plane.

Pratt, Ellen. *Amy and the Cloud Basket*. Chapel Hill, N.C.: Lollipop Power, 1975.

Amy McClune lived in the town of Pan. Only the men caught clouds and put them in baskets, until Amy showed the town that she could catch the clouds as well as the men.

Reavin, Sam. *Hurrah for Captain Jane*. New York: Scholastic Book Services, 1971.

Jane fantasizes about being the first woman captain of an ocean liner.

————. *Jelly Beans for Breakfast*. New York: Parents' Magazine Press, 1968.

Two little girls dream of things they will do, including traveling to the moon.

Rockwell, Harlow. *My Doctor*. New York: Macmillan, 1973.

A woman proves to be a very good doctor.

Rothman, Joel. *I Can Be Anything You Can Be*. New York: Scroll Press, 1973.

This book shows that a little girl can become anything a little boy can.

Saul, Wendy and Abigail. *Butcher, Baker and Cabinetmaker: Photographs of Woman at Work*. New York: Thomas Y. Crowell, 1978.

Written about women of all ages and all walks of life working in nontraditional occupations.

Speare, Elizabeth Geroge. *The Witch of Blackbird Pond*. Boston: Houghton Mifflin, 1958.

The heroine rebels against bigotry and her puritanical surroundings, which lead to a witch hunt and trial.

Surowiecki, Sandra Luca. *Joshua's Day*. Chapel Hill, N.C.: Lollipop Power, 1977.

Joshua lives in a one-parent home. His mother, who is a photographer, takes him to a day care center where he interacts with both boys and girls.

Taves, Isabella. *Not Bad for a Girl*. New York: M. Evans and Co., 1972.

When Sharon Lee is asked to join the Little League, the people of her village are upset.

Thayer, Jane. *Quiet on Account of Dinosaur*. New York: Morrow, 1964.

Jane is interested in dinosaurs and becomes a famous scientist.

Wolde, Gunilla. *Tommy and Sarah Dress Up*. Boston: Houghton Mifflin, 1972.

Tommy and Sarah dress up and act out many different roles.

Yashima, Taro. *Crow Boy*. New York: Viking Press, 1955.

Chibie was scorned by his classmates for six years until a male teacher took time to discover his uniqueness as a person.

Young, Eleanor R. *Fathers, Fathers, Fathers*. Minneapolis: T. S. Denison, 1971.

This story presents the father's role. It uses simple illustrations of men of differing nationality and occupation.

Zolotow, Charlotte. *William's Doll*. New York: Harper and Row, 1972.

William more than anything wants a doll, but his male relatives think that's "sissy." William's grandmother finally understands that he wants a doll to practice being a father and gives him a doll.

*Science*

Asimov, Isaac. *ABC's of the Earth*. New York: Walker and Co., 1971.

An alphabet book about the environment. Goes beyond traditional ABC books in scope.

————. *ABC's of the Ocean*. New York: Walker and Co., 1970.

An alphabet book that goes from aquaculture to zooplankton!

Balestrino, Philip. *Hot as an Ice Cube*. New York: Thomas Y. Crowell, 1971.

This book describes how everything in the world has heat in it—even an ice cube. It also contains experiments to show that there is heat in all things.

Barton, Byron. *Wheels*. New York: Thomas Y. Crowell, 1979.

A creative story about the invention of the wheel and its progress through history. Good for stimulating invention, also imagining what the world would be like without wheels.

Brenner, Barbara. *Bodies*. New York: E. P. Dutton, 1973.

This book looks at all kinds of bodies—all shapes, colors, and sizes. It shows the differences and similarities in all of them and stresses the uniqueness in everyone.

Cole, Joanna. *Find the Hidden Insects*. New York: Morrow, 1979.

This book illustrates how and why insects protect themselves. It may spark investigations of how other animals hide in their own habitats.

Pike, Tillis S., and Joseph Levine. *Gravity All Around*. New York: McGraw–Hill, 1963.

Tells what gravity is and poses pictorial questions for children to answer. (How is gravity helping in each picture—a boy playing basketball, woman pouring milk.) Also has experiments for the child to do.

Pringle, Lawrence. *Natural Fire: Its Ecology in Forests*. New York: Morrow, 1979.

Pringle brings children to a new understanding of the ecological balance in nature.

Selam, Millicent. *You and the World Around You*. Garden City, N.Y.: Doubleday, 1963.

Story describes stars, plants, trees, and animals. It gives the child a perspective of himself in his environment. Good pictures to stimulate discussion.

Simon, Mina, and Howard Simon. *If You Were an Eel, How Would You Feel?* Chicago: Follett, 1963.

Poetically expresses the characteristics of certain animals. A novel way of describing animals—what they look like and what they do.

Spier, Peter. *Noah's Ark*. New York: Doubleday, 1977.

An intricate and descriptive picture book that shows many animals and where they live and what they eat.

Walther, Tom. *A Spider Might*. New York: Scribner, 1978.

This unique and exciting book about people and spiders blends science and humor.

Wolf, Barbara. *Evening Gray, Morning Red: A Handbook of American Weather Wisdom*. New York: Macmillan, 1976.

Before the days of weather reports, people predicted weather by the skies. Rhymes about weather are given and explained in this interesting text.

# INDEX

| *Annual Goals* | *Activity* | *Curriculum Area* | *Page* |
|---|---|---|---|
| | Listen Before You Move | Listening | 360 |
| | Music and Movement | Movement | 480 |
| | Painting to Music | Art | 454 |
| | Weighty Movements | Movement | 478 |

## LANGUAGE SKILLS

| | | | |
|---|---|---|---|
| To improve expressive language | Best and Worst | Expressing Language | 335 |
| | Bookstore | Dramatic Play | 488 |
| | Bring Me | Expressing Language | 336 |
| | Di-Vergent | Expressing Language | 335 |
| | Dress Up and Tell | Dramatic Play | 492 |
| | Ideas | Expressing Language | 334 |
| | Interviews | Expressing Language | 339 |
| | My Shoes | Expressing Language | 334 |
| | Panama | Dramatic Play | 491 |
| | Treasure Hunt | Expressing Language | 338 |
| | What Shall We Make? | Dramatic Play | 495 |
| To increase vocabulary | Barefoot | Outdoor Play | 530 |
| | Object File | Listening | 354 |
| | Rhyming Words | Expressing Language | 340 |
| | Room Shapes | Mathematics | 425 |
| | Symptoms | Health and Safety | 439 |
| | Synonyms | Expressing Language | 339 |
| | Will It Fit? | Mathematics | 427 |
| To follow directions | Be the Teacher | Social Studies | 390 |
| | Body Maneuvers | Movement | 479 |
| | Listen Before You Move | Listening | 360 |
| | Obstacle Course | Large Motor Play | 515 |
| To interpret body language | Feelings | Expressing Language | 342 |
| | Who Am I? | Dramatic Play | 491 |
| To improve breath control | Bird-in-a-Hole | Science/Discovery | 401 |
| | Pinwheel | Science/Discovery | 403 |
| To increase understanding | Class Book | Reading Readiness | 380 |
| | Color Words | Expressing Language | 342 |
| | Feelings | Expressing Language | 342 |
| | Opposite Lotto | Reading Readiness | 375 |
| | Synonyms | Expressing Language | 339 |
| | Traveling | Expressing Language | 344 |
| | Visual Analogies | Reading Readiness | 377 |

## THINKING AND REASONING

| | | | |
|---|---|---|---|
| To increase attention span | Color Concentration | Reading Readiness | 372 |
| | Treasure Hunt | Expressing Language | 338 |
| To improve cause and effect reasoning | Balance It | Large Motor Play | 519 |
| | Bird-in-a-Hole | Science/Discovery | 401 |
| | Contour Maps | Science/Discovery | 401 |
| | Corrugated Collage | Art | 446 |
| | Crayon Rubbing | Art | 448 |
| | Creature | Art | 448 |
| | Dress Up and Tell | Dramatic Play | 492 |
| | Gelatin | Science/Discovery | 400 |

| *Annual Goals* | *Activity* | *Curriculum Area* | *Page* |
|---|---|---|---|
| | Listening Obstacle Course | Listening | 361 |
| | Magnets | Science/Discovery | 398 |
| | Mixing Colored Water | Science/Discovery | 403 |
| | Perspectives | Reading Readiness | 373 |
| | Pinwheel | Science/Discovery | 403 |
| | School Moods | Art | 447 |
| | Shoe Store | Dramatic Play | 487 |
| | Smell Cues | Health and Safety | 436 |
| | Temperature | Science/Discovery | 400 |
| | Texture Paint | Art | 449 |
| | Texture Playdough | Art | 449 |
| | Torn Paper Flowers | Art | 445 |
| | Vibrations | Music | 466 |
| | Water Tones | Listening | 355 |
| | What Shall We Make? | Dramatic Play | 495 |
| | What Would You Do If? | Health and Safety | 438 |
| | What's Missing? | Reading Readiness | 373 |
| | Who Has Been Here? | Social Studies | 387 |
| To increase logical reasoning | Bring Me | Expressing Language | 336 |
| | Measure It | Mathematics | 430 |
| | Title | Listening | 362 |
| | Will It Fit? | Mathematics | 427 |
| To improve classification skills | Classify It | Reading Readiness | 379 |
| | Match 'em | Reading Readiness | 376 |
| | Picture Shapes | Mathematics | 424 |
| | Pick-a-Pair | Small Motor Play | 504 |
| | Room Shapes | Mathematics | 425 |
| | Sorting | Small Motor Play | 500 |
| | Taste Sort | Science/Discovery | 408 |
| | Texture Playdough | Art | 449 |
| To improve sequencing skills | Comics | Reading Readiness | 379 |
| | Going to the Beach | Listening | 358 |
| To improve color concepts | Shape Pictures | Mathematics | 419 |
| To make predictions | Magnets | Science/Discovery | 398 |
| | Measure It | Mathematics | 430 |
| | Mixing Colored Water | Science/Discovery | 403 |
| | Pace It Off | Mathematics | 430 |
| | Pinwheel | Science/Discovery | 403 |
| | Temperature | Science/Discovery | 400 |
| | Who Has Been Here? | Social Studies | 387 |
| To increase problem-solving skills | Follow That Line | Reading Readiness | 370 |
| | Gelatin | Science/Discovery | 400 |
| | Mixing Colored Water | Science/Discovery | 403 |
| To improve decision making | No Name | Dramatic Play | 494 |
| | Title | Listening | 362 |

## MATHEMATIC SKILLS

| | | | |
|---|---|---|---|
| To improve number concepts | Abacus | Mathematics | 412 |
| | Counting Songs | Music | 469 |
| | Cuisenaire Rods | Mathematics | 414 |
| | Time Cards | Mathematics | 416 |

| *Annual Goals* | *Activity* | *Curriculum Area* | *Page* |
|---|---|---|---|
| To improve measurement concepts | Areas | Mathematics | 420 |
| | Jump over the Creek | Outdoor Play | 526 |
| | Measure It | Mathematics | 430 |
| | Pace It Off | Mathematics | 430 |
| To improve spatial concepts | Contour Maps | Science/Discovery | 401 |
| | From Your House to Mine | Social Studies | 393 |
| | Pace It Off | Mathematics | 430 |
| To improve shape concepts | Areas | Mathematics | 420 |
| | Little Shadows | Mathematics | 422 |
| | People Shapes | Mathematics | 423 |
| | Picture Shapes | Mathematics | 424 |
| | Room Shapes | Mathematics | 425 |
| | Shape Pictures | Mathematics | 419 |
| To improve size concepts | Areas | Mathematics | 420 |
| | Object Sizes | Mathematics | 425 |
| | People Shapes | Mathematics | 423 |
| | Room Shapes | Mathematics | 425 |
| | Will It Fit? | Mathematics | 427 |
| To improve time concepts | Time Cards | Mathematics | 416 |

## SOCIAL SKILLS

| | | | |
|---|---|---|---|
| To take turns | From Your House to Mine | Social Studies | 393 |
| To increase sharing skills | Solutions | Social Studies | 385 |
| To broaden concepts of families | Animal Families | Social Studies | 384 |
| | Photograph Story | Social Studies | 389 |
| | Roles | Social Studies | 390 |
| To increase survival skills | Emergency Room | Dramatic Play | 487 |
| | Smell Cues | Health and Safety | 436 |
| | Symptoms | Health and Safety | 439 |
| | What Would You Do If? | Health and Safety | 438 |
| To improve self-help skills | Lock Box | Small Motor Play | 502 |
| To increase awareness of roles people play | Audiologist | Dramatic Play | 489 |
| | Bookstore | Dramatic Play | 488 |
| | Be the Teacher | Social Studies | 390 |
| | Cast It | Dramatic Play | 486 |
| | Circus | Dramatic Play | 486 |
| | Connections | Dramatic Play | 488 |
| | Dentist | Dramatic Play | 485 |
| | Doctor's Office | Dramatic Play | 485 |
| | Emergency Room | Dramatic Play | 487 |
| | Eye Doctor | Dramatic Play | 490 |
| | Photograph Story | Social Studies | 389 |
| | Shoe Store | Dramatic Play | 487 |
| | Visitor | Social Studies | 388 |
| | Who Am I? | Dramatic Play | 491 |
| To cooperate with peers | Audiologist | Dramatic Play | 489 |
| | Color Concentration | Reading Readiness | 372 |
| | Eye Doctor | Dramatic Play | 490 |

| *Annual Goals* | *Activity* | *Curriculum Area* | *Page* |
|---|---|---|---|
| | Connections | Dramatic Play | 488 |
| | Creature | Art | 448 |
| | Di-Vergent | Expressing Language | 335 |
| | Hands and Feet | Social Studies | 385 |
| | Our Town | Social Studies | 384 |
| | Solutions | Social Studies | 385 |
| | Treasure Hunt | Expressing Language | 338 |
| | What Would You Do If? | Health and Safety | 438 |
| | Who Has Been Here? | Social Studies | 387 |

**FEELINGS**

| | | | |
|---|---|---|---|
| To express feelings | Best and Worst | Expressing Language | 335 |
| | Feelings | Expressing Language | 342 |
| | My Books | Reading Readiness | 380 |
| | Share Your Feelings | Social Studies | 392 |
| | | | |
| To increase feelings of group belonging | Bookstore | Dramatic Play | 488 |
| | Class Book | Reading Readiness | 380 |
| | Connections | Dramatic Play | 488 |
| | Dress Up and Tell | Dramatic Play | 492 |
| | Flannel Board Stories | Reading Readiness | 374 |
| | Hand/Foot Painting | Art | 458 |
| | Hug Tag | Outdoor Play | 531 |
| | I'm Thinking Of | Social Studies | 392 |
| | No Name | Dramatic Play | 494 |
| | Our Town | Social Studies | 384 |
| | Panama | Dramatic Play | 491 |
| | Share Your Feelings | Social Studies | 392 |
| | Slings | Dramatic Play | 494 |
| | Traveling | Expressing Language | 344 |

**AWARENESS**

| | | | |
|---|---|---|---|
| To increase body awareness | Balance It | Large Motor Play | 519 |
| | Barefoot | Outdoor Play | 530 |
| | Be It | Movement | 474 |
| | Body Maneuvers | Movement | 479 |
| | Body Parts | Social Studies | 386 |
| | Circus | Dramatic Play | 486 |
| | Hand/Foot Painting | Art | 458 |
| | Hands and Feet | Social Studies | 385 |
| | Jump over the Creek | Outdoor Play | 526 |
| | Little Shadows | Mathematics | 422 |
| | Movement Exploration | Movement | 474 |
| | My Shadow | Art | 456 |
| | My Puzzle | Small Motor Play | 503 |
| | Rag Doll | Movement | 476 |
| | Relaxation Stories | Movement | 476 |
| | Slings | Dramatic Play | 494 |
| | Symptoms | Health and Safety | 439 |
| | Throwing Games | Small Motor Play | 506 |
| | Variations on Crawling | Large Motor Play | 512 |

| *Annual Goals* | *Activity* | *Curriculum Area* | *Page* |
|---|---|---|---|
| | Variations on Hopping | Large Motor Play | 513 |
| | Weighty Movements | Movement | 478 |
| To improve self-concept | Interviews | Expressing Language | 339 |
| | My Puzzle | Small Motor Play | 503 |
| To increase awareness of individual differences | Hand/Foot Painting | Art | 458 |
| | I'm Thinking Of | Social Studies | 392 |
| To increase awareness of moods | Painting to Music | Art | 454 |
| | School Moods | Art | 447 |
| To increase knowledge of foods | Taste Sort | Science/Discovery | 408 |
| To increase awareness of physical needs | Cast It | Dramatic Play | 486 |
| | Slings | Dramatic Play | 494 |
| To increase awareness of hearing needs | Audiologist | Dramatic Play | 489 |
| To increase awareness of visual needs | Eye Doctor | Dramatic Play | 490 |
| To increase awareness of other cultures | Panama | Dramatic Play | 491 |

# 15

# *Needs: Intellectual*

Watching Phillip, you would guess him to be one of the youngest children in the class, yet he is actually one of the oldest. He rarely has much to say, and he seems to play at things rather than with them. Everything seems so hard for him. The other children notice and call him "dumb" and "stupid." Maybe he'll grow out of it. Is this your imagination or is Phillip really slow?

Can you remember how you felt in school when you didn't know the answer and the teacher called on you even though your eyes were down? You hadn't done your homework or you weren't paying attention, and then you were asked to go to the blackboard. Did you feel stupid or ashamed? That's how Phillip may feel. He may have a mental impairment—intellectual needs.

A mental impairment is traditionally defined subaverage intellectual function combined with poor adaptive behavior, both of which are apparent at an early age. This definition assumes that retardation is a generalized phenomenon that can be classified and is permanent. The prognosis sounds dim, but by reorienting your thinking, it is possible to be realistic and even a bit optimistic. When children's intellectual growth does not keep pace with physical growth and chronological age, they have intellectual needs. Realistically, children with a mental impairment need you to use a variety of teaching methods over a longer period of time to help them learn. As they get older, there will be some things they may not be capable of learning. A watered-down kindergarten program isn't the answer. You need a program designed to meet these children's individual strengths and needs.

## CLASSIFICATION OF INTELLECTUAL NEEDS

The classification of intellectual needs is determined in part by the child's level of intellectual functioning, the intelligence quotient or IQ. On the Stanford-Binet, average intellectual functioning is represented by a score of 100. Those with IQs over 100 are brighter than average, while those with IQs less than 100 are not as bright. From the bell-shaped curve shown below, you can see that 50 percent of all the people in the United States have IQs between 90 and 110. About sixteen percent fall between 79 and 89. We sometimes call these children slow learners.

Percent of population in various IQ ranges

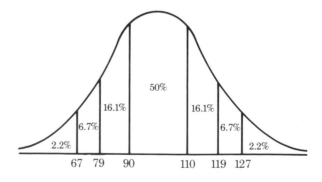

Based on David Wechsler, *The Measurement of Adult Intelligence* (Baltimore, Williams and Wilkins, 1944).

It is unlikely that you will notice them during the preschool years. They will probably graduate from high school, but will rarely go on to higher education. Below 79, children are usually categorized as having some delay.

*Mild* delays are often not noticed during the preschool years, although you may begin to suspect something as you watch these children. The most obvious signs are that they are slower to talk than other children, may seem immature, and may also have been slower to walk (after fifteen months). A four-year-old with a mild delay will act more like a three-year-old. These children may be classified *educable mentally handicapped* (approximate IQ 50–75).

Even at a preschool age, *moderately* affected children show noticeable delays in both mental development, especially speech and language, and motor development. They may need assistance in self-help skills. These children may not be toilet trained at the preschool level, or if they are, may not be able to manage taking off and putting on their clothes alone. In some cases, these children will look different from other children (if, for example, they have Down's syndrome). In other cases they won't. A four-year-old will act more like a two-year-old. Most likely, parents will know that this child is mentally impaired. These children may be classified as *trainable mentally handicapped* (approximate IQ 30–55).

*Severely* affected children (approximate IQ 20–35) show marked delays in all areas of development and, at the preschool level, have few or no communication skills. It is unlikely that these children would be mainstreamed into a regular classroom. These children do profit greatly from preschool education, but their needs are generally best met in programs designed for their developmental level.

Children who are *profoundly* retarded (IQ below 20–25) show gross retardation in all areas and usually need nursing care.

It may seem that intelligence quotients alone are the easiest way to determine if children are mentally impaired, but most professionals agree, especially for young children, that a test score in and of itself is not enough. It is important to know how the child functions in his world.

Because the tests are considered reliable within about five points and the choice of cutoff point varies, you will find some overlap in the range of scores. About nine children out of every hundred have some degree of mental impairment. If you go back to the bell-shaped curve, you will find that seven of the nine children will be between 67 and 79, and two below 67.

The concept of *mental age* is useful for teaching purposes. If you are given an IQ, you can figure out the mental age. You can estimate if you are given only a classification and know the chronological age. Ages should be converted to months to make the arithmetic easier.

$$IQ = \frac{Mental\ Age}{Chronological\ Age} \times 100$$

$$50 = \frac{?}{48\ months} \times 100$$

The mental age equals 24 months.

If you have a child who is four years old (48 months) and is classified as moderately retarded or trainable, this child is developing at about half the normal rate and will function much like a two-year-old. A child who is classified as having a mild delay is functioning at about three-fourths the normal rate. Such a four-year-old will be more like a three-year-old.

When children with mental delays are mainstreamed, they are often placed with younger children, which makes their delays less obvious. A mildly delayed four-year-old may be placed in a class with three-year-olds. Unless the child is unusually large, this is often a good solution for all. As this child will perform at a level closer to his mental age than his chronological age.

## CHILDREN'S NEEDS— TEACHING GOALS

Related annual goals may be grouped under broad categories called "teaching goals." Outlined under each teaching goal below are the most important needs of children with intellectual needs. A child may have some or all of these needs, and additional needs as well. Suggestions on what you might consequently teach them are included. Often, a course of action is implicit in the description of the need.

### Language Skills

Language, both expressing and receiving, is probably this child's weakest area. This child has both a smaller vocabulary, and uses simpler sentence structures than his peers. His language may be difficult to understand and used less frequently than other children in the class. As he is developing more language skills set aside time to repeat simple songs and stories. Use rhyming to develop vocabulary. Give the child practice following one and two step directions.

### Thinking and Reasoning Skills

By definition children with intellectual needs have fewer skills in this area than their peers as well as less resources to develop these skills. Begin with simple yet necessary concepts such as colors and numbers. Point out similarities and differences within classification systems (for example, cars and trucks both have wheels). Increase attention span by programming for what the child likes and praising the child for staying with projects to completion; initially this may require your staying with the child as well.

### Motor Skills

These children are relatively better at large motor activities than small motor ones. However, motor activities in general often lack smoothness and flow. These children need practice with activities that require stopping, starting, and turning corners—for example, running an obstacle path. Activities that require the use of alternating sides of the body such as riding a tricycle or marching are difficult, but also need practice. Fine motor skills can be practiced in conjunction with eye-hand coordination activities. These are necessary prewriting skills. Using clip type clothes pins builds finger strength, and art activities are a way to work on small motor coordination.

### Awareness

All children need to learn about themselves. These children will take more time to learn the labels of their body parts. Use songs as well as direct questioning to teach this. Develop a more positive self concept by pointing out to this child and others in the room what this child *can* do and how much he *has* learned.

### Guidelines

Because it is more difficult for children with mental delays to learn, it is more important that you become aware of how children learn in order to meet the needs of these children.

1. Use as many of the senses in teaching as possible. Even if you are teaching concepts that are primarily visual, like colors, have children reinforce the visual with other sensory experiences.
   See the red ball.
   Sit on the red square.
   Add red food coloring to the finger paint.
   Eat a red tomato.
   Listen to a red fire truck.
   These children, like most children, don't learn the first time around, so teach the same concept in different contexts.
2. Keep going over the same concept until they have *overlearned* it. Because these children may easily forget, review information until it is firmly established.
3. Teach a concept for a short time each day for many days, rather than for a long period of time on fewer days. Spaced practice is always more

effective than massed practiced as those who "cram" for an exam know.
4. Because it is difficult for these children to learn, determine the learning value of specific materials and use those which are most efficient or those that teach two necessary skills at one time. For example, buttoning sequences where children must duplicate a pattern of colors teaches both buttoning, a necessary self-help skill, and color concepts.
5. Generalizing is usually very difficult for these children. When you teach concepts try to make them as close to the setting where they will be used as possible and as real as possible. Keep activities relevant, short, and to the point. Be wary of cute shortcuts. One school I visited decided to teach children to say "three-teen" instead of thirteen because it was easier. Some of those children are now about "three-teen" and their peers make fun of them when they tell how old they are.
6. When teaching these children, use many examples. If you use only one example when teaching the concept *red*, it is likely that the children who learn this one particular "red" will deny other "reds."
7. In general, teach from simple to complex. Where appropriate, simplify information, but

Children with developmental needs must have many first-hand experiences. For example, they need to discover that water splashes when they jump in it.

not to the point that it loses its meaning. If children are still having problems, do a task analysis. A task analysis is breaking a task down into its component parts, sequencing these, and then teaching them. A great deal has been written on the use of task analysis. However, if you understand the basic principles involved in a task, you can do the task analysis yourself. Start with something the child must do frequently, like putting on a coat. If the children still have problems, review your analysis for both order and possible missed steps. Change a few things and try again.

Following is a sample task analysis, including a filled-in chart that shows the child's progress.

8. In some cases, the technique of backward chaining is useful. Using the example of putting on the coat from Figure 15–1, you would offer the most help with the first steps and the least help with the last. The first thing you would expect the child to do by himself is Step 8 (zip up the coat). This means the child gets some satisfaction for task completion instead of needing help to finish. (Backward chaining is easier when the component parts are of equal difficulty.)

9. Be sure to reinforce appropriate behavior. Set your sights realistically though. Reinforce effort and steps accomplished toward a goal. Don't wait until the goal is accomplished or the child may lose motivation.

10. Avoid a watered-down program. Don't try to teach these children the whole curriculum at a lower, simpler level. Rather, concentrate on what is important for these children. What skills will be essential later for the children, that need a base developed now?

**Figure 15–1** Task Analysis and Tracking Chart

| | M | T | W | TH | F | M | T |
|---|---|---|---|---|---|---|---|
| 1. Take coat off hook. | PH | VH | VH | VH | NH | NH | NH |
| 2. Put coat on floor inside up. | PH | PH | VH | VH | NH | NH | NH |
| 3. Stand at neck of coat. | PH | PH | VH | VH | VH | NH | NH |
| 4. Bend over. | PH | PH | PH | VH | VH | NH | NH |
| 5. Put hands in armholes. | PH | PH | PH | VH | VH | NH | NH |
| 6. Flip coat over head, pushing arms into arm holes. | PH | PH | PH | PH | VH | VH | VH |
| 7. Start zipper. | PH | PH | PH | PH | VH | VH | VH |
| 8. Zip up coat. | PH | PH | VH | VH | VH | NH | NH |

Be sure to praise the child for his efforts

Key: PH = physical help
　　　VH = verbal help
　　　NH = no help

11. Let children with intellectual needs progress at their own rates, not those of the other children in the class. Gear the rate toward the mental age rather than the chronological age.

## CURRICULUM ADAPTATIONS

Adapting the curriculum, in general, consists of simplifying tasks, focusing on essential tasks and omitting others, and including tasks that other children may learn at home.

### Expressing Language, Listening, and Reading Readiness

Like all children, those with intellectual needs depend on communicating with others to have their needs met. They need to develop language skills to make this possible.

1. Work on vocabulary. Start with a nucleus vocabulary that focuses on the child. Teaching body parts teaches not only vocabulary but body awareness as well. Next focus on the family, followed by clothing, health care (toileting, food safety), and some aspects of both the school and home environments. Emphasize nouns and verbs first. They are essential for communicating needs.

2. Encourage these children to talk. It sometimes helps to give the cues for subjects to talk about. Pictures taken during field trips can be used later to help children talk about what happened on the trips. The children can also sequence these pictures. At first, make the sequence obvious.

    Picture 1: Getting into the cars
    Picture 2: Arriving at the orchard
    Picture 3: Eating apples at the orchard
    Picture 4: Taking off coats back at school; carrying the apples

3. Start with firsthand experiences, not abstractions. If you are going to set up a grocery store in the dramatic play area, take a field trip to one first or tell parents about your plans and encourage them to take the child.

These children usually need a longer period of "readiness" before they can apply skills. It is important to build a solid base. This requires patience on your part. You can't push them before they are ready, and you must not quit because you decide they will never learn. First establish basic skills, then use these skills to teach integration or higher level skills.

1. Concentrate first on auditory and visual identification. Don't assume that these children can

label all the sounds and objects in their environment. Then work on discrimination skills. Once identification skills have been established, work on visual and auditory memory. For example, have children first match alphabet letters, then label them by name or sound.

2. Once some concepts have been mastered, move on to higher level skills. For example, have children classify objects by color once they understand the colors.

3. Sitting for the sake of sitting, although helpful to the teacher, is not a useful skill for the child. Teach the child to use readiness materials while they are waiting. This will also alleviate the long-term problem developmentally delayed children typically have with leisure time.

At the beginning, use short, simple stories that have a familiar theme. Remember, the group experience may be new to the child.

1. Animal stories with big pictures and few words, alphabet books, and those with simple rhymes are good.

2. It may be helpful to cue the child into a specific concept by asking the child to listen for the item while you read the story. For example, before reading the story *Caps for Sale*, ask the child to listen for who sold the caps. It may also be helpful to discuss the meaning of some words beforehand. Establish that caps are hats, for example, since many of these children have generalization difficulties.

Fingerplays can help teach concepts, can improve fine motor coordination, and can keep children interested and occupied. Using fingerplays also engages the tactile mode for learning and may make the necessary repetition less monotonous.

1. Use fingerplays to teach basic concepts, such as numbers: "Counting Kittens," "Ten Fingers," "Five Little Girls," "One, Two, What Shall I Do?"

2. Use fingerplays to follow stories, field trips, and other activities: "Roly-Poly Caterpillar," "Elephant Song," "The Windshield Wipers."

### Social Studies

Like all children, those with intellectual needs should learn about the community in which they live. When you teach units in this area, concentrate on roles the children may need to know or can readily identify with.

1. Discuss the roles of police, firefighters, and mail personnel. Go on field trips to see them at work, then follow up with role playing.

2. Inevitably these children are tested by psycholo-

By using a flannel board story to teach the names of animals, the teacher can vary the complexity of the story to meet the child's ability and can invite the child to participate in the process.

gists or educational diagnosticians. Help them learn about these roles. Have them play games in a one-on-one situation with a teacher or an aide.

3. Be sure to value *all* occupations and jobs, not just prestigious ones. These children may eventually have a nonprestigious job.

### Science/Discovery

Science for children with mental impairments should be basic. It should focus on firsthand knowledge and give information that is relevant for their future learning and well-being.

1. Use field trips, especially those dealing with nature and the environment.

2. Discuss the seasons and the predictable changes that occur with the changes in nature. Discuss how the seasons affect clothing and activities.

3. Encourage these children to test simple cause and effect reasoning. State a relationship and have the child test it. "The color is darker if you

press harder" may be obvious to you, but these children may not realize they cause the change systematically.

4. Plant a garden for firsthand experience with growth and the necessary conditions for growth.

## Mathematics

Although children with mental impairments may never learn calculus, they do need a foundation in basic mathematical skills to function in society.

1. Teach number concepts, such as counting, with real objects that can be moved or touched. Count children, boys, girls, blocks, chairs, and tables, or use an abacus.
2. Try to choose math experiences that also teach other skills. (Using real objects will help the child's motor development.) Pegboards are useful for facilitating small motor skills while teaching counting and one-to-one correspondence. They can also be used to teach sequential patterns, and design duplication.

## Health and Safety

It is important for intellectual needs children to make good health habits part of their routine. They may have to be taught some of the things that other children come to school knowing: (toileting, washing hands, blowing and wiping their nose, eating, grooming).

1. Teach safety skills. Emphasize dangers with the greatest likelihood of occurrence and those that are most dangerous, such as traffic lights or poison.
2. Concentrate on building good food habits. (Often these children may have the habit of sitting in front of the television while eating potato chips and drinking soft drinks.) Help children learn about healthy snacks.
3. Role play with the children about what to do if they get lost.
4. Break complex skills down into simple tasks that the child can do. Teach the necessary skills in different curriculum. Toileting, for example, involves the ability to dress and undress oneself, so be sure to teach buttoning and snapping as part of fine motor skills.

## Art

Art for children with mental delays should focus on the process not the product. It is important to keep in mind that, especially for these children, the final product may be inconsequential.

1. Use a variety of art media.
2. Cutting is often difficult—it may be helpful to use

"easy grip" or "training" scissors with a loop or a spring handle. These can be obtained from many school supply companies. As alternatives, have children tear materials or consider using precut materials.

## Music

Music can be used in a variety of ways with children who have intellectual needs. Repetition makes it easier for children to learn the songs. Teach the parents the songs so the child can hear and sing them at home as well as in class.

1. Use music to teach basic concepts, such as numbers and colors.
2. Music can be used to expand a child's vocabulary and to increase auditory memory.
3. Music paired with movement encourages children to move and releases energy. In creative movement, there is no right or wrong. You may have to discuss the necessary elements first. (Quiet music means move slowly.) Don't expect a lot of interpretation.
4. Music can also be used to help children establish a rhythm pattern. However, be careful *not* to encourage a rhythm pattern if the child has a habit of swaying or rocking.
5. Using songs that call children by name, you can increase self-esteem and a sense of group belonging.
6. Songs may need to be sung slower than usual (especially those with movements) so that these children can participate.

## Dramatic Play

Dramatic play allows playing without judgment. It is a way to make strange experiences more familiar and is a good way to teach appropriate behavior.

1. Set up a play store (department, grocery, pet). Play through the essential features, visit a real store, and then refine the play. Use it for a week or more. Setting it up for one or two days isn't enough for these children.
2. Playing with other children in this area might also provide the child with information about how roles are played in society. Some children with special needs are assumed to have few demands beyond their physical needs. They are given little realistic feedback. Feedback is necessary for their development. It can be realistic without being judgmental.
3. Play usually should be fairly concrete with realistic props. These children are less imaginative than their peers. Have a lot of props available to facilitate play: (a garage, for example, needs cars, trucks, a block structure, rope, hose, and gas pumps).

## Small Motor Play

When you plan for small motor play, you need to think of the skills this child is going to need to find a job and work, even though that may seem too far off in the future to worry about. It takes these children longer to learn skills. Since abstract reasoning is difficult for them, it is important that you build on other, more concrete skills. Because fine motor skills are necessary for most self-care, more time and space needs to be devoted to them.

1. Start with beginning grasping and manipulation. Be sure to use a variety of objects so that the child can practice many styles. Encourage the child to use the pincer grasp (thumb and forefinger apposition).
2. Use many different activities that require fine motor skills (form boards, pegboards—rubber ones for strengthening finger muscles—plastic blocks that fit together). Start with relatively large, preschool-size objects. Gradually add more pieces and smaller objects. Use this opportunity to teach color and number skills also. Have children sort and group various materials.
3. Code your sorting and matching tasks by number. (Use *1* for easy tasks, *2* for more difficult, and so on.) This means that all the children can do the same activity but at different levels.
   *1* Sort identical objects out from a mix, round beads from crayons or paper clips from rubber bands.
   *2* Group the same objects by size, big from small paper clips or big nuts and bolts from small ones.
   *2* Sort the same objects in different colors, red from green round beads or red from white leggos.
   *3* Group the same objects with differing shapes, round from square from cylindrical red beads.
   Within each step you can make the task more difficult by adding more objects, colors, sizes, and shapes. Start with two items and work up to perhaps ten. A more difficult version would be grouping objects by color, size, or shape.
   *4* Have a mix of objects that can be grouped in two or more ways. At first demonstrate the system and have the child follow it. Later let the child group and regroup on his own. A mix of large and small paper clips, large and small rubber bands, and large and small beads (of varying colors, and shapes) may all be sorted into two containers, as large and small.
4. Provide materials and activities that require the use of two hands: clapping, lacing beads onto string or pipe cleaners, lacing cards with various sized holes (some large and easy to string, others small), snap-construction toys.
5. Provide puzzles at different levels of difficulty. Children with mental delays often have trouble putting pieces in the corresponding holes because of delayed eye-hand coordination. Puzzles with pegs attached to individual pieces are easier to manipulate. ("Push pins" can also be used as "knobs.")
6. Provide activities that require different motions of each hand. (One example is Jack-in-the-Box, where a child must hold the box with one hand while turning the knob with the other. Many times children with cognitive delays have difficulty with this task. It is easier for children to do the same thing with both hands or to use only one hand. They will naturally gravitate toward easier tasks.
7. Often it is harder for children with delayed development to hold a pencil or crayon. Larger ones are easier to grip. Provide a variety of pencils, crayons, and brushes of different sizes.

## Large Motor Play

Large motor skills help develop stamina and increase body coordination and awareness. Game skills (kicking, running, throwing, catching, jumping, batting) involve the necessary large motor skills. It is probably unwise, however, to expect these children to participate in organized games. The stress of winning and losing may only point out lack of skill rather than encouraging skill development.

1. Emphasize basic skills and the variations: walking forward, backward, sideways, fast, slow.
2. These children are often below average in physical stamina. They tend to just sit or stand and watch. They need to be strongly encouraged daily to participate in active games.
3. Use large, light-weight blocks, which are easier to manipulate.
4. Some children with mental impairments (such as

Children must learn to control large muscles before they can master fine control. Toys are an enjoyable way for them to practice.

Down's syndrome) are hypotonic, or have floppy muscle tone. This directly affects both large and small motor skills. To accommodate this use a variety of activities at different levels of difficulty, such as walking sideways and skipping.

## Transition

Transitions can be used to teach colors, numbers, and body awareness. This time can also be used to promote independence and prevocational skills.

1. Have a sign in–sign out board. Use this for roll call some days. Either have the children find their own name tag and put it on and take it off the board, or have them move cards from one side to the other. This reinforces name recognition and independence as the children learn to do it more fully.
2. These children are likely to need more help with toileting and dressing. Dismiss them at a time when they can get the maximum amount of help.
3. Use this time to reinforce concepts the child has learned.
4. Allow enough time for self-help activities, so the child can be successful. It is easy for this child to get distracted and for you to feel rushed when others are waiting.

## CHILD STUDY TEAM REPORT

### *Josie E.*

In attendance: Mrs. E.; Mrs. C., Speech and Language Clinician; Mr. I., Infant Stimulation Program; Mrs. R., preschool teacher.

Josie E. is a three-year ten-month-old girl who was diagnosed as having Down's syndrome at birth. She and her mother have attended an infant stimulation program for developmentally delayed children and their families since the child was six months old. Both the staff at the program and Josie's parents feel she is now ready to go to a preschool for part of her educational program.

Josie lives at home with her parents. Her mother is expecting her second child in three months. Mrs. E. has been able to spend a great deal of time with Josie, both in the infant stimulation program and at home, where she carries through the therapist's suggestions. She is concerned that Josie's development may suffer after the arrival of the baby. Yet, at the same time, she wants to be able to spend time with her new baby.

The last psychological testing done on Josie indicates that both cognitively and socially, she scores much like a slow learner, functioning on the borderline for educable mentally handicapped, with a full scale IQ of 75 on the Stanford-Binet Intelligence Scale. Josie's verbal and nonverbal intelligence scores were comparable, placing her at a mental age of approximately two years, seven months, which is fifteen months lower than her chronological age. Her social age was slightly higher, as measured by the Vineland Social Maturity Scale (with Mrs. E. as informant), which placed her at the two-year ten-month level.

Josie has been receiving speech and language therapy at the infant stimulation program for about eighteen months. Recent language testing has been completed on the Peabody Picture Vocabulary Test.

Josie demonstrated receptive knowledge of common nouns and verbs. Her receptive language age was two years, ten months. On the Zimmerman Preschool Language Scale, an auditory comprehension age of two years nine months was attained, and verbal abilities were measured at two years eleven months. During therapy, Josie has demonstrated that she is familiar with and can name common nouns and verbs and is able to express herself in three- or four-word phrases and sentences. Josie is currently working on understanding and using adjectives, pronouns, and positional words correctly. Articulation therapy is also ongoing.

The physical therapist and occupational therapist are providing Mrs. E. with a home program for Josie. Josie received direct therapy from them until her progress and Mrs. E.'s interest in following through at home enabled Josie to be dismissed. Emphasis has been on improving the quality of Josie's movement, and reducing her tactile defensiveness. The therapists both commented on Josie's eagerness and her confidence in attempting difficult motor tasks.

The staff from the infant stimulation program emphasized Josie's need for concrete experiences to facilitate both learning and remembering. For example, songs have helped Josie identify body parts and perform simple body movement. They also reported Josie has demonstrated a beginning knowledge of shapes, sizes, and colors. The staff has also been working on auditory, visual, tactile, and taste identification and discrimination in order to help Josie use all her senses in new learning experiences.

The staff at the program would like Josie and Mrs. E. to attend one morning a week, and Josie to attend a preschool class for two-to-three-year-olds three mornings a week. In this way, Josie can continue to receive speech and language therapy and can begin to establish some peer relationships that would enhance her development. The staff feels this can best be accomplished by involvement in both types of programs and that staff interaction is essential.

Mrs. E. would like Josie to begin preschool soon so that the child does not feel she is being sent to school because of the new baby. She also cautioned the preschool staff that Josie is prone to respiratory infections and should wear a hat and scarf when outside on chilly days. She added that Josie loves to look at books and dress up and has enjoyed the activities in language therapy and the infant stimulation program.

## INDIVIDUALIZED EDUCATION PROGRAM

NAME ___Josie E.___ DOB __10 / 1 / 78__

AGE ___3-10___ GRADE ___Preschool___

SCHOOL ___Peter Rabbit Pre-School___

PARENTS/GUARDIANS ___Mr. & Mrs. E.___

ADDRESS ___267 Hope Street___

PHONE ___853-1490___

On __9/6/82__, the IPRD Committee
    (Date)
met to review all current data and
recommends Level __I__ placement.

Date of new review ___1/15/83___

Exceptionality: ___Mentally handicapped___

Present at meeting:

Parents ___Mrs. E.___ Representative of District/Agency ___Mrs. R., preschool___

Others: Name/Position ___Mrs. C., Sp. & Lang. Clinician___ ___Mr. I., Infant Stim Program___

### CURRENT TEST DATA

TEST/DATE/RESULTS

| Psych. | / 6/82 / | Borderline mentally handicapped; social age slightly higher. |
| Sp. & Lang. | / 7/82 / | Uses 3–4 word phrases; identifies common nouns and verbs |
| PT/OT | / 5/82 / | Ongoing home program and assessment. |

Recommended Special Services (Hrs/Wk):

| Speech and Language Therapy | / | 1 hr./wk. |
| Infant Stimulation | / | 1 hr./wk. |
| Occupational/Physical Therapy | / | Home program |

Total Hours/Week:

Special Education Classroom ___2___

Regular Classroom ___6___

The committee has determined the following learning strengths and needs to be reflected in the IEP:

| STRENGTHS | NEEDS |
|---|---|
| Social age (relatively) | Receptive & expressive |
| Expressive language (nouns | language (adjectives, |
| and verbs) | pronouns and prepositions) |
| Eager to learn/try motor | Quality of movement |
| tasks | Tactile defensiveness |

STUDENT    Josie E.    DATE    9/16/82

GOAL    To improve expressive language

PARENT SIGNATURE _____

TEACHER SIGNATURE _____

| INSTRUCTIONAL OBJECTIVES | EDUCATIONAL METHODS | Begin | End | Eval. | Name | Position |
|---|---|---|---|---|---|---|
| | | DATE | DATE | | PERSONS RESPONSIBLE | PERSONS RESPONSIBLE |
| Given a visual stimulus, Josie will be able to describe it using a four–five word sentence with three–four parts of speech 4/5 trials. | Peek Pictures, Ideas, Flannel Board Stories, Puppets, Dress Up and Tell | 9/16 | 1/15 | | Mrs. R. | Teacher |
| Given a dramatic play area, Josie will use 4–5 word sentences with her peers during 60% of language sample. | Telephone, Shoe Store, Picnic, Traveling | 9/16 | 1/15 | | Mrs. R. | Teacher |
| Josie will receptively* and expressively* identify 5/6 of the following prepositions: in; on; under; through; beside; over on five consecutive trials over a two-week period. | Cat and Mouse, Obstacle Course, Controller, Robot | 9/16 | 1/15 | | Mrs. R. | Teacher |
| Josie will receptively and expressively identify 10 of the following adjectives when presented four at a time: big; little; happy; sad; red; yellow; green; blue; orange; black; white; purple; empty; full; rough; smooth; fast; slow, on five consecutive trials over a two week period. | Object sizes, Expressions, Texture Playdough, Fast and Slow, Soap Sticks, Mixing Colored Water, Colored Fingernails | 9/16 | 1/15 | | Mrs. R. | Teacher |

*receptively—by responding appropriately to: Show me the one that is <u>on</u> the box. or Put the book <u>on</u> the table.

*expressively—by answering the question: Where is the book?

STUDENT _____ Josie E. _____    DATE _____ 9/16/82 _____

GOAL _____ To improve body awareness _____

PARENT SIGNATURE _____    TEACHER SIGNATURE _____

| INSTRUCTIONAL OBJECTIVES | EDUCATIONAL METHODS | Begin | End | Eval. | Name | Position |
|---|---|---|---|---|---|---|
| | | | DATE | | PERSONS RESPONSIBLE | |
| Josie will use her whole hand surface, including fingertips, fingers, and palms, when participating in finger painting, playdough, clapping (songs and fingerplays) sand; water table on 5 consecutive occasions over 2-week period. | Texture Playdough, Nature Feely Board, Mixing Colored Water, Cereal Balls, Hand/Foot Painting | 9/16 | 1/15 | | Mrs. R. | Teacher |
| Josie will receptively and expressively identify the following body parts: 10/12; head, eye, nose, mouth, ear, shoulder, arm, leg, foot, knee, finger, hair, on 3 consecutive occasions over 2-week period. | Movement Songs, Puppet Hand/Foot Painting | 9/16 | 1/15 | | Mrs. R. | Teacher |
| Josie will be able to vary rate as fast/slow of physical movement while walking, crawling, jumping, rolling on floor, and clapping in 3/3 trials. | Rhythm Walk, Variations on Crawling, Walking, Jumping, Rolling | 9/16 | 1/15 | | Mrs. R. | Teacher |

STUDENT ___Josie E.___

GOAL ___To cooperate with peers___

DATE ___9/16/82___

PARENT SIGNATURE ___

TEACHER SIGNATURE ___

| INSTRUCTIONAL OBJECTIVES | EDUCATIONAL METHODS | DATE Begin | DATE End | Eval. | PERSONS RESPONSIBLE Name | Position |
|---|---|---|---|---|---|---|
| Josie will participate in parallel play in the dramatic play corner on 5 observed occasions. | Circus, Picnic, Shoe Store, Scrambled Eggs | 9/16 | 1/15 | | Mrs. R | Teacher |
| Josie will name her classmates with 80% accuracy.* | Name songs, Name games | 9/16 | 1/15 | | Mrs. R | Teacher |
| Josie will choose a partner for activities requiring ''a buddy'' on 5 observed occasions. | Soap Sticks, Painting to Music, Telephone, Changes, Hug Tag | 9/16 | 1/15 | | Mrs. R | Teacher |

*This would depend on number of children in the class.

# GLOSSARY

**Adaptive physical education** Physical education activities that are changed to meet the needs of the delayed or impaired child.

**Down's syndrome** A form of mental retardation present at birth. Can be visually identified by characteristic "Asian" eyefolds and the simian crease in the palms of the hands. This diagnosis is confirmed by a genetic workup. These children have 47 instead of the usual 46 chromosomes.

**Encephalitis** A viral infection of the brain that can cause permanent damage.

**Hydrocephalus** The condition of having excessive cerebrospinal fluid within the brain that can permanently damage brain tissue. This condition can result from a spinal injury or may be present at birth.

**Karyotype** The process of analyzing the chromosome number and composition. This is used to determine the diagnosis and whether the cause is genetic.

**Meningitis** A bacterial infection of the brain and its covering membranes. Severe cases can result in mental retardation.

**Mental retardation** Significantly subaverage general intellectual functioning existing concurrently with deficits in adaptive behavior and manifested during the developmental period (according to the *Manual on Terminology and Classification in Mental Retardation* by the American Association on Mental Deficiency.)

**Microcephalus** A condition in which the brain itself is underdeveloped (fewer brain cells), characterized by a smaller-sized head and a forehead that slants away from the face.

**Multihandicapped** A person who has several major disabilities (e.g., cerebral palsy and blindness that are not part of a specific syndrome).

**Phenylketonuria (PKU)** A hereditary metabolic disorder in which a child lacks the specific enzyme to break down phenylalanine, causing mental retardation. With early detection and a special diet, this retardation can be prevented.

**Prevocational skills** Basic skills (self-help, fine motor, social skills) necessary for admission to a vocational program.

**Primary handicap** A handicap designated as the major one when children have several. (Such a designation is often required by programming guidelines.) When mental retardation is one of several handicaps, it is usually considered to be the primary one.

**Task analysis** Breaking down tasks into their component parts and ordering those parts.

# TEACHING RESOURCES

In some situations you may want or need additional information. There are many national as well as regional, state, and local organizations that can help you. The following annotated list of national organizations should be useful in helping you decide where to get the information you need.

American Association on Mental Deficiency
5101 Wisconsin Avenue, N.W.
Washington, DC 20016
Physicians, educators, administrators, social workers, psychologists, students, and others interested in the general welfare of mentally retarded persons and the study of cause, treatment, and prevention of mental retardation.

American Institute for Mental Studies
Vineland, NJ
Private research and demonstration center for the diagnosis, treatment, education, and care of children with brain-related handicaps.

Down's Syndrome Congress
1640 West Roosevelt Road, Room 156E
Chicago, IL 60608
Parents, educators, and health professionals interested in promoting the welfare of persons with Down's syndrome. Advises and aids parents with possible solutions to needs of the Down's syndrome child. Acts as a clearinghouse on Down's syndrome information.

Directory of State and Local Resources for the Mentally Retarded
Secretary's Committee on Mental Retardation
U.S. Department of Health, Education and Welfare
Washington, DC 20201
A directory of resources available on the state and local level.

National Association for Retarded Children
2709 Avenue "E"
East Arlington, TX 76011
Does not make referrals, but supplies general information about programs, facilities, institutions, and careers for the retarded.

National Association of Private Residential Facilities for the Mentally Retarded
6269 Leesburg Pike, Suite B-5
Falls Church, VA 22044

Facilities that serve mentally retarded and other developmentally disabled persons. Includes other groups interested in the field of private residential programming.

National Institute for Continuing Education in Developmental Disabilities
New York, NY

Holds twenty seminars a year covering information on the latest methods and techniques in the field of developmental disabilities.

One to One
1 Lincoln Plaza
1900 Broadway
New York, NY 10023

Develops community-based alternatives to institutions for the retarded and disabled. Provides grants, interest-free loans, technical assistance, and support to nonprofit agencies.

Retarded Infants Service
386 Park Avenue South
New York, NY 10016

Service agency devoted to the physical well-being and development of the retarded child and the sound mental health of the parents. Helps families with retarded children with all aspects of home care, including counseling, Home Aide Service, and consultation.

Share, Inc.
P.O. Box 1342
Beverly Hills, CA 90213

Individuals organized to raise funds for the mentally retarded under the direction of the Exceptional Children's Foundation. Projects include preschool training and special education classes for mentally retarded children not accepted by public schools; an infant development program; and a residential home for the retarded.

# BIBLIOGRAPHY

Buscaglia, Leo. *The Disabled and Their Parents: A Counseling Challenge.* Thorofare, N.J.: Slack, 1975.

Dempsey, John. *Community Services for Retarded Children. The Consumer-Provider Relationship.* Baltimore, MD: University Park Press, 1975.

Grossman, Herbert J., ed. *Manual on Terminology and Classification in Mental Retardation.* 3rd. ed. Washington, DC: American Association on Mental Deficiency, 1973.

Isaacson, Robert. *The Retarded Child: A Guide for Parents and Friends.* Niles, Ill.: Argus Communications, 1974.

Karnes, Merle B. Conference Chairman, June B. Jordan, and Rebecca F. Dailey, eds. *Not All Little Wagons Are Red—the Exceptional Child's Early Years.* Arlington, Va.: Council for Exceptional Children, 1973.

Koch, Richard and Kathryn J. Koch. *Understanding the Mentally Retarded Child: A New Approach.* New York: Random House, 1975.

Koch, Richard, and James C. Dobson. *The Mentally Retarded Child and His Family: A Multidisciplinary Handbook.* New York: Brunner/Mazel, 1976.

Love, Harold D. *The Mentally Retarded Child and His Family.* Springfield, Ill.: Charles C. Thomas, 1973.

Molloy, Julia S., and A. M. Matkin. *Your Developmentally Retarded Child Can Communicate.* New York: John Day, 1975.

Nichtern, Sol. *Helping the Retarded Child.* New York: Grosset and Dunlap, 1974.

Noland, Robert L., ed. *Counseling Parents of the Mentally Retarded: A Sourcebook.* Springfield, Ill.: Charles C. Thomas, 1970.

Perske, Robert. *New Directions for Parents of Persons Who Are Retarded.* Nashville, Tenn.: Abingdon, 1973.

*Biography/Autobiography/Fiction*

Buck, Pearl S. *The Child Who Never Grew.* New York: John Day, 1950.

Buck's own struggle to live with having produced a mentally retarded child, her decision to institutionalize the child, and her experience with how societies differ in treatment of the exceptional individual.

Frank, John Paul. *My Son's Story.* New York: Knopf, 1952.

A father's story of his first child, John Peter, the problems that lead to a diagnosis of mental retardation, and the child's institutionalization. The story tells the effects on the family, the financial and emotional demands, and the search for a suitable institution. Several chapters by the mother round out the book.

Rivera, Geraldo. *Willowbrook.* New York: Vintage Books, 1972.

The story of an institution for the mentally retarded in New York state; explores the thoughts of the parents who have children in that institution and the plights of misplaced children. The book points out how parents are actively fighting for their children's rights.

Rogers, Dale Evans. *Angel Unaware.* New York: Jove Publications, 1977.

The true story of the actress's mentally retarded daughter born with Down's syndrome, who lived only two years. It is a religion-based explanation of why children are born with this defect.

Stigen, Gail. *Heartaches and Handicaps*. Palo Alto, Calif.: Science and Behavior Books, 1976.

Stigen's personal reactions and experiences when her first child was diagnosed mentally retarded. Invaluable hints, ideas, and opinions are given on the following topics: services, where to go for help, social workers, special education, sibling rivalry, carpools, Special Olympics, religion, and the endless meetings.

Terese, Robert, and Corrine Owen. *A Flock of Lambs*. Chicago, Ill.: Henry Regnery Company, 1970.

How the authors learned to understand, teach, and care for mentally retarded children. The text follows their efforts to provide meaningful employment and lifelong living arrangements for retarded individuals.

# BIBLIOGRAPHY FOR CHILDREN

## Awareness

Anders, Rebecca. *A Look at Mental Retardation*. Minneapolis: Lerner Publications, 1976.

The book touches lightly on the facts of mental retardation while focusing on the problems and feelings of the retarded and the importance of acceptance.

Clifton, Lucille. *My Friend Jacob*. New York: E.P. Dutton, 1980.

The relationship between seventeen-year-old, mentally retarded Jacob and eight-year-old Sammy is sensitively portrayed. This book is a must for children and adults to better understand the feelings of the mentally disabled.

Grollman, Sharon. *More Time to Grow. Explaining Mental Retardation to Children: A Story*. Boston: Beacon Press, 1977.

About Carla and her brother Arthur and their family's acceptance of children's different rates of development. It suggests activities for children, and provides guidelines and annotated resources for adults.

Hirsch, Karen. *My Sister*. Minneapolis: Carolrhoda Books, 1977.

The narrator expresses mixed emotions of happiness and jealousy as he describes his mentally impaired sister's individuality and capabilities.

Larsen, Hanne. *Don't Forget Tom*. New York: Thomas Y. Crowell, 1974.

Tom, a mentally handicapped child, is usually happy. But when he can't do all of the things his brothers and friends manage to do, he becomes jealous and angry.

Ominsky, Elaine. *Jon O.: A Special Boy*. Englewood Cliffs, N.J.: Prentice-Hall, 1977.

Although the introduction is inaccurate, the rest of the book portrays a Down's syndrome boy's joys and frustrations while coping with daily life.

Rodowsky, Colby F. *What About Me?* New York: Watts, 1976.

Dorrie begins to understand her feelings about her younger brother, Freddie, who is affected by Down's syndrome.

Smith, Lucia B. *A Special Kind of Sister*. New York: Holt, Rinehart and Winston, 1979.

Sarah's mixed feelings toward her retarded brother.

Sobol, Harriet Langsam. *My Brother Steven Is Retarded*. New York: Macmillan, 1977

Beth tells about herself and her retarded brother Steven—about the good times they have together and the times when she is angry or upset or sad because of Steven. She explains what it is like to be a part of a family where one person is retarded.

## Appropriate Books

Aliki. *My Five Senses*. New York: Crowell, 1962.

A simple, informative book about the delight of discovery through seeing, hearing, smelling, tasting, and feeling.

Allen, Robert. *Numbers. A First Counting Book*. New York: Platt and Munk, 1968.

A book with big clear photographs of familiar objects.

Ginsburg, Mirra. *The Chick and the Duckling*. New York: Macmillan, 1972.

About a leader, the Duckling, and a follower, the Chick. Whatever Duckling does, Chick does, until he realizes that he can't do all that Duckling can do. Chick learns to be content to be himself.

Jensen, Virginia Allen, and Dorcas Woodbury Hallar. *What's That?* New York: Collins, 1978.

The children can feel Little Rough, Little Spot, and their friends during their adventures.

Johnson, John Emil. *My First Book of Things*. New York: Random House, 1979.

A short colorful book about a little boy and all the things he has. The drawings are large and realistic.

Krauss, Ruth. *The Growing Story*. New York: Harper and Row, 1947.

A little boy sees everything growing and wonders if he is growing too. When his pants and warm coat are brought out again after being stored for the summer, he realizes that they are too small and that he has indeed grown.

Philipson, Morris. *Everything Changes*. New York: Pantheon, 1972.

This book begins by telling what seeds and eggs grow into, then it says how people change and that change is good.

Reiss, John J. *Colors*. Englewood Cliffs, N.J.: Bradbury Press, 1969.

A good first book for learning colors. Each color has several pages.

———. *Numbers*. Scarsdale, N.Y.: Bradbury Press, 1971.

A bold, colorful book of numbers from 1 to 20, then by 10s to 100 and 100s to 1,000.

Gibbon, David. *Kittens*. New York: Crescent Books, 1979.

A photographic book of kittens and things they like to do. A short phrase accompanies each page.

# INDEX

| *Annual Goals* | *Activity* | *Curriculum Area* | *Page* |
|---|---|---|---|
| | Texture Classification | Science/Discovery | 406 |
| | Tracing Pictures | Art | 446 |
| To improve tactile memory | Nature Feely Board | Science/Discovery | 404 |
| To improve discrimination of smells | Food Sense | Science/Discovery | 405 |
| To improve taste discrimination | Food Sense | Science/Discovery | 405 |
| To improve sensory integration | Body Parts | Social Studies | 386 |
| | Colored Fingernails | Art | 457 |
| | Counting Songs | Music | 469 |
| | Listen Before You Move | Listening | 360 |
| | Movement Songs | Music | 468 |
| | Musical Colors | Music | 470 |

## LANGUAGE SKILLS

| | | | |
|---|---|---|---|
| To improve expressive language | Dress Up and Tell | Dramatic Play | 492 |
| | Sentences | Expressing Language | 333 |
| | Telephone | Expressing Language | 338 |
| | Who Are You? | Health and Safety | 441 |
| To increase vocabulary | Rhyming Words | Expressing Language | 340 |
| | Seasonal Clothing | Health and Safety | 435 |
| To follow directions | Color Graphs | Small Motor Play | 499 |
| | In and Out | Movement | 478 |
| | Ladder Walk | Outdoor Play | 529 |
| | Listen Before You Move | Listening | 360 |
| | Obstacle Course | Large Motor Play | 515 |
| | Sandwich Tricks | Mathematics | 418 |
| To interpret body language | Feelings | Expressing Language | 342 |
| To improve breath control | Blowing Bubbles | Outdoor Play | 531 |
| | Bubble Machine | Outdoor Play | 527 |
| | Straw Painting | Art | 450 |
| To increase understanding | Feelings | Expressing Language | 342 |

## THINKING AND REASONING SKILLS

| | | | |
|---|---|---|---|
| To increase attention span | Color Lotto | Reading Readiness | 369 |
| | Red Light/Green Light | Health and Safety | 434 |
| To improve cause and effect reasoning | Blowing Bubbles | Outdoor Play | 531 |
| | Cornstarch Playdough | Science/Discovery | 402 |
| | Dress Up and Tell | Dramatic Play | 492 |
| | Dyeing Macaroni | Art | 446 |
| | Mixing Colored Water | Science/Discovery | 403 |
| | Nature Feely Board | Science/Discovery | 404 |
| | Red Light/Green Light | Health and Safety | 434 |
| | Seasonal Clothing | Health and Safety | 435 |
| | Shoe Store | Dramatic Play | 487 |
| | Straw Painting | Art | 450 |
| | Torn Paper Flowers | Art | 445 |
| | Tracing Pictures | Art | 446 |

| *Annual Goals* | *Activity* | *Curriculum Area* | *Page* |
|---|---|---|---|
| To increase logical reasoning | Matrix | Reading Readiness | 374 |
| | Scavenger Hunt | Reading Readiness | 371 |
| To improve classification skills | Classify It | Reading Readiness | 379 |
| | Food Lotto | Science/Discovery | 407 |
| | Nutty Sort | Science/Discovery | 407 |
| | People Pictures | Mathematics | 415 |
| | Place Mat Collage | Art | 458 |
| | Sorting | Small Motor Play | 500 |
| | Texture Classification | Science/Discovery | 406 |
| To improve sequencing skills | Buttoning Sequences | Small Motor Play | 504 |
| | Day Play | Dramatic Play | 490 |
| | Scrambled Eggs | Science/Discovery | 404 |
| To improve color concepts | Color Scavenger Hunt | Outdoor Play | 531 |
| | Colored Fingernails | Art | 457 |
| | Musical Colors | Music | 470 |
| | Shape Pictures | Mathematics | 419 |
| To make predictions | Food Sense | Science/Discovery | 405 |
| | Mixing Colored Water | Science/Discovery | 403 |
| | Noisy Toss | Large Motor Play | 517 |
| | Pouring Peanuts | Small Motor Play | 507 |
| | Scrambled Eggs | Science/Discovery | 404 |
| | Straw Painting | Art | 450 |
| To increase problem-solving skills | Mixing Colored Water | Science/Discovery | 403 |

## MATHEMATIC SKILLS

| | | | |
|---|---|---|---|
| To improve number concepts | Abacus | Mathematics | 412 |
| | Counting Cherries | Mathematics | 413 |
| | Counting Songs | Music | 469 |
| | Hidden Objects | Mathematics | 416 |
| | Peg Design | Mathematics | 417 |
| | People Pictures | Mathematics | 415 |
| | Spacy Dots | Mathematics | 415 |
| To improve measurement concepts | Areas | Mathematics | 420 |
| To improve spatial concepts | Letter Collage | Art | 460 |
| | Spacy Dots | Mathematics | 415 |
| To improve shape concepts | Areas | Mathematics | 420 |
| | Carpet Shapes | Mathematics | 417 |
| | Inside Out | Mathematics | 422 |
| | Musical Colors | Music | 470 |
| | Pockets | Mathematics | 417 |
| | Sandwich Tricks | Mathematics | 418 |
| | Shape Pictures | Mathematics | 419 |
| To improve size concepts | Areas | Mathematics | 420 |
| | Inside Out | Mathematics | 422 |
| | Object Sizes | Mathematics | 425 |
| | Pouring Peanuts | Small Motor Play | 507 |
| To improve time concepts | Day Play | Dramatic Play | 490 |

| *Annual Goals* | *Activity* | *Curriculum Area* | *Page* |
|---|---|---|---|
| **SOCIAL SKILLS** | | | |
| To increase survival skills | Red Light/Green Light | Health and Safety | 434 |
| | Seasonal Clothing | Health and Safety | 435 |
| | Who Are You? | Health and Safety | 441 |
| To improve self-help skills | Buttoning Sequences | Small Motor Play | 504 |
| | Counting Cherries | Mathematics | 413 |
| | Lock Box | Small Motor Play | 502 |
| | Pouring Peanuts | Small Motor Play | 507 |
| To increase awareness of roles people play | Audiologist | Dramatic Play | 489 |
| | Circus | Dramatic Play | 486 |
| | Day Play | Dramatic Play | 490 |
| | Eye Doctor | Dramatic Play | 490 |
| | Patient in the Hospital | Social Studies | 388 |
| | Shoe Store | Dramatic Play | 487 |
| To cooperate with peers | Audiologist | Dramatic Play | 489 |
| | Changes | Reading Readiness | 372 |
| | Color Scavenger Hunt | Outdoor Play | 531 |
| | Eye Doctor | Dramatic Play | 490 |
| | Hug Tag | Outdoor Play | 531 |
| | Robot | Listening | 360 |
| | Share Your Feelings | Social Studies | 392 |
| | Telephone | Expressing Language | 338 |
| To cooperate with adults | Who Are You? | Health and Safety | 441 |
| **MOTOR SKILLS** | | | |
| To improve large motor coordination | Noisy Toss | Large Motor Play | 517 |
| | Obstacle Course | Large Motor Play | 515 |
| | Target Bounce | Outdoor Play | 524 |
| | Variations on Crawling | Large Motor Play | 512 |
| | Variations on Rolling | Large Motor Play | 512 |
| | Variations on Walking | Large Motor Play | 515 |
| To improve small motor coordination | Color Graphs | Small Motor Play | 499 |
| | Lock Box | Small Motor Play | 502 |
| | My Puzzle | Small Motor Play | 503 |
| | Nutty Sort | Science/Discovery | 407 |
| | Sorting | Small Motor Play | 500 |
| To improve eye-hand coordination | Alphabet Line | Reading Readiness | 367 |
| | Bubble Machine | Outdoor Play | 527 |
| | Classify It | Reading Readiness | 379 |
| | Clay | Art | 451 |
| | Dyeing Macaroni | Art | 446 |
| | Letter Collage | Art | 460 |
| | Noisy Toss | Large Motor Play | 517 |
| | Nuts and Bolts | Small Motor Play | 505 |
| | Peg Design | Mathematics | 417 |
| | Pockets | Mathematics | 417 |
| | Pouring Peanuts | Small Motor Play | 507 |
| | String Painting | Art | 451 |
| | Target Bounce | Outdoor Play | 524 |

| Annual Goals | Activity | Curriculum Area | Page |
|---|---|---|---|
| | Throwing Games | Small Motor Play | 506 |
| | Torn Paper Flowers | Art | 445 |
| To improve balance skills | Balancing | Large Motor Play | 517 |
| | Flopsy | Movement | 480 |
| | Ladder Walk | Outdoor Play | 529 |
| To encourage creative movement | Flopsy | Movement | 480 |

### CREATIVITY

| | | | |
|---|---|---|---|
| To encourage creativity | Clay | Art | 451 |
| | Mood Montage | Art | 453 |
| | String Painting | Art | 451 |
| To encourage creative problem solving | Body Parts | Social Studies | 386 |
| | Hands and Feet | Social Studies | 385 |
| To stimulate curiosity | Cornstarch Playdough | Science/Discovery | 402 |

### FEELINGS

| | | | |
|---|---|---|---|
| To express feelings | Feelings | Expressing Language | 342 |
| | Share Your Feelings | Social Studies | 392 |
| To increase feelings of group belonging | Color Scavenger Hunt | Outdoor Play | 531 |
| | Dress Up and Tell | Dramatic Play | 492 |
| | Flannel Board Stories | Reading Readiness | 374 |
| | Hand/Foot Painting | Art | 458 |
| | Hug Tag | Outdoor Play | 531 |
| | My Song | Music | 469 |
| | Share Your Feelings | Social Studies | 392 |

### AWARENESS

| | | | |
|---|---|---|---|
| To increase body awareness | Balancing | Large Motor Play | 517 |
| | Body Mural | Art | 454 |
| | Body Parts | Social Studies | 386 |
| | Body Sounds | Listening | 356 |
| | Cave Exploration | Outdoor Play | 528 |
| | Changes | Reading Readiness | 372 |
| | Circus | Dramatic Play | 486 |
| | Colored Fingernails | Art | 457 |
| | Flopsy | Movement | 480 |
| | Hand/Foot Painting | Art | 458 |
| | Hands and Feet | Social Studies | 385 |
| | In and Out | Movement | 478 |
| | Ladder Walk | Outdoor Play | 529 |
| | Mixed-Up People | Art | 456 |
| | Movement Songs | Music | 468 |
| | My Puzzle | Small Motor Play | 503 |
| | My Song | Music | 469 |
| | Place Mat Collage | Art | 458 |
| | Robot | Listening | 360 |
| | Throwing Games | Small Motor Play | 506 |

*Part* **2**

# *Activities for Meeting Children's Special Needs*

# *Introduction*

During the last few years, since mainstreaming has become prevalent, teachers have been called upon to use more care than ever in planning their work. In choosing activities for your class, you will have to analyze the needs, strengths, likes, and dislikes of each child. Although some of the children in your class will have special needs and problems, you will want to choose activities that teach concepts, develop skills, and satisfy the needs and interests of *all* the children in your class.

The activities in this book are presented in terms of the particular needs they meet. They are organized both by curriculum areas and by goals. This makes them easily accessible to your programming needs.

At the beginning of each curriculum area is an index to the activities in that chapter. The activities are organized by the goals that they implement. When activities have more than one goal, they appear in the index under each goal. For example:

CHAPTER 16   EXPRESSING LANGUAGE

# INDEX

| Goal | Activity | Page |
|------|----------|------|
| To improve expressive language | My Shoes | 000 |
| To encourage creativity | My Shoes | 000 |

The index is followed by an introduction that explains how this particular curriculum area fits into the total preschool program. Next is a discussion of long-term goals that are most easily met; for example:

CHAPTER 19    SOCIAL STUDIES:    To encourage creative problem solving
To increase awareness of roles people play
To broaden concepts of families

These teaching goals are followed by particular strategies that are most useful with special needs children. For example:

CHAPTER 20    SCIENCE/DISCOVERY
Children with VISUAL needs will need plenty of opportunity to touch the equipment and materials you have available. Be sure to provide time for this and use realistic props to help these children learn. Be sure to include materials that magnify.

The organization of the activities section, which follows teaching strategies, is designed to aid you in record keeping as well as day-to-day programming.

## ACTIVITIES AND RECORD KEEPING

In addition to designing a curriculum and choosing appropriate materials for the children in your classroom, you will want to develop a record-keeping system that helps you identify children with special needs and chart their progress. When you think about developing or refining your record keeping, first decide why you need to keep the records. If, for example, your goal is to find out what activity areas your children like or dislike or which particular children play together, the following form might be useful.

Put a check in the appropriate column for each child.

Time____
Date____

| Children's Names | Art | Dramatic Play | Small Motor Table | Blocks | Books | Locker Area | Wander-ing | Other | Comments |
|---|---|---|---|---|---|---|---|---|---|
| Aaron Misha Natalie Samantha And so on | | | | | | | | | |

Make the form correspond to the areas in your room. Be sure to allow for children who are in transit and in other places. When you have adapted the form, make about 50 copies. Use them 3 or 4 times a day during freeplay for 2 or 3 weeks. If you keep the forms on a clipboard in a convenient place, you will be most likely to use them. This should take only 2 or 3 minutes once you have learned the children's names. It helps to put the lists in alphabetical order by children's first names.

After a week, put all the forms together, and a pattern should emerge. You can tell who plays together and in what areas, and if you observe frequently enough, you can see how long children stay in each area. Begin to develop a profile about children's likes and dislikes (how much or how little time they spend in different areas). Use the following weeks to refine your skills and verify hunches. When you feel confident about the data, let the results influence your teaching. For example, if you have not observed Natalie in the Dramatic Play Area, try to set it up to entice her. You might even talk with her about it.

Such a record is also useful at the beginning of a parent-teacher conference. Because the record has nothing to do with quality of performance, it is nonthreatening to parents and provides information about their child's activities during the day. Use this type of chart at the beginning, middle, and end of the year to track how the children have changed. It is also useful in evaluating the interest level of the activities you have chosen.

Knowing where children are, how long they stay at various activities, and who they play with is useful, but it is only a beginning. From this chart and other observations, you probably will have unconsciously labeled some children as "needs more observation." This may be because they do things better than or not as well as their peers, or because their skills seem to be uneven or to fluctuate greatly.

If you want to concentrate on the children's levels of skill, a checklist may help you quantify and focus your observations. Start with general areas.

| Children's Names | Sensory Skills (Auditory) | Sensory Skills (Visual) | Language Skills | Thinking and Reasoning Skills | Math Skills | Social Skills | Motor Skills | Crea-tivity | Feel-ings | Aware-ness |
|---|---|---|---|---|---|---|---|---|---|---|
| Chu Dene José Marsha Tom | | | | | | | | | | |

Key 1 Above average
2 Average
3 Seems inconsistent
4 Needs work

Thinking about the activities you plan in these areas is useful for future programming. For example, if you play a game and decide that Chu does not know her colors, you may decide just to work on naming colors. But if you label your observations "Sensory Skills (Visual)," you may be more likely to recognize that she cannot identify or discriminate colors. This approach will make the activities you select more appropriate and perhaps more varied, because you can work on specific skills instead of conducting a general drill. The overall index at the back of the book uses these general categories as well as the activities that are useful in the assessment and improvement of skill levels.

In areas where you find children are inconsistent or need work, break down the behavior into smaller pieces. For example, if you think a child needs practice in visual or reading readiness skills, plan activities in the following areas:

| Child's Name | Date / Quality | Activity | Page | Date / Quality | Activity | Page |
|---|---|---|---|---|---|---|
| Visual identification | | | | | | |
| Visual discrimination | | | | | | |
| Visual memory | | | | | | |
| Visual closure | | | | | | |
| Visual association | | | | | | |
| Visual comprehension | | | | | | |
| Visual sound | | | | | | |

Key   Date: the date on which you try the activity
      Quality:   1   Activity done quickly, easily accurately
                 2   Activity completed accurately, but with some difficulty and repetition
                 3   Activity completed with many errors
                 4   Activity not completed
                 5   Activity not attempted
      Activity:   the name of the activity you used
      Page:   the page in the book on which the activity you used appears

Before you pick the activities you will use, return to the first chart and see where the child spends his time and what he likes to do. The trick is to figure out how to teach what the child needs to learn in such a way that he will want to learn it. This is where the activities and the indexes come in.

The indexes at the end of the chapter in Part 1 list all the activities that are designed for children with a specific set of needs. For example, all the activities in the book designed for children with LEARNING needs are listed at the end of that chapter. In Part 2, the indexes at the beginning of the curriculum areas list the activities within those areas by goal. The overall index at the end of the book lists all the activities in the book that are designed to meet a particular goal and specifies the curriculum area for each activity. To use these indexes effectively, you must think about and plan your teaching program.

## USING ACTIVITIES IN THE IEP

If a child has an Individual Educational Plan (IEP), look at the annual goals in the plan, locate these goals and related ones in the index, and use the activities listed to expand the IEP.

If you must write an IEP, read Chapter 4, then use the goals and activities in Part 2 to help you write the plan. To adapt the specific activities to an IEP format use the following example:

# BUTTONS

**GOAL**   To improve small motor coordination
           To improve tactile discrimination
**OBJECTIVE**   The child will pair the buttons.
**MATERIALS**   12 pairs of buttons                    a bowl
                an egg carton or ice cube tray         a blindfold

The goal is already stated as an annual goal. The objective and materials become an instructional objective. And an appropriate evaluation is added: Given an egg carton, 12 pairs of objects, and a blindfold, the child will correctly match 10 of the 12 pairs of objects.

You have now generalized the activity and added an evaluation. Look up other activities that also increase tactile discrimination and generalize them. You now have not only the IEP but also a variety of activities you can use to implement it.

Some of the activities in this book are familiar ones given a twist to make them especially useful for children with special needs (e.g., Circus, Animal Families). Others are new activities designed with a special need in mind (e.g., Audiologist, Slings). However, if you refer to the goals at the beginning of the activities, you will see that each activity meets needs and helps develop skills in all the children in the class. Feel free to adapt these activities to suit your needs, and use them as a springboard to make up your own. If you want more ideas for activities, an annotated bibliography of activity books is given at the end of the book.

There are many by-products of a good activities program. While the main purpose of the activities is to teach specific concepts and skills, they also can increase the children's awareness of their own strengths and needs and the differences between themselves and others. If materials are stored conveniently, the children can learn independence by getting things and putting them back instead of depending on others to do these tasks. They also can gain practice in making choices, deciding what activities they want to participate in and for how long. As they put things away, they can practice sorting and classification skills. And since there are limits to how many children can participate in an activity at one time, children also can learn about sharing and taking turns.

As a teacher of children with special needs, you have much to keep in mind. Because you have the strengths and needs of all the children in your class to consider, you must find activities that give extra to special needs children but are appropriate and enriching to all. You must use the school as a world in which all the children belong and have appropriate work to do. But, most of all, you must remember that you are a model for all the children. Your behavior toward the special needs children—your acceptance, consideration, and respect—will speak louder to the class than anything you deliberately set out to teach. I hope these varied activities will be a stimulating resource for your teaching programs.

# 16

# *Expressing Language*

# INDEX

| *Goal* | *Activity* | *Page* |
|---|---|---|
| To interpret body language | Body Language | 344 |
| | Body Noises | 345 |
| | Feelings | 342 |
| To follow directions | Directions | 343 |
| | Locomotion | 340 |
| To improve auditory discrimination | Rhyming Words | 340 |
| | Telephone | 338 |
| To improve visual association | Color Words | 342 |
| To improve visual comprehension | Bring Me | 336 |
| | Peek Pictures | 337 |
| To increase logical reasoning | Bring Me | 336 |
| To improve spatial concepts | Cat and Mouse | 342 |
| To encourage creativity | Ideas | 334 |
| | My Shoes | 334 |
| | Traveling | 344 |
| To encourage creative problem solving | Di-Vergent | 335 |
| | Treasure Hunt | 338 |
| To express feelings | Best and Worst | 335 |
| | Feelings | 342 |
| To increase feelings of group belonging | Traveling | 344 |
| To increase body awareness | Body Language | 344 |
| | Body Noises | 345 |
| To improve self-concept | Interviews | 339 |
| To cooperate with adults | Interviews | 339 |
| To cooperate with peers | Directions | 343 |
| | Peek Pictures | 337 |
| | Telephone | 338 |
| To increase attention span | Treasure Hunt | 338 |

Two of the major tasks children face during their preschool years are developing a vocabulary large enough to express their wants and needs and to enable them to understand the wants and needs of others, and learning the rules that govern how language is used.

Young children need concrete language experiences. They need field trips and other opportunities to develop firsthand their understanding of the connection between words and objects or actions. Because of overprotection and logistic problems, children with special needs often lack these experiences.

All children need to learn language skills. To teach these skills to children with special needs, you may need to develop new techniques or use a different emphasis.

## EXPRESSING LANGUAGE GOALS

- To improve expressive language. Create opportunities for children to talk, reinforce them when they use language appropriately, be a good language model, and listen when children are speaking.
- To increase vocabulary (general [verbs, nouns, adjectives, adverbs, pronouns,] and specific [colors, numbers, time, feelings]). This is probably best done through firsthand experiences, labeling, and asking well-timed questions.
- To increase understanding. Ask questions, give directions, expand the meaning of words that children already know (orange is a color and also a fruit). If you repeat back what a child says while expanding it, he learns new grammatical structures and vocabulary.

  > CHILD: Big truck.
  > TEACHER: Yes, that is a big, red truck. Can you bring it over here so that we can look at it?

- To interpret body language. Since so much of communication depends on not just words, but how they are said and in what context, children should become aware at an early age of their own body language and gain some skills in interpreting others' body language.

## TEACHING STRATEGIES

Children with SPEECH AND LANGUAGE needs must concentrate on the development of underlying inner language skills by participating in many firsthand experiences. If children are reluctant to speak, create a need for them to talk: Instead of asking these children yes/no questions ("Do you want to play with the blocks today?"), use the form "Where do you want to play today?" to elicit more speech. For children who need work on specific speech sounds, read stories and ask questions that require them to use those sounds.

Children with HEARING needs must practice talking; encourage them to attempt this even if their speech is not always understandable. Because they are more dependent on body language than others, they need to fine-tune their abilities to interpret it. These same skills are also useful in speech reading and signing.

Children with VISUAL needs usually depend on verbal skills to find objects or to ask others to find what they need. They need practice in giving and following directions.

Children with PHYSICAL needs may not be as mobile as others. They need practice in asking for what they want, especially if they cannot reach it. They particularly need to learn to give precise directions.

Children with ADJUSTMENT, LEARNING, and HEALTH needs require a vocabulary that helps them verbalize feelings and increases their understanding of situations they may face.

CULTURALLY DISTINCT children need work developing a Standard English vocabulary that will help them play with peers and communicate with the teacher.

Children with INTELLECTUAL needs learn more slowly than other children, so they will need extra repetitions of vocabulary and extra help in generalizing words to apply to a variety of situations.

GIFTED AND TALENTED children can expand their vocabulary and language skills to dictating stories that either you write down or they record on an audio tape.

# SENTENCES

**GOAL**   To improve expressive language

**OBJECTIVE**   The child will respond to questions using complete sentences.

**MATERIALS**   None

**PROCEDURE**   During group time tell the children that you are going to ask them questions and that, according to the rules for this game, they cannot use just the words *yes*, *no*, or *maybe*, but must answer with a complete sentence.

> TEACHER: Is your name Susan?
> SUSAN: Yes, my name is Susan.
> TEACHER: Would you like to play in the block area today?
> SUSAN: No, I would like to use the easel.

When the child has answered the question or completed a sequence, the child is then free to go.

**COMMENT**   When children use only *yes*, *no*, or *maybe* as responses, they lose a chance to practice language. If you have children who are uncomfortable with this activity, question them at the end when you can give them more attention, the group is smaller, and they can benefit from having heard the answers given by their classmates. *Especially good for* SPEECH AND LANGUAGE and CULTURALLY DISTINCT: These children may not be comfortable talking and need practice in language usage. Helps children with INTELLECTUAL needs who need more practice than other children to learn the same amount of information.

# IS–IS NOT

**GOAL**   To improve expressive language
　　　　　To increase understanding

**OBJECTIVE**   The child will state what is or is not his name.

**MATERIALS**   None

**PROCEDURE**   Go around the class and have each child state what *is* and *is not* his name: "My name is Jay. My name is not Lynn." When children have the idea, begin to joke with them and have them correct you: "Sam is a cow!" "No, Sam is not a cow. Sam is a boy." Be sure to use the negations:

> is/is not
> has/has not
> does/does not
> same/not the same
> need/need not

Once children realize that negations are more than *no*, begin to introduce some of the less absolute words that allow for exceptions, such as:

| | |
|---|---|
| some | almost |
| sometimes | always |
| more | often |
| less | many |

"Some of the children in this class are girls."

**COMMENT**   Children develop the idea of a negative before the idea that something is different; that is, it is easier for children to learn the same/not the same than it is to learn the same/different. They also find absolutes easier to understand than less definite terms. *Especially good for* ADJUSTMENT needs: provides a vocabulary that can help these children express what they do or do not want to do and helps them define their behavior in nonabsolutes. "Sometimes I sit in my locker and sometimes I play with the other children." These same skills are important for LEARNING needs.

# MY SHOES

**GOAL**    To improve expressive language
To encourage creativity

**OBJECTIVE**    The child will tell an imaginative story at least three sentences long about a familiar object.

**MATERIALS**    Common objects:

| | | |
|---|---|---|
| shoes | winter coat | roller skates |
| socks | bathing suit | bicycle/tricycle |

**PROCEDURE**    During group time, discuss the difference between animate and inanimate objects and have children imagine what objects might feel if they had feelings. Give them an example: "Make believe you are your shoes."

> I have pretty buckles and I am red. This morning I was sleeping in a dark closet when someone turned on a bright light and stepped on me. I creaked a little, but that didn't stop her. She put me on and ran down a flight of stairs. I then was stood on in the kitchen for twenty minutes. Finally, there was some relief. . . .

**COMMENT**    These imaginings can be dramatic, if you feel in the mood, or simple sequences to create awareness of daily routines. *Especially good for* GIFTED AND TALENTED: helps them take another point of view creatively. If you use a simpler form and ask relevant questions, children with LEARNING needs can improve body awareness and awareness of time sequences. Using the shoes as an example, you might ask: "What color are you? What do you look like? Where does Susy put you on? Then where do you go?"

# IDEAS

**GOAL**    To improve expressive language
To encourage creativity

**OBJECTIVE**    The child will need at least three uses for an object.

**MATERIALS**    Common objects with few details, such as:

| | | |
|---|---|---|
| blocks | a plate | a simple article of clothing |
| a book | a chair | such as a scarf or a |
| a cup or glass | a table | sock |

**PROCEDURE**    Choose an object and ask the children to identify it. First ask them to describe the usual uses for the object. Then ask them to think of different ways to use the object. (The block could keep the door open; you could paint a face on it and use it as a doll, step on it to reach something, and so on.)

**CONTINUATION**    Show the children pictures of objects from traditionally threatening places, such as a doctor's office or hospital. Have children think of different uses for these objects. Start with tongue depressors and flashlights, then work your way up to dentist's drills and needles for shots.

**COMMENT**    Tell children to think of lots of ways to use the objects, ways that are different from how people usually use them. Be sure not to judge responses as silly or dumb or to allow other children to do that. *Especially good for* GIFTED AND TALENTED: encourages many varied responses. HEALTH needs can use this game in the waiting room or in new and threatening environments.

# DI-VERGENT

**GOAL**   To improve expressive language
To encourage creative problem solving

**OBJECTIVE**   The child will name at least two ways in which life would be different without a particular thing.

**MATERIALS**   None

**PROCEDURE**   Have a discussion about something (wheels, electricity, paper, and so on). Start off simply. Ask the children to name things they have or use. Then ask them to imagine what it would be like if we didn't have _____, or what it would be like if the sun didn't set, for example.

**CONTINUATION**   Expand this concept to have children think about how life would be different if they didn't have hands, eyes, ears, and so on, scrupulously avoiding any references that could hurt or offend a child with special needs. Pose questions as to how they could do certain things and learn ways of compensating. Where appropriate, have children demonstrate what they would do.

**COMMENT**   Start with events and objects that the children are familiar with and that are easy and obvious. By demonstrating what they would do in certain situations, children become aware of what it is like not to have a full range of movement. This also helps show them ways they can help others. *Especially good for* GIFTED AND TALENTED: helps focus problem solving. Children with sensory needs, such as HEARING, VISUAL, and PHYSICAL, might share with others how they compensate as well as get some ideas from the other children. In order to begin, you might comment on and praise these children for the ways they compensate. For example, "Joan has a great way of looking for things when her locker gets rearranged. Can you show the class how you search for things? What is she doing? Now, if you were in the dark and wanted to find a special toy, how would you do it?" Perhaps even blindfold a child to demonstrate the search. Ask for new ideas.

# BEST AND WORST

**GOAL**   To improve expressive language
To express feelings

**OBJECTIVE**   The child will state the best thing and the worst thing that happened to him the preceding day or weekend.

**MATERIALS**   None

**PROCEDURE**   During group time, give each child (or a designated smaller group of children) an opportunity to talk about the best and worst things that happened to him the day before. As children's time lines are not very well defined, they may relate events from longer ago than asked for. The variety of comments may be tremendous:

| WORST | BEST |
|---|---|
| Mother and father's getting divorced | Going out to dinner |
| Coming to school | Watching a special TV show |
| Falling down | Having a special food |
| Being alone and scared at night | Daddy's coming home |
| A sister's birthday | |
| Being spanked | |
| Being teased or yelled at | |

As you might guess, these topics, brought up by one or two children, can lead to general discussions about the concerns of all children.

**COMMENT**    Children are surprisingly candid about and responsive to this. With the help of a sensitive teacher to make sure the children don't hurt each other's feelings, the activity provides a safe place for children to talk about their "worst" things without shame or ridicule. They learn that all people have best and worst things, including you, if you are willing to share these. *Especially good for* ADJUSTMENT needs: These children can bring sensitive subjects up and talk about them without being judged or belittled. GIFTED AND TALENTED children and those with LEARNING needs can share their feelings and gain perspective on how others feel. Children with HEALTH needs can share concerns and fears but might also learn that "worst" things are relative and it doesn't always help to dwell on them and forget the "best."

# CONTROLLER

**GOAL**    To improve expressive language
To increase vocabulary
To increase understanding

**OBJECTIVE**    The child will give instructions that can be carried out by the teacher or another child.

**MATERIALS**    None

**PROCEDURE**    Have the child be the controller of a robot (another child or the teacher). His job is to tell the robot what to do. You should be the first robot. If the directions are unclear ("Robot walk"), send back a message: "That does not compute. Robot needs to know whether to walk forward, backward, or sideways." The feedback will help children expand their vocabulary and become more specific in their speech.

**COMMENT**    *Especially good for* CULTURALLY DISTINCT: builds vocabulary. (The robot can compute only English [or only Spanish], depending on your goals.) Children with HEALTH and PHYSICAL needs can learn precision in asking for what they need.

# BRING ME

**GOAL**    To improve expressive language
To increase logical reasoning
To improve visual comprehension

**OBJECTIVE**    The child will get a requested object or state that he couldn't bring it.

**MATERIALS**    None

**PROCEDURE**    The teacher requests various objects, and the child must either get the object or say, "I'm sorry, I can't bring you _____ because _____."

| CHILD COULD BRING | CHILD COULDN'T BRING |
|---|---|
| block | wall |
| shoe | floor |
| piece of paper | sky |
| | sun |

When the children get the idea of the game, the child who can't bring the requested item can name something he can bring.

**COMMENT**   This is a request game that requires some logical reasoning skills to play. This is a great time to have a sense of humor. *Especially good for* GIFTED AND TALENTED: increases creative thinking. When you make requests, keep the ability level of the children in mind so that they don't become frustrated. HEALTH or PHYSICAL needs don't have to actually bring the objects, just state whether or not it is possible.

# PEEK PICTURES

**GOAL**   To improve expressive language
To improve visual comprehension
To cooperate with peers

**OBJECTIVE**   The child will label or describe one aspect of the picture after two opportunities to look at it.

**MATERIALS**   shoe box with a hole in one end, a 3½-inch slot in the lid, and a 2″ × 2″ window in the lid covered with cellophane to let in light
pictures (about 3″ × 3″) of varying complexity, mounted on poster board and pasted on Popsicle sticks for ease in getting in and out

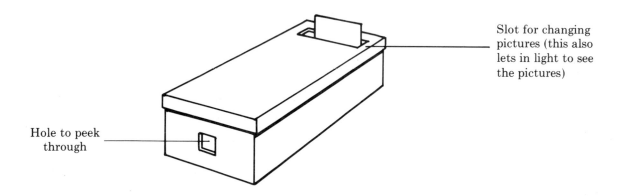

Slot for changing pictures (this also lets in light to see the pictures)

Hole to peek through

**PROCEDURE**   Cut a small hole in one end of a shoe box, a slot in the lid at the opposite end, and a window to let in light. Place a picture in the slot. This game is played in pairs. Have one child take a peek and describe what he sees to the other. Each child can peek and add a statement about what he sees.

**CONTINUATION**   Use pictures of objects. Have one child give a functional definition of the object, (e.g., it's something you drink out of) and the other child guess what it is. Encourage children to tell a story about the picture.

**COMMENT**   Putting the picture in a shoe box adds an element of surprise and a sense of secrecy to the picture. *Especially good for* SPEECH AND LANGUAGE needs: Choose objects that emphasize speech sounds children need to work on and encourage the children to talk with peers. Children with HEALTH needs could use this easily made activity at home. To increase a sense of group belonging and to help children with HEARING needs identify classmates by name, put a picture of each child in the box, then point to the child and match the picture to a printed name or sign.

# TELEPHONE

**GOAL**    To improve expressive language
To improve auditory discrimination
To cooperate with peers

**OBJECTIVE**    The child will talk to another child on the phone without seeing him.

**MATERIALS**    2 telephones
pictures (2 sets)
divider that stands on a table

**PROCEDURE**    Borrow telephones from the telephone company or make them from string and tin cans. Place the telephones on both sides of the divider and encourage children to talk with each other. If they do not talk spontaneously, you need to add some props or a procedure for encouraging them. Give each child an identical set of pictures; have one child describe the picture he is looking at so that the other child can find the picture.

**COMMENT**    *Especially good for* SPEECH AND LANGUAGE and LEARNING needs: isolates the auditory aspect of language, encourages precision in language usage, and teaches how to communicate using only auditory cues. A good starting place for ADJUSTMENT needs, who may find it easier to communicate without being face to face. For VISUAL needs, use objects that can be felt and described rather than pictures. If INTELLECTUAL needs have problems with this activity, use very simple pictures and take down the divider so that they can see. Dialing is a good fine motor activity for PHYSICAL needs.

# TREASURE HUNT

**GOAL**    To improve expressive language
To encourage creative problem solving
To increase attention span

**OBJECTIVE**    The child will follow the directions and guess what the treasure is.

**MATERIALS**    A small object that can be hidden in the classroom, like:

a pair of scissors        a book
a crayon        a paintbrush

**PROCEDURE**    Hide an object in the room and then give children verbal directions to follow to find the object.

It is near something that is large and red.
It is on something soft.
You would go by it on your way to the bathroom.

As children get closer to the treasure, make the directions more specific. Continue to give hints as they guess what the treasure is.

CHILD: Is it a doll?
TEACHER: No, it's larger than a doll.

**CONTINUATION**    Once the children know how to play this game, you can play verbally, just giving clues and answering questions rather than actually hiding something. ("I'm thinking of something that is square and red.") Increase the complexity of the hiding place or object to increase attention.

**COMMENT**    *Especially good for* LEARNING needs: combines verbal and motor responses. For GIFTED AND TALENTED, make either the directions or the clues very difficult. For VISUAL needs, use texture clues and locate the object in familiar areas of the room.

# INTERVIEWS

**GOAL**    To improve expressive language
To cooperate with adults
To improve self-concept

**OBJECTIVE**    The child will answer questions in front of a group of children.

**MATERIALS**    A play microphone

**PROCEDURE**    Do a takeoff on some of the popular talk shows: "Good morning, today is Tuesday, February 2, and we are delighted to have as our guest today Miss Katie Ying. Katie, can you tell our listeners some of the things that you really like to do? Do you have any favorite foods? . . . "

**COMMENT**    Be sure to have a "mike" as a prop. You might even explain that this is Katie's first appearance and she might be a bit shy. *Especially good for* SPEECH AND LANGUAGE needs: Make the questions easy at first, until the children feel more comfortable. GIFTED AND TALENTED have the opportunity to talk about particular interests they have and want to share. For HEALTH needs, provides opportunity to be the center of attention and set the topics of discussion. ADJUSTMENT needs are likely to enjoy the attention, yet are cooperating with adults in a positive way.

# SYNONYMS

**GOAL**    To increase vocabulary
To increase understanding

**OBJECTIVE**    The child will label an object or concept in at least two different ways.

**MATERIALS**    Pictures or objects that have more than one name (see synonyms below)

**PROCEDURE**    Define synonyms—words that mean the same thing but sound different. Then present children with the objects or pictures of the objects, and see how many synonyms they can think of. It is not important that these be synonyms in a dictionary sense. The point is for the children to know that one object can have several different names. Start with objects in your classroom and community:

| | |
|---|---|
| rug/carpet/floor covering | store/shop |
| chair/seat | street/road |
| couch/sofa/davenport | bed/cot |
| scissors/shears | |

Then work on familiar concepts:

| | |
|---|---|
| small/little/tiny | sharp/pointed |
| near/close | |

**COMMENT**    Children need to know that objects often have several names even in the same language. *Especially good for* CULTURALLY DISTINCT and SPEECH AND LANGUAGE needs: The synomym may be easier to say for children who have problems with particular speech sounds. (The child who has trouble saying *s* may find *couch* easier than *sofa*.) VISUAL needs depend on having good vocabularies because they can't see gestures. GIFTED AND TALENTED can learn vocabulary by figuring out synomyms for difficult words and putting the words and synomyms into categories.

# RHYMING WORDS

**GOAL**    To increase vocabulary
To improve auditory discrimination

**OBJECTIVE**    The child will give at least one rhyming word for the one the teacher presents.

**MATERIALS**    None

**PROCEDURE**    Define rhyming words—words that end with the same sound. Give lots of examples before asking the children for words. Read a story or go over a familiar fingerplay that uses rhyming words. Then start with a familiar word that ends with a common rhyme and make a list of the rhyming words the children generate. List both real and nonsense words. Praise the children for finding a real rhyme, even if it is a nonsense word, but point out that it isn't a real word.

| ACE | DARE | HEAD | BUMP |
|-----|------|------|------|
| brace | scare | read | stump |
| trace | stare | bread | lump |
| pace | care | dead | jump |
| place | bare | tread | grump |

| COW | COT | IT | BED |
|-----|-----|-----|-----|
| now | hot | bit | fed |
| how | got | fit | led |
| pow | pot | hit | red |
| plow | shot | lit | sled |

Without slowing the children down too much, use the opportunity to expand the children's vocabularies by asking them to define the words. Have all the children repeat the rhyming words quickly and slowly.

**CONTINUATION**    Children who enjoy playing with words can make a "Have You Seen" book of rhyming words they can illustrate. Have you seen a:

|  |  |
|--|--|
| red bed | bare mare |
| plow cow | fake cake |

**COMMENT**    This is a good way to dismiss children. As each one leaves, ask the child to give a word that rhymes with yours ("José, give me a word that rhymes with cat." "Sat." "Sally, another word." "Hat.") *Especially good for* GIFTED AND TALENTED: They can learn about the structure of language and use the continuation activity to further explore parts of words as well as rhyming. INTELLECTUAL needs can profit from being part of the group and repeating words with the others while learning the concept of rhyming. For HEARING needs, first pick a word the children can picture, such as *bed*; then go to *red* and *sled* and demonstrate *led*. In this way these children can learn to attend to initial sounds and to guess what is said even if they only pick up the ending. They can add these words to their speaking vocabularies by learning the endings and then mastering the initial sounds. Children with SPEECH AND LANGUAGE needs can practice words with the group and learn vocabulary as well.

# LOCOMOTION

**GOAL**    To increase vocabulary
To follow directions

**OBJECTIVE**    The child will follow the directions given.

**MATERIALS**   None

**PROCEDURE**   As the children take an imaginary walk around the room or outdoors, call out commands, such as:

> *Stop.*
> There is a *big* step—go *up* it.
> Oh, the sidewalk is *hot*—tiptoe *fast*.
> There is a *little* step—go *down* it.
> Wait—listen.
> OK—walk *forward*.
> Stop. There is a wall—walk *sideways*.
> Oh, there is a *small* hole—trace it with your hand—now, wriggle through it.
> Lean *back* against the wall and relax.
> Take a deep breath.
> Sit down.

**COMMENT**   *Especially good for* VISUAL needs: These children depend on verbal directions to find things and move safely. LEARNING needs can learn about spatial relations, following directions, and self-control. Also good for running off energy.

Giving and following precise directions is difficult. Begin with an adult as one of the participants, and as children become more skillful, have them give each other instructions.

# CAT AND MOUSE

**GOAL**    To increase vocabulary
To improve spatial concepts

**OBJECTIVE**    The child will verbally describe the path to the hidden mouse.

**MATERIALS**    a doll house or structure
toy mouse
toy cat

**PROCEDURE**    Tell the children a story in which you are a cat and there is a mouse hiding from you. First let the children hide the mouse. Then verbally trace your search for the mouse while the children move the cat in response to your directions. "I'm looking in the house in the bedroom under the bed." (If caught, the mouse can escape and hide again.) Be dramatic if that is your style. As children get the idea, have a child be the escaping mouse. Be sure to discuss the speed at which he is moving. Quiz children on *how* as well as *where* they are moving; for example, "I'm tiptoeing up the stairs."

**COMMENT**    *Especially good for* LEARNING needs: gives needed work in both spatial awareness and sequencing. For CULTURALLY DISTINCT, gives practice with prepositions and builds vocabulary. You can test SPEECH AND LANGUAGE needs for their grasp of spatial concepts and ability to follow directions by having a child move the cat as you direct.

# COLOR WORDS

**GOAL**    To increase understanding
To improve visual association

**OBJECTIVE**    The child will name an associated word and tell why it occurred to him.

**MATERIALS**    None

**PROCEDURE**    Teach the children the game of word associations. ("I'll say a word and I want you to tell me what other words you think of.") For example:

> red: fire, hot, tomatoes, anger
> blue: water, cool
> green: grass, leaves
> pink: soft
> white: snow, uniforms
> black: night, cat
> yellow: lemon, sun

**COMMENT**    If children don't say some of the obvious words you want to explore, say, "It reminds *me* of . . . ." *Especially good for* VISUAL needs: Helps children who may never see color to develop associations with color words others use to convey feelings and moods. GIFTED AND TALENTED children can explore this concept in more depth and see how many things they can think of that are usually one color.

# FEELINGS

**GOAL**    To increase understanding
To interpret body language
To express feelings

**OBJECTIVE**   The child will state a socially acceptable response to what the child in the picture wants to do.

**MATERIALS**   Pictures of children who are experiencing an emotion, such as:

      angry         excited
      happy         sad

**PROCEDURE**   Cut out pictures or make pictures of children who are experiencing an emotion and label that emotion. Show the pictures to the children and have them make some choices about what the child in the picture wants to do; for example: Sherry is angry! Does she want to read a book or kick a ball? Sit still or run fast? Go to sleep or go outside? As children get the idea, have them contribute suggestions about what the children might want to do. Talk about the implications of the suggestions made. Teach children it's good for them to express their emotions, both negative and positive, but that they need to learn to express them in a way that doesn't hurt others.

**CONTINUATION**   Expand this activity to have children focus on situations that are either happy or sad. In a small group you might ask children what they do when they are happy or sad. Ask children what they might like you or another adult or child to do for them; "If you were sad at school, would you like me to hold you on my lap or just sit beside you?"

**COMMENT**   *Especially good for* ADJUSTMENT AND LEARNING needs: They are working at getting in touch with their developing feelings. GIFTED AND TALENTED may also profit from verbalizing and concentrating on their feelings; INTELLECTUAL needs often have a hard time connecting expressions and feelings with appropriate behavior. As HEARING needs have to concentrate on visual cues, point out all the examples of body language in the pictures (such as clenched fist, tension).

# DIRECTIONS

**GOAL**   To increase understanding
          To cooperate with peers
          To follow directions

**OBJECTIVE**   The child will give directions that allow his partner to duplicate a table arrangement without seeing it.

**MATERIALS**   Two sets of objects, such as:

| | |
|---|---|
| one large red block | a table divider, high enough so |
| one small red block | that the children cannot see |
| two small animals (duck, cow, rabbit, etc.) | across it |

**PROCEDURE**   Have two children sit across the table from each other with the table divider in the middle. One child arranges his materials and then gives directions so that the other child can make an identical arrangement. When this has been completed, the children check and see how similar the arrangements are. Help the children understand what is wrong if the arrangements don't match.

**CONTINUATION**   Start with three objects. As the children improve in giving and following directions, add more objects that introduce other dimensions, such as color and size.

**COMMENT**   This activity encourages children to use spatial as well as identity terms. *Especially good for* LEARNING needs: Teaches spatial concepts. VISUAL needs learn to follow verbal instructions to find things they cannot see and to give clear and intelligible descriptions. CULTURALLY DISTINCT can learn vocabulary and use of prepositions.

# TRAVELING

**GOAL**    To increase understanding
To encourage creativity
To increase feelings of group belonging

**OBJECTIVE**    The child will play with the props and compare features of each mode of travel.

**MATERIALS**    Props for various modes of travel:

| HIKING | TRAIN |
|---|---|
| knapsack | engine |
| hiking boots | caboose |
| dehydrated food | dining car |
| | engineer's hat |
| CARS | |
| cars with steering wheel | PLANES |
| maps | cockpit |
| sandwiches | caps |
| | trays of food |
| BOATS | airplane |
| flags | |
| boat | |
| life preservers | |

**PROCEDURE**    Have the children play with the props. Then talk about them with the children and compare characteristics.

**COMMENT**    *Especially good for* SPEECH AND LANGUAGE needs: Emphasize the vocabulary as well as information about various modes of travel. For HEARING needs, add more visual props, such as pictures of boats and trains to set the mood. For VISUAL needs, add props that can be felt, such as seat belts or a fan. For PHYSICAL needs, emphasize how movement takes place and have children classify modes of travel for ease in short and long distances. For CULTURALLY DISTINCT, be sure to include modes of travel that these children are familiar with (motorcycles, buses, carts and horses, and so on) while you are expanding knowledge and language skills in this area. For GIFTED AND TALENTED, have your travelers adapt to a variety of conditions—the atmosphere of the moon, jungles, deserts, crowded cities, and so on. Have children come up with creative solutions to travel problems and a rationale for their suggestions.

# BODY LANGUAGE

**GOAL**    To interpret body language
To increase body awareness

**OBJECTIVE**    The child will guess what another child's emotion is from his body language.

**MATERIALS**    Masks:
full-face Halloween mask          paper bags with holes for the eyes

**PROCEDURE**    Have a child put a mask on his face. Ask the child to portray a specific emotion and have the other children guess what emotion it is. As the children guess the emotion, ask them the basis for their guess (clenched fists—anger; open arms—joy). Once agreement is reached on the emotion being portrayed, have them decide how the child's face will look. Then take off the mask and see if they have guessed correctly.

**CONTINUATION**    Have a child portray an emotion behind a screen that allows only the head to show and let the others guess how the body looks.

**COMMENT**    *Especially good for* HEARING needs: These children depend more than others on visual cues. When they are role playing a particular emotion, ADJUSTMENT and LEARNING needs (who tend to have emotional outbursts) can develop a sense of how their body feels. This awareness is the first step in learning to control one's behavior.

# BODY NOISES

**GOAL**    To interpret body language
         To increase body awareness

**OBJECTIVE**    The child will make at least five different noises using at least three different parts of the body.

**MATERIALS**    None

**PROCEDURE**    During group time, ask the children if they can make a sound with their hands, fingers, feet, or mouth. As you ask about each body part, see how many different sounds you can get from the group.

**CONTINUATION**    You might help the children classify the sounds as happy, sad, angry, and so on. As they become more proficient at this, you might even request that a child make "an angry sound with his feet," a "happy sound with his hands," and so on.

**COMMENT**    *Especially good* for LEARNING and ADJUSTMENT needs: increases awareness of the body and body language and provides a socially acceptable release for emotions.

# 17

# *Listening*

## INDEX

Listening is an important part of communication. It is usually part of a process that also includes talking (expressing language) and seeing (reading readiness.) Although all these skills are usually used together, it is helpful to separate them for the purpose of developing and strengthening skills in a given area—especially when you are planning programs for children with special needs.

Children are most likely to develop good listening skills if you are a good model. If you are always willing to repeat what you say, children learn *not* to listen the first time around. And when you are listening to a child, LISTEN.

Start off with brief periods when children are expected to listen. Vary your method of presentation to include just listening (when you give directions), listening paired with visual cues (as in stories) and listening while doing something physical (using rhythm instruments or dancing).

## LISTENING GOALS

- To improve auditory identification (getting meaning from what is heard). The child learns to identify a fire alarm, running water, or other familiar sounds. The ability to identify specific sounds allows the child to get more cues about his environment.
- To improve auditory discrimination (distinguishing between likenesses and differences). The child learns to distinguish between a fire alarm and a jingle bell (gross discrimination) or the *p* and *b* sound (fine discrimination).

    Once children can identify a variety of sounds, they begin to make finer distinctions. They may know that the teacher is calling roll, but they must listen carefully to know whether to respond to Kenny or Penny. You can use rhyming words to sharpen the child's ability to identify similar and dissimilar parts of words, and build vocabulary at the same time.
- To improve auditory memory (remembering what is heard). This includes long-term memory (the story of *Whistle for Willie* that you read last week) and short-term memory (the directions you just gave about who could get their coats). In addition to remembering what was said, children must learn to remember in proper sequence (the days of the week and months of the year).
- To improve auditory closure (filling in obvious missing pieces of speech, e.g., "Sugar and spice and everything _____"). This involves the use of grammatical rules (parts of speech, tense, pronouns, and so on) and picking out speech patterns and rhyming words. Children learn what category of word is missing as well as particular words. They know the question "We swim in the _____?" might be answered by *pool* or *lake* but not *her*, as the sentence requires a noun, not a pronoun.
- To improve auditory association (understanding what is heard in the context of past experience and knowledge). This is a fairly high-level process that uses analogies (at night it is *dark*, in the day it is _____), categorization and classification skills, and the ability to associate behaviors with words. (What do you do when you hear the fire alarm?) It also involves generalizing about how things are alike and different. (How are a bell and a siren alike? How are they different?)
- To improve auditory comprehension (bringing together all the previously learned skills and using them to understand and focus what is being stated). This involves being able to think up a title for a story or make up a relevant beginning or ending of a story. The more complex the material, the more difficult the task.

## TEACHING STRATEGIES

Children with SPEECH AND LANGUAGE needs must have a lot of practice listening to gain the language skills they need. Some of these children have articulation problems because they do not listen accurately and their speech reflects what they hear or they don't have good speech models.

Those with HEARING needs require special help in this area. Because of the hearing loss, they need to learn to use any residual hearing that is available to them. Some of these children prefer seeing or touching to listening as a way of learning. Utilize these skills together at first, then gradually help the child refine the auditory skills that are available to him.

Children with VISUAL needs are more dependent than others on using auditory cues. Especially those skills related to auditory memory and association. Children who are blind may miss the non-verbal qualities of attending and eye contact as well as the ability to reflect someone's thoughts and respond to his questions.

For children with a high activity level, such as many of those with LEARNING needs, having to *just* listen may be seen as close to punishment. Since these children are easily distracted, be sure you aren't competing with outside noises or an uncomfortable physical environment. This also is important with CULTURALLY DISTINCT children who may be learning a second language or trying to master the fine discrimination of a first one.

Children with ADJUSTMENT needs may have learned to tune out their environment because it seemed irrelevant or scary. They will need your help in learning to tune you in.

To the extent that children with PHYSICAL needs have been restricted in the variety of listening experiences they have had, they may need help in this area, primarily in connecting sounds to possible sources and in comprehending the relationship. This is also true for children with HEALTH needs. In both cases, adults often forget that there may be so much attention to other areas of learning that listening is neglected, or that although children listen, they may not understand what they hear.

Children with INTELLECTUAL needs will spend most of their time during the preschool years mastering the skills of auditory identification and discrimination. You should provide many opportunities for practicing these skills. GIFTED AND TALENTED children, if they have developed the prerequisite skills, need to be challenged with more auditory association and comprehension skills.

# NOISY STEPS

**GOAL**    To improve auditory identification

**OBJECTIVE**    The child will step on the picture of the object in response to the sound.

**MATERIALS**    tape and tape recorder
pictures of things that make sounds

**PROCEDURE**    Make picture cutouts and tape them to the floor or a piece of sturdy cloth. Use pictures of animals or sound makers (clock, tuning fork, bell, telephone). As the sound is made, the child steps on the picture of that object. Some children can make the sounds while others move, or you can use a tape recording of the sounds.

**CONTINUATION**    This also can be played like "Twister"; that is, the child puts a different body part on each picture of an object as the sound of the object is made.

**COMMENT**    *Especially good for* LEARNING needs and CULTURALLY DISTINCT: uses auditory, visual, and tactile senses.

# MAGICIAN

**GOAL**    To improve auditory identification

**OBJECTIVE**    The child will make the noise requested by the teacher and identify at least two noises made by classmates.

**MATERIALS**    None

**PROCEDURE**    The teacher plays the magician and "changes" a child into a noise-making object by whispering into the child's ear what object he is to be. The child then pretends to be the object by making the noise, and the other children guess what the object is. Possible objects or situations include the following:

| | |
|---|---|
| farm animals | food cooking |
| musical instruments | outside noises |
| vehicles | inside noises |

**COMMENT**   *Especially good for* SPEECH AND LANGUAGE and LEARNING needs: enjoyable substitute for classroom drilling to improve auditory skills. Add details to give VISUAL needs environmental cues about what is happening. (For example, beat a real drum. Ask where you might see a drum: in a band, a parade, a concert.) The use of pictures along with the sounds can help clarify sounds for HEARING needs.

# SOUND EGGS

**GOAL**   To improve auditory identification
To improve auditory discrimination

**OBJECTIVE**   The child will find the pairs of containers that sound the same.

**MATERIALS**   Five pairs of containers (these could be plastic eggs; orange juice or milk cartons; oatmeal boxes; and so on—nothing transparent)
materials that make a sound (enough for two containers):

| | |
|---|---|
| rice | paper clips |
| dried beans/peas/lentils | pebbles |
| sugar | bells |
| macaroni | |

**PROCEDURE**   Partially fill each pair of containers with a different kind of small object. Mark the bottoms of the pairs of containers with pairs of numbers or letters so that the child can check to see that he has made a pair. Ask the child to shake the containers and identify the pairs by sound.

**CONTINUATION**   Have open containers and see if by looking at these the children can figure out what is inside the pairs of closed containers. Explore cause and effect: Does it sound the same when the quantity in each container is different? Does it depend on how hard you shake the container?

**COMMENT**   *Especially good for* SPEECH AND LANGUAGE and auditory LEARNING needs: provides training in fine auditory discrimination.

# SOUND AND TELL

**GOAL**   To improve auditory identification
To localize sound

**OBJECTIVE**   The child will identify the sound.

**MATERIALS**   a screen (could be a rectangular table on its side)
a paper bag for each child in the class
a noisemaker (an object from class or one brought from home), such as:

| | |
|---|---|
| whistle | dishes |
| two blocks | bell |
| spoon | pen that clicks |
| timer | scissors |

**PROCEDURE**   Ask each child to bring a noisemaker from home or to find an object in the classroom that makes a noise. Give each child a bag in which to hide the noisemaker. Have each child go behind the screen and make the sound. The other children guess what it is. Then have the child make the sound so that all can see.

**CONTINUATION**   Discuss the properties of objects that make noise and those that do not. Classify noises as loud, soft, sharp, and so on. Have children make noises with various body parts behind the screen. The other children can then guess how the sound was made.

**COMMENT**   *Especially good for* CULTURALLY DISTINCT and SPEECH AND LANGUAGE needs: these children may have difficulty talking in front of the group and will enjoy an opportunity to participate, with few language demands. VISUAL needs can refine auditory skills; if other children use the noisemakers in various parts of the room, they can practice locating as well as identifying sound.

# LISTENING WALK

**GOAL**   To improve auditory identification
        To improve auditory memory

**OBJECTIVE**   The child will identify a sound he hears on the walk and describe the sound and what made it in a group discussion.

**MATERIALS**   None

**PROCEDURE**   Before you take the children outside, ask them to listen carefully and identify sounds, but not to talk to each other during the walk. Tell them to try to figure out what is making each sound. When they return, have them describe and imitate the sounds and ask other children to decide what might have made the sounds. For example, the child might say, "I heard a peck, peck, peck. What is it?" rather than "I heard a bird."

**CONTINUATION**   To increase auditory discrimination, be sure to have the children describe the sound, not what made it. For variety or in bad weather, you might try an inside walk. Reading some of the *Noisy Books* by Margaret Wise Brown is a good follow-up activity.

**COMMENT**   *Especially good for* VISUAL needs: increases sound awareness, ability to identify, and memory. Vary the walk by having the children first walk making a lot of noise and then very little noise and compare what they hear. LEARNING and ADJUSTMENT needs can work off a little energy during the walks.

# SOUND CUES

**GOAL**   To improve auditory identification
        To improve auditory association

**OBJECTIVE**   The child will identify the sound and what actions the sound describes.

**MATERIALS**   tapes of sounds
        tape recorder

**PROCEDURE**   Record a variety of sounds. Have the children identify the sounds. Then have them decide where they might hear each sound and what might be happening. Indoor sounds that might be used include the following:

mixer: cooking
vacuum: cleaning

toilet flushing: going to the bathroom
washing machine: washing clothes

This can also be done with street noises, such as:

brakes: stopping
engine: starting
siren: emergency/fast car
whistle: police officer

**COMMENT** *Especially good for* VISUAL needs: uses auditory sounds as cues for what is happening in the environment. For HEALTH needs, use hospital sounds; be sure to include some happy ones.

# LETTER DAY

**GOAL**  To improve auditory identification
To improve visual identification
To improve tactile identification

**OBJECTIVE**  The child will identify the letter through vision, hearing, and touch.

**MATERIALS**  letters of the alphabet made of sandpaper
objects that begin with each letter

**PROCEDURE**  Pick a letter of the alphabet. The first letter of the child's name is a good one to use. Expose the child to that letter in as many ways as you can. With the letter P, for example:

Trace a sandpaper letter *P*.
Feel your breath with your hand as you say *P*.
Point to *P* in a group of letters.
Think of words that start with *P*.
Make cookies in the shape of *P*.
Eat *p*retzels for snack.
Read a "*P*eanuts" story.
Play the *p*iano.

**COMMENT**  You can do this with any letter. Granted, *X* is a challenge! If you plan to do all the letters, start with the vowels and leave the most difficult consonants until last. *Especially good for* SPEECH AND LANGUAGE needs: concentrate on problem sounds. Children with LEARNING needs can learn using all their senses. CULTURALLY DISTINCT can expand vocabulary as they practice speech sounds. INTELLECTUAL needs are helped by repetition.

# SAY IT

**GOAL**  To improve auditory discrimination
To improve auditory memory

**OBJECTIVE**  The child will correctly imitate the sound the teacher makes.

**MATERIALS**  None

**PROCEDURE**  During group time, say various words or sentences and have the children imitate you. Using the same words, change your voice pitch, intonation, speed, or stress.

|  | SENTENCE | VARIATIONS |
|---|---|---|
| TEACHER: | I like juice. | normal |
|  |  | loud |
|  |  | soft/whisper |
|  |  | fast |
|  |  | slow |
|  |  | puckered mouth |
|  | I | stress |
|  | like | stress |
|  | juice. | stress |
|  |  | raise for a question |
|  |  | hold your nose |

As the children change their voices, verbalize for what you (they) did. "Great, you all said it as loud as I did."

**CONTINUATION**  Have some children change their voices and the other children imitate them. Again, ask them to identify the change. Make longer, more challenging sentences.

**COMMENT**  *Especially good for* SPEECH AND LANGUAGE needs: gives practice in voice control and speech rhythms in a group situation. For VISUAL needs, be sure to explain situations where these voices are most often used so that children will understand when they are appropriate (shouting at sports events, talking softly in church). They also need the practice in memory skills, as they are so dependent on them. HEALTH and PHYSICAL needs can participate because there is no physical exertion. CULTURALLY DISTINCT can have fun playing with language without fear of criticism while getting needed practice.

# WHISPER

**GOAL**  To improve auditory discrimination
To improve auditory memory

**OBJECTIVE**  The child will act out the originally whispered task.

**MATERIALS**  None

**PROCEDURE**  This is a takeoff on the party game "Telephone." Pick a command such as "Touch your head." With the children sitting in a circle, whisper this to the first child, have the first child whisper to the second child, and so on around the circle until the child at the end performs the task requested.

**CONTINUATION**  As the children improve, increase the length of the task so that they must remember longer commands (e.g., "Go to the door and open it; then come back and sit down").

**COMMENT**  Be sure to have a sense of humor about this. *Especially good for* SPEECH AND LANGUAGE needs: Children can see the outcome of misarticulation in a fun way. Children with LEARNING needs can translate words into actions while being part of a group.

# SOUND BINGO

**GOAL**  To improve auditory discrimination
To improve auditory association

**OBJECTIVE**  The child will identify the letter by its sound (b—"bah" as in ball).

**MATERIALS**   Bingo cards with letters rather than numbers

**PROCEDURE**   Using a regular bingo game format, call sounds instead of letters. A few letters will have to be eliminated, as they sound the same as others (e.g., c and k), unless you give words that start with that sound. The children circle the letter for each sound as it is called out. The winner is the first child to circle every letter in a row, column, or diagonal. But continue until all children win.

**CONTINUATION**   You can also call out words and have the children circle the initial sound, for example, apple: A.

| B | I | N | G | O |
|---|---|---|---|---|
| a | u | r | p | o |
| s | h | b | c | i |
| w | x | free | v | g |
| m | j | n | l | d |
| e | f | g | t | z |

**COMMENT**   *Especially good for* SPEECH AND LANGUAGE needs and CULTURALLY DISTINCT: a fun way of increasing listening skills while learning letter sounds. Ask GIFTED AND TALENTED to give examples of words that could start with the sound given.

# WHERE IS IT/WHO IS IT?

**GOAL**   To improve auditory discrimination
        To localize sound

**OBJECTIVE**   The child will point to the general area in which a child is walking.

**MATERIALS**   None

**PROCEDURE**   Have the children sit facing a wall with their eyes shut. Ask one child to walk to a specific area of the room. As he is walking, tell the children to listen and then point to the area where he has walked. Then have them open their eyes and check if they are right.

**CONTINUATION**   As the children's ability to localize sound increases, see if they can name the area of the room where the walker is instead of pointing (e.g., the dramatic play area, the construction area). This is difficult because the children have to remember the various parts of the room and visualize their locations.

Another adaptation is to have the children try to identify the walker by the sound of the footsteps. Help with some initial questions: "What kind of shoes is this child wearing? Is the walk heavy or light, fast or slow?" (Do this on a bare floor.)

**COMMENT**   *Especially good for* VISUAL needs: gives the kinds of auditory cues these children depend on for information. It is reassuring for HEALTH and PHYSICAL needs to be able to listen and tell when someone is coming if they are not able to move around. This activity helps them learn to do so.

# OBJECT FILE

**GOAL**   To improve auditory discrimination
        To increase vocabulary

**OBJECTIVE**   The child will sort objects according to initial sounds.

**MATERIALS**    small objects
shoe boxes
felt letters

**PROCEDURE**    Use this activity to teach initial consonant sounds. Place many small objects in the center of a table. Mark shoe boxes with felt cutouts of letters representing the appropriate sound. Have the children sort the objects into their appropriate boxes.

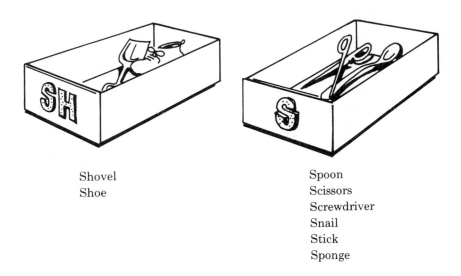

Shovel                          Spoon
Shoe                            Scissors
                               Screwdriver
                               Snail
                               Stick
                               Sponge

Objects can also be sorted by function.

| TOOLS | TABLEWARE | |
|---|---|---|
| screwdrivers (various sizes | plates | napkin |
| hammer | cups | glasses |
| pliers | knife | saucer |
| wrench | fork | |
| stapler | spoon | |

**COMMENT**    This activity is used in the same way a picture file might be used. *Especially good for* VISUAL, SPEECH AND LANGUAGE, and HEARING needs and CULTURALLY DISTINCT: can be used with or without language and provides tactile as well as visual cues to the objects. Be sure to add language practice by talking about the objects and their uses. Have GIFTED AND TALENTED classify and reclassify objects into groups based on function.

# WATER TONES

**GOAL**    To improve auditory discrimination
To improve cause and effect reasoning

**OBJECTIVE**    The child will state whether the tapped glasses sound the same or different.

**MATERIALS**    Water glasses with varying amounts of water in them that can be tapped

**PROCEDURE**    Fill glasses with different amounts of water. Allow the children to explore the glasses and the sounds they produce. Help them discover the relationship between the amount of water and the pitch. Then see if they can arrange the glasses by pitch.

**CONTINUATION**    Have blindfolded children match the glasses and put them in order of pitch from high to low.

**COMMENT**    *Especially good for* VISUAL and SPEECH AND LANGUAGE needs: A way of fine-tuning listening skills as well as learning about pitch. Helps GIFTED AND TALENTED draw generalizations about amounts of water and pitch and then experiment to check the results.

# BODY SOUNDS

**GOAL**    To improve auditory discrimination
To increase body awareness

**OBJECTIVE**    The child will decide which words for body parts have the same beginning sound.

**MATERIALS**    None

**PROCEDURE**    Name a part of the body and then ask the children to name a part (or choose between two parts that you name) that has the same beginning sound or letter.

> toe: teeth, tongue
> eye: elbow, eyebrow, ears
> leg: lips
> hair: hand, head
> finger: fingernails, foot
> arm: ankle
> knee: knuckles

**CONTINUATION**    Have children name things in the room that have the same initial sound.

**COMMENT**    *Especially good for* SPEECH AND LANGUAGE needs: teaches vocabulary and listening skills using real objects. Real objects, especially parts of the body, make the learning more relevant for INTELLECTUAL and HEARING needs. Be sure to do this activity several times.

# TAPE IT

**GOAL**    To improve auditory discrimination
To improve self-concept

**OBJECTIVE**    The child will identify his own voice and that of at least one classmate.

**MATERIALS**    a tape recorder
a blank cassette

**PROCEDURE**    Over the course of several days, have children talk into the tape recorder for a minute or two about what they are doing. When everyone in the class is on tape, have a small-group listening time when the children try to guess who is talking.

**CONTINUATION**    Send this tape to a child who has been out of school for a long time or to a child who has moved.

**COMMENT**    Have the children state who they are after they talk; keep a list of the order in which the children speak so that you know for sure who is talking. *Especially good for* HEALTH needs: These children can contribute to and enjoy this activity at home and perhaps even send in a return tape. The activity also benefits VISUAL needs, who depend on auditory cues. If the tape is sent home

Listening is an active process that can be both intense and fun.

with the child and if the parents are given the order in which the children spoke, the child can practice identifying the voices at home.

# WHO'S THERE?

**GOAL**    To improve auditory discrimination
To improve self concept
To cooperate with peers

**OBJECTIVE**    The child will identify other children by listening to their voices.

**MATERIALS**    None

**PROCEDURE**    During group time, select a child to be the listener and have him turn his back to the group. Point to a child in the group. This child can say, "John, I want to be your friend." Let the listener guess who it is. If he is wrong, have the other child say, "No, I am not Anita." Then have the child add a statement about something that they like to do together or about the listener, such as, "I like to play blocks with you." Keep the activity going until the listener guesses who it is.

**COMMENT**    This activity is good because both children actively participate and the longer it takes the listener to guess, the more positive things this child can learn. *Especially good for* VISUAL needs: These children may depend on auditory cues to identify classmates. LEARNING needs: focuses on auditory skills while getting positive things said about him.

# ANIMAL SOUNDS

**GOAL**    To improve auditory memory

**OBJECTIVE**    The child will identify the animals by the sounds made.

**MATERIALS**    Pictures of animals

**PROCEDURE**    Show children pictures of animals and have them make the sounds the animals make.

|   |   |
|---|---|
| geese: hiss | sheep: baa |
| bees: buzz | cows: moo |
| cats: meow | dogs: bark |
| ducks: quack | horses: neigh |
| roosters: cook-a-doodle-doo | pigs: oink |
| snakes: sss | |

**CONTINUATION**    Sing "Old MacDonald Had a Farm." Old MacDonald can have a *house* for pet sounds or even a *zoo* for wild animal sounds.

**COMMENT**    *Especially good for* SPEECH AND LANGUAGE needs and CULTURALLY DISTINCT: teaches animal sounds and names. Use pictures to make the association easier. Also useful for HEARING needs if there is enough residual hearing to identify the sounds.

# DRUMBEATS

**GOAL**    To improve auditory memory
To improve auditory association

**OBJECTIVE**    The child will repeat the pattern.

**MATERIALS**    A drum, a piano, or hands

**PROCEDURE**    Beat the drum, strike a note on the piano, or clap in a specific pattern. Have the children repeat the pattern.

**CONTINUATION**    Make the patterns progressively more difficult by making them longer and varying the rhythms, but be sure there is always a recognizable, repeated pattern.

**COMMENT**    *Especially good for* SPEECH AND LANGUAGE and LEARNING needs: helps develop a feel for patterns of sound instead of just isolated sounds. Helps VISUAL needs have fun while learning longer and more complex auditory patterns. For HEARING needs, use dramatic movements to accompany the beat (large hand spread before clap, hand lifted high above drum or piano), so these children will pick up the visual, if not the auditory, aspect of the pattern.

# GOING TO THE BEACH

**GOAL**    To improve auditory memory
To improve sequencing skills

**OBJECTIVE**    The child will remember during group discussion at least three items that he is taking on a trip to the beach.

**MATERIALS**    flannel board
pictures of objects children would be likely to take

**PROCEDURE**    Discuss the beach and what people do there. Then play the game "I am going to the beach and in my suitcase I'm going to take *a swimsuit.*" The child must repeat the sentence and add another item. If children have trouble thinking of a suitable object, suggest two items to choose from (e.g., a ski cap and a beach ball). As each child chooses, place the chosen picture on the board, which would look something like this:

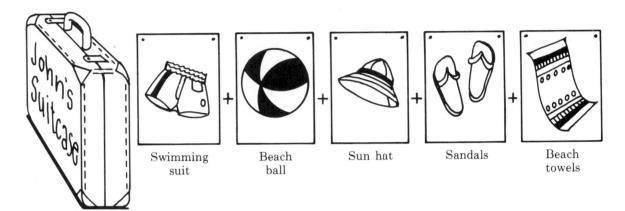

| Swimming suit | Beach ball | Sun hat | Sandals | Beach towels |

When the children stop naming items, take the cards down and see how many they can remember. When that becomes easy, see if they can remember the pictures in the order in which they were hanging.

**CONTINUATION**    The class can go for a picnic and pack their lunches. Then see if the children remember to eat everything they brought. The class can pack for a trip to the jungle, desert, North Pole, hospital, and so on. Encourage children to discuss why certain items are necessary.

**COMMENT**    *Especially good for* CULTURALLY DISTINCT: exposes children to a variety of situations and at the same time increases memory skills. For VISUAL needs, use real objects and a real suitcase when possible. HEALTH needs might remember things they took to a hospital, such as a toothbrush, pajamas, and so on, that are common to all children. Wait to call on GIFTED AND TALENTED until some of the more obvious items have been mentioned.

# JOHNNY HEAR, JOHNNY DO

**GOAL**    To improve auditory memory
To improve self-concept

**OBJECTIVE**    The child will repeat what is done or said.

**MATERIALS**    None

**PROCEDURE**    Adapt the concept of "Monkey See, Monkey Do" to (child's name) *hear*, (child's name) *do*.
Example:

> Johnny hear: clap, clap (teacher)
> Johnny do: clap, clap (child)
> Tony hear: Hello (teacher)
> Tony do: Hello (child)

**CONTINUATION**    This is a good activity to use at the beginning of a large group time or as a way of dismissing children individually from the group. (Add: "Tony, you can go.") You can also make this a visual activity by using *see* instead of *hear* and using actions instead of sounds.

**COMMENT**    *Especially good for* CULTURALLY DISTINCT and SPEECH AND LANGUAGE needs: requires children to listen, singles them out by name, and allows them to participate in front of the group without much talking.

# ROBOT

**GOAL**     To improve auditory memory
To cooperate with peers
To increase body awareness

**OBJECTIVE**     The child will follow the directions that are given.

**MATERIALS**     None

**PROCEDURE**     Pick a child to be the robot and command the child to do certain things:

Walk forward three steps.
Walk to the block corner and sit on a block.
Touch your toes.

**CONTINUATION**     As the children become more adept, give more complicated tasks and allow another child to take the role of the controller. At first you may need to teach the controller how to give clear and simple directions.

**COMMENT**     *Especially good for* LEARNING needs: Children can be active while learning to listen first and do just what the directions say. Good practice for PHYSICAL needs if directions are appropriate. For INTELLECTUAL needs, use simple one-step directions.

# LISTEN BEFORE YOU MOVE

**GOAL**     To improve auditory memory
To follow directions
To improve sensory integration

**OBJECTIVE**     The child will follow at least a two-step direction.

**MATERIALS**     None

**PROCEDURE**     During transition times, dismiss the children with two- or three-part directions.

All those wearing blue may touch their nose and then get their coat.
All those wearing red shoes can jump twice and get their coat.

**COMMENT**     It is important to use transitions as a time of learning. *Especially good for* LEARNING needs: gives practice following directions; can be used frequently and varied to avoid boredom. For HEARING needs, use pictures (e.g., blue) and act out the directions (e.g., touch your nose). For VISUAL needs, use items that children can recognize by feeling (e.g., buttons, shoelaces, fuzzy sweaters). INTELLECTUAL needs should be given simple directions. Start with one-step directions (For example, "Stan, touch your nose with your finger and then get your coat." If necessary, wait until he has touched his nose to tell him to get his coat.) GIFTED AND TALENTED should be given more complex directions.

# RHYMING PICTURES

**GOAL**     To improve auditory closure

**OBJECTIVE**     The child will match the pictures of objects whose labels rhyme.

**MATERIALS**     Pictures of objects, some of which rhyme

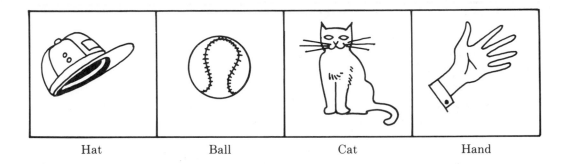

Hat   Ball   Cat   Hand

**PROCEDURE**   Make picture cards in which the name of the first object rhymes with one of the three other pictures on the card. See if the child can pick out the rhyming ones by looking at the pictures. Write the words on the back rather than the front of the pictures. That way, you have two games: When the children can read, they can match the words to the pictures.

**CONTINUATION**   As the children get better at the game, make the words more difficult.

**COMMENT**   *Especially good for* SPEECH AND LANGUAGE and HEARING needs: gives visual cues for an auditory task. GIFTED AND TALENTED can expand their language skills. HEALTH needs can easily do this activity at home, and the game can be geared to the ability of the child.

## FAST AND SLOW

**GOAL**   To improve auditory association
To improve sensory integration

**OBJECTIVE**   The child will beat a slow or fast pattern.

**MATERIALS**   A piano, drums, or hands

**PROCEDURE**   Using a percussion instrument, teach the concepts "fast" and "slow" by playing different rhythm patterns. Have the children move to the beat. Show the children pictures of things that go fast or slow and have them beat out the rhythm.

**COMMENT**   Having the children move helps generalize the learning experience. *Especially good for* SPEECH AND LANGUAGE, HEARING, and LEARNING needs: teaches the regulation as well as the identification of speed and rhythm.

## LISTENING OBSTACLE COURSE

**GOAL**   To improve auditory association
To improve cause and effect reasoning

**OBJECTIVE**   The child will go through the course, using sound echoes.

**MATERIALS**   an obstacle course of large cardboard boxes
a blindfold

**PROCEDURE**   Randomly place large cardboard boxes in an area. Have the child go through the area either clapping his hands or stamping his feet to determine the location of the boxes. He can also hear when he is getting close to the wall.

**COMMENT**   *Especially good for* VISUAL needs: These children depend on auditory skills for locating obstacles. GIFTED AND TALENTED may enjoy the challenge if the principles are explained.

# SOUNDS

**GOAL**    To improve auditory association
             To improve classification skills

**OBJECTIVE**    The child will identify and classify the sound.

**MATERIALS**    tape recorder
                  batteries/cord and socket
                  tape with sounds:

| HOUSE SOUNDS | OUTSIDE SOUNDS | WARNING SOUNDS |
|---|---|---|
| toilet flushing | transportation sounds | fire alarm |
| water running | leaves crunching | car horn |
| alarm clock ringing | birds chirping | train whistle |
| cooking | bells ringing | fire siren |
| door slamming | digging | shout |

**PROCEDURE**    Have the children listen to these sounds. See if they can identify each sound and say where they might hear it. Discuss what is happening and what, if anything, they should do.

**COMMENT**    Learning and visual needs: develops a connection between sounds, what is going on in the environment, and what it means to the child.

# TITLE

**GOAL**    To improve auditory comprehension
             To increase logical reasoning
             To improve decision making

**OBJECTIVE**    The child will choose an appropriate name for the story.

**MATERIALS**    A made-up story or a story with the title hidden

**PROCEDURE**    Read or tell the story to the class. Explain that it has no title and that you want their help in deciding on the title. Ask them to suggest titles and then to explain why they think the title they suggested would be a good one. If they forgot obvious features of the plot, point out the omissions.

**CONTINUATION**    Use increasingly complex stories.

**COMMENT**    Appropriate titles require high-level reasoning skills, so this activity is *especially good for* GIFTED AND TALENTED. It can be used to help LEARNING and VISUAL needs focus on the major theme of the story.

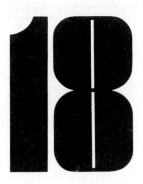

# Reading Readiness

## INDEX

| *Goal* | *Activity* | *Page* |
|---|---|---|
| | Opposite Lotto | 375 |
| | Visual Analogies | 377 |
| To increase visual comprehension | Class Book | 380 |
| | Comics | 379 |
| | My Books | 380 |
| To improve tactile discrimination | Sandpaper Letters | 367 |
| To interpret body language | Expressions | 368 |
| | Matching Faces | 370 |
| To increase understanding | Class Book | 380 |
| | Opposite Lotto | 375 |
| | Visual Analogies | 377 |
| To improve cause and effect reasoning | Perspectives | 373 |
| | What's Missing? | 373 |
| To increase logical reasoning | Matrix | 374 |
| | Scavenger Hunt | 371 |
| To improve classification skills | Classify It | 379 |
| | Match 'em | 376 |
| To improve sequencing skills | Comics | 379 |
| | Natural Sequencing | 377 |
| To increase problem-solving skills | Follow That Line | 370 |
| To improve eye–hand coordination | Alphabet Line | 367 |
| | Classify It | 379 |
| | Fishing for Faces | 368 |
| To express feelings | My Books | 380 |
| To increase awareness of feelings | Matching Faces | 370 |
| To increase body awareness | Changes | 372 |
| To increase attention span | Changing Objects | 371 |
| | Color Concentration | 372 |
| | Color Lotto | 369 |
| To cooperate with peers | Changes | 372 |
| | Color Concentration | 372 |
| | Follow That Line | 370 |
| To increase feelings of group belonging | Class Book | 380 |
| | Flannel Board Stories | 374 |

Educators are becoming more and more interested in and concerned about reading and reading readiness, although there is no agreement on a method for teaching readiness. There is agreement, however, that the teacher is more important than the method used. Your enthusiasm for reading and valuing it as a skill are more important than the way you decide to teach it. For children with special needs, reading can be a wonderful discovery or an albatross.

## READING READINESS GOALS

- To improve visual identification (labeling objects or letters that one sees). Children learn that objects have consistent labels and that these labels stand for or symbolize the objects.
- To improve visual discrimination (distinguishing among various objects by looking for similarities and differences). In order to read, children need to be able to make fine distinctions between letters and words, but before they can do this, they must learn to distinguish between different shapes and colors. Then they move on to an exercise such as:

    Find the one that is the same as the first one:

    > p      d      b      p      j      g

- To improve visual memory (remembering what has been seen). This includes long-term memory (remembering in June the color of their snowsuit) and short-term memory (closing their eyes and remembering the color of the shirt they are wearing). In addition to remembering what they've seen, children must also learn to remember things sequentially. Because the sequence in which letters appear determines what word is formed (*mat* v. *tam*), remembering sequentially is an essential reading skill.
- To improve visual closure (recognizing objects or pieces of visual information without seeing the whole thing). For example, it is possible to recognize a rabbit even if it is missing an ear. Eventually, children learn how to look at word configurations instead of looking at only the individual letters in each word.
- To improve visual association (understanding what is seen in the context of past experience and knowledge). If you show children a snow scene and ask them about the temperature, they will tell you it is cold. This skill includes the ability to abstract the function of things: Children can pair a lamp and a flashlight based on their function of giving light.
- To increase visual comprehension (bringing together the previously learned skills and using them to interpret visual information). If you show children a picture and ask them, "What's happening in this picture?" they use visual comprehension to tell a story about it. This skill includes summarizing the main points or ideas of something that has been read.

    Teaching visual skills is a broad process that includes: field trips, followed by stories dictated by the children to help them recall trips; and the recording of children's interpretations of pictures.

## TEACHING STRATEGIES

Children with SPEECH AND LANGUAGE needs may be reluctant to participate in reading readiness. Negative feelings about language often carry over to this area. These children may need to be encouraged and rewarded for participation.

Children with HEARING needs may profit if you devote extra programming time to visual readiness skills, since they may learn more easily by reading than by listening. Reading readiness skills are the same skills required for speech reading.

Children with VISUAL needs may need a very individualized reading readiness program. Create the need for vision and encourage children to refine the visual skills they can use. Have large-print books on your bookshelves for those who can learn to read print. For children who will use braille, emphasize the development of tactile rather than visual skills.

Children with LEARNING needs are likely to need more practice than others in readiness skills. These skills are frequently difficult for them, and your initial concern about their development may arise from their performance in this area. Plan activities that intrigue them while teaching the necessary skills at the same time.

Reading can broaden the range of experiences that is available to children with PHYSICAL or HEALTH needs.

Children with ADJUSTMENT needs may find the readiness program less threatening than field trips and oral language. They can expand their knowledge at a time when other options are not available. Be sure to allow them plenty of time to do these activities.

CULTURALLY DISTINCT children will need extra help, especially if English is not their native language or if reading is not a valued part of their culture.

Children with INTELLECTUAL needs also require a lot of time to practice reading readiness skills. These skills may well be learned in conjunction with such necessary small motor skills as patterned eye movement (left to right), following a line of print with a finger, and turning pages. Have the children work on them for as long as it takes to attain mastery. But do this in short periods and be sure prerequisite skills have been attained before going on to more difficult tasks (that is, visual identification before discrimination or memory skills).

GIFTED AND TALENTED children may be early readers. Educators think early reading results from a combination of the child's maturity, his personal interest, and a conducive environment. Your classroom is part of this environment and should provide support and encouragement for children to read whenever they are ready.

# ALPHABET LOTTO

**GOAL**   To improve visual identification
To improve visual discrimination

**OBJECTIVE**   The child will match the letters.

**MATERIALS**   An alphabet lotto game, as described below

**PROCEDURE**   Divide pieces of posterboard (9″ × 12″) into six rectangles (4″ × 4½″). Print a letter of the alphabet (not necessarily in order) in each rectangle. Make four cards with different letters on each.

| D | N | A |
|---|---|---|
| Z | Q | G |

| Y | F | B |
|---|---|---|
| P | L | R |

| M | U | H |
|---|---|---|
| C | S | I |

| E | W | K |
|---|---|---|
| J | T | O |

Cut 24 4″ × 4½″ pieces, also out of posterboard. Print one letter on each rectangle.

Put individual matching letters into a box to draw from so that you can play a game of lotto. (As our alphabet has 26 letters, 2 will be missing. Make two sets, omitting different letters from each one.)

If children are having trouble matching particular letters, design cards to meet these problems. For example, with lower case letters, make a card with reversible lines and curves.

| b | q | p |
|---|---|---|
| z | g | d |

To expand the letter concept, make the following lotto combinations:

| Board | Cards |
|---|---|
| Printed upper case | Printed upper case |
| | Printed lower case |
| | Script upper case |
| | Script lower case |
| | Picture with initial letter sound |

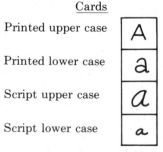

With all these combinations, there will be five cards for each letter on the board.

**CONTINUATION**     This can be played as a matching game by a child alone.

**COMMENT**     Because all children need to learn letters, this game is adaptable to many special needs. *Especially good for* SPEECH AND LANGUAGE and HEARING needs: These children can both match the letters and make the speech sounds associated with them. Add the finger spelling alphabet to match with the letters for HEARING needs and script letters for GIFTED AND TALENTED. Since the game is easy to make, parents can make it for a HEALTH needs child to use at home. Use particular configurations of letters to help LEARNING needs who tend to confuse similar letters, such as *b* and *d*. For VISUAL needs, make letters of felt or sandpaper. If the children will become braille readers, the braille alphabet can be used and matched to the sandpaper letters.

# SANDPAPER LETTERS

**GOAL**     To improve visual identification
To improve tactile discrimination

**OBJECTIVE**     The child will trace the letter with his index finger. The child will name the letter. The child will then name an object that starts with that letter.

**MATERIALS**     sandpaper          glue
cardboard          pictures

**PROCEDURE**     Cut the letters of the alphabet out of sandpaper and glue each on a cardboard square. Glue on the back a picture of something that begins with that letter. Have the child trace the letter with his index finger as you talk about the structure of the letter. ("This is the letter A. It has three straight lines. One, two, three. The third connects the first two in the middle.")

**COMMENT**     *Especially good for* HEARING and LEARNING needs: The tactile mode reinforces the visual one. For VISUAL needs, have an object for the child to manipulate and associate with the letter if possible.

# ALPHABET LINE

**GOAL**     To improve visual identification
To improve visual discrimination
To improve eye–hand coordination

**OBJECTIVE**     The child will find the requested letter and put it on the clothes line.

**MATERIALS**     clothesline                marking pen
26 or more wooden          paper
clothespins                pictures

**PROCEDURE**     Print a letter of the alphabet on each clothespin. Have the children put the alphabet on the clothesline in the appropriate order or put up each letter as you call it out, depending on the children's ability and your goals.

**CONTINUATION**     Print the letter on a separate piece of paper, and collect pictures that children can sort by initial sound. Have the children match the paper letters to the clothespins, then hang the letters. The same can be done with the pictures. Have more advanced children make words with the clothespins. (For that you'll need some duplicate letters.)

**COMMENT**     Because this activity can be used in a variety of ways, it can benefit many different children. *Especially good for* PHYSICAL and INTELLECTUAL needs: develops finger strength while teaching the alphabet. GIFTED AND TALENTED can practice fine motor skills and put together words. Useful for HEALTH needs because the materials are common and, in addition to teaching the alphabet, are portable and can be used in a variety of situations.

# EXPRESSIONS

**GOAL**    To improve visual discrimination
To interpret body language

**OBJECTIVE**    The child will choose the expression that matches your expression.

**MATERIALS**    Cards with pictures of various facial expressions

**PROCEDURE**    Make cards with a variety of expressions. Write on the back the feelings they represent.

Happy                Sad                Angry                Surprised

Make an expression and see if the children can match a card to your expression. Then ask the children to make the expression themselves.

**CONTINUATION**    Have the children think of events that might have influenced your expressions. Ask them what someone might do in these situations.

**COMMENT**    This activity is *especially good for* HEARING needs: These children may depend on body cues to interpret emotions. (When you add the continuation, use pictures to help clarify the events that are related to the expression.) Gives needed practice to LEARNING needs, who often misinterpret body cues. Children with ADJUSTMENT needs receive help in identifying their emotions, learning appropriate behavior, and recognizing similar feelings in others.

# FISHING FOR FACES

**GOAL**    To improve visual discrimination
To improve eye–hand coordination

**OBJECTIVE**    The child will match the faces he catches to a face on a poster.

**MATERIALS**    matching pairs of pictures of faces        a shoe box
construction paper        a poster-sized piece of paper
paste        a stick (fishing pole) with a string at the
paper clips        end, to which a magnet is tied

**PROCEDURE**    Paste one of each pair of faces on a small piece of construction paper and attach a paper clip at the neck. Put the faces in the shoe box. Paste the remaining faces on the poster. Have the children use fishing poles to fish for the faces in the box. Ask the children to match the face they have "caught" to the same face on the poster.

**CONTINUATION**    The children can fish for numbers, letters, or even fish (then count the catch). If you actually want to put fish in water, make them out of plastic and use waterproof marker for the face.

**COMMENT**    *Especially good for* HEARING needs: helps these children learn to focus on the small details they may need some day for speech reading. LEARNING and ADJUSTMENT needs can discuss the facial features (smile v. frown) while practicing fine motor skills. For PHYSICAL needs: the activity can be done sitting or standing, and it gives fine motor and visual discrimination practice.

# COLOR LOTTO

**GOAL**   To improve visual discrimination
To improve visual memory
To increase attention span

**OBJECTIVE**   The child will match the first set of colors to the second set.

**MATERIALS**   Squares of primary (red, blue, yellow) and secondary (green, orange, purple) colors made into a lotto set

**PROCEDURE**   First play lotto with primary and secondary colors. Be sure to label the colors for the children. When children can match these colors, make up a shade and tint lotto by having cards for six shades each of red, blue, and so on. Either paint these yourself and cover with transparent paper or use origami paper. Shade and tint colors require much finer visual discrimination than primary colors. Shade discrimination is also a good way to focus attention.

**CONTINUATION**   Place one set of lotto cards at one side of the room and the other at the opposite side. Show the children a card and have them select the one that is just like it and bring it to you. To increase the difficulty, use the shades and tints or two colors.

**COMMENT**   *Especially good for* HEARING needs: These children depend on the ability to make fine visual distinctions. For INTELLECTUAL needs, use the primary and secondary colors to teach matching skills. LEARNING needs can improve visual memory and work off a little energy as they walk, hop, or jump across the room to get the matching color.

Games that require children to know colors, recognize patterns, count spaces, and take turns are enjoyable ways to teach reading readiness skills.

# FOLLOW THAT LINE

**GOAL**   To improve visual discrimination
To increase problem-solving skills
To cooperate with peers

**OBJECTIVE**   The child will make a pattern.

**MATERIALS**   poster board
markers (red, black, green)

**PROCEDURE**   Cut poster board into 3″ × 3″ squares and arrange these squares in a pattern on a large table or the floor. This is for your ease in drawing. Using black, red, and green markers, draw a pattern of lines, stopping and starting colors, and using straight and curved lines. The child then can build a track with the cards in a variety of patterns, for example:

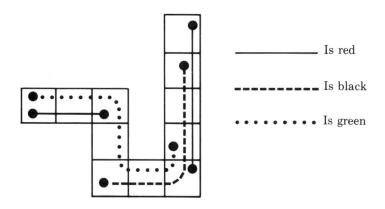

_____ Is red

- - - - - - - - - Is black

. . . . . . . . . Is green

Your patterns can be much longer than this one and ultimately more complex.

**CONTINUATION**   The more squares you have, and the more colors and patterns, the more complicated the task is. It is also more challenging when children must make a designated pattern. Making the letter H, for example, requires a lot of problem solving.

**COMMENT**   *Especially good for* LEARNING *and* HEARING *needs:* requires visual discrimination as well as planning. GIFTED AND TALENTED can be challenged to make more complex patterns. Small group projects require interaction and an agreed upon strategy.

# MATCHING FACES

**GOAL**   To improve visual discrimination
To increase awareness of feelings
To interpret body language

**OBJECTIVE**   The child will match his face to the one made by the teacher or a peer in the mirror.

**MATERIALS**   A large mirror

**PROCEDURE**   Sit in front of a large mirror with one or two children. Make a face and have them imitate it. Start with obvious faces: Really turn the corners of your mouth down, stick out your tongue, raise your eyebrows, and so on. Encourage the children to make the faces. Discuss how they feel when they make each face. Have them touch their faces with their hands to see if they can not only see, but feel a difference. Have them experiment with tension and relaxation in their faces.

**CONTINUATION**   Talk about the relationship between how someone looks and feels. Discuss how the way a person looks might affect our behavior toward him.

**COMMENT**    *Especially good for* LEARNING and HEARING needs: Both need to learn better use of visual cues to interpret their own and other people's moods. ADJUSTMENT needs can profit from becoming aware of the nonverbal aspects of their own behavior as well as that of others.

# CHANGING OBJECTS

**GOAL**    To improve visual memory
To increase attention span

**OBJECTIVE**    The child will return three objects to their original order after they have been rearranged.

**MATERIALS**    objects
a screen

**PROCEDURE**    Put three objects in a row and ask the children to look at them. Put a screen in front of the objects and rearrange them. Ask the children to put them in the original order.

**CONTINUATION**    As the children improve, increase the number of objects and their similarity.

easy: cup/doll/block
harder: red block/blue block/green block
hardest: red stocking cap/red baseball hat/red ski cap

For more variation, take one object away and have the children name the missing object.

**COMMENT**    *Especially good for* HEARING and LEARNING needs: helps develop a good visual memory. Benefits PHYSICAL and HEALTH needs because it requires little physical skill and can easily be done in the school or hospital. For these children, you might use objects that are familiar in medical practice (tongue depressor, little flashlight, stethoscope, Bandaid) if you think it will help them. For CULTURALLY DISTINCT, choose items these children are familiar with that others may not be, for example, chopsticks, a rice bowl, or a ceramic soup spoon. This gives everyone a chance to learn and these children something to share.

# SCAVENGER HUNT

**GOAL**    To improve visual memory
To increase logical reasoning

**OBJECTIVE**    The child will find the pictured object in the classroom.

**MATERIALS**    Pictures of objects in the room or duplicates of these objects

**PROCEDURE**    Give the children cards with pictures of objects that are in the room (red block, baby doll's shoes, piece of yellow paper). Have them leave the card behind while they find the item (or items). The children will then bring back the item and see if it matches.

**CONTINUATION**    Encourage children to think before they look for the object and to explain where in the room they think it will be and why. You might even time the hunt to encourage efficiency and to teach a little math.

**COMMENT**    *Especially good for* HEARING and LEARNING needs: helps children not only remember but generalize a visual image to a real object. For INTELLECTUAL needs: use real objects rather than pictures. Until the children get the idea, they may have to take the object with them. Keep the objects simple at first while the children learn the process, then gradually introduce pictures geared to their ability level.

# CHANGES

**GOAL**   To improve visual memory
To increase body awareness
To cooperate with peers

**OBJECTIVE**   The child will name or point to the change.

**MATERIALS**   None

**PROCEDURE**   Use a small group, or have children pair up. One child closes his eyes while the child who is "it" changes something about his appearance (for example: unties shoe, rolls up pant leg, removes glasses, or unbuttons shirt). The first child must name or point to the change.

**CONTINUATION**   As the children improve, encourage them to make more subtle changes.

**COMMENT**   *Especially good for* HEARING needs: These children depend on noticing and remembering subtle visible changes to gain information. Because this game allows the child who is "it" to be in control of the change and to be part of the group, it is good for children with HEALTH or PHYSICAL needs. For INTELLECTUAL needs, have children make major changes (e.g., take off a shoe).

# COLOR CONCENTRATION

**GOAL**   To improve visual memory
To increase attention span
To cooperate with peers

**OBJECTIVE**   The child will remember where the matching color is.

**MATERIALS**   A set of cards with matching pairs of colors on one side

**PROCEDURE**   This is a variation of the game "Concentration." Lay out the cards face down. Each child takes a turn and chooses two cards. The objective is to turn over two cards that are the same color.

**CONTINUATION**   As children become more proficient, add shades of colors. You can use a regular deck of cards for numbers, or pairs of pictures of any kind. The more cards you add, the more difficult the activity becomes.

**COMMENT**   *Especially good for* HEARING and LEARNING needs: reinforces visual skills. The activity can be individualized to meet the interests of different children. If, for example, a GIFTED AND TALENTED child is interested in dinosaurs, play the game with pictures of dinosaurs. The more detailed the pictures, the more difficult the game becomes. Children with HEALTH needs might enjoy playing this with parents or siblings.

# WHAT IS IT?

**GOAL**   To improve visual closure

**OBJECTIVE**   The child will identify the object.

**MATERIALS**   pictures of familiar objects
a large envelope

**PROCEDURE**   Put a picture of a familiar object in an envelope. Pull it out slowly until part of the picture is exposed. Have the children guess what it is. Keep exposing more of the picture until it is correctly identified. Encourage the children to guess and to give you the reasons for their guesses.

**COMMENT**    Be sure to start with pictures of simple, familiar objects. *Especially good for* HEARING needs: helps these children identify something from only a glimpse when they miss verbal descriptions. Can be used to encourage creative problem solving, especially with GIFTED AND TALENTED children.

# PERSPECTIVES

**GOAL**    To improve visual closure
To improve cause and effect reasoning

**OBJECTIVE**    The child will identify the view he is shown and sort the pictures correctly.

**MATERIALS**    Pictures of familiar objects from many perspectives

**PROCEDURE**    Draw or photograph familiar objects or people from different perspectives (above, below, side), and have the children put all the pictures of the same object together. Discuss with the children why different parts can or cannot be seen from different perspectives and what cues can be used to identify objects.

**COMMENT**    This is a difficult task for most young children, although by age 5 some will be able to do it. GIFTED AND TALENTED children may enjoy the challenge of learning to recognize parts of objects and the idea of seeing things from different points of view. You might follow this by asking them about perspectives in their artwork.

# WHAT'S MISSING?

**GOAL**    To improve visual closure
To improve cause and effect reasoning

**OBJECTIVE**    The child will name the missing part.

**MATERIALS**    pictures that have parts missing
broken toys

**PROCEDURE**    Provide a set of pictures that are not complete. Ask the child, "What is missing?" If he does not notice, give him clues (e.g., "How do you think this rabbit will see?") Pictures that might be used include:

> face with one eye
> house with no door
> car with three wheels
> doll with one arm
> fork with two tines

**CONTINUATION**    You might follow this by looking at broken toys (those with missing pieces) and discussing what happened to the toy and whether it can be fixed or what can be done to compensate for the lost piece.

**COMMENT**    *Especially good for* HEARING and LEARNING needs: fine tunes visual skills. SPEECH AND LANGUAGE needs can learn vocabulary words as well as practice language skills. For GIFTED AND TALENTED, make the missing pieces more subtle—a door handle, instead of a door, missing.

# FLANNEL BOARD STORIES

**GOAL**    To improve visual association
To increase feelings of group belonging

**OBJECTIVE**    The child will participate in the story telling process.

**MATERIALS**    flannel board
flannel board story pieces (these are easy to make: trace figures from a coloring book on pellon and cut them out)

**PROCEDURE**    Pick a relatively simply story with a few central characters. (Animals work well.) Make felt or Pellon characters (they have more body if you use two pieces of felt with webbing between). Tell the story and have the children put up the pieces as you talk about them.

**COMMENT**    *Especially good for* HEARING and INTELLECTUAL needs: It is easy for them to follow the central theme. Both VISUAL and LEARNING needs profit from manipulating the figures and participating in the story telling process. GIFTED AND TALENTED may use the flannel board pieces to generate their own stories.

# MATRIX

**GOAL**    To improve visual association
To increase logical reasoning

**OBJECTIVE**    The child will state which piece is missing.

**MATERIALS**    flannel board
felt shapes, 1 large and 1 small of each of the following:
red triangle, circle, square, and rectangle
green triangle, circle, square, and rectangle
blue triangle, circle, square, and rectangle
yellow triangle, circle, square, and rectangle

**PROCEDURE**    Set up a 3 × 3 matrix on a flannel board.

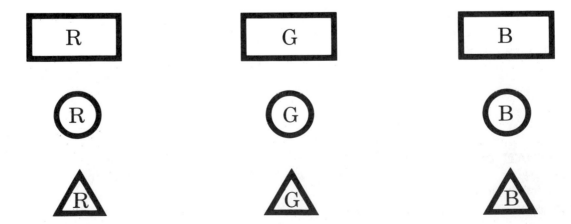

Have the children close their eyes while you remove one piece. Ask them which piece is missing and how they know. If you remove the center piece, their reasoning should be "It has to be a circle because horizontally there are only circles, and it has to be green because vertically all the shapes are green." This is a thinking, not a memory game. The more complex 3 × 8 matrix (the 8 columns are arranged into 4 groups of matching large and small shapes) looks like this:

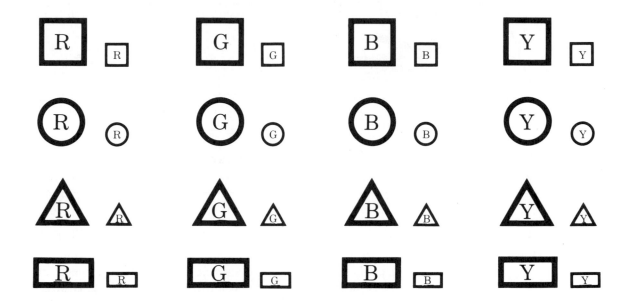

**CONTINUATION**  Work progressively from 3 × 3, to 4 × 4, to 3 × 6, to 3 × 8, to 4 × 8 matrices. You can make a variety of activities using the matrix principle.

**COMMENT**  After children learn the thinking, they can play with each other and create their own matrix. *Especially good for* INTELLECTUAL needs: at first they can use the pieces for color and shape identification and later explore the reasoning. For VISUAL needs, use different textures to make the shapes. Practice in reasoning and in experiencing spatial relations will help these children learn to move around skillfully.

# OPPOSITE LOTTO

**GOAL**  To improve visual association
To increase understanding

**OBJECTIVE**  The child will correctly place or match the cards.

**MATERIALS**  A lotto game of opposites, homemade or bought

**PROCEDURE**  Make a lotto game of a board and individual cards requiring the children to match opposites.

**CONTINUATION**   Write the words on the back so that eventually, if you cut up the board, the children can match opposite words.

**COMMENT**   *Especially good for* CULTURALLY DISTINCT and SPEECH AND LANGUAGE needs: builds vocabulary and teaches the concept of "opposite" in a visual rather than auditory way. GIFTED AND TALENTED children can use the continuation activity. They can also think of new ideas for cards and, with help, draw the pictures for these cards.

# MATCH 'EM

**GOAL**   To improve visual association
To improve classification skills

**OBJECTIVE**   The child will match the pictured items by their function.

**MATERIALS**   A series of cards with pictures of objects that can be matched by function but that do not look the same, for example:
pictures of clothes to be matched with pictures of the body parts on which they are worn: feet—shoes/boots/slippers; upper body—coat/sweater/jacket; head—football helmet/stocking cap/Easter bonnet; and lower body—jeans/slacks/skirt.
animals and their young: chicken/chick; cow/calf; sow/piglet; mare/colt; ewe/lamb; cat/kitten; and dog/pup.
objects that have similar uses: lamp/flashlight/candle; car/boat/airplane; cup/mug/glass; stuffed chair/rocking chair/ladder-back chair; book/newspaper/magazine; and canopy bed/crib/twin bed.

**PROCEDURE**   Draw these cards or make them with pictures cut out of magazines or advertisements and glued on poster board. Have the children match the cards appropriately.

**CONTINUATION**   Print the words on the back of the cards. As the children learn to read, they can play the same game with the words, then check themselves by using the pictures.

**COMMENT**   *Especially good for* SPEECH AND LANGUAGE and HEARING needs: increases functional generalization skills and vocabulary. For GIFTED AND TALENTED, encourage the use of the continuation activities. Add other dimensions to the matching: For example, include wild animals with farm animals or add pictures of the food that the animals eat. For CULTURALLY DISTINCT, add appropriate regional clothing and objects to match the ones that are used in the classroom. It will broaden the experience of all children to realize that, functionally, forks and chopsticks are similar.

# NATURAL SEQUENCING

**GOAL**     To improve visual association
                    To improve sequencing skills

**OBJECTIVE**     The child will put the pictures in order.

**MATERIALS**     Pictures of a naturally occurring sequence

**PROCEDURE**     Make pictures of naturally occurring sequences, for example:

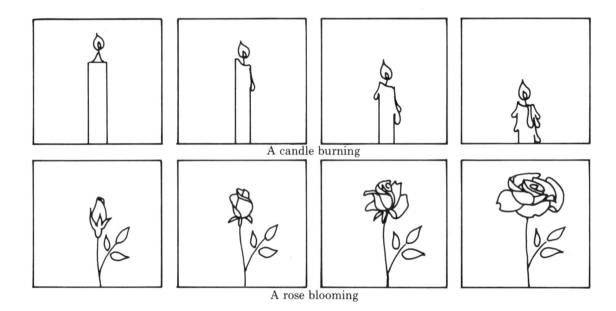

A candle burning

A rose blooming

Have the children order these pictures.

**COMMENT**     Be sure the pictures do not always show objects going from big to little. You do not have to be a terrific artist to make these, provided you pick concepts that are simple to illustrate. However, pictures are available commercially. *Especially good for* HEARING needs: a good follow-up after a field trip. These children tend to see things individually, without developing the connections language allows. This activity, combined with verbal discussion, may have to be used in place of a field trip for PHYSICAL or HEALTH needs.

# VISUAL ANALOGIES

**GOAL**     To improve visual association
                    To increase understanding

**OBJECTIVE**    The child will complete the analogy by filling in the blank correctly.

**MATERIALS**    large cards, divided in quarters
small cards to cover one quarter of each large card

**PROCEDURE**    Make large cards with blobs of different colors, a completed pair in the two top squares and half a pair in the lower left. Each card should illustrate a "color analogy": red is to pink as blue is to ——————— (light blue). Make a series of small cards of different colors.

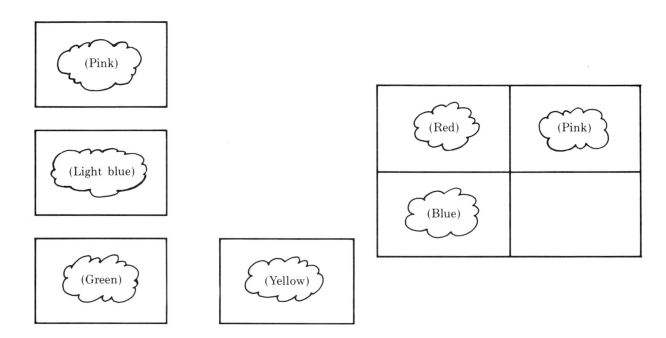

Have the child pick a card to complete the analogy. Talk about the analogy and help the child figure out what makes the two pairs analogous.

**CONTINUATION**    Provide as many analogies as you can. Here is another example:

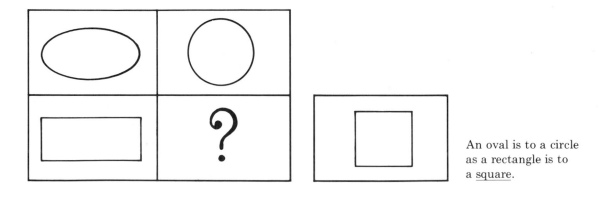

An oval is to a circle as a rectangle is to a <u>square</u>.

**COMMENT**    *Especially good for* HEARING needs: Much adult thinking is by analogy, and it is important for the child to learn this first by sight, then to generalize it. GIFTED AND TALENTED children can profit by learning this skill early, as it enables them to make sense of activities they read or hear about, but have not experienced.

# CLASSIFY IT

**GOAL**    To improve visual association
To improve classification skills
To improve eye–hand coordination

**OBJECTIVE**    The child will classify the objects in at least two different ways.

**MATERIALS**    miniature cars    small animals of different colors
miniature airplanes    boxes

**PROCEDURE**    Using 2 or 3 boxes, explain a classification system to the children and have them use it. If necessary, put one or two objects in the box first. The children then continue the system. For example:

| | | |
|---|---|---|
| airplanes | not airplanes | (2 boxes) |
| red | not red | (2 boxes) |
| cars | airplanes | animals (3 boxes) |

**CONTINUATION**    Any small objects that are classifiable can be used. When the children have mastered your system, have them make up their own systems for classification and tell you what they are, or start another system yourself, and have the children figure it out for themselves.

**COMMENT**    *Especially good for* VISUAL needs: Tactile cues can be used to sort. Make the activity more creative for GIFTED AND TALENTED by having them see how many different ways objects can be categorized and by increasing the number of categories. INTELLECTUAL needs can start out with simpler classifications—red and blue, for example—and can use fewer objects. To work on fine motor skills for PHYSICAL needs, use small objects or any that the child can manipulate.

# COMICS

**GOAL**    To increase visual comprehension
To improve sequencing skills

**OBJECTIVE**    The child will put the comic strip pieces in a logical sequence.

**MATERIALS**    a simple comic strip (4 or 5 pictures) cut apart    clear contact paper
heavy paper    (to put over pieces)
glue    envelopes (for storage)

**PROCEDURE**    Glue the comic strip on heavy paper, cover it with clear contact paper, and cut into frames. Number the backs in order. Keep the frames in envelopes when not in use. The children can help make these and trade them with other children, or you can prepare them ahead of time. Ask the children to put the frames in the proper sequence and explain what is happening in the comic strip.

**CONTINUATION**    Leave out the final picture and have the children make up an ending for the story.

**COMMENT**    Be sure to pick comics that have an obvious sequence. *Especially good for* LEARNING needs: an amusing way to practice sequencing. For HEALTH needs, can be easily done and made at home. GIFTED AND TALENTED can be challenged by using more difficult comic strips and creating several endings.

# MY BOOKS

**GOAL**   To increase visual comprehension
To express feelings

**OBJECTIVE**   The child will make a book about his feelings.

**MATERIALS**   construction paper        crayons
magazines              paste or glue

**PROCEDURE**   After the children decide what feelings they want in their book, they can cut pictures from magazines or draw their own pictures to illustrate the feelings. Some suggestions are:

> My Angry Book
> I Love It When, . . .
> I Want to Cry When . . .
> I Wish Other People Wouldn't . . .

**CONTINUATION**   As children become more aware of their feelings, talk with them about socially acceptable ways of expressing these feelings, one of which is to write about or draw them.

**COMMENT**   Children can make more than one book. *Especially good for* ADJUSTMENT and LEARNING needs: The first step in learning to control feelings is to become aware of them. Encourages the use of books as a way of venting emotions. GIFTED AND TALENTED can be encouraged not only to draw or paste pictures that illustrate their feelings, but also to write (or dictate to the teacher) about their feelings.

# CLASS BOOK

**GOAL**   To increase visual comprehension
To increase understanding
To increase feelings of group belonging

**OBJECTIVE**   The child will contribute a page to the book.

**MATERIALS**   several newspapers          scissors
magazines                  a loose-leaf or ring binder
blank paper $8\frac{1}{2}'' \times 11''$         a paper punch
paste or glue

**PROCEDURE**   Choose newspapers and magazines that have some articles relevant to children. Have the children clip a story they like, paste it on a page, and illustrate it in their own way.

**CONTINUATION**   If there is enough interest to continue this project, begin to classify the stories (e.g., people, animals, places).

**COMMENT**   This is a nice activity to do before group parent-teacher meetings as parents too can see their children as part of the group. *Especially good for* GIFTED AND TALENTED: especially interesting for early readers. Children with HEALTH needs can develop a valuable interest in newspapers and magazines. These publications are usually available, and the other necessary materials can be brought.

# Social Studies

## INDEX

| *Goal* | *Activity* | *Page* |
|---|---|---|
| To improve visual closure | I'm Thinking Of | 392 |
| To improve taste discrimination | Food Forms | 391 |
| To improve sensory integration | Body Parts | 386 |
| To follow directions | Be the Teacher | 390 |
| To improve cause and effect reasoning | Food Forms | 391 |
| | Who Has Been Here? | 387 |
| To make predictions | Problems | 386 |
| | Who Has Been Here? | 387 |
| To improve spatial concepts | From Your House to Mine | 393 |
| To take turns | From Your House to Mine | 393 |
| To increase sharing skills | Solutions | 385 |
| To express feelings | Share Your Feelings | 392 |
| To increase body awareness | Hands and Feet | 385 |
| | Body Parts | 386 |
| To increase awareness of individual differences | I'm Thinking Of | 392 |

Social studies in the preschool is designed to help children better understand and function in the world in which we live. During these years children are developing their sense of values and attitudes about themselves, other children, and adults in the family and community.

Social studies is an area for specific activities and learning, but also one where watching and modeling are important. For example, children in the process of learning to take turns wonder whether or not they will actually get their turn if they postpone it or let someone in ahead of them. If they *do* lose their turn, they will be less likely to take turns in the future. Children may wonder how to talk to a child who stutters. They will probably use your behavior as a model.

Children can also learn through social studies about the situational aspects of behavior. Behavior that is appropriate in one situation is not necessarily right in another. Shouting in the play yard is fun and suitable; shouting in the classroom is not OK.

Field trips are one of the most common ways of making abstract ideas more concrete to young children. Where field trips are impractical, resource people can be invited to visit. Resource media such as film, television, records, or tapes can also be used. Social studies should also be taught through the more informal organization and decision-making of each day; deciding what to name the new goldfish, what to do when someone knocks down the blocks, and how to share special materials are all part of the social learning that occurs at this age.

## SOCIAL STUDIES GOALS

- To encourage creative problem solving. Living and working with others, children have to learn to compromise. Young children know about "yes" and "no" and "mine," but they need to be taught ways of taking turns, sharing, and developing rules that all can abide by. They also need to have some knowledge of exceptions to rules and why and how these exceptions are made. As we live in a world of diminishing resources, children need to learn about conservation and the interaction between people and their environment (e.g., We burn wood to get heat. If we burn less wood, it will be cooler. What do we do? Put on warmer clothes.)

- To increase awareness of roles people play. A basic sense of economics—the concept that things usually cost money and that people work at a variety of occupations to get this money—can be learned at a young age. People's occupations require different skills and preparation. Children can begin to learn which occupations sound interesting to them and which would be suitable for them, taking into consideration any limitations their special needs might present.
- To broaden concepts of families. Children start out very egocentric, believing that all children are like them and all families are like their families. They need to become aware of individual and family differences without making judgments that "different" is "bad." Learning about the functions of families and the roles they play, including an international perspective if possible, can be the beginning of citizenship.
- To increase feelings of group belonging. All children need to feel as though they are part of the class. It is important that they become aware of themselves both as unique human beings and as people who are similar to, as well as different from, others. Children can learn that they are all members of the class even though some of them are boys and others girls, some like art and others don't, and some wear glasses and others don't.
- To cooperate with adults. When children enter preschool, they may have had little experience with adults other than their parents. They need to broaden their experience with the roles that adults play as well as the authority structure that exists. Unilateral authority is not the goal; the goal is an adult model that is sensitive to children's needs and makes only necessary rules. However, those rules made are enforced. Children need to trust, respect, and cooperate with adults.
- To cooperate with peers. If this is the children's first school experience, they may have had little experience with peers other than siblings. Some children learn how to get along with each other easily, without conscious effort on the teacher's part; others need to be taught this just as much as they need math and language skills.

## TEACHING STRATEGIES

Children with SPEECH AND LANGUAGE needs can work on broadening their language skills through field trips, followed by language experience stories. The language and approach skills for sharing and taking turns can also be emphasized.

Like those with SPEECH AND LANGUAGE needs, children with HEARING needs can profit from firsthand experiences, followed in the classroom by visual aids to clarify and generalize these experiences. Because of weak language skills, these children may need to be taught nonverbal ways of approaching other children, and others must be made aware that that is what is happening.

Children with VISUAL needs must be exposed to role models who wear glasses and use other optical devices. They need to be encouraged to use the correctable vision they have and even to learn the skills to explain to others why these particular devices help them. For those with little vision, the use of records and tapes can help them expand their social world.

Children with LEARNING needs must be encouraged to use a variety of solutions to problems: they have a tendency to get stuck and require practice and guidance. The skills of taking turns and sharing are especially useful.

Children with ADJUSTMENT needs may have fewer social skills and perhaps even an unwillingness to approach others. The classroom and community need to become familiar and safe places for them. Do a lot of preparation for field trips as well as follow-up.

Social studies is a way children with PHYSICAL needs can learn about places that may not be accessible to them; although with creative problem solving, the number of places can be diminished. Children can go on field trips. They can also become more familiar with the human resources the community provides, through class visitors.

Children with HEALTH needs may be aware of the medical aspects of the community, but this knowledge should be expanded and put into perspective. These children also need to develop approach skills in addition to methods of keeping in touch with peers when away from school (telephone, visits after school, and so on).

CULTURALLY DISTINCT children have the opportunity to share the knowledge of their culture as well as learn about other cultures. Socially acceptable behavior differs among cultures, so it's important to be nonjudgmental and to teach social skills that will help the child get along in the school environment.

Children with INTELLECTUAL needs can learn about their environment by building on familiar experiences. Begin with their immediate surroundings of family and school, then expand to the larger community.

Social studies provides enrichment opportunities for GIFTED AND TALENTED children and practice in developing social skills, which usually are not advanced. These children can explore areas in greater depth and learn skills for working with children who cannot do so.

# ANIMAL FAMILIES

**GOAL**    To encourage creative problem solving
To broaden concepts of families

**OBJECTIVE**    The child will role play one member of an animal family.

**MATERIALS**    None

**PROCEDURE**    Create an animal family. Provide role-playing situations with this family at play on all fours. Include climbing, balancing, and other skills. Also include some misbehavior, sibling rivalry, or typical peer quarrels in the role-plays. Have the children make up endings for the situations. Help them to form conclusions about the consequences of their actions.

**CONTINUATION**    Talk about the similarities and differences between animal families and people families. Expand this idea to the environment where these animals live.

**COMMENT**    The children may become very attached to their animal family. You can use this activity to help solve immediate classroom crises. *Especially good for* CULTURALLY DISTINCT. They can identify with a variety of family styles that are all acceptable. GIFTED AND TALENTED can be encouraged to learn more about the subtle differences between animals. SPEECH AND LANGUAGE needs can be part of a family and even practice sounds, yet not have a great need for language.

# OUR TOWN

**GOAL**    To encourage creative problem solving
To increase feelings of group belonging

**OBJECTIVE**    The child will construct a block structure within his boundaries.

**MATERIALS**    masking tape
blocks
block accessories

**PROCEDURE**    In the block corner, use masking tape and map out a road and plots. Assign each child a plot and have children construct buildings. Ask children to decide what kinds of buildings (houses, restaurants, hospitals, firehouses, gas stations, apartments) their community needs and who is going to build them. Try leaving the construction style up to each child. Pose questions, such as "Where would someone go if they got sick?" Expand the children's ideas if necessary. Emphasize group problem solving and a sense of community spirit.

**CONTINUATION**    This is most successful if you can expand the block area and leave the structures up for several days.

**COMMENT**    This encourages parallel play, yet keeps firm boundaries about what is each child's territory. *Especially good for* LEARNING and ADJUSTMENT needs: The boundaries are clearly established and all the children know what they are to do. VISUAL needs can feel the edges of their plot; put their blocks in a tray to make it easier for them to build a structure if necessary. Encourage GIFTED AND TALENTED not only to build, but to help assess the needs of the community and try to encourage their classmates to cooperate. Light blocks, or perhaps small ones, might make it easier for HEALTH and PHYSICAL needs to participate.

# SOLUTIONS

**GOAL**    To encourage creative problem solving
To increase sharing skills

**OBJECTIVE**    The child will state at least two things he could do.

**MATERIALS**    None

**PROCEDURE**    Pick situations that the children might encounter at school or in the community but give them a twist (just for interest). For example:

> What would you do if:
> You wanted to swing but all the swings were occupied by spacemen?
> You wanted to play with the blocks but the block corner was full of sea horses?
> You wanted a drink but there was a long line of ghosts ahead of you?

Encourage the children to develop ways of sharing materials, even with spacemen.

**COMMENT**    Encourage creative as well as practical solutions. Children can learn to develop a variety of solutions as well as a plan to carry them out. This is *especially good for* GIFTED AND TALENTED children as it encourages unusual solutions. LEARNING needs could be encouraged to solve verbally situations that they have trouble with at a behavioral level. For HEARING needs, pick situations you can either picture or role play. This is also good for SPEECH AND LANGUAGE needs. In all cases be sure to provide the needed language.

# HANDS AND FEET

**GOAL**    To encourage creative problem solving
To increase body awareness

**OBJECTIVE**    The child will place the objects appropriately.

**MATERIALS**    flannel board
pictures of hands and feet
a variety of small pictures that will adhere to the flannel board:

| | |
|---|---|
| keys | socks |
| spoons | boots |
| mittens | slippers |
| rings | shoes |
| gloves | swim fins |

**PROCEDURE**    Have the children pick a picture and place it on the flannel board near the hands or the feet.

**CONTINUATION**   This can be expanded to deal with the function of hands and feet as well.

| | |
|---|---|
| picture of a lake: | how do you get there? |
| puzzle: | how do you do this? |
| pen: | how do you write with this? |

Discuss what might be hard to do without hands and feet and how handicapped people compensate. You might tie this into a dramatic play activity.

**COMMENT**   *Especially good for* HEARING needs: It does not require speech. INTELLECTUAL needs might find this activity easier on a one-to-one basis. PHYSICAL needs, especially the child with a broken limb, might talk about what it is like not to have the use of hands or feet. Discussions like this, however, must be approached with care. You might start by talking about how well the child performs certain tasks, then *ask* the child whether or not he wants to tell the others how he learned. Encourage GIFTED AND TALENTED to find many different ways of compensating.

# PROBLEMS

**GOAL**   To encourage creative problem solving
        To make predictions

**OBJECTIVE**   The child will state at least two solutions to given problems.

**MATERIALS**   Drawings of problem situations:
        a cat caught up in a tree
        two children fighting over a toy
        a child locked out of his house

**PROCEDURE**   Show the children the pictures and have them generate as many different solutions as they can.

**CONTINUATION**   Present the situations verbally and have the children act out the solutions.

**COMMENT**   The objective here is not to find *the* solution, but for children to realize that there are many solutions. Also, be sure to help children think through the implications of the solutions by asking them questions like "what would happen then?" after they have given solutions. *Especially good for* CULTURALLY DISTINCT: The social context of the problem can be addressed, and you can discuss why different solutions would be better under some circumstances than under others. AD-JUSTMENT and LEARNING needs can be helped to work through problems verbally and to discuss feelings others might have without actually encountering a situation where emotions might run strong.

# BODY PARTS

**GOAL**   To encourage creative problem solving
        To improve sensory integration
        To increase body awareness

**OBJECTIVE**   The child, when shown a picture of a body part, will perform an activity with that part of the body.

**MATERIALS**   Cards with pictures of body parts

**PROCEDURE**   Hold up pictures of body parts. Have children perform activities with that part of their body (e.g., legs—run, kick; arms—wave; head—nod; hands—clap; and so on).

**CONTINUATION**   Hold the pictures up more than once and encourage the children to think of other things to do with that body part. Make the exercise more difficult by adding body parts such as elbow, knee, waist, ankle, and wrist, or have the children make the distinction between using one and using both arms, legs, feet, and so on.

**COMMENT**   *Especially good for* SPEECH AND LANGUAGE and HEARING needs: does not require speech to participate; GIFTED AND TALENTED can find *another* use or a less obvious body part. For VISUAL needs, the body parts can be named instead of shown. INTELLECTUAL needs may need to be shown the part on their own body as it is named. Call on these children for the most obvious parts; after one child illustrates the behavior, have all the children do it. PHYSICAL and HEALTH needs can increase body awareness as long as you choose body parts that they can use.

# WHO HAS BEEN HERE?

**GOAL**   To encourage creative problem solving
To make predictions
To improve cause and effect reasoning

**OBJECTIVE**   The child will describe who would make the designated foot prints and give a reason for his choice.

**MATERIALS**   a variety of shoes in different sizes:
baby shoes            high heels
sneakers              hiking shoes
baseball spikes
water-based paint
paper ($8\frac{1}{2}'' \times 11''$)

**PROCEDURES** Make footprints with the shoes by putting the bottom of the shoes in paint, then printing each one on a sheet of paper. Make at least four footprints with each pair of shoes. Start by showing the children footprints that are about the size they would make. Ask them to arrange the prints as if someone were walking. Ask the children to describe the size of the person and where the person might be going. Have the children walk on the prints to see if the spacing is right; help them correlate size of footprints with spacing. Then help the children view the prints of speciality shoes and decide under what conditions they would be most useful.

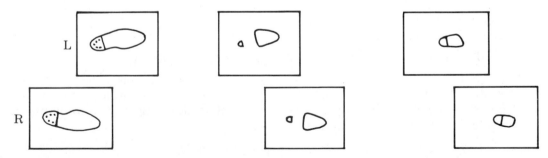

**CONTINUATION** You might follow this with dramatic play about a shoe store; the children can pick out shoes or ask for shoes for a specific occasion.

**COMMENT** *Especially good for* GIFTED AND TALENTED: The thinking skills are both challenging and fun. You might have these children design shoes for various environments (swamp v. desert). CULTURALLY DISTINCT and SPEECH AND LANGUAGE needs can learn what different shoes are called. Be sure to include shoes from a variety of places—moccasins, thongs, clogs, and so on. For HEARING needs, have the actual shoes that the children can match to the prints. That will make the relationship more obvious. For VISUAL needs, in addition to the actual shoes, use textured paint so the children can feel the prints as well.

# PATIENT IN THE HOSPITAL

**GOAL**   To increase awareness of roles people play

**OBJECTIVE**   The child will participate in the game and discuss the roles of the people the "patient" comes in contact with.

**MATERIALS**   None

**PROCEDURE** Adapt the song "The Farmer in the Dell" to your specific purposes relative to the medical profession.

> There's a child who is sick,
> There's a child who is sick.
> Hi Ho the Office O.
> There's a child who is sick.

"There's a child going to the doctor" and "There's a child going to the hospital" can also be used. In the following stanzas, the child chooses a mother, the mother chooses a father, the parents choose a doctor, and the doctor chooses a nurse. Then,

> They all stand together,
> They all stand together.
> Hi Ho the Office O.
> Until the child gets better.

**COMMENT**   Depending upon which member of the medical profession you think the child will encounter, you can add speech therapist, occupational therapist, and physical therapist. To be most effective, this game should be preceded by a discussion of what the various members of the medical profession do.

*Especially good for* HEALTH and PHYSICAL needs: They encounter many members of the health profession and this activity helps make it fun rather than threatening. For SPEECH AND LANGUAGE needs, mention the speech and language therapist; for INTELLECTUAL needs, add the occupational therapist; for ADJUSTMENT needs, include a psychologist, counselor, or family therapist. For HEARING needs have an audiologist. Also add pictures of the people for the children to hold or a significant piece of equipment (stethoscope) or a uniform (nurse's cap).

# VISITOR

**GOAL**   To increase awareness of roles people play
      To cooperate with adults

**OBJECTIVE**   The child will state what the adult does in the community.

**PROCEDURE**   Invite adults from the community to come into the class. Pick people who are comfortable with children. Have them talk briefly about what they do and answer the children's questions. Choose people who will broaden the children's understanding of the community, as well as reduce sex role stereotyping. For example:

| | |
|---|---|
| photographer | Red Cross staff |
| businessman/woman | waitress/waiter |
| welcome wagon staff | male nurse |
| female medical doctor | female lawyer |
| plumber | female engineer |
| builder | real estate agent |
| construction worker | farmer |
| musician | computer programmer |

**CONTINUATION**   This can be followed by a field trip to visit that person at work, as well as by dramatic play in the classroom incorporating that theme.

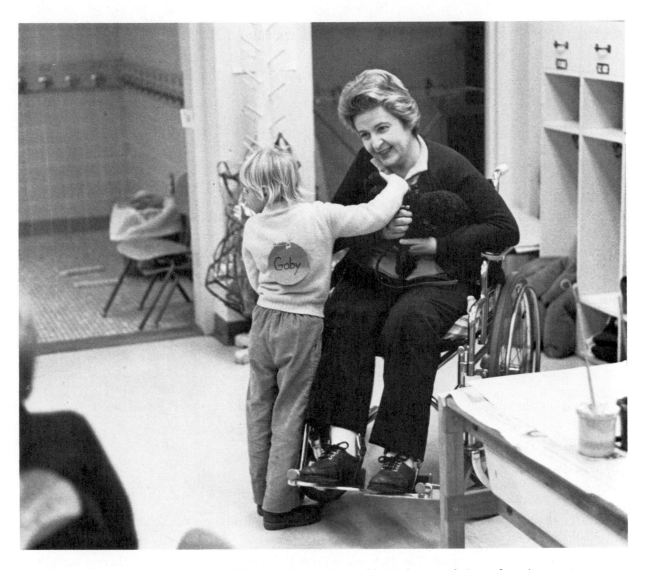

Classroom visitors offer opportunities for children to ask questions and learn about people in a safe environment.

**COMMENT**   Children, especially those with limitations, often have a restricted view of the community. This activity can extend their understanding and make them feel safer in the community. SPEECH AND LANGUAGE needs can learn the vocabulary of the professions. Be sure to include visitors who use skills and methods children with VISUAL and HEARING needs can identify with. For CULTURALLY DISTINCT, have role models and guests from other cultures. This is a way of making the community, which may be less accessible to PHYSICAL and HEALTH needs, more available and understandable. Choose visitors to challenge GIFTED AND TALENTED children; if possible, have guests talk with small groups or meet with these children after a large-group presentation.

## PHOTOGRAPH STORY

**GOAL**   To increase awareness of roles people play
To broaden concepts of families

**OBJECTIVE**   The child will state at least two roles the person in the picture is playing.

**MATERIALS**    Pictures of several familiar people, including teachers in your school and even
yourself, in a variety of roles:

| | |
|---|---|
| a teacher with the children in the class | a daughter with her mother |
| a mother with her own children | a sibling with brothers and sisters |
| a wife with her husband | a student taking a course |

**PROCEDURE**    Use pictures of males and females, and be sure to include pictures of children and
the roles they play. Note the similarities and differences among the roles that children and adults
play. It is important at the beginning to use pictures of familiar people so that children understand
the concept of multiple roles.

**CONTINUATION**    Expand this to include some different occupations: the President of the United
States and an astronaut are also husbands, fathers, sons, and siblings.

**COMMENT**    Children begin to gain a perspective on adult roles. *Especially good for* HEARING
needs: The pictures aid in setting the framework for the discussion. PHYSICAL and HEALTH needs
can see their role as patient as being only one of the roles they play, and the medical personnel as
playing more familiar roles. SPEECH AND LANGUAGE needs and CULTURALLY DISTINCT can increase
vocabulary as they learn about roles, as well as broaden their concepts of what people do. GIFTED
AND TALENTED can learn about roles in a way that expands their options and increases their knowledge of what people do, without creating sex role stereotypes.

# BE THE TEACHER

**GOAL**    To increase awareness of roles people play
To cooperate with adults
To follow directions

**OBJECTIVE**    The child will imitate the teacher by giving directions to the children.

**MATERIALS**    None

**PROCEDURE**    During group time, pick one child to help you give instructions. He can model you
by directing his classmates. Be sure to give specific directions: "Turn the lights off, then on again.
Then go to the block area and be sure the blocks are put away."

**COMMENT**    *Especially good for* ADJUSTMENT and LEARNING needs, who don't like to clean up or
who have difficulty during these times. Be sure to talk to them about how they feel, especially
when others are reluctant to clean up. For GIFTED AND TALENTED, discuss ways of talking to others
and how one can be in charge and yet not demanding. Help them build leadership and social skills.

# ROLES

**GOALS**    To broaden concepts of families

**OBJECTIVE**    The child will state at least three roles he has in the family.

**MATERIALS**    Flannel board and felt or Pellon figures:

| | |
|---|---|
| 2 boys | 2 women |
| 2 girls | older man |
| 2 men | older woman |

**PROCEDURE**  Have a group discussion about the variety of roles that children play. Use flannel board figures to help clarify these roles for the children. Explain such roles as:

brother/sister, stepbrother/stepsister  
boy/girl  
daughter/son, stepdaughter/stepson  
nephew/niece  
grandson/granddaughter  
grandfather/grandmother  

friend  
cousin  
man/woman  
husband/wife  
father/mother, stepfather/stepmother  

Also explain that one person can play many roles. Be sure to include all the relationships that children in your classroom might have. When the children have identified their various roles, describe roles to see if the children can guess who you are talking about. "I'm thinking of a girl who has one sister who is younger than she is and no brothers. Who am I thinking of?"

**CONTINUATION**  Some children might be interested in developing a family tree.

**COMMENT**  *Especially good for* CULTURALLY DISTINCT: They can realize that all children have a variety of roles. For ADJUSTMENT needs who are going through family changes, discuss roles that change with a changing situation (marriage, birth, separation, death) and those that don't change (your mother is still your mother even if she no longer lives with your father). GIFTED AND TALENTED may enjoy expanding this concept to roles beyond the family, such as student and occupational roles.

# FOOD FORMS

**GOAL**  To broaden concepts of families  
To improve cause and effect reasoning  
To improve taste discrimination  

**OBJECTIVE**  The child will identify food in different forms and state who in a family eats it in those forms.

**MATERIALS**  
a variety of whole foods  
baby food jars of the same foods  
a scraper  
a masher  

a baby food grinder  
a knife  
a hot plate  

**PROCEDURE**  Pick one or several foods (carrots and apples are traditional favorites, peaches and squash also work well). Have the children feel the food, whole and cut up into different shapes.

CARROT  
whole    curls (cut long and thin  
pieces       and put in ice water)  
coins    cubes (cut at an angle)  

Put some of the carrots in a saucepan to cook. (It's fun to cook whole carrots as well as cut-up ones. Set a timer and have the children see which is softer after a specified time period.) When the carrots are cooked, experiment again with different forms:

whole    coins    mashed  
purée (if you have a blender)  
ground (in baby food grinder)  

Compare these to baby food in jars. Discuss the taste of the different forms and how some are the same or almost the same and others different. Experiment by adding salt. Talk about who would eat the various forms (babies who don't have teeth, children getting permanent teeth, and people with braces or false teeth) and why (variety, need, or individual preference).

**COMMENT**   *Especially good for* HEARING needs as they have problems generalizing and CULTURALLY DISTINCT as they may lack experience in actually seeing one food in this many different forms. Allow VISUAL needs to feel and to taste the changes. For SPEECH AND LANGUAGE needs, be sure to add the vocabulary about the states of foods—soft, hard, crisp, mushy, and so on. HEALTH needs can broaden categories of food they may or may not eat and understand what a "soft" diet means.

# SHARE YOUR FEELINGS

**GOAL**   To increase feelings of group belonging
To cooperate with peers
To express feelings

**OBJECTIVE**   The child will share a feeling with his classmates.

**MATERIALS**   None

**PROCEDURE**   After the children have discussed feelings and expressions, ask them to share a feeling with the other children. For example, love. Some ways the children might share this are to hold hands, kiss, hug, say "I love you," and so on.

**CONTINUATION**   As children become more comfortable with this activity, have them tell others how they feel during the experience.

**COMMENT**   At first, older children might feel self-conscious doing this activity, but if you demonstrate and encourage them, they are usually willing to follow. Young children often have trouble expressing positive feelings. *Especially good for* LEARNING and ADJUSTMENT needs: This is a structured way of obtaining positive interaction. For HEARING needs, stress visual and tactile expression of feelings. For VISUAL needs, use auditory and tactile modes. For PHYSICAL needs, demonstrate how these children can be touched as well as other ways to share feelings. Be sure to include wide cultural variations in the expression of feelings so CULTURALLY DISTINCT can share feelings as well. SPEECH AND LANGUAGE needs can develop a vocabulary to express feelings, yet the activity does not necessarily demand its use. Encourage GIFTED AND TALENTED to use a variety of ways to share feelings. INTELLECTUAL needs can feel part of the group and express feelings as well. HEALTH needs, because of restrictions, frequent absences, and not feeling well, need help expressing feelings with peers and knowing that they are valued members of the class.

# I'M THINKING OF

**GOAL**   To increase feelings of group belonging
To improve visual closure
To increase awareness of individual differences

**OBJECTIVE**   The child will guess the object or person.

**MATERIALS**   None

**PROCEDURE**   This is a variation of the game "Twenty Questions" but is used as a teaching tool to help children realize when they don't have enough information;

> TEACHER: I'm thinking of someone with brown hair. Who am I thinking of?
> CHILD: Me.
> TEACHER: I could be thinking of you, but you can't be sure. Listen. I'm thinking of someone with brown hair and a plaid shirt. Who am I thinking of?
> CHILD: Sam.

TEACHER: I could be thinking of Sam, but who else has brown hair and a plaid shirt?
CHILD: Tom.
TEACHER: Listen then. I'm thinking of . . .

**CONTINUATION**    As children become better observers, encourage them not to guess until they have enough clues. If they are having trouble with the idea of the game, ask them to guess *all* of the children it could be. As you give clues, have the children eliminate classmates verbally until only one child is left. You can also play this game by having the children guess objects in the room.

**COMMENT**    This activity creates a sense of group belonging; children learn that they are all both similar to and different from each other. The activity is not demanding: Children can participate either verbally or nonverbally. Be sure not to pick out stereotypic characteristics; don't say, "I'm thinking of someone in a wheelchair" for a child with a PHYSICAL impairment. Do say, however, that you are thinking of someone with blue eyes even when the child has VISUAL needs. She still has eyes. Comment also on particular things children like to do. If, for example, a child with AD-JUSTMENT needs likes to play in the dramatic play area, remind others of that by saying, "I'm thinking of someone who likes to play in the dress-up corner." You can talk about someone who is not there, such as a child with HEALTH needs, and discuss how you miss this child and others when they are absent. You can take this opportunity to reward a child, such as one with LEARNING needs, by saying, "I'm thinking of someone who is sitting still." Make the clues more subtle to help children with HEARING needs develop the skills of classifying and observation they will need. GIFTED AND TALENTED children can be given two or three characteristics to consider at one time: "I'm thinking of someone who has blond hair, who likes to paint, and whose last name starts with J."

# FROM YOUR HOUSE TO MINE

**GOAL**    To cooperate with peers
To take turns
To improve spatial concepts

**OBJECTIVE**    The child will trace a path from his house to a friend's house.

**MATERIAL**    A simple laminated map of the community that includes the school and the children's houses. (Each house should have a child's name or picture on it.)
crayons
tissue

**PROCEDURE**    Set the map on a table with several crayons beside it. Encourage the children to pick a friend and work together to trace a path from one child's house to the other child's house. Use the tissue to erase the crayon.

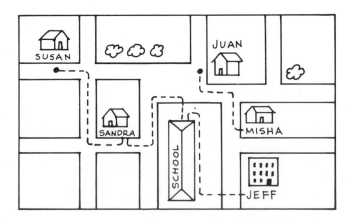

**CONTINUATION**   Map out field trips so the children know where they are going relative to the school.

**COMMENT**   This is a way of increasing understanding of the community and spatial relations, as well as the ability to work with others. *Especially good for* LEARNING, HEARING, and SPEECH AND LANGUAGE needs: The potential for use of language is great, but the demands for its use are not. Encourage GIFTED AND TALENTED to use alternative routes and make more complicated maps. For HEALTH needs, talk about visiting those who are ill. This might be followed by a walk to an ill child's house. If appropriate, singing a familiar song would be fun. Be sure to talk about some disease's being contagious.

# Science/Discovery

## INDEX

| Goal | Activity | Page |
|------|----------|------|
| To increase problem-solving skills | Gelatin | 400 |
| | Mixing Colored Water | 403 |
| To stimualte curiosity | Cornstarch Playdough | 402 |
| | Look Closer | 408 |
| To improve visual identification | Look Closer | 408 |
| To improve visual discrimination | Food Lotto | 407 |
| | Nutty Sort | 407 |
| To improve visual association | Food Lotto | 407 |
| To improve tactile discrimination | Food Sense | 405 |
| | Nature Feely Board | 404 |
| | Texture Classification | 406 |
| To improve tactile memory | Nature Feely Board | 404 |
| To improve discrimination of smells | Food Sense | 405 |
| | Wiggly Worms | 406 |
| To improve taste discrimination | Food Sense | 405 |
| | Taste Sort | 408 |
| To improve sensory integration | Popcorn | 402 |
| To improve breath control | Bird-in-a-Hole | 401 |
| | Pinwheel | 403 |
| To improve sequencing skills | Scrambled Eggs | 404 |
| To improve spatial concepts | Contour Maps | 401 |
| To improve small motor coordination | Nutty Sort | 407 |
| To increase knowledge of foods | Taste Sort | 408 |

When children study sciences, they should be learning not only about the world we live in, but about how to learn as well. To accomplish this double purpose, teachers must stimulate the children's natural curiosity, help them become keen observers, and show them that the process of solving a problem is as important as the answer.

An early understanding of scientific principles can help children become better problem solvers and increase their independence as they grow. We all use scientific principles in our daily lives (leverage, dissolving solids in liquids, and the use of heat to change the state of matter). If children can understand some basic principles, they will be able to apply them in different situations (prying open a tin of cocoa, sweetening tea, and cooking food). All children can learn to use scientific knowledge to expand the range of what they can do.

Children with special needs are limited in their ability to explore the world. These limitations are often exacerbated by overprotective adults who restrict their activities, provide too much help, and give answers without giving the children a chance to work out solutions for themselves. Since it is especially important for children with special needs to become good problem solvers, their presence in the classroom presents a challenge to the teacher.

## SCIENCE/DISCOVERY GOALS

- To improve cause and effect reasoning. Science is one area in which our actions have fairly predictable results. Children can learn about cause and effect by experimenting and then asking themselves why solution A worked while solutions B, C, and D did not.
- To make predictions. Help the children to figure out how they intend to solve the problem and to predict the effects of their actions before actually doing them.
- To improve classification skills. Children can begin to see how things are connected and to understand functional relationships (leaves and trees, a section of orange and a whole orange).
- To increase problem-solving skills. Encourage children to ask "how" questions and then stimulate them to find the answers instead of telling them. After they have done this several times, they can begin to generalize what they have learned and can start to make connections between theoretical and practical knowledge.
- To stimulate curiosity. Present an interesting problem (e.g., an uneven balance) and stimulate the children to ask questions. ("What would you like the scale to do? Do you want it even, or you want one side to be higher than the other?")

## TEACHING STRATEGIES

Children with SPEECH AND LANGUAGE and HEARING needs can learn through science how sounds are made and which parts of the body are involved in making various sounds. They can learn to use objects such as a feather or a pinwheel to observe the effects of their breath. Children with HEARING needs can learn how hearing aids work by using microphones and by playing with the balance on a stereo and the volume on tape and record players.

Children with VISUAL needs will need more opportunity to touch the equipment and materials you have available. Be sure to provide time for this and use realistic props to help these children learn. Be sure to include materials that magnify.

Children with LEARNING needs can gain much in the way of firsthand experience and needed sensory integration. They can also gain from an approach that emphasizes experimenting and keeping data. The children can learn to learn.

Children with PHYSICAL needs may want to concentrate on some of the more mechanical aspects of science. They can learn how to lift things using a pully, how to reach with a pole or a magnet, and how to hold open a door.

The lives of children with HEALTH needs, perhaps more than other lives, are linked to medicine and scientific discoveries. Their understanding of the scientific process can help them look at the implications of taking medicine v. not taking it, for example. They can also explore and learn about their body and how it functions. Choose to discuss parts of the body that are related to the needs of the children in your class.

Children with ADJUSTMENT needs may find this area nonthreatening and appreciate the discovery-based approach. The children can respond to questions with actions and sometimes discuss cause and effect relationships.

Science may help explain some differences among cultures to CULTURALLY DISTINCT children. Children can explore basic genetics and make a family tree. They can also look at the colors and textures of skin and hair.

For children with INTELLECTUAL needs, be sure to repeat experiments and do variations on the themes that you choose. If you plan activities that can be used at different levels, these children can participate.

GIFTED AND TALENTED children can be encouraged to explore their environment in a realistic way, as well as expand to theoretical concepts. They can begin to explore a more abstract aspect of science. They can also learn to use reference materials at their level to encourage independence in problem solving. Present problems that are inherently interesting from the children's perspective. Encourage them to observe closely what they do while solving a problem. Help the children learn to apply, in an increasingly general way, what they have learned by teaching them to see a pattern of principle (general) and application (particular) in each science activity.

# MAGNETS

**GOAL**    To improve cause and effect reasoning
To make predictions

**OBJECTIVE**    The child will predict which objects will be attracted by the magnet and which ones will not, before using the magnet.

**MATERIALS**    magnets of varying sizes, shapes, and strengths    assorted nonmetal objects
assorted metal objects    stick

**PROCEDURE**    Give the children a variety of magnets and materials to experiment with. Ask them to sort objects according to the objects' response to the magnet. As they begin to understand the idea, ask the children to predict whether or not specific objects will be attracted by the magnet. Teach them to modify objects so that they will be attracted to the magnet (e.g., put a paper clip on a small piece of paper).

**COMMENT**    *Especially good for* GIFTED AND TALENTED: allows them to explore the properties of materials and to make predictions and verify them. For PHYSICAL needs, add to the materials a magnet on the end of a stick. This helps eye–hand coordination and teaches the children to use a tool as an extension of their arm to get things they can't reach. Have them try picking up paper clips on the floor while sitting in a chair.

# PLANTING SEEDS

**GOAL**    To improve cause and effect reasoning
To make predictions

**OBJECTIVE**    The child will help plant the seeds, help put the signs on the pots, and make predictions about how well each plant will grow.

**MATERIALS**    seeds    water
soil    signs
pots    paper (to graph results)
crayons

Science must be a "hands on" experience for children. To understand how plants grow, children need to participate in planting, tending, and harvesting.

**PROCEDURE**   Plant seeds in three large pots. Make signs to indicate the condition under which the seeds will try to grow, measure the plants each day, and then graph the results.

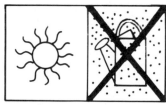
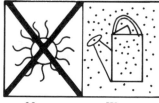
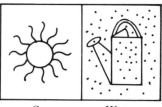

Be sure to put several seeds in each pot, as some seeds may not grow even under ideal conditions. This is a good lead-in to a discussion of what conditions people need in order to live. If you want to continue this analogy, use different types of seeds requiring varying amounts of water and sun.

**COMMENT**   Try using large pots containing several seeds instead of an individual pot for each child; there are always some plants that just don't grow. Be sure to choose seeds with a short germination period (rye grass, beans) or the children might become discouraged or forget about the project before the seeds come up. *Especially good for* HEALTH needs: helps these children by showing variations in growth. This is an easy project to do at home if the children duplicate the sun/water condition: Send a sprouted seed home to a child who is absent for a long time and compare the growth between the school and home plant. HEARING and LEARNING needs profit from the signs used as reminders of the conditions under which the plants are grown. You might even use different colored pots as an added cue (e.g., yellow for sun/no water, black for water/no sun, red for sun-/water). For CULTURALLY DISTINCT, plant seeds of plants familiar to them that serve the same purpose of understanding growth and its requirements. Be sure to eat the results if possible!

# TEMPERATURE

**GOAL**  To improve cause and effect reasoning
To make predictions

**OBJECTIVE**  The child will make predictions about the influence of specific events on the various temperatures.

**MATERIALS**  several large thermometers
empty containers
containers of liquids that vary in
temperature

ice cubes
a hot plate (if you have the staff to
supervise)

**PROCEDURE**  Have a table set up with thermometers, empty containers, a container of water, a container of ice cubes, and a hot plate if you are using one. Encourage the children to find out what happens if they add one ice cube to a cup of room-temperature water, two ice cubes, and so on. See if the children can grade (order) liquids by temperature and then check their results with the thermometer. Be sure the liquids don't get too hot to touch.

**COMMENT**  This is a better small than large group activity. *Especially good for* GIFTED AND TALENTED: uses prediction skills and allows the children the independence of checking their own work. LEARNING, HEALTH, and PHYSICAL needs learn that thermomenters can take the temperatures of liquids as well as people. To emphasize the differences in temperature, have the children draw the levels of mercury on a chart.

# GELATIN

**GOAL**  To improve cause and effect reasoning
To increase problem-solving skills

**OBJECTIVE**  The child will state the changes that take place in the gelatin during the activity.

**MATERIALS**  fruit-flavored gelatin
hot water
cold water

ice cubes
fruit

**PROCEDURE**  Following the directions on the package, make gelatin with ice cubes. Emphasize vocabulary like cold, hot, boiling, ice, melt, thicken, powder, liquid, and solid. Add fruit at various stages in the thickening process and discuss sinking and floating. Make the gelatin in two batches, one with ice and one with cold water, to discover which thickens first. Plan to have the gelatin for snack or lunch.

**COMMENT**  *Especially good for* HEALTH needs: can be done at home. GIFTED AND TALENTED can compare making gelatin with both cold water and ice by timing both processes and predict when the gelatin will be thick enough so that the fruit floats instead of sinking, and make a chart showing how their predictions compare with what actually happens. HEARING needs, who often miss verbal sequences, can profit from seeing the process in all its stages. Encourage VISUAL needs to stir the gelatin at various stages to learn more about the change from a powder to a liquid and the thickening process as the gelatin turns to a solid. If you make a batch just for these children, they can stir it with their fingers.

# BIRD-IN-A-HOLE

**GOAL**    To improve cause and effect reasoning
To improve breath control

**OBJECTIVE**    The child will blow the bird into its nest.

**MATERIALS**    a stick
a bird (made from anything light enough to be blown easily: Ping-Pong ball, plastic ornament, and so on)
a box with a hole in the side (bird's nest)
string

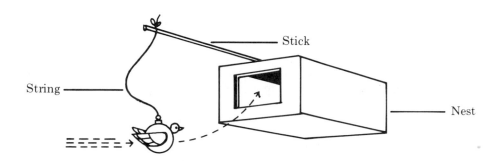

**PROCEDURE**    Tie the bird to the stick with string and attach the end of the stick to the box (see illustration). Be sure to make the string on the bird long enough so that it can get through the hole. Have the children blow the bird into its nest.

**COMMENT**    This takes more breath control than power. Start with a short string and lengthen it to make the activity more difficult. *Especially good for* HEARING and SPEECH AND LANGUAGE needs: visually demonstrates breath control. Encourages HEALTH needs to gain more breath control. GIFTED AND TALENTED may enjoy helping to make the project and discovering that the bird will arc like a swing and that the farther out the bird, the longer the string has to be.

# CONTOUR MAPS

**GOAL**    To improve cause and effect reasoning
To improve spatial concepts

**OBJECTIVE**    The child will match the contours of the classroom or playground area to the map.

**MATERIALS**    papier-mâché        water
cardboard        a container
crayons

**PROCEDURE**    Have the children choose an area of the classroom (e.g., blocks, dramatic play) or playground and draw it on cardboard with crayons. Discuss with the children what in their drawing stands up from the surface (tables, swings, and so on). Have the children use the papier-mâché to make their drawing reflect these contours. As children learn more about the mathematical concept of relative size, do the activity again, this time measuring the space and dividing the cardboard into quarters for placement of objects.

**COMMENT**    Especially good for VISUAL needs: If these maps are done accurately, they are a useful way for children to explore the environment by comparing the model to reality. As LEARNING needs often have problems with spatial orientation, this can increase their knowledge of their surroundings. GIFTED AND TALENTED can profit from the measuring aspect of the project.

# CORNSTARCH PLAYDOUGH

**GOAL**    To improve cause and effect reasoning
To stimulate curiosity

**OBJECTIVE**    The child will explore the properties of cornstarch in its various states.

**MATERIALS**    water        tea leaves
cornstarch    food colors
beet juice

**PROCEDURE**    Have the children help mix a box of cornstarch with a little water to make a play-dough. You can leave it white or tint it. You might try some natural dyes like beet juice or tea leaves. Help the children talk about the process and the different states of the playdough. Give them the vocabulary they need to do this. Allow children to add too much as well as too little water to see what happens.

**COMMENT**    Unless children are allergic to corn, the playdough is edible. *Especially good for* HEALTH needs: Playdough can easily be made in bed on a tray. VISUAL and HEARING needs can explore the properties of this very strange playdough through their available senses. Good for PHYSICAL and INTELLECTUAL needs, as the playdough requires little strength or coordination to manipulate. ADJUSTMENT needs may find a soothing, yet intriguing medium.

# POPCORN

**GOAL**    To improve cause and effect reasoning
To improve sensory integration

**OBJECTIVE**    The child will discuss how popcorn changes states.

**MATERIALS**    popcorn        salt
popcorn popper    bowl
butter

**PROCEDURE**    Make popcorn in a forced-air popper or one with a plastic lid so that the children can see the corn pop. Talk about the different senses used.

hear: pop
see: kernel to fluffy popcorn
taste: popcorn
smell: while it pops
feel: kernel and popped corn

Discuss the role of heat in this change. Try the popcorn with and without salt and butter. Show how the butter, too, changes states when heated.

**COMMENT**    Be careful to avoid accidents when popping corn with children. The popper gets very hot. It is also easy for children to choke on a piece of popcorn. Learn the Heimlich maneuver—all teachers should know it. *Especially good for* VISUAL, HEARING, and LEARNING needs: The children use all their senses. They can see and feel the corn before and after it is popped, smell it while it is popping, listen for the pops, and eat the popped corn. SPEECH AND LANGUAGE needs can listen for the first and last pop and, with CULTURALLY DISTINCT, can learn the vocabulary associated with the change of state.

# MIXING COLORED WATER

**GOAL**   To improve cause and effect reasoning
To make predictions
To increase problem-solving skills

**OBJECTIVE**   The child will be able to mix the water and food coloring and predict what color will be made.

**MATERIALS**   water                                    measuring cups
clear plastic glasses or                 spoons
  clear trays with separate sections     food coloring
eye dropper

**PROCEDURE**   Mix food coloring and water in clear glasses or trays. Emphasize vocabulary about specific colors as well as the relationship between the intensity of colors and the amount of food coloring used. Have children predict what will happen before they do any mixing. Encourage them to count the number of drops they use of each color. With help, they can learn to chart this.

**COMMENT**   *Especially good for* GIFTED AND TALENTED: allows them to consider reasons for the change of color. LEARNING, INTELLECTUAL, and PHYSICAL needs learn colors while practicing a fine motor skill.

# PINWHEEL

**GOAL**   To improve cause and effect reasoning
To make predictions
To improve breath control

**OBJECTIVE**   The child will blow hard and softly on the pinwheel and predict how fast the pinwheel will turn.

**MATERIALS**   pinwheels        tape
paper            string (to suspend paper)

**PROCEDURE**   Have children blow pinwheels hard and softly. Then have them blow the pinwheels to make a suspended piece of paper move. Tell them to take away the pinwheels and blow directly on the paper from the same distance. Compare the results.

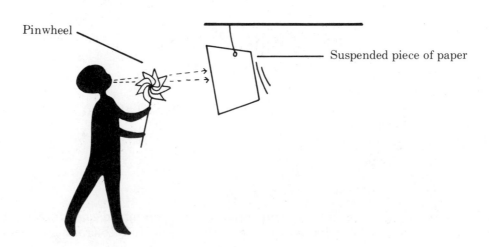

Pinwheel

Suspended piece of paper

Use other methods of moving air, such as a hand-held or electric fan (be sure fingers can't touch the blade) or blowing through a tube or funnel. Be sure to keep the paper as a visual sign, though. Encourage children to predict the differences in movement. See if they can figure out how to make the pinwheels move toward them and away from them and how the shape and size of the paper affects how much it moves.

**COMMENT**    Especially good for HEARING and SPEECH AND LANGUAGE needs: visually demonstrates breath control and the force of the air in blowing. GIFTED AND TALENTED can test predictions about the direction in which the pinwheels will move as well as the movement of air. HEALTH needs can be encouraged to breathe deeply and become more aware of breath control.

# NATURE FEELY BOARD

**GOAL**    To improve cause and effect reasoning
To improve tactile discrimination
To improve tactile memory

**OBJECTIVE**    The child will identify the object by touch.

**MATERIALS**    objects from a nature walk          cardboard
glue

**PROCEDURE**    On a nature walk, help the children pick up objects, such as nuts, sticks, stones, and leaves. When you get back to the class, glue each of the objects onto a separate, small piece of cardboard. Have the children feel the objects while blindfolded and try to remember what they are and where they were found. Discuss with the children why certain things are found in specific places. Classify the objects found (e.g., from trees, green things, and so on).

**COMMENT**    *Especially good for* VISUAL needs: teaches these children to explore the environment without seeing it and then to review what they have learned. Be sure to discuss with these children where things are likely to be found and why: "The leaf was under the tree because it fell from one of the branches" (look up at a branch). This helps HEARING needs not only increase their tactile skills, but also see where things occur naturally, especially if they have missed the verbal references. VISUAL, INTELLECTUAL, and HEALTH needs can help make the feely board. You can make the board more relevant by reminding them of where they found the objects or by drawing pictures for a visual reference. Helps LEARNING needs by integrating the sense of touch with the memory of where the objects were found.

# SCRAMBLED EGGS

**GOAL**    To make predictions
To improve sequencing skills

**OBJECTIVE**    The child will scramble an egg and eat it. He will also put the sample egg, bowl, and scrambled egg in the right order.

**MATERIALS**    1 egg per child          pepper
electric fry pan          cup
water          fork
salt          teaspoon

**PROCEDURE**    Have a group of three or four children make scrambled eggs. At each stage of the procedure, have children predict what will happen. Allow each child to crack his own egg into a cup; stir it; add salt, pepper and 1 teaspoon of water; put it in an electric fry pan; scramble it with a fork; put it on a plate; and then eat it for a snack with the other children in the group. When finished, show them:

> an egg in the shell
> an egg beaten in the dish
> an egg scrambled

Have the children put these different states in the correct sequence and discuss the differences between them and the effect of heat on the egg.

Cook other foods that change properties with heat and discuss the effects. It's always fun to make vegetable soup or applesauce.

**COMMENT** Children who will not otherwise eat eggs will often eat the eggs that they cook. *Especially good for* SPEECH AND LANGUAGE and INTELLECTUAL needs: Give a play-by-play description of what the children are doing while they are doing it. LEARNING needs can get fine motor practice by using half of the broken shell to pick out the yolk and/or beating the egg longer with a fork, eggbeater, or whip to see how the yellow changes color as more air is beaten in. Allow HEARING needs to watch the sequence, or draw that sequence for them, before they begin.

# FOOD SENSE

**GOAL**   To make predictions
To improve tactile discrimination
To improve taste discrimination
To improve discrimination of smells

**OBJECTIVE**   The child will identify different foods by smell, taste, and/or feel.

**MATERIALS**   small pieces of familiar food
paper cups
foil

**PROCEDURE**   Put each variety of food in a separate paper cup, preferably a kind you can't see through.

> Smell: Cover the paper cup with foil that has a few holes in it.
> Touch: This can be done in a variety of ways. Choose the one that works best for you:
> > Ask the children to close their eyes (most will peek) or blindfold them.
> > Hold the cup above their eye level.
> > Have them feel behind a screen.
> Taste: Place a piece of food in the children's mouth or have the children do that—most children want to see before they taste.

Help children describe aloud the qualities of the food they are handling (e.g., "It smells sweet," "feels wet," and so on). Help them guess what the food is without seeing it.

Repeat this activity with fresh fruits and vegetables. Use it as a way of broadening children's food experiences.

**COMMENT**   This can be used as a snack activity for a day. Check if any LEARNING needs children are on the Feingold diet because this may restrict the food you can use. Also, be sure to check for allergies, especially among HEALTH needs. Omit any forbidden foods from the trays. Be sure to talk about foods that the children can have, rather than dwelling on those they cannot. *Especially good for* CULTURALLY DISTINCT: Introduce foods that are familiar only to them as well as foods new to them but familiar to the others. For LEARNING needs, sensory integration is valuable in learning about new foods. VISUAL needs profit from a more structured approach of smelling, touching, and tasting various foods. You might have the whole food available to touch. For HEARING and SPEECH AND LANGUAGE needs who are uncomfortable speaking, or INTELLECTUAL needs who lack the necessary vocabulary and also need to learn to make the part/whole association, have a tray with an example of each of the foods in the cups, for example, a whole pineapple, a whole orange, and an uncut apple. This way the children can touch and also point to the food even if they cannot label it.

# TEXTURE CLASSIFICATION

**GOAL**  To improve classification skills
To improve tactile discrimination

**OBJECTIVE**  The child will be able to sort objects into the categories of hard, soft, smooth, and rough.

**MATERIALS**  four shoe boxes
a set of objects with different textures: hard, soft, smooth, and rough (at least 3 items of each texture). Examples:

| HARD | SOFT | ROUGH | SMOOTH |
|------|------|-------|--------|
| wood | foam rubber | sandpaper | satin |
| metal | piece of blanket | burlap | plastic pen |
| rock | yarn | brush | glossy paper |

**PROCEDURE**  Have the children sort the objects into the shoe boxes. When they can do this accurately, have them do it blindfolded. Then have them label things in the classroom that are hard, soft, rough, smooth, and so on.

**COMMENT**  Use two categories first; when these have been mastered, use all four. The best blindfolds are half-face Halloween masks that have the eyes covered. These stay on and don't seem to scare the children. *Especially good for* VISUAL needs; refines both tactile discrimination and classification skills. Initially, for HEARING, INTELLECTUAL, and LEARNING needs, use only two categories; first, state the names of the objects and have the children repeat them, then categorize the objects as hard, soft, rough, or smooth. Add more objects (cotton balls, velour fabric, sponge, hard plastic, and so on) to aid generalization. Once the idea of classification has been understood, add more classes of texture and more subtle differences.

# WIGGLY WORMS

**GOAL**  To improve classification skills
To improve discrimination of smells

**OBJECTIVE**  The child will sort the worms by smell.

**MATERIALS**  rubber fishing worms (available as bait at sporting goods stores; get different colors and different fruit smells, such as cherry and blueberry.)
a large box
a shoe box for each color worm

**PROCEDURE**  Put a variety of rubber fishing worms in a large box. First, allow the children to sort them by both color and smell. As they gain skill, blindfold the children and have them sort the worms by smell only. When they take off the blindfold, they can check the colors.

**COMMENT**    This is also an interesting tactile experience. *Especially good for* VISUAL needs: combines rather subtle smelling with touch. These children usually need to use olfactory cues to determine where they are and to help identify many things in their environment. LEARNING and HEARING needs can improve sensory integration by using their senses of smell and vision with the tactile experience.

# FOOD LOTTO

**GOAL**    To improve classification skills
To improve visual discrimination
To improve visual association

**OBJECTIVE**    The child will match the sets of pictures correctly.

**MATERIALS**    A lotto game with 3 sets of pictures of fruit:
1. 2 identical pictures of each fruit
2. a picture of a whole fruit to be matched with a picture of the same fruit cut in half
3. a picture of a whole fruit to be matched with a picture of the same fruit in a different state (e.g., apple/applesauce; orange/orange juice; and cherries/cherry pie)

**PROCEDURE**    Start with a traditional lotto game in which children match the identical pictures of fruit. Then have the children match the second set and finally the third set. The same idea can be used with vegetables. Show the fruits as they grow (e.g., orange tree, grape arbor).

**COMMENT**    You can draw the pictures yourself or find a parent or friend to do it. Otherwise, you or the children can cut them out of magazines. While all children may have trouble recognizing the source of unfamiliar foods, this activity is *especially good for* HEARING needs, who have difficulty grasping verbal generalizations, and CULTURALLY DISTINCT who might be encountering many new foods and food sources. For INTELLECTUAL needs, actually make applesauce and orange juice before using the lotto.

# NUTTY SORT

**GOAL**    To improve classification skills
To improve visual discrimination
To improve small motor coordination

**OBJECTIVE**    The child will sort the nuts by type.

**MATERIALS**    a variety of nuts in their shells        nut crackers
(walnuts, peanuts, pistachios, and so on)        nut picks
a large bowl

**PROCEDURE**    Put the nuts in a large bowl. Have the children sort them into piles of similar nuts. Label these, both verbally and in writing. Crack the nuts and have them at snack time.
*Note*: Be sure none of the children is allergic to nuts!

**COMMENT**    Especially good for CULTURALLY DISTINCT: may give them a chance to try a new food. PHYSICAL and INTELLECTUAL needs can develop fine motor skills and finger strength while cracking and shelling the nuts.

# TASTE SORT

**GOAL**    To improve classification skills
To improve taste discrimination
To increase knowledge of foods

**OBJECTIVE**    The child will taste the food and classify it correctly.

**MATERIALS**    foods with distinct textures          plates
(soft, crunchy, juicy and chewy)    eating utensils

**PROCEDURE**    Give the children a variety of small pieces of food. Have them chew the samples and then sort the foods according to texture. You can expand the activity by providing whole foods for the children to sort after tasting the samples or by adding a new set of categories, such as taste (sweet, salty, sour and bitter).

**COMMENT**    Use this activity in place of a snack, it gives an opportunity to introduce a variety of different food tastes. *Especially good for* CULTURALLY DISTINCT: introduces new foods and teaches categorizing of food into groups different from the traditional groups of fruit, vegetable, and so on. For LEARNING needs, it improves classification skills and sensory integration while providing the built-in reward of the food. Encourage parents of HEALTH needs to do this activity at home and have children sort the food into what they can and cannot have. GIFTED AND TALENTED may be able to sort the food into the four basic food groups and, within those groups, into crunchy, juicy, sweet, salty, and so on. They may then discover that some groups are more alike than others. You can help them discover how the texture of food changes with its state: An apple is crunchy, but applesauce is soft.

# LOOK CLOSER

**GOAL**    To improve classification skills
To stimulate curiosity
To improve visual identification

**OBJECTIVE**    The child will state something about an object that is not noticeable to the naked eye.

**MATERIALS**    magnifying glass
objects with appearances that change when magnified:
fabric in which you can see the weave
a painted picture that shows the brush strokes
tissues
a grain of oatmeal

**PROCEDURE**    Arrange the objects on a table and have the children look at them under a magnifying glass. When the children learn what to look for, have them explore the room and themselves (their hair, pores, clothes) with the magnifying glass and then group their findings.

**COMMENT**    *Especially good for* VISUAL needs: A good way to use residual sight; teaches the idea of magnification: If something is too small to be seen, there are ways to make it bigger. HEARING needs can fine-tune the visual discrimination skills so vital to speech reading.

# *Mathematics*

# INDEX

Mathematics is more than counting or computing. Math skills include grouping or classifying objects; understanding relative relationships of size, shape, and order; measuring; problem solving; and estimating. All children need math concepts to function in today's world.

## MATHEMATICS GOALS

- To improve number concepts. All children must learn to count, match numbers, and understand that numbers stand for quantities.
- To improve shape concepts. Recognizing shapes is both a part of math and a prereading visual discrimination skill.
- To improve size concepts. Understanding relative size and the vocabulary that goes with it is a necessary math skill.
- To improve measurement concepts. Start by measuring the children themselves. Then measure distances and quantities, as in cooking.

## TEACHING STRATEGIES

For children with SPEECH AND LANGUAGE needs, in addition to working with and naming numbers and shapes, emphasize the vocabulary that goes with the firsthand experiences of learning math: taller, shorter, more, less, equal, the same, one more, one less.

Children with HEARING needs, who may not easily understand words, need many examples of math concepts with which to associate the words. They need to use numbers, identify likenesses and differences, and group and classify objects using visual and tactile skills to reinforce the auditory.

Children with VISUAL needs must learn math concepts with three-dimensional objects before they can be expected to generalize these concepts to two-dimensional ones. Use natural situations and real objects: two crackers, ten raisins. Use pegs to count. Help children feel round balls and square boxes. Then, perhaps, use sandpaper outlines of circles and squares. Help children pace off and count distances to and from various places in the room: five steps from the locker to the circle area compared with ten steps from the locker to the blocks. Help make math both real and useful to these children.

For children with LEARNING needs, teach math skills through as many senses as possible. Give the children two cookies: They can count them, see them, hear you say there are two, and then consume them—one at a time! Using real materials and situations, help children develop a sensorimotor awareness of math on which later to build abstract concepts.

Children with ADJUSTMENT needs may feel comfortable with math because it requires little social interaction. Math skills can be used to help these children feel like part of the group. Incorporate math skills into turn-taking, sharing, and discussions about likenesses and differences.

Because the tendency to overprotect children with HEALTH needs may have deprived them of valuable experiences, these children must develop an experiential basis for math skills. Don't start with rote memorization; have the children learn by using various materials. When they take medication, have them count the number of pills they take (they should know this for safety) and the sips of water. Make math real and relevant for these children.

Children with PHYSICAL needs must learn math concepts that relate to size, distance, and speed. It is important for these children to be able to estimate distances and especially the time it takes to travel a given distance. Size concepts help them understand where they will and won't fit; they also learn that like other children, they are growing.

Children with INTELLECTUAL needs must have a strong sensorimotor foundation on which to build math skills. Use real objects that can be touched and manipulated. Count with pegs or an abacus, but also count boys, girls, chairs, tables, and blocks before you count dots.

CULTURALLY DISTINCT children need math skills like all others; perhaps they could teach the other children to count in a different language.

For GIFTED AND TALENTED children at this age, math holds great potential for learning that is not limited by the inability to read. Help children establish basic number concepts; then expand these to include language skills, for example, two, a pair, a duo, a duet. Help them count and classify objects in a variety of different ways. Teach measuring and estimating skills. Be sure to help boys and girls equally, since too often stereotyping discourages girls from developing strong math skills.

# ABACUS

**GOAL**    To improve number concepts

**OBJECTIVE**    The child will move the designated number of beads.

**MATERIALS**    a large abacus (or rods with nuts on them, suspended from a frame)
several small abacuses for individual work

**PROCEDURE**    Ask the children to count the beads, as well as move specific numbers of beads.

**COMMENT**    *Especially good for* HEARING, INTELLECTUAL, and LEARNING needs: The children must physically move the beads, and they can visually check their work. VISUAL needs get tactile feedback by actually moving the beads and checking their count. GIFTED AND TALENTED can use the abacus to progress to higher-level math skills if they are ready.

# MATCHING DOTS

**GOAL**    To improve number concepts

**OBJECTIVE**    The child will match the dot card to the corresponding number card.

**MATERIALS**   cards numbered 1 through 10
cards with up to 10 dots

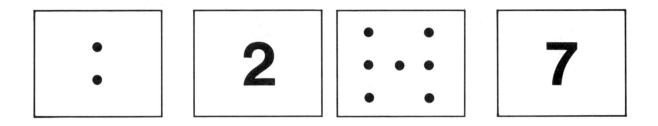

**PROCEDURE**   Have the children match the cards.

**CONTINUATION**   Add cards that have other shapes or pictures on them (small animal stickers, for example) to help the children learn that the number doesn't change with the shapes or their placement on the page.

**COMMENT**   Children can do these activities on their own or with an aide; they require no verbalization. Do, however, emphasize the language concept "equals." *Especially good for* HEARING and LEARNING needs: utilizes visual cues to teach number concepts. For VISUAL needs, use sandpaper numbers and buttons or shapes. Use shapes other than dots because dots may be confused with the braille configurations for numbers.

## COUNTING CHERRIES

**GOAL**   To improve number concepts
To improve self-help skills

**OBJECTIVE**   The child will button the designated number of cherries.

**MATERIALS**   a felt cherry tree        glue
red buttons            scissors

**PROCEDURE**   Sew 10 red buttons on a piece of green felt that has been cut to look like a tree. Sew or glue a second piece of felt over the first and cut slits where the buttons are. Ask children to make a cherry tree with six cherries (i.e., button six buttons) and so on. (See page 414.)

**COMMENT**   This activity not only gives help in counting but promotes the self-help skill of buttoning. *Especially good for* LEARNING, INTELLECTUAL, VISUAL, and PHYSICAL needs: gives practice in motor coordination as well as number concepts.

1st piece

2nd piece
(now on top of first piece)

# CUISENAIRE RODS

**GOAL**    To improve number concepts
To improve eye–hand coordination

**OBJECTIVE**    The child will arrange the rods in ascending order by size.

**MATERIALS**    A set of cuisenaire rods (drinking straws that vary by ½ inch in length)

**PROCEDURE**    Cuisenaire rods are useful for teaching a variety of math skills. They can be counted, sorted by color or length, arranged in a sequence, or even used to build designs. Try taking a piece out of a sequence to see if the children can put it back.

**CONTINUATION**    Using the rods as models, draw designs on sheets of paper and see if the children can fill in the designs.

**COMMENT**    The cuisenaire rods are small. I would not use them with 2- and 3-year-old children or any children who might swallow them (especially children with INTELLECTUAL or ADJUSTMENT needs). The principle is sound, however. A 1-inch rod is difficult to swallow and easy to make by cutting dowels into sections. *Especially good for* HEARING and LEARNING needs and GIFTED AND TALENTED: The rods provide visual number cues, require manipulation, and have potential for teaching higher-level math skills.

# NUMBER TAPPING

**GOAL**    To improve number concepts
To improve auditory memory

**OBJECTIVE**    The child will state the number of taps made.

**MATERIALS**    piano          drum
table          tambourine

**PROCEDURE**    Have a child tap a number or tap it yourself. Have the class state the number or hold up the right number of fingers, or call on one child to answer.

**COMMENT**    For interest, as well as to meet the needs of the children in your class, clap your hands or tap on different objects, such as the piano, a knee, a table, a drum, a tambourine, and so on. *Especially good for* VISUAL and LEARNING needs: requires integration of auditory, tactile, and verbal skills to learn number concepts. For HEARING needs, tap dramatically so that the children can use visual as well as auditory clues.

# PEOPLE PICTURES

**GOAL**    To improve number concepts
To improve classification skills

**OBJECTIVE**    The child will arrange (sort) the pictures in a way designated by the teacher.

**MATERIALS**    Pictures of people of various ages and both sexes:

| | |
|---|---|
| infant | 22-year-old |
| toddler | 40-year-old |
| 7-year-old | 60-year-old |
| 15-year-old | |

**PROCEDURE**    Ask the children (1) to arrange the pictures in order by age; (2) to pick out the oldest and the youngest; (3) to count the number of boys, of girls, and the total number of people; and (4) to guess what kinds of things each person might like to do.

**COMMENT**    Children often confuse size and age. (I once supervised a very tall student teacher in kindergarten, who introduced me to the class as her teacher. Several children promptly told me that wasn't possible because I wasn't big enough!) *Especially good for* CULTURALLY DISTINCT and INTELLECTUAL needs: This is a way of helping children gain a perspective on age as well as size concepts; they learn that age and size don't always go together.

# SPACY DOTS

**GOAL**    To improve number concepts
To improve spatial concepts

**OBJECTIVE**    The child will group together cards that are numerically equal to the card given to him by the teacher.

**MATERIALS**    A set of 3 cards for each number between 2 and 10. Each card of a set should have an equal number of dots, with different dots arranged in a different pattern on each card.

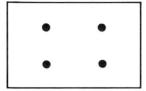  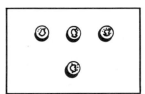

**PROCEDURE**    Have the children match cards with equal numbers of dots.

**CONTINUATION**    Have the children tell you where the markings are on the card (e.g., center, right-hand side, top half).

**COMMENT**    *Especially good for* LEARNING needs: Spatial configuration sometimes distracts the child from the concept of numbers. A good activity for HEARING needs because it requires almost no verbal communication. This is not a good way to teach INTELLECTUAL needs, but once these children have mastered a number concept, this is a good way for them to learn the generalization. For VISUAL needs, use sandpaper shapes rather than dots, or tape pennies to the cardboard.

# TIME CARDS

**GOAL**   To improve number concepts
To improve time concepts

**OBJECTIVE**   The child will match cards with the clock face.

**MATERIALS**   cards with times written on them
a set of cards with corresponding times shown on a clock face

**PROCEDURE**   Have the children match the number cards with the clock-face cards. Start with the easier times and gradually move to the more difficult ones.

**CONTINUATION**   After several children have learned to tell time, you can make a lotto game using this idea.

**COMMENT**   This is a rather difficult abstract concept. It will be too advanced for most 3-year-olds. *Especially good for* GIFTED AND TALENTED: They may be interested in learning how to tell time, as will HEALTH needs, who are often concerned about the passage of time and when things will happen.

# HIDDEN OBJECTS

**GOAL**   To improve number concepts
To improve visual memory

**OBJECTIVE**   The child will find the correct quantity of the designated object.

**MATERIALS**   familiar objects
pictures of the same familiar objects on numbered cards

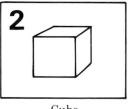   

Cube          Leaf          Rubber band          Key

**PROCEDURE**   Hide a variety of familiar objects. Give each child one of the cards and have him find the correct number of objects.

**CONTINUATION**   Just show the children the cards—they then must remember both the object and how many to find.

**COMMENT**   Encourage children to help each other and double-check the numbers. If you have a large number of children, have them work in pairs. *Especially good for* SPEECH AND LANGUAGE, LEARNING, and HEARING needs: requires the children to translate visual cues into action, but does not require speech. For VISUAL and INTELLECTUAL needs, glue an actual object on the card and use sandpaper numbers, or use the actual number of pictures to correspond to the number requested.

# PEG DESIGN

**GOAL**    To improve number concepts
To improve visual discrimination
To improve eye–hand coordination

**OBJECTIVE**    The child will reproduce the design.

**MATERIALS**    pegboards
pegs

**PROCEDURE**    Make a design on a pegboard, geared to the ability of the children who will reproduce it. Quiz the children as they reproduce the design and encourage them to count the spaces and the number of pegs.

**CONTINUATION**    Add pegs, colors, and more complex designs as the children become more competent.

**COMMENT**    This can be an easy or a very difficult activity. *Especially good for* LEARNING, INTELLECTUAL, and HEARING needs: uses objects to teach number concepts and requires practice in small motor skills at the same time.

# CARPET SHAPES

**GOAL**    To improve shape concepts

**OBJECTIVE**    The child will sit on the designated shape.

**MATERIALS**    Carpet scraps

**PROCEDURE**    Cut out large shapes from carpet remnants or samples (indoor-outdoor carpet works well, as it does not unravel). Have the children sit on these shapes during group time. Once a general pattern has been established, you can instruct the children to find a specific shape and sit on it.

**COMMENT**    When you want the children to sit in a circle, use the shapes as a spacing technique. Tape a circle on the floor or rug and have the children put their shapes on the tape. If there are children you don't want to sit together, arrange the shapes on the tape and then tell Ruben to sit on the triangle and Cathy on the rectangle. *Especially good for* INTELLECTUAL needs: uses a routine to teach a necessary skill. Helps LEARNING and ADJUSTMENT needs learn self-control skills, while teaching shapes.

# POCKETS

**GOAL**    To improve shape concepts
To improve eye–hand coordination

**OBJECTIVE**    The child will put the matching shape in each pocket.

**MATERIALS**    a board                       tagboard shapes to match the pockets
different-shaped felt pockets

**PROCEDURE**   Staple felt pockets onto the board. Make smaller tagboard shapes that will fit in these pockets. Have the children put the shapes in the appropriate pockets.

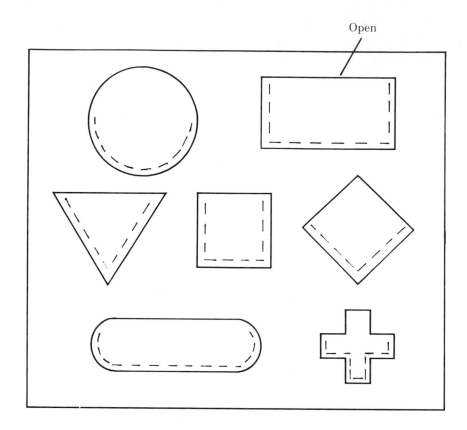

**CONTINUATION**   Blindfold children who find this easy so that they must feel both the shapes of the pockets and the tagboard shapes.

**COMMENT**   *Especially good for* INTELLECTUAL, VISUAL, PHYSICAL, and LEARNING needs: They must use visual and tactile cues to complete the activity and practice motor coordination to get the shapes in the pockets.

# SANDWICH TRICKS

**GOAL**   To improve shape concepts
To follow directions

**OBJECTIVE**   The child will eat the designated shape.

**MATERIALS**   Sandwiches

**PROCEDURE**   Cut sandwiches into geometric shapes. Give each child a separate piece of a whole sandwich. Have the children put the sandwiches back together as if they were puzzles, and then direct them to eat the pieces shape by shape (square, triangle, large rectangle, and so on).

**COMMENT**   Make the filling a sticky one, such as peanut butter, so that the bread stays together (jelly and honey are pretty messy). *Especially good for* INTELLECTUAL needs: requires little fine motor manipulation and has a built-in reward system. VISUAL needs can feel the sides of sandwiches to determine the shape; be sure to give them plenty of time.

# SHAPE PICTURES

**GOAL**　To improve shape concepts
　　　　To improve color concepts

**OBJECTIVE**　The child will connect the designated shapes using a crayon or marker.

**MATERIALS**　A ditto containing several arrangements of various types of small shapes (triangles, circles, squares). Within each arrangement, all the shapes of one type, when connected, should form a letter or shape.

**PROCEDURE**　Have the children connect the shapes with a crayon and then name the design.

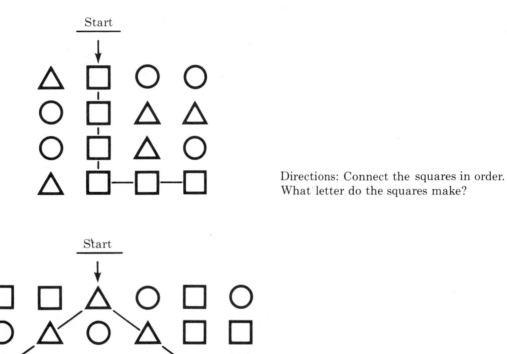

Directions: Connect the squares in order. What letter do the squares make?

Directions: Connect the triangles so that they make a triangle.

**CONTINUATION**　This can also be done with colors (connect all the red circles). Be sure to have the children count the shapes and colors when they are finished.

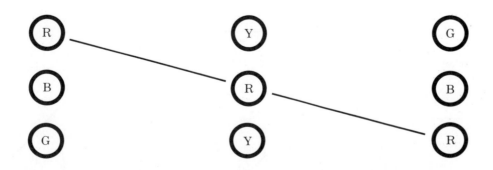

**COMMENT**　*Especially good for* GIFTED AND TALENTED: can require some higher-level cognitive skills while giving practice in fine motor coordination. For INTELLECTUAL and PHYSICAL needs (if they have fine motor difficulties), use few shapes on the page. This is an easy activity to send home to children who are absent from school, especially those with HEALTH needs.

# AREAS

**GOAL**   To improve shape concepts
To improve size concepts
To improve measurement concepts

**OBJECTIVE**   The child will cover the given shape with building pieces.

**MATERIALS**   building pieces made of white poster board
shapes made of red poster board

**SAMPLE PIECES:**

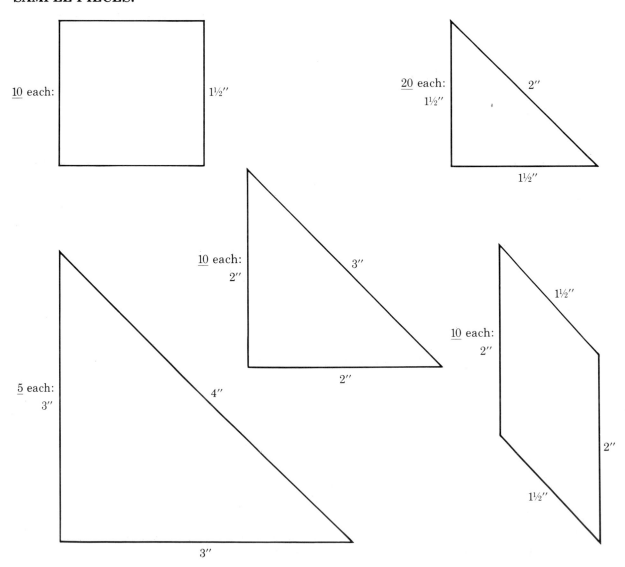

**SAMPLE SHAPES:**

**PROCEDURE**    Using a combination of building pieces, outline a variety of shapes on the red poster board and cut them out. Then have the children cover a shape with the building pieces. Encourage them to find a number of different ways to cover the same shape. Have them measure the area according to the number of pieces they have used to cover it.

**COMMENT**   This activity can be used at several different levels by varying the complexity of the shapes and the challenges you pose. *Especially good for* children with INTELLECTUAL needs: Use simple shapes and use the materials as a puzzle. For VISUAL and PHYSICAL needs, glue sandpaper to the shapes and use a felt board. This makes the building pieces less slippery and gives more tactile feedback. For GIFTED AND TALENTED, use this to teach measuring and have the children see how many different ways they can use the pieces to cover the shapes.


# TOUCH SHAPES

**GOAL**   To improve shape concepts
To improve tactile discrimination

**OBJECTIVE**   The child will identify the shapes by touch.

**MATERIALS**   shapes cut out of materials with pronounced tactile qualities (felt, sandpaper, and so on)
cardboard
glue

**PROCEDURE**   Glue the shapes on cardboard and see if the children can identify them. When they can do this by sight, blindfold them and see if they can do it by touch.

**CONTINUATION**   Give the children 3 different cards (2 of which are the same shape) and see if they can figure out, using only touch, which one doesn't belong. They may need a further clue. "Which one is a different shape?" This becomes more difficult when items that are the same shape differ in texture, and the children have to realize that the texture clue is misleading.

**COMMENT**   *Especially good for* VISUAL and HEARING needs: teaches children to use tactile skills in reasoning.


# INSIDE OUT

**GOAL**   To improve shape concepts
To improve size concepts
To improve visual discrimination

**OBJECTIVE**   The child will name the large and small shapes and put them together.

**MATERIALS**   Large tagboard geometric shapes with smaller shapes cut out of them (old wallpaper sample books also work).

**PROCEDURE**   Have the children find the small shape that fits inside the large one.

**COMMENT**   *Especially good for* INTELLECTUAL and LEARNING needs: increases awareness of relative position, size, and shape and improves motor coordination.


# LITTLE SHADOWS

**GOAL**   To improve shape concepts
To increase body awareness
To improve eye–hand coordination

**OBJECTIVE**     The child will duplicate with his hands the shape made.

**MATERIALS**     Slide projector or strong light

**PROCEDURE**     Using your hands and arms in front of the light, make shapes (circles, squares, triangles) that make shadows on the wall. Have the children duplicate the shapes with their hands while naming the shapes.

**CONTINUATION**     Make animal shapes with your hands and have the children guess what animal it might be. Then have them make up their own animal shapes.

**COMMENT**     *Especially good for* LEARNING needs: uses an unusual medium to teach shapes; the children can respond verbally as well as through their own movements. GIFTED AND TALENTED will benefit from the fine motor practice while being creative by making up animals.


# PEOPLE SHAPES

**GOAL**     To improve shape concepts
          To improve size concepts
          To cooperate with peers

**OBJECTIVE**     The child will be able to form a shape with the bodies of his classmates.

**MATERIALS**     Pictures of shapes

**PROCEDURE**     Discuss shapes. Hold up a picture of a shape and pick one child as "shaper." Have him choose the children he needs to make the shape and have them lie on the floor in that shape.

  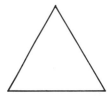

**CONTINUATION**     Have the child change the shape by adding or removing children. If you don't have the space for this activity, the children can use wooden clothespins to build shapes.

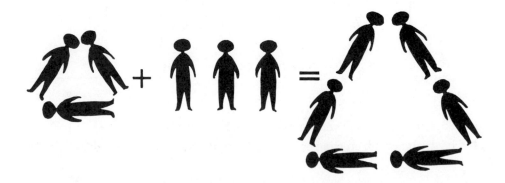

**COMMENT**     *Especially good for* HEARING and LEARNING needs: uses both tactile and visual cues to teach shapes and sizes. Benefits GIFTED AND TALENTED because it requires planning and abstract reasoning.

# PICTURE SHAPES

**GOAL**   To improve shape concepts
To improve visual comprehension
To improve classification skills

**OBJECTIVE**   The child will sort the pictures according to shape.

**MATERIALS**   Pictures mounted on cards of common objects (record, house, ice-cream cone), with definite shapes

**PROCEDURE**   Have the children sort the pictures according to shape.

**CONTINUATION**   As they become more proficient, have them find a particular shape in a picture containing several shapes. Initially, help the children see the shapes by showing them the various shapes and asking them to find a given shape within the picture. The children can also make a shape collage.

**COMMENT**   *Especially good for* HEARING and LEARNING needs: requires visual generalization and application of knowledge of shapes to pictures of real objects. With GIFTED AND TALENTED, use more difficult pictures that require some searching to find an unusually placed or inconspicuous shape.

# WHAT DOESN'T BELONG?

**GOAL**   To improve shape concepts
To improve classification skills
To improve visual association

**OBJECTIVE**   The child will identify the object that doesn't belong.

**MATERIALS**   Three objects or pictures that go together for some reason, and a fourth that doesn't.

**PROCEDURE**   Have the children pick out the object or picture that doesn't belong. Encourage them to talk about how they arrived at their decision. For example:

The circle doesn't belong; the other shapes are all made up of straight lines.

**CONTINUATION**   If the children can read, have them pick the word that doesn't belong among 4 words:

| | | | |
|---|---|---|---|
| cat | dark red | shirt | table |
| dog | light red | *pants* | chair |
| *canary* | *yellow* | sweater | sofa |
| bear | pink | jacket | *scissors* |

These distinctions can be made quite challenging.

a      f      G      t

(G is a capital letter.)

**COMMENT**   *Especially good for* LEARNING and HEARING needs: teaches both visual discrimination and classification. For VISUAL needs, use three-dimensional objects or felt letters and shapes.

# ROOM SHAPES

**GOAL**   To improve shape concepts
          To improve size concepts
          To improve classification skills
          To increase vocabulary

**OBJECTIVE**   The child will find objects in the room that are the designated shape.

**MATERIALS**   None

**PROCEDURE**   This is probably most fun as a thinking game.

> TEACHER: I'm thinking of something in this room that is square.
> CHILDREN: The record player.
> TEACHER: No, the record player is square, but that is not what I'm thinking of. The square I'm thinking of is red.

The process continues as the children make more guesses.

**CONTINUATION**   When children can classify objects in the room by two-dimensional shapes, introduce three-dimensional shapes and their names (for example: square, cube; triangle, pyramid; circle, sphere).

**COMMENT**   At first, accept anything that is the right shape and ask the children to find more things of that shape. *Especially good for* GIFTED AND TALENTED: can require fairly high-level problem solving. Helps LEARNING needs learn to translate auditory information into a visual representation. Can be used to make any room familiar to HEALTH needs (doctor's office, hospital, and so on) as the children realize these rooms have common objects. For HEARING needs, as you name a shape, hold up a card with that shape or draw it on the chalkboard, so the children are sure to be looking for the right shape.

# OBJECT SIZES

**GOAL**   To improve size concepts

**OBJECTIVE**   The child will order objects according to size.

**MATERIALS**   at least 3 different sizes of an object: measuring spoons and cups, for example
                a water table or sand table

**PROCEDURE**   Place sets of 3-dimensional objects on the water table or sand area. Ask the children to point to or give you the objects in order of size. Help children explore the relative sizes of objects through pouring and measuring. Give them examples for comparisons: "It takes 4 of the smallest cup to fill the big one." Arrange the objects in order of size (measuring cups are easy), and give the children another set to match to the first. When this has been mastered, add a slightly different set to be matched. (Measuring spoons will do in this case.) Have the children arrange the sets from the largest to the smallest. Then stagger the arrangement so that it looks something like this:

½ cup          ¼ cup          1 cup          ⅓ cup

1 teaspoon     ¼ teaspoon     1 tablespoon   ½ teaspoon

See if the children can remember the relative sizes by having them place the objects in the proper order again.

**CONTINUATION**   Have the children measure cornmeal, beans, or other materials. Once children understand the relative size concept, give them some containers that are deceptive (a tall thin container that holds the same amount as a short fat one).

Objects that can be manipulated help children develop beginning math skills. Blocks, for example, can be counted, stacked, or even placed in a row to measure something else.

**COMMENT** *Especially good for* HEARING, SPEECH AND LANGUAGE, LEARNING, and INTELLECTUAL needs: a "hands-on" experience with size that encourages discovery, exploration, and lots of discussion. Encourage GIFTED AND TALENTED to make predictions about relative size and then to check if they were right.

# MATCHING RODS

**GOAL**    To improve size concepts
To improve measurement concepts
To make predictions

**OBJECTIVE**    The child will match the 2 sets of rods.

**MATERIALS**    a piece of cardboard
different lengths of rods, dowels, or drinking straws
glue

**PROCEDURE**    Make an ordered set of rods by gluing rods, dowels, or drinking straws of various lengths to cardboard. Arrange one set of rods by length and another set randomly:

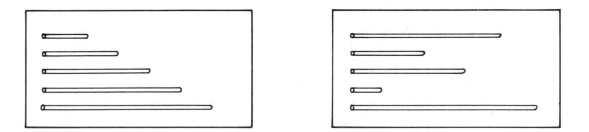

You can then teach size progression and the concepts "same" and "different" and "long" and "short." Have the children match the unattached rods to the ones that are glued down. Be sure to place the rods far enough apart so that the children can put the unattached rods between the ones that are attached.

**CONTINUATION**    After the children match the rods correctly, have them predict which length rod will be matched by each unattached rod and then check out this prediction. Be sure to include language skills ("Yes, that one's the same length" or "No, that one is longer.") Have the children duplicate on the table the pattern of the rods on the board and then check their arrangement with the rods attached to the board.

**COMMENT**    This can be made easier by adding a vertical piece at the left side so that the children can push the pieces up against that end. You can also make use of different colored rods.

*Especially good for* VISUAL, HEARING, LEARNING, and PHYSICAL needs: helps teach sequencing and measurement concepts both visually and tactilely while giving practice in fine motor skills.

# WILL IT FIT?

**GOAL**    To improve size concepts
To increase vocabulary
To increase logical reasoning

**OBJECTIVE**    The child will answer the question correctly.

**MATERIALS**    None

**PROCEDURE**   Use written questions or think up questions about the relative sizes of common objects. Ask the children how these objects would fit together. Have some questions that are easy, some that are silly, and some that are challenging, depending on your children's needs: "Will an elephant fit in a refrigerator?" "Will an orange fit under my chair?" "Can you hold a baby in your hand?" "Can you put a ball in a closet?"

**COMMENT**   The more ridiculous the questions, the better the children like them. Do, however, choose some that can be tested in the classroom. *Especially good for* SPEECH AND LANGUAGE and LEARNING needs: requires the children to use language and process knowledge in an enjoyable, non-threatening way. For GIFTED AND TALENTED and CULTURALLY DISTINCT, use the size to expand vocabulary subtly while increasing logical reasoning skills.

# TOPLESS POPCORN

**GOAL**   To improve measurement concepts

**OBJECTIVE**   The child will measure the distance from the popcorn popper to the designated piece of popcorn on the sheet.

**MATERIALS**   popcorn popper          double sheet
                popcorn                 measuring tape

**PROCEDURE**   Place a popcorn popper in the middle of a clean sheet; have the children sit around the edge. Make popcorn, leaving off the top of the popper. After the popcorn has popped, move the hot popper away and have the children measure the various distances the popcorn has popped.

**COMMENT**   This is a good rainy day activity. If the actual measurement gets cumbersome with a large group, have each child measure the distance to the kernel closest to him first. You might experiment with various types of measurement (i.e., two hands v. 10 inches v. one block). Don't use feet to measure if you expect to eat the popcorn, and be careful to watch for choking. *Especially good for* HEARING and LEARNING needs: uses all the senses—hear the popcorn pop; see how it pops; smell the popcorn; feel it, both before it pops and after; and then, after measuring, taste it. A good way to teach orientation skills to VISUAL needs: There is the built-in reward of eating the popcorn when the children have found it.

# ARM'S LENGTH

**GOAL**   To improve measurement concepts
          To increase body awareness

**OBJECTIVE**   The child will choose which graph represents longer arms and legs and which represents shorter arms and legs.

**MATERIALS**   paper        pencils
                bar graph    dolls

**PROCEDURE**   Measure each child's arms and legs. Record the measurements on a bar graph large enough to chart the actual lengths. Compare the children with each other and with dolls. Emphasize measurement vocabulary: long, short, feet, inches.

**COMMENT**   There is often a lot of social stigma attached to being short or tall; don't compare heights. Measuring body parts seems to avoid stigmatizing children, yet provides the same match and body awareness experience. *Especially good for* HEARING needs: There are visual representations of the lengths. PHYSICAL needs can participate and be part of the group whether or not the limbs function.

## CEREAL BALLS

**GOAL**  To improve measurement concepts
To improve sensory integration
To cooperate with peers

**OBJECTIVE**  The child will make the recipe.

**MATERIALS**  honey          measuring cups
peanut butter     large bowl
coconut          small bowl
cereal           mixing spoon

**PROCEDURE:**  Write the recipe on large paper:

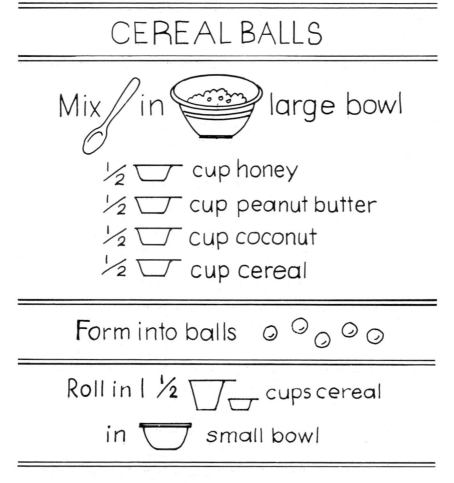

Mix honey, peanut butter, coconut, and ½ cup cereal.
Put remaining cereal into cereal bowl.
Scoop peanut butter mixture out, form into balls,
and roll in cereal. (½ cup dry milk can be added
if children seem to need this.)

Encourage the children to take turns as they work.

**CONTINUATION** Make other recipes.

**COMMENT** Be sure to discuss the concept fully. Use alternative measurements ($2\frac{1}{4}$ cups instead of $\frac{1}{2}$ cup). Talk about foods that are good for you and that taste good. *Especially good for* CULTURAL-LY DISTINCT: If traditional recipes are brought in, the culture can be shared as well as the food. VISUAL, HEARING, and LEARNING needs can profit from participating in the processes. They can see the recipe, see and feel the measuring cups, feel the batter as it's stirred, and then taste the results. Be sure to show the children with VISUAL needs how to feel the containers to see if they are full. Give the children with SPEECH AND LANGUAGE needs a play-by-play description of the process. Note: Be sure to check if any children have allergies, especially to peanut butter.

# MEASURE IT

**GOAL** To improve measurement concepts
To increase logical reasoning
To make predictions

**OBJECTIVE** The child will use at least three different measuring instruments.

**MATERIALS** Objects to measure with (yardsticks, books, and so on)

**PROCEDURE** Ask the children to measure the distance to a specific place, such as the door to go outside. Suggest a variety of methods of measuring:

| | |
|---|---|
| pacing | body lengths |
| foot in front of foot | yardstick |
| hands | books |

As the children get the idea, encourage them to think up new techniques. Chart the various measurements.

**CONTINUATION** As the children improve in this skill, have them estimate relative measurements: "If the door is two body lengths, how many hands will it be?"

**COMMENT** *Especially good for* GIFTED AND TALENTED: stimulates creativity, facilitates problem solving, and explores different ways of measuring. HEALTH and PHYSICAL needs: can make predictions of length in a variety of places and can think of ways they can measure. As these children may get more tired than others, learning to estimate distance relative to their stamina is an important skill. ADJUSTMENT needs may be willing to predict distance and talk about this relative to being part of the group.

# PACE IT OFF

**GOAL** To improve measurement concepts
To improve spatial concepts
To make predictions

**OBJECTIVE** The child will estimate the number of paces it takes to reach the object.

**MATERIALS** Objects in various parts of the room

**PROCEDURE** During group time or with a small group, name objects or areas in the room. Have the children estimate how many paces it will take to get to the designated place. While one child walks, have the others count. Write down the estimate as well as the result. Once some results have been obtained, discuss the relative distances of objects:

> We know the easel is six paces.
> Is the fish tank closer or farther?
> Right, farther.
> Now, is four paces likely to get us there?
> Good, let's see where we are with nine paces.

**CONTINUATION**   This can be done outside, but the numbers will be larger.

**COMMENT**   Have children use a standard pace and not shift to a giant leap or baby step at the end to make the numbers fit. *Especially good for* LEARNING needs: increases spatial awareness while working with number skills. A good way for HEALTH needs to explore a different space in a familiar way. In a doctor's office, the children might estimate the paces to the receptionist's window, the magazines, and so on. GIFTED AND TALENTED can be encouraged to predict the number of paces and then check their prediction.

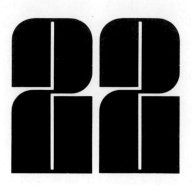

# *Health and Safety*

# INDEX

| Goal | Activity | Page |
|---|---|---|
| To improve identification of smells | Smell Cues | 436 |
| To improve expressive language | Who Are You? | 441 |
| To increase attention span | Red Light/Green Light | 434 |
| To cooperate with adults | Who Are You? | 441 |
| To encourage creative problem solving | What Would You Do If? | 438 |
| To increase body awareness | Symptoms | 439 |

Health and safety are areas of study as well as states of being. When young children become aware of what it means to be healthy and have the knowledge and vocabulary to describe their symptoms, there is less likelihood of serious, undetected illness. When they have learned to recognize signs of danger and act appropriately, the environment will be much less threatening to them. It is important for all children to refine their awareness and skills in both these areas: Only healthy and safe children are free to enter into your program fully.

## HEALTH AND SAFETY GOALS

- To increase survival skills. Health and safety patterns must be conscientiously taught to special needs children. This includes teaching ways of compensating for their needs and being aware of ways to be safe and healthy.
- To improve cause and effect reasoning. For children to learn to make good judgments about what is and is not safe for them to do, they must learn to think through the implications of actions *before* they decide to do something and then evaluate the consequences in terms of whether or not it is a safe thing to do.
- To increase vocabulary. Children must learn a vocabulary to help them better express how they feel, how to respond to questions, and how to ask for and get the information they need if they are lost.

## TEACHING STRATEGIES

Children with SPEECH AND LANGUAGE needs may have to work on the vocabulary that is part of health and safety. At first, understanding is enough (e.g., "Show me what you do when you see a red light"). Next, work on the vocabulary to go with the actions. As children learn more body parts, help them say more than "I don't feel good."

Those with HEARING needs may miss the warning sounds of car horn, fire alarm, and shouting. They need to learn to recognize and respond quickly to visual signals of danger. At an early age, they need to have signs and words that are descriptive of feelings and body parts they can't point to if they cannot tell others how they feel.

Children with VISUAL needs are often more sensitive to auditory signals than to visual ones. They may not see another child riding a tricycle toward them, or the traffic light, or the swing in motion. They need to learn to use both their residual vision and their hearing to compensate. They need to work on labeling body parts and developing a vocabulary to explain how they feel. They need to be able to feel rashes and cuts if they cannot see them (be sure they have clean hands to do this).

Children with LEARNING needs must practice not only seeing but also responding appropriately to safety signals. This is a time when obedience is important and self-control stressed. These children need help working on their health needs. Because their behavior is so variable, they are often unaware of how they feel or are so changeable that they are not taken seriously until their symptoms become obvious to all.

Children with PHYSICAL needs may not move as fast as others and need to refine skills of speed and distance for their own safety. If they have a prosthetic device or braces, they need to be aware of any irritation or pain that develops, or they might have to do without these aids until the irritation clears up. Children who lack sensation in some body parts must learn to deal with conditions they may not feel, such as sunburn, getting wet, and so on.

Children with HEALTH needs often have recurring episodes of sickness. They can help prevent these episodes by learning to recognize their symptoms and/or avoiding situations that are likely to cause them difficulty. This in turn will help them toward independence.

Children with INTELLECTUAL needs have a wide variety of needs and may be less able than others at this age to evaluate situations relative to health and safety. It is your responsibility to evaluate the classroom situation and to see that the environment itself is made safe for them. Start making good health and safety practices part of their routine; for example, wash hands after toileting and before eating, and dress appropriately for the weather (this may mean telling them to take off their coats on a warm afternoon outside).

Children with ADJUSTMENT needs may temporarily forget some health and safety rules and may need reminders. Take care to keep these routines part of the program. Children who are less responsive to the environment need more help in choosing clothing that is appropriate for the weather and in responding to safety cues.

CULTURALLY DISTINCT children may have recently come from another climate and need some acclimation to the new one. If they speak another language, teach them early what the safety signs mean for their behavior, whether or not they can understand or say the appropriate words. Different cultures have different standards for what is acceptable and safe behavior. Be sure to emphasize class rules and enforce them in your classroom. Children can learn to operate under two sets of rules, providing they are consistent.

GIFTED AND TALENTED children tend to be curious about a great many things and, at this age, lack the judgment to determine which exciting things are safe and which are dangerous. They need help in making this distinction. They must learn to develop a pattern of checking with adults before finding out such things as whether or not you can really swallow a penny, and if detergent makes your mouth foam as it does the water in the sink. They also need feedback on how to report their feelings if they are sick and a clear understanding that this is not the time to be creative.

# RED LIGHT/GREEN LIGHT

**GOAL**    To increase survival skills
To improve cause and effect reasoning
To increase attention span

**OBJECTIVE**    The child will stop when red is held up and go when green is held up.

**MATERIALS**    Red and green pieces of paper

Safety rules can be taught at an early age. These children know where the tricycles can be ridden, and a barrier has been set up in case some children forget.

**PROCEDURE**  Adapt the traditional game of red light/green light by having the children walk when you hold up a piece of green construction paper and stop when you hold up a piece of red paper. Once children learn the process, increase the time between changes from red to green, and make some times very short so the children must pay close attention.

**CONTINUATION**  This can be done with any type of motor activity (clapping, hopping, waving, and so on). Outside, you can have someone be traffic director and regulate the tricycles with red and green "lights."

**COMMENT**  This is an important safety concept for the exceptional child to learn early. *Especially good for* HEARING needs: They depend on visual cues to know when to cross streets. INTELLECTUAL needs require more practice than others to learn; use this activity frequently and make the situation as close to the real one as possible. For LEARNING needs, hold up the red paper for what seems like a long time to help them practice waiting for the light to change. For PHYSICAL and HEALTH needs, use the red light to stop the activity for a few moments if the pace seems too fast, or add a piece of yellow paper (caution) to slow things down a bit. For VISUAL needs, start by saying "stop" and "go"; then turn this into a listening game. Blindfold half the children. Instead of looking at colors, these children wait until they hear their classmates move and say "go" before they move, then listen for quiet and the word "stop." This then becomes an auditory discrimination task.

## SEASONAL CLOTHING

**GOAL**    To increase survival skills
To increase vocabulary
To improve cause and effect reasoning

**OBJECTIVE**    The child will state in what season various items of clothing are worn and why.

**MATERIALS**    Articles of clothing or pictures of them

**PROCEDURE**    Have the children sort the clothes or pictures into piles by season. Have fabric swatches to sort also.

| SPRING | SUMMER | FALL | WINTER |
|---|---|---|---|
| long pants | swim suit | long pants | snowsuit |
| sweater | shorts and sleeveless top | jacket | mittens |
| jeans | cotton | kneesocks | boots |
| flannels | eyelet | knit | fur |
| terrycloth | terrycloth | gabardine | wool |
| | | | velvet |

Be sure to agree that some clothes for cool weather can be worn in spring or fall or all seasons. It is the reasoning that matters.

**CONTINUATION**    Add pictures of events to be classified as well.

| SPRING | SUMMER | FALL | WINTER |
|---|---|---|---|
| trees bud | people swim | school starts | animals hibernate |
| birds build nests | people take | leaves change colors | snow falls |
| wind blows | vacations | apples and pumpkins are harvested | trees drop leaves |

**COMMENT**    *Especially good for* CULTURALLY DISTINCT: They need to learn clothing needs and the predictability of seasonal change, especially if they have moved from another climate. For VISUAL and INTELLECTUAL needs, use actual clothing and sort it into boxes. When questions arise, have the child try on the clothing and comment on it as well. ("When you put mittens on, I can't see your hands. Mittens keep your hands warm"). Helps LEARNING and ADJUSTMENT needs learn about themselves in relation to their environment. PHYSICAL and HEALTH needs can learn to use clothing for protection from the elements as well as protection from brush burns from falling.

# SMELL CUES

**GOAL**    To increase survival skills
To improve cause and effect reasoning
To improve identification of smells

**OBJECTIVE**    The child will state what the smell is, what the situation might be, and what he should do after smelling the container.

**MATERIALS**    Small containers, each holding a cotton ball saturated with a familiar-smelling substance (paint, food, perfume, and so on)

**PROCEDURE**    Have the children guess what the smells are, in what situations they would find them, and how they should respond. For example:

> paint, wet paint, don't touch
> food, mealtime, set table
> gasoline, danger, leave
> ammonia, cleaning time, pick up toys
> perfume, going out, say good-bye

A variety of behaviors is possible in all these situations.

**CONTINUATION**   Do this activity several times during the year just to teach the children the process. Tell the children to smell, not taste. Use substances that have familiar smells and are safe to ingest (food works well). Move on to smells of dangerous substances. Be very clear that these are dangerous and not for tasting. Obviously, this needs close supervision.

**COMMENT**   *Especially good for* VISUAL needs: They need as many nonvisual cues as possible about what is going on in their environment. Because of visual associations, these cues are meaningful to us; they aren't necessarily meaningful to the visually impaired child, who may not recognize that a situation is dangerous when others do. GIFTED AND TALENTED are often more curious about their environment than others. They must learn that there are some things they cannot experiment with.

# WARNING SIGNS

**GOAL**   To increase survival skills
To improve cause and effect reasoning
To improve visual discrimination

**OBJECTIVE**   The child will demonstrate appropriate behavior when the sign is held up.

**MATERIALS**   Pictures of familiar warning signs (stop, yield, railroad crossing, one way, traffic lights, and so on)

**PROCEDURE**   Introduce the various warning signs; be sure to include the ones near your school. Discuss with the children what the signs mean and what the children should do when they see them. Have the children demonstrate the correct behavior when you hold up the signs.

**CONTINUATION**   Use these signs outside in the play yard to direct traffic flow. Be sure to change the locations frequently so children really do have to look. Follow this with a walk in the community.

**COMMENT**   *Especially good for* HEARING and LEARNING needs: They need visual stimulation and practice to develop good safety patterns. For SPEECH AND LANGUAGE needs, be sure to add the vocabulary that reminds the children what they are doing.

# WARNING SOUNDS

**GOAL**   To increase survival skills
To improve cause and effect reasoning
To improve auditory identification

**OBJECTIVE**   The child will state what he should do when he hears a specific sound.

**MATERIALS**   A tape recording with warning sounds

**PROCEDURE**   Make a tape recording of various warning sounds a child might hear and have him identify them. Include a broad range of sounds:

| | |
|---|---|
| fire alarm | truck's beep (when backing up) |
| fire siren or whistle | shouts |

| | |
|---|---|
| police siren | bell buoy |
| train whistle | calling a name |
| car horn | fog horn |
| oven timer | "timber" (tree falling) |
| microwave timer | "fore" (golfers) |
| clothes dryer timer | "careful" |
| telephone sound when left off the hook | "watch out" |

When the children can identify these sounds, have them name a sound and tell where they might hear it and what they should do when they hear it.

**COMMENT** *Especially good for* VISUAL needs: They depend on auditory cues for their safety. HEALTH and PHYSICAL needs can use the cues to determine what is happening in the environment, whether or not they can see what is going on.

# WHAT WOULD YOU DO IF?

**GOAL**   To increase survival skills
To improve cause and effect reasoning
To encourage creative problem solving

**OBJECTIVE**   The child will think of at least two solutions to a problem.

**MATERIALS**   None

**PROCEDURE**   Think of a variety of problems a child might encounter and ask the children:

What would you do if
you cut your finger?
you smelled smoke or saw a fire?
you broke a glass?
you got lost?
you fell down and couldn't get up?

The usual response will be to tell an adult. Continue questioning the children ("What if there weren't an adult around?") or, as the children solve the problem, change the situation slightly ("I'd go outside." "What if the doors were locked?") Try to get children to think of as many solutions as possible, because in a true emergency, paths may be blocked. Discuss the implications of various solutions.

**CONTINUATION**   Have the children role play these situations.

**COMMENT** *Especially good for* SPEECH AND LANGUAGE needs: encourages problem solving in a situation where language may make the solution easier. HEARING needs may need to demonstrate how they can solve problems with limited language skills. They will probably need encouragement and guidance to figure this out. It is especially important for them to know what to do when lost, because they will be scared as well. This child may not hear his name being called if he wanders away. PHYSICAL needs must learn to solve problems such as this within their ability to move and act independently. Perhaps GIFTED AND TALENTED children can be asked for solutions last, after some of the easier ones have been done. Try placing restrictions on them, such as not being able to speak or walk, to see how they might help others solve these problems.

# SYMPTOMS

**GOAL**    To increase survival skills
To increase vocabulary
To increase body awareness

**OBJECTIVE**    The child will state what his symptoms are.

**MATERIALS**    None

**PROCEDURE**    Help the child develop the vocabulary to describe his symptoms and to give some information on the degree of the "hurt."

### VOCABULARY

| BODY PARTS | MEDICAL TERMS |
|---|---|
| tummy, stomach | vomit, throw up |
| head | dull pain |
| arms, legs | sharp pain |
| knee, neck | sore |
| | swollen, puffy |
| **DEGREE TERMS** | dizzy |
| a little | cut |
| a lot | blood, bleeding |
| small, little | hot, cold |
| large, big | |

Role play situations in which a child who is "hurt" tells you or another child what's wrong. Decide what to do in the case of various symptoms (dizzy—lie down; cut—wash it; swollen part—put ice on it; and so on).

**COMMENT**    This is useful information to teach a child *before* he becomes ill. *Especially good for* HEALTH and PHYSICAL needs: Be sure to include specific terms these children may use, depending upon their specific needs. For SPEECH AND LANGUAGE needs, emphasize vocabulary. With GIFTED AND TALENTED, help them realize that when one is not role playing, the objective is to be accurate, not creative.

# TRAFFIC SIGN HUNT

**GOAL**    To increase survival skills
To improve auditory memory
To improve visual discrimination

**OBJECTIVE**    The child will correctly verbalize what to do in response to each sign shown.

**MATERIALS**   story
traffic signs

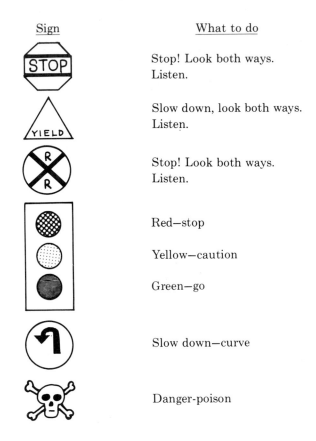

| Sign | What to do |
|---|---|
| STOP | Stop! Look both ways. Listen. |
| YIELD | Slow down, look both ways. Listen. |
| R R (railroad) | Stop! Look both ways. Listen. |
| (traffic light) | Red—stop |
| | Yellow—caution |
| | Green—go |
| (curve) | Slow down—curve |
| (skull and crossbones) | Danger-poison |

**PROCEDURE**   This is an adaptation of the bear hunt. Start "walking" by putting your palms on your thighs in a rhythm.

Anyone want to go on a traffic sign hunt? OK, let's go. Close the gate (close with hand motions). We're coming to a corner. I see a sign (hold up a stop sign). What do you think it is? A stop sign! What do we have to do? (Stop. Hold up palms toward children.) OK, look both ways. (Look.) No cars. Let's cross the street. Hurry. (Increase beat of hand.) You don't wander across streets, but you don't have to run either. Oh, what's this? This is a railroad crossing sign. (Hold up.) See the tracks. Be very careful. Look both ways. Are the gates up or down? Listen, do you hear anything? Are there any lights flashing? OK, let's cross. Look again and let's go. Oh, there really are a lot of signs to look at when you go for a walk. What's this one? (Hold up yield sign.) What shape is that? What should we do? It's a little like a stop sign; we don't have to stop, just slow down (slow rhythm) and look around. If we see anyone, then we have to stop. Look, do you see anything? Hey, I see an elephant. Do we have to stop? Yep. The elephant has the right of way. We have to yield. Go very slowly. OK, he's gone. That was a nice rest. I wonder what other kinds of signs we'll see. Hey, that one has lights. It's green and yellow and red. What is it? (Hold up traffic light.) We have the green; now what do we do? We can go. I am beginning to get tired; how about you? No, well, ah, there is another sign. That's for a curve. Lean left or you'll get off the road. Do you think we're on a mountain? Let's slow down. Oh, what's that sign? (Hold up skull and crossed bones sign.) Danger. Let's get out of here. As fast you can, lean right, hurry back over the curve. Now, oh, there's the light; what color is it? Red. Stop. OK, now it's green; let's go. There's the yield; is there anything coming? (Look.) We're OK, good, keep going. What will it be next? Oh, the railroad. Stop. Look. Listen. Any trains? Let's go. Hurry, oh, there's the stop sign; everybody stop. Look, let's go. Open the gate; shut it. Whee, it's good to be back here in our classroom.

**COMMENT**   Use your imagination and be dramatic. The kids love it, especially when you go fast at the end. *Especially good for* children with HEARING needs as it helps them understand what is going on during trips. ADJUSTMENT needs can participate, yet it is not as demanding as individual questions might be. For LEARNING needs, the activity can be repeated and it uses visual, tactile, and auditory skills. For VISUAL needs, describe the signs and allow the child to touch them. Describe what you might be listening for.

# WHO ARE YOU?

**GOAL**   To increase survival skills
To cooperate with adults
To improve expressive language

**OBJECTIVE**   The child will respond with his first and last name to the question "Who are you?" or "What is your name?"

**MATERIALS**   None

**PROCEDURE**   As a way of dismissing children from the group, ask each child "Who are you?" When children can respond to this question, ask them where they live, then what their phone number is. You can vary this within the group, depending on what each child has learned.

**COMMENT**   Your ultimate goal here is to have children who may get lost practice saying who are they are, and so on, as a way of getting back to their parents. In order to practice this, have a guest ask the children the questions so they get some practice with strangers. *Especially good for* HEARING and SPEECH AND LANGUAGE needs: If the children's speech is not clear, see if you can teach them to write the requested information; CULTURALLY DISTINCT, ADJUSTMENT and INTELLECTUAL needs may be unwilling or unable to respond to these requests. If that is so, put it on a card or write this information in the child's shoe or coat (if winter), have the child show it to you on request.

# *Art*

# INDEX

| *Goal* | *Activity* | *Page* |
|---|---|---|
| To express feelings | Painting a Feeling | 452 |
| To increase feelings of group belonging | Hand/Foot Painting | 458 |
| To increase awareness of individual differences | Body Mural | 454 |
| | Eye–Hair Collage | 455 |
| | Hand/Foot Painting | 458 |
| | Hand Plaster | 455 |
| | Mixed-Up People | 456 |
| To increase awareness of moods | Mood Colors | 453 |
| | Mood Montage | 453 |
| | Painting to Music | 454 |
| | School Moods | 447 |
| | Soap Sticks | 455 |

Through art activities, children can explore materials and express themselves in a visual form. Unlike work with movement or music, they can look back at past art work and see change. Although art activities usually result in a product, the process is most often more important than the final outcome.

Art provides a lifelong means of expressing feelings and gaining enjoyment that is essential for children with special needs. It allows these children to be a part of the group while, at the same time, expressing their feelings and creativity without being judged as different or strange.

## ART GOALS

- To improve cause and effect reasoning. Through art, children can control a small part of their world. They can learn that when they do something one way, they get a certain result; if they change their method, the result changes. Art is important because it is one of the few areas in which children this age can act on their own.
- To encourage creativity. Art is a process of creation by the children. No two pictures should be the same, as no two children are the same. Encourage the children to do what *they* want, not what *you* want. Children's art doesn't have to look like something or be anything except a creative experience.
- To increase body awareness. Through art, children can learn more about themselves and their bodies. They can gain first hand experience by feeling the difference between finger paint and glue, as well as finding out what each does. They can also begin to learn what techniques work best with what materials. As long as the emphasis is on the process of making the art and not the final product, children with special needs are sure to learn more about themselves.
- To improve eye–hand coordination. Children can develop better control over their fine motor skills by seeing what happens as they learn to use materials in their art activities. With practice, children can perfect art techniques and further develop their eye–hand coordination.

## TEACHING STRATEGIES

Children with SPEECH AND LANGUAGE needs may become so absorbed in art that they forget their reluctance to talk; they may discover that they want to talk about or explain their work. Art provides an alternative to verbal expression but can also be used to create the need for it.

Children with HEARING needs can refine visual skills while playing beside other children in a way that does not demand high-level language skills. They can learn by watching what others do and seeing what they make while still choosing and using materials in their own way.

Children with VISUAL needs may need obvious boundaries for work on paper, such as a thick black line marking the outside of the paper, but given that and an emphasis on process, there are few limitations on what these children can do. Three-dimensional materials such as clay and play-dough are particularly good because the children can feel the results.

Children with LEARNING needs find in art an emotional release and an opportunity to integrate the visual and tactile senses and make a creation that will not be judged by others as right or wrong.

Encourage children with ADJUSTMENT needs to use art as a way of expressing feelings. Strong feelings can be expressed through the use of bold colors, pounding clay, and tearing paper. Draining angry feelings in these ways helps the children keep themselves in control.

Children with HEALTH needs may express concerns and fears through art that they are unable or unwilling to express with words. When their large motor activities must be limited, art can be used as an alternative way of releasing energy and emotions.

Children with PHYSICAL needs can use art to express feelings, increase body awareness, and practice necessary motor skills. Through art, the children can see, for example, how a limb moves through space. The children can use this information to make changes while still moving at their own pace in an activity of their choice. The process can be one of experimentation and learning rather than drill or exercise.

CULTURALLY DISTINCT children can handle new and varied materials. They can experiment with techniques and learn about the properties of materials. They can exert their unique skills and interests on the art media yet at the same time be part of the group.

Children with INTELLECTUAL needs can use art to practice fine motor skills; they can see and even feel how they are growing in this area. Through manipulation of various art media, they can learn about color, shape, and size.

Encourage GIFTED AND TALENTED children to invent new ways of using materials and to refine methods they have used before. You can help them to create with a purpose in mind without your using adult standards to judge how well that purpose is met. These children can define problems, seek solutions, and grow in creative ability.

# TORN PAPER FLOWERS

**GOAL**   To improve cause and effect reasoning
To improve eye–hand coordination

**OBJECTIVE**   The child will make a picture by tearing and pasting paper.

**MATERIALS**   a pot or vase of flowers            construction paper
colored paper scraps            paste and crayons

**PROCEDURE**   Show the children the flowers. Discuss the parts that make up the flower (stem, petals, leaves, and so on). Show the children how to tear and paste paper petals and other flower parts. (If flowers aren't interesting to the children in your class, make something that is.) Once the children know the technique, allow them the freedom to make *their* flower. Use crayons to complete details.

**COMMENT**   *Especially good for* ADJUSTMENT and LEARNING needs: Tearing is a frustration release and helps eye–hand coordination. PHYSICAL and INTELLECTUAL needs can practice tearing and produce a picture without refined coordination. Show GIFTED AND TALENTED and older children how to curl the torn paper around a pencil so that it curls away from the paper to give depth.

# TRACING PICTURES

**GOAL**    To improve cause and effect reasoning
To improve tactile discrimination

**OBJECTIVE**    The child will trace the shape with his fingers.

**MATERIALS**    paper          glue
crayons     sand

**PROCEDURE**    Have the children draw a simple shape (circle, triangle, square), pattern, or picture (kite, table, cup, balloon, maze) on heavy paper. Tell the children to put glue around the outline and then sprinkle sand on it. Point out where the sand stays and where it doesn't. When the glue is dry, shake off the excess sand and have the children trace the object with their fingers or lightly color in the object using the sand as a boundary.

**CONTINUATION**    Once the children are good at this, have them trace and color the picture blindfolded.

**COMMENT**    Help younger children avoid ending up with puddles of glue that take days to dry! *Especially good for* VISUAL needs: They have created a tactile picture they can use. For PHYSICAL and INTELLECTUAL needs, put the sand in a salt shaker.

# CORRUGATED COLLAGE

**GOAL**    To improve cause and effect reasoning
To improve eye–hand coordination

**OBJECTIVE**    The child will make a collage on the corrugated paper.

**MATERIALS**    a 6″ × 9″ or larger piece of corrugated paper (such as a box divider or packing separator)

a variety of yarns          glue or paste
cloth materials          Popsicle sticks
pipe cleaners

**PROCEDURE**    Have the children make collages with a piece of corrugated paper, some glue, and the materials to be glued. Help the children see that the glue goes naturally into the corrugations, where it is easy to glue the yarn, but where it is much more difficult to glue the cloth.

**COMMENT**    As the children gain experience and better motor control, you might have them try doing this blindfolded, more as a sensory experience than an art activity.

*Especially good for* VISUAL needs: gives a definite tactile boundary to their work. Can require substantial problem solving from GIFTED AND TALENTED if you want them to do more than just experience the media.

# DYEING MACARONI

**GOAL**    To improve cause and effect reasoning
To improve eye–hand coordination

**OBJECTIVE**    The child will dye the macaroni.

**MATERIALS**    a variety of shapes of macaroni          vinegar
(wagon wheels, flat noodles, spirals,     paper cups
shells, and so on)          spoons
food coloring          wax paper

**PROCEDURE**    Put water in paper cups with food coloring and a little vinegar (vinegar makes colors brighter but plain water works too). Have the children place macaroni in the dyes. Help them discover that:

1. Macaroni becomes darker the longer it is left in the dye.
2. Macaroni becomes soggy with time

Take the macaroni out with a spoon and put it on wax paper to dry.

**CONTINUATION**    String the dyed macaroni pieces or make a macaroni collage.

**COMMENT**    *Especially good for* INTELLECTUAL needs: emphasize the colors while dyeing the macaroni and the fine motor skills while using the spoon and stringing. Although VISUAL needs may not be able to see the color change, they can feel the change in texture and the three-dimensional quality of the collage and enjoy stringing the macaroni.

# SCHOOL MOODS

**GOAL**    To improve cause and effect reasoning.
To increase awareness of moods

**OBJECTIVE**    The child will draw a picture depicting the two moods.

**MATERIALS**    Photographs of the school in the sun and in the rain

**PROCEDURE**    During group time, show the children pictures of the school, one taken on a sunny day, the other on a dark and rainy day. Encourage the children to talk about the pictures—not which one they like or don't like, but how they feel when they look at the pictures and what they see that is the same and what they see that is different in both pictures. Have the children contrast the photographs by folding a paper in half and drawing and coloring the school on a rainy day on one side of the paper and on a sunny day on the other.

**COMMENT**    Talk about the colors the children used in each picture and the differences in how they feel on sunny days and rainy days. *Especially good for* HEARING needs: teaches how to use visual, environmental cues for information. Offers GIFTED AND TALENTED the opportunity to be creative and use cause and effect reasoning.

# STRING MOBILE

**GOAL**    To improve cause and effect reasoning
To improve eye–hand coordination

**OBJECTIVE**    The child will create a string picture that can be hung as a mobile.

**MATERIALS**    string
glue or cornstarch
waxpaper

**PROCEDURE**    Soak the string in glue or cornstarch and have the children arrange it on wax paper. When the string dries, take it off and hang it up as a mobile.

**CONTINUATION**    Have the children put the string on tissue or construction paper and hang it as a string picture. For a 3-dimensional mobile, wrap the string around an inflated balloon; when the string is dry, pop the balloon.

**COMMENT**    When you hang the mobiles, have them low enough so that the children can feel them. *Especially good for* VISUAL needs: The project can be felt. Gives LEARNING needs practice in eye–hand coordination while exploring a different texture. Project is nondemanding for HEALTH needs and can be taken home and hung as a reminder of school if they are absent long. Requires few language skills for CULTURALLY DISTINCT yet allows the children to be part of the group.

# CREATURE

**GOAL**   To improve cause and effect reasoning
To encourage creative problem solving

**OBJECTIVE**   The child will make a creature and describe the environment in which it lives.

**MATERIALS**   papier-mâché made with newspaper, wheat paste, and water (see below)
balloons

**PROCEDURE**   Tear the newspaper into very small pieces and pour a little boiling water over it. Stir until it forms a pulp. Cool. Then add about 6 tablespoons of wheat paste for every 2 cups of pulp. Mix first with a spoon, then with the hands. Let the children mold the papier-mâché into some creaturelike form. Covering an inflated balloon with papier-mâché is a good way for the children to begin. Talk about this creature during the process so that the children think about how it moves (crawls, walks), what and how it eats, where it lives, and so on. See if they can adapt the creatures to the environment they create.

**CONTINUATION**   When the creatures are dry, you might encourage the children to use the construction area to build a house for them.

Finger puppets can be made the same way. (Don't forget the finger hole.) They can then be painted, dressed, and used in the dramatic play area.

**COMMENT**   Precede this activity by discussing people and animals and how they are adapted to their environments (a monkey's tail is for climbing; polar bears are white [protective coloration]; a cheetah is fast). Another good activity to precede this one is paper tearing, a great rainy-day tension reliever. Keep the torn paper for the papier-mâché (encourage small pieces). The papier-mâché process is as much fun as the product.

*Especially good for* GIFTED AND TALENTED: fosters problem solving as well as cause and effect reasoning. Helps PHYSICAL needs think about adaptations to the environment: Wheelchairs, prosthetic devices, and crutches are all adaptations.

# CRAYON RUBBING

**GOAL**   To improve cause and effect reasoning
To improve sensory integration

**OBJECTIVE**   The child will rub with a crayon paper placed over the textured articles to reproduce a pattern.

**MATERIALS**   paper                      masking tape
thick crayons              objects with various textures

**PROCEDURE**   Talk about various surfaces that the children touch and how they would describe them (soft, furry, scratchy, and so on), then about surfaces that they see (shiny, hairy, has ridges or patterns), and then about the two combined (something that feels bumpy, looks rough). Demonstrate rubbing techniques to the children. Either have them go around the room and find their own textures to rub or provide a variety of textured objects on a table. Tape the corners of the paper to the table with the object under it. The tape keeps the paper from moving as the children rub. Write the names of the article rubbed on the other side of the paper. During group time, ask the children to look at the papers and guess what article was rubbed. (The name on the back helps for those "creative" rubbings.)

**COMMENT**    *Especially good for* LEARNING needs: helps integrate the senses. GIFTED AND TALENTED can predict how a rubbing will look and then see if they were right. Develops finger strength in PHYSICAL needs without requiring fine coordination.

# TEXTURE PLAYDOUGH

**GOAL**    To improve cause and effect reasoning
To improve tactile discrimination
To improve classification skills

**OBJECTIVE**    The child will classify the playdough as rough, smooth, soft, or grainy.

**MATERIALS**    Playdough made with flour, salt, oil (recipe follows)

**PROCEDURE**    Make playdough one of two ways:
1. 7 parts flour to 1 part salt (1 tbsp. or so of vegetable oil)
2. 2 parts flour to 1 part salt (1 tbsp. or so of vegetable oil)

Discuss the difference in texture.

**CONTINUATION**    Vary the texture of the playdough; use 7 parts flour to 2 parts salt; 7 parts flour to 3 parts salt; 7 parts flour to 4 parts salt; 7 parts flour to 5 parts salt; and 7 parts flour to 6 parts salt to see how well the children can make tactile discriminations. Color code the different mixtures if necessary.

**COMMENT**    Have the children help make the playdough so that they can see the difference in the quantities of flour and salt. Help them verbalize: the more flour, the smoother the dough; the more salt, the grainier it is. *Especially good for* HEARING and VISUAL needs: develops and refines tactile discrimination skills. For GIFTED AND TALENTED, develops cause and effect reasoning and classification skills.

# TEXTURE PAINT

**GOAL**    To improve cause and effect reasoning
To improve visual discrimination
To improve tactile discrimination

**OBJECTIVE**    The child will describe the texture of the paint.

**MATERIALS**    Add texture to easel paint with one of the following:

flour: lumpy (don't stir it too much)          sawdust: rough
sugar: shiny, grainy (use right away)          salt: shiny, grainy, (table or Epsom
syrup: sticky                                               salt)
sand: gritty                                                 salad oil: oily

**PROCEDURE**    Have the children experiment with various textures.

**CONTINUATION**    Adding the same materials to finger paint changes the texture and expands not only the visual, but also the tactile experience of painting.

Try finger painting with whipped Ivory Flakes, frosting, pudding, mashed potatoes, or cooked spaghetti with food coloring for added stimulation of the senses of smell and/or taste.

**COMMENT**    You might experiment with making different colors and different textures on the same day:

> red: rough—sawdust
> blue: oily—salad oil
> yellow: lumpy—flour

*Especially good for* HEARING and VISUAL needs: They can experience both tactile and visual changes of a familiar substance. For ADJUSTMENT and LEARNING needs, the finger painting especially releases tension and provides sensory integration. All the changes give GIFTED AND TALENTED practice in cause and effect reasoning.

# STRAW PAINTING

**GOAL**    To improve cause and effect reasoning
To improve breath control
To make predictions

**OBJECTIVE**    The child will make a straw painting.

**MATERIALS**    watery tempera paint
paper
straws

**PROCEDURE**    Make very watery tempera paint. Put a small amount of paint on the paper and have the children create a picture by blowing the paint around on the paper with a straw.

**COMMENT**    Help the children see the different effects of blowing hard and softly and for a short time and a long time. *Especially good for* HEARING, SPEECH AND LANGUAGE, HEALTH, and INTELLECTUAL needs: gives experience in blowing and breath control. The paint helps children control their breath by allowing them to see the effects of it. For ADJUSTMENT and LEARNING needs, this visual sign helps their ability to control their breath, to make predictions about where the paint will go, and to integrate the two of these.

# FOOT PAINTING

**GOAL**    To encourage creativity
To increase body awareness

**OBJECTIVE**    The child will paint a picture with his feet.

**MATERIALS**    buttermilk
paper
powdered tempera paint

**PROCEDURE**    Have the children sit on the edge of their chairs around a large piece of paper (or in front of an individual-sized piece). Pour a small quantity of buttermilk on the paper and sprinkle over it some tempera paint powder. Encourage the children to paint with their toes as well as with their whole bare foot.

**COMMENT**    Be sure to have a portable tub and towels available for washing and drying feet. Make this an outside activity in warm weather.

*Especially good for* LEARNING and ADJUSTMENT needs: helps release frustrations and increase awareness of the feet. For VISUAL and HEARING needs, stimulates creativity with an area of the body that is rarely used outside of walking. For HEALTH and PHYSICAL needs, this activity is fun, not taxing, involves little skill, and increases awareness of body parts.

# WIRE SCULPTURE

**GOAL**   To encourage creativity
To improve eye–hand coordination

**OBJECTIVE**   The child will create a wire sculpture.

**MATERIALS**   varying lengths of easily bendable wire
Styrofoam

**PROCEDURE**   Encourage the children to make sculptures by twisting, coiling, looping, and bending the wire and by joining it to additional pieces of wire. The children can stick the wire through the Styrofoam for added stability.

**CONTINUATION**   Add pipe cleaners, different sizes of wire, paper clips, safety pins, and so on to encourage further creativity.

**COMMENT**   Buy wire that can be coiled easily with bare hands, but holds its shape once bent. The telephone company may give this to you free—theirs is even color coded. *Especially good for* PHYSICAL and VISUAL needs: emphasizes the sense of touch. Allows HEALTH needs to have a lot of control over the medium. An inexpensive and nonmessy home activity.

# STRING PAINTING

**GOAL**   To encourage creativity
To improve eye–hand coordination

**OBJECTIVE**   The child will make a string painting.

**MATERIALS**   pieces of string, yarn, or cord of   two or three colors of tempera paint
various thicknesses approximately   in pie pans
two feet long   paper

**PROCEDURE**   Give the children a variety of pieces of string, cord, or yarn, show them how to dip it in the paint, and allow them to make a design by applying the paint on paper with the string.

**COMMENT**   If very thick paint is used, the children will be able to feel the ridges the string makes. The children can also match the ridges to the thickness of string used. Help children identify differences in techniques: for example, holding string taut between two hands v. holding one end and swirling.

*Especially good for* VISUAL needs: These children can participate in a creative visual process and can feel the picture when it is dry. For PHYSICAL and INTELLECTUAL needs, put the yarn or string through an empty spool to make it easier to grip. Focus on naming colors if this is appropriate.

# CLAY

**GOAL**   To encourage creativity
To improve eye–hand coordination

**OBJECTIVE**   The child will mold the clay.

**MATERIALS**   dry clay   rolling pins
water   blunt knife

**PROCEDURE**   Make, or have the children make, clay from powder. Vary the amount of moisture with the strength and motor skills of the children (more moisture—easier to manipulate). Encourage the children to use rolling pins and blunt knifes as well as hands to hold the clay. If you want, allow the clay to dry and paint it, or fire it in a kiln and paint it.

**COMMENT**   Be sure to allow adequate time for exploration. *Especially good for* INTELLECTUAL and PHYSICAL needs: builds finger strength and coordination, and the clay consistency can be varied with the needs of the children. An emotional release for ADJUSTMENT and LEARNING needs.

# PAINTING A FEELING

**GOAL**   To encourage creativity
To express feelings

**OBJECTIVE**   The child will paint a picture that depicts a feeling.

**MATERIALS**   paper
paint in vibrant colors and somber colors

**PROCEDURE**   Have a discussion about feelings. Talk about being happy, sad, angry, and scared. Have the children think of imaginary situations, or ones they might have been in, where these

When easels are brought outside on a bright day, children may discover that their feelings change.

feelings are appropriate. You might read a story on emotions. (See bibliographies.) Then have the children choose an emotion they are going to paint (write it on the back of the paper they are going to use).

**COMMENT**   Be sure not to judge the children's comments even if the situations sound bizarre. Differentiate between feelings and behavior. It is OK to feel angry; it isn't OK to throw rocks.

> Feeling: I was angry when my mother came home from the hospital with my baby brother.
> Behavior: I threw a rock in my brother's crib when my parents brought him home from the hospital. (This example might give them ideas!)

*Especially good for* CULTURALLY DISTINCT, LEARNING, ADJUSTMENT, and HEALTH needs: creates an awareness of feelings and a sense that it is OK to feel the way they do. Provides an avenue for expressing feelings.

# MOOD MONTAGE

**GOAL**   To encourage creativity
To increase awareness of moods

**OBJECTIVE**   The child will create a mood montage.

**MATERIALS**   pictures and/or magazines     scissors
crayons     paper
glue or paste

**PROCEDURE**   Give the children the pictures, magazines, and crayons. Have them pick a mood or feeling, find pictures that match or create that mood, and paste the pictures on pieces of paper. They can use the crayons to personalize and finish the pictures.

**CONTINUATION**   This project can be done on separate pieces of paper to form a book or on a big piece to form a wall mural that is a group project.

**COMMENT**   Encourage the children to talk about their picture. *Especially good for* ADJUSTMENT and LEARNING needs: creates awareness of moods and of some of the situations in which these moods may occur. Have INTELLECTUAL and PHYSICAL needs rip out the pictures or use adapted scissors without finger holes.

# MOOD COLORS

**GOAL**   To encourage creativity
To increase awareness of moods

**OBJECTIVE**   The child will choose an appropriate color theme for the picture.

**MATERIALS**   a short story
tempera paint or crayons
paper

**PROCEDURE**   Read (or tell) the class a story with a definite mood. Have the children draw pictures about the story in dark and/or light colors.

**CONTINUATION**   A discussion of colors and how the children feel about them could follow. Let the children choose the colors that represent their mood, but make sure the stereotypic colors are available.

**COMMENT**   The illustrations of the book should help set a mood too. Discuss some of the color stereotypes (fire engine red—hot; sky blue—cool; clean white—aseptic, sterile; and so on).

*Especially good for* HEARING needs: helps them learn to use visual, environmental cues for information. May help ADJUSTMENT needs to realize that people have moods, that situations can create moods, and that moods are OK.

# PAINTING TO MUSIC

**GOAL**    To encourage creativity
To improve sensory integration
To increase awareness of moods

**OBJECTIVE**    The child will paint an interpretation of the music.

**MATERIALS**    music that has a specific theme    paint
paper    paintbrushes

**PROCEDURE**    Begin with a story or discussion of the theme (e.g., the circus). Show pictures and discuss the sights, sounds, smells, and mood of the theme. Then play the record and have the children paint the picture the music helps them "see." (For older children, simply play a passage and ask them to close their eyes and imagine a story or a scene.)

**CONTINUATION**    Finger painting to music can be a tremendous tension release, especially if you start with strong, vigorous music and finish with softer, gentler music.

**COMMENT**    Be sure to talk with the children about their choice of color, size of drawing, and so on. Experiment with a wide variety of music. *Especially good for* LEARNING needs: helps to integrate the senses. Serves as an energy release for ADJUSTMENT needs and tickles the imagination of GIFTED AND TALENTED. Requires little hand coordination for PHYSICAL needs. Helps VISUAL needs to interpret auditory stimuli, with concentration on the process of painting, not on the final result. For CULTURALLY DISTINCT, choose music that is typical of their particular region or cultural group.

# BODY MURAL

**GOAL**    To increase body awareness
To increase awareness of individual differences

**OBJECTIVE**    The child will paint his silhouette.

**MATERIALS**    butcher paper    scissors
paintbrushes    paint
crayons

**PROCEDURE**    Have the children trace silhouettes of each other with crayons on one large sheet of paper and paint in their own silhouettes. Hang this on the wall in one piece or have the children cut their pictures out. Point out similarities and differences among the children.

**COMMENT**    Hanging the piece as a whole may enhance the children's sense of belonging to the group. *Especially good for* CULTURALLY DISTINCT, INTELLECTUAL, and SPEECH AND LANGUAGE needs: increases vocabulary and body awareness if you refer to the body parts as you or a child traces them. For LEARNING and ADJUSTMENT needs, discuss the body parts and what they do as well as similarities and differences among the children. For VISUAL needs, use a heavy black marking pen to mark the outline of the body so it is easier to see. If necessary, help the children cut out the body; as you label the parts, the children can paint them with textured paint so that they can feel them.

# EYE–HAIR COLLAGE

**GOAL**  To increase body awareness
To increase awareness of individual differences

**OBJECTIVE**  The child will produce an art project using colors the same as his eye and hair colors.

**MATERIALS**  magazines      paste
scissors      paper

**PROCEDURE**  Help the children find magazine pictures that contain the same colors as their hair and eyes. The children can cut or rip out the pictures and then paste them on a sheet of paper with their name in the center to make an eye–hair collage. A color photograph of the child may also be placed in the center.

**COMMENT**  Discuss similarities and differences among the children. *Especially good for* HEAR-ING, ADJUSTMENT, and LEARNING needs: teaches colors and individual differences using visual cues instead of words. These differences can be found in all children, not only those who are labeled as special.

# HAND PLASTER

**GOAL**  To increase body awareness
To increase awareness of individual differences

**OBJECTIVE**  The child will make a print of one hand.

**MATERIALS**  plaster of paris
tin pie pans

**PROCEDURE**  Make the plaster of paris according to the directions and put it in a pie pan or other suitable container. Help the children put their hand quickly into the mixture with a down-ward motion and then slowly take it out (have them practice the motions first). Put the children's name on the underside of the pan, so you'll know whose hand it is.

**COMMENT**  When the plaster hands are dry, have a discussion about similarities and differ-ences. Have the children try to find the hand that fits; encourage them to make descriptive state-ments about those that don't ("My fingers are longer." "This hand is bigger.")

*Especially good for* SPEECH AND LANGUAGE and LEARNING needs: helps these children recognize that all children have hands that are unique and that there are words to describe the differences among them. For VISUAL needs, gives a new kind of tactile awareness of the differences among peo-ple's hands. These children can feel the imprint and, if the other child is willing, feel the hand that made it.

# SOAP STICKS

**GOAL**  To increase body awareness
To increase awareness of moods

**OBJECTIVE**  The child will decorate another child's face.

**MATERIALS**  colored soap sticks (available commercially)
mirror

**PROCEDURE**    Have the children use the soap sticks to paint other children's faces. Have the painted children look in the mirror. Talk about the relationship between colors and moods.

**COMMENT**    This activity can be done with grease paint, but soap sticks are great because they wash off faces, chairs, and clothes in a minute. *Especially good for* LEARNING and ADJUSTMENT needs: helps children become more aware of their own moods and those of others.

# MIXED-UP PEOPLE

**GOAL**    To increase body awareness
    To increase awareness of individual differences

**OBJECTIVE**    The child will put pieces of a picture together to reassemble a picture of a body.

**MATERIALS**    magazines
    cardboard
    paste

**PROCEDURE**    Cut pictures of whole people out of magazines and paste them on cardboard. Then cut the pictures into six parts (two arms, two legs, trunk, and head). Have the children put these pieces together to make a whole person. When they can put these in the right order, give them pieces that are the correct body parts but from different people.

**CONTINUATION**    Discuss concepts of relative size (the head is smaller than the trunk). The second part of the activity requires more generalization skills as the body pieces really do not fit together.

**COMMENT**    *Especially good for* INTELLECTUAL needs: These children often have trouble with knowledge of body parts. For LEARNING and ADJUSTMENT needs; use as part of an overall awareness program. For HEARING needs, develops language and generalization skills.

# MY SHADOW

**GOAL**    To increase body awareness
    To cooperate with adults

**OBJECTIVE**    The child will cut out his shadow and decorate it.

**MATERIALS**    large paper
    a bright light
    a marking pencil

**PROCEDURE**    Tack a large piece of paper on a wall. Have each child stand in front of the paper with the light behind him so that he will cast a shadow. Trace the shadow and then have the child cut it out and decorate it.

**CONTINUATION**    When on the playground, point out the children's shadows made by the sun and talk about the differences in their sizes.

**COMMENT**    With 3-year-olds, trace the shadow yourself. As the children develop better skills, have them trace each other. (You may have to pick a dark day or pull the blinds to get a good shadow.)

*Especially good for* ADJUSTMENT and HEARING needs: These children can see the process and the product while becoming more aware of the environment. Have GIFTED AND TALENTED help figure out where to set up the paper and light to produce a more "true" shadow and to play with the distortions.

# PUPPET HANDS

**GOAL**  To increase body awareness
To improve expressive language
To improve small motor coordination

**OBJECTIVE**  The child will carry on a conversation through his own hand puppet and/or with a classmate's.

**MATERIALS**  A washable felt marker

**PROCEDURE**  Have the children make a fist with the thumb on the outside. With the felt marker, draw a face on the index finger and thumb of the children's hand; help them move their hand to make the puppet talk.

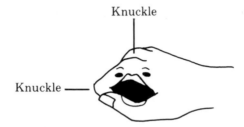

Knuckle

Knuckle ——

**COMMENT**  Children who may not ordinarily be willing to talk are often willing to talk through a puppet. If necessary, give the children a subject to talk about.

*Especially good for* SPEECH AND LANGUAGE needs: Because these children are often criticized for their speech, the puppets may increase their willingness to talk. ADJUSTMENT needs will often express emotions in this way that they cannot express in other ways. HEALTH needs can learn this skill at school and then use these puppets (with another's help in drawing them) in solitary play at home.

# COLORED FINGERNAILS

**GOAL**  To increase body awareness
To improve color concepts
To improve sensory integration

**OBJECTIVE**  The child will color his fingernails different colors and follow a set of commands with the designated finger.

**MATERIALS**  Washable colored felt markers

**PROCEDURE**  Have the children color each fingernail of one hand a different color. Tell the children what to do with each finger:

Shake the finger with the yellow on it.
Hide the finger with the red on it.
Put the finger with the green on it on your nose.

**CONTINUATION**    As the children become more adept have them use both hands. Adapt common fingerplays for movement of specific fingers.

**COMMENT**    Washes off easily with soap and water. *Especially good for* LEARNING needs: teaches not only color concepts but also sensory integration. For INTELLECTUAL needs, keep the commands very simple ("Show me the red one"). Encourage SPEECH AND LANGUAGE and ADJUSTMENT needs to talk with the puppets. Make no judgments about the way they talk; encourage them. HEALTH needs can play this anywhere.

# PLACE MAT COLLAGE

**GOAL**    To increase body awareness
To improve visual association
To improve classification skills

**OBJECTIVE**    The child will make a categorical food collage.

**MATERIALS**    pictures of food          construction paper
clear contact paper     glue

**PROCEDURE**    Have the children sort pictures of food cut from magazines (according to your specific goals and the children's ability) and glue these on place-mat-size pieces of construction paper. When finished, cover the place mats with clear contact paper so that they can be wiped off.
    Some suggestions for categories follow:

| | |
|---|---|
| fruits | vegetables |
| meats/fish | dairy products |
| favorite foods | foods I'm allergic to |
| "junk foods" | foods grown in our garden |
| foods from other cultures | nonfood pictures |

**COMMENT**    *Especially good for* HEALTH needs and CULTURALLY DISTINCT: helps the children increase their knowledge of how specific foods meet nutritional needs. INTELLECTUAL needs can sort pictures of food from pictures of things that are not food.

# HAND/FOOT PAINTING

**GOAL**    To increase body awareness
To increase awareness of individual differences
To increase feelings of group belonging

**OBJECTIVE**    The child will create an art project using hands or feet.

**MATERIALS**    tempera paint
paper

**PROCEDURE**    Paint the palms of the children's hands or the soles of their feet. Allow them to press their hands on or walk on a large sheet of paper.

**COMMENT**    Doing this outside may be wise. (The paint will wash off the grass and sidewalk if the children walk there.) Discuss the uniqueness of hand and foot prints. To help create a sense of group belonging, make this into a class mural and identify each child's foot and/or hand prints.

*Especially good for* INTELLECTUAL needs: The task is easy; the result is unique. Have GIFTED AND TALENTED and VISUAL needs use magnifying glasses to find the differences and similarities among the prints.

# SALT PUTTY BEADS

**GOAL**   To improve eye–hand coordination
To improve measurement concepts

**OBJECTIVE**   The child will help make and string salt putty beads.

**MATERIALS**   salt                    toothpicks
flour                   yarn
water                   wooden spoon
food coloring

**PROCEDURE**   Have the children make the putty:

> 1 1/3 cups salt
> 1 cup flour
> 2/3 cup water
> food coloring—optional

Mix with wooden spoon, then hands. Make beads by rolling putty between palms. Before the beads dry, punch a hole in the center with a toothpick or skewer (depending on how large you want the hole). Allow beads to dry. They can be strung with heavy thread or yarn into bracelets, necklaces, ornaments, and so on.

**CONTINUATION**   Encourage creativity by having the children paint the dry beads.

**COMMENT**   Discuss the relationship between the amount of putty rolled and the size of the bead. *Especially good for* LEARNING needs: They can see, handle, and string the beads they make. PHYSICAL needs benefit because the activity requires two hands and is not taxing. If they have problems stringing the beads, use pipe cleaners or drinking straws instead of string. For VISUAL needs, when measuring the ingredients, use 1/3 cup twice, instead of 2/3 of 1 cup, to teach the children to feel when a cup is full by putting their finger on the rim. HEALTH needs can wear the beads at home and talk with others about school.

# STICK PUPPETS

**GOAL**   To improve eye–hand coordination
To increase awareness of roles people play

**OBJECTIVE**   The child will make a puppet with a tongue depressor.

**MATERIALS**   tongue depressors        cloth
glue                     gauze pads
cotton balls             crayons
marking pen

**PROCEDURE**   Encourage the children to make puppets of their choice by gluing materials on the tongue depressor. Children decorate only the top half of the tongue depressor and use the bottom half to hold the puppet.

**CONTINUATION**    Encourage the children to use the puppets in the dramatic play area.

**COMMENT**    Discuss the way doctors use tongue depressors. Before children make the puppets, discuss why doctors look at throats and how far the tongue depressor goes in.

   *Especially good for* SPEECH AND LANGUAGE, HEARING, and HEALTH needs: familiarizes the children with tongue depressors, which they may encounter frequently, and then allows them to control the use of the tongue depressor for a change.

# LETTER COLLAGE

**GOAL**    To improve eye–hand coordination
   To improve visual discrimination
   To improve spatial concepts

**OBJECTIVE**    The child will identify the designated letters.

**MATERIALS**    letters of the alphabet ($1\frac{1}{2}''$ or larger)
   construction paper
   paste or glue

**PROCEDURE**    Give each child a variety of letters to paste and discuss the letters as the child is making the picture.

   That's an *A*.
   That's *A* like in *apple*.
   Can you find a letter that is in your name?

**CONTINUATION**    Use letters that have a texture (made of felt, cloth, sandpaper, and so on) to make this a tactile experience. If the children can differentiate vowels and consonants, make the vowels a rough texture and the consonants a smooth one or vice versa. Discuss the differences between vowels and consonants.

**COMMENT**    Discuss how to hold the paper so that each letter is right side up if possible. If that is impossible, help the children discover why. Use the letters to talk about various spatial relationships:

   The *A* is beside the *C*.
   The *F* is between the *K* and *Z*.
   The *O* is above the *R*.

   *Especially good for* SPEECH AND LANGUAGE needs: allows these children to work on letter and sound concepts during an art project. LEARNING needs can work on spatial relations as well as visual and tactile discrimination. Textured letters provide tactile as well as visual feedback for VISUAL and HEARING needs. For INTELLECTUAL needs, use fewer letters and concentrate on those that the children are learning in other situations. Encourages CULTURALLY DISTINCT to learn prepositions and letters. Encourage the children to learn the alphabet in two languages if this is appropriate.

# Music

# INDEX

| *Goal* | *Activity* | *Page* |
|---|---|---|
| To improve number concepts | Counting Songs | 469 |
| To improve shape concepts | Musical Colors | 470 |
| To increase feelings of group belonging | My Song | 469 |
| To increase body awareness | Movement Songs | 468 |
|  | My Song | 469 |
|  | Rhythm Walk | 464 |

Music is enjoyable to most children. It can be soothing or stimulating, it can promote social activity, and it can be used anytime or anywhere. Traditionally, music has not been integrated with the rest of the curriculum. It has been restricted to a "music period" and taught without any goal beyond the vague one of teaching children music. But music can be used to meet a number of educational needs. Music activities can teach and/or reinforce skills that are part of other curriculum areas, such as recognizing colors and shapes, counting, and rhyming, but teaching goals must be specific and related to individual needs and differences. Music is fun, and it will make the children want to use their bodies, their minds, and their creative energy.

## MUSIC GOALS

- To increase sense of rhythm. Awareness of rhythm for moving and speaking is important and is perhaps most easily developed using music. In addition children can gain better control of their breath through phrasing music as well as by holding notes and emphasizing sounds.
- To improve auditory discrimination and memory. Learning the words to songs, as well as figuring out and remembering rhythm patterns and pitch, aids in developing auditory skills.
- To improve cause and effect reasoning. As children learn to use their voices and play instruments, they can learn causal relationships—for example, beating a drum harder makes it sound louder.
- To improve sensory integration. Music can easily be paired with both movement and art to help children interpret moods and respond to activities with more than one sense.
- To increase body awareness. By singing about and using specific body parts, children become more aware of their body and what it does. They can participate in music in so many ways that all children can feel part of the group whether or not they can sing, move, or listen with their peers.

## TEACHING STRATEGIES

For children with SPEECH AND LANGUAGE needs, music can provide a nonthreatening atmosphere for using expressive language. Through music, you can encourage these children to attempt speech and to imitate other children and adults. Include songs and activities that concentrate on special letters or sounds they are having trouble producing. Provide them with musical instruments that encourage tongue and mouth movement. Use music to teach these children that talking and singing are fun.

By definition, music is primarily an auditory experience. For children with HEARING needs, music activities have to be changed to include experiences that will mean something to them and will allow them to participate. Make sure to include visual cues for these children—clap the rhythm, stamp feet, and so on. Encourage them to watch the other children. Use loud songs or ones with dissonant sounds. Take the top off the piano so that they can watch it play. Let them feel vibrations. Use creative movement activities that allow them to experience rhythm. Have another child or an adult move with them. Introduce them to songs on an individual basis, going over the vocabulary with the help of pictures. Make music a good release for emotions, not an emotionally frustrating experience.

For children with VISUAL needs, music can be used to enhance listening skills and auditory discrimination. These children may have difficulty moving around, but moving to music is an excellent way to give them an awareness of their body in relation to the environment. Remove obstacles that might be in the way.Give the children boundaries they trust, such as two adults who can cue them when their movements are too large. Have other children be their movement partners, or just have the visually impaired children move while sitting. Use music to help them learn to localize sound and distinguish one voice from another. Let them feel vibrations of instruments and voices. Sound will be vital in the life of these children, so use music to train their hearing.

Make sure LEARNING needs children understand what is expected of them. Give visual and movement cues, if possible, to help them understand. Use high interest activities. Repeat lessons but vary the activities. Music can help these children improve muscle coordination. Go slowly, however, and build towards integration. Let the children hit pot lids before you expect them to clap their hands. Program activities that use as many senses as possible and be aware of the children's reactions. If one activity does not work, try another one.

Take the PHYSICAL needs children's limitations into consideration when programming. If children cannot move their legs, make sure to include some creative movement activities with everyone sitting. Teach them to move their wheelchair to music. If children cannot move their hands, include stomping instead of just clapping. Put the children on the floor with the others. Pick the children up and dance with them. Program quiet activities in with active ones so as not to overtire the children. Do not exclude them; if you can't modify an activity to include them, pick a different activity or find something they can do (work the record player, play the flute, and so on).

Use music to teach ADJUSTMENT needs children to relax (play soft music at rest time) and to release feelings (have them beat a drum if they are angry). Provide plenty of movement and large motor activities to help them express pent-up emotions.

With INTELLECTUAL needs children, expect to repeat a lot. These children may choose to sing one or two songs over and over. Use simple, concise directions. Do not expect a lot of imagination; encourage the children to imitate others if necessary. In creative movement, give them a part they are familiar with and understand. If costumes are part of the experience, provide realistic ones. Start with large motor activities and encourage the children to move their whole body by stimulating them with bold music. Gradually work on small motor skills.

Send home copies of songs so that parents can sing them at home with the HEALTH needs children. Send home tapes of new songs you teach while the children are not in school. Include copies of the words so they can know the song when they return to school. Music can provide a good transition between home and school. Provide some restful activities so as not to tire the children. Have the class send home a musical greeting to ill children. Use music to keep the children involved with the class.

For GIFTED AND TALENTED children, music can provide a challenge and a good outlet for creativity. Encourage them to lead songs, interpret music through painting, learn to play instruments, and create dances. Do not tie these children down; music is the medium for giving children the freedom to explore themselves and the world around them.

CULTURALLY DISTINCT children can help to broaden your music program while they become more a part of the group. Learn simple songs in other languages and use musical instruments from other lands. Play records of music with interesting rhythms that are distinct features of foreign cultures, as well as records with rhythms that are distinct features of our culture (jazz, spirituals, and so on).

# RHYTHMIC PATTERNS

**GOAL**   To increase sense of rhythm
To improve auditory memory

**OBJECTIVE**   The child will reproduce the rhythmic pattern.

**MATERIALS**   None

**PROCEDURE**   Clap a simple, short, rhythmic pattern dramatically. Have the children clap the pattern back to you. As they gain skill, make the patterns longer and more complex. Clap the number of letters in a child's name and have the children guess who it could be.

**COMMENT**   Use clapping as a way of dismissing the children from group time. Individualize the patterns based on each child's skill.

*Especially good for* HEARING needs: uses a visual sign to teach rhythm. Good auditory training for VISUAL needs. SPEECH AND LANGUAGE and LEARNING needs can use both visual and auditory cues to develop rhythm and memory skills.

# MOOD SONGS

**GOAL**   To increase sense of rhythm
To improve cause and effect reasoning

**OBJECTIVE**   The child will state how specific songs should be sung (loud/soft, fast/slow, high/low).

**MATERIALS**   None

**PROCEDURE**   Choose songs that have specific moods: lullabies, action songs, holiday songs, funny songs. Have the children talk about the songs, how they should be sung, and why. Have them sing one. Then have them sing it a "wrong" way (e.g., a loud lullaby). Discuss how they feel while they are doing this and why songs have distinctive moods.

**CONTINUATION**   Expand the activity to include movement as well as music.

**COMMENT**   *Especially good for* ADJUSTMENT and LEARNING needs: They learn to become more aware of and to control their moods.

# RHYTHM WALK

**GOAL**   To increase sense of rhythm
To increase body awareness

**OBJECTIVE**   The child will move in time with the beat.

**MATERIALS**   Drum or piano

**PROCEDURE**   Set up a path around the room (or outside) and have the children walk to the beat that you play. Vary the beat and see if the children can change with you. (Until they get the idea, warn them before changing: "Listen, I'm going to change now. Is it faster or slower?") Sometimes beat slowly enough for it to become a balancing activity.

**COMMENT**   This can be done with any instrument, but percussion instruments are preferable because the children can see as well as hear the beat.

*Especially good for* SPEECH AND LANGUAGE needs: reinforces the rhythmic aspect of speech. Be sure HEARING needs can see you as you strike the instrument; do it dramatically. For VISUAL needs, put up a string path as a guide if necessary. For PHYSICAL needs, keep the beat slow; have the children roll the wheels of the wheelchair or use a walker or crutches in a rhythmic pattern. ADJUST-MENT needs can be part of the group yet are not required to interact much.

# DIRECTOR

**GOAL**  To increase sense of rhythm
To improve cause and effect reasoning
To improve breath control

**OBJECTIVE**  The child will follow the visual and auditory directions given.

**MATERIALS**  None

**PROCEDURE**  Pretend that you are the director of an orchestra and teach the children some of the simpler hand signals: soft—palms toward them (up and down); loud—palms toward you (large gesture); slow—waving slowly (circular); fast—waving fast (circular); expand—pass arm in front of body parallel to floor; staccato—cut in the air (vertically). Your signals don't have to be the actual signals, but you and the children should agree on their meanings.

Start out using words like me, me, me, me; la, la, la, la; see, see, see, see. Then go to 2 or more syllables. Names are always fun: Ja—expand (use horizontal hand movement) mie—staccato (vertical hand movement).

**CONTINUATION**  This can be used for a rhythm band, but instruments are far more difficult to control than voices.

**COMMENT**  *Especially good for* SPEECH AND LANGUAGE needs: uses an enjoyable group experience to teach voice control. CULTURALLY DISTINCT can learn the responses without necessarily knowing the language. HEARING needs can utilize the visual hand cues to respond.

# INSTRUMENTS

**GOAL**  To improve auditory discrimination
To improve auditory memory

**OBJECTIVE**  The child will name the instrument being played out of his sight.

**MATERIALS**  a screen
a variety of instruments:

| | |
|---|---|
| tambourine | drum |
| flute | bells |
| triangle | |

**PROCEDURE**  This progressive activity is designed to increase listening skills throughout the year and is done in a variety of steps. Begin with instruments that differ widely in sound production (tambourine, flute, triangle, drum). Have the children play the same instrument after you demonstrate it. Next, ask the children to imitate the sounds after you play the instruments. Then place the instruments in front of the screen; as the children watch, put an instrument behind the screen and play it. Ask the children to imitate and identify the sound. When they can correctly identify the sound, place two instruments behind the screen, play one of them, and have the children identify the sound. As they get better, use three, then four instruments.

**CONTINUATION**  Add instruments that are more like each other; three bells, high, medium, and low; a series of percussion instruments; and so on. Record instruments on a tape. Play it, accompanied by pictures at first, eventually, eliminate the pictures.

When musical instruments are available, children can experiment with sound while fine tuning their auditory discrimination skills.

**COMMENT**    *Especially good for* SPEECH AND LANGUAGE needs: The progression, instruments, and pace can be varied with the needs of the children. Label the instruments for VISUAL and HEARING needs; allow them to feel the instruments and play them in freeplay before this group experience.

# VIBRATIONS

**GOAL**    To improve auditory discrimination
To improve cause and effect reasoning

**OBJECTIVE**    The child will state the relationship between the vibrations and the sound.

**MATERIALS**    tuning forks
guitar or autoharp
stretched rubber bands

**PROCEDURE**    During small group time, strike a tuning fork and then put it in water. Let the children see the vibrations it makes. Then put the fork in water without striking it so that the children can see that the fork itself doesn't make the ripples. Then allow them to feel the vibrations on various parts of their bodies. Try to have at least two different tuning forks so that they can see, hear, and feel a difference.

Allow the children to feel the vibrations of the strings on a guitar; have them note the relative sizes of the strings. Encourage them to experiement with plucking stretched rubber bands of various thicknesses.

**CONTINUATION**   Demonstrate and then have the children make guitars with cigar boxes and different thicknesses of rubber bands. You might take the front off a piano (preferably an old one) and let the children feel the vibrations as the notes are played.

**COMMENT**   Help the children become aware that they also make vibrations in order to make sounds. Have them talk while holding their hand on their vocal cords.

*Especially good for* VISUAL, HEARING, and LEARNING needs: gives auditory, visual, and tactile representations of sound. SPEECH AND LANGUAGE needs can learn more about how speech is produced. GIFTED AND TALENTED can vary the size and tension of rubber bands to learn about pitch.

# WHERE IS IT?

**GOAL**   To improve auditory discrimination
To improve cause and effect reasoning

**OBJECTIVE**   The child in the middle will point to the child in the circle who made the noise.

**MATERIALS**   a variety of instruments, one for each child
a blindfold or mask

**PROCEDURE**   Have the children sit in a circle. Give each one an instrument. Make sure children sitting beside each other have different noisemakers. Have one child make a noise. Have a blindfolded child in the center of the circle point to the place he thinks the sound came from. If he is almost right but can't quite find the right place, take off the blindfold and have him look at all the instruments in the area to help him figure out who made the noise.

**CONTINUATION**   You might have the child in the middle try to localize the other children's voices by having them say a particular sentence, such as "Who am I?" As the children acquire skill, they should be able to identify classmates by voice alone. If they have trouble, give some clues ("I have red hair" "My name starts with *R*").

**COMMENT**   Have children who are really good guess the instrument also. Be sure to change instruments frequently. You may want to split the class into two groups (at opposite ends of the room) to decrease the possibility of confusion.

*Especially good for* VISUAL needs: develops listening skills and helps the children to recognize their classmates from auditory cues alone. For LEARNING, HEALTH, and PHYSICAL needs, improves spatial concepts and gives practice identifying and localizing sounds.

# BONNIE

**GOAL**   To improve auditory discrimination
To improve sensory integration

**OBJECTIVE**   The child will squat on every other *Bonnie*.

**MATERIALS**   None

**PROCEDURE**   Sing the song "My Bonnie Lies over the Ocean" with everyone standing. Each time you sing the word *Bonnie*, if the children are standing, they squat; if they are squatting, they stand.

**CONTINUATION**   The principle can be used with any song that has a repetition like this one.

**COMMENT**    This is a lot easier to do than it sounds on paper. It is a good way to add variety and work off a little energy. *Especially good for* SPEECH AND LANGUAGE and LEARNING needs: teaches children to recognize a specific sound and then do a movement. For variety, change the movement. Have PHYSICAL needs raise and lower a hand instead of standing and squatting.

# SEQUENCING SONGS

**GOAL**    To improve auditory memory

**OBJECTIVE**    The child will remember at least 3 items in the sequence.

**MATERIALS**    None

**PROCEDURE**    Sing songs that require the children to remember a particular sequence. As you reach that part, pause to see if they can remember the sequence without your help. For example, when you sing "Old MacDonald Had a Farm," pause after "and on his farm he had a _____."

**COMMENT**    *Especially good for* SPEECH AND LANGUAGE needs: They are part of a group language experience as they are developing memory skills. For LEARNING, INTELLECTUAL, and HEARING needs; pair the words with pictures if the children have trouble remembering the words alone.

# MOVEMENT SONGS

**GOAL**    To improve sensory integration
    To increase body awareness

**OBJECTIVE**    The child will follow the motions stated in the song.

**MATERIALS**    None

**PROCEDURE**    Sing the song: "Put Your Finger in the Air."* Once you know the song, help the children explore their bodies by putting their finger on their knee, cheek, shoulder, ankle, and so on. Then go on to various other combinations like "Put your nose on your shoulder, on your shoulder." In the third line, you need to be creative and have a rhyme in mind: "Put your nose on your shoulder, leave it there until you're older."

　　Other songs designed to increase body awareness include:
　　　　"Heads, Shoulders, Knees, and Toes" (Tune: "Oats, Peas, Beans")
　　　　"My Head, My Shoulders, My Knees, My Toes" (Tune: "Mulberry Bush")
　　　　"Where Is Thumbkin?"
　　　　"Clap Your Hands"
　　　　"The Hokey Pokey"

**CONTINUATION**    Have children sing these songs with their eyes closed.

**COMMENT**    *Especially good for* LEARNING, VISUAL needs, and CULTURALLY DISTINCT: teaches body parts, uses both auditory and tactile senses, and provides an opportunity to experience success and a sense of group belonging. INTELLECTUAL needs will profit from the repetition.

---

*"Put Your Finger in the Air," words and music by Woody Guthrie, © 1954 Folkways Music Publishers, Inc., New York. Folkways Record FP5.

# MY SONG

**GOAL**   To increase body awareness
To increase feelings of group belonging

**OBJECTIVE**   The child will look at the named child while singing.

**MATERIALS**   None

**PROCEDURE**   Sing songs in which you can substitute the name of a child from your group, or adapt a song to include a name. Have the children stand up as the class sings about them.

### BINGO

There was a farmer had
a son and Michael
was his name—O.
M-I-C-H-AEL
M-I-C-H-AEL
M-I-C-H-AEL
And Michael was his
name—O.

### PAW-PAW PATCH

Where, oh where is pretty
little Sherry?
Where, oh, where is
pretty little Laura?
Where, oh, where is
handsome Juan?
They're in the block
corner, picking up blocks.

### HEY BETTY MARTIN

Hey, Mary Ball
tippy toe tippy toe.
Hey, Mary Ball
tip toe fine.

### WHO HAS RED ON?

G.L. has a red shirt,
red shirt, red shirt
G.L. has a red shirt
in school today.

**COMMENT**   These songs are great at the beginning of the year when children are getting to know each other. Also use them when you are trying to get a group together and you have a few wanderers ("Hey, Jamie Deiner, come join us").

*Especially good for* ADJUSTMENT needs: helps them feel part of the group and unique at the same time. If children with HEALTH needs have been absent, this provides an easy way to refresh their memory of the children's names without embarrassment. For INTELLECTUAL needs, use throughout the year as a reminder of other's names.

# COUNTING SONGS

**GOAL**   To improve sensory integration
To improve number concepts

**OBJECTIVE**   The child will count from 1 to 10.

**MATERIALS**   None

**PROCEDURE**   Sing the song "Ten Little Indians" and variations of it: "Ten Little Pennies," "... Buttons," "... Children," "... Pencils," "... Chairs," and so on. When you use large objects, tap them; put small ones in a can. Be dramatic; forget where you are in the middle of the song and have the children figure out the next number by counting the objects.

**CONTINUATION**   Once the children improve their number concepts of 1 to 10, have them sing the song using the numbers from 10 to 20.

**COMMENT**  *Especially good for* INTELLECTUAL needs: Sing slowly; this will reinforce the other ways you are working on number concepts. Have GIFTED and TALENTED count by 2s.

# MUSICAL COLORS

**GOAL**  To improve sensory integration
To improve shape concepts
To improve color concepts

**OBJECTIVE**  The child will name the color and the shape he lands on.

**MATERIALS**  A variety of colored shapes, one for each child, mounted on cardboard and placed in a circle

**PROCEDURE**  Play music and have the children move around the outside of the circle of colored shapes. When the music stops, have the children sit on the nearest shape. Ask them to name the color and the shape. If you want to make this a game, eliminate those who do not know. Remove some of the shapes (probably the easiest ones) so that again the number of colored shapes matches the number of children, and start the music again. Continue until only one child is left. The longer the children last in the game, the more colors and shapes they know.

**CONTINUATION**  As the children become more competent, you can use shades of colors (pink, violet, and so on) and more difficult shapes (oval, cross, and so on). As they circle around the shapes to the music, have the children move like various animals. Use numbers and letters instead of colors and shapes.

**COMMENT**  This is an adaptation of musical chairs based on color/shape recognition but without the mad scramble: There is a place for everyone.

*Especially good for* LEARNING needs: They must listen for an auditory cue and then move to a visual shape. INTELLECTUAL needs can learn shapes and colors if you are careful to stop the music when they are near the simpler shapes. This can be adapted for PHYSICAL needs so they do not have to sit down or move fast.

# Movement

## INDEX

Movement helps children become aware of their body. This awareness in turn can help them express feelings and moods, improve self-control, and learn how to relax at will. It is important for exceptional children to learn to relax, since many disabilities are worsened by tension. These children are frequently placed in tension-producing situations, such as visits to doctors, physical therapists, audiologists, or having to take endless batteries of tests. Movement exploration teaches children to discover their own best ways both to relax and to work off excess energy. Movement activities help develop rhythm and balancing techniques (putting the arms out may make it easier to balance on one foot). They can provide sensory integration and offer an opportunity for creativity and expression.

Movement can be integrated with other activities, especially music, and done in small or large groups. It is important not to judge movements as being silly or awkward, and to see movement of all kinds as being equally appropriate for both boys and girls. The more freely and easily a child can move in the world, the more opportunities he will have for exploration and active involvement with materials of all kinds.

## MOVEMENT GOALS

- To increase body awareness. Before children can control motions they need to know how to make them and how this feels. Movement exploration allows children to compare their body when it is tight and tense to when it is limp and relaxed and to compare an open, stretched position to a curled position.
- To encourage creative movement. In addition to becoming more aware of their bodies, children can, through movement, become a tree in the wind, a flower ready to bloom, or a fish swimming against the current. By actually acting out their interpretations of these events, they can learn about nature and themselves.
- To relax at will. Children must learn to relax in a conscious way since tension is related to the occurence of episodic illnesses. Children often have their most difficult times when tension is high. If children can learn to relax during these times, the situation is often eased. Children with special needs face tense situations more frequently than other children.
- To increase sensory integration. By pairing movement with other activities, such as music and art, children can learn to more fully understand both experiences. They can interpret music as

they explore the relationship of loud music to expansive movements, whether or not they have the language skills to express their feelings.

## TEACHING STRATEGIES

Children with SPEECH AND LANGUAGE needs must increase their body awareness and learn to recognize when they are tense. Many speech problems increase under tension; therefore, children with language needs rarely talk under conditions of stress. They need to learn to recognize and deal with these situations at an early age.

Children with HEARING needs also often retreat under stress. As the sense of balance is located in the inner ear, these children's sense of balance may be impaired and they probably need extra experience learning how to move without falling. These children benefit especially from individualized activities in which they are neither right nor wrong.

Children with VISUAL needs need to spend a lot of time on orientation and mobility skills. They must learn a variety of ways of moving safely. With creative movement activities, they can enjoy learning these skills.

Children with LEARNING needs can use movement to increase sensory integration, express emotions, and learn to control their body. Creative movement activities should be geared to their individual needs.

Children with ADJUSTMENT needs can be part of the group; movements that might at other times be thought unusual could at this time be considered creative. As long as there is no right or wrong, these children can participate and learn about their body, discover how to relax, and perhaps find some ways to work through feelings.

Children with HEALTH needs can learn to express feelings and concerns that they may not have the words for. They can learn body control and ways to move that are optimal for them.

Children with PHYSICAL needs may be limited in their ability to move. If this is the case, they need to develop those muscles they *can* use, so they can use them to compensate for those they cannot use.

CULTURALLY DISTINCT children will discover that movement is universal. These activities provide a place for them to share and to be with others while learning more about their own body.

Children with INTELLECTUAL needs can profit from the work on body awareness. They may not have the most creative interpretations, but for them the practice moving and the opportunity to be part of a nonjudgmental group is far more important than that.

GIFTED AND TALENTED children can take advantage of the creative opportunities in movement to express themselves through their body. As their motor needs are closer to their chronological age than to their mental age, this may give them the opportunity to be more like the other children.

# BE THE BODY

**GOAL**  To increase body awareness

**OBJECTIVE**  The child will assume the same position as the cardboard body.

**MATERIALS**  cardboard (enough to cut out a child-size body)
scissors
brads

**PROCEDURE**  Cut parts of a body out of cardboard and fasten them together at the joints with brads. First, have the children lie on the body and assume its positions. Work up to playing a game with the body in which one child arranges the cardboard body parts and another assumes that body configuration. Be sure to tell the children what they are doing: "Good, you raised your right arm."

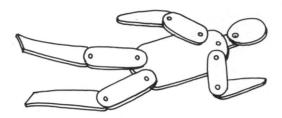

**CONTINUATION** This can be a group time activity if you arrange the body and have all the children assume its positions.

**COMMENT** LEARNING and HEARING needs: allows these children to both see and feel the positions of the body. VISUAL needs can feel the body and assume the same position. Be sure to label the body parts for SPEECH AND LANGUAGE needs. CULTURALLY DISTINCT may need the body parts labeled in two languages.

# BE IT

**GOAL** To increase body awareness
To encourage creative movement

**OBJECTIVE** The child will use his body to show how an object moves.

**MATERIALS** Pictures of objects that move:

| | |
|---|---|
| airplanes | wind mills |
| trains | helicopters |
| birds | worms |
| kites | |

**PROCEDURE** Show the children the pictures and discuss how they might make their body move like the objects in the pictures. Encourage creativity by pointing out differences in the children's interpretations and by not making judgments.

**CONTINUATION** On another day, dismiss the children from group time by having them fly like a bird to the art table and so on.

**COMMENT** Have an appropriate way to stop the children's movements: airport, train station, heliport. *Especially good for* LEARNING needs: requires children to integrate visual and auditory stimuli and translate them into active, physical movement. For GIFTED AND TALENTED, use some unusual objects, and for CULTURALLY DISTINCT, use objects from a variety of cultures. HEARING needs can use the pictures and translate these into movements. Help these children if their movements are initially inappropriate. For VISUAL needs, discuss the object and how it moves (fast, slowly, in air, on water, overland) to broaden the children's experiences.

# MOVEMENT EXPLORATION

**GOAL** To increase body awareness
To encourage creative movement

**OBJECTIVE** The child will move in response to the directions given.

**MATERIALS** None

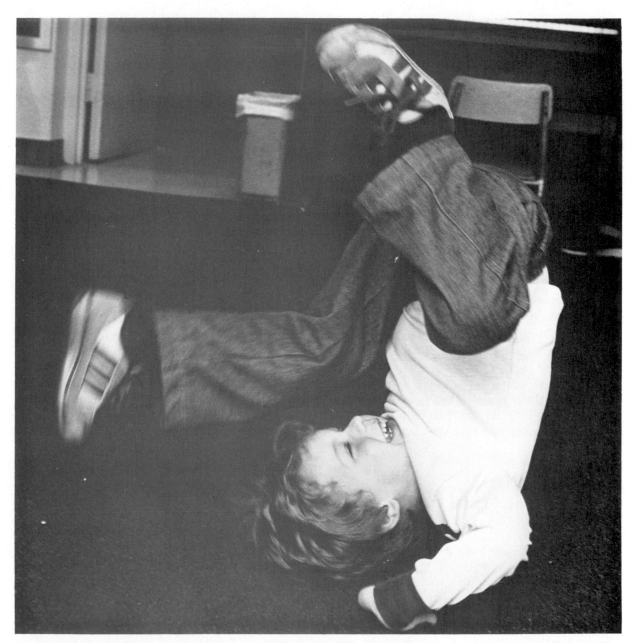

Children learn about their bodies by experimenting. For some children movement is easy and fun; for others it is difficult.

**PROCEDURE**    Ask the children to move in unusual ways, such as:

Use any 3 parts of your body to move across the floor:
  1 hand, 2 feet
  2 hands, 1 foot
  1 hand, 2 knees
Hold your feet with your hands and pretend they are connected: How many ways can you move across the floor?
Can you move across the floor without touching your feet on the ground?

**COMMENT**    After one child has responded to a request, see if other children can respond to the same request in a different way. *Especially good for* PHYSICAL needs: These children may be very skillful in following the directions. With discussion, others may become aware of the problems of not being able to use one or more limbs. Challenge GIFTED AND TALENTED by calling on them last or for particularly difficult situations. For HEARING needs, use pictures of the body parts or demonstrate which parts can be used.

# RAG DOLL

**GOAL**   To increase body awareness
To relax at will

**OBJECTIVE**   The child will move in a loose, relaxed manner.

**MATERIALS**   Rag doll

**PROCEDURE**   Show the children a rag doll and demonstrate how it moves. Start with the children lying down and show them what happens to the rag doll when the legs and arms are lifted. Then go around the class and check out your collection of "rag dolls." Raise limbs an inch or two and see how floppy children can be. (Don't drop a leg very far or the children will tense!)

**CONTINUATION**   As the children learn to relax lying down, see if they can gain skill in locating just the muscles they need; that is, they can sit up while keeping their arms and head relaxed. Then have them try standing. Eventually add music.

**COMMENT**   Tension increases pain, so anything you can teach children about relaxing is useful. It will be especially helpful to those who will be going through scary or painful medical experiences, but most children find *all* contact with dentists and doctors an occasion for tension. *Especially good for* HEALTH needs: helps these children handle continual contact with the doctors. LEARNING and ADJUSTMENT needs often become so wound up that they lash out and cannot gain control of their bodies. This activity can help them regain control. GIFTED AND TALENTED can enjoy the challenge of learning to relax specific body parts as well as the fun and creativity of being a floppy dancer.

# RELAXATION STORIES

**GOAL**   To increase body awareness
To relax at will

**OBJECTIVE**   The child will relax his body while listening to the story.

**MATERIALS**   None

**PROCEDURE**   Have the children lie down and shut their eyes. Tell them a story while they listen and relax. The actual content of the story may vary with what your class has done and the experiences your children are familiar with. An example follows:

> There was a little boy who was tired, but he couldn't go to sleep; he had the wiggles. Every time a part of him was tired, another part would start to wiggle, and he'd giggle, and then he couldn't go to sleep. So he decided to tell himself a sleepy story. He started with his toes and said, "Toes, don't wiggle," but they kept wiggling. Then he said, "Toes, we're going to the beach and we are going to walk through so much sand that you'll be glad not to wiggle." And he walked and he walked and he walked and finally he was so tired that he sat down and his toes weren't wiggling. They were too tired. His ankles were tired and so were his knees. They felt heavy. Even his legs felt heavy. It just felt nice to be sitting down. Maybe even lying down. Oh, stretch out. . . . Umm. Rest your head back, get comfortable, close your eyes. . . . Oh, relax those tired feet again, all the way up the leg. Now your hip. Now your middle. Let your shoulders touch the floor if they want to; your elbows too. Now your hands. Uncurl your fingers. Even that little finger is heavy. Now let's check on the way back up. The wrists, elbows, and shoulders are all heavy and relaxed. Move your head up and lay it down; roll it a little to find a comfortable place. Open your mouth. Now close it. Yawn. Close your eyes.

Pause. Breath deeply. Pause. You're waking up. Roll your head, open your eyes. Sit up and wiggle just a little.

**COMMENT**   The relaxation portion of this is best spoken in a slow, placid monotone. At first, make your pauses short. As the children gain skill, increase the length of the pauses and incorporate some visual images. *Especially good for* SPEECH AND LANGUAGE needs: The vocabulary for the body parts is useful; the ability to relax is valuable when it becomes voluntary. For VISUAL needs and perhaps LEARNING needs who may not know the body parts, lightly touch the parts as you talk or have someone else do that. ADJUSTMENT needs can increase their body awareness and voluntary muscle control. HEALTH and PHYSICAL needs can increase body awareness and learn a skill to decrease pain. GIFTED AND TALENTED can enjoy the visual images they imagine while being part of the group and learning a valuable skill.

# MIRROR MOVEMENT

**GOAL**   To increase body awareness
To improve sensory integration

**OBJECTIVE**   The child will both lead and follow the body movements of his partner.

**MATERIALS**   None

**PROCEDURE**   Pair up the children and have them face each other. Pick one child in each pair to be the first "mover." Start out with very slow movements. The second child should follow the movement in a mirrorlike fashion. (If child A raises the left hand, child B raises the right hand.) Encourage a variety of movements after the children understand the procedure.

**CONTINUATION**   Have the children use movements that are slightly faster, more complex, and subtler.

**COMMENT**   This should be a nonjudgmental activity that provides for a variety of levels of participation. Even if children choose just to stand and have their partners stand, they are in fact mirroring each other. *Especially good for* ADJUSTMENT needs: encourages a sense of belonging and an acceptance of peculiar movements. This helps LEARNING needs to increase body control. Have VISUAL needs lightly touch their partner's hands to follow the movements. For PHYSICAL needs, restrict the limbs used to those that children can control. Some children may have to sit in order to free their arms for movement.

# TEMPO

**GOAL**   To increase body awareness
To improve sensory integration

**OBJECTIVE**   The child will change the speed of his movements as the tempo of the music changes.

**MATERIALS**   Drum or piano

**PROCEDURE**   Have the children lie down on the floor, spaced so that they can stretch and not touch each other. As they are lying there, tell them that you want them to listen to the beat and move according to how fast or slow the beat is. They can move any body parts they want in any way as long as they remain in one place on their back. Start with a slow beat so you can watch and make comments to the children about their movements. Then abruptly go to a fast beat. If they move with you, get finer gradations to your changes.

**COMMENT**   This activity can be used to quiet excited children. *Especially good for* LEARNING needs who have problems moving between these two states. VISUAL needs can pick up the mood as well as the movement. For PHYSICAL and HEALTH needs, pace your periods of vigorous beat so that the children don't become too tired. Emphasize the quality of the movement.

# WEIGHTY MOVEMENTS

**GOAL**   To increase body awareness
To improve sensory integration

**OBJECTIVE**   The child will follow the movements as directed.

**MATERIALS**   records
record player

**PROCEDURE**   Talk to the children about the way they move. Talk about the weight of their movements. Ask them to stomp across the floor, then tiptoe across the floor. Have them label which was light and which was heavy. Have them demonstate other heavy and light movements. Then have them combine heavy and light movements in a rhythmic fashion using heavy movements to accent the beat (light, light, heavy, light, light, heavy). Add music and see if they can accent the beat with their movements.

**COMMENT**   *Especially good for* SPEECH AND LANGUAGE needs: emphasizes the rhythmic nature of movement, especially as it is paired with music. CULTURALLY DISTINCT: Add rhythm patterns that are more familiar and representative of a particular culture. The broadening of the rhythm patterns is great for GIFTED AND TALENTED, as they can learn more about music and movement.

# IN AND OUT

**GOAL**   To increase body awareness
To follow directions

**OBJECTIVE**   The child will crawl through the designated holes.

**MATERIALS**   a refrigerator-size box          clear contact paper
paints or colored tape

**PROCEDURE**   Make holes in the box in a variety of geometric shapes that are the right size for the children to crawl through. Paint or tape the borders of these shapes with different colors inside and outside. Cover the paint with clear contact paper so that it doesn't come off on clothes. Ask the children to go in one place and come out another: "Go in the blue triangle and come out the red circle." You may need a skylight so that colors can be seen from the inside.

**CONTINUATION**   Vary the movements the child must make: crawl using arms only, one arm and one leg, blindfolded, and so on. Discuss how easy and how difficult these different ways are.

**COMMENT**   *Especially good for* INTELLECTUAL, LEARNING, and VISUAL needs: Children can feel the shapes while doing a motor task. (If the child can't see the colors, leave color out of the directions.)

# MOVING BALLOONS

**GOAL**   To increase body awareness
To follow directions

**OBJECTIVE**   The child will follow the directions given.

**MATERIALS**  Balloons

**PROCEDURE**  Show the children several balloons, then blow them up. Talk about what happens if you do different things to a balloon (tie it in the middle and pinch off the end; blow it up until it pops, if you are comfortable doing this; let the air out fast, then slowly, stopping sometimes). Then have the children pretend their bodies are balloons. Talk them through the process of being blown up, then have them slowly let the air out. Have them let it out fast, and so on.

**CONTINUATION**  Once children are familiar with this activity, have small groups of children be one balloon by joining hands and being blown up and deflated together.

**COMMENT**  Having a variety of shapes and sizes of balloons encourages creativity in children. *Especially good for* LEARNING and ADJUSTMENT needs: allows energy release in a controlled way. For PHYSICAL and HEALTH needs, you can regulate the amount of exertion by the directions you give.

# CIRCLES

**GOAL**  To increase body awareness
     To increase feelings of group belonging

**OBJECTIVE**  The child will be part of at least three different types of circles.

**MATERIALS**  None

**PROCEDURE**  Have the children sit down in a circle. Then discuss how many different ways they can make circles as a group. (Standing, holding hands, kneeling, bending down, feet together. If they join hands and lean back, they can have a circle of feet inside a circle of hands.)

**CONTINUATION**  You might ask the children to make big and small circles or to make circles using just their own body. You can also suggest other shapes

**COMMENT**  *Especially good for* ADJUSTMENT and HEALTH needs: These children can be part of the group, yet the activity is not demanding. For children with VISUAL, HEARING, and LEARNING needs, this experience lets them feel geometric shapes they usually only see.

# BODY MANEUVERS

**GOAL**  To increase body awareness
     To encourage creative movement
     To follow directions

**OBJECTIVE**  The child will move in response to the directions given.

**MATERIALS**  None

**PROCEDURE**  Start by having the children follow some fairly simple directions. See if they can make their bodies as small as possible, then as large as possible (discuss the effect of a deep breath on this). Then have them crawl under a chair or stretch to reach something very high (a real object). Have them pretend they are crawling through a small hole or a tunnel that turns periodically; climbing up a steep, rock-faced mountain; walking on a high, thin wire; and so on.

**CONTINUATION**  Introduce other factors for children to adapt to: The tunnel gets muddy; a wind comes up; they see a bear.

**COMMENT**  *Especially good for* LEARNING needs: requires the integration of auditory information into movement. GIFTED AND TALENTED children can be challenged by the conditions under which these maneuvers must be performed.

# FLOPSY

**GOAL**   To increase body awareness
To encourage creative movement
To improve balance skills

**OBJECTIVE**   The child will perform the designated activity.

**MATERIALS**   A mattress

**PROCEDURE**   Put an old mattress or piece of 5-inch foam on the floor, preferably in the center of a piece of carpet. Have the children jump, roll, walk, and so forth on the mattress. Encourage them to experiment by doing these activities on the floor and then on the mattress.

**COMMENT**   This is a very good rainy or snowy day activity. *Especially good for* INTELLECTUAL and HEALTH needs: The motion helps lung drainage for children with respiratory problems. ADJUSTMENT and LEARNING needs can use the energy release. Balance practice is great for HEARING needs.

# TENSE ME

**GOAL**   To increase body awareness
To relax at will
To follow directions

**OBJECTIVE**   The child will tense and relax the designated body parts.

**MATERIALS**   None

**PROCEDURE**   Have all the children lie or sit on the floor. Sitting is easier at the beginning because both you and they can see better. Have them make a tight fist or muscle in one arm and feel that arm with their other hand. Then tell them to see how loose (relaxed) they can make that arm. Again have them feel it with their other hand. Discuss the difference in feeling. Next move to the face and have them make their face "tight" ("tight" and "loose" or "floppy" seem to work better than the words "tense" and "relaxed"). Again, ask them to feel their faces, this time with both hands. They might even look in the mirror. Then have them see if they can relax by wiping away the tightness with their hands.

**CONTINUATION**   See if the children can learn to isolate parts of their body and tense just that part: Can they tense the right arm and keep the right fist relaxed? This is more difficult.

**COMMENT**   Before children can voluntarily relax, they need to learn the feeling of what relaxation is. Otherwise, they won't know what they are striving for. *Especially good for* HEALTH, ADJUSTMENT, and LEARNING needs: It is important for these children to develop the ability to relax voluntarily. Repeated practice of this activity will help SPEECH AND LANGUAGE needs and CULTURALLY DISTINCT, who may not participate in activities if they are tense or do not feel part of the group. For some PHYSICAL needs, learning to be aware of tension and to control it may make a difference in their long-term ability to move.

# MUSIC AND MOVEMENT

**GOAL**   To encourage creative movement
To improve sensory integration

**OBJECTIVE**   The child will move in a way that is appropriate to the mood of the record.

**MATERIALS**   record player
a record

**PROCEDURE**  Start with a fairly well-known, obvious, familiar selection such as the song "Toyland" from *Babes in Toyland*. Tell the children a story about a toy shop and have them discuss the various toys that might be there. Ask them to close their eyes and picture the toys. Then play the record and have them *be* the toys.

**CONTINUATION**  Use other themes that children can relate to, such as a parade, the circus, and so on.

**COMMENT**  If you think the children might not be familiar with the toys or other themes discussed, precede the activity with a field trip. *Especially good for* LEARNING and ADJUSTMENT needs: an energy release. CULTURALLY DISTINCT will find this a way of integrating new experiences and sharing music from their culture. Encourage GIFTED AND TALENTED to respond creatively to the music and to discuss how they feel as they move. Choose slower paced music for PHYSICAL and HEALTH needs.

# MOVING COLORS

**GOAL**  To encourage creative movement
To increase awareness of moods

**OBJECTIVE**  The child will move in a way that expresses his reaction to the color.

**MATERIALS**  cards of various colors
pictures of objects of various colors

**PROCEDURE**  Hold up a color card and ask the children how the color makes them feel. Have them name objects that could be that color. Show them pictures of significant objects that are traditionally that color.

red: stop signs
fire engines
orange: safety hats and vests
yellow: sun
blue: water
white: uniforms
snow
green: grass
trees

Then have them move creatively to the color cards as you hold them up. Note the differences in how children move in response to a color. There is no right or wrong interpretation.

**CONTINUATION**  Coordinate this activity with an art section on color. Add music to enhance the mood. Place colored cellophane over the projector and turn down the light to create a whole atmosphere of color.

**COMMENT**  *Especially good for* HEARING needs: These children need to use any visual cues available to interpret mood. Once an individual color–mood link has been formed, it can be used as a shorthand way to make children with LEARNING and ADJUSTMENT needs aware of what level of activity is appropriate.

# Dramatic Play

## INDEX

| Goal | Activity | Page |
| --- | --- | --- |
| To improve cause and effect reasoning | Dress Up and Tell | 492 |
| | Shoe Store | 487 |
| | What Shall We Make? | 495 |
| To improve sequencing skills | Day Play | 490 |
| To improve decision making | No Name | 494 |
| To improve time concepts | Day Play | 490 |
| To increase survival skills | Emergency Room | 487 |
| To cooperate with peers | Audiologist | 489 |
| | Eye Doctor | 490 |
| | No Name | 494 |
| To improve eye–hand coordination | What Shall We Make? | 495 |
| To encourage creativity | Puppets | 492 |
| | Who Am I? | 491 |
| To encourage creative problem solving | Connections | 488 |
| To increase body awareness | Circus | 486 |
| | Slings | 494 |
| To increase awareness of hearing needs | Audiologist | 489 |
| To increase awareness of physical needs | Cast It | 486 |
| | Slings | 494 |
| To increase awareness of visual needs | Eye Doctor | 490 |
| To increase awareness of other cultures | Panama | 491 |

Dramatic play is spontaneous, self-expressive play through which a child can learn to understand himself and his relation to others and to the world around him. In dramatic play children construct a world in which they can make up for defeats and frustrations and experiment with different ways of working out fears, feelings, and uncertainties. Dramatic play can help the exceptional child grow in social understanding and cooperation; it provides a controlled emotional outlet and a means of self-expression. Because it involves the whole child—body, mind, emotions, and experience—dramatic play is an exciting curriculum area where much can be accomplished.

You, the teacher, can use dramatic play as an index to measure the growth and development of children. Through observations you can assess small and large motor coordination, speech development, social–emotional growth, and concept formation.

There are developmental progressions in dramatic play; young children who have not had much experience playing with others often play alone or next to another child in a parallel fashion. As children grow older, they demonstrate increased language skills, attention span, and subject matter. Dramatic play becomes more complex; children begin to play cooperatively and form loose groups. These groups are formed with a purpose, and members of the groups are assigned various roles. Some division, however fleeting, of leader and follower appears.

## DRAMATIC PLAY GOALS

- To increase awareness of roles people play. Children with special needs encounter many people in the medical and helping professions. It is important that they learn what these people do as well as have the opportunity to work through some of the feelings they have about these people and the procedures they use. Dramatic play offers a safe opportunity to do that.
- To increase feelings of group belonging. Children can participate in dramatic play at many different levels. They can play alone or with other children. If they choose, they can just play beside others, or they can organize a group that has a purpose and everyone in the group a particular responsibility in helping to attain that purpose. They can choose roles that meet their individual interests and needs.
- To improve expressive language. Children who cannot participate in certain experiences because of their special needs can do so vicariously through dramatic play. Encourage them to learn the expressive language to talk about the experience as well as increase the scope of their knowledge.

## TEACHING STRATEGIES

This area is one that allows children with SPEECH AND LANGUAGE needs to work on language skills without fear of judgment. They can practice situations before encountering them, as well as work through sensory motor experiences they have had. If speech is difficult, they can use puppets, talk on the telephone, or dress up and pretend they are another person. Above all, encourage them to talk.

Help children with HEARING needs act out situations that they are likely to encounter. Use as many props as you can, and keep them realistic. Help the children learn what to do in a given situation through dramatic role play. First, set up the situation at school so they can practice appropriate behavior. Then, if possible, have a related field trip. Act out the situation again in school as reinforcement, and have the children show you what they have learned.

Children with VISUAL needs, like those with HEARING needs, require many props in order to participate fully. Choose props that can be easily identified by feel. If you keep the props in the same place, it will be easy for these children to find the ones they need.

For children with LEARNING needs use the dramatic play area to help them become more aware of roles and feelings. Help them express caring and happy feelings as well as sad, angry, and unhappy ones. As holidays and special events are often stressful for these children, playing them through may help.

This area has great potential for helping children with ADJUSTMENT needs work through their fears and anxieties about specific issues. Under your guidance they can play with other children, free from threatening demands. If talking directly about situations produces anxiety, have the child pretend to be someone else or talk through a puppet.

Children with HEALTH and PHYSICAL needs are often restricted as to what they can and can't do. Help them experience some of the can'ts vicariously by using their imaginations in dramatic play. Also help them work or play through situations that they find scary. Use full-length mirrors to increase body awareness.

Children with INTELLECTUAL needs may need a dramatic play area filled with familiar materials; try starting with a housekeeping area to which you gradually add more materials. Provide simple, realistic props for them to practice using.

Dramatic play is a way of learning about other cultures. Let CULTURALLY DISTINCT children share firsthand some of the ways they do things that might be different. Have them show slides or use travel folders to help children get the feel for another area. This is also a good way to teach CULTURALLY DISTINCT children about our culture.

Provide GIFTED AND TALENTED children with enough props to create ideas but not so many that they stifle creativity and problem solving.

# DENTIST

**GOAL**   To increase awareness of roles people play

**OBJECTIVE**   The child will play the roles of both dental office personnel and patient.

**MATERIALS**   Props for a "dentist's office":

| | | |
|---|---|---|
| dental floss | cups of water | lab coat |
| tongue depressors | pretend drill | chair |
| cloth for around neck | small mirrors | table |

**PROCEDURE**   Set up a dentist's office. Allow children to play the dentist, dental hygienist, nurse, receptionist, patient, parent of patient, and so on. Encourage them to talk about their concerns. Also talk about why it is important to go to the dentist.

**CONTINUATION**   Precede this with a trip to a dentist's office and follow it with some information on teeth and food. Talk about the care of the teeth and oral area as well as its function in speech.

**COMMENT**   Be sure that all materials that are likely to be in children's mouths are clean. *Especially good for* ADJUSTMENT, HEALTH, and LEARNING needs: They may be fearful of trips to the dentist; this might help them work through some of those concerns and control their fears. For children with SPEECH AND LANGUAGE and HEARING needs, discuss the function and importance of teeth in speech. Add a listening tape of the dentist's office. This will help VISUAL needs and others because the sounds are often frightening, especially when children can't see what is making them. With GIFTED AND TALENTED and CULTURALLY DISTINCT, emphasize the role of dentists and that both men and woman can be dentists.

# DOCTOR'S OFFICE

**GOAL**   To increase awareness of roles people play

**OBJECTIVE**   The child will pretend to be the doctor, nurse, or patient.

**MATERIALS**   Props for a doctor's office:

| | |
|---|---|
| stethoscope | flashlight (without batteries) |
| syringes (without needles) | tongue depressors |
| dolls | lab coat |

**PROCEDURE**   Set up the dramatic play area like a doctor's office. Have the children examine "sick" dolls and/or classmates. Be sure to include information on routine procedures, such as immunization and regular checkups, in addition to sick calls.

**COMMENT**   This will probably be a familiar situation since most of the children have been to the doctor for a checkup. Introduce this with a story or visit from a doctor. Be sure to discuss why people go to doctors.

*Especially good for* ADJUSTMENT and LEARNING needs: They may be afraid of doctors. HEALTH needs may want to have lots of time to be the doctor—in control for a change. Be sure to leave time for this. For GIFTED AND TALENTED, use more complicated props and give more information on procedures.

# CAST IT

**GOAL**   To increase awareness of roles people play
To increase awareness of physical needs

**OBJECTIVE**   The child will put a cast on either a doll or a classmate.

**MATERIALS**   plaster tape (available at most drug stores)     water
scissors without points     dolls
broken chicken bone

**PROCEDURE**   Talk about broken bones: show one from an animal and talk about what a cast does for a bone. Set up the dramatic play area with plaster tape (just soak it in water to use it), a bucket of water, and dolls. First, have the children experiment with a doll. Then, if you want, have them put a cast on a thumb or finger. The cast will slip off, but you might feel more secure if you have some blunt-nosed fingernail scissors so you can cut off any stubborn ones. Discuss with the children that breaking bones hurts, but casting doesn't.

**CONTINUATION**   If most of the children put casts on their thumbs, you can make an art project out of decorating the casts.

**COMMENT**   You might warn parents about this project so they will know their child's thumb isn't really broken when he wears his cast home.

It is possible that any child in your class may have to have a cast put on. Children who know how and why casts are put on and taken off are less fearful when they need an actual cast, especially children with PHYSICAL, HEALTH, LEARNING, and ADJUSTMENT needs. VISUAL and HEARING needs and CULTURALLY DISTINCT gain more understanding of the process involved by doing it themselves as they realize it really doesn't hurt. For GIFTED AND TALENTED children, talk at length about how casts work and why they are necessary.

# CIRCUS

**GOAL**   To increase awareness of roles people play
To increase body awareness

**OBJECTIVE**   The child will participate in at least one event.

**MATERIALS**   Props for a circus:
hats     balance beam
scarves     stuffed animals
costumes     mats

**PROCEDURE**   Encourage children to cooperate in developing circus acts using the props.

**CONTINUATION**   Read a story about the circus and talk about animal trainers, acrobats, tightrope walkers, and so on. Be sure to have this activity if there is a circus in town.

**COMMENT**   See that there are plenty of different acts so all the children can participate at an appropriate level. *Especially good for* GIFTED AND TALENTED: They could help to organize the circus. SPEECH AND LANGUAGE, PHYSICAL, HEARING, VISUAL, HEALTH, CULTURALLY DISTINCT, LEARNING, and

INTELLECTUAL needs can show the things they do well in an informal atmosphere without a formal audience.

# EMERGENCY ROOM

**GOAL**    To increase awareness of roles people play
To increase survival skills

**OBJECTIVE**    The child will play the role of either the doctor or the patient.

**MATERIALS**    An emergency room set-up:

| | |
|---|---|
| table | paper |
| chairs | pencils |
| bandages | lab coat |

**PROCEDURE**    Set up the dramatic play area as an emergency room. During group time, talk about the reasons for going to the emergency room: a broken bone a bad cut or burn, as opposed to a headache or a cold. Talk to the children about what would be likely to happen: someone would ask for their name and insurance number, and they would have to wait. Also discuss what they could do while they wait, what the doctor might do, and the possibility that they would not know the doctor.

**COMMENT**    The purpose of this is really to familiarize the child with a set of procedures so that the fear of the emergency room is not added to the medical problem if they should have to go. Try to have an element of realism as well as creativity. See this as a variation on the doctor's office, although the element of time, the reasons for going to the emergency room, and the other people in the waiting room are different.

*Especially good for* HEALTH needs: They are more likely than others to go to an emergency room; GIFTED AND TALENTED can consider when and why it is appropriate to go to the emergency room rather than to the doctor's office.

# SHOE STORE

**GOAL**    To increase awareness of roles people play
To improve cause and effect reasoning

**OBJECTIVE**    The child will select and buy a pair of shoes appropriate for his stated purpose.

**MATERIALS**    Shoes for different purposes:

| | | |
|---|---|---|
| baseball shoes with cleats | walking shoes | shoes with steel toes |
| running shoes | clogs | baby shoes |
| high heels | winter slippers | golf shoes |
| ballet slippers | sandals | bowling shoes |
| toe shoes | boots | thongs |
| hiking boots | | |

**PROCEDURE**    During group time, discuss with the children the functions of shoes and how some situations require certain kinds of shoes. Have some examples and talk about how these shoes make it easier. Use obvious examples:

> steel toes: won't hurt if something gets dropped on the toes
> baseball cleats: get better traction running, less likely to slip
> sandals: cooler

Once children have grasped the idea, have them use it in dramatic play to choose the shoes they need.

**COMMENT**   This activity not only teaches the principles of buying and selling but also teaches specialized ways of coping with environments. *Especially good for* GIFTED AND TALENTED: They can use the concept of shoes to think through requirements of various roles. For INTELLECTUAL needs, have the children pair up the shoes after several pairs have been taken out. For HEARING needs, provide pictures of the people or places where the shoes might be used. If these pictures are pasted to the boxes, the children can help put the shoes away.

# BOOKSTORE

**GOAL**   To increase awareness of roles people play
To improve expressive language
To increase feelings of group belonging

**OBJECTIVE**   The child will pretend he is buying and selling books.

**MATERIALS**   Props for a bookstore:

| | |
|---|---|
| books | cash register |
| "money" | bags |

**PROCEDURE**   Set up a bookstore in your room with a collection of children's books that can be categorized by the pictures on the front; use books about the country, animals, people, and so one. Encourage children to look over the selection and ask for the books they want. Be sure some children are clerks and some consumers.

**COMMENT**   *Especially good for* SPEECH AND LANGUAGE needs and CULTURALLY DISTINCT: fosters interest in books and language, allows choice, and encourages role playing. Encourage GIFTED AND TALENTED to use their ability to read (if they can) to aid in the selection of books.

# CONNECTIONS

**GOAL**   To increase awareness of roles people play
To increase feelings of group belonging
To encourage creative problem solving

**OBJECTIVE**   The child will make one statement about what will happen when a connection is cut.

**MATERIALS**

| | |
|---|---|
| string | wide marking pen |
| 8″ × 8″ squares of construction | tape |
| paper of various colors | scissors |

**PROCEDURE**   Pick a familiar place (e.g., the children's school) and draw a large picture of that place. Help the children think through the places in the city or services they are dependent upon. As each is mentioned, write the name on a piece of paper, attach string with a piece of tape, give this to a child, and secure the other end of the string to a central location in the picture. (See illustration on page 489.)

Talk about what each connection signifies. Then take a pair of scissors and cut one string (e.g., electric). Ask the children how the school would be different without electricity and what they could do to compensate: no lights—use flashlights or candles.

**CONTINUATION**   Use other familiar places like the fire department, hospital, department store, and so on.

**COMMENT**   Children can even use their homes and talk about it with their parents. It's important that children see the interdependency of services as well as the alternatives for services, if

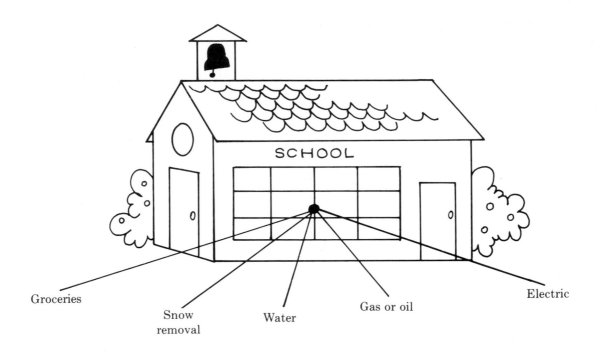

necessary. *Especially good for* GIFTED AND TALENTED: may give them another perspective on community relations and should challenge their creative problem solving capacity. HEALTH and ADJUSTMENT needs can do this with any environment as a way of becoming more familiar with that environment. For CULTURALLY DISTINCT, talk about different environments and how connections are not necessarily the same in all places.

# AUDIOLOGIST

**GOAL**     To increase awareness of roles people play
To cooperate with peers
To increase awareness of hearing needs

**OBJECTIVE**    The child will play the role of either the audiologist (ear doctor) or the patient.

**MATERIALS**    Props for an audiologist's office:
bells
ear muffs
a box with knobs
buzzers

**PROCEDURE**    During group time, introduce the concept of an audiologist and what he does. Talk about how and why people get their hearing tested. Then explain that there is an audiologist's office set up in the dramatic play area. Use a box with knobs on it; bells, buzzers, or anything that makes noise; and ear muffs for earphones. Have the children "test" each other's hearing. They can raise a hand when they hear a noise.

**COMMENT**    Use this activity to prepare all the children to have their hearing tested by a nurse or an audiologist. *Especially good for* SPEECH AND LANGUAGE and HEARING needs, for whom this procedure is common: allows these children to work through any feelings they may have about the procedure. For ADJUSTMENT, CULTURALLY DISTINCT, HEALTH and PHYSICAL, VISUAL, and INTELLECTUAL needs, playing through the experiences should make actual testing less fearful and increase cooperation, which in turn should increase the accuracy of the test results. GIFTED AND TALENTED can be challenged to help find bells that vary in loudness and perhaps help set up the area.

# DAY PLAY

**GOAL**    To increase awareness of roles people play
To improve sequencing skills
To improve time concepts

**OBJECTIVE**    The child will enact a sequence of appropriate activities.

**MATERIALS**    Props for the activities of a day:

| | |
|---|---|
| kitchen | family room |
| bedroom | bathroom |
| living room | |

**PROCEDURE**    Talk about the different times of the day and the activities that go with them. Set up centers designated as specific parts of the day and have the children rotate from center to center until they have completed a whole day. Have them play different roles (themselves, mother, father, sibling) and discuss who gets up first, what or who wakes them, and what they do first. Emphasize that family patterns are different.

**COMMENT**    This can also be done with a small group of children playing out different parts of the day and others guessing the part. *Especially good for* ADJUSTMENT and LEARNING needs particularly at the beginning of of the school year if children are having difficulties adjusting to school: helps in arranging the day's activities in the proper sequence and putting them into perspective. This is also a good way to teach routines to INTELLECTUAL needs.

# EYE DOCTOR

**GOAL**    To increase awareness of roles people play
To increase awareness of visual needs
To cooperate with peers

**OBJECTIVE**    The child will play the role of either the eye doctor or the patient.

**MATERIALS**    Props for an eye doctor's office:
vision chart (the chart the children will be tested with) or a similar homemade vision chart
card with a "three-legged table" to be matched to the chart (see illustration)
glasses
frames
mirror
index card
pointer

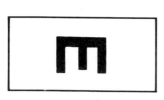

Card

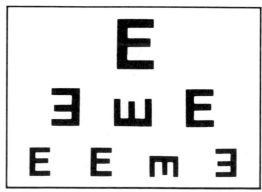

Chart

**PROCEDURE**    During group time, discuss eye doctors and what they do. Explain that you have set up the dramatic play area as an eye doctor's office. Encourage one child to be the doctor and point to the letters, another to be an assistant and help with glasses and the testing process. Have the children match the card to the chart to become familiar with the procedure. Have them talk about these roles and how they feel about them.

**COMMENT**    Follow this with vision screening by a nurse or other qualified person. This activity teaches children how doctors help people to see better and may also identify some children with vision needs. *Especially good for* VISUAL needs: They probably know the process and can help others work through any feelings they might have about it. Allow HEARING and INTELLECTUAL needs to watch the process for a few minutes, then help them through the procedure, if necessary. For ADJUSTMENT, CULTURALLY DISTINCT, LEARNING, HEALTH, PHYSICAL, and SPEECH AND LANGUAGE needs, playing through the experience should make the actual testing easier and less frightening, and the results more accurate. Encourage GIFTED AND TALENTED to experiment with the relationship between distance and seeing, and have them find where in the room they can no longer see accurately. They can then measure this distance.

# WHO AM I?

**GOAL**    To increase awareness of roles people play
To encourage creativity
To interpret body language

**OBJECTIVE**    The child will act out in pantomime the role suggested by the hat.

**MATERIALS**    Characteristic hats:

| | | |
|---|---|---|
| firefighter's hat | fishing hat | baseball hat |
| police officer's hat | cowboy hat | baby's bonnet |
| hardhat | woman's hat | rain hat |
| stocking cap | football helmet | sun bonnet |

**PROCEDURE**    Show the collection of hats to the children. Have them figure out what person would wear each hat and act out that person's role in pantomime. At first use hats that are specific to one role, then use some to broaden ideas; that is, a woman's hat could be worn by a mother, teacher, secretary, or lawyer. Talk about the characteristics of the hats that make them suitable for the people who wear them.

**COMMENT**    This is an amusing way to talk about community helpers because it uses one clue and leaves the rest to the child. You can also talk about the purpose of the hats. *Especially good for* HEARING and LEARNING needs: requires the child to use one clue to identify a role, then act out that role so others can figure out what it is. If necessary, allow VISUAL needs to feel the hats. Have GIFTED AND TALENTED analyze the subtle differences among similar hats (football helmet, motorcycle helmet, bicycle helmet).

# PANAMA

**GOAL**    To increase feelings of group belonging
To improve expressive language
To increase awareness of other cultures

**OBJECTIVE**    The child will state at least two similarities and two differences between the place where he lives and the place set up in the dramatic play area.

MATERIALS    travel pamphlets      records
                   picture books      traditional costumes

PROCEDURE    Set up the dramatic play area with the materials listed above. During group time, discuss the ways the children in your class are similar to and different from children who live in a different place. Discuss things like location, language, families, food, geography, school, size, clothing, transportation, and weather. Try to make these ideas as concrete as possible, yet not stereotypic. Encourage the children to play games and act as children in the different place might act.

CONTINUATION    Use this activity as part of a unit on travel and invite a visitor from another place.

COMMENT    Choose places based on your resources and the composition of the class. *Especially good for* GIFTED AND TALENTED: a way of expanding their environment. CULTURALLY DISTINCT can share experiences or learn with the class about other places.

# PUPPETS

GOAL    To increase feelings of group belonging
           To improve expressive language
           To encourage creativity

OBJECTIVE    The child will interact with others using puppets.

MATERIALS    puppets
                   improvised stage

PROCEDURE    Provide the children with a variety of puppets. (Sock puppets often are best because the children can make them themselves and move them easily.) Allow the children to choose and act out their feelings. If they need help, ask open-ended questions: Set the stage, but don't write the script. Encourage the expression of feelings.

CONTINUATION    Give children a "theme" to use and props. Your setting the stage may make this experience more relevant and meaningful to the special needs of some of the children.

COMMENT    *Especially good for* SPEECH AND LANGUAGE needs: They are often willing to talk through a puppet when they are self-conscious about speaking themselves. ADJUSTMENT and LEARNING needs can become more in touch with their feelings through using puppets. CULTURALLY DISTINCT and HEARING needs can participate in a nonthreatening way and be part of the group.

# DRESS UP AND TELL

GOAL    To increase feelings of group belonging
           To improve expressive language
           To improve cause and effect reasoning

OBJECTIVE    The child will dress up and tell others where he is "going" and why he chose those clothes.

MATERIALS    Clothes for dress-up:

| | | |
|---|---|---|
| dresses | scarves | sweaters |
| shirts | ties | boots/shoes |
| pants | hats | slippers |
| skirts | gloves | nightshirts/gowns |
| blouses | blazers | pajamas |
| shorts | jackets | robes |

Be sure there is variation in the above items (e.g., cotton and wool skirts) so children can dress for a season and an occasion. Have enough clothes that go together so the children really can make an outfit.

**PROCEDURE**    Have the children dress up. Before they start, encourage them to think about where they plan to "go" and what clothes meet the occasion. At the beginning you may want to ask them about their choices. "Your dress is very light and doesn't have any sleeves. Do you think this is a summer or a winter party?" Don't tell them the answer, but do help them see relevant characteristics. If at first they don't seem to realize the connections, talk further. "If you wore this dress in the winter, your arms would be bare and they might get cold. What could you put on so that wouldn't happen?"

Provide a variety of clothes so that children can dress up and experiment with roles.

**CONTINUATION**   If possible, take pictures of the children and write what they say on the back.

**COMMENT**   Keep adding a variety of clothes so children can come back to this activity. *Especially good for* SPEECH AND LANGUAGE and HEARING needs: They can think about what they want to say as they dress, and say a lot or a little. For VISUAL needs, point out the tactile features of the clothes—weight of fabric, length of sleeves, and style—and help them see why these are relevant features before they are asked to tell about them. As this is primarily a reasoning exercise, they could even request another child to bring them an article of clothing they describe. LEARNING, HEALTH, and INTELLECTUAL needs can gain practice in self-help skills while dressing up. Be sure to have some clothing that a child with PHYSICAL needs can put on easily. Encourage GIFTED AND TALENTED and CULTURALLY DISTINCT to expand their knowledge through this activity. Add clothing that is unusual—safari outfit, wetsuit, and so on. Have them write detailed stories about an outfit.

# SLINGS

**GOAL**   To increase feelings of group belonging
To increase body awareness
To increase awareness of physical needs

**OBJECTIVE**   The child will list at least three things that are hard to do with only one arm.

**MATERIALS**   A piece of material or scarf for each child, large enough to be made into a sling

**PROCEDURE**   During group time, talk about what it is like to have only one arm. (Some children are born with only one arm, others break their arms, and so on.) Have the children guess what things are difficult to do with just one arm, and encourage them to participate in activities in the dramatic play area, with one arm in a sling. At the end of the period, help the children who participated to talk about the feelings and difficulties they had. Most children, especially younger ones, will become frustrated and take the sling off. That's fine, but be sure to use their experience of frustration to make your point.

**COMMENT**   The point will be stronger if you put the dominant arm in the sling. *Especially good for* GIFTED AND TALENTED: They can increase their perception of what kinds of changes having only one arm might make. SPEECH AND LANGUAGE, CULTURALLY DISTINCT, PHYSICAL, and HEALTH needs can build vocabulary, practice speech, and get in touch with their feelings.

# NO NAME

**GOAL**   To increase feelings of group belonging
To cooperate with peers
To improve decision making

**OBJECTIVE**   The child will suggest a name for the doll.

**MATERIALS**   A doll that has not been in the classroom before

**PROCEDURE**   During group time, show the children the doll. Explain that it is new to the room and doesn't have a name. Ask the children how they think you should go about naming the doll—not what, how. Note their suggestions; then suggest that if they want, they can play with this doll in the dramatic play area. (You may have to regulate the number of children that can be there at any one time.) At the end of the day the class can actually name the doll or make suggestions that will be finalized the following day. When the group meets again, talk about the method used to reach a decision as well as the decision reached. Then ask them about their own names and why they think their parents chose those names.

**CONTINUATION**   This activity can be used for a class pet or any other thing in the classroom that can be named.

**COMMENT**   *Especially good for* SPEECH AND LANGUAGE needs: They can participate using language in a decision-making process. GIFTED AND TALENTED and ADJUSTMENT needs can be part of a group and learn skills in compromising during decision making.

# WHAT SHALL WE MAKE?

**GOAL**   To improve expressive language
To improve cause and effect reasoning
To improve eye–hand coordination

**OBJECTIVE**   The child will make an appropriate piece of doll's clothing.

**MATERIALS**

| linen | corduroy | needles |
|-------|----------|---------|
| wool | gabardine | patterns |
| gingham | knit | scissors |
| cotton | denim | pins |
| chiffon | velvet | tape |
| vinyl | fur | thread |

**PROCEDURE**   Have patterns for doll clothes (be sure to have patterns appropriate for both boys and girls). Have the children choose a pattern, then pick the material to make the desired clothing. Help the children pin or tape on the pattern, cut it out, and sew up the seams with a large needle and heavy thread. Talk about their choices of material relative to the style and weather, when it will be worn, and so on.

**COMMENT**   If the children are young, 2- and 3-year-olds, it may be enough for them to just choose the material and cut it out. A parent volunteer could do the sewing. *Especially good for* LEARNING and CULTURALLY DISTINCT: They can practice motor skills while building reasoning skills that could help them be more responsive to the environment. For HEARING needs, add pictures of the seasons (or specific occasions), have them match the material to the picture, then continue with the project. GIFTED AND TALENTED can be encouraged to make up a story about the occasion for which the clothing is worn.

# *Small Motor Play*

## INDEX

All children need to develop the small muscles of the body. These are the muscles necessary to pick up tiny objects, to draw pictures, to cut with scissors, and to perform many self-help activities such as buttoning and snapping. Small motor skills are often used in conjunction with vision. These eye–hand coordination skills also demand practice. Writing, craft activities, and many sports are dependent upon the development and refinement of the small muscles of the body.

## SMALL MOTOR PLAY GOALS

- To improve small motor coordination. Through practice children will develop the skills they need to use their small muscles smoothly.
- To improve tactile discrimination. This is especially important for children who are limited in the use of one or more of their senses.
- To improve eye–hand coordination. The ability to integrate vision and touch is an important skill for writing and cutting as well as games that involve balls.
- To increase body awareness. Small motor skills give children information about their bodies and physical activities that are difficult or easy for them to do.
- To improve self-help skills. Many of the skills required for independence in daily living require the mastery of small motor skills (e.g., pouring liquids, cutting food, buttoning, and so on).

## TEACHING STRATEGIES

Children with SPEECH AND LANGUAGE needs must develop and practice the small motor skills associated with speech, such as breath control and lip and tongue movements, in addition to those necessary for visual discrimination, writing, and self-help. When these children are practicing fine motor skills, be sure to talk with them about what they are doing.

One of the primary ways the child with HEARING needs contacts his world is through touch. It is important that this child refine that sense to gain as much information as possible. Fingerplays are particularly good, because the child can be part of a group while learning skills he needs for sign language.

Children with VISUAL needs require a great deal of practice in the small motor skills. Because these skills often involve eye–hand coordination, these children may have to learn ways of compensating as well as refining their residual vision. The tactile avenue is a good one for this child to learn from as the child can use this in conjunction with vision.

Children with LEARNING needs must practice skills such as snapping, tying, and buttoning which use body parts in coordination and which help increase the child's independence.

Children with ADJUSTMENT and LEARNING needs often have difficulty learning small motor skills. It is important that these children be encouraged to use and develop these skills without being pushed to the point of frustration.

As these activities are easily adaptable for quiet play, children with HEALTH needs can use them to pace their day. Since they have probably spent a lot of time in small motor play, try to think of variations and new materials that will keep them interested.

You may have to think up variations for children with PHYSICAL needs as well; because of physical limitations, they may already have mastered many small motor skills. To adapt activities to individual difficulties, use lightweight objects that are easily manipulated or materials that tolerate some degree of error but still work, such as blocks with bristles, which can be placed half on and half off and still stay, instead of blocks which must be correctly placed or they do not stay.

Children with INTELLECTUAL needs must devote more time than other children to small motor activities. They need simple activities and lots of practice, perhaps they could begin by just grasping small objects and letting go when they want to. Especially in the beginning, use relatively large objects with few pieces; program for success. Try to include as many self-help skills as you can.

Having children in the class who are CULTURALLY DISTINCT can add variety to your small motor activities. These children need practice, as the others do, but they may be able to introduce some new skills to the class. A small loom, new materials to touch and classify, and new games can all add interest.

GIFTED AND TALENTED children will perform small motor skills much like their peers. Their ability to plan and structure materials may be advanced, so provide a lot of materials and a wide variety to enhance creativity. But be sure that these children get the practice they need in small motor skills.

# BUTTONS

**GOAL**  To improve small motor coordination
To improve tactile discrimination

**OBJECTIVE**  The child will pair the buttons.

**MATERIALS**  12 pairs of buttons　　　　　　　　a bowl
an egg carton or ice cube tray　　　a blindfold

**PROCEDURE**  Collect pairs of buttons that feel different from each other. Put one button of each pair in an egg carton or ice cube tray section and put the other button in a bowl. Have the children match up the pairs while blindfolded.

**CONTINUATION**  This same procedure can be used with fabric, textured wallpaper discs, or small objects. If you have more than two objects that match, you can also teach number concepts.

**COMMENT**   Especially good for VISUAL and HEARING needs: By using small objects that are difficult to hold and feel at the same time, the child practices fine motor skills while learning tactile discrimination.

# FEELY BAG

**GOAL**   To improve small motor coordination
To improve tactile discrimination

**OBJECTIVE**   The child will identify an object by feeling it.

**MATERIALS**   several soft bags
objects that can be identified by feel:

| | |
|---|---|
| glasses or cups | cars and trucks |
| blocks | doll furniture |
| balls | dishes |

**PROCEDURE**   Make several large drawstring bags out of soft pliable fabric such as cotton knits, old sheets, or socks. Place an object in a bag and have the children feel through the bag to figure out what the object is. Use only one object per bag.

**COMMENT**   Almost anything in your room that will fit in the bag and has obvious tactile features will do. *Especially good for* LEARNING, PHYSICAL, and VISUAL needs: requires the children to use only their sense of touch to identify the object. As their skill increases, be sure the objects have to be felt systematically to be identified. CULTURALLY DISTINCT, SPEECH AND LANGUAGE, and HEARING needs may have to have a duplicate set of items on a tray so they can either point to the object or feel it while seeing it. This way children who don't know the names of specific objects can participate, and you are not limited to choosing only the most common objects. You can direct them to feel for specific features.

# COLOR GRAPHS

**GOAL**   To improve small motor coordination
To follow directions

**OBJECTIVE**   The child will color the designated square a specific color.

**MATERIALS**   paper with squares drawn on it
crayons

**PROCEDURE**   Draw a pattern of squares on a piece of paper for each child. Then give the children directions:

> Color the first two squares green. Color the next square red. Color the next three squares yellow . . .

Be sure the children color from left to right to coordinate with reading readiness skills. You can have them skip a square or color it white. Have them describe the pattern to you using both color and number.

**CONTINUATION**   Have the children repeat the pattern after you have established it. You can do the same thing with beads and a string and introduce the concept of size as well.

**COMMENT**   It is sometimes more fun to call this a train, with each square a car. *Especially good for* LEARNING and INTELLECTUAL needs: Information is presented at a relatively slow rate using auditory directions or a visual model; the children then perform a motor task. For VISUAL needs, use textured fabric or wooden beads of various shapes and sizes.

# TACTILE GAMEBOARD

**GOAL**   To improve small motor coordination
To follow directions

**OBJECTIVE**   The child will play the game with some of his classmates.

**MATERIALS**   a cookie sheet or jellyroll pan          magnets
string or 20–30 toothpicks                  paper plates
glue                                                          felt dots

**PROCEDURE**   Make a tactile gameboard by gluing the string or toothpicks to the pan in a ladderlike track. Use magnets as markers. You can make a variety of games this way. To make a simple counting game, make a spinner out of a paper plate and use felt dots to signify the number of spaces to move.

**CONTINUATION**   Children can play the game blindfolded.

**COMMENT**   You can paste felt or yarn on commercially available games to make them tactile. *Especially good for* VISUAL needs: allows these children to play games with their classmates that they might not otherwise be able to play. HEARING and LEARNING needs might profit from the added cues as well as following simple visual and tactile directions.

# SORTING

**GOAL**   To improve small motor coordination
To improve classification skills

**OBJECTIVE**   The child will sort common objects by category.

**MATERIALS**   three containers for each child
objects that can be sorted into two categories:

| OBJECTS | CATEGORY A | CATEGORY B |
|---|---|---|
| buttons | rough | smooth |
| | two holes | four holes |
| silverware | forks | knives |
| | big spoons | little spoons |
| shapes | squares | circles |

**PROCEDURE**   Anchor three containers to a board. (Coffee cans with lids work well. Vary the size of the can to the objects to be sorted.) Set the containers in a row and put the objects to be sorted in the middle container. Then have the children sort the objects into the two empty containers.

Sorting games combine classification skills and small motor development. The tongs provide further challenge.

**CONTINUATION**   Have children sort objects into categories such as: furniture, animals, fruits, vegetables, vehicles, and kitchen utensils.

**COMMENT**   Children can work side by side if you select the objects carefully to meet individual abilities. *Especially good for* HEARING, LEARNING, and PHYSICAL needs: uses motor skills paired with the cognitive task of classifying. For INTELLECTUAL needs, use simple objects with obvious differences that are large enough to be handled easily and few enough so the task can be completed (i.e., blocks and rubber balls). For VISUAL needs, choose objects that are visually very different (black and white objects) or those which have tactile cues. For GIFTED AND TALENTED, add more containers so there are more possible categories (large squares, small squares, large circles, small circles). Encourage children to classify objects in a variety of different ways (size and shape).

# LOCK BOX

**GOAL**   To improve small motor coordination
To improve self-help skills

**OBJECTIVE**   The child will perform all of the possible tasks.

**MATERIALS**   A busy board lock box

**PROCEDURE**   Make or buy some busy boards. All require fine motor skills, but some teach more needed skills and are more intriguing than others. My most successful one was a "lock box." It has a variety of locks and keys (attached by strings so they don't get lost). Use a combination lock to be really challenging. Put pictures inside so the children see something when the doors open.

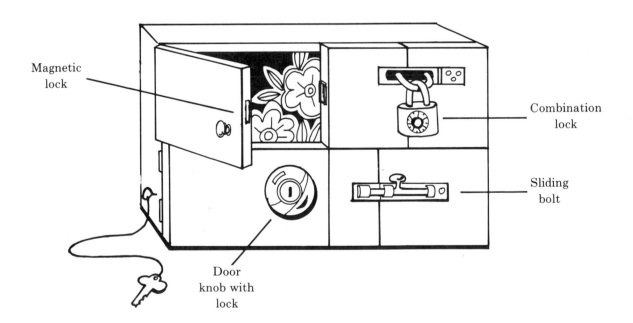

**CONTINUATION**   Use busy boards to teach different skills by changing what opens and closes the doors and which skill is called for.

**COMMENT**   With this particular busy box, children might get into locked places if they had a key, but they might also get *out* of a locked bathroom. *Especially good for* children with INTELLECTUAL needs: Use very simple locks until they develop the small motor skills and logic. Use locks that requires finger strength and wrist rotation for children with PHYSICAL needs. Those with HEALTH needs can borrow a box like this to play with at home, or perhaps the parents might use yours as a model and make one. Use more difficult or intricate locks—combination and those with keys cut on both sides—to challenge GIFTED AND TALENTED.

# MY PUZZLE

**GOAL**  To improve small motor coordination
To increase body awareness
To improve self-concept

**OBJECTIVE**  The child will put the puzzle together.

**MATERIALS**  An 8″ × 10″ picture puzzle of each child

**PROCEDURE**  Take pictures of all the children in class. (Black and white is fine; color is expensive.) Keep a small picture for each child's locker or a class collage. Have an 8″ × 10″ enlargement of each child made, laminate it or cover it with clear contact paper, and glue it to heavy cardboard. Draw lines on the back and cut it with heavy scissors or a jigsaw. No matter how you cut it, it will fit back together. (Put the child's initials on each piece so the children can put the puzzles back together if they get mixed up.)

**CONTINUATION**  You can use this procedure with any picture. Make puzzles with pictures of handicapped children to spark discussion.

**COMMENT**  This project becomes a lot less expensive if you know someone with a darkroom who will print the pictures. *Especially good for* SPEECH AND LANGUAGE needs: Have them talk about themselves and their body parts. For VISUAL needs (if there is any residual vision), have the picture developed with higher-than-usual contrast so the features stand out. HEARING and LEARNING needs will enjoy seeing a picture of themselves emerge from a visual discrimination exercise. At first, as you might for INTELLECTUAL needs, cut the picture in only three or four pieces. As the children become proficient at putting the puzzle together, cut it into more pieces. For children with PHYSICAL needs, you might make a frame for the picture so it is more easily contained. For HEALTH needs, GIFTED AND TALENTED, and CULTURALLY DISTINCT, point out their uniqueness as individuals and their similarities as group members.

# FEELY BOX

**GOAL**  To improve tactile discrimination

**OBJECTIVE**  The child will be able to match the objects by feeling in the box and looking on the tray.

**MATERIALS**  a closed shoebox with a hole big enough to put a hand through
a tray
two sets of common objects (comb, crayon, cup, key, and so on)

**PROCEDURE**  Make a feely box out of a shoe box and put the common objects in it. Have a similar set on a tray so the child can compare them to the objects he felt in the box. Point to an object on the tray and have the child pull the matching object from the box.

**COMMENT**  The second set of objects allows the child to participate without using speech. As the children become better at this, make the objects more similar. Although similar to the feely bag, this activity has different goals and process. Here the child is limited to small objects which he feels with one hand; in feely bags, the child feels larger objects one at a time through the bag. *Especially good for* HEARING, VISUAL, LEARNING, CULTURALLY DISTINCT, and SPEECH AND LANGUAGE needs: Language is not necessary to participate, yet there is an opportunity to use language while working on tactile skills.

# PICK-A-PAIR

**GOAL**   To improve tactile discrimination
To improve classification skills

**OBJECTIVE**   The child will match the textures.

**MATERIALS**   Materials of different textures:

| | | |
|---|---|---|
| cardboard | flannel | felt |
| sandpaper | sponge | nylon |
| corduroy | dotted swiss | wool |
| silk | ultrasuede | fake fur |

**PROCEDURE**   Cut pieces of fabric of different textures in two. Place one piece on a tray and the other in a bag. Ask the child to match the pieces.

**CONTINUATION**   Have the children classify the textures in some way: woven—not woven, soft—hard, rough—smooth, and so on.

**COMMENT**   *Especially good for* VISUAL needs: It is good preparation for reading braille if this is necessary. GIFTED AND TALENTED are challenged by a tactile classification project.

# GRADING SANDPAPER

**GOAL**   To improve tactile discrimination
To improve cause and effect reasoning

**OBJECTIVE**   The child will be able to arrange pieces of sandpaper in order from roughest to smoothest.

**MATERIALS**   small pieces of sandpaper of different grades from coarse to fine
pieces of wood

**PROCEDURE**   Ask the children to put the pieces of sandpaper in order by grade. Start with rather obvious variations in texture.

**CONTINUATION**   As the children learn to make the distinctions, have them do it blindfolded, and make the gradations more subtle.

**COMMENT**   Have some extra sandpaper and some pieces of wood to experiment with so the children see the uses of the various grades. Discuss how long it takes to get the wood smooth (the coarser the sandpaper, the shorter the time). Sanding wood is also a small motor process. *Especially good for* VISUAL and HEARING needs who may depend more than others on making fine tactile discriminations to get information about their environment: It is important for them to learn appropriate ways of feeling things and saving the information gained.

# BUTTONING SEQUENCES

**GOAL**   To improve tactile discrimination
To improve self-help skills
To improve sequencing skills

**OBJECTIVE**   The child will continue the sequence.

**MATERIALS**   Pieces of fabric of different colors and/or textures with a button and a button hole.

**PROCEDURE**   Decide on the shape you want to use and cut shapes out of different fabrics (e.g., felt, leather, velvet, cotton, wool, terrycloth).

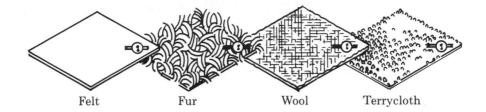

Felt        Fur        Wool        Terrycloth

Put a button on one end and a button hole on the other. Finish the edges so they don't ravel. (Felt is good to use because it doesn't have to be finished and you can just make a slit for the button hole.) Button the materials together in a sequence and have the children copy it. They can use both visual and tactile skills for this.

**CONTINUATION**   Make a color sequence by using fabrics in different colors.

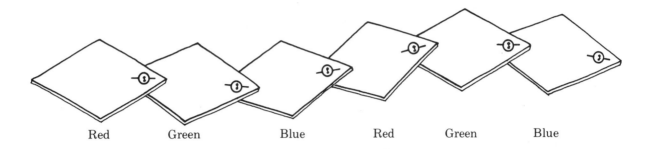

Red        Green        Blue        Red        Green        Blue

Or make the activity slightly more complex by using Velcro, large hooks and eyes, snaps, and so on as fasteners. Have children count the length of the sequence and the sizes and shapes of fabrics, too.

**COMMENT**   *Especially good for* VISUAL, HEARING, and LEARNING needs: teaches sequencing, a reading readiness skill, and self-help at the same time. For PHYSICAL needs, make the materials large enough for the child to handle, and be sure to use a fastener he can work. Experiment with Velcro, large hooks, and other fasteners. For INTELLECTUAL needs, first let the child practice just the buttoning or fastening; then use a simple repeating pattern like red, white, red, white.

# NUTS AND BOLTS

**GOAL**   To improve tactile discrimination
To improve eye–hand coordination
To improve visual discrimination

**OBJECTIVE**   The child will screw the correct size nut on the bolt.

**MATERIALS**   matching nuts and bolts
bowls

**PROCEDURE**   Put bolts in one bowl and nuts in another. Provide a third bowl for the bolt with the nut on it. Use wing nuts if possible because they are easier to turn. At first, use sizes that vary greatly, such as $\frac{1}{4}''$, $\frac{1}{2}''$, and $1''$. As children become more proficient, add in-between sizes.

**CONTINUATION**   Blindfold the children and see if they can match the nuts and bolts by feeling alone. As children get proficient, have them count the number of tries it takes to get a correct fit (i.e., see if they can change from trial and error to "guessing").

**COMMENT**   Be sure to have the same number nuts as bolts so children will find the ones that really match. *Especially good for* LEARNING, VISUAL, HEARING, and INTELLECTUAL needs: utilizes visual and tactile senses and gives practice in fine motor coordination.

# FOLLOW THAT LIGHT

**GOAL**    To improve eye–hand coordination

**OBJECTIVE**    The child will make his light follow the teacher's light.

**MATERIALS**    Two flashlights

**PROCEDURE**    Turn on two flashlights. Give one to a child and keep the other. (This works best in a dimly lit room or on the chalkboard.) Make simple designs with the light on the wall, floor, or ceiling, and have the child follow them. As the skill improves, make the patterns more complex and faster.

**COMMENT**    This is a good activity for a dreary, rainy day; it's also a good one for children to play at home with parents or older siblings. *Especially good for* LEARNING and HEARING needs: it is a novel way to develop eye–hand coordination; matching at a distance helps spatial relations. It is a nontaxing game for HEALTH needs to play at home or in the hospital.

# VELCRO TOSS

**GOAL**    To improve eye–hand coordination

**OBJECTIVE**    The child will hit the target from increasingly greater distances.

**MATERIALS**    Velcro-covered ping-pong ball
dart board with Velcro pieces attached (glued or stapled)

**PROCEDURE**    Have the children toss the ping-pong ball at the target and see if they can get it to stick. As their skill increases, increase the distance they stand or sit from the target. Have them toss both underhand and overhand.

**COMMENT**    The Velcro areas on the target can be made larger or smaller depending on the children's needs. *Especially good for* PHYSICAL and HEALTH needs: The balls are light; the child doesn't get tired; and the activity can be played sitting, standing, or lying down.

# THROWING GAMES

**GOAL**    To improve eye–hand coordination
To increase body awareness

**OBJECTIVE**    The child will participate in various throwing games.

**MATERIALS**    objects to throw, such as a ball or bean bag
targets

**PROCEDURE**    Have the children participate in the various types of throwing activities listed below. Discuss how it feels, where they can throw objects and where they shouldn't, and which objects are harder to throw and which are easier. Allow them to add their own suggestions.

> texture ball throw: use a sponge or texture ball (whiffle ball); the children begin with underhand tossing to a person close by. Gradually extend distance, and graduate to overhand throwing.
> texture ball tag: Divide the class into teams and play dodge ball outside.
> texture ball basketball: use a shoe box with the bottom removed. Tape it to the wall for an indoor game.

ring toss game: a variation of horseshoes with rubber rings, this game requires a different set of throwing skills.

beanbag toss: toss bags through large holes in a target; also use like indoor horseshoes.

paper throw: crumple paper into balls and shoot them into a wastebasket.

softball throw: proceed from underhand to overhand, and increase distance.

tennis ball throw: this game becomes more difficult as the ball bounces; cup hands together and catch ball.

milk carton toss: use plastic milk bottles or cartons stacked in pyramids. Knock the structure down with a softball or tennis ball.

bucket throws: use a bucket or wastebasket for catching utility balls, softballs, or hardballs. First set the bucket on the floor, then on raised chairs and boxes.

empty box throw: place a bottomless cardboard box on its side on a chair or ledge. The object is to throw a ball through the box without hitting the sides.

tennis toss-back: throw a tennis ball high against a brick or cement wall and catch it before it bounces (an outside activity).

pitch back: use a pitch-back net for close throwing.

pole throw: use different lengths of poles or dowling for throwing. Do this outside and measure the distances.

football: use straight throws and running throws. Throw the ball into boxes.

one-legged throws: stand on one leg and throw various balls at targets. Use stuffed bags suspended on a line for targets.

sponge throw: the target is cardboard with holes of various sizes. Use suspended hula hoops for target practice.

**COMMENT**   These are good outdoor activities. Be sure to assign retrievers for the throwers, and be aware of safety needs all the time. *Especially good for* LEARNING and PHYSICAL needs: there tosses build strength and coordination. For INTELLECTUAL needs, start with the easier tasks. With GIFTED AND TALENTED, encourage them to make predictions about how far they can throw various objects and then measure the actual distances.


# POURING PEANUTS

**GOAL**   To improve eye–hand coordination
To make predictions
To improve self-help skills

**OBJECTIVE**   The child will pour the substances without spilling them.

**MATERIALS**   a tray of plastic measuring pitchers and bowls
a large container
peanuts, dried beans, or split peas

**PROCEDURE**   Have the children practice pouring from the large to the smaller containers. Ask them to make predictions about the size relationships among the containers and how much each will hold relative to the others. Name the containers and their parts (handle, lip, pitcher, glass) as well as the sizes (1 cup, 2 cups, 1 quart.)

**CONTINUATION**   As children gain competence, have them pour liquids and eventually their own juice or milk.

**COMMENT**   It's a good idea to start with substances that don't produce much mess when spilled. *Especially good for* PHYSICAL and INTELLECTUAL needs: They both may need extra help in small motor coordination; self-confidence is gained through increasing independence. For VISUAL needs, teach the children to place the lip of the pitcher in the glass with the pitcher itself just touching the rim. Have the children place their finger in the glass to check how full it is.

# PING-PONG BLOW

**GOAL**  To increase body awareness
To improve breath control

**OBJECTIVE**  The child will blow the ball along the path.

**MATERIALS**  a ping-pong ball
blocks
straw

**PROCEDURE**  Make a path with blocks on a table and have the children blow the ping-pong ball along the path. They can blow with their mouths alone or use a straw.

**CONTINUATION**  To make the task more difficult, use a rope or toothpick path; this requires better breath control.

**COMMENT**  Encourage the children to try to move the ball along the path; if they decide it is a contest to see how hard they can blow, add a few more twists and turns to the path. *Especially good for* HEARING and SPEECH AND LANGUAGE needs: shows visually what they are doing with their breathing, even if they can't hear the distinctions. Improves the breath control of HEALTH needs.

# Large Motor Play

## INDEX

| Goal | Activity | Page |
|---|---|---|
| To improve tactile discrimination | Feeling Track | 519 |
| To follow directions | Maze | 516 |
| | Obstacle Course | 515 |
| To improve cause and effect reasoning | Balance It | 519 |
| To make predictions | Noisy Toss | 517 |
| To improve number concepts | Maze | 516 |
| To improve time concepts | Timed Race | 519 |
| To cooperate with peers | Seesaw | 520 |
| To improve eye–hand coordination | Noisy Toss | 517 |

Using and developing the large muscles of the body is one of the tasks of early childhood. Some people feel that the large muscles, especially the lateral muscles of the chest, must be developed before smaller muscles, such as the muscles of the hands, can be effectively used. Muscles must be used in order to develop properly. Since children with special needs are often overprotected, they may need extra encouragement and plenty of opportunities to develop their large muscles at school. In particular, children need to develop the skills of balance, rhythm, and coordination. They need to participate in activities that expose their muscles to demanding tasks. We should resist the temptation to do too many things for children with special needs and allow them to participate in enough resistance and power activities to develop strength.

To help children develop appropriate large motor skills, you need time, space, and the proper equipment. Outside, children can creep best in concrete or ceramic culverts. Inside, they need free floor space for this purpose. Climbing requires a jungle gym or ladderlike arrangement. As their sense of balance improves, children progress from walking, to walking on a balance beam, to riding tricycles, and to rollerskating. You should provide space and objects for children to push, pull, carry, and lift. Children also need to jump, slide, and swing.

## LARGE MOTOR PLAY GOALS

- To improve large motor coordination. To carry out activities smoothly, children need to practice large motor skills so that coordination becomes natural. With age, these skills need to be refined.
- To increase body awareness. Children need to learn to control their body and move it in ways they desire. They need to learn their strengths and limitations: what is easy and what is hard for them to do.
- To improve balance skills. All antigravity postures require balance. Walking, running, cycling, and dancing require children to learn how to handle their body and how to compensate when

they lose balance. These are dynamic balance activities. Also be sure to include static balance activities, such as holding positions and objects without losing balance.

## TEACHING STRATEGIES

For children with SPEECH AND LANGUAGE needs, be sure to supply words for what they are doing in the large motor area to help reinforce strengths and sensory integration.

Children with HEARING needs may need to develop their sense of balance with games that require starting, stopping, and turning.

Children with VISUAL needs must learn how to tell where they are. They need to develop safe ways of moving through unknown spaces. This requires the combination of large motor, auditory, and tactile skills. They also need encouragement and a safe place to practice these skills.

Children with LEARNING needs can use large motor activities as a way to release excess energy, as well as a way to increase body awareness. Encourage them to practice large motor skills until they achieve the necessary coordination.

Like children with LEARNING needs, those with ADJUSTMENT needs can use large motor activities to vent energy and to feel part of a group. Large motor activities often have a loose organization that allows individualization. Take advantage of this for these children.

Those with HEALTH needs must develop as much strength and endurance as they can. Respect their limits but encourage them to participate.

Children with PHYSICAL needs may need the upper-body strength of a gymnast to move from the wheelchair to the toilet. Give these children the opportunity to develop upper-body strength or whichever skills serve their needs.

Children who are CULTURALLY DISTINCT may not need special help in large motor play. But be sure to help them learn the vocabulary for what they are doing while they are doing it.

Children with INTELLECTUAL needs may not be as proficient as other children in this area since their large motor development may be slow. Be sure to plan activities for them that are not demanding.

For children who are GIFTED AND TALENTED, large motor play may be an opportunity to gain perspective. Although they may be able to conceptualize better than others, their ability to carry out activities will be close to that of others their own age. Help them accept that they may be better at some things than at others.

# CRASHING

**GOAL**    To improve large motor coordination
  To increase body awareness

**OBJECTIVE**    The child will roll on the cylinder, stopping himself with his hands.

**MATERIALS**    a cylinder or barrel sturdy enough to support the weight of a child and large enough so that the child is about an arm's length off the floor when on top of the cylinder.
  pieces of carpet

**PROCEDURE**    Cover the cylinder or barrel with pieces of carpet. The children lie over the cylinder on their stomach and roll toward the floor, catching themselves with their hands.

**COMMENT**    This is one of few activities that develop the lateral chest muscles, which are important for both large and small muscle development. *Especially good for* LEARNING and VISUAL needs: provides a way to develop the lateral chest muscles in preparation for the fine motor skills. PHYSICAL needs will develop strength by pushing themselves off the floor.

# VARIATIONS ON CRAWLING

**GOAL**    To improve large motor coordination
To increase body awareness

**OBJECTIVE**    The child will participate in the various crawling activities.

**MATERIALS**    record player and record
materials for an obstacle course:
    yarn        boxes
    boards    chairs

**PROCEDURE**    Have the children participate in various types of crawling activities. Have the children:

crawl to music and imitate animals (horse, turtle, and so on)
crawl through on obstacle course made of boxes or chairs
crawl in timed races that follow yarn trails
crawl through holes in boxes or hula hoops partially buried in the ground
crawl up one side of a seesaw board, maintain balance as board tips down, and then
   crawl down the board to the ground (be sure to have an adult as a spotter)
crawl forward and backward on a board propped between two steady pieces of furniture (e.g., chairs)

Discuss what each type feels like, how it is different from crawling normally, what animals crawl on four legs, and which surfaces are easier to crawl on.

**COMMENT**    This is an activity for both indoors and outdoors. When crawling outside, clear the area of harmful objects. *Especially good for* LEARNING, INTELLECTUAL, and PHYSICAL needs: Crawling is a basic skill, and the variations can be geared to the abilities of the individual children involved. Have GIFTED AND TALENTED children add to your variations on crawling and discuss when and why they might use these variations. VISUAL needs might find this a safe way to explore a new environment.

# VARIATIONS ON ROLLING

**GOAL**    To improve large motor coordination
To increase body awareness

**OBJECTIVE**    The child will participate in the various rolling activities.

**MATERIALS**    None

**PROCEDURE**    Have the children participate in various types of rolling activities. Ask them to:

roll with hands extended over the head, feet together
roll with hands extended over the head, feet clasping ball or towel
roll with hands at sides of body
roll around an obstacle course of pillows
roll with one hand above the head, one at side
roll down a hill or incline
roll in circles while someone holds their ankles

Discuss how each type of rolling feels for the children, which types are easier for keeping balance, and what new ways they can think of to roll.

**COMMENT**    These rolls are good for rainy days or as outdoor activities on the grass. Be sure to clear the area of rocks or other potentially harmful objects. *Especially good for* LEARNING, VISUAL and INTELLECTUAL needs: easy, a good energy release, and develops necessary muscles.

# VARIATIONS ON HOPPING

**GOAL**   To improve large motor coordination
To increase body awareness
To improve balance skills

**OBJECTIVE**   The child will participate in various hopping activities.

**MATERIALS**   Hopping stones made of tiles or cut-up oilcloth or tablecloths

**PROCEDURE**   Have the children participate in various types of hopping activities. Discuss what each type of hopping feels like to them. Have them:

> hop on their left foot
> hop on their right foot
> hop as quietly as they can
> hop as loudly as they can
> hop as high as they can
> hop as low as they can
> hop as far as they can on one foot; on two feet
> hop in one direction as far as they can on their left foot, and hop back on
>     their right foot
> hop and change feet
> hop holding someone's hand

**CONTINUATION**   Play a hopping game by having patterns of tiles set out and having the children hop on the tiles in an obstacle course fashion according to your directions.

**COMMENT**   For 2- or 3-year-olds, hopping itself may be a challenge; for 4- and 5-year-olds, the more complex variations are fun. *Especially good for* HEARING *and* LEARNING needs: They can practice balance as well as large motor skills. For GIFTED AND TALENTED children, you may introduce counting the number of hops.

# VARIATIONS ON JUMPING

**GOAL**   To improve large motor coordination
To increase body awareness
To improve balance skills

**OBJECTIVE**   The child will participate in various jumping activities

**MATERIALS**   None

**PROCEDURE**   Have the children participate in the various styles of jumping.

> jumping together: one child faces another and holds hands; they jump together to
>     the count of ten.
> jumping line: children jump back and forth over a line a given number of times.
>     (Variations: one-foot jump, backward jump.)
> stair jump: children jump from step to a line on the floor.
> standing jump: children jump forward for a distance from standing position.
> hopscotch: lay out course and teach rules; children practice.
> snake jump: children crouch in squat position and jump up as far as possible.
> kangaroo jump: with feet together, elbows bent, and hands away from body, chil-
>     dren do knee bends and jumps three times.
> rabbit jump: children squat low on heels, palms down, and fingers pointing forward,
>     and simulate rabbit jump with feet coming forward between hands.

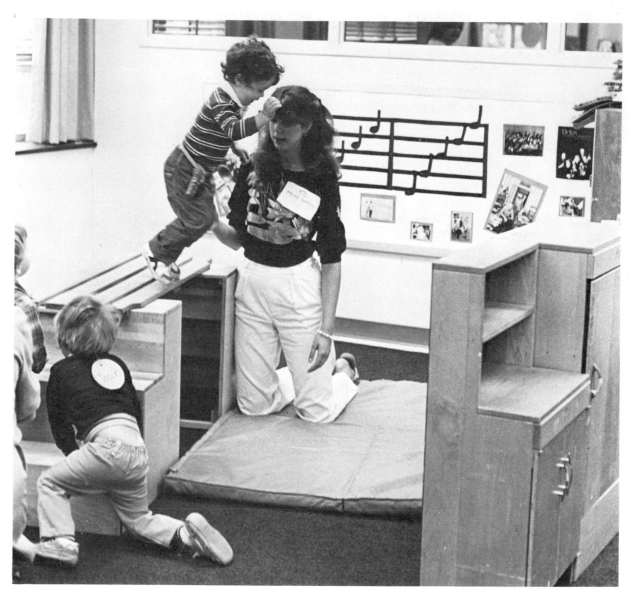

Children master a skill by practicing the skill and its variations.

mattress jump: use partially filled air mattress; children jump forward and backward without falling (use on a rug with spotters).

simple jump rope: children jump forward and backward to count of ten, lifting both
feet at once.

pole jump: vary height according to ability of each child; children jump over pole.

jumping jacks: children do these exercises as in physical education classes.

jumping an obstacle course: children jump a box, jump rope, jump another box,
jump hopscotch one way, jump on one foot three times, and jump rope ten times
(or some variation of this).

Discuss how each style of jumping feels and how long the children could do it.

**COMMENT** *Especially good for* LEARNING needs: a good energy release on a rainy day. For
HEALTH needs, increases drainage of the lungs. For VISUAL needs, let the child feel the object to be
jumped over before jumping, especially when the activity is done in pairs.

# VARIATIONS ON WALKING

**GOAL**     To improve large motor coordination
To increase body awareness

**OBJECTIVE**     The child will participate in various walking activities.

**MATERIALS**     None

**PROCEDURE**     Have the children participate in various types of walks.

> barefoot walk: children walk through mud, sand, rocks, and concrete and describe the sensations involved.
> forward walk: children walk a straight or curved path to target and back. Record time. (Variation may include walking up and down steps.)
> backward walk: children walk backward through a predetermined course with a rope for guidance. Record time. (Variation may include walking backward up and down steps.)
> walking sideways: children walk to the right one step at a time, crossing their left foot over their right foot. Reverse the step when moving to the left. If the children are in a circle or two circles facing each other, the activity requires less space and can be done in the classroom. As a long line it can be more like follow the leader.
> ostrich: children bend forward at waist, grasp ankles, and walk forward while keeping knees stiff and stretching neck in and out.
> duck: children do a deep bend and place hands behind their back; they walk forward one foot at a time, but remain in bent-knee position.
> arm walk: children lie flat on floor, push up entire body with arms, keeping knees straight, and walk forward with arms while feet drag behind.
> seesaw walk: children walk up one side of the board, balance while board tips down, and continue walking down to the end. Be sure to have an adult beside the board, as this walk can be dangerous.

Discuss what ideas the children have for variations and how each walk feels to them; that is, could they do the walk for a long or short time and was it hard to keep their balance.

**COMMENT**     These are good rainy day activities and fun ways of getting from group to individual centers. *Especially good for* INTELLECTUAL needs: helps refine a skill in an enjoyable way. LEARNING needs can practice coordination and walk off energy.

# OBSTACLE COURSE

**GOAL**     To improve large motor coordination
To follow directions

**OBJECTIVE**     The child will complete the obstacle course in the correct sequence.

**MATERIALS**     barrels
boxes
boards, and so on

**PROCEDURE**     Set up an obstacle course either inside or outside. The course can be simple or complex, depending on the age and past experience of the children, but should require a variety of physical skills. Give the children directions for completing the obstacle course:

> Run over to the box, roll the ball to the wall, then wriggle under a ladder, crawl through the barrel, creep around the chair, and walk to the rug.

**COMMENT**    *Especially good for* INTELLECTUAL needs: Keep the course simple and relatively short or allow the children to stop in the middle. For GIFTED AND TALENTED, make a complex course and have them go through it several times using different movements. For VISUAL needs, use a rope as a guide through the course. In addition, give auditory cues, for example: "You're getting close to the tunnel now, get down on your hands and knees and crawl though the tunnel." (Others might enjoy trying this blindfolded.) For SPEECH AND LANGUAGE needs, give a play-by-play description of their location and actions: "Good, you're crawling through the tunnel, now you're walking around the chair." For LEARNING needs, use arrows; don't depend on the children's remembering how to go through the course in the correct sequence. For HEARING needs, also use arrows and add line drawings of the necessary postures as visual cues.

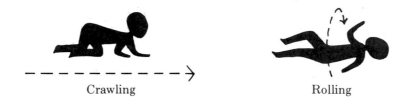

Crawling                Rolling

For PHYSICAL needs, adapt the course requirements or make the course in two sections, one of which these children can accomplish. If the children can use their arms but not their legs, have a nonwalking course with limited variation in the height of the equipment. For HEALTH needs, time their trip through the course and see if they can complete it in a specified amount of time at a comfortable pace (it's not a race).

# MAZE

**GOAL**    To improve large motor coordination
To follow directions
To improve number concepts

**OBJECTIVE**    The child will follow the numbers through the maze, doing the appropriate movements.

**MATERIALS**    A set of large cards (manila-folder paper is a good material)

**PROCEDURE**    Put a number and a picture of a child doing a motion on each card. Place these around the room on the floor so that the children can move through the course.

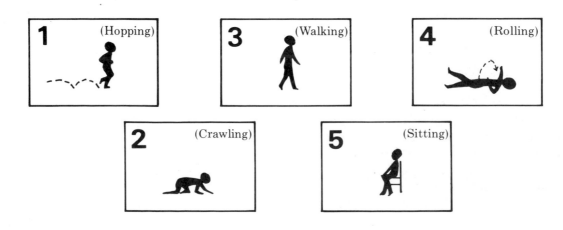

**COMMENT**   Vary the numbers and motions to meet the needs of the children. This is a fun way of getting them into a group after a breaktime, or, if you change the last card, having them leave a group. *Especially good for* LEARNING and HEARING needs: combines visual directions with a motor activity.

# NOISY TOSS

**GOAL**   To improve large motor coordination
To improve eye–hand coordination
To make predictions

**OBJECTIVE**   The child will state what object he hit on the target and the sound it makes.

**MATERIALS**
| | |
|---|---|
| tennis balls or beanbags | a pan lid |
| cardboard or plywood | bucket |
| foam | screws |
| bells | |

**PROCEDURE**   Using a large piece of cardboard or plywood with attached objects that make a noise when hit, make a target for children to throw tennis balls or beanbags at.

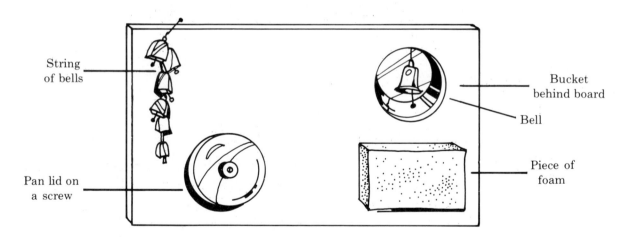

**COMMENT**   Be sure to include vocabulary about directions: up, down, right, and left. *Especially good for* LEARNING and VISUAL needs: gives auditory as well as visual feedback. Because the targets are relatively far apart, PHYSICAL needs and INTELLECTUAL needs are able to predict which target they will hit.

# BALANCING

**GOAL**   To increase body awareness
To improve balance skills

**OBJECTIVE**   The child will walk between the lines.

MATERIALS    two lines of tape on the floor
balance beam
ladder

PROCEDURE    Start with lines of tape about 9 inches apart and 7 feet long. Have the children walk between them without stepping outside of them. As the children become more proficient, place the lines closer together. When the lines are 4 inches apart, substitute a balance beam.

CONTINUATION    After the children become proficient, curve the lines:

or:

COMMENT    *Especially good for* INTELLECTUAL, HEARING, and LEARNING needs: helps them develop more control over their movements. VISUAL needs may need to walk barefooted so that they can feel the tape. For those who can see well enough, use high-contrast colors.

# VARIATIONS ON BALANCING

GOAL    To increase body awareness
To improve balance skills

OBJECTIVE    The child will walk the length of the balance beam without help and following the directions given.

MATERIALS    lumber, 1" × 6" × 8', for walking board
balance beam, 2" wide
balance beam, 4" to 5" wide

PROCEDURE    When children can walk between taped lines with some degree of success, have them try walking the 1" × 6" board with the following variations:

walk forward, with help, on walking board that is placed on floor; then without help
walk backward
walk sideways
walk forward and back, turn without stepping off
walk holding an object in hands
walk slowly down the board touching heel against toe
walk backward the same way
walk forward without looking at feet
walk backward without looking at feet
touch hand to the board
touch knee to the board

CONTINUATION    Once the children can do these activities on the walking board, use the balance beam, first the 4" side on the floor, then on the stand; for those with a great sense of balance, use the 2" side.

COMMENT    *Especially good for* HEARING and LEARNING needs: Both groups need practice on balance skills. VISUAL needs may require more assistance at the beginning and may need a feel for the board before they can do it independently. For HEALTH needs, this is a good way to increase body awareness. Balance beams or some variation of them are easily made and portable.

# FEELING TRACK

**GOAL**   To increase body awareness
To improve tactile discrimination

**OBJECTIVE**   The child will describe the textures.

**MATERIALS**   a board about 2′ × 6′
materials of various textures, about 2′ × 1′, attached to the board sequentially:

| | |
|---|---|
| wood | foam padding |
| carpet | sand put on wet paint and allowed to dry |

**PROCEDURE**   Cover the entire board with the textured materials. Blindfold the children and have them walk across the board barefoot and describe what they feel.

**COMMENT**   Children rarely use their feet in this way, so it is good to remind them their feet are useful not only for walking, but also for giving environmental cues. *Especially good for* VISUAL and HEARING needs: teaches them to be aware of their whole body as a source of tactile information. Be sure to discuss the textures and label them for SPEECH AND LANGUAGE needs.

# TIMED RACE

**GOAL**   To increase body awareness
To improve time concepts

**OBJECTIVE**   The child will move to a particular place in a specified amount of time.

**MATERIALS**   A timer

**PROCEDURE**   Have several children line up in a row (indoors or outdoors); explain that you want them to walk (crawl, wriggle, and so on) to a designated spot in a specified amount of time. For example, they could try to walk 30 feet in one minute. This is slow! If you have a timer that rings, it is fun to set it and have them listen to it tick; the ticking is rhythmic and increases their awareness of time as they move.

**CONTINUATION**   During group time, have children estimate how long various things will take to see how exact their concept of time is. (You might do this before attempting the activity, especially with younger children.) Once children have some understanding of relative time, incorporate different movements; for example, have children walk to the spot in one minute and hop back in one minute to see how they plan their time.

**COMMENT**   *Especially good for* LEARNING and ADJUSTMENT needs: teaches self-control as well as awareness of time. For HEALTH and PHYSICAL needs, choose speeds based on the children's abilities. Be sure to note that fast is not always best.

# BALANCE IT

**GOAL**   To increase body awareness
To improve balance skills
To improve cause and effect reasoning

**OBJECTIVE**   The child will predict which objects will be hard to balance and which will be easy and test his predictions.

**MATERIALS**   A variety of objects:

| | |
|---|---|
| books | paper plates |
| rubber bands | paintbrushes |
| crayons | feathers |

**PROCEDURE**   Demonstrate how to balance objects on the head. Ask children to predict which objects will be easy to balance and which will be hard. Then have them balance the objects to see if their predictions were correct. Have them try to sit, stand, walk (fast and slowly), while balancing the objects.

**COMMENT**   *Especially good for* PHYSICAL, LEARNING, and VISUAL needs: helps them develop and improve posture and spatial awareness. For GIFTED AND TALENTED, use more challenging objects; ask them to predict how long they can balance an object or whether or not they can sit down twice without having it fall off.

# SEESAW

**GOAL**   To improve balance skills
  To cooperate with peers

**OBJECTIVE**   The child will alternate performing a motion with a partner.

**MATERIALS**   None

**PROCEDURE**   Have the children find partners (if there are size differences, don't have drastically different-sized children pair up) and hold hands facing each other. One child does a deep knee bend while the other stands straight. Then they reverse. The children continue the activity in rhythm.

**COMMENT**   Balance skills are invaluable. *Especially good for* LEARNING and ADJUSTMENT needs: allows them to be part of the group while doing an activity. You may have to physically move VISUAL needs and also give them verbal directions at first.

# *Outdoor Play*

# INDEX

| Goal | Activity | Page |
|---|---|---|
| To improve cause and effect reasoning | Balloon Badminton | 528 |
| | Blowing Bubbles | 531 |
| | Picnic | 530 |
| To increase visual identification | My Yard | 527 |
| To improve tactile discrimination | Barefoot | 530 |
| | Cave Exploration | 528 |
| To increase vocabulary | Barefoot | 530 |
| To follow directions | Ladder Walk | 529 |
| To improve breath control | Blowing Bubbles | 531 |
| | Bubble Machine | 527 |
| To improve color concepts | Color Scavenger Hunt | 531 |
| To make predictions | Balloon Badminton | 528 |
| To improve measurement concepts | Jump over the Creek | 526 |
| To cooperate with peers | Color Scavenger Hunt | 531 |
| | Hug Tag | 531 |
| | Variations on Throwing | 526 |
| To improve balance skills | Freeze | 528 |
| | Ladder Walk | 529 |

Outdoor play is an integral part of most preschool programs, yet one which often receives little planning. Because children with special needs often take longer to learn new skills or to learn to compensate for their disabilities, it is essential that you take advantage of all the learning opportunities you have. This means you can no longer consider an outside play period as an unstructured recess, but as a time for the children to learn things they cannot learn inside a classroom: the feel of the wind, the sound of leaves crunching underfoot, or running as far as they can. The less competitive the activities are, the better, so the children have the opportunity to learn what they themselves can do. They can learn to measure their own progress over time instead of constantly comparing their achievements with those of other children.

The amount of time that can be spent outside varies with the climate. Use your outdoor time for active play and also as a time to expand learning. When the weather is mild, give a new slant to some traditional activities. Move the casels outside to water paint; use large chalk to draw murals on the concrete (the rain will do your clean-up if you time it right). Be outside in a constructive way. Have a picnic for lunch or at juice time. Have a rest or quiet time outside and listen to the sounds. Outside adds another dimension to learning.

## OUTDOOR PLAY GOALS

- To improve large motor coordination. Both large and small motor coordination require practice. Large motor coordination, in particular, often requires space that is available outside only.

- To improve eye–hand and eye–foot coordination. The ability to coordinate vision with motion is important. Games with balls (throwing, catching, and kicking) help children develop these skills.
- To increase body awareness. Children need to learn about themselves in relation to the outdoors. The added space that outdoors provides allows children to learn more about their bodies. They can find out how far they can ride a tricycle without getting tired. They can learn how to release their energy in ways that being indoors doesn't allow.
- To increase feelings of group belonging. Because many outdoor groups are loosely organized and not demanding, it is easier for children with special needs to be part of these groups. They can also participate in some of the more structured ball and running games, if the rule is that all children must be chosen before anyone gets a second turn.
- To improve cause and effect reasoning. Children need many opportunities to discover the properties and interrelationships of materials—being outdoors provides some of these. For example, if a child wears a hat outdoors on a windy day, the hat may be blown away. Children need to know how far they can run and how heat and cold affect this distance; they need to learn that they can slip more easily when it's raining; and they need to learn the differences between moving in open spaces and in confined ones. They can learn how things grow by planting a garden and by seeing what happens when grass is cut.

The activities in this section are designed for outdoors. Notes are made in other sections on how to adapt other activities for outside play; some of the activities in this section can be done inside if you have a siege of inclement weather.

## TEACHING STRATEGIES

Outdoors is a great place for children with SPEECH AND LANGUAGE needs to learn about breath control. They can see and feel the effects of the wind's blowing the grass, leaves, and themselves. They can even blow against the wind.

For children with HEARING needs, the chance to work on balance skills is invaluable. Because little language is required in this area, they can fit in easily.

For VISUAL needs, outdoors may be a challenge. With the change of temperature, glasses sometimes fog up, so have tissues handy to wipe them off. Children's glasses are made so they won't shatter; the danger is they will fall off and break. For very active children, a safety strap minimizes this problem. For low-vision and blind children watch for safety concerns. Be sure that paths for moving vehicles are well delineated and that there is a low fence around swings, seesaws, and other moving equipment so that children cannot accidentally walk into them.

Help children with LEARNING needs develop smoother, more efficient coordination while learning to use the space available to run off excess energy.

Help children with PHYSICAL and HEALTH needs regulate their activities so they don't become too tired. This is especially important during very cold or hot weather. You may even want to be sure they are among the last children to go outside. When feasible, try to have some quieter activities also—books or puzzles on a blanket, easels, and so on.

Children who are CULTURALLY DISTINCT may be unfamiliar with some of the outdoor equipment. If these children climb the fence instead of the jungle, help them down and show them how to use the other climbing equipment available.

It is important that children with INTELLECTUAL needs use the time outdoors to be both active and with the other children. They may need your encouragement to explore the materials available to them outside. Be sure they try a variety of activities.

GIFTED AND TALENTED children will function more like their chronological age than their mental age on most of the outdoor activities. This is a good opportunity for them to be part of the group, participate in group games, and perhaps even have others help them learn a particular skill.

# TARGET BOUNCE

**GOAL**   To improve large motor coordination
To improve eye–hand coordination

**OBJECTIVE**   The child will bounce the ball on the target.

**MATERIALS**   tape
ball

**PROCEDURE**   Tape a target on the ground, large at first and progressively smaller as children become more skillful. Have the children stand about three feet on either side of the target and bounce the ball to each other, hitting the target.

**COMMENT**   When done inside, this activity is a lot more controllable if the children sit in chairs. Have them see how often they can catch the ball and/or hit the target. *Especially good for* PHYSICAL needs: Modify the size of the ball and the target so that they can participate; helps develop upper body strength. INTELLECTUAL needs will benefit from the practice in coordination. For VISUAL needs, use either a large ball or one that has a bell inside.

# VARIATIONS ON BOUNCING

**GOAL**   To improve large motor coordination
To improve eye–hand coordination

**OBJECTIVE**   The child will bounce the ball in a variety of ways.

**MATERIALS**   8″ or 10″ balls

**PROCEDURE**   Have the children bounce the ball with 1 hand (at the beginning 2 hands may be necessary). Then encourage them to:

> bounce the ball low
> bounce the ball higher
> bounce the ball as high as their waist
> bounce the ball with their right hand
> bounce the ball with their left hand
> bounce the ball and change hands
> bounce the ball and walk at the same time

**CONTINUATION**   Have the children bounce the ball to another child.

**COMMENT**   The purpose of this activity is to develop control and coordination, not speed and strength. *Especially good for* LEARNING needs: develops coordination and releases energy. Good for HEALTH and PHYSICAL needs because it is self-paced and you can think up variations that fit the children's needs. ADJUSTMENT needs can develop large motor skills yet not be required to interact with others unless they choose to do so.

# VARIATIONS ON RUNNING

**GOAL**   To improve large motor coordination
To increase body awareness

**OBJECTIVE**   The child will run in a variety of ways.

**MATERIALS**  Material to make a path:
  tape          yarn
  rope          cones
  string

**PROCEDURE**  Have the children run outside and try the following variations:

  run slowly without touching anyone
  run fast without touching anyone
  run without touching anyone and stop on the signal
  run and change direction on the signal
  run as quietly as possible
  run as noisily as possible
  run as lightly as possible
  run as heavily as possible
  run, stop, run in a different direction
  run a course marked with tape, string, or rope to indicate the need to
    change direction
  run, walk, run; see how long the children can alternate between the two
  run slowly and talk to a friend

**COMMENT**  These variations help children refine skills as well as build endurance. *Especially good for* SPEECH AND LANGUAGE needs: talking while running helps them use language and also creates awareness of how exercise influences breath. LEARNING needs can practice coordination in large motor skills. HEARING needs can practice the variations that involve changing directions. For VISUAL needs, run slowly with the children holding their hand; then gradually increase speed. If the children feel comfortable, gradually remove your support but continue to talk to them as you run beside them.

# PARACHUTE GAMES

**GOAL**  To improve large motor coordination
  To increase feelings of group belonging

**OBJECTIVE**  The child will participate in group games.

**MATERIALS**  a parachute (use a sheet if a parachute is unavailable)
  ball

**PROCEDURE**  Have a group of children hold onto the outside of the parachute and raise and lower it. When they lift it high enough, have one child run under it to the other side before the parachute touches him. Or, place a ball in the center of the parachute and have the children try to keep the ball in motion without its falling out. Or, mushroom sit: When the parachute is held up high, have the children step in two steps, pull the parachute over their heads, and sit on the edge of the parachute; it will form a dome. These games require both individual coordination and group timing.

**COMMENT**  *Especially good for* LEARNING and HEARING needs and CULTURALLY DISTINCT: They can be part of the group without needing a high level of verbal skill. As the children all hold on to the parachute, VISUAL needs can sense the rhythm through their hands.

# PICTURE RELAYS

**GOAL**   To improve large motor coordination
To increase feelings of group belonging

**OBJECTIVE**   The child will participate in a team relay race.

**MATERIALS**   Pictures of different ways of moving

**PROCEDURE**   Show the children the pictures you have made and ask a child to demonstrate the movements. Then give each team 3 cards face down. Have each team get the same 3 cards, but not in the same order. Start the race. Emphasize the different movements rather than winning or losing. Stress that speed is one aspect of the race, but quality of movement is also important.

**COMMENT**   *Especially good for* HEARING needs: They can see a picture of the movement before doing it. Be sure they aren't the first ones to do the action if you aren't sure they understand it. For PHYSICAL needs, make up a movement you are sure these children can do and include it in the relay. The specific movements you pick will depend on the children's skills. To encourage LEARNING needs to translate the pictures into actions, make up some unusual pictures and compare the children's positions to the ones in the pictures.

# VARIATIONS ON THROWING

**GOAL**   To improve large motor coordination
To improve eye–hand coordination
To cooperate with peers

**OBJECTIVE**   The child will participate in various throwing experiences.

**MATERIALS**   8″ or 10″ ball          15″–24″ wastebasket
tennis ball          hula hoops

**PROCEDURE**   Have the children participate in various types of ball throwing activities. Discuss the differences in skill required between large and small balls. Have the children try the following variations:

> throw the ball as high as they can
> throw the ball as low as they can without hitting the ground
> throw the ball as far as they can
> throw the ball softly to another child
> throw the ball in a high arc to another child
> throw the ball into a round wastebasket from 2′ to 5′ away
> throw the ball through the hula hoops from varying distances

Encourage children to measure the distances they throw and make a graph, or count the number of times they can catch the ball while throwing with another child.

**COMMENT**   As most throwing activities require a partner to catch, this activity is *especially good for* ADJUSTMENT, LEARNING, HEARING, CULTURALLY DISTINCT, and GIFTED AND TALENTED needs: develops both coordination and social skills. VISUAL needs can also participate in the throwing although the eye–hand coordination demands practice. For blind children, use balls with bells inside.

# JUMP OVER THE CREEK

**GOAL**   To improve large motor coordination
To increase body awareness
To improve measurement concepts

**OBJECTIVE**   The child will jump over the "creek" without touching the edges.

**MATERIALS**   Yarn, string, rope, or tape

**PROCEDURE**   Make your "creek" on the ground with two strings 6″ apart. Have the children jump across. At first, increase the distance by 3″, then by 1″ as it becomes more difficult. Have the children make graphs of how far they jump.

**CONTINUATION**   This is fun to do a few times throughout the year so the children can measure their progress. This game can also be used with one string to see how high the children can jump.

**COMMENT**   Be sure this doesn't become competitive; let each child try to jump further than he has before. *Especially good for* LEARNING and HEARING needs: develops large motor skills and shows a highly visual representation of distance. This will intrigue GIFTED AND TALENTED and allow them to practice the needed skill of measuring.

# BUBBLE MACHINE

**GOAL**   To improve eye–hand coordination
To improve breath control

**OBJECTIVE**   The child will blow bubbles and catch at least five, using a pincher movement.

**MATERIALS**   bubble mixture
bubble wand

**PROCEDURE**   Have some children blow bubbles and other children pop them, using a pincher (thumb–finger opposition) movement.

**COMMENT**   A good activity on a warm day, because it can get damp and a bit wild! *Especially good for* HEARING and SPEECH AND LANGUAGE needs: both need to be more aware of their own breath control. This gives them a visual response to how hard or soft they are blowing. INTELLECTUAL needs can profit from both the breath control and the practice of fine motor skills.

# MY YARD

**GOAL**   To improve eye–hand coordination
To increase visual identification

**OBJECTIVE**   The child will identify at least 3 things he sees.

**MATERIALS**   a yard of string for each child          small sticks or long nails
several magnifying glasses of different sizes     a hammer

**PROCEDURE**   On a warm, sunny, dry day cut pieces of string a yard long, and get small sticks or long nails. Have the children pound these in the ground and attach the string. Give the children a magnifying glass and have them explore their "yard." Their "yard" is a circle with a 1 yard *radius*. At first you may have to help them see the little things: how one blade of grass looks covered with dew. If the ground is damp, have the children sit on something.

**COMMENT**   *Especially good for* PHYSICAL needs: allows them to make discoveries without too much physical exertion. HEALTH needs can also enjoy this, but check for allergies to grass, which are usually worse just after the grass has been cut. GIFTED AND TALENTED can be encouraged to explore different degrees of magnification while they keep looking for more things. VISUAL needs who can profit from magnification can participate in this project. Be sure to draw the analogy between glasses and magnifying glasses: different ways to help people see.

# BALLOON BADMINTON

**GOAL**    To improve eye–hand coordination
To improve cause and effect reasoning
To make predictions

**OBJECTIVE**    The child will hit the balloon with the racket.

**MATERIALS**    balloons
badminton rackets

**PROCEDURE**    Have children hit balloons (under-inflated ones break less easily) alone or with another child. As they become more proficient, add a net. Help them make predictions about how far or how often they can hit the balloon. Explore the causal relationships between how hard they swing, the angle of the racket, and where the balloon goes.

**COMMENT**    If children have difficulty with the racket, have them practice without it. *Especially good for* PHYSICAL needs: requires skill but not strength. The practice in coordination is helpful. HEALTH needs could play this game in bed or in a chair. To make the activity less competitive, have children keep track of how many times they can hit the balloon instead of counting how many times the other children miss. Hitting the balloon as hard as he can in a restricted area is a good variation for LEARNING or ADJUSTMENT needs who may have some excess energy to work off.

# FREEZE

**GOAL**    To increase body awareness
To improve balance skills

**OBJECTIVE**    The child will stop and maintain his position until he is unfrozen (touched).

**MATERIALS**    Drum, gong, or record and record player

**PROCEDURE**    Have the children move in a way you name, or allow free movement (walk, hop, crawl, skip). Play some music or beat a drum or gong, then stop suddenly. At the silence, the children should freeze in their position. You might initially call out "freeze" until they get the hang of it. As you unfreeze the children (by touching them), talk about the positions they are in. ("You're really doing a good job standing on one foot. I thought you might melt before I got here.")

**COMMENT**    *Especially good for* LEARNING and VISUAL needs: increases awareness of self in space and what positions are easy and difficult to hold. To adapt this for HEARING needs, use a visual signal for the "freeze." If you aren't sure the children can hear you, blink lights (if inside) or wave hands while making a noise. As there are often balance problems associated with hearing needs, this activity provides good practice.

# CAVE EXPLORATION

**GOAL**    To increase body awareness
To improve tactile discrimination

**OBJECTIVE**    The child will go through the "cave" and feel the various experiences set out for him.

**MATERIALS**    a "cave"                  water
pudding                shaving cream
rubber worms           cornstarch mixed with water
ice                    Ivory Snow Flakes beaten with water

**PROCEDURE**    Construct an obstacle course; string a rope continuously through the course as a guideline and have the children go through the course blindfolded. Place a knot at each stopping place and have the children feel something and try to guess what it is. Use the materials suggested above or others that might occur to you. (Put the pudding before the water so the hands can be cleaned.) During group time, show the children the various setups, discuss how they felt, and pass them around for further exploration. This can easily become a haunted house at Halloween. For effect, add an audiotape with "haunted" sounds.

**COMMENT**    *Especially good for* VISUAL, LEARNING, and HEARING needs: These children need to improve both tactile discrimination and the vocabulary for it. If you have PHYSICAL needs in your class, be sure to supply a guide if necessary. This is also a good adaptation for INTELLECTUAL and ADJUSTMENT needs who may have difficulty following the procedure or who may be reluctant to take the risk involved in reaching into the substances.

# LADDER WALK

**GOAL**    To increase body awareness
To improve balance skills
To follow directions

**OBJECTIVE**    The child will walk between the rungs of a ladder.

**MATERIALS**    A ladder

**PROCEDURE**    Lay a ladder on the ground and have the children walk its length. See if they can do it taking only one or two steps between each rung. This can be part of an obstacle course. To make it more difficult, raise the height of the ladder or have the children hold something in both hands as they walk. This is also useful for teaching following directions and number concepts (i.e., "Walk over three rungs, then turn around and come back.") As the children learn such concepts as half, they can stop halfway. Other movements, such as combining hands and feet and walking sideways and backwards can add variation and change the level of skill. Children can also try this blindfolded, but be sure to have a spotter.

Outdoor equipment enables children to experiment with balance and large motor coordination.

**COMMENT**    *Especially good for* LEARNING and INTELLECTUAL needs: They learn not only to balance but also to adapt their strides to the distance between the rungs of the ladder. Varying directions is also helpful. For VISUAL needs, the orientation skills are useful, but double-check with the orientation and mobility specialist (if there is one working with the children) for specific techniques to use.

# BAREFOOT

**GOAL**    To increase body awareness
To improve tactile discrimination
To increase vocabulary

**OBJECTIVE**    The child will talk about how various textures feel on his feet.

**MATERIALS**    Blindfold (a half-face Halloween mask with the eye holes covered works well)

**PROCEDURE**    When it is warm enough, allow the children to go barefoot outside. Ask them to describe the feel of sand, grass, mud, gravel, cement, wood, and so on on their feet. As the children walk in different areas, talk about how the feelings change underfoot: cold/hot, soft/hard, wet/dry, round/pointed, and so on. As children say things like "It hurts," try and help them figure out what properties of a substance make it hurt (i.e., sharp, hard, or hot). Bring samples of what was walked on into your group and have a discussion about the experience. Have the children feel the same substances with their hands and talk about the difference. Be sure to check the area first for broken glass or other objects which might hurt children's feet.

**CONTINUATION**    Set up a structured area outdoors with a variety of substances to walk through. Put blindfolds on the children and see if they can identify the substances.

**COMMENT**    *Especially good for* VISUAL needs: builds vocabulary, especially if you discuss where certain textures might be felt (the road vs. the grass). LEARNING and HEARING needs can practice tactile integration with verbal skills in describing only what they have felt. SPEECH AND LANGUAGE needs and CULTURALLY DISTINCT can build vocabulary and practice specific speech sounds; GIFTED AND TALENTED can be encouraged to think about footware for specific movements on different textures. (Use baseball shoes, golf shoes, running shoes, tennis shoes, swim fins, and snow shoes as examples.)

# PICNIC

**GOAL**    To increase feelings of group belonging
To improve cause and effect reasoning

**OBJECTIVE**    The child will talk about what one takes on a picnic.

**MATERIALS**    Props for a picnic:
blanket              dishes
picnic basket        food

**PROCEDURE**    Arrange to have a picnic snack. Use large-group time to discuss what you will need to bring and do: something to sit on, picnic basket, dishes, food and drink; who is going to carry these; and why some foods are good to take and others are not. If possible, have the children prepare at least part of the picnic. Be sure to talk about what you would and wouldn't take with you and why. Have your picnic outdoors if it is warm enough; if not, do it indoors.

**COMMENT**    This is a firsthand experience that can help the children generalize from the known procedures at lunch or snack to those required when food is carried to another place to be eaten.

*Especially good for* SPEECH AND LANGUAGE and HEARING needs and CULTURALLY DISTINCT: They can add this to their repertoire of experiences.

## BLOWING BUBBLES

**GOAL**     To improve cause and effect reasoning
To improve breath control

**OBJECTIVE**     The child will blow bubbles and explain the relationship between how he blows and the kind of bubble that forms.

**MATERIALS**     cups
water
liquid dishwashing detergent

vegetable dye
straws

**PROCEDURE**     Put a drop or two of detergent in a cup, add vegetable dye if you wish, and have children blow bubbles through a straw. Be sure the children know the differences between blowing and sucking.

**COMMENT**     Encourage children to blow hard, softly, fast, and slowly, and talk about the difference in the bubbles. *Especially good for* SPEECH AND LANGUAGE, HEARING, and INTELLECTUAL needs: All need to practice breath control. Blowing bubbles is fun in itself and gives the children a chance to develop a needed skill while feeling part of a group.

## HUG TAG

**GOAL**     To increase feelings of group belonging
To cooperate with peers

**OBJECTIVE**     The child will hug another child.

**MATERIALS**     None

**PROCEDURE**     This is a tag game. When one child is "it," he tries to tag the other children. Children are safe if they are hugging someone when they are tagged. They may not hug the same person two successive times.

**COMMENT**     This is a twist on a familiar game. It is great fun, active, and encourages social behavior. *Especially good for* HEARING, and LEARNING needs: pairs visual and tactile input. Encourage VISUAL and SPEECH AND LANGUAGE needs to talk before and during the hug so they practice speech and are not startled. Approach this cautiously with ADJUSTMENT, HEALTH, and PHYSICAL needs—make the hugs gentle and nonthreatening. Great for CULTURALLY DISTINCT and GIFTED AND TALENTED because they are part of a group and hugs are universal. Encourage INTELLECTUAL needs to approach others as well as respond to being approached.

## COLOR SCAVENGER HUNT

**GOAL**     To increase feelings of group belonging
To improve color concepts
To cooperate with peers

**OBJECTIVE**     The child will find an object that is the same color as each of the colors on his card.

**MATERIALS**    A card with four different colors

**PROCEDURE**    This is a scavenger hunt with a twist. The children don't have to find specific objects, but rather objects that are specific colors. Have children work in pairs. Give each pair a card with four colors and have them bring back one thing that is each of those colors. For example, use a card with the colors green, red, white, and yellow: green—leaf or grass; red—flower, paint chip, or block; white—pebble or paper; and yellow—dandelion. This can also be done inside, but it creates a lot of confusion if the group is large. You might consider allowing the children to just name the objects, not bring them back.

**COMMENT**    *Especially good for* HEARING and LEARNING needs: requires the children to translate visual cues into an object that can be found. To help them participate, have INTELLECTUAL and PHYSICAL needs work with others in pairs. For VISUAL needs, use cards that have texture cues (rough—tree bark; flexible—grass; hard or sharp—stone).

# *Awareness*

# INDEX

This activity area is designed to help all children become aware of the implications of special needs. The goal is for children to better understand how these needs affect a child and how children can interact with each other in light of these needs. To begin with, children must become aware of others' situations. Stories can be of some use, but as we all know, children learn best by doing. The following activities are designed to help children feel, on a short-term basis, what it might be like to have a special need.

Once the child has begun to be aware of the condition of others, it is the skill of a sensitive teacher that determines the long-term outcome of this awareness. Children look to you as a model. If you pity children with special needs or are overprotective or condescending toward them, the children will react the same way.

You may need some time to look over these activities and see which ones you feel comfortable with and which ones you want to reconsider later in the year. If there are activities that you feel uncomfortable with, don't use them, but let them jog you into thinking up activities you can use.

These activities are important for *all* children. For example, a child in a wheelchair cannot be expected to have any more idea of what it is like to have a visual impairment than can any other child in your class.

These activities are not easy; they are not part of the everyday curriculum. They require special planning and thinking on your part. They also have special payoffs—to you and to all the children in your class. You will have helped these children learn to view things from another's perspective early in life, without making judgments about that person's being good or bad.

# TALKING

**GOAL**   To increase awareness of speech and language needs
**OBJECTIVE**   The child will state how he feels when others can't understand him.
**MATERIALS**   None

**PROCEDURE**   In a small group give a child a specific thing to say and then tell him how he has to use his mouth. For example:

> Keep your teeth clenched while you talk.
> Keep your lips closed.
> Keep your tongue behind the lower teeth.
> Keep your mouth open.

Have the children continue trying to make themselves understood until they experience some frustration and can empathize with the child who has a speech problem. Discuss how it feels to the child when others don't understand his speech.

**COMMENT**   This activity helps children learn about the function of the various parts of their mouths in speech. It may be useful in helping an insensitive child gain understanding of speech problems. It can be varied by having an individual child talk into a tape recorder, then listen to himself.

# TONGUE TWISTERS

**GOAL**   To increase awareness of speech and language needs

**OBJECTIVE**   The child will state how he feels after saying a difficult "tongue twister" fast.

**MATERIALS**   None

**PROCEDURE**   Teach children some tongue twisters, then encourage them to say them fast. This often results in both laughter and the realization that some things are difficult for all of us to say. For example:

> The bootblack brought the book back.
> Beth brought a big blue bucket of blueberries.
> Big black bugs buckle and bulge beneath the big blue bundle.
> Betty Balder bought some butter for her bread batter.
> Greek grape growers grow great grapes.
> Peter Piper picked a peck of pickled peppers.
> Suzy sells seashells down by the seashore.
> The sixth sheik's sixth sheep's sick.
> Red roosters read riddles rapidly.

**CONTINUATION**   Have children make up their own tongue twisters. It is a good language exercise.

**COMMENT**   This is good for awareness and, done slowly, for practicing specific initial sounds.

# NO WORDS

**GOAL**   To increase awareness of speech and language needs
   To increase awareness of hearing needs
   To increase awareness of other cultures

**OBJECTIVE**   The child will state how he feels when he has trouble talking and/or when others don't understand.

**MATERIALS**   None

**PROCEDURE**    Have a discussion about how animals and people communicate without using words.

> bees: dance to help other bees find honey
> dogs: bark, wag tails
> birds: chirp
> people: gesture

Give one child in the class instructions for a task the group must perform. Have him get the other children to carry out the task without using words. Initially all the children could do the same thing—for example, go to the bathroom and wash their hands. As the children get better at this, you could give more difficult tasks.

**COMMENT**    Discuss the differences between using nonverbal "language" and words, especially in relation to how long it takes to convey information without words. Lead this into a general discussion of communication and how difficult it is to express yourself when you don't know the right words to say. Point out examples of nonverbal body language people use.


# MUFFLES

**GOAL**    To increase awareness of hearing needs

**OBJECTIVE**    The children will discuss how it feels to have trouble understanding speech while playing together.

**MATERIALS**    ear muffs or cotton balls
record player or tape recorder
records or tape

**PROCEDURE**    Set up the dramatic play area in the usual way. Have the children wear ear muffs or put cotton balls in their ears and tell them to whisper while playing instead of talking out loud. You can add to the effect by having a record or tape player in the background to make it even harder to hear the speech. Follow this activity with a discussion at group time. Start your discussion by talking very softly while the music is playing. When the children get restless and frustrated, go back to your normal style. Talk about how hard it is to cooperate with others and to pay attention when you can't hear.

**COMMENT**    Children can begin to better understand the implications of not being able to hear.


# VOICELESS ROLL CALL

**GOAL**    To increase awareness of hearing needs

**OBJECTIVE**    The child will respond to his name in an appropriate way.

**MATERIALS**    None

**PROCEDURE**    Call roll, but mouth the names instead of speaking them out. Use your regular form for response. Discuss how difficult this is, especially how hard it is to keep looking.

**CONTINUATION**    When the children get the idea, tell them voicelessly what activities are available and ask them to make choices.

**COMMENT**    You may have to practice a bit before you are comfortable calling roll this way. Children with severe visual needs will not be able to participate in this activity.

# FINGER SPELLING LOTTO

**GOAL**  To increase awareness of hearing needs

**OBJECTIVE**  The child will match the letters of the alphabet with the appropriate finger spelling letters.

**MATERIALS**  alphabet lotto cards with Ameslan signs for each letter (example of signs in glossary of chapter on hearing needs)

**PROCEDURE**  Make a lotto game using the letters of the alphabet and the manual signs for those letters.

**CONTINUATION**  At dismissal time, call the children by making the sign for the first letter of their names, or hold up a picture of the appropriate sign for each.

**COMMENT**  This activity teaches the manual alphabet—a new way of communicating—to hearing children.

# CHARADES

**GOAL**  To increase awareness of hearing needs
To increase awareness of other cultures

**OBJECTIVE**  Without using words, one child will act out his object or action for the others to guess.

**MATERIALS**  pictures of people, animals, or objects
pictures of someone doing something:

| | |
|---|---|
| getting a drink | going outside |
| getting a cookie | getting in the car |
| putting on a coat | |

**PROCEDURE**  Give the child a picture of what he is to pantomime. Be sure to give hints and suggestions to both actors and guessers until the children catch on.

**CONTINUATION**  Expand your discussion to include children who can speak but who speak another language.

**COMMENT**  Encourage awareness of nonverbal communication and how hard it is to communicate without speech.

# SPECIAL DOLLS

**GOAL**  To increase awareness of hearing needs
To increase awareness of health needs
To increase awareness of physical needs

**OBJECTIVE**  The child will play with the doll.

**MATERIALS**  To make a doll with hearing aid:

| | | |
|---|---|---|
| rubber or vinyl dolls | small plastic box (size | heavy needle |
| hearing aid | proportionate to doll's size) | bias tape |
| ear molds | waxed thread | snap |
| bag to hold aid | plastic T-shaped plug (game | felt |
| | parts are ideal) | |

1. Heat the needle and make hole in doll's ear, enlarge with heated needle to accommodate the shaft of the plug.
2a. Make a hole in the shaft of the plug with the needle.
2b. Push the waxed thread through the hole in the shaft and knot.
3. Make holes in the box with the heated needle; open the box and insert ends of string through holes and knot.
4. Make slots in the top of the box with heated needle.
5. Cut rectangle of felt large enough to make bag for box, sew on three sides, leave top open.
6. Cut two strips of bias tape—one long enough to reach around the doll (side) and the other long enough to reach from the doll's waist in front over the doll's shoulders to the waistline in back doubled (top).
7a. Sew the side strip to one side of the bag.
7b. Sew one half of the snap to the other end and the other half to the bag.
7c. Sew the ends of the top strip to the top of the bag.
8. To assemble: Place box in bag on doll's chest; slip (top) bias tape strip over the doll's head; and wrap (side) strip around doll *through* loop made by (top) strip and snap on the other side.

To make a doll with casts:

| | |
|---|---|
| flour paste | plastic bags |
| newspaper | $\frac{1}{2}''$ diameter dowel (or Primary pencil if long enough) |
| paper towels | |

1. Mix flour/water paste to a thin consistency.
2. Cover the area of the doll on which the cast is to be built with plastic.
3. Cover the plastic with $1\frac{1}{2}''$ strips of newspaper dipped in the paste mixture.
4. If applying hip/leg casts, after covering the plastic with one layer of newspaper, force the doll's feet apart and brace them with the dowel.
5. Continue to apply strips of newspaper until three layers have been applied and the dowel is covered.
6. Use $1\frac{1}{2}''$ strips of paper toweling to form a fourth layer.
7. Allow to dry at least two days.

To make a doll with leg braces:

| | |
|---|---|
| tin (tuna or cat food cans work fine) | Velcro |
| leather | aluminum tubing |
| felt | paper fasteners |
| waxed thread | shoes to fit the doll |
| heavy needle | |

1. Use tin snips to cut four strips of tin to the desired size (width and length).
2. Trim heavy rim from tin can.
3. Shape the tin around the doll's leg(s), thigh, and calf.
4a. Cut aluminum tubing to desired length. Flatten ends and drill two holes approximately $\frac{1}{2}-\frac{3}{4}''$ from the tip on each end.
4b. Place strips in position on the outside of the top band. Drill hole through tin to match the holes in the aluminum strips.
4c. Fasten strip to tin with paper fasteners.
4d. Repeat procedure for lower band but drill only one hole at the appropriate height from the bottom strip to secure the lower band. Secure with paper fasteners.
5. Wrap leather around the outside of both bands. Stitch in place using waxed thread. Leather should extend beyond the front edge far enough to overlap the ends.

6a. Cut felt and cover the inside of the band. Edges of felt should extend to cover the tin edges.
6b. Glue felt in place.
7. Sew Velcro to the ends of the leather to finish the closing.
8. Attach the braces to doll shoes with paper fasteners.

**PROCEDURE**  During group time introduce the doll to the group. Explain the doll's need briefly to the children. Then ask a child to take the doll to the doll corner to be included with the others. Encourage conversation about the doll, what it can and can't do as well as the other dolls, and how the children feel about the doll. Be sure not to make judgments if they don't like the doll. Some children probably won't.

**CONTINUATION**  Once you get the idea of constructing these dolls, make more.

**COMMENT**  It is important that the dolls are attractive and don't appear to be broken. For example, don't use a doll with a missing arm to represent an amputee. It is just a broken doll and should be treated like one. Because children often use dramatic play to work through feelings and practice roles, these dolls offer children the opportunity to practice interacting with their classmates who have special needs.

(Development of and directions for these dolls were done by Marilyn Little, graduate student in Individual and Family Studies, College of Human Resources, University of Delaware, as part of her thesis requirements. Used with permission of Marilyn Little.)

# MOVING IN THE DARK

**GOAL**  To increase awareness of visual needs

**OBJECTIVE**  The child will show how he can move safely in the dark.

**MATERIALS**  None

**PROCEDURE**  Make up a story about a child who has to go some place in the dark and is afraid of hitting his head. Have the children think of ways he could move so that he won't be hurt, then demonstrate these.

Log roll

Crab walk

Hold hands in front

Duck walk

Hitch

**COMMENT**  This activity helps children become aware of their heads in space and illustrates the problem of moving when you can't see.

# SIMULATED GLASSES

**GOAL**   To increase awareness of visual needs

**OBJECTIVE**   The child will be able to state what he sees using various types of glasses.

**MATERIALS**   glasses frames or sunglasses        gauze
half-face Halloween masks        cellophane
adhesive tape

To simulate visual conditions, you can use inexpensive sunglasses or the Halloween masks. When you cover the eye holes put the cellophane over the inside opening or make sure the sticky side of the tape faces outward.

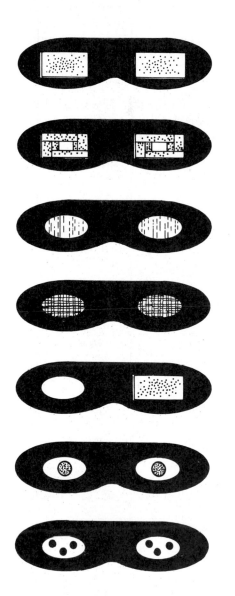

Blindness
Adhesive tape over openings
(sticky side of tape should face
outward)

Tunnel vision
Adhesive tape over edges of
openings

Low vision with light perception
Masking tape over openings

Cataracts
Gauze over openings

Loss of stereo vision
Adhesive tape over one opening
(also demonstrates problem
of wearing a patch)

Peripheral vision only
Adhesive tape circles on
cellophane in center of
openings

Blind spots
Small adhesive tape circles on
cellophane over openings

**PROCEDURE**   Have children talk about what they can and cannot see with the glasses. Encourage them to wear the glasses and then do what they usually do during the day. Talk with them about what is easy to do with the glasses and what is difficult.

**CONTINUATION** Have children use magnifying glasses and binoculars and talk about the changes these make in what they see. This may lead to a discussion about what a child with visual needs can or cannot see.

**COMMENT** With your help children can progress from being aware of what the visual needs child can see or not see to the implications this has at home and in school.

# WHO IS IT?

**GOAL** To increase awareness of visual needs

**OBJECTIVE** The child will identify a classmate by touch.

**MATERIALS** A blindfold

**PROCEDURE** Blindfold one child and have him touch another child. You will have to give some guidance at first on the appropriate ways to touch another person. You might even guide the child's hand to feel the length of hair, type of shoes and clothes, facial features, and so on. Help the child by telling him what to feel for:

> Let's see. Who has long, straight hair, and is wearing a long-sleeved blouse, a sweater that buttons down the front, a pleated skirt, knee socks, and tie shoes?

**CONTINUATION** To improve auditory discrimination, have the child identify a classmate through sounds instead of by touch.

**COMMENT** This activity gives children the experience of seeing" with their hands as children with visual needs do. It also shows them some of the difficulties such children face.

# NOISY TASKS

**GOAL** To increase awareness of learning needs

**OBJECTIVE** The child will state how it feels to work in a noisy environment.

**MATERIALS** record
record player
noisemakers

**PROCEDURE** Have the children do some task that requires a lot of concentration (coloring intricate designs, lacing a paper plate) Tell them you want them to do this task as fast as they can without making mistakes Time them (2 minutes is about right). Spend another 2 minutes in the same activity, either before or after, but provide as many distractions as possible: Turn the lights on and off; talk loudly to an aide; bang some things together; open and shut the door; stomp around; and so on. Have the children count how many holes they laced or squares they colored under each set of circumstances. You could graph the results for the whole class if you choose. Talk with the children about how easy or difficult it was for them to work with lots of distractions. Then explain to the class that for some children even small distractions prevent them from working well.

**CONTINUATION** If the occasion arises, help the children think back to this activity as a reminder of how difficult it is to work with distractions.

**COMMENT** You could expand this to include other kinds of distractions, such as the TV at home.

# CUTTING CARDBOARD

**GOAL**   To increase awareness of learning needs
To increase awareness of physical needs

**OBJECTIVE**   The child will state his feelings about cutting the cardboard.

**MATERIALS**   scissors
heavy cardboard

**PROCEDURE**   Draw intricate designs on cardboard and have the children try to cut out the design. Given children's scissors and the coordination of children this age, this task will be difficult. Discuss how the children feel about not being able to accomplish this task and relate it to how hard it is for them to cut out even simple designs on paper. Discuss that some things are easy and some hard for all children. Talk about how it feels to do things that are hard. Ask, for example, how they felt while attempting the task: if they wanted to leave and do something else; wanted to get help from the teacher; wanted to talk to their friends; and so on. Have them talk about which things are easy and hard for each of them and how they can help each other do difficult tasks (don't do it for someone, but don't tease, tell them to hurry up, and so on).

**COMMENT**   This activity will help children gain some insight into the frustrations that result from attempting a task that is a little beyond their abilities.

# PENS

**GOAL**   To increase awareness of learning needs
To increase awareness of physical needs

**OBJECTIVE**   The child will draw a picture or design with a ball-point pen refill.

**MATERIALS**   ball-point refills
paper
large chalk

**PROCEDURE**   Have children draw a picture or copy a design with a ball-point pen refill that is not in a pen, or have them use very large chalk to color a very small design. Talk with them as they are drawing about what they are making and how easy or difficult the tools make it. Then expand this to include children who, even with regular crayons or markers, find it hard to draw.

**COMMENT**   Be sure the refills are closed at the top so children don't go home with ink all over them. Children can learn how difficult some fine motor tasks can be for others.

# FAST TALK

**GOAL**   To increase awareness of learning needs
To increase awareness of intellectual needs

**OBJECTIVE**   The child will state how he feels when directions are given too fast for him to follow.

**MATERIALS**   None

**PROCEDURE**   At the end of a time when you would normally give children directions, give those directions quite rapidly. To make the point, give two- or three-step directions. Speak as fast as you can. Talk with the children about how they feel when they can't follow or keep up.

**CONTINUATION**   Sing a song with motions so fast that the children have difficulty keeping up, or play a 33⅓ record at 45 RPM. (Be sure this doesn't sound too funny as it may then become just a joke.)

**COMMENT**  It is important that children learn that even though children try hard, it is very difficult for some of them to keep up.

# MY DAY

**GOAL**  To increase awareness of adjustment needs

**OBJECTIVE**  The child will help the teacher plan a special event.

**MATERIALS**  None

**PROCEDURE**  Have a celebration on each child's birthday or some other designated day, and have the child help you plan for his favorite things. Be sure the choices are ones you can actually follow through on; do you want fingerpaint or easel paint provided, or are you willing to have either? Encourage the child to set up the dramatic play area, blocks, pick the snack; plan a parade, a picnic, and so on.

**COMMENT**  This activity is good for all children. It can be used to highlight their uniqueness and to help them develop a sense of belonging. Include their favorite activities (in some blend that is teachable), and try to indicate to the class why a child might choose certain activities and reject others.

# NEW DOLL

**GOAL**  To increase awareness of adjustment needs

**OBJECTIVE**  The child will tell how he feels about the new doll.

**MATERIALS**  A child-size (4′) doll dressed in typical clothes

**PROCEDURE**  Bring the doll into the classroom and give it special privileges: Let it sit beside you during group time, point out how well it is dressed and how special it is, but don't let the children touch it for fear they will break it or get it dirty. When they do touch it, tell them how careful they must be. Have some "presents" for the new doll—clothes, books, and so on. Then discuss with the children how they feel about this new doll, and its privileges and whether or not they want the doll to visit again. Discuss ways of dealing with these feelings.

**CONTINUATION**  Have a baby visit. Discuss the good and bad points of new babies. Read stories on this subject. (See Children's Bibliography—Needs: Adjustment Chapter.) Discuss how having a baby is different from having a doll (more time consuming, messier, and so on).

**COMMENT**  Children appreciate a chance to talk about their feelings of neglect when they have a new sibling or family member who has a special need.

# SAD

**GOAL**  To increase awareness of adjustment needs

**OBJECTIVE**  The child will draw a picture of a situation in which he felt sad.

**MATERIALS**  paper
crayons

**PROCEDURE**   Have children make a book of drawings of situations in which they were sad (or angry, unhappy, or mad.) When most of the children have had time to put in several entries, have a group discussion and talk about how children might feel if a lot of sad things happened at one time, how hard it would be to be happy, and how they might even be scared and expect sad things to happen. Talk about what children can do to make themselves feel better when they feel sad.

**CONTINUATION**   Go on to talk about situations in which children feel happy, but help them to realize that feeling really sad may keep them from enjoying things that usually make them happy. You might want to have the child dictate a few sentences for his book to go along with the pictures.

**COMMENT**   Helps all children realize that everybody, including adults, has some "down" days.

# GET WELL CARDS

**GOAL**   To increase awareness of health needs

**OBJECTIVE**   The child will make a get well card.

**MATERIALS**   paper
crayons or paint

**PROCEDURE**   Have the children make drawings or paintings of their choice on a folded piece of construction paper. They can make either two pictures (front and inside of card), or one picture with a written message (dictated to teacher).

**CONTINUATION**   Have children talk about how it feels to be sick, how they feel sending the card, and how the child getting the card will feel when he gets it.

**COMMENT**   Make the first card for a specific child; then start a collection so you will always have a card to send when the occasion arises. After a while, the children may notice that certain members of the class are sick more often than others.

# MEDICAL TOOLS

**GOAL**   To increase awareness of health needs

**OBJECTIVE**   The child will match the equipment shown to the correct body part.

**MATERIALS**   Pictures of pieces of medical equipment and the parts of the body where these are most commonly used:

| | |
|---|---|
| throat: tongue depressor | arm: blood pressure cuff |
| throat: throat swab | eyes, ears, throat: small flashlight |
| knee: rubber hammer | lungs, heart: stethoscope |
| arm: intravenous system | bottom: needle and syringe |

**PROCEDURE**   Have the children match the pictures of medical equipment to pictures of the appropriate body parts. This often leads to discussion about doctors and medical procedures.

**CONTINUATION**   If possible, have a doctor visit the class and demonstrate the equipment.

**COMMENT**   Be sure to use the equipment the children in your class are most likely to encounter. This activity should help make all children's contact with the medical profession less frightening, and also help them realize that some of their classmates must see doctors more frequently than they do.

# NOT TO EAT

**GOAL**   To increase awareness of health needs

**OBJECTIVE**   The child will state which of the substances are edible and which are not.

**MATERIALS**   A variety of substances, some edible (milk, peanut butter, nuts) and some not, (soap, playdough, sand)

**PROCEDURE**   Put the substances on a table and talk about which ones the children can eat and which ones might make them sick. Then talk about individual differences in things people can't eat. Children with allergies, for example, must avoid some foods. Mention the particular allergies of children in your class.

**COMMENT**   Children must learn which food they can and cannot eat and that some children cannot eat some foods that are good for others. They may not be able to eat some food they really like. Discuss the temptation of "sneaking" these foods and the implications of that behavior.

# TIRED

**GOAL**   To increase awareness of health needs

**OBJECTIVE**   The child will name some activities he doesn't want to do when he's tired.

**MATERIALS**   None

**PROCEDURE**   Encourage children to run or jump very actively until they are tired (they could run or jump in place if the weather is bad). Then have them list the activities they wouldn't want to

Awareness can lead to understanding and knowledge of how to interact with others. These girls had no difficulty figuring out how to play together on the glider.

do right away (run more, climb fast, ride a tricycle, and so on) and those they would do (quiet activities like listening to a story or record). Talk about how children differ in how easily they get tired and how it isn't fun to play actively when you're tired.

**COMMENT**    All children know how it feels to be tired, they need to learn that others may feel tired when they don't. Encourage children to tell each other when they are tired and suggest things they can still do together.

# CREEPERS

**GOAL**    To increase awareness of physical needs

**OBJECTIVE**    The child will move around the classroom on the creeper or dolly.

**MATERIALS**    Several creepers, mechanic's dollies, or anything on wheels, several inches from the floor and propelled by the children's hands and feet

**PROCEDURE**    Have the children explore the room from the dolly and see how tired they get, what they can and can't reach, and how their body feels after a while. After the novelty has worn off, discuss with the children the limitations involved in moving around this way.

**COMMENT**    It is important to have children stay on the dolly long enough to realize the limitations.

# MITTENS

**GOAL**    To increase awareness of physical needs

**OBJECTIVE**    The child will state how he feels when trying to pick up objects with mittens on.

**MATERIALS**    mittens
a variety of small objects

**PROCEDURE**    Have the children bring mittens to school or provide them. They can be worn throughout the day or used just to demonstrate fine motor skills such as stacking small blocks, interlocking shapes, eating snacks, stringing beads, coloring, and so on. Have children discuss how they feel after the day's activities. If they take the mittens off, ask why and discuss how they felt before and after.

**COMMENT**    Through this activity all children become more aware of how useful their fingers are. They also gain an appreciation of the difficulties faced by children with fine motor coordination problems.

# WHEELS

**GOAL**    To increase awareness of physical needs

**OBJECTIVE**    The child will point to the wheels in each of the pictures.

**MATERIALS**    Pictures of things with wheels

**PROCEDURE**    Have the children discuss the function of wheels and encourage children to experiment moving on or using things with wheels. If you happen to have shelves on wheels, have the children compare moving those shelves with shelves not on wheels. When you are outside, keep the wheels of a tricycle or wagon from turning by putting something through the spokes and discuss how this affects its movement. Be sure to include a wheelchair. Talk about brakes as well.

**COMMENT**   All children can learn about the functions wheels play in moving.

## BUTTONING

**GOAL**   To increase awareness of physical needs
To increase awareness of intellectual needs

**OBJECTIVE**   The child will button tiny buttons quickly.

**MATERIALS**   Infant clothes and doll clothes with small buttons

**PROCEDURE**   Have children try to button and unbutton infant clothes. Time the children to see how fast they can do this. Then have them try the clothes on a doll (make sure it's a tight fit). Encourage the children to keep trying, and discuss how they feel when they get frustrated.

**COMMENT**   All children often get frustrated in the process of learning self-help skills, but these skills are especially difficult for children with intellectual needs to master.

## FOREIGN LANGUAGES

**GOAL**   To increase awareness of other cultures

**OBJECTIVE**   The child will be able to recognize when speech is in English and when it is not.

**MATERIALS**   None

**PROCEDURE**   Sing or play a record of a familiar song in a foreign language. Ask children what the words mean and discuss how some words are the same or similar in several languages. Then teach the English. "Frère Jacques" is one of the most common ones; there are many holiday songs that are appropriate. Discuss with the children how hard it is to listen and pay attention when you don't understand.

**CONTINUATION**   If there are Spanish or French TV or radio stations in your area, turn them on for the children.

**COMMENT**   All children can appreciate language problems facing non-English speakers.

## HOLIDAYS

**GOAL**   To increase awareness of other cultures

**OBJECTIVE**   The child will act out how his family celebrates a special holiday.

**MATERIALS**   None

**PROCEDURE**   Talk with children about how their families celebrate particular holidays. Then choose one or two children each day to act this out for the group. Include different holidays and birthdays. Be sure to discuss feelings, excitement, and expectations. Discuss how fine it is that families have different ways of celebrating as well as different holidays that are celebrated.

# INTERNATIONAL SNACK

**GOAL**    To increase awareness of other cultures

**OBJECTIVE**    The child will taste the snacks.

**MATERIALS**    An international snack including:

    flour tortillas     pupu
    fondue     crepes
    Irish soda bread     grits
    pita bread

**PROCEDURE**    As one activity for the day, make a snack that is foreign. Start with something that is familiar but borrowed, like pizza and tacos, and move on to less familiar foods. Discuss what the foods are made of and where they come from, then eat them. Use parents and grandparents as a resource.

**CONTINUATION**    Have an international pot luck dinner. Encourage families to come and share. Then take pictures of the families (if you can afford it) as a way of sharing. (Be sure to use a broad definition of the word family; to include stepparents, grandparents, aunts, uncles, and cousins.)

**COMMENT**    Helps children think of "different" as "special" rather than "bad."

# LINGO'S

**GOAL**    To increase awareness of other cultures

**OBJECTIVE**    The child will name the object in both languages.

**MATERIALS**    Objects labeled in two languages

**PROCEDURE**    Label objects in the room with bilingual signs. For example:

    bathroom: baño
    clock: reloj
    chalkboard: pizarra
    books: libros

Discuss the fact that people don't all use the same language.

**CONTINUATION**    Read a story that has some foreign words. Teach a simple song in another language.

**COMMENT**    The actual language you choose will probably depend upon the nationalities of children in your class and/or your own background.

# FURTHER READINGS

## CHILD DEVELOPMENT

Any of the following books would be useful in helping you decide whether or not your expectations for children are age appropriate.

Ambron, Sueann. *Child Development.* 3d ed. New York: Holt Rinehart and Winston, 1981.

Bee, Helen L., and Sandra K. Mitchell. *The Developing Person: A Life-Span Approach.* New York: Harper and Row, 1980.

Dworetzky, John P. *Introduction to Child Development.* St. Paul, Minn.: 1981.

Fein, Greta G. *Child Development.* Englewood Cliffs, N.J.: Prentice-Hall, 1978.

Fong, Bernadine, and Miriam Resnick. *The Child: Development Through Adolescence.* Menlo Park, Calif.: Benjamin/Cummings, 1980.

Gander, Mary J., and Harry W. Gardiner. *Child and Adolescent Development.* Boston: Little, Brown, 1981.

Gardner, Howard. *Developmental Psychology: An Introduction.* Boston: Little, Brown, 1978.

Hanson, Richard A., and Rebecca Reynolds. *Child Development: Concepts, Issues and Readings.* St. Paul, Minn.: West, 1980.

Helms, Donald B., and Jeffrey S. Turner. *Exploring Child Behavior.* 2nd ed. New York: Holt, Rinehart and Winston, 1981.

Klopp, Claire, B., and Joann B. Krakow. *The Child Development in a Social Context.* Reading, Mass.: Addison-Wesley, 1982.

Lawton, Joseph T. *Introduction to Child Development.* Dubuque, Iowa: Wm C. Brown, 1982.

Lefrancois, Guy R. *Of Children: An Introduction to Child Development.* 3d ed. Belmont, Calif.: Wadsworth, 1980.

Leve, Robert. *Childhood: The Study of Development.* New York: Random House, 1980.

Mussen, Paul, John Conger, and Jerome Kagan. *Essentials of Child Development and Personality.* New York: Harper and Row, 1980.

Papalia, Diane E., and Sally W. Olds. *A Child's World: Infancy Through Adolescence.* 3d ed. New York: McGraw-Hill, 1982.

Schickedanz, Judith A., David I. Schickedanz, and Peggy D. Forsyth. *Toward Understanding Children.* Boston: Little, Brown, 1982.

Smart, Mollie S., and Russell C. Smart. *Children: Development and Relationships.* 4th ed. New York: Macmillan, 1982.

Travers, John F. *The Growing Child.* Glenview, Ill.: Scott, Foresman, 1982.

Watson, Robert I., and Henry Clay Lindgren. *Psychology of the Child and Adolescent.* 4th ed. New York: Macmillan, 1979.

Yussen, Steven R., and John W. Santrock. *Child Development: An Introduction.* 2nd ed. Dubuque, Iowa: Wm C. Brown, 1982.

## ACTIVITY BOOKS

Arnold, Lois B. *Preparing Young Children for Science: A Book of Activities.* New York: Schocken, 1980.

Focuses on observation and comparison skills for children from 4 to 8 years.

Baratta-Lorton, Mary. *Workjobs: Activity-centered Learning for Early Childhood Education.* Menlo Park, Calif.: Addison-Wesley, 1975.

Activities that promote discovery and exploration through play are provided. Format includes necessary materials, directions for the activities and ideas for getting started as well as for follow-up discussions. *Workjobs for Parents* uses the same philosophy with activities designed for the home.

Brown, Sam, ed. *Bubbles, Rainbows and Worms: Science Experiments for Preschool Children.* Mt Rainier, Md.: Gryphon House, 1981.

Includes learning activities that children can do themselves and additional explanations for teachers of the scientific principles involved.

Collier, Mary Jo, Imogene Forte, and Joy MacKenzie. *Kid's Stuff.* Nashville, Tenn.: Incentive Publications, 1969.

A kindergarten and nursery school activity book for language arts, science, social studies, math, art, and music.

Croft, Dorien J., and Robert H. Hess. *An Activities Handbook for Teachers of Young Children.* Boston: Houghton Mifflin, 1980.

Structured activities to use in a variety of curriculum areas.

Cromwell, Liz, and Dixie Hibner. *Finger Frolics: Fingerplays for Young Children.* Mt. Rainier, Md.: Gryphon House, 1976.

A collection of fingerplays to use with young children.

Curtis, Sandra. *The Joy of Movement in Early Childhood.* New York: Teachers College Press, 1982.

Uses photographs to show various stages in motor activities such as walking and running, and then gives specific games and activities to evaluate and facilitate movement in children.

Debelak, Marianne, Judith Herr, and Marth Jacobson. *Creating Innovative Classroom Materials for Young Children.* New York: Harcourt Brace Jovanovich, 1980.

A wealth of ideas for making creative yet inexpensive classroom materials.

Fiarotta, Phyllis. *Snips and Snails and Walnut Whales: Nature Crafts for Children.* New York: Workman Publishing, 1975.

An activity book for making crafts with natural materials.

Flemming, Bonnie Mack, and Darlene Suftley Hamilton. *Resources for Creative Teaching in Early Childhood Education.* New York: Harcourt Brace Jovanovich, 1977.

A large, topically-arranged resource book with a multitude of curriculum ideas for use in the classroom.

Forte, Imogene, Mary Ann Pangle, and Robbie Tupa. *Center Stuff for Nooks, Crannies and Corners.* Nashville, Tenn.: Incentive Publications, 1973.

A more advanced activity book for use with kindergarten children.

Jacobson, Willard J., and Abby Barry Bergman. *Science for Children: A Book for Teachers.* Englewood Cliffs, N.J.: Prentice-Hall, 1980.

Gives an in-depth view of topics and information as well as how to translate this knowledge to a useable form for children.

Kaplan, Sandra Nina, JoAnn Butom Kaplan, Sheila Kunishima Madsen, and Bette Taylor Gould. *A Young Child Experiences: Activities for Teaching and Learning.* Pacific Palisades, Calif.: Goodyear Publishing, 1975.

Includes projects that make use of scrounge materials.

Machado, Jeanne M. *Early Childhood Experiences with Language Arts.* Albany, N.Y.: Delmar Publishers, 1975.

A rich resource of planned experiences, creative activities, and ideas for teaching the language arts to young children. An excellent storehouse of ideas easily adapted to most children.

Miller, Mabel Evelyn. Kindergarten Teachers' Activities Desk Book. Englewood Cliffs, N.J.: Prentice-Hall, 1974.

Contains many activities, projects, ideas, and games to help children learn.

Nocera, Sona D. *Reaching the Special Learner Through Music.* Morristown, N.J.: Silver Burdett, 1979.

Addresses the role of music in special education, as well as gives characteristic learning styles and needs of various groups of special needs children. Includes songs, poems, and stories.

Pile, Naomi. *Art Experiences for Young Children.* New York: Macmillan, 1973.

Stresses creative art activities that allow for different ages and experiences.

Russell, Helen Ross. *Ten-Minute Field Trips.* Chicago, Ill.: J G Ferguson, 1973.

A teacher's guide for using the school grounds for environmental studies.

Sharp, Evelyn. *Thinking Is Child's Play.* New York: Avon, 1970.

Gives a series of classification games based on Piaget theory and arranged developmentally.

Vernazza, Marcelle. *Complete Handbook of Kindergarten Music Lesson Plans and Activities.* West Nyack, N.Y.: Parker Publishing, 1981.

Through step-by-step, easy-to-follow lesson plans offers a complete music program designed specifically for kindergarten children. The lesson plans include the materials needed, the objective or musical focus, directions and activities, and, in some cases, ways of continuing the lesson. The activities are easily adaptable to children with various disabilities and will turn any group of children into music enthusiasts. Creative movement and listening can be easily incorporated.

Watrin, Rita, and Paul Hanly Furfey. *Learning Activities for the Young Preschool Child.* New York: Van Nostrand, 1978.

Emphasizes activities that are appropriate and functional for toddlers. The activities are divided by curriculum area.

Willson, Robina Beckles. *Creative Drama and Musical Activities for Children: Improvised Movement, Games, Action Songs, Rhymes and Playlets.* Boston: Plays, 1979.

Makes music a language experience by helping children become more aware of their own voices and the control they have over them.

Zaslavsky, Claudia. *Preparing Young Children for Math: A Book of Games.* New York: Schocken, 1979.

Over 100 math games arranged by difficulty.

## I N D E X

**VISUAL SKILLS**

**CREDITS**

Page 97 *The Joy of Signing* by Lottie Riekehoff, copyright 1978 by the Gospel Publishing House.

All other line art by Paige Hardy & Associates, Inc.

Photographs: Pages 28, 57, 79, 86, 118 (right), 118 (left), 137, 164 (top left), 164 (top right), 192, 198, 244, 273, 304, 389, 426, 469, and 475 by Pat Childs; 5, 9, 13, 17, 21, 31, 49, 51, 61, 80 (bottom), 82, 110, 136, 142, 163, 169, 172, 220, 222, 247, 279, 302, 342, 357, 369, 399, 435, 452, 493, 501, 514, 529, and 545 by John Deiner; 80 (top), HBJ Photos; 4 by Bob Herbert; 165 (bottom left) by Noella Horton; 164 (bottom left), 164 (bottom right), 165 (top left), and 165 (top right) by Ron Horton; 135, 191, 218, 224, 276, and 306 by Charlie Miller.